The Crash of a Civilization

The Crash of a Civilization

KANCHAN BANERJEE

PRABHAT PRAKASHAN

Published by

PRABHAT PRAKASHAN PVT. LTD.
4/19 Asaf Ali Road,
New Delhi–110 002 (INDIA)
e-mail: prabhatbooks@gmail.com

ISBN 978-93-5521-240-5
THE CRASH OF A CIVILIZATION
by Kanchan Banerjee

Edition
2025

Price
₹ 995 (Rupees Nine Hundred Ninety-Five Only)

Printed at
Sita Fine Arts, Delhi

The Dharmic tradition of India dictates that people are obligated to perform some duties as yajñá to fulfil the *rnas*: *Pitri rna, Rishi rna, Deva rna,* and *Nri rna*. The *Deva rna* is fulfilled via personal *adhyatmic* practices. This book serves my *rnas* to the *Pitris* – our ancestors, especially the *khastriyas*, the protectors, for whom we are still living and following our heritage for millennia. To serve my *rnas* for the *Rishis* – the sages and teachers because of whom I know and write. And finally, to perform the *Nri rna* towards the people who are around us because of whose contributions we live in the society.

FOREWORD

Prof. Ved Nanda

There is no dearth of books, mostly by historians and political scientists, describing, analyzing, and assessing the grim story of India during the 800 years of foreign domination until the country gained independence in 1947. This, indeed, was a dark period when Indian society suffered myriad atrocities.

What does this book add? The book is special, and an important contribution as Kanchan Banerjee brings a fresh and lively perspective to this era. He relates the comprehensive and detailed story, going back to pre-Islamic Arabia's history, attacks from Huns and numerous other invasions, and the Islamic rule, followed by the British occupation, up to present-day India. He paints a realistic picture of plunders, massacres, and the destruction of temples, educational institutions, and industries. Banerjee's focus, however, is not on history per se, but the impact of the major actors and events that shaped this history, as he concludes that the Islamic rule, the colonial subjugation, missionaries' misguided zeal, and Marxists' slant on India's past accomplishments, have sought to destroy the Indian civilization.

Kanchan Banerjee is eminently suited to undertake this study. As a student of science, he verifies and rigorously analyzes the facts before drawing any inferences and conclusions. He engaged with the Muslim community and had firsthand experience of communist movements while in his native West Bengal, India. After moving to the United States, he became a prominent student leader. He is a journalist, and a voracious reader, and a proud Hindu and Indian-American. This book is a product of his experience, research, and reflection.

He finds the colonists' equating Dharma with "Hinduism" and "religion" as "one of the biggest tragedies in the history of humankind and the mind of the conscious Hindu." He considers the "left-liberals," whom he calls "Neo-Colonists" or for short, the "Neo-Cols," who are bent upon eradicating the historical contribution of the Hindus from mathematics and science to language and health, as well as the spiritual traditions, as a serious threat to India's integrity, security, and progress. Thus, despite the upheavals India has faced and continues to face, Banerjee asserts that the country's core, which is "all-inclusive, multi-dimensional, and plural," still remains intact.

Banerjee is an engaging storyteller. Although his historical account is aimed at demonstrating the adverse impacts of foreign domination on the Indian civilization, through stories, he brings the history to life, whether he is describing Zoroastrianism, Judaism, Christianity, or broader Abrahamic religions and belief systems, Arab deities, Arabic and Islamic terminologies, or different sects of Islam.

His stories on dating Indian historical events and on historic centers of learning – 21 including Takshila, Nalanda, and Kashi-Varanasi – are riveting and eye-opening. So are his accounts of the British rule and the events leading to India's partition, the controversy about the destruction of Nalanda University, the story of Mongol Emperor Genghis Khan's life and adventures, and the origin of the name Afghanistan.

Banerjee is concerned at this critical time that so many Indians are naïve about their past history and indifferent about their future. Noting that Hinduism and Hindutva are "misunderstood, misused, and misappropriated," he says the book is designed "to create awareness among our next-gen [of] how much history has been concocted by the neo-cols to keep the Indians feeling inferior, passive, selfish, and ashamed about their tradition and heritage and their ancestors."

Banerjee concludes with an uplifting message: "India is rising again to give the light of peace and harmony to the world," but millions of people must want it, work for it, and dedicate themselves to the cause. He leaves with a question to the reader – what would be your role in it?

Padma Bhushan Prof. Ved P. Nanda is a Professor at the Sturm College of Law and former Vice Provost of the University of Denver, Colorado. He is the Past President of the World Jurist Association, former Vice President and counselor of the American Society of International Law, and a member of the United States Institute of Human Rights advisory council.

❑

FOREWORD

Prof. Saradindu Mukherji

It is a bold attempt to offer interesting ideas on various themes that have shaped the evolution of human society over the millennium. Kanchan Banerjee being a "non-historian," has done an admirable job in offering a scholarly survey of various landmarks in history that have deeply impacted – mainly harmed Bharat/India. Unfortunately, with many of the historians in Nehruvian India being propagandists, there was little scope for scientific history. No wonder even school students lost interest in such studies. Unfortunately, little has been done to scrap the unacceptable and offer a more satisfying academic agenda. The constructive ideas offered by public intellectuals during the Ayodhya movement proved the practical value of authentic history and the critical role of honest scholars. Banerjee admits that in writing this, he is doing his duty to his ancestors – our Rishis, and conveying a message – a wake-up call to contemporary society.

He covers a wide spectrum of issues from pre-Islamic Arabia to the university campus in our own times. In between, he traces the rise and spread of the monotheistic creeds and how Christianity and Islam being basically predatory in nature, adversely affect others. Next, he shows how all these forces, along with the other hegemonic forces – the democratic Western world and the Chinese Communists – seek to dominate India.

If the Indian society often fails to take on both the internal and international challenges more effectively, it is because of the ever-increasing clout of the "secularists," no matter who runs the administration. Banerjee explains this well. To get out of this rut, the Hindu society must equip itself with sound knowledge and imbibe a practical approach in facing up to the myriad problems. He makes deft use of legends, anecdotes, and other source materials to make a convincing case. He does well in explaining the much-used terms like idol, beef-up, RIP, adjectives such as "Great" for Alexander and Akbar, the atrocious statement of Manmohan Singh, a Sikh refugee from Islamic Pakistan on the "first claim on our resources by the Muslims of India" and various such matters. A nation that is systematically brain-washed in glorifying religious fanatics like Tipu Sultan, Titu Meer as "freedom fighters" and encouraged to ignore the likes of Shivaji, Subhas, Savarkar, and Syama Prasad can't avoid self-flagellation. India needs an objective historical narrative. It is no point smothering the well-known fault lines. Myopic vision actually cripples society.

The ravages inflicted by the barbarian invaders on our society and people that decimated our famous academic centers have been delineated well. Banerjee sketches the course of the freedom movement, the growing strength of communal/separatist movements, and the mindset that nurtured it, leading to the partition and its horrible consequences. The partition of India was a major victory of the Islamic ummah and a crushing defeat for the Hindu nation. Exchange of population could have permanently solved one of our major problems. Banerjee ends on an optimistic note saying India "is rising again." There is much to commend the author in his maiden venture.

Prof. Saradindu Mukherji, formerly of Delhi University. Member, Indian Council of Historical Research. Ministry of Education, Government of India.

❑

INTRODUCTION

Shri Uday Mahurkar

Many Indian spiritual giants, including Swami Vivekanand and Shri Aurobindo and visionary thinkers like Veer Savarkar, predicted a century ago that India would one day become a Vishwaguru, a global leader of true spirituality and human values cutting across all lines. On the last page of his epic work ' Hindutva', which defined the counters of Indian nationalism in 1923, Savarkar says that a day will come when the world will have to face the force of Hindutva but also predicts as to how Hindus or India would behave with those who accept its superiority. He says India's terms of dealing with them won't be different from what has been said in Geeta or what Lord Buddha had preached. So, in the end, one who is often reviled as divisive, talks of Vasudhaiva Kutambakam, interpreted today it means that when India becomes a Superpower and a Vishwaguru, it will not exploit smaller nations economically and militarily like Superpowers do now but treat them according to the laws of humanity because the world, after all, is one large family.

Kanchan Banerjee's book, with its wide grasp of comparative religions, the problems faced by Indians and humanity over the past 2,000 years, and the possible solutions that Indian culture and spirituality have to these problems is like a guide or a reference book to understanding as to how India will become a Vishwaguru. India and its people are in dire need of such understanding though they are poised to attain their goal under the visionary leadership of Prime Minister Narendra Modi, who is discovering the true strength of Bharat by tapping the latent talent of the people and throwing open to them the fields of individual advancement, removing the cobwebs of minority vote-bank politics and reaching out to ancient Indian wisdom even while embracing modern technology with all the might.

For, divisive forces in the form of followers of alien ideologies like communism and Pan-Islamism continue to bedevil the country on one hand while on the other hand, materialistic pursuits based on approval or even encouragement of life, based on an obsession with sex, intoxicants, and violence in the form of, amongst others, films on OTT platforms pose a challenge to the Indian way of life. How India will meet these challenges is a question one would ask, along with another question as to how India will become a Vishwaguru with this overdose of materialistic pursuits creeping into its society.

Even while being sure of India's final destiny, Banerjee is rightly concerned about the lack of sense of history in a vast section of Indians due to distortions in history caused by the writings of the neo-colonists and communists. His concern is that a Romila Thapar still has some kind of hold over a section of Indian minds as against the rise of an RC Majumdar (both known historians with the former representing the Left narrative and the latter representing the nationalist narrative).

One would ask how can Banerjee, a student of science and not history, can undertake and execute such a forceful project based on the world as well as Indian history and culture and also come out with solutions? Well, academic qualification is not the only prerequisite to writing a good book. A lot depends on one's inclination, passion, commitment, and intelligence, which Banerjee has had in ample measure being nurtured in the nationalist orientation and atmosphere and then later becoming a journalist fighting for nationalist causes.

Though lengthy in terms of the range of its contents, the book is quite engaging as Banerjee has written it in a gripping manner. His pen journey takes the reader through the histories of Abrahamic religions, India's foreign domination, and its resultant sufferings after achieving greatness in the Chanakya and post-Chanakya era as demonstrated by the development of great places of learning based on ancient Indian knowledge and wisdom like Nalanda, Takshila and Kashi also lesser-known but equally important names like Bikrampur, Nagarjunkonda, and Pushpgiri. Many of these great places of ancient Indian learning are not known to most Indians even today, and that shows the hard work that Banerjee put in writing this book.

I am sure anyone fired with the thirst to know India's evolution over the centuries in comparison to the evolution of other cultures and its great contribution no less than its sufferings under foreign domination will find this book a great asset, and so would those patriotic Indians who wish to see India emerging as a Vishwaguru and a Superpower in the future—wishing great success to the book.

Shri Uday Mahurkar is a renowned author, political analyst, and journalist. He was a senior deputy editor of the India Today group. Recently he has been appointed as the Information Commissioner by the Government of India. His most recent book is 'Veer Savarkar: The Man Who Could Have Prevented Partition'.

PROLOGUE

What inspired me to write this book? First of all, this is not a history book but rather an assessment of the impact of historical events in India. I know that the academics would frown that I don't have a Ph.D. or even a bachelor's degree in history; I am not even an academic in a college! Though I've taught Computer Science-related subjects in several institutes, I am not an academic in the popular sense.

Established historians such as Romila Thapar have criticized well-known scholars for writing on history, claiming they do not understand using historical sources. Anyone who is not a certified historian attempting to write on history is typically discredited – for example, Romila Thapar criticized the researchers and scholars like Sitaram Goel and Arun Shourie.[1]

I am neither a historian nor a 'scholar'; what are my credentials? I am a person of science.

History is not an exact science. Interpretation is a major factor in the whole process. In addition, it is commonly said that 'the victors write history'. In 1891, US Senator George Graham Vest said, "history is written by the victors and framed according to the prejudices and bias existing on their side."[2]

But is that true? It is also said that the lens of the interpreter interprets history. This may have some truth in it.

There are two parts to past events that combine to form what is known as 'history': (1) fact and evidence, (2) interpretation and conclusion. Maharaja Vikramaditya Hemu rose to challenge the Mughals and Pathans. There is enough verifiable evidence to accept this as 'fact'. Now the interpretation: many Muslims may feel that Hemu was an infidel and anti-Muslim who dented the Islamic rule in Delhi. In contrast, Hindus may take pride in the fact that Hemu was a great hero. But there is something beyond interpretation: cause and effect, meaning, the outcome and impact of these events, and lessons learned. So the impact and lessons learned are critical outcomes of knowing facts about our past; that is why we study history, and that is the purpose of this book.

History is not a science, and it is subject to change based on new evidence. Today, knowledge is no more the monopoly of a few academicians. Knowledge has been liberated. Soon, we may see many professions, such as history, getting replaced by crowd-sourced research similar to many scientific studies through global participation. And finally, there are some collective truths beyond interpretations; that is why India's motto is *'Satyameva jayate'*. The 'triumph of truth' is ushered faster when knowledge is democratized, and that is what is happening now. The democratization of knowledge means equal access to information and knowledge.

Not everyone has the skill and aptitude to seek all knowledge; that's why specialization happens. People doing original research in history and archeology is one thing and knowing or learning history from the researchers and scholars is another thing. Anybody can read history books and logically compare available evidence to their own conclusion, and they do not need a historian to hold their hands. This is especially true during the digital era. I've read several hundred books and research works sitting at home, thanks to COVID-19, www.

archive.org, and other online sources. Earlier, you had to sit in a library for hours to study these books (if you found them in the first place). I can see high-resolution photos of many archeological sites and understand the facts based on evidence using my own faculties.

Scientific research involves hypothesis and proof or disproof via a process. If it is proven through experiments, which can be verified anywhere by anybody, it becomes a theory. The outcome of science is measurable and predictable.

On the other hand, history is putting together potential evidence and coming to a conclusion based on logic and common sense. Of course, there is a methodology and process. All knowledge acquisition processes have some basic prerequisites. In history, the challenge is multifold; apart from the 'he said she said' and interpretations based on cultural and other biases, the evidence can be proven totally wrong. But what makes history authentic is seeking the truth, which is very difficult, but the easy part is it can be achieved in many cases using common sense and logic.

So, the audacity I have to write on history comes from my search for truth and inquisition as a person of science. In computer science, logic and analytical skills are fundamental. When I looked at the way our history has been written, common sense told me that many assertions do not make sense, and I started studying history. As a student, I found plenty of disconnects.

As a matter of fact, historians should appreciate that people with science backgrounds are reviewing the history written in the past. This may bring a new dimension since scientists do not generally have cultural and ideological biases while doing research, and historians should welcome it for aiding in their search for truth.

I began writing this book during the onset of the global pandemic Covid-19. The cursed lockdown came as a blessing in disguise to enable me to do research and write. Thanks to technology, most of the books I have read are online, including texts written even from the 6th century CE till today. I did not even have to go to libraries or listen to the lectures of perhaps biased history professors. I think I am fortunate not to be influenced by vested interest groups.

After I started writing, since the text size had become too large, I have decided to split the content into two books. We expect the next (2nd) book to be published soon and invite the readers to look for it in advance.

This book takes the reader on a journey through pre-Islamic Arabia's history to India's last Mughal 'emperor', Bahadur Shah Zafar. From Clive to Churchill, from Deoband to Jamat, and then from M.N. Roy, Rajani Palme Dutt to Yechuri and JNU – all part and parcel of the set of stories that impacted millions and changed India's future.

This book addresses a circular connection between Marxists, Islamists, Missionaries, and the Western and Chinese hegemony to destabilize India's progress.

The second book amicably addresses several social maladies of Hindu Society, including casteism – its history and impact. It also studies and demonstrates a multifaceted understanding of various aspects of the Hindu system, the Hindus, and Hindu society in an attempt to empower both. It proposes specific courses of correctional activities for the people and the leaders of the land for the progress of the world's only continuous civilization, the Hindu Civilization, by treading on the path of Dharma instead of selectively following the ritualistic activities and ceremonies and mimicking and experimenting with Western ideas of secularism, theology, communism, etc.

Our worldview is created by our upbringing, environment, and societal impacts. What people see around them is colored by the glasses that they wear. Our 'believer self' is what prompts us to pick our action options. For example, if one thinks that the world is only for them to enjoy – they would exploit everything and everybody, including nature as well as their family and neighbors; whereas if you subscribe to the idea of co-existence, in becoming a cooperative being, your actions will show some compassion and a degree of sacrifice. Every engagement of yours will have a co-evolving impact on others in the world.

Many core ideas and terminologies of India do not always have an English equivalent. Initially, we will use Western and colonial terms such as religion, spirituality, worship, philosophy, etc., to make it easy for the reader to connect with Indian ideas. As we get deeper into the book, we will introduce, define, and contrast Indian terminologies. Also, terms such as Hindu, Indian, Bharat, and India are also going to be used interchangeably.

Materialism, atheism, and spiritualism – each dimension of human experience guide people to behave and live life in a certain way. It so happened that though India has never shied away from new ideas from around the world, including materialism, its core is all-inclusive, multi-dimensional, and plural. For India, the relationship between worldly and non-material is balanced, having no barrier between the sacred and the secular, material and the spiritual. And that is the true heritage of India. Almost all other nations have lost or are in the process of losing their original affinities, heritage, and cultural value systems. Even after confronting innumerable invasions and assaults on her geography, history, and intellect, India has remained relatively firm on her ideas, culture, and heritage for centuries. And to date, the Indian natives mostly remain in this core value system, which involves having faith in the interconnectedness of the entire creation. That is India's ultimate version of spirituality. The people who are carrying this legacy forward are called the Hindus. And the complex socio-spiritual system that evolved on this soil is called the 'Hindu System', which includes all human endeavors, excellence and virtuosity, universal wellbeing, and further evolution of individuals and societies. If there is one nation and one race on earth that is the embodiment of pluralism, it is India. The Hindus of India and the global population of India-inspired cultural value system (Hindus, Buddhists, etc., all over the world) cannot and should not be expressed with the term 'Hinduism', but rather the term 'Hindu System' does justice to it.

The number of languages India speaks, the variety of food habits, clothes, festivals, and modes of worship in different parts of India are difficult to experience anywhere else. Yet India is abused by the world academics and media every day, every hour, to showcase the gutters and the slums. Many academics' full-time job is to denigrate India. A multi-billion dollar propaganda machinery is operating in India supported and nourished by anti-Hindu foreign-funded machines. This 'intelligentsia' incessantly decimates India's pluralism and diversity, misusing democratic values and freedom. It could be petrodollar, Euro, or US Dollar – the intent and purpose are the same – Communist, Christian Missionary, Islamic Fundamentalism, or Western and Chinese hegemony; each force has been extraordinarily active for decades. The past Indian Governments not only turned a blind eye to these divisive plans and activities but, in many cases, have been complicit, and the resulting impact has been devastating. We shall explore these in detail as we move along.

Of all the tragedies of the Indian society, including creating a rigid caste system out of the hugely misunderstood Jati and Varna system and destruction of learning Institutions, temples, and industries, the most devastating one was equating the 'Hindu system of sustenance' that is 'Dharma' with 'religion' by the colonists. Indians have given philosophy, a knowledge system, and action plan to salvage the world from hatred, wars, diseases, and all forms of sufferings; to provide the world with the means to efficiency and perfection for individuals and societies in the formulation of Dharma and Yoga. Dharma represents principles, whereas Yoga is the means. Much of contemporary literature, journalism, and even text on religions written by the Hindus prove that most Hindus don't even understand the profound meaning and relevance of Dharma today. Dharma has been juxtaposed and placed with the 'religions' of the world, mostly Abrahamic ones whose inherent tendency is exclusivism and have a history of horrific destruction of native cultures and causing deaths of millions through crusades and jihads. And this idea of 'religion' has been drilled into the Hindus' heads. It has been imprinted in their DNA; hence many have begun acting like the Abrahamic followers when it comes to dharmic practices, including caste discrimination. The extremely complex 'Hindu System' which has evolved for over a few millennia, was much misunderstood and misinterpreted by the unqualified colonials and other foreigners who came to India with vested interests – they imposed a Missionary and colonial term to Dharma – 'Hinduism' or 'Hindu Religion'! This is one of the biggest tragedies in the history of humankind and the mind of the conscious Hindu. Hindus today have been reduced to begging for fundamental human rights and mercy in the world of hatred and racism, where other religious groups are looking only to grow influence by increasing the numbers of followers and their territory.

At present, India faces many social problems, just like any other society. Some of these problems, such as caste, superstitious beliefs, mistreatment of women, are related to their social practices; these have to do with broken and corrupt social systems, not an unnatural state of a very ancient civilization and culture. The older a society is, the more complex the challenges are, especially if it has to go through massive disruptions due to foreign interventions. Casteism (yes, Europe had a caste system[3] and Christians also have a caste system[4]), corrupt religious leaders and practices, corrupt politicians, and many other such challenges are faced by all major nations, including India. But those who do not accept the many facets of the Hindu heritage would only point to those deficiencies to simply toss away all the great things Hindus have already given to the world and many more they are yet to offer.

Human life is multi-dimensional. Each person lives in a physical, mental, and intellectual state. It so happened that the Hindu seers added the fourth dimension – the *adhyatma*, loosely translated as the 'subject beyond the body and matter', a similar yet broader concept than 'spirituality', and the person pursuing life towards the goal is called *adhyatmic*.

According to Judith Brown, '(Jawaharlal), Nehru tried to graft the best of British institutions and values onto a country largely resistant to them… Nehru failed in his dream of creating a new India, uniting the values of East and West'.[5] Nehru is also believed to have said that he was the 'last Englishman to rule India'.[6]

It was Sri Aurobindo who foresaw a civilizational challenge over 100 years ago, and Indian leaders like Jawaharlal Nehru not only failed to understand and act on it but worked to the detriment of India. He said:

"The movements of the nineteenth century in India were European movements, they were colored with the hues of the West. Instead of seeking strength in the spirit, they adopted Europe's machinery and motives, the appeal to humanity's rights or the equality of social status and an impossible dead level which nature has always refused to allow. Mingled with these false gospels were a strain of hatred and bitterness, which showed itself in the condemnation of Brahminical priestcraft, the hostility to Hinduism, and the ignorant breaking away from the hallowed traditions of the past. What was true and eternal in that past was likened to what was false or transitory. The nation was in danger of losing its soul by an insensate surrender to European materialistic aberrations. Not in this spirit was India intended to receive the mighty opportunity which the impact of Europe gave to her. When the danger was greatest, a number of great spirits were sent to stem the tide flowing in from the West and recall her to her mission; for, if she had gone astray, the world would have gone astray with her."[7]

Nehru has been explicit that he did not have much faith in India's spiritual heritage. Raja Rao, a journalist and thinker, had an experience with Nehru who quoted this in reply to Rao's query to him about Nehru's view on India's ancient heritage:

'Why Siva and Parvati, Sri Krishna!"

Three thousand years of that and where's that got us—slavery, poverty.'

'And incomparable splendour, even today.'

'What, with twenty-two-and-a-half years of life expectancy and five pice per person per day of national income? We've had enough of Rama and Krishna. Not that I do not admire these great figures of our traditions, but there's work to be done. And not to clasp hands before idols while misery and slavery beleaguer us.'[8]

So, when a person of this worldview (atheist and socialist) occupies the highest position in the Indian government, one can imagine the outcome. Certain forces were spread in India in the name of secularism by people like Nehru. They are now trying to discredit the so-called 'Hindutva' movement. They're a hideaway opposition to any type of nationalistic movement or Hindu identity assertion, which they term as 'communalism'. A true Hindu culturally cannot be divisive and violent except for the purpose of self-defense. A Hindu, from childhood, chants or hears others chanting *'Sarve bhavantu sukhina, sarve santu nirāmayāḥ'* – meaning 'let everybody be happy and healthy'. No one can pull out even one instance of hateful invasion by Hindus from the history books. There are no examples of attempts to forced conversion by Hindus anywhere in the Hindu tradition, and there is no example of denoting other races or sects as evil or 'infidel'.

So, who are these accusers? They call themselves the 'left-liberals'. But, as we go deeper into history in this book, we will find out these so-called liberals are essentially fundamentalists of their own ideology. They're cooperating with fundamentalist religious forces, who have plans to destroy the dharmic fabric of India or Bharat, the habitat of the 'tolerant Hindus'! Their support from various international communities in the West, Middle East, and China is very well-known. They are the new incarnation of the colonists today. They work to influence the minds of people, the Indian society and affect people's relation to the land – let us call these people the **Neo-Colonists** or, in short, the ***NeoCols***. Just like parasites, bacteria, and viruses, they take over living organisms and eventually severely injure and kill the prey.

The NeoCols wanted and still want to wipe off the historical contributions by the Hindus in building every pillar of the current civilization, from mathematics and science to language and health, as well as the spiritual traditions that made Yoga the tool to evolve an individual and a society to higher levels of consciousness and living. For the NeoCols to gain a foothold and finally control the Indian social, economic, and political systems, they deliberately denigrate and ridicule anything great about the Indian civilization – by intentionally nitpicking on the aberrations and disproportionately exaggerating the facts. They have attempted to obliterate the millennia-old Indian pride, just like the British did. Why? To come to power using alternative political and social systems and keep their control in all critical spheres of society and polity, including academia and media. These persons and groups act as the Godfathers of humanity. They stifled the incredible power of India's traditions because they knew very clearly that if the age-old universal ideals were to come back, it would cost their friendship with communism dearly. They also found it convenient to shake hands with the forces inimical to the Hindus, namely the Islamists and the missionaries, to serve their mission to propagate, even if it means suicide and self-destruction!

The world's sectarian 'belief systems' called 'religions', colonialism, imperialism, racism, communism, and fascism – are all fruits of the same tree bearing fruits of exclusivity. They all have a common thread – long history of exploitation, violence, and destruction of societies and cultures to control people's lives and stay in power.

Hindus face multitudes of challenges, some of which may seem insuperable. But deep-rooted in India's Dharmic system, the Indian mind can solve them all amicably. The bare minimum requirement is to understand the utility and strength in Indian heritage by its inheritors – the leaders, the policymakers, and people at large.

NeoCols are the biggest threat to India's integrity, security, and progress. Every Indian need to know that and understand the implications and what they ought to do to avert a civilizational disaster in the making again. Alien ideologies such as communism and religious fundamentalism of 'my way or the highway' must be understood, confronted, and defeated.

Time has come that the global domination in the economy, whether by the West or China, must be understood by the policymakers, and the Government of India must act decisively with precision surgery of the threats and proper rehabilitation of the sick society, polity, industry, and economy.

Maya Angelou, the great American poet and civil rights activist, once said: "History, despite its wrenching pain, cannot be unlived; however, if faced with courage, need not be lived again."[9] Most Hindus are either ignorant or are in cowardly denial of their past, especially about Islamist onslaughts, colonialism, and communism and their impact on India. They are happy with the status quo to have a 'good' life and do not want to be bothered about the nation's past or the future from which they take everything for granted. As we get deeper into the history later, we will find that Islamic, especially Turko-Mongol barbarian invaders, slew Hindu rulers, converted, raped, killed Hindus by the millions, erected gates made of heads of slain Hindus, and sold them (the Hindus) in their slave markets. They destroyed thousands of great architectural sites, including between 20 to 60 thousand temples [10], many a time usurping these structures to build mosques or tombs over the ruins of the original structures. People are oblivious to the destruction of India's educational institutes and industries by the Islamists and colonists and their role in creating the horrific present-day state of what we know as the caste system (details will be discussed in the next book). They are unaware of the silent work of the termite called communism on the foundation of Indian society and polity. They must understand the root cause of the downtrodden society, discrimination, and poverty, whereas the Indian seers always preached harmony and peace. The muted impact of the largely discarded ideology of communism on the foundation of Indian society and polity will be exposed in this book.

Swami Vivekananda, in his famous speech in Chicago on September 11, 1893, said:

'Sectarianism, bigotry, and its horrible descendant, fanaticism, have long possessed this beautiful earth. They have filled the earth with violence, drenched it often with human blood, destroyed civilization and sent whole nations to despair. Had it not been for these horrible demons, human society would be far more advanced than it is now'.[11]

This book intends to create awareness and explore possible means to prevent sectarian movements unleashed by various foreign ideologies in India.

References

1. "Communalism in the Waiting of Indian History", People's Publishing House, Delhi 1987 (1969), p. 15–16.
2. Phelan, Matthew, "The History of 'History Is Written by the Victors' ", Slate, 26 Nov, 2019. https://slate.com/culture/2019/11/history-is-written-by-the-victors-quote-origin.html
3. Edward Alsworth Ross, "Principles of Sociology", 1920 http://www.archive.org/stream/principlesofsoci00ross?ui=embed#mode/2up

4. Fuller, C. J. (March 1976). "Kerala Christians and the Caste System". Man. New series.
5. Brown Judith M., "Nehru: a political life", Yale University Press, p. 407.
6. Wolpert, Stanley, "Nehru: A tryst with destiny", Oxford, 1997 p. 373.
7. Paranjape, Markand, Asiatic Democracy – The Penguin Sri Aurobindo Reader, Penguin Press, 1999, p. 16.
8. Rao, Raja, "The Meaning of India", Penguin Random House, India, 2020.
9. Maya Angelou, "On the Pulse of Morning", 1967.
10. Sita Ram Goel; Arun Shourie; Harsh Narain; Jay Dubashi and Ram Swarup. "Hindu Temples – What Happened to Them", (Vol I & II) Voice of India, 1990.
11. https://www.artic.edu/swami-vivekananda-and-his-1893-speech

❑

PRELUDE

Legend goes like this:

In a place near modern Ujjain, a shepherd boy attending cattle suddenly discovered a mound. He then proclaimed, “I am the judge, and I will settle all your disputes.” He was adept at settling many disputes of people far and beyond with perfect judgment. Every time he sat on that mound, he was no longer the same – he even looked different!

The then king of Ujjain came to know about it, and upon inquiring, he learned that underneath the mound was the legendary ‘Judgment seat of Vikramaditya’.[1]

They excavated the place and found a black marble throne supported by thirty-five stone angels. He ordered the throne to be placed in his palace so that he could sit on it and give the right judgments. One day, when the king was about to sit on this throne, one of the marble angels on the throne transformed into a real angel and said to the king, “Stop, do you think that you are worthy enough to sit on the judgment seat of Vikramaditya? Is your heart as innocent as that of the shepherd boy?” The king sensed that his heart was definitely not as pure and innocent as the shepherd boy. As soon as he admitted, the angels flew away, carrying the throne into the sky, forever.

The story (*Complete Works of Sister Nivedita,* Volume 3) may be fictional. Still, we can infer from this story that India had reached the pinnacle of civilizational prosperity and glory during that time where the highest degree of morality, ethics, and a justice system had evolved.[2][3]

Let us take a historic quick peek into India during the Gupta period (319 CE–543 CE),[4] the Golden Period of India. The fourth Emperor Chandragupta II also was known as Rajadhiraj Vikramaditya[5] and was the king of Ujjain from 375 CE until 415 CE.

India was a 'must visit' place on earth back in those days. Otherwise, why were travelers, pilgrims, and invaders alike attracted to her? Many globetrotters came from faraway places, defied extreme odds through deserts, mountains, oceans, and forests to reach India. We only hear of a few of them, those that made it – or reached their destiny. Others either never completed their journey alive or were simply forgotten in history.

Here is a short list of the famous foreign travelers to India:

1. Megasthenes, Greece (302 BCE)
2. Faxian, China (405 CE–411 CE)
3. Hiuen Tsang from China (630–645 CE)
4. Hui'Chao from Korea (726 CE)
5. Al Beruni from Persia (1024–1030 CE)
6. Marco Polo from Italy (1292–1294 CE)
7. Ibn Batuta from Morocco (1333–1347 CE)
8. Nicolo Conti from Italy (1420–1421 CE)
9. Afanasy Nikitin from Russia (1469–1472 CE)
10. Vasco Da Gama from Portugal (1497–99, 1502–03, 1524 CE)
11. Domingo Paes from Portugal (1520–1522 CE)

12. Captain William Hawkins led the English East India Company's first expedition to India in 1609.

Among the missed missions are:

1. Christopher Columbus Italy, 1492
2. Amerigo Vespucci Italy 1497

Faxian (Fa Xian or Fa-Hsien) was one of the most famous Chinese travelers who visited India. During the rule of Chandragupta II in 400 CE,[6] he came to India and widely traveled the country for over a decade. He first traveled to Peshawar, the western part of the country (currently in Pakistan), and far south-east, Tamralipta, a great port city in Bengal, one of the easternmost regions of Bharat.

He had noted that the majority of Hindus were rich in general, and there existed great social harmony. He did not come across any untoward incident or experience any difficulty while he was traveling through India. Even the highways were safe, and no robberies took place. There were Dharmashalas (charitable rest houses) next to the highways for travelers. There were hospitals for the poor, and free medicine and food were given to all. He had this to say about Indian society: "It might have been built not by men but by gods."[7] We will later find out how the NeoCols have given us a false narrative that during Sher Shah's time, he built the GT Road and various road services as noted above!

By then, the great towering figures such as Mahavir, Buddha, Chanakya, Charaka, Aryabhatta, Susruta, Patanjali, Nagarjun, Kalidasa, and Panini – had all completed their life's mission, leaving behind incredible impacts on the civilization. They became part of the civilizational memories like the other great ones before them – Ram, Sita, Krishna, Draupadi, Ahalya, Lopamudra, Agastya, et. al.

A new chapter began in Indian history towards the end of the 5th century CE.

The majestic Himalayas stood fast as the protector of the land, yet some people managed to invade India and capture some of its legendary riches. The Kidarite Huns, or the 'Red Huns', attacked Northwest India, especially Punjab, around 390-410 CE and took over the remnants of the Kushan Empire.[8]

Another Hun tribe called the Alchon Huns repeatedly attacked India during the Gupta Period between 480 CE and 528 CE[9], first led by Toramana and then Mihirkula. They occupied Kashmir, Afghanistan (Gandhara), and parts of Punjab. They were barbaric tribes and much cruel by nature, who destroyed many Buddhist monasteries and temples and killed thousands of monks. Mihirkula was known to be very sadistic, and he never smiled – some called him 'the Indian Nero'.[10]

The civilization needed mighty forces to defeat the Huns.

As the Gupta kings brought great prosperity to India, so did the Malwa Kingdom (present-day Madhya Pradesh). In a great battle, Alchon Hun king Toramana was defeated by Malwa king Prakashadharma and Gupta king Bhanugupta.[11][12] His son Mihirakula was defeated in 528 CE by Gupta king Narasimhagupta, and he may have been supported by Malwa king Yashodharaan.[13] But the invasions of the Huns inflicted severe damage to the great Gupta Empire and the Malwa Kingdom, and thus the economy of the entire country.

After being defeated in the Great War, Mihirkula was captured by the Gupta soldiers. In King Puru's story, we have read how he wanted to be treated by Alexander – as 'the way a king should be treated by a king', but Narasimhagupta did the exact opposite of that. Mihirkula was brought to the court of the King. A man who was a sadistic, brutal killer of thousands of people, who never smiled in his life – was made to beg for his life. Though Mihirkula was somewhat of a benevolent king for his people and King Narasimhagupta could have forgiven him, but Mihirkula's cruelties had shown no limits. He was given capital punishment. The king's mother, a kind-hearted lady observing the situation, asked her son Narasimhagupta to forgive Mihirkula and let him go.[14][15] The king could not ignore his mother's order and set him free. But the barbarian that Mihirkula was, upon being set free, recollected some of his soldiers and took many people captive before he left for Kashmir. He killed many of these captives near the river Sindhu. He then begged shelter from the Prince of Kashmir. Monsters do not always appreciate kindness, so he then kills the prince and takes over Kashmir. But destiny had it; soon after that, he died during an expedition.[16] Perhaps as a repentance for the sins of Mihirkula, his younger brother Pravarasena (530-590 CE) came to Kashmir and took over the reign of Kashmir,[17] and he is supposed to have built the city of Srinagar as the Kingdom of Kashmir.[18]

There is no trace of the Huns in India today – they became a part of the great 'Ocean of Humanity called Bharat' as stated by the great poet Rabindranath Tagore. Later, the Greeks who tried to conquer India had to return after experiencing strong resistance by the Indians.

India was a global leader in trade during the time of the Guptas.[19] Some manufacturing hubs in India were notable from those times. Paithan (Near Aurangabad, Maharashtra) was the capital of the Satavahana Kingdom. Nasik, Pataliputra, and Varanasi are among the other famous manufacturing hubs. They produced, collected, and packaged many products that were 'luxury' goods for the rest of the world. These included silk, fur and leather goods, iron products, ivory, pearl, and spices. What was otherwise a peaceful and prosperous country was not only inflicted with violent attacks by the Huns, it also suffered a severe blow on the trade resulting in a loss of revenue from these products from all over India. It is said that back in the days, India alone shared almost 30% of the global trade.[20]

In 627 CE, Chinese pilgrim and traveler Xuan Zang reportedly had a dream that convinced him to journey to India. He went to Kashmir in 631 CE[21] and later traveled throughout India. According to him: "Concerning the ordinary people, although they are naturally light-minded, yet they are upright and honorable. In money matters, they are without craft, and in administering justice, they are considerate. ... They are not deceitful or treacherous in their conduct and are faithful to their oaths and promises. In their rules of government, there is remarkable rectitude, whilst in their behavior, there is much gentleness and sweetness…."[22] He further stated that in Bharat, "Roads are safe for travel – not infested with *robbers*. The Government lets the people alone, and is popular."[23]

By then, India was known as the proverbial 'golden bird' for its wealth and prosperity. Some say that the Romans gave this epithet to India during the first century. And some suggest that it was Mahmud Ghazni, the invader, sarcastically but truthfully called Indians 'golden sparrows'. It is hard to pinpoint the original source today, by the reasons for the Romans to give such a name to India, if true, is natural. Trade of India with the rest of the world until the 10th century CE (time of the invasions) was unparalleled. It is said that Emperor Vespasian summoned the Romans not to import Indian luxury goods in exchange for precious gold and banned the usage of gold for the exchange of goods, which drained the country's economy. It appears that in those days 'India ran a large trade surplus with the Roman Empire,' and Pliny, the famous Roman historian (23CE–79 CE) wrote: "Not a year passed in which India did not take fifty million sesterces away from Rome." which "caused trade imbalance, implied a continuous drain on gold and silver coin, causing shortages of these metals in Rome".[24]

Thus Mark Twain wrote:

"This is indeed India! the land of dreams and romance, of fabulous wealth and fabulous poverty, of splendor and rags, of palaces and hovels, of famine and pestilence, of genii and giants and Aladdin lamps, of tigers and elephants, the cobra and the jungle, the country of a hundred nations and a hundred tongues, of a thousand religions and two million gods, cradle of the human race, birthplace of human speech, mother of history,

grandmother of legend, great-grandmother of tradition, whose yesterdays bear date with the mouldering antiquities of the rest of the nations — the one sole country under the sun that is endowed with an imperishable interest for alien prince and alien peasant, for lettered and ignorant, wise and fool, rich and poor, bond and free, the one land that all men desire to see, and having seen once, by even a glimpse, would not give that glimpse for the shows of all the rest of the globe combined."[25]

Italian explorers Amerigo Vespucci (1454–1512 CE), Vasco Da Gama (1460–1524 CE), and many other explorers from Europe were looking to find new wealth sources. They were the Portuguese, the Dutch, the French, and the British. Among these countries, the British were one of the world's major colonial forces during the 18th, 19th, and first part of the 20th century.

Britain lost America as its major colony in 1776 CE. They had been looking for new colonies to support the extravagant lifestyle of their aristocrats and feed their poor. The sixth Mughal king, Aurangzeb, died in 1707 CE. Eventually, the British East India Company under Robert Clive, with the support of some aristocrats of Bengal, overthrew and slew the then king (Nawab) of Bengal Siraj-Ud-Doula in 1757 CE, transformed the trading outfit of Britain, the East India Company, into a governing force. Within a few decades, they had colonized entire India.

Britain took control of not only governance but also the livelihood of Indians. They slowly established British judicial, educational, commercial, and industrial systems, replacing the indigenous ones and reducing the native Indians to 'kala aadmi' or 'black slaves' as they did with the Africans by bringing them as slaves to America in several other places.[26] Indians also were called 'bloody nigger', or 'devilish nigger' [27] by the British.

In 1857, the British saw the first major uprising by the Indians in the form of a military revolt (Sepoy Mutiny, 1857). By 1947, Britain was out of India after looting everything they could lay their hands on, leaving behind a crippled society, a ravaged economy, and a bunch of 'brown sahibs' to govern the country embodied in Pandit Jawaharlal Nehru, the first appointed Prime Minister of India. While Mountbatten was 'doing his job' the plan he had to implement was in the best interest of Britain. The partition was to ensure there is no 'all-powerful Indian Nation stretching with Iran and the Middle East as its neighbors. Partition would also mean having a foothold in the newly created weak Pakistan, which is even today clouted by the Western powers including the UK and the USA.' [28]

Churchill was a self-declared Hindu hater and Islam sympathizer because the latter was also an Abrahamic faith.[29][30] We will discuss that subject in detail later in the book. Initially, Churchill, then Opposition leader in the British Parliament, opposed the idea of independence of India, later understood the clever design and said: 'If I could achieve Dominion status for Hindustan and Pakistan, the whole country would be behind us'.[31][32]

The onset of radical Islam and neo-pan-Islamism's appearance was fueled by the British working closely with the clergies and Islamist groups. The formation of the Deoband School for the propagation of Islam in India was actively supported by the British. Several Muslim leaders, including Muhammad Zafarullah Khan, who was actually working hand in hand with the British, eventually led to the formation of the Muslim League, which sowed the seed of Muslim separatism. Finally, India got divided.[33][34]

Until the early 1800s, there was no separate institutionalized identity of India's spiritual traditions, such as the Jains, the Sikhs, and the Buddhists. First, due to the limitation of understanding Indian systems and traditions and later, to implement the division within the Hindu communities and sects, the colonists hatched a sinister plan of compartmentalizing the Hindu society and creating separate identities for these traditions. They came up with terms such as Buddhism,[35] Jainism, Sikhism,[36] and Hinduism. And then Hindus were divided into a rigid caste design[37], which later came to haunt the society. Post-independence, the NeoCols continued this relay race of dividing along religious and racial lines by concocting terms like Brahminism, Manuvad, Dalit, and other such divisive ideas.

After India's partition and independence, the Khalistani separatist movement was created with active support from the Islamist-Military state Pakistan, which cost many lives, and India almost lost the entire state of Punjab.[38][39] The state of Jammu and Kashmir initially remained independent during the partition but later officially joined India. Again, inspired by Islamist expansionism, a large part of Kashmir was infiltrated and occupied by Pakistani forces. They have long been engaged in a proxy battle in Kashmir using terrorism.

Part of the challenge for the new generation of Indians to understand India's current socio-political problems in light of the geopolitical issues is that they have been taught a history of the Hindus as a conquered meek nation. Almost a lone voice, an eminent post-independence scholar, author, and researcher Sita Ram Goel noted:

"In the process, Indian history has become a history of foreign invaders – Aryans, Iranians, Greeks, Parthians, Scythians, Kushans, Arabs, Turks, Persians, Portuguese, Dutch, French, and British – rather than a history of the greatest civilization which the world has known, and later on of Hindu heroism which fought and ultimately frustrated all foreign invaders.

It was this version of Indians history which gave a good conscience to the British imperialist while he pulverised Hindu society, plundered Hindu wealth and poured undisguised contempt on Hindu culture. It was this version of Indian history which emasculated Hindu society and emboldened the residues of Islamic imperialism to stage street riots and then walk away with precious parts of the Hindu homeland, thus consolidating an aggression which had not succeeded even though mounted again and again for more than a thousand years. It is this version of India's history which is being invoked by the fifth-columns of Islam, Christianity, and Communism, each of which looks forward to a final conquest of this country with the help of foreign finances and, if need be, foreign firearms. And it is this version of India's history which is being promoted by power-hungry politicians who woo the Muslim vote-bank while they divide Hindu society into mutually hostile camps."[40]

We will soon explore how various Islamist movements and institutions were established between the mid-1800s and early 1900s with active support from the British. Post-independence, the support came from the communists and finally from the NeoCols. A massive effort that the NeoCols have put forth to inflict injury and create holes in the collective civilizational memory by well-oiled machinery to erase these memories. A global networking web with numerous funding sources is at work in India for its missions to break apart, dominate and impose their ideologies on society and the polity.[41] To understand the current affairs in these circles, one must know the history of foreign forces in India. The following chapters will explore two non-native religious belief systems, Christianity and Islam's history, colonialism, and communism that severely impacted India.

References

1. Sister Nivedita, "Judgement Seat of Vikramaditya". https://estudantedavedanta.net/completeworks-SisterNivedita_3.pdf
2. Chandragupta II emperor of India, Britannica.
3. https://www.britannica.com/biography/Chandragupta-II
4. Singh, Upinder, "A History of Ancient and Early Medieval India – From the Stone Age to the 12th Century", Pearson Education, 2008, pp. 42–43.
5. Gupta Dynasty, Microsoft Encarta Online Encyclopedia 2009 http://encarta.msn.com

6. Sharma, Tej Ram, "Personal and Geographical Names in the Gupta Inscriptions", Concept, 1978, p. 49.
7. Sen, Tansen (2006), "The Travel Records of Chinese Pilgrims Faxian, Xuanzang, and Yijing", Education About Asia, 11 (3): pp. 24–33.
8. Fa-Hien's Views on India | Indian History, S. Geetha, History Discussion. https://www.historydiscussion.net/history-of-india/fa-hiens-views-on-india-indian-history/6515
9. Ghosh, Amalananda (1965). Taxila. CUP Archive. pp. 790–791. Abraham Eraly (2011). The First Spring: The Golden Age of India.
10. Saroja, "Kashmir Crisis: Unholy Anglo-Pak Nexus", Kalpaj Publications, 2010.
11. Ojha, N.K., "The Aulikaras of Central India: History and Inscriptions", Arun Publishing House, 2001.
12. Salomon, Richard, "New Inscriptional Evidence For The History Of The Aulikaras of Mandasor". Indo-Iranian Journal. 1989, p. 32.
13. Sagar, Krishna Chandra, Foreign influence on ancient India Unknown Binding – Import, Northern Book Center, 1992.
14. Majumdar, Ramesh Chandra, "Ancient India", Motilal Banarsidass. 1977, pp. 242–244.
15. Louis Renou; Jean Filliozat (1957). "Political history of India from the earliest times to the 7th century A.D. ", 1957, p. 176–183.
16. Majumdar, Ramesh Chandra, "Ancient India", Motilal Banarsidass. 1977, pp. 242–244.
17. Dani, Ahmad Hasan; Litvinsky, B. A., History of Civilizations of Central Asia: The crossroads of civilizations, A.D. 250 to 750. UNESCO.1996, p. 169.
18. Stein, M. A., "Kalhana's Rajatarangini: A chronicle of the kings of Kashmir". Motilal Banarsidass. 1989, pp. 439–441.

19. Gupta Empire Trade, The Indian History http://theindianhistory.org/Gupta/gupta-empire-trade.html
20. The World Economy: Volume 2: Historical Statistics, Angus Maddison, OECD Publishing, https://www.stat.berkeley.edu/~aldous/157/Papers/world_economy.pdf
21. Parthasarathi, Prasannan (2011), "Why Europe Grew Rich and Asia Did Not: Global Economic Divergence, 1600–1850", Cambridge University Press, p. 45.
22. "History through the Eyes of . . . Xuanzang: Indian Life, 7th Century AD", Randall Stephens, HistSociety. http://histsociety.blogspot.com/2010/08/history-through-eyes-of-xuanzang-indian.html
23. Thomas T. Allsen, "The Royal Hunt in Eurasian History", p. 182, University of Pennsylvania Press https://www.upenn.edu/pennpress/book/14223.html
24. John Colville's Diary Entry of 23rd February 1945.
25. "The Dollar's Long Tail" The Free Library. 2011 Al Bawaba (Middle East) Ltd. 16 Oct. 2021
26. https://www.thefreelibrary.com/The+dollar%27s+long+tail-a0275994968
27. Twain, Mark, "Following the Equator" (1897) Ch. XXXVIII http://www.gutenberg.org/files/5811/5811-h/5811-h.htm
28. Naoroji, Dadabhai, "Remembering Our leaders", Volume 6, p. 6, 1996.
29. Mitra, Dinabandhu, Neel Darpan, 1860: 1st Act, 3rd scene; 5th Act, 2nd scene (https://www.gutenberg.org/files/54027/54027-h/54027-h.htm)
30. Pachauri, S.K., Mountbatten in India and 15th August 1947, *Proceedings of the Indian History Congress;* Vol. 68, Part One (2007), pp. 889-894 (6 pages) [https://www.jstor.org/stable/44147897]
31. Bose, Mihir, "A Hatred for Hindus", History Today Volume 66 Issue 12, December 2016 https://www.historytoday.com/hatred-hindus

32. Bose, Mihir, "Why did Winston Churchill hate the Hindus and prefer the Muslims?", Quartz India, April, 4, 2017 https://qz.com/india/948392/why-did-winston-churchill-hate-the-hindus-and-prefer-the-muslims/
33. "Was Britain divided about Indian independence, 1930-47", Churchill Archive for Schools. https://www.churchillarchiveforschools.com/themes/the-themes/key-developments-in-british-and-empire-history/was-britain-divided-about-indian-independence-1930-47/the-sources/source-9
34. Frankel, Francine R., "When Nehru Looked East: Origin of India-US Suspicion and India-China Rivalry", Oxford, 2020, p.39.
35. https://drive.google.com/file/d/1OxMBfg7FQk8fYioJq9BOtJX5gCkZP9tU/view
36. Note by Sir Zafarullah Khan on Dominion Status. MSS EUR F125/135. British Library. 1940. pp. 117–150.
37. Missions: Buddhist Missions, Encyclopedia.com https://www.encyclopedia.com/environment/encyclopedias-almanacs-transcripts-and-maps/missions-buddhist-missions
38. Mandair, Arvind-Pal Singh, "Sikhism: A Guide for the Perplexed", University of Michigan, 'Sikhism is not an indigenous term but a colonial construct', 2013 p. 5.
39. Heth, Ben, "The Impact of European Colonialism on the Indian Caste System", Swansea University, 2012 https://www.e-ir.info/pdf/30280 (E-International Relations)
40. Zeeba T Hashmi, "Pakistan's involvement in the Khalistan Movement", Daily Times, 15 October, 2015 https://dailytimes.com.pk/98062/pakistans-involvement-in-the-khalistan-movement/
41. "Nurtured by Pakistan: Canada's leading think tank exposes Khalistani extremism and its Pak sponsors", Times Now

News, 10 September, 2020 https://www.timesnownews.com/india/article/nurtured-by-pakistan-canada-s-leading-think-tank-exposes-khalistani-extremism-and-its-pak-sponsors/650484

42. Goel, Sita Ram, "Heroic Hindu Resistance to Muslim Invaders – 636 AD to 1206 AD", 2009, Voice of India
43. Singh, R.S.N., "Know the Anti-Nationals", Lancer Publisher, 2021.

❑

ACKNOWLEDGEMENTS

It was an uphill task for me to write the book since this is the first one. I'm indebted to a few individuals for which I could complete the book. First of all, well-known writer and journalist Shri Uday Mahurkar encouraged me to write the book. Vedic scholar and Indologist Vamadev Shastri (Dr. David Frawley) gave me much guidance. As a historian, Dr. Saradindu Mukherji has guided me a lot. Dipanjan Biswas and Abhinava Goswami helped me in the editing process.

I'm also deeply grateful to my wife Haimanti for regular feedback and for patiently supporting me for this many months of the journey. So, thanks to all for this successful completion of the first book.

CONTENT

CHAPTER

1

MIDDLE EASTERN HISTORY AND DIFFERENT FAITHS

Was Zarathustra an Iranian, Greek or Indian Yogi?
Who are the Parsis?
What is the connection between Iran, Arya and Aryan?
Was Iran part of the Vedic civilization?
Is Shah title Hindu or Muslim?
What is Paganism and is it dead?
What are the Abrahamic religions?
Was Jesus in India?

Let us begin our journey by taking a quick look at the Middle East, the birthplace of three religions: Judaism, Christianity, and Islam. Religiously and culturally, all three have the same Biblical root, the oldest one being Judaism. These are called Abrahamic religions, after the earliest figure found in Biblical literature – Abraham (Abram). However, it is often overlooked that many different religious practices existed, and people worshiped many deities[1][2] throughout the Middle East until the advent of Islam. But even before that, we had many 'Pagan' practices and a prominent tradition called Zoroastrianism.

There was a 'prophet' named Mahābād and is believed to have lived long before Zoroaster.[1a] Others called him *Hooshang, the 'first human'.*

Indologist William Jones wrote in 1799:

"...in the opinion of the best informed Persians, who professed the faith of Hu'shang (Hooshang), distinguished from that of Zera'tusht, the first monarch of Iran and of the whole earth was Maha'ba'd, a word apparently Sanscrit, who divided the people into four orders – the religious, the military, the commercial, and the service – to which he assigned names unquestionably the same in their origin with those now applied to the four primary classes of the Hindus.

They added that He received from the creator, and promulgated among men, a sacred book in a heavenly language, to which the Muselman author gives the Arabic title of Desatir, or Regulations, but the original name of which he has not mentioned; and that fourteen Maha'ba'ds had appeared or would appear in human shapes for the government of this world: now when we know that the Hindus believe in fourteen Menu's (Manu's) or celestial personages with familiar functions, first of whom left a book on regulations, or divine ordinances, which they hold equal to the Veda, and the language of which they believe to be that of the Gods, we can hardly doubt, that the first corruption of the purest and oldest religion was the system of Indian Theology, invented by the Brahmans and prevalent in these territories, where the book of Maha'ba'd or Menu is at this hour the standard of all religious and moral duties."[3]

Zoroastrianism

Zoroastrianism is one of the oldest traditions, which has barely managed to survive the onslaughts of time and conquests, besides India's Vedic traditions, especially in the Middle East. Zoroastrianism is named after the founder Zoroaster or Zarathustra. He is known as Zartosht or Zardosht in Middle

Persian, Zarhust in Parthian, and Zartosht in modern Persian. These sun-worshipping people inhabited mainly today's Iran, which was also called Persia, an exonym. Many followers of this tradition in Iran had to flee the country during the Islamic invasions, and some took refuge in western India, especially in Gujarat and Maharashtra.[4] With time they have become an integral part of the Indian culture and are known as 'Parsis' (meaning the people of Persia) today.

Are you familiar with characters such as Jayadratha and Yudhishthira from Mahabharata? Does Zarathrustra sound like a familiar name such as Jayatustha, Jayashtita or Jayashtira or even Japastjitah? It feels like an echo of the past!

How it all Began – The Story

At the age of thirty, one day, Zarathustra planned to perform the *'haoma'* ceremony. (Avestan *haoma* is similar to Vedic soma, both words derived from the Proto-Indo-Iranian word *'sauma'*,[5] which is akin to Vedic 'homa', the sacrificial ceremony). He went to fetch the water from the sacred river *Daiti*. After taking a dip in the river, while coming out of the water he had a vision of *'Vohu Manah'* (meaning Good Mind or Good Thought or Good Purpose). After this, *Vohu Manah* guided him to the six *Amesha Spentas,* great immortal divine beings emanating from the Supreme Being – *Ahura Mazda.*

He shared this incident of the vision and experience with many but was not much appreciated by people because they did not believe this, as his revelations challenged their local traditions. His cousin Maidhyoimana gladly accepted his ideas and became his follower. But after twelve years of hard work in this mission to convince people, not much changed. Then he left his home and arrived in a new country which was ruled over by King Vistaspa (Vishtaspa). One day Zarathustra was debating with the local religious scholars about creation and the creator, and the king and queen witnessed it. The king was so impressed with Zarathustra that he embraced his philosophy. Once, the king's favorite horse had major health issues and was miraculously healed by Zarathustra, making the king very happy. Later the king made Zarathustra's teachings an official 'religion' of the kingdom.[6]

According to some, Zarathustra was a Kashmiri Brahmin yogi.[7][8]

The river *Daiti* is located in Kashmir, which is called the 'land of the Rsis/Rishis' (sages). According to Prof. Dr. Philip G. Kreyenbroek, Professor and Director of Iranian Studies at Georg-August University of Göttingen (1996–2017), the 'new country' mentioned above where he was preaching was none other than the Balkan or Greece. [9] During the Christian missions in the early days of Christianity, the so-called 'Paganism' was destroyed along with all their cultures everywhere. Perhaps that's why there is no trace of Zoroastrianism left in Europe. However, the Zoroastrian culture flourished in Persia until the advent of Islam in the 6th and 7th centuries.

Some historians date the origin of Zoroastrianism to as early as the 2nd Millennium BCE. Others suggest Zarathustra's lifetime to be around the 6th century BCE.[10] While another group asserts that he may have lived around the 10th century BCE and reformed and reorganized the age-old Indo-Iranian (perhaps Vedic) traditions and formulated which later was called Zoroastrianism by the West.[11]

It is generally accepted that after Zarathustra's death, the Achaemenid Empire or the First Persian Empire became the home of his teachings around 675 BCE.[12] Later it spread across many parts of the Middle East. During its peak, the Achaemenid Empire covered a vast area from the Balkans (Greece) and Eastern Europe to the Middle East.

Zoroastrians call their tradition *Mazdayasna* where *Ahura Mazda* is the creator-God and the most revered deity. *Ahura* means Lord, and *Mazda* means wisdom. *Yasna* means worship or devotion. Thus, *Mazdayasna* means 'devotion to Lord

Mazda' – the essence of the Zoroastrian religion.[13] *Zend Avesta* is the main Scripture, written in the old Avestan language, akin to Vedic Sanskrit in grammar, lexicon, and even vocabulary, as we will learn soon.

A concept called *'Amesha Spenta'* is presented in the Avesta, referring to the seven great 'immortal' divine entities emanating from *Ahura Mazda*. A similar idea is present in Hindu iconography, where the Sun is riding a chariot harnessed by seven horses, representing the seven colors of light. There are several variations of the term, such as *'Ameshaspand'* (eternal spand or vibration), *'Mahraspand'* (similar to maha-spand or great vibration), and *'Amahraspand'* (amar-spand immortal vibration?). *Spand* is vibration in Sanskrit and could be related to the idea of *'spandan'* (the state of vibration) during the creation of the physical universe according to Hindu cosmology. Hindu cosmology suggests that the universe was created via vibration and the primordial sound of *Aum*.

In the expression of *Amesha Spenta*, similar to *amesha* it is *hamesha* in Persian, which means always or forever, or immortal. Spenta represents seven G*athas* as the revelations of Zarathustra, which means furthering, strengthening, bounteous, and holy.[14]

Each of the seven *Amesha Spenta* described in *Gathas* is meant for moral qualities each follower of their tradition is supposed to follow, including good thoughts, words, and deeds; each individual is expected to imbibe in oneself the qualities of an Amesha Spenta.

In the Vedic tradition, among the seven *'hotars'* present during the worship or *homa* (oblation and offering in the fire), the presiding priest is called *hotṛ*. In the *Rigveda:*

तवाग्ने होत्रं तव पोत्रमृत्वियं तव नेष्ट्रं त्वमग्निदृतायतः ।
तव प्रशास्त्रं त्वमध्वरीयसि ब्रह्मा चासि गृहपतिश्च नो दमे ॥२॥

"Thine is the Herald's task and Cleanser's duly timed; Leader art thou, and Kindler for the pious man. Thou art Director, thou the ministering Priest: thou art the Brahman, Lord, and Master in our home." — *Rigveda 2.1.2*

Based on the hymn above, there are seven priests: *hotṛ, potṛ, neṣṭṛ, agnīdh, prashāstṛ* (meaning the *maitrāvaruna*), and *adhvaryu*.

Below is a list of the seven *hotars* mentioned in the Avesta:

Gathic name	Approximate meaning
Spəṇta Mainyu	Holy/Creative Spirit/Mentality
Vohu Manah	[Good] Purpose
Asa[Vahista]	[Best] Truth / Righteousness
Xšaθra [Vairya]	[Desirable] Dominion
[*Spanta] Armaiti*	[Holy] Devotion
Haurvatāt	Wholeness
Amərətāt	Immortality

Similar to the Vedic cosmological ideas such as manifest and manifest destiny, these seven divine beings in the Avesta are the foremost seven primordial beings before the creation, and they officiated the entire creation.

In practice, the *Amesha Spenta* represents qualities and moral practices to be strived by human beings to emulate their spirit. It is also a similar concept, such as the 108 or 100 names of *dev* and *devi* in Hindu spiritual practices, where each name represents a unique quality that devotees praise and try to emulate. Thus, Spentas are to be achieved in one's life through good thoughts and deeds and assimilate the qualities.

Persian and Avestan history is like amber preserving prehistoric life and elements in fossil form, preserving much of the civilizational information found in the language (ancient Persian and Avestan), architecture, and inscriptions.

From the similarities of language (Avesta and Sanskrit), rituals, and spiritual practices, it is clear that Zoroastrianism has origins in the Vedic traditions, especially connected to Kashmir. *Gatha* is the Avestan term for seventeen Avestan hymns. Like the Vedic hymns, they are arranged in five different *'chhandas'* (as in the Vedas) or meters, which collected Zarathustra's revelations and teachings as *Zenda* or *Zend*. Also, in Sanskrit, *gatha* means story, often singing the praise of a person while telling the story.

Some more examples of Sanskrit and Avestan connections:[15]

English	Sanskrit	Avestan
Army	séna	haena
Chant	stotra	zaothra
Community Person	aryamán	airyaman
Cosmic Order	rta	arstat/arta
Divine	deva	deva
Demon	rákshas	rakshas
Gold	hiranya	zaranya
Immortality	amaratta	amaretat
Lord	ásura	ahura
Priest	hótar	zaotar
Sacrificial offering	yajñá	yasna
Sacred Drink	sóma	haoma
Sovereignty	ksatra	khshathra
Thirst	trsna	trsna

A Sanskrit term for water *'apa'* is *Āb* (plural *Ābān*) in the Middle Persian-language. In the Avestan language, it was apas or 'the waters'. An ancient cosmological divine entity in Iran, *Anahita* (the full original form is *Arədvī Sūrā Anāhitā*), is the deity of "the Waters" and also associated with fertility, healing, and wisdom. In Sanskrit, the name 'Ārdrāvī śūrā anāhitā' (आर्द्रावी शू रा अनाहिता) means "of the waters, mighty, and immaculate". Similar to Sarasvatī, Anāhitā nurtures crops and herds, representing a divine river. The spiritual hymn text called Yasht described the river as: "great in bigness as all these waters which flow forth upon the earth" (Yasht 5.3), [16] very similar to the river Sarasvatī.

According to William Jones, there were Hindu rulers in Iran, and their language (Persian) was heavily influenced by Sanskrit. Was he talking about a greater Vedic civilization of a forgotten era?

He wrote:

"Thus has it been proved by clear evidence and plain reasoning that a powerful monarchy was established in Iran long before the Assyrians, or Firdausi, government; that it was in truth a Hindu monarchy, (p. 92) ... long before the Tartars and Arabs had rushed from their deserts, and returned to that very country, from which in all probability they originally proceeded, and which the Hindus had abandoned in an earlier age, with positive commands from their legislators to revisit it no more."[17]

On the origin of the Persian language, he wrote:

"Having twice read the works of Firdausi with great attention, since I applied myself to the study of old Indian literature, I can assure you with confidence that hundreds of Parsi nouns are pure Sanscrit, with no other change than such as may be observed in the numerous bhashas, or vernacular dialects, of India; that very many Persian imperatives are the roots of Sanscrit verbs and that even the moods and tenses of the Persian verb substantive, which is the model of all the rest, are deducible from the Sanscrit by an easy and clear analogy: we may hence conclude that the Parsi was derived, like the various Indian dialects, from the language of the Brahmans; and I must add, that in the pure Persian I find no trace of any Arabian tongue,..."[18]

Arya, Aryan, Iran, Persia

Nations have their native names (endonym) and names given to them by other nations or conquerors (exonym). Bharat was the name of what is now called India as it was called so by the Greeks, and later, it was adopted by the rest of the western world. Similarly, Iran was called Persia. The first Persian Empire known in history around the 5th century BCE was the Achaemenid Empire, and the emperor was Cyrus II. The Greeks addressed the Emperor with the title Pérsēs, Persikḗ or Persís.[19] Most likely, the origin of the emperor and his subjects were called Pārsa in the Persian language. The Pars tribe gave its name to the region where they lived (the modern-day Fars or Pars province). In Latin, the name for the whole empire was Persia, while the Iranians called their nation Iran or Iranshahr. Their language was called Persian, which later became Farsi, being very prominent in the Indian subcontinent. Farsi was brought to India mostly by the invaders.[20]

The term *airyānąm* (different from Vedic deity Āryaman) is found in Avesta, and Iranians have called themselves Arya since the time of Zarathustra. The name of the country thus became Iran at some point in history. They are also called 'Arians' as 'Arian', which is distinctly different from the Caucasian idea of Aryan (discredited Aryan Invasion Theory). The word Arya is present in the Vedas, the Ramayana and Mahabharata, and other ancient literature. In Vedic Sanskrit tradition, Arya stands for noble, nobility, and distinguished. Two examples from the Rig Veda (the oldest of the Vedas):

मूर्धा दिवो नाभिरग्निः पृथिव्या अथाभवदरती रोदस्योः।
तं त्वा देवासोऽजनयन्त देवं वैश्वानर ज्योतिरिदार्याय॥

mūrdhā divo nābhir agniḥ pṛthivyā athābhavad aratī rodasyoḥ |
taṃ tvā devāso 'janayanta devaṃ vaiśvānara jyotir id āryāya ||

-Rig Ved 01.059.02

Meaning: The forehead of the sky, earth's center, Agni became the messenger of earth and heaven. Vaisvanara, the deities produced thee, devata, to be a light unto the Arya.

प्राग्नये तवसे भरध्वं गिरं दिवो अरतये पृथिव्याः।
यो विश्वेषाममृतानामुपस्थे वैश्वानरो वावृधे जागृवद्भिः॥

prāgnaye tavase bharadhvaṃ giraṃ divo arataye pṛthivyāḥ |
yo viśveṣām amṛtānām upasthe vaiśvānaro vāvṛdhe jāgṛvadbhiḥ ||

-Rig Ved 07.005.01

Meaning: Bring forth your song of praise to mighty Agni, the speedy messenger of earth and heaven, Vaisvanara, who, with those who wake, hath waxen great in the lap of all the immortal devatas.

The word 'Aryan' was probably used first about 2400 years ago during the reign of the third Achaemenid king, Darius I. The inscription at Naqsh-e Rostam, near Persepolis in Iran, reads: "I am a Persian, the son of a Persian, an Aryan, of Aryan family". [21] In this case, Arya refers to a family of nobility.

Since the age of Zoroaster and especially during the Sassanid empire, Iranian people have called their country (endonym) variously Arya (Aryana), Iran, Iranzamin, Aryaman, and Iranshahr. Iran or Aryana is synonymous with the 'Land of Aryans'.[22] In the old Iranian language, aryānām waiǰah means 'expanse of the Aryans' or simply Iranians. In new Persian, the term is *eran-wez,*[23] which represents the homeland of the original Iranian people. The extended version of Avesta called *Vendidad* mentions "sixteen perfect lands". Again, it is similar to the Indian *Aryavarta*. Some also think that the original land of Airyanem Vaejah was related to Kashmir ("lies west of Kālakavana, east of Adarsana, south of the Himalayas and north of the Vindhyas," which includes a good part of modern-day Kashmir as well).[24][25][26] If this were to be true, then no doubt Zarathursta has a strong connection with Kashmir.

In Iran, an ancient metropolis called Naqsh-e Rostam has a group of ancient rock reliefs from the Achaemenid dynasty (550–330 BCE). There are four large tombs, including of King Darius I, which has many inscriptions. These inscriptions interestingly connect to both, the term 'Arya' or 'Aryan' and Sanskrit language.

One inscription reads: "I am Darius the great king, king of kings, king of countries containing all kinds of men, king in this great earth far and wide, son of Hystaspes, an Achaemenian, a Persian, son of a Persian, an Aryan, having Aryan lineage".

The most interesting one is: *"Adam darayavaush khshaya-thiya vazraka khshayathiya/khshayathi-yanam... parsa parsahya puthra ariya ariyachithra"*, which translates to: "I, Darius, the great king, the king of kings... a Parsi, the son of a Parsi, an Aryan of Aryan family."[27][28]

Though the Persians resisted Islamic conquest, also known as the 'Arab Invasion of Iran' for many years, they finally succumbed in 651 CE as the Sasanian Empire fell.

Many years later, in 1935, with a decree of the head of the country, Reza Shah Pahlavi, the Shah of Iran, officially renamed the country permanently from Persia to the Islamic Republic of Iran.

William Jones is credited with introducing the Aryan Invasion Theory (1786) based on his linguistic studies, which suggested that the so-called Indians came from outside into this region, especially to India. However, if we carefully read his writings (Works of William Jones), it is clear that he was convinced that India influenced many nations, including Iran. About 75 years later, people like Max Mueller used the idea of 'Aryan Race'. Today most scholars have discarded this imaginary theory and support the 'Out of India' or 'Indigenous Aryans theory' (IAT) idea, which means that Indian people went to major parts of the world bringing their ancient culture and science, mathematics, etc.

Shah Title

Shah in Persian meant 'very large'. The title Shah (shansha or shahenshah) for the emperor was started by the founder of the Sasanian Empire, Ardashir I, around 224 CE (in Persian — šāhān šāh ī ērān; now the extinct Parthian language in Iran used šāhān šāh ī aryān for the same).

People with the last name Shah in India are found mostly in Gujarat and Rajasthan states, especially among the Jains. In Gujarati, 'Shah' means merchant and may have been derived from the Sanskrit Sadhu (honest), which is Sahu in Prakrit. Sahu, Sahai, and Saha are also similar last names. The Parsis do not use Shah in India as a last name. Though some Indian Muslim rulers used the term Shah as their last name, it was to denote an 'emperor' as in Sher Shah, Bahadur Shah, etc. Today, it is rare to find Muslims using this last name.

Bedouin and Arab

Zarathustra's followers were also called the Behdin (probably related to the nomadic Bedouin tribes). The term is still in use, and it means 'the good religion'.[29] Beh was Weh in Persian, which means good, Din is related to Persian den or Daena, meaning religion. In Zoroastrian tradition, Behdin represents an individual who is formally 'baptized' into religion in a ceremony called Navjote.

The term Bedouin becomes 'badawi' in Arabic, meaning 'desert dwellers'. There were other names as well for the Bedouins. The Assyrians used *Arabaa*, and the current day Bedouins still call themselves *Arabaa*. This confirms that the land of Arabia did not have any great settlement, such as a city or state; they were nomadic. Islamic scriptures such as the Quran referred to them as A'rab. One of the many meanings by which the Collins dictionary refers to an 'Arab' is a street urchin or a 'waif left to roam the streets',[30] wherein waif means an orphan, outcast, and a stray being. According to Nehada Barkat, one meaning of the word 'Arab' is 'nomad'. She also suggested that the Arabic language originated from Nabataean Aramaic script and has been used since the 4th century CE.[31]

Vedic and Zoroastrian Influence on Abrahamic Faiths

Is it possible that Indian, Vedic, or Hindu ideas in an untraceable past trickled into the world of 'religions' as some would say 'Hinduism is the Mother of all religions'? Or, for that matter,

Vedic culture was prevalent in the greater part of the planet, and what today we see as various 'religions' are residues of that hazy past of human history?

There are some similarities between the Vedic traditions and Abrahamic religions. *Avatar* and Messiah, Mukti and Salvation, *paap* and *punya* – sin and righteousness – are a few examples. These are misappropriations and took different forms and meanings from original ideas. The idea of karma got a new form in 'sin' of three kinds. Canon Cheyne, a scholar on the *Old Testament*, noted: "The threefold division of sins into those of thought, word and deed in Ps. XVII 3-5 is thoroughly Zarathustrian. ...A knowledge of this great religion is necessary to the full equipment of an Old Testament scholar,...had it (Judaism) not come into contact with Zarathustrianism, Israel would historically speaking have struggled in vain to satisfy its greatest religious aspirations."[32] The later-day Zoroastrians evolved these ideas along with the angel, reward and punishment and resurrection, etc. It is also very much possible that the idea of hell and heaven, reward and punishment, entered India via the Abrahamic traditions in reverse feedback into Indian traditions.

Now let's head towards ancient Babylon.

The Mesopotamian kingdom known as the Chaldean Kingdom was also called the New Babylonian kingdom, founded by Nabopolassar in 626 BCE and had its own 'Babylonian Religion'.[33]

King Nebuchadnezzar was considered the best king of that dynasty, and Babylonia had its golden period during his reign. In 587 BCE, he conquered and destroyed the Jewish holy center Jerusalem, and many Jewish people were exiled in Babylon. About a century later, the famous Persian Emperor Cyrus conquered Babylonia and liberated the Jews around 550 BCE. While Cyrus came from Zoroastrian tradition, he did not impose it on the Jews. He encouraged them to follow their own religion and helped them rebuild the Temple of Solomon in Jerusalem. However, the Zoroastrian thoughts impacted the

Jewish beliefs and practices. Mary Boyce noted, "This was only one of the many liberal acts recorded of Cyrus, but it was of a particular moment for the religious history of mankind; for the Jews entertained warm feelings thereafter for the Persians, and this made them more receptive to Zarathushtrian influence."[34] As a matter of fact, the Jewish people even regarded Cyrus as a messiah despite the fact that he was not a Jew. According to Isaiah 42:1-4, the Jewish god *Yahweh* is quoted as "Cyrus will bring forth justice to the nations,...He will not fail...till he has established justice in the earth."

An ancient text called the *Book of Tobit* is part of the Catholic and Orthodox biblical scriptures estimated to be written in 100 CE. The idea of 'Seven Spirits' – Amesha Spentas – is present in the *Book of Tobit*.[35]

It appears that the Abrahamic traditions picked Indian ideas via Zoroastrian practices, which influenced Judaism, especially during the rule of Cyrus after their 'Babylonian exile'. The non-Vedic concepts such as heaven and hell, Messiah, Judgment Day, etc., have been key features of all three Abrahamic religions, philosophies, and theologies, including Second Temple Judaism, Gnosticism, Greek philosophy, Christianity, and Islam as modified Zoroastrian concepts. In Hebrew, the title *HaMashiac*h means "The Anointed One", which is believed to be the origin of the trimmed term *Messiah*. We can feel an echo of *Amesha Spenta or hamesha here.*

A side note: the letter S is the letter H in Avestan and other languages. Later, when we try to find the source of the word Hindu, we will visit the term Sindhu which became Hindu as spoken by the people in those days. We have a great example of the Sindh (currently in Pakistan), which is reminiscent of the era when the land was called Sindh following the Sindhu (Indus) river. Typically it is said that the people on the eastern side of the river Sindhu were called Hindus. But the existence of Sindh makes an exception. The people are called Sindhi, and the language is also Sindhi. A great example is the Yasna

Haptaŋhāiti, which in the Avestan language means "Worship in Seven Chapters", comprising a set of seven hymns.

Paganism

Every civilization and people all across the globe developed nature worship and animistic traditions. Animism entails that various entities in Nature – land, water, air, mountains, rivers, forests, etc., and plants and animals – all possess a unique spiritual essence. And thus develop a culture and tradition to respect, revere, and protect the same. Like all other parts of the world, the Middle East and Europe had many different societies following various religious practices and deities (including the Graeco-Roman religions and deities) until the Christian forces confronted them with Islam in the Middle East. The Western theologians called their practices 'polytheism' or the belief in many 'gods' as opposed to Abrahamic 'monotheism' or the belief in 'one and only God'.

Initially, the term pagan was used for the 'religion of peasantry',[36] but later, it developed to include 'unknown' religious practices or groups other than Christianity as they worshipped 'false gods' – including 'Hinduism'.

Paganism was used as a derogatory term against any 'non-believers' of the Abrahamic belief systems. Christians also used other words for them, such as Hellene, a gentile (originally used by the Israelites to refer to non-Israelites as gentile may also mean a non-Jewish person), and heathen. According to the *Merriam-Webster dictionary*, the word heathen means a) an unconverted member of a people or nation who does not acknowledge the God of the Bible and b) an uncivilized or irreligious person.

Centuries of persecutions by Christian missionaries and Islamic iconoclasts could not completely decimate the so-called Pagans. Today there is a movement to revive these old cultures called Neo-Paganism, and these traditions have muc in common such as worship of Nature. Initially, the practices of what was later called 'Hinduism' were also looked down upon as Paganism and sometimes was called Satanism.[37]

Today, all native, indigenous, and ethnic cultures and traditions fall under the term Pagan, which is no longer derogatory. However, the term heathen is still used as a derogatory term,[38] mostly by Christians.

Abrahamic Religions and Belief Systems

In the Middle East, the story was vividly set in the Garden of Eden. In this story of the creation of humanity, God creates the first two humans, Adam and Eve. Every one of the Middle Eastern Abrahamic faiths believes that humanity descended from this pair of original man and woman. They fell from grace when they ate the forbidden apple. This is referred to as the 'original sin', which is a foundational theory of Christianity – but not as much in Judaism and Islam. In the original *Hebrew Bible*, also called *Tanakh*, humans were created in the Image of God. Later, Adam and Eve's story came into being – Adam was created from dust, and Eve from Adam's rib to be his companion. Upon committing the original sin – they had to obey God forever as repentance of their sin. Every devout Christian is expected to believe this theory.

According to the Hebrew Bible, in the *Book of Genesis*, the most famous Bible story in the early time was the Great Flood. The story is very well known. Noah was supposed to be the last patriarch before the 'great flood'. He is credited with the 'first tiller of the soil' and the 'inventor of wine'. Biblical patriarchs refer to the twenty male ancestor figures starting from Adam to Abraham. The Genesis story describes that 'God' ordered Noah to build a huge ship or 'ark' to save his family, mankind, and the land animals during the upcoming great flood. This ship was called 'Noah's Ark'. Although no evidence of the said Ark could be found, and the Bible does not give any geologic information, all people of Abrahamic faith firmly believe in this story.

The story goes like this:

The ninth-generation patriarch after the great flood and Noah was Terah. They had three sons, namely Abram, Nahor, and Haran. Abram was married to Sarai, but she was not able to conceive. When Abram was 99 years of age, an oracle came that Abram's new name was to be Abraham, which according to the Bible meant "a father of many nations",[39] and Sarai was to be known as Sarah, who was now 90. Further instructions came from God that he was going to give a son to them. Abraham laughed at it since they were too old to have any child. But after that oracle, a miracle happened. Suddenly Abraham and Sarah were surrounded by a large number of people in the household. And appeared Ishmael or Isaack, who was 13 and circumcised.

According to some other sources, due to her inability to bear children, Sarah had asked their Egyptian housemaid Hagar to bear the child with Abraham.

According to the biblical literature (Genesis 1–11), God created the world in 6 or 7 days between 6984 BCE[40] and 3616 BCE[41], and God also created the first human couple, Adam and Eve, supernaturally. All human beings are born from this couple. Most Christians reject the Darwinian evolutionary theories, such as any connection of the human race with primates or proto-humans. Based on the scriptures, the timing of this creation of the 'first couple' was around 6000 years ago.[42]

Adam, in Hebrew, means Earth. 'I am' is *Aham* in Sanskrit, in Zend *Azem,* and in old Persian, it's *Adam*. It seems that there might be some Vedic connections. But the 'first woman' Eve is more mysterious. In Hebrew, she is *Chavah*, which means 'to breathe', or *Chayah* means 'to live or to give life'. Eve came much later via other European languages. Eve was created from the rib of Adam, and her name is linked to 'evil', blaming her for the evil brought into the world due to the sin of eating from the Tree of Knowledge. The medieval commentator Rashi (Rabbi Solomon ben Isaac, 1040 CE–1106 CE) explained: The name Chavah is a derivative of the Hebrew word Chayah, meaning 'living one".[43] Chavah embodies not only the essence of life itself, but it also has the creative ability to grant that life. They were born according to the Abrahamic faiths around 5000 years ago. However, according to modern science, modern humans are at least 300,000 years old; [44] therefore, the Biblical creation theory is not aligned with genetics and genealogy.

One Albert Perry was an African-American who lived in South Carolina. His Y chromosome has revealed the contemporary genealogical and genetic assertion of modern human's age around 200,000 years. Michael Hammer, a geneticist at the University of Arizona in Tucson, based on Albert Perry's 'unusual Y chromosome' conducted some experiments. Hammer's research revealed that his subject Albert Perry did not descend from the genetic Adam as noted in Genesis. His distinct Y chromosome pointed at separation in his male lineage from all the other males about 338,000 years ago.[45]

On the other hand, Constantine Samuel Rafinesque, an American biologist, suggested the possible connection with Indian law giver Manu and Noah:

"Our Noah is thus NH (pr NOE) which the Jews since pronounced NUH, and even Mnuh! Exactly the same name as given him by the Hindus! And all meaning repose, with many collateral meanings, lawgiver, collecting people, assembly humanity...The laws of M'nu are preserved by the Hindus: to him is also ascribed the substance of the Vedas, and the whole Mosaic history till near his own death. But the Hindus have many M'nus; Adam and Seth were such, by the names of Adimo and Satya."[46]

Judaism

Abraham or Ibrahim became the common patriarchal ancestor of all three belief systems developed in the Middle East, namely Judaism, Christianity, and Islam. Abraham was the founding father of the oldest one among these Abrahamic beliefs; he had great abridging power between the Jewish people (the Hebrews) and their storm and warrior God YHWH or Yahweh, the God of Israel. In ancient times the sun was used as a symbol to identify YHWH. According to J. Glen Taylor:

"...many of these same Israelites considered the sun a symbol or icon of Israel's God, Yahweh. Yet early Israel was far more developed than we might guess from this; the same evidence that points to Yahweh as having a consort (or wife) and being symbolized by the sun, also points to an understanding of Yahweh as an abstract, non-anthropomorphic deity. In short, many early Israelites combined various notions about Yahweh that we would call 'orthodox' and 'pagan'. " [47]

Scholar Mark Smith also supported the above: "Indeed it has been alleged that in the final decades of the Judean Monarchy, the temple solar cult reflected other foreign influence or the indigenous cult of the sun deity."[48] Was the influence from Zoroastrianism or some Vedic remnants?

In Christianity, Abraham is the 'role model', and in Islam, the order of the prophets starts with him. Descendants of Ishmael are called Ishmaelites, and the Arab Muslims relate to him as their original ancestor. Abraham's son was Isaac, and Isaac's son Jacob was also called Israel; the Israelites connect their ancestry to him.

Between 930 BCE and 720 BCE, the current land of Israel had two distinct parts – the Kingdom of Israel (or Samaria), also called 'House of Joseph' and Judah to the south. As noted earlier, there were many deities throughout the region – sometimes, the male deity was with a female consort. For example, *Yahweh* was the deity of Israel, and goddess *Asherah* in Judah was the head of a pantheon of many other deities.

The Jewish people kept their traditions alive for centuries through many struggles. However, the name Judaism came much later. Jewish people call themselves Yehudah (Yehudi) or Judah, which collectively represents their religious practices, history, legal system, and culture.

There were three distinct Jewish sects.

The Pharisees were the largest sect in Israel and the most popular sect in Judea. They developed the rabbinic movement, which eventually became the mainstream tradition of Judaism.

The Sadducees mostly belonged to the priestly, aristocratic, and military classes. They believed in free will, rejected oral law, and focused on temple worship.

The Essenes were a minor sect who abstained from temple worship in Jerusalem and believed in an afterlife. They were voluntarily living in poverty and performing various purification rituals. Many Essenes avoided marriage and led a celibate life. Jesus Christ, Thomas, John, and all other apostles are believed to have been born in this sect,[49] connecting to the Vedic heritage.[50]

According to Canadian historian Steve Mason, "the Essenes were a *'long-established association of celibate males'* located in Judaea and living in towns and villages west of the Dead Sea. Mason references nevertheless apparently married Essenes, in contradiction to the claims regarding their monastic virtues and dislike of women, which, Mason suggests, is simply Josephus fibbing, but who knows? They *actively* (my assertion) recruited male volunteers."[51] This sounds similar to practices of the Buddhist tradition in monasteries.

And, there were the Zealots, not as significant, also called the Fourth Philosophy (modern term zealot may have roots to this sect). Their philosophy was that a Zealot must act on behalf of God, who would punish their nation otherwise. Zealots vowed to root out all offenders.

While there are several streams of Judaism in practice today, the common belief is that God revealed the commandments to Moses on Mount Sinai, which later became the *Torah*.

There are about 15 million Jews worldwide, and Israel, their homeland, has over 7 million people.[52] *Sabbath* or resting holiday for the Jews is Saturday.

A footnote about God's praise in Abrahamic religions has become most prominent in Islam: "may blessing of Allah and peace be upon him (Prophet)" and 'Allah Hu' is most likely a borrowed term from the Jewish tradition. *'Hakodesh baruch hu'*, which means "The Holy One, Blessed Be He (God)".[53]

There are many theories about the presence of Jewish people in India. Based on Aristotle's statement, some even suggest that Jewish people are originally from India. Others suggest that the so-called 'lost tribe of the Jewish people' was in India.[54]

According to the Israeli scholar of early Christianity and Judaism David Flusser, the story of Abraham has many similarities with some stories from the Upanishads. According to him: "One can easily discover parallels in the Upanishads to the Abraham legend".[55]

Hananya Goldman (Head Librarian, Sami Shamoon College of Engineering) has discussed this Vedic and Zoroastrian influcnce and connection with Judaism.[56] According to him: "...Tamil loan words in the Bible, and the idea that Hebrew speakers were exposed to Tamil and Sanskrit words by the sea-trade with southern Arabia in the tenth to sixth centuries BCE. He cites David Fusser's belief in the possible Indian origins of the Midrash, explaining Abraham's discovery of divine unity, reflecting fundamental teaching of the Upanishads. This transmission may have occurred in the 2nd century BCE, coinciding with possibly new Jewish religious thinking, emphasized by the Essenes. Whatever other transmission situations occurred, one clear way was the Seleucid Empire that had originally encompassed Afghanistan, with access to India."

He also noted:

"The story of a contest between three of Darius' bodyguards on what is the world's most powerful force is of Persian origin (truth is the giveaway as this was one of the chief virtues of Zarathustra religion). The story, nevertheless, is similar to a rabbinic story on Abraham's discovery of the truth of YHWH

Given this, Goodman holds that Abraham's discovery of YHWH has its basis in a Persian story confirming thereby an earlier statement in these papers that the Bible is a Near Eastern/ Middle Eastern compilation. A similar Indian story concludes the comparisons (pages 35-36). He also points to Philo's knowledge of Indian philosophy, as well as Megasthenes, whom Philo writes on, with references to the Brahmins as philosophers. Such philosophers, Goodman believes, were connected to the Essenes. D. Dennis Hudson points to the similarities of ideas on body pollution and the rituals to deal with such pollution between Hinduism and Judaism.... The Qumran text The Manuel of Discipline instructs its readers that they are of the light or the darkness, providing choice, but this again is from Zarathustra."[57]

Christianity

We all know that Western history has been written mostly by European historians, many of whom were devout followers of the Christian belief system. The history we read about Alexander is based on textual materials as evidence which were written much later than his supposed lifetime. Peter Green noted that most primary sources are lost, and the historicity of Alexander is established based on a few surviving inscriptions and fragments.[58] While the lives of Abrahamic prophets such as Moses, Abraham, or Isaack are passed as historical events, *Ramayana* and *Mahabharata* of the Hindus are treated as 'mythological' texts. Many devout but ignorant Hindus also call these great epics 'mythologies' without knowing that 'mythology' means an 'imaginary story' or 'false story' and is a Christian-colonial invention. 'Myth' has a relationship with the Sanskrit word *mithya* – which means false. So, basically, 'mythology' really denotes false or made-up stories.

During the early biblical time, Judah was called Judea or Judaea, located in mountainous southern Palestine. During the 1st century CE, Judea was the center of many cultures.

According to Flavius Josephus, an ancient historian, there were many different Judaic sects, including Pharisees, Sadducees, Essenes, and Zealots.[59] There was much fighting among these sects, giving rise to several religious leaders such as Yohanan ben Zakkai, Hanina ben Dosa, etc. This finally led to unrest in the region in the 1st century BCE. The religious text *Mishnah* was first compiled into the written form of the 'Oral Torah'. The Jewish concept of a *Messiah* or a 'future anointed leader' who would recover the lost glories of the 'Israelite kingdom of God' from the foreign rulers was introduced.

This is how the history of Christianity has been presented to the world:

During this time, there was the biblical *"Kingdom of the House of David"* where the predicted *Messiah* would descend from the *Abrahamic* (Jews and Christian faiths) lineage.

Joseph was the descendent of King David in Judea, and he was the fiancé of Mary, a native Jewish of Nazareth in Judea. One night she was fast asleep, and suddenly Angel Gabriel appeared in her dream. Heavenly lights surrounded Gabriel. He told Mary, almost whispering to her – "you are going to be a mother soon and will give birth to a son. His name will be Jesus, who is the 'Son of God'". Mary shared this experience with Joseph in the morning, who did not believe it. That night, Gabriel appeared to Joseph, told him the same thing, and said that 'he (Jesus) would save people from their sins.'

The Roman emperor was conducting a census in that region, and Mary and Joseph were ordered to go to a town called Bethlehem, which was their hometown. Pregnant Mary could not walk that far, so she was put on a donkey. After their long journey to Bethlehem, they could not find a place to stay. Joseph sensed that Mary might give birth at any time. Finally, the inn's owner suggested they stay at their stable where there were many animals. Shortly after, Mary gave birth to a beautiful child. Gabriel appeared again – but this time to the shepherds who were tending to their cattle. Gabriel told them about the birth of Jesus, who would be their 'Savior and *Messiah*'.

The Three Wise Men who 'traveled from afar eastern country' saw a bright star shining on the sky. They felt that the 'Messiah King' was born, and then they followed the star and reached the stable in Bethlehem where Jesus was born. They knelt and worshipped the 'Savior.' So, the Savior Jesus Christ became the Lord of the Christians, and Christianity spread to the whole world afterward.

Although a majority of the scholars and historians support the existence of a historical Jesus, the conclusions are mostly based on biblical literature, especially the Gospels. There are some who doubt if he existed at all,[60][61] while others dispute his actual timeline.[62]

Christianity, a post-Judeo Abrahamic belief system, is based on the life, death, and teachings of Jesus Christ. His coming as a Messiah was prophesized in the Hebrew Bible, which is commonly called the *Old Testament*, and later was chronicled in the modern Bible, called the *New Testament*. According to some historians, Jesus was a Galilean Jew.[63]

The primary theological proposition is that Jesus was born in Nazareth, a city in the Northern District of Israel, and he was a first-century Jewish preacher and religious leader. He was also referred to be a Rabbi, a Jewish priest, and a teacher. He is said to have debated with contemporary Jewish scholars on God and religious practices. He also showed miracles and performed healings. Christians believe he is the incarnation of and a Messiah (the Christ) as prophesied in the Old Testament.

He was arrested while preaching, as he was becoming increasingly popular and had gathered many followers. He was first tried by the Jewish authorities (Sanhedrin Court), who then handed him over to the Roman authorities.[64] The trial of Christ was presided over by the governor of Judea province Pontius Pilate, who served under the Roman emperor Tiberius.

This event's timing is still debated and is said to have happened between 26/27 CE and 36/37 CE. The trial gave the verdict – crucifixion of Jesus. He was just 33 years old, as calculated in biblical literature.[65] Crucifixion was a common practice for executing criminals with death sentences in those days. Christians believe that he had risen from the dead after the crucifixion, also called anastasis and resurrection. His followers formed the early Church of Christ.

The basic common belief among various sects of Christianity has been these:

Jesus is the 'son of God'. He ministered and preached a new creed; he was then persecuted and was put to death on the cross. He sacrificed his life on behalf of all the 'sinners' to save them, and later rose from the dead for the salvation of mankind. His life and messages, which were delivered orally called 'parables', were later recorded in the Gospels (good news) as the Bible (New Testament) compiled by his followers Matthew, Mark, Luke, and John (called saints by the Christians). The New Testament was created on the foundation of the Jewish Old Testament.

The practices of Judaism between the construction of the 'Second Temple' in Jerusalem in 516 BCE and its destruction in 70 CE by the Romans is called the sect of 'Second Temple of Judaism'. The Hebrew Bible, synagogue, and the rise of Christianity happened during this period. The idea of 'Christianity' came into existence in the first century CE in the Roman province of Judea as the 'Second Temple of Judaic sect'.[66]

The initial followers of Christ, called apostles, took Christianity to various parts of the world, including Europe, Anatolia, and the Levant, which covered roughly today's Syria, Lebanon, Jordan, Israel, Palestine, and a large part of Turkey; also, parts of Greece and Mesopotamia, Egypt and Ethiopia.

The fall of Jerusalem in 70 CE ended temple-based Judaism,[67] and Christianity found a distinct identity and prominence. The Christians had major conflicts with the

Jewish leaders, and Christianity was, in a way, forbidden. Finally, Emperor Constantine decriminalized and legitimized Christianity in his Roman Empire by the Edict of Milan in 313 CE. He later convened 'Nicaea's Council' in 325 CE to bring about consensus among various sects through an assembly representing all Christendom, and by 380 CE Christianity became the Roman Empire's state religion and started to spread rapidly.

Jesus in India Story

Some people still question if Jesus is a historical figure or not. Perhaps today it is an irrelevant subject to discuss, but one can take up a more exciting topic – Jesus's India connection. First of all, what is the 'lost years' of Jesus? In various Christian literature and Gospels, details of the life of Jesus are noted, except the years between the age of 12 through 29. Luke 2: 52 says, "And Jesus increased in wisdom and stature, and in favour with God and man".[68]

As noted earlier, Jesus was most likely born in the sect called Essene. The founder of the Theosophical Society, Helena Blavatsky, suggested that Jesus had secretly been trained by the Essenes [69] and later left the community and became a traveling healer.[70]

The 2nd President of the Theosophical Society, Annie Besant, suggested that Jesus was sent "to be trained in an Essene community" and went to an "Essene monastery" in Egypt, where he was "fully instructed in the secret teachings which were the real fount of life among the Essenes".[71]

Many suggest that Jesus spent 18 years of his 'hidden years' in India. According to them, he was exposed to Hindu-Buddhist training and studied and practiced Indian spiritual methods under the tutelage of Hindu/Buddhist Gurus; then went back and preached his teachings, which are supposed to be Indian/Vedic. Some suggest that he stayed in Varanasi, Puri, etc., – spiritual locations.

Was it at all possible for Jesus to visit India from Judea, thousands of miles away? Yes, via the Silk Route, it was very much possible.

Some say that Jesus survived the crucifixion and moved to the Himalayan region in India again. There is a tomb called Rozabal Tomb in Srinagar, Kashmir; according to legends, it is said to be of Jesus. [72]

Some others are more specific, saying that he was initiated by the Nath Sampraday (sect) suggested by Bijoy Krishna Goswami, a Guru from the same sect.

The whole discussion started while the entire world was shocked after a book was published by the Russian journalist and adventurer Nicolas Notovich in 1894. His book *La vie inconnue de Jesus Christ* (Life of Saint Issa) claimed that during his missing 18 years, he went to India and Tibet and studied under Hindu and Buddhist spiritual masters.[73]

He apparently traveled to a monastery in Tibet and saw scrolls documenting the visit of Saint Issa or Jesus. A large number of scholars, especially Christians, disputed and rejected the assertions of Nicolas as a hoax and unfounded.

An American preacher and scholar, Levi H. Dowling, wrote a book called *The Aquarian Gospel of Jesus the Christ* (1908). In this book, he claimed that during the missing years, Jesus traveled across India, Tibet, Persia, Assyria, Greece, and Egypt.[74]

Nicholas Roerich, a Russian theosophist, and philosopher, also visited Lhasa in 1925 and supported the revelations of Nicolas Notovich.[75]

Later two Indian monks visited the same monastery and were said to have verified the veracity of Nicolas, including Swami Trigunatitananda and Swami Abhedadananda of the Ramakrishna Order. Several Hindu Gurus also eulogized Jesus, including the founder of ISKCON, Srila Prabhupad, Yuketswar Giri, Puri Shankaracharya, and Paramhansa Yogananda.

The BBC also produced a documentary called 'Jesus in India' that explored these possibilities and suggested that Jesus was a Buddhist Monk.

Recently several books have been published including, *Jesus Lived in India: His Unknown Life Before and After the Crucifixion* (2001) by Holger Kersten, *The Fifth Gospel: New Evidence from the Tibetan, Sanskrit, Arabic, Persian, and Urdu Sources About the Historical Life of Jesus Christ After the Crucifixion* (2006), and *The Venus Blueprint: Uncovering the Ancient Science of Sacred Spaces*, a book by Richard Merrick, 2012. These books also talk about the life of Jesus in India and Tibet, but the evidence is still scanty.

What are the implications of these assertions that Jesus was a Yogi or, for that matter, lived in India and learned under the tutelage of Hindu Gurus? First of all, it may give a free license to Christian missionaries to convert innocent Indian people suggesting Jesus be one of their own Gurus or even Avataras. While India has innumerable sages and saints with great spiritual heights, Jesus would become one of many hundreds of such saints. Why should Hindus need another one who, if the assertions are true, is a foreign student first and an ascetic later? However, many Hindus pay respect to Jesus, at least during Christian holidays.

On the other hand, some Christian evangelists also play tricks to convert in large numbers by using Hindu symbolisms such as wearing saffron, using Aum on the cross, etc. That is not any reflection of 'Yogi' or a 'Buddhist' monk Jesus!

When we look at the current state of Christianity, it is clear that it is a rudimentary form of Hindu Bhakti Yoga. Some relic of Puja is there. Ash Wednesday, Baptism, etc., may have similarities with Vedic rituals. Some Gospel teachings are very close to Buddhist ideas as well. But that's all; it is exclusivism embedded in the system. There is not much for a Hindu to celebrate about it, and most Christians disagree with this idea. Some groups promote Isha-ism or Yogi-Isha form of

Jesus, give Jesus-like attributes to Saint Thomas (like a twin), but eventually, they practice some form of Christianity. They do not allow any other Hindu deities to accompany Jesus. Even if they do, like the 'Divine Life Society' which was founded by Paramhansa Yogananda, the exhibition of Jesus gets prominence over the faces of Yogic or Hindu tradition Gurus. So, the only thing remains that for those who want to promote this idea tha Jesus was a Yogi, it is fair to ask them to put efforts to reset reform their ideas and practices significantly to reflect true Yoga tradition. If Jesus was a Yogi, learned it from India, i would be ironic that many Christian leaders and churches are against yoga!

Christianity, being one of the most prominent 'religions' played a very distinct role in many societies. After mos forms of Paganism were destroyed, in the wild wild West where Darwinism had taken a deep foothold, which preached 'survival of the fittest', in the absence of a viable form of ethica system, Christianity became a veritable window of opportunit for people for morality, ethics, social empowerment. Even th African slaves found some solace in Christianity though the were transplanted from their native lands and cultures. With al the imperfections and problems the church has created, it ha also done much good for the people, especially the ones devoi of any deep spiritual heritage apart from the Pagans. One ca imagine if there was no Christianity and no churches in the Wes what would fill the vacuum of destroyed native cultures. One c the reasons the destructive ideology of communism came int being is due to lack of a higher spirit in the pure materialisti philosophies and ideologies. But how about India? India, th land of Dharma, does not need to learn morality and ethics fro others and, of course, yoga and divinity.

Before the British came to India, none of the Hindu sec such as Shaivites, Vaishnavas, Shaktas, Naths, or Tantriks we identified separately from the Hindu system. No distinct form identity for Jainism, Buddhism, or Sikhism was made – becau they are part of the great Yogic heritage where key concepts such as Yoga, Dharma, Karma, Reincarnation, etc. are intertwined. Buddha was born in the Hindu tradition and even preached from the Upanishads. The 10th Sikh Guru Govind Singh formed Khalsa to fight Islamic aggression. The same was the case with the Nath sampradaya. But in recent days, some NeoCols are pushing more for this separation, sometimes giving the feeling that the Sikhs are closer to Islam or their interactions with Islam were very close; hence they are separate from the Hindus.[76]

But the mystery remains – if Jesus started preaching at the age of 30 after his return to his homeland, then he had just three years to propagate his ideas to the world, and yet he became so popular and famous would in itself be a miracle!

References

a. "Dabestan-e Madaheb (School of religious doctrines) -- parts 3-13". www.avesta.org

. Hoyland, Robert G. (2002), "Arabia and the Arabs: From the Bronze Age to the Coming of Islam", Routledge,

. Teixidor, Javier (2015), "The Pagan God: Popular Religion in the Greco-Roman Near East", Princeton University Press,

. "Works of William Jones", London Printed For G. G. And J. Robinson, Pater-Noster-Row And R. H. Evans (Successor To Mr. Edwards), No, 26, Pall-Mall. Mdccxcix (1799). (p. 88)

. Parsi Communities, Early History, Encyclopaedia Iranica. Iranicaonline.org (2008-07-20).

. Houben, Jan E. M. "The Soma-Haoma problem", Electronic Journal of Vedic Studies. 9/1a. May 4, 2003.

. Shabazi, A. Shapur, "Goštāsp", Encyclopedia Iranica, Vol. 11, Costa Mesa: University of California Press, 2003, pp. 171–176.

Himanshu Bhatt, "Zoroastrianism and Hinduism", Hindupedia http://www.hindupedia.com/en/Zoroastrianism_and_Hinduism#cite_note-6

8. P.N.K. Bamzai, "Koshur Samachar, Kashmiri Pandits and Saraswat Brahmins", Kashmiri Blogs https://www.kashmirblogs.wordpress.com/2009/02/09/kashmiri-pandits-and-saraswat-brahmins/amp/
9. Interview with Prof. Dr. Philip G. Kreyenbroek, Professor and Director of Iranian Studies Georg-August University of Göttingen (1996-2017); https://en.mehrnews.com/news/140392/Zarathustra-s-message-seems-to-have-impressed-Greeks-Prof-Kreyenbroek
10. Foltz, Richard, "Religions of Iran: From Prehistory to the Present", London: Oneworld publications, p. 10–18.
11. O'Brien, Patrick Karl editor. "Atlas of World History", Concise Edition. 2002, p. 45.
12. "BISOTUN iii. Darius's Inscriptions". Encyclopaedia Iranica.
13. Amesha Spenta, Britannica. https://www.britannica.com/topic/amesha-spenta
14. Ibid
15. "The Relationship of Vedic Sanskrit and Avestan" (Old Persian), San Jose State University. https://www.sjsu.edu/faculty/watkins/sanskritavestan.htm
16. Lommel, Herman. "Anahita-Sarasvati". Asiatica: Festschrift Friedrich Weller Zum 65. Geburtstag. Leipzig: Otto Harrassowitz. 1954, pp. 405–413.
17. Henry George Liddell; Robert Scott (eds.). "Lexicon of the Greek Language". Oxford. 1882, p. 1205.
18. "Works of William Jones", London Printed For G. G. And J. Robinson, Pater-Noster-Row And R. H. Evans (Successor To Mr. Edwards), No, 26, Pall-Mall. Mdccxcix (1799). p. 83
19. Ibid. p. 80-81.
20. Bennett, Clinton; Ramsey, Charles M. "South Asian Sufis: Devotion, Deviation, and Destiny". A&C Black. 2012. p. 18.

21. J. P. Mallory, "In Search of the Indo-Europeans", 1991. p. 125.
22. Inscription of Darius the Great at Naqsh-e- Rostam https://www.cais-soas.com/CAIS/Languages/aryan/inscription_of_dariush_grt_rstm.htm
23. ERAN-WEZ, Encyclopedia Iranica. https://iranicaonline.org/articles/eran-wez/
24. Baudhayana Dharmasutra, 1.1.2.10
25. Agarwal, Vishal "Is there Vedic evidence for the Indo-Aryan Immigration to India" Dialogue July-September, 2006, Volume 8 No. 1. http://www.asthabharati.org/Dia_Jul%2006/Vish.htm
26. "Vasistha Dharma Sutra" (oldest sutras ca. 500–300 BCE) I.8-9 and 12-13.
27. "I Am Darius", Parsiana. https://www.parsiana.com/current-issue/articles.aspx?id=YtNsF2zng3o=&issue=73
28. "Naqshe Rustam", Heritage Institute http://www.heritageinstitute.com/zoroastrianism/naqsherustam/page2.htm
29. "Behdin The Good Religion", Iranica Online http://www.iranicaonline.org/articles/behdin-the-good-religion
30. "Arab", Collins Dictionary. https://www.collinsdictionary.com/us/dictionary/english/arab
31. Nehed Barakat, "Let's banish the term 'Arab world'. What does it mean anyway?", The Guardian, 18 April, 2018 https://www.theguardian.com/commentisfree/2018/apr/18/lets-banish-the-term-arab-world-what-does-it-mean-anyway
32. Cheyne, Canon, "The Origin and Religious Contents of the Psalter", Kegan Paul, Trench, Trubner & Co., 1891.
33. Dougherty, Raymond Philip, "Nabonidus and Belshazzar: A Study of the Closing Events of the Neo-Babylonian Empire". Wipf and Stock Publishers, 2008

34. Mary Boyce, "Zoroastrians — Their Religious Beliefs and practices", Psychology Press, 2001.
35. Fitzmyer, Joseph A., "Tobit", Commentaries on early Jewish literature. de Gruyter, 2003, p. 50, 55–57.
36. Owen Davies. "Paganism: A Very Short Introduction". Oxford University Press. 2011, pp. 1–2.
37. KB Napier, Hinduism — "Satanic to its core", Christian Doctrine, 25 September, 2015 http://www.christiandoctrine.com/christian-doctrine/anti-god-beliefs/1513-hinduism-satanic-to-its-core.
38. Hobson, Archie, "The Oxford Dictionary of Difficult Words". Oxford University Press. 2004. p. 203.
39. Genesis 17:5 Parallel Verses, Bibleref https://www.bibleref.com/Genesis/17/Genesis-17-5.html
40. Hales, William, "New Analysis of Chronology and Geography, History and Prophecy", vol. 1, 1830, p. 210–215.
41. "Young's Analytical Concordance of the Holy Bible", 1879, 8th Edition, 1939—entry under 'Creation', quoting William Hales New Analysis of Chronology and Geography, History and Prophecy, Vol. 1, 1830, p. 210.
42. Creationism, PBS https://www.pbs.org/faithandreason/intro/evolucrea-frame.html
43. Sara Esther Crispe, "Chavah: Mother of All Life", https://www.chabad.org/theJewishWoman/article_cdo/aid/335943/jewish/Chavah-Mother-of-All-Life.htm
44. Neubauer, Simon; Hublin, Jean-Jacques; Gunz, Philipp (2018-01-01). "The evolution of modern human brain shape". Science Advances. 4 (1)
45. Colin Barras, "The father of all men is 340,000 years old", New Scientist, 6 March 2013 https://www.newscientist.com/article/dn23240-the-father-of-all-men-is-340000-years-old/
46. Rafinesque, C. S. (Constantine Samuel), "The American Nations: or, Outlines of Their General History, Ancient

and Modern" (2 volumes; Philadelphia: C. S. Rafinesque, 1836) Oxford University. p. 104.

47. Was Yahweh Worshiped as the Sun? Israel's God was abstract, but he may also have had a consort, J. Glen Taylor, Biblical Archaeology Review 20:3, May/June 1994.
48. "The Near Eastern Background of Solar Language for Yahweh", Mark S. Smith, Journal of Biblical Literature, Vol. 109, No. 1 (Spring, 1990), pp. 29-39 , Published By: The Society of Biblical Literature
49. Wilkin, Stanley, "Bit by bit uncovering reality: Jesus, Essenes, the True Teacher". University of London, 2019.
50. Dahan Levi, Fida Hassnain, "The Fifth Gospel: New Evidence from the Tibetan, Sanskrit, Arabic, Persian, and Urdu Sources About the Historical Life of Jesus Christ After the Crucifixion", (2006)
51. Wilkin, Stanley, "Bit by bit uncovering reality: Jesus, Essenes, the True Teacher". University of London 2019.
52. www.jewishdatabank.org
53. "JPS Dictionary of Jewish Words", by Joyce Eisenberg and Ellen Scolnic, (Philadelphia, 2001). (The Joys of Hebrew, by Lewis Glinert (New York, 1992)
54. Weil, Shalva. (1991) "Beyond the Sambatyon: the Myth of the Ten Lost Tribes", Tel-Aviv: Beth Hatefutsoth, the Nahum Goldman Museum of the Jewish Diaspora.
55. David Flusser, "Judaism and the origins of Christianity", Magnes Press, Hebrew University. 1988, p. 650.
56. Goodman, Hananya, "Between Jerusalem and Benares: Comparative Studies in Judaism and Hinduism", State University of New York Press 1994, p. 35- 40.
57. Ibid.
58. Green, Peter, "Alexander of Macedon", P. xxii–xxviii; Penguin Books, 1974.

59. Whealey, Alice, "Josephus on Jesus: The Testimonium Flavianum Controversy from Late Antiquity to Modern Times",. Peter Lang Publishing, 2003.

60. Lataster, Raphael, "There was no Jesus, there is no God: A Scholarly Examination of the Scientific, Historical, and Philosophical Evidence & Arguments for Monotheism", 2013.

61. Waugh, Rob, 'Jesus never actually existed at all' controversial French author argues, Metro, 12 April 2017 https://metro.co.uk/2017/04/12/jesus-never-actually-existed-at-all-controversial-french-author-argues-6571007/

62. Alvar Ellegård, "The Myth of Jesus 1992; Jesus: One Hundred Years Before Christ". A Study in Creative Mythology, 1999.

63. Vermes, Geza (1981). "Jesus the Jew: A Historian's Reading of the Gospels". Philadelphia: First Fortress.

64. "Who killed Jesus?", BBC, 18 September, 2009. https://www.bbc.co.uk/religion/religions/christianity/history/whokilledjesus_1.shtml

65. Humphreys, Colin J.; Waddington, W. G. (March 1985). "The Date of the Crucifixion". Journal of the American Scientific Affiliation. p.37.

    "From twelve to thirty then are "Jesus' silent years," which does not denote he was silent. It means the Evangelists remain silent about what Jesus did." ... "Only Luke reports that Jesus was in the Temple when he was twelve, apparently for his bar mitzvah (2:42), and that he began his public ministry when he was "about thirty years of age" (3:23). What did Jesus do from age twelve to thirty?"

66. Based on regnal years of Darius I, brought down in Richard Parker & Waldo Dubberstein's Babylonian Chronology 626 B.C.–A.D. 75, Brown University Press: Providence 1956, p. 30.

57. Khan Academy, “Judaism, an introduction” https://www.khanacademy.org/humanities/ap-art-history/introduction-cultures-religions-apah/judaism-apah/a/judaism-an-introduction

58. James H. Charlesworth, “The Historical Jesus: An Essential Guide”, 2008

59. H. P. Blavatsky, “*Isis Unveiled: A Mastery-Key to the Mysteries of Ancient and Modern Science and Theology*” (2 vols, Pasadena, CA: Theosophical University Press, 1976 [1877]), p. 133.

70. ibid p. 144

71. Annie Besant, “*Esoteric Christianity: Or the Lesser Mysteries*" (5th edn.; Adyar, Madras, India: Theosophical Publishing House, 1901-1950), p. 97.

72. Miller, Sam, “Tourists flock to ‘Jesus’s tomb’ in Kashmir”, BBC News, 27 March 2010. http://news.bbc.co.uk/2/hi/programmes/from_our_own_correspondent/8587838.stm]

73. Gandhi, Virchand R. (translator), “The Unknown Life of Jesus Christ”. Kessinger Publishing. 2003.

74. Dowling, Levi H., “The Aquarian Gospel of Jesus the Christ” (original publication 1908) pp.12 and 65.

75. Roerich, Nicholas, “Altai-Himalaya” by Nicholas Roerich www.roerich.org

76. Khan, Hammad, “Adityanath’s Nath Yogi tradition has a history of pluralism, close ties to Islam”, Scroll.in, 7 October, 2018.

https://scroll.in/article/896582/a-far-cry-from-adityanaths-hindutva-the-nath-yogi-tradition-has-a-history-of-religious-pluralism

❑

CHAPTER

2

CHRISTIANITY IN INDIA

When did Christianity first come to India ?
What is a Crusade?
How many people died worldwide due to Crusades?
What is Inquisition?
Who started the Goa Inquisition and how many people died?
Who was Xavier? A saint or a monster?
What are the key impacts of Christian missionary activities in India?
What is the difference between belief system, religion and dharma?
How many countries have Christian majority?
What is the difference between God, Ishwara and Bhagwan?
Was Alexander and Akbar really 'Great'?
Was 'Mother' Teresa truly a saint?

Early Period

When did Christianity arrive in India? Who brought it? The presence of Christianity in India is almost as old as the religion is. It is said that during the lifetime of Jesus, 12 people firmly believed in him called the Apostles or the first followers. One of them was Judas Thomas. A born Jew who doubted the resurrection of Jesus as told in the New Testament but was later convinced that he was the Savior (hence he was called the 'doubting Thomas'). Though the evidence is scanty, legend says that he, along with some traders, arrived in northwest India – his dreamland. After spending some time there due to a threat of invasion by a local king, he got on a boat going to India's Malabar Coast. He ended up landing in the southern coastal area of India, namely Kerala, in a flourishing port called Muziris, along with a Jewish trader where many other Jews lived, in 50 or 52 CE. The mentioned place corresponds to modern-day North Paravur and Kodungalloor. Thomas started preaching the 'gospel' (teachings of Jesus) to the locals. He founded several churches, including Malankara Church along both sides of the Periyar River, where he preached the gospel throughout the Malabar Coast. The Oriental Orthodox autocephalous (independent) or the Malankara Orthodox Syrian Church, also known as the Indian Orthodox Church, is the descendant of Thomas' original Malankara Church. This is believed to be the beginning of Christianity in India.[1]

Christians regard Thomas as the 'patron saint' of Indian Christians. In 72 CE, he is said to have been murdered by the locals in Myalpur, near Madras, and was declared a 'martyr.'[2] This incident suggests his conflict with locals, perhaps for conversion activities! The Saint Thomas Cathedral Basilica, also known as the San Thome Church, is located on St. Thomas Mount near Mylapore, Chennai, Tamil Nadu. This church was built on St. Thomas's tomb, which was first built in the 16th century by the Portuguese and rebuilt in the 19th century.

The 'Saint Thomas Christians' believe that he established seven church communities in Kerala. Thomas baptized around thirty-two Brahmin families, out of which eight were given the highest status. The Pakalomattom family was given the privilege of Thomas for providing new *metrans* or bishops for the Church. The membership of these old families has been an indicator of Kerala's social status in the Christian community.

These communities were reserved in their evangelica conversion activities due to caste barriers. They kept stric genealogical preservation, refused to accept any 'lower caste Hindus into their fold, and practiced endogamy.

It is a widespread belief that the locals, mostly Hindus an some Jews, welcomed Thomas. But the story was not as clea since there were conflicts with the locals in the very beginning The evidence of this matter is found in the *Hymns of Sain Ephrem* edited by Lamy *(Ephr. Hymni et Sermones, IV),* whic shows clear hostile thoughts expressed by the early Christians

"It was to a land of dark people he was sent, to clothe then by Baptism in white robes. His grateful dawn dispelled India' painful darkness. It was his mission to espouse India to the One Begotten. …Thomas works miracles in India, and at Edess Thomas is destined to baptize peoples perverse and steeped i darkness, and that in the land of India."[3]

Ephrem was a Syriac Christian deacon and a fourth-centur theologian, and a hymnographer in Syriac language.

A common historical misconception is that India's earlies Christians were the 'Syrian Christians' of Kerala who cam to India from Syria after the Arab Invasion. In Kerala, th 'Syrian Christians' were known as Nasrani (Nazarenes; Gree *Nazoreans*), meaning from the birthplace of Jesus of Nazareth.[4

The name 'Syrian Christian' was given by the Dutc colonists in India when they encountered these 'Old Christians, and they called the contemporary Portuguese converts 'Latin Christians. According to George Joseph, the term 'Syrian' ha nothing to do with the country, Syria.[5] It was probably derive from 'Cyrus', the king of Persia (559–529 BCE), who conquere Babylon and permitted the Jewish people to return to Judea thus emancipating them. Early Jewish converts to Christianit believed that Cyrus resembled Jesus, and Syrian or Cyrian wa synonymous with the term Christian.

Many of these converted Christians in India retained Hind practices such as *annaprasan* (first staple food to the child ritual bath after funeral activities, and eating vegetarian while mourning, and even keeping the sacred thread. They solemnized marriage ceremonies like the Hindus along with their caste lines.[6] However, to not lose social status and identity as Christians, the practice of endogamous marriages became prevalent. Like the Hindu caste structure, they established 'Church sabhas' to deploy controlling activities such as disgrace, ostracism, and ex-communication. They ensured to keep distinct social identities through dress, etiquette, food, and professions.

Many think that the Yoga tradition of India influenced Jesus. And many believe that the lost years of his life were his time spent in India with the Yogis.[7] Another theory is that after he was crucified, some of his disciples took him down from the cross and healed his wounds with medicine. He was kept hidden for a while. After a few days, he reappeared, which Christians call the 'resurrection.' He then moved to secret places so as not to be captured again. There is a grave of Christ in Kashmir, which many believe was his final hiding and resting place.[8] Others think that he was never crucified.[9]

A relationship of the fundamental teachings of Christianity with Dharmic ideas such as Ahimsa (non -violence)[10] is attributed to Christ. And there are observations that the teachings of Jesus are nothing but of Buddha.[11]

But the political powers in Rome and Constantinople used Christianity to control people and to accumulate power. Later we will see that the Communists used similar tactics to brainwash and manipulate people into Marxist-Leninist doctrines – the goal of which is no different than a religious conquest.

Crusades

According to the *Merriam-Webster dictionary*, crusade means "any of the military expeditions undertaken by Christian powers in the 11th, 12th, and 13th centuries to win the Holy Land from the Muslims". The Crusades were initiated or supported by the Latin Church, or the Western Catholic rites, originating in Europe. The language used was Latin for liturgical rites also known as Roman Rites. Different Christian institutions also used the crusades to destroy paganism and the so-called heresy or blasphemy. But above all, initially, these wars were among various rival Roman Catholic forces for political and territorial gains. While there are debates among the historian about the proper understanding of the term crusade – it wa primarily used for 'armed pilgrimages to Jerusalem'[12] Catholic campaigns to recover the Christian holy land with the promise of spiritual gains. Others used the term for any and every 'holy war' initiated by the Catholic forces.

After the advent of Muhammad and Islam, the first people to have a direct ideological and territorial conflict during their conquests were the Christian powers. There were numerou 'holy wars' which the Christians called Crusades, and th Muslims called it Jihad. These wars went on for many year between 1095 CE and 1271 CE. Many such battles wer initiated to gain control over Jerusalem' – which is claimed a the 'holy city' or 'holy land' by all three Abrahamic faiths.

Pope Urban II declared the First Crusade in 1095 CE, when he gained Byzantine Emperor Alexios I's military support to fight the Turks. He also received tremendous support from al across Europe. Thousands joined the bandwagon, partly wit the promise of the 'mass assertion into heaven at Jerusalem' an many economic benefits. While the Christian powers controlle much of the territories gained through the crusades, it came t an end in 1291 when Acre city in Israel was under siege and fe to the Mamluk Sultanate that established itself as an Islami caliphate.

Crusades continued for many more centuries, but large scale battles did not occur anymore after the fall of Acre Between the 14th–16th century, some of the crusades wer against the Protestant Christians. Finally, in 1699 CE, th crusades virtually ended with the war of the 'Holy League

Pope Innocent XI organized an alliance of various Papal States - the Roman Empire, the Polish Lithuanian Commonwealth, and the Venetian Republic for the Holy League in 1684 to fight the Islamic Ottoman Empire. Later, the Tsardom of Russia also joined the league. After the Ottoman Empire's defeat, a treaty was signed to end the war, after which the Ottomans lost much control of central parts of Europe.

The death toll of various crusades is estimated anywhere between one million to nine million between 1095 CE and 1291 CE, the height of the Crusades. John Hittel suggested, *"In the two centuries of this warfare, one million persons had been slain, but it had not been without some compensations."* [13]

John M. Robertson noted, *"It is a reasonable calculation that in the two centuries from the first Crusade to the fall of Acre (1291), there had perished, in the attempts to recover and hold the Holy Land, nine millions of human beings, at least half of them Christians. Misery and chronic pestilence had slain most; but the mere carnage had been stupendous."* [14]

Inquisitions

Apart from the Crusades, another common fateful and sad history in Christianity is 'Inquisition' or 'Holy Inquisition.' It was conducted by a group of institutions within the Catholic Church. It meant 'a period of prolonged and intensive questioning or investigation', simply put, a set of inquiries to combat heresy. Heresy in Christianity denotes the denial or doubt of a Christian faith's core doctrine defined by one or more Christian churches. In reality, the Inquisition was about suspicion, inquiry, prosecution, and punishment.[15] Inquisition was introduced in France in the 12th century to control dissent from the Church, and by the 1500s, it became much more pervasive, first in the European countries during the 'Spanish Inquisition' and then throughout the world, and especially due to Protestant and Catholic conflicts. Christian forces in Spain and Portugal played a major role and administered courts for

Inquisition in their Empires in Europe, the Americas, and Asia. Peruvian and Mexican Inquisitions destroyed native cultures and traditions by enforcing Christianity on the native population and the Jewish and Muslim converts.[16][17] The usual punishment for any suspicion of heresy or blasphemy was imprisonment for a few years to life. But more cruel punishments were meted out to millions with death sentences. The ultimate punishment of heresy was execution, done via death by burning or 'burning at stake' after the convicted ones were handed over to the authorities, such as a magistrate. The local laws were then applied, which had severe punishments for 'religious crimes' like sacrilege.[18][19]

The churches used to form tribunals for the accused and suspects, deployed torture, extracted forced confessions. Inevitably, they would be convicted for heresy. The Jesuits and the Portuguese Colonies' administrators would go to the colonies on behalf of the 'Holy Office of Catholic Church' to enforce the Inquisitions.[20]

In 1494, Pope Alexander VI bestowed the title of "Catholic King and Queen" on Ferdinand and Isabella of Spain to recognize their service and defense of the Catholic faith in Spain; hence they became Catholic Monarchs.

Throughout Europe, Jews and 'pagans' were converted to Christianity. For example, in 1497, a large number of Jews and others were forced to accept Christianity.[21]

But under the rule of the new Portuguese emperor Ferdinand, the inquisitions were enacted against these converts, especially the 'Crypto-Jews' to be spied upon and or investigated for heresy. There was a massacre of these so-called 'conversos' or 'Marranos' in Lisbon in 1506.[22] The Portuguese Inquisition held its first *auto-da-fé*, or the burning of a heretic by the Spanish Inquisition in 1540, a forced 'public penance' for the heretics. The Portuguese Inquisition expanded its scope of operations from Portugal to its colonial possessions, including Brazil, Cape Verde (located at the westernmost point of continental Africa), and Goa, the westernmost city of India. Other inquisitions were imposed on South American countries, such as the *Lima Inquisition* and the *Brasil Inquisition* under the Lisbon tribunal. With these inquisitions taking place, many Jews and other non-Christians fled from Portugal to the Americas and India for fear of persecution.[23]

Goa Inquisition

Gaya is a very ancient sacred city for the Hindus in the state of Bihar, which is as sacred as Kashi or Varanasi. Similar to Gaya, Goa, in a way, was the 'Gaya of the West'. Goa was considered the holiest city in the Indian west and had hundreds of temples and spiritual practice places. In the Puranas, it was called by various names such as *Gove, Govapuri,* and *Gomant*.[24]

The Delhi Sultanate captured Goa in 1312 after plundering and ravaging the city of Govapuri and demolishing numerous Hindu shrines.[25][26]

After the arrival of the Portuguese Christians in Goa, Daman, and Diu – the three coastal cities and islands in Western India were identified by the Europeans as the 'Rome of the Orient' because of a large Christian population and churches.

We will get to the story of Goa a little later. Indian ships were superior worldwide till the British people landed in India around the 1700s.[27] Poverty and lack of opportunities in Europe had drawn many explorers to India's 'new world'. Today we get news of piracy in the oceans now and then. But these pirates were abundant in the 13th and 14th centuries since there were no laws in the Indian Ocean for maritime travels.

After the discovery of the 'India Run', the sea route to India from Portugal by Vasco Da Gama, the Kingdom of Portugal used to send a fleet of ships to the Goa region, which was called Armad, in the early 1500s. Apart from official business, the captains and sailors of these ships also adopted piracy to make extra money from other vessels in the same water.[28]

The Portuguese pirates were also notoriously known as Armad (Armada), today called Harmads, who frequented the Bay of Bengal as well. Armads used to attack the trading ships both to and from India for loot. But the image of Portuguese people started to change once some explorers took a task on them to reach India for a bigger fortune, including creating colonies. This idea was inspired by John II, the King of Portugal (1477 CE), who decided to drop dependency on the local feudal lords for his treasury. During this time, the gold and slave trade in Africa was prevalent. John also wanted to explore the extremely profitable Spice Trade into Asia, which the Republic of Venice (Italy) had a monopoly over. John pushed and deployed his naval assets for this purpose.[29][30]

One of the first explorers sent on these expeditions by the King of Portugal was Vasco da Gama. Vasco da Gama was born in a small city of Portugal in an aristocratic military family. He later joined the military, rose in the ranks rapidly, and set out on his voyage in 1497 CE. First, he reached Cape Verde and then made his way to Cape of Good Hope in South Africa to Mozambique, Mombasa (Kenya), Malindi, and finally reached Calicut in southern India.

In those days, traders from other parts of the world had to pay customs and taxes for goods bought and sold to the authorities.

The story goes like this:

The Hindu king (son of King Mana Veda, name unknown), belonging to the Samoothiri (Zamorin)[31] dynasty, was ruling at that time. Calicut, now Kozhikode, was an important trading port. Upon hearing that a king's envoy from Portugal had arrived, as per tradition and protocols, he was given a grand reception with a procession of over 3000 armed soldiers and guards. Vasco da Gama wanted to meet with the king, but it was not granted. The local representative of the king asked him what the purpose of his arrival was. The reply was that they came "in search of Christians and spices." Gama was asked to send gifts to the king. But the gifts were not valuable enough

– no gold, silver, or precious stones, which was the norm those days. Hence the royals were not at all impressed. At that time, there were many Arab and Muslim merchants in that region. Finding da Gama as their rival, they informed the authorities that they were just pirates and not 'royal ambassadors' of any kind. Disappointed, Gama requested to keep a group of his men there to sell their remaining merchandise upon his departure. He did not get permission; instead, he was asked to pay customs duty for his goods in gold. Local authorities detained Gama's agents as security for payments. Gama failed to pay up, and an angry Gama kidnapped some of the locals, including some soldiers and fishermen, and left the land within three months after his arrival.

He was more successful in Calicut during his 2nd expedition. He took up the third and final expedition in 1524 when King John III appointed him as the Portuguese colonies' Viceroy in India.

In the meantime, came more expeditions one after another by Pedro Álvares Cabral, Francisco de Almeida, and by 1515 CE, Goa was entirely under Portuguese rule. Before their settlement in Goa, Daman, and Diu, the Portuguese came as traders in southern India.

The Portuguese captured Goa from the Bijapur Sultanate in 1510 CE. The Portuguese leader Afonso de Albuquerque defeated the ruler Yousuf Adil Shah and took over the territory,[32] following which the then Portuguese governor in India, Afonso de Albuquerque, turned Goa into an urban metropolis. He introduced radical reforms like mixed marriages between the Portuguese and Indians, contributing to Goa's Indo-Portuguese religio-cultural legacy. Trade was as important a part of their Indian engagements as carving out spheres of Christian influence among the local population. In fact, the major Portuguese factories on both the western and eastern coasts of India were established with the primary objective of establishing a commercial monopoly with the East Indies (as India was called in those days) alongside religious advancements.

The Goa Inquisition was, in a way, a Crusade against the converted local New Christians, along with the Sephardic or Hispanic or Spanish Jews, Hindus, and Muslims. The so-called 'Saint' Xavier heard the stories of converted Goans not following Christianity properly. In a letter he sent from his headquarters in Malacca in Malaysia on May 16, 1546, he requested the Inquisition from the King of Portugal John III to establish the Portuguese Empire's Catholic Church on Indian subjects. The Inquisition was established in 1560 together with the Portuguese Empire and the Jesuits in Portuguese colonies in India, mainly Goa, which continued until it was abolished in 1820.

In 1542 CE, the first Jesuits (a member of the Society of Jesus, a Roman Catholic order of priests founded by St. Ignatius Loyola, St. Francis Xavier, and others in 1534, to do missionary work: Oxford dictionary) arrived in India, led by Francis Xavier co-founder of the new Society of Jesus. Francis was born i Javier (Xavier in old Spanish) in Spain. He came to Goa in 154 for Jesuit missionary work. They were sent by King John III of Portugal to help on religious issues in the Portuguese Empire under the 'Padroado Arrangement' in the mid 15th century.[33] The first Christian seminary called 'Holy Faith' was established by them, and later they renamed it to "St. Paul's College." He was invited to head Saint Paul's College, which became the first Jesuit headquarters in Asia in 1556.[34]

Evidently, the first printing press landed at this Jesuit College and began printing in 1556 CE. It was initially going to Ethiopia via India, and it ended up staying in India and aided in promoting Christianity. It was later used tactfully for the mission of the church.[35]

Xavier wreaked havoc in the lives of Indians, and he destroyed numerous places of worship by requesting the Inquisition (the infamous Goa Inquisition) before he even ved in India.[36] The tomb of Francis Xavier, who died in 52, lies in the Igreja do Bom Jesus in the old City of Goa in glass casket and innocuously 'worshipped' by the 'devotees'. t is believed that the Goa Inquisition was one of the most widespread ones in the history of Christianity.

During the Goa Inquisition, thousands of people who did not accept Christianity or were not Christians, which included mostly Hindus, were burnt alive, sometimes in public. French traveler Dellon personally witnessed the atrocities and terror of the priests. In his book, published in 1687, he gave a detailed account of the horror.[37]

Hindus lost all rights to live in the Portuguese-administered region. Hundreds of Hindu temples were destroyed – leaving behind a long dark chapter in Indian history involving Christians and Portuguese colonialism. The Inquisition came to an end in 1820. But Goa remained under the occupation of the Portuguese ost-India's independence from the British. In 1961, the Indian overnment annexed it to India via military intervention.[38] As ne of the innumerable crimes of Christendom's atrocities, can te Vatican acknowledge and apologize and stop conversion aivities for good as repentance?

Colonial Christian Missionary Impacts onIndia

Generally, in India, the standard view for colonialism and missionary activities are clubbed together since they went hand in hand.[39]

Many, including educated Indians, accept the fact that the British did much good to India, and there are some truths in these suggestions.

First of all, while India lost its freedom to British colonial power, it also brought an end to India's mostly tyrannical Muslim rule. However, towards the end of their rule, Britain had partnered with the Muslim leaders to weaken and divide India via people like the rabid Islamist Muhammad Zafarullah Khan, a member of the Executive Council of the Viceroy of India.[40]

Around the early 18th century, India fell behind the rest of the world in its power of innovation due to the invasions and destruction of its great institutions of learning during the period of Islamic aggression and occupation as well as colonial impositions.[41] As a result, Europe became the new innovation hub in the world.

Colonists improved the roadways and postal system and introduced railways and bridges. It helped modernize India with industrial developments, setting up printing presses – though often, these were built upon the demolition of indigenous industries. The English language was also an essential introduction to India for global communication. English schools, predominantly Christian Missionary were established after destroying India's indigenous school system, which was more available than even today.[42]

The colonists established the schools – initially to educate their children and then later creating 'clerks' out of the Indians who attended these schools, which would later aid them to better rule the country. India, till today, has not recovered from the losses in their education system created by people like Macaulay, which still carries remnants of colonial influence over the Indian minds.[43]

In the meantime, Christian churches were built in many cities across the country, initially for the colonists' use. Once the ploy to convert the natives came into play, many, especially people from the 'educated' classes, began to convert to Christianity. A classic example is the famous Bengali poet Michael Madhusudan Dutta. But there was not much impact of these conversion efforts since the number of Christian converts remained relatively low in India.

But for the last few decades, numerous Christian Missionary groups have been very active in conversion work in various states such as Tamil Nadu, Andhra Pradesh, etc. Their main targets are the tribal people and so-called 'Dalits' or the lower caste Hindus. Decades back, various states in the northwestern region of India, including Nagaland and Mizoram, were significantly impacted by Christian missionary work.

One can find firsthand information about the English schools during the British rule from none other than Swami Vivekananda, who studied at the General Assembly's Institution, later renamed the Scottish Church College. The afore-mentioned 'aristocrat Indians' sent their children to these schools. Vivekananda studied Western logic, Western philosophy, and European history. He passed the Fine Arts examination in 1881 and completed his Bachelor of Arts degree in 1884 from there. Here is what he said about this education system in 1897:

"The child is taken to school, and the first thing he learns is that his father is a fool, the second thing that his grandfather is a lunatic, the third thing that all his teachers are hypocrites, the fourth that all the sacred books are lies! By the time he is sixteen, he is a mass of negation, lifeless and boneless. And the result is that fifty years of such education has not produced one original man in the three Presidencies. Unless we correct the way we educate our kids, there is no hope. This system is designed to generate aliens and stupid protagonists." [44]

Fifty years before the advent of Vivekananda, Macaulay had written in a letter to his father how the British school system was not just an arbitrary development but was a planned and designed activity of the British minds. Here is the text of the letter Macaulay wrote to his father Zachary Macaulay on October 12, 1836:

"My dear Father, ...Our English schools are flourishing wonderfully. We find it difficult, indeed at some places impossible, to provide instruction for all who want it. At the single town of Hoogley fourteen hundred boys are learning English. The effect of this education on the Hindoos is prodigious. No Hindoo who has received an English education ever continues to be

sincerely attached to his religion. Some continue to profess it as a matter of policy. But many profess themselves pure Deists, and some embrace Christianity. The case with Mahometans is very different. The best-educated Mahometan often continues to be a Mahometan still. The reason is plain. The Hindoo religion is so extravagantly absurd that it is impossible to teach a boy astronomy, geography, natural history, without completely destroying the hold which that religion has on his mind. But the Mahometan religion belongs to a better family. It has very much in common with Christianity; and even where it is most absurd, it is reasonable when compared with Hindooism. It is my firm belief that, if our plans of education are followed up, there will not be a single idolater among the respectable classes in Bengal thirty years hence. And this will be effected without any efforts to proselytise, without the smallest interference with religious liberty, merely by the natural operation of knowledge and reflection. I heartily rejoice in this prospect.... "[45]

Even today, there is a myth that these missionary schools are some of the best schools in India, and many Indians spend fortunes sending their children to these schools. While the children may not convert to Christianity, their mindset is developed as the colonists – no deep respect for their ancient heritage, thus creating many NeoCols. Today, there are hundreds of schools in India that are not convent or missionary and provide an excellent education to all young people. But a section of Indian parents is still hooked to the colonial school system for no real reason.

The Current State of Christianity in the World

There are many denominations among the Christians, the largest four being Catholicism (more than 50% or 1.3 billion), Protestantism (38% or about one billion), Eastern Orthodox Church (230 million), and Oriental Orthodox (62 million). The total number of Christian believers in the world is about

2.5 billion, of which 26% are in Europe, 37% in the Americas, 24% in Sub-Saharan Africa, and about 13% in the Asia Pacific region. Christians make up just about the same proportion of the world's population today (32%) as they did a century ago (35%).[46] According to a 2011 report by Pew Research Center's Forum on Religious and Public Life:

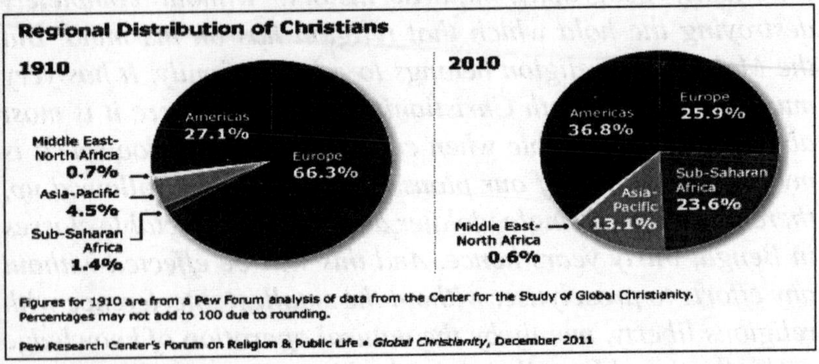

About 63% of Christians live in Europe and the Americas and are in the majority. In 1910, the number was 93%. Also, the proportion of the Christian population dropped from 95% in 1910 to 76% in 2010 in Europe and from 96% to 86% in the Americas as a whole.

Nearly half (48%) of all Christians live in the ten countries, which include the United States, Brazil and Mexico in North and South America, Russia and Germany in Europe, the Philippines and China in Asia-Pacific and Nigeria, the Democratic Republic of the Congo and Ethiopia in sub-Saharan Africa.

Some interesting facts about the Christian population, who constitute 1/3rd of the global demography, are as follows:

Though Christianity was originated in the Middle East and North African region, only 13 million or 4% of the world population residing there are Christians.

A Muslim-majority country Indonesia has more Christians than all 20 countries in Middle East-North Africa combined. (11% or about 30 million)

In about 158 countries (2/3rd of all countries in the world) and territories, the majority population is Christian.

About 90% of Christians live in countries where Christians are the majority; only about 10% of Christians worldwide live as minorities.[47]

China has almost 100 million Christians, according to several sources. According to Pew, by 2050, India will have a 2.2% Christian population.[48] According to 2011 census data, India's Christian population has not changed much in terms of the total population percentage, and total Christians were about 28 million or 2.3%.[49] However, various evangelical sources suggest that the official numbers are underestimated. Part of the reason they give is alleged 'Dalit' Christians by the Government agencies do not count backward class Hindus who have been converted in large numbers to Christianity, and the process continues. According to them, the percentage of Christians in India is 5-6%, and the total number is between 60 and 84 million.[50]

Common Christian-Colonial Terms (Wrongly) used by Hindus

The nearly 200 years of colonial and Christian missionary presence in India has severely impacted Indian society, thought processes, as well as the world view of millions of Western-educated, communist-influenced academics, and media professionals. As a result, many colonial, Christian, and Western concepts have found a permanent place in Indian vocabulary that influences the thought process of the educated Indians. Below are some examples of such concepts which can be corrected once understood.

Hindu Religion

The influence of the Western theological system was so powerful that even masters like Raja Ram Mohan Roy and Vivekananda had to use their terms to express and explain the Hindu system and its distinct features. One such incredibly impactful term is 'Hindu Religion' or Hinduism. This has a long-term effect on the Hindu psyche. It helped to cut Hindus off from the original ideas of their tradition, and they began to look at everything that is Hindu through the prism of the colonists and missionaries. Thus, Christianity's influence came upon them, and a profound and multifaceted term Dharma has been equated with 'religion'. The idea of Dharma (which will be elaborated in the second book), which is universally applicable to every person no matter what religion, race, or tradition they belong to, was destroyed.

God

It is strange that the word "God" was not used in any Judeo-Christian scripture or literature, including Hebrew and Aramaic, until very recently. Yet so much conflict takes place around the world in the name of this very 'God'. This 'God' is, in reality, a European contribution.

The term "God" generally refers to the Jewish, Christian, and Islamic 'creator being' and represents El YHVH (Yahweh), God, and Allah, respectively.

The name of what is referred to as 'God', used before the 6th century CE, was Jehovah (JeHoWah). In the Aramaic language, which is said to have been spoken by Jesus, the term used was *Alaha*, and the Assyrian Christians use the word Ĕlāhā (Elohim). [51] According to linguists, the origin of the term 'God' is the Proto-Germanic word guđan. In Proto-Indo-European language, the root was ǵhau*(ə)*, which meant "to call" or "to invoke".

The Gothic language translations of parts of the Bible, written in the 4th century CE, are called the *Silver Book* (Codex Argenteus). Although the term god was not capitalized initially, the Gothic translators had Greek influence since the names of Greek deities such as Theos or Deus were capitalized. English texts from early days have been influenced by Christianity and, just like the usage of personalization of names in general, used 'God' with capital G, whereas they used 'gods' for non-Abrahamic deities of the so-called polytheistic religions.

One interesting piece of information to note is that even though Islam is called a 'monotheistic' religion, certain sects believe that Allah has 99 names.[52] While others say that 'all good names belong to Allah'.

What is the image of God in Abrahamic faiths? Michelangelo's classic 16th-century painting (Sistine Chapel fresco Creation of the Sun and Moon) shows a muscular old man with grey hair and a beard with an angry face and eyes.[53]

Hindus should understand that 'God' represents neither *Isvara* or *Ishwar* nor *Bhagwan*, nor their deities such as Durga, Ganesh, Saraswati, or for that matter, Ram or Krishna. Instead of the Dharmic system playing a key role in defining other systems, the Abrahamic system and concepts have been imposed on the Hindu system, a typical colonists' pattern. More details will be presented later on this.

To the Hindus, *Ishwar* means the all-pervasive Supreme Being, which is ubiquitous and all-knowing. The word 'God' is a very limited term. In the Vedic and Hindu heritage, various aspects of the Supreme Being are represented through various deities termed d*evas or devatas* and d*evis*, a whole different concept than the idea of God or god/goddess. But Hindus use the term god/goddess interchangeably and thus forget the original meaning of both Isvara and *devas* and *devis*.

Recently some Hindus came up with a new idea for God – 'Generator, Operator (Preserver) and Destroyer' which is an effort to match with the Christian idea of Trinity, which may have also been partially borrowed from the idea of Hindu Trinity of 'Brahma, Vishnu, Shiva'.

'The fear of god' which had no place, has also crept into the Hindu tradition, like Christianity and Islam – perhaps as a reaction to these religions or just due to pure confusion. An example of this introduction of fear is that if one does not follow a particular deity, one will get punished (e.g., *Satyanarayan Katha* in Eastern India). If you perform worship, you will be rewarded. It is to the researchers to figure when this corruption happened but has not been part of the Dharmic culture in its proper form.

Rest in Peace – RIP

There is a common trend, especially among educated Hindus, to use the word RIP, especially on social media when someone dies. It is the Abrahamic tradition that people need to be buried after they die. There would be a 'Judgment Day' based on their deeds, whether they followed a lifestyle which is supposed to be obeyed by the adherents (the Prophet and the holy book and religious dictums). If they were positively verified, they would go to eternal heaven, else in eternal hell. Until then, they have to 'rest in peace' in their graves. Whereas, Hindus cremate the dead so that their bodies' material elements are back to the five essential elements and their *atman* take a journey towards the next life until they attain *'mukti'*. The 'Judgement Day' theory and eternal hell or heaven were coercive ideas for people to follow their religion. Hindus must learn to consciously avoid using RIP and many other such ideas given to them by the Abrahamic and colonist systems.

Idol

The original meaning of the word 'idol' is 'false' god. According to Abrahamic doctrines, a false god is a deity who or which is worshipped falsely out of ignorance, and it possesses no such authority or capability as may be professed. This characterization is mainly for the Jews' YHWH, for the Christians' 'God', and the Muslims' 'Allah'. Jews, Christians, and Muslims interpret it as the 'only and real' God, the supreme creator, and the principal object of the Abrahamic faith. Others' are not only false but illegitimate, non-functioning in terms of authority, which is used as a definition of "idol".[54]

In the Abrahamic traditions, including Judaism, the portrayal of God in any kind of human or statue form is not permissible. It is called aniconism. For example:

"Do not have any other gods before Me. Do not represent [such] gods by any carved statue or picture of anything in the heaven above, on the earth below, or in the water below the land. Do not bow down to [such gods] or worship them. I am God your Lord, a God who demands exclusive worship. Where My enemies are concerned, I keep in mind the sin of the fathers for [their] descendants, to the third and fourth [generation]. But for those who love Me and keep My commandments, I show love for thousands [of generations]." (Exodus 20:3-6)

"[Therefore,] do not make yourselves false gods. Do not raise up a stone idol or a sacred pillar for yourselves. Do not place a kneeling stone in your land so that you can prostrate yourselves on it. I am God your Lord." (Leviticus 26:1)

And thus, the practice of iconoclasm or breaking of these 'false idols' became prevalent in these faiths, which took extreme form during Islamic conquests. The *Quran* says:

'Believers fight for the cause of Allah, while disbelievers do battle for the cause of idols. So fight the minions of the devil' (IV, verse 76).

'Fight against them until idolatry is no more' (II, 193).

'Idolatry is worse than carnage' (II, 217).

It's evident that the concept of iconoclasm was developed in the Middle East with the advent of the Abrahamic religions. Christianity had many 'iconoclastic' movements. The temples, symbols, and images of Pagan deities were destroyed. Many British Christians in India took the 'idols' out from ruined temples. Many times, they were stolen into a museum for multiple purposes.[55] Apart from financial benefits, another important purpose it served is to show the superiority of

Christianity, that these deities were false and had no powers. Also, it was a show of the conquerors to display their superior power and status.

Hindus worship their deities for the divine presence in many forms, most of the time having many human-like features and sometimes as simple as a rock or carved monolith. The divine power is expected to manifest, and the act of manifestation is called *'murtha'*, and the image is called *'murthy'* or *'murti'*. It can be a human-like form using stone, clay, or even a painting envisioned by a devotee. Every time a Hindu uses the word 'idol', they are unknowingly imposing the Abrahamic idea on their great deities and undermining the original ideas of their dharmic traditions. Hindus could use the terms most appropriate – *murthy*, *vigraha*, *pratima*, or simply 'deity' in English.

Worship

Thanks to the English language, the term 'worship' is being used universally for any act or service to divinity. Hindus and Christians alike use the term frequently. But in vernacular languages, people in India do use the appropriate terms.

Let's explore the meaning of the word 'worship'. The dictionary defines worship as – 'the state of being worthy; worthiness'. According to the Germanic sources, the older version of 'worship' in the Anglo-Saxon language was 'weorþscipe', which meant worthiness, dignity, nobleness; glory, fame; and later it assumed new meanings: 'to venerate', 'honour shown to an object',[56] *"worthiness* or *worth-ship"* – to give, worth to something.[57] In the New Testament, the word used for 'to worship' is *proskuneo* which means 'to bow down to gods or kings'.[58]

In Judaism, the original name of the supreme divine being was Yahweh, the God of the Israelites, whose name was revealed to Moses, but after the 3rd century BCE, the use of the term became very limited. By then, Judaism was no more a local religious group, and they started to use the word *Elohim* for god, and in the synagogues, the word, *Adonai* or 'my Lord' and *Kyrios* or 'Lord' was used. Today, the Jewish people have at least six different words related to the praise of the creator god. [59] Most Christians consider the Church Services such as prayers and singing hymns as offering worship to God.

In Islam, the term *salata* or *ṣalāh* is commonly called *namāz* or the five times daily ritual prayer and constitutes one of the five pillars of Islamic faith and practice. The term 'worship' is not permitted in Islam since it may be directed to an object or action and not exclusively to Allah.[60]

The Hindus use many different words to connect with the divinity – *homa, puja, archana, arati, prarthana, kirtan, bhajan, upasana* etc., – these are not the Western and Abrahamic concepts of 'worship'. More details of these will be presented in the 'Understanding Hindu Dharmic System' section in the next book.

AD & BC

Today, for day-to-day activities, we use the Western Gregorian Calendar, virtually a Christian Calendar. It was named after Pope Gregory XIII, who introduced it in 1582 CE. For describing the dates and years, the labels 'AD' and 'BC' are typically used to describe a period in history using Gregorian calendars, sometimes unconsciously and unaware of the meaning of these abbreviated words.

Before introducing the Gregorian Calendar, the Julian Calendar was used, which was replaced by the current one because it did not correctly capture the 'tropical year' of 365 days, the time it takes the earth to circle once around the Sun.

Roman statesman Julius Caesar introduced the Julian calendar around 45 BCE in the form of *Ab urbe condita,* which in Latin means 'from the founding of the City', that is Rome (753 BCE), abbreviated as AUC.

AD stands for Anno Domini – in Latin, it means "in the year of the Lord", and later it is also interpreted as 'in the year of Our Lord'. The full phrase in Latin goes something like, *"anno Domini nostri Jesu Christi"*. Though many non-Christians have reverence for Jesus Christ, most don't see Jesus as their 'Lord'. BC denotes Before Christ. An increasingly greater number of people today use the term CE or 'Common or Current Era' and BCE 'Before Common or Current Era'.

A good number of people in the Indian subcontinent are also using the Hindu Calendar Vikrama Samvat or VS, also called the Vikrama calendar, and is the official calendar of Nepal. According to popular legend, Emperor Vikramaditya of Ujjain established the Vikrama Samvat era after defeating the Śakas around 57 BCE. There are also regional calendars in the Indian subcontinent, such as Tamil, Punjabi, and Bengali calendars. *Bangabda* is such a calendar that King Shashanka of Bengal started. The Bengali era is called Bengali Sambat (BS) or the Bengali year *Bangabda.* It began in 593/594 CE. Efforts have been made to give credit for this calendar to Akbar, who was born several years after the introduction of Bangabda in 594 CE.[61][62] As per some historians, King Shashanka introduced it.

Mythology

Mythology has roots in the Sanskrit term *mithya* or false. While accepting *Old* and *New Testaments* as factual and historical, the colonists and missionaries would tag ancient Indian texts such as *Ramayana* and *Mahabharata* as mythology in the lines of ancient Greek literature. Hindus should call them epics or *'itihasa'*. Or simply call them by their names, including the *Puranas*.

Beef Up

While the debate on beef-eating has been a hot subject, especially by the Indian Marxists, the majority of Hindus, even those who eat meat, less than 2% of them consume beef.[63] Yet, many Hindu journalists and writers use the term 'beef up' indiscriminately to express weight or strength to something. By doing so, they influence the subconscious of the population, especially the youth going to English medium schools in India.

Alexander and Akbar, the 'great'

Most historians in the West use 'Alexander the Great', to describe Greek conqueror Alexander III of Macedon. Though physical evidence is sparse, mostly the literary sources elaborate on his conquests. He was not the only conqueror in the world, but his conquest ended after his encounter with India. Many Indians know about King Puru's dialogues (Porus) with Alexander after being captured by the latter. Alexander's ambitious adventure missions caused anywhere between 2.5 million to 3.5 million deaths.[64]

This has also been the case with Mughal ruler Akbar – some called him 'Akbar the Great'; though he was relatively a better ruler for non-Muslims than other Kings in Delhi, he too had many vices. It is very clear from the fact that in 1578 CE, he assumed the title 'Ghazi' similar to his grandfather Babur. Ghazi means a person who participates in *ghazwa* or Jihad as military expeditions and raids to conquer a non-Muslim land, as exemplified by Muhammad with 17 such ghazw or ghazwa.[65]

The title Akbar assumed in 1578 CE:

'Emperor of Islam, Emir of the Faithful, Shadow of God on earth, Abul Fath Jalal-ud-din Muhammad Akbar Badshah Ghazi (whose empire Allah perpetuate), is a most just, most wise, and a most God-fearing ruler'. [66]

Though Akbar was too young and scared to behead Maharaja Hemu in his unconscious state, Akbar's guardian Bairam Khan wanted him to earn the title of Ghazi by smiting Hemu's neck.

We will learn more about Akbar's Islamism later.

For some strange reason, Indians are also fond of calling a conqueror 'great' – probably due to the epigenetics and psychological consequence of people from all conquered nations. But it is abnormal for people not to change their thought processes, images of conquerors and put them in the right place in history. However, later we will present how India witnessed the NeoCols' attempt to whitewash the conquerors' horrendous past, even the most brutal ones such as Babur and Ghazni; it has become a natural habit of them to call anyone 'great' other than their own great ones such as Vikramaditya, Chandra Gupta, Bappa Raval, Shivaji, etc. Indian kings rarely conquered another nation, killing thousands and destroying civilizations, yet why the same Indians call invaders 'great' is a subject to ponder.

'Mother' Teresa of Calcutta

Noble Peace Prize and posthumous sainthood were given to Mary Teresa Bojaxhiu from Albania. But for what? Was she a saint or simply an icon of Christian Missionary conversion machinery?

The well-invested story *Something beautiful of God*, a 1969 documentary by the BBC, started the propaganda. Many Hindus have touched her feet and taken pride in meeting her, and proudly published their photographs together. Unfortunately, due to biased media and the convoluted thinking of many Hindus, they don't even think that something could be wrong with this personality because the Christian world has given her 'sainthood' and a Nobel Prize, a rare feat! A parallel is easy to draw between Xavier (who was responsible for large-scale massacres of non-Christians and destructions in Goa) and Teresa (conversions and death of poor and destitute without proper medical treatment) regarding India's Hindus' ignorance and idiocy!

Teresa had 517 missions in 100 countries at the time of her death, and with millions of dollars worth of assets, it was just conversion machinery and network.

In his 1994 documentary *Hell's Angel* on UK's Chanel 4, Christopher Hitchens figured Teresa was no saint, just an evangelist and a Christian Missionary to convert suffering children and people to Christianity.[67] "There is something beautiful in seeing the poor accept their lot, to suffer it like Christ's Passion. The world gains much from their suffering," Teresa once told Christopher Hitchens. Christopher pointed in his documentary, "Here is a Western woman who has forsaken her life, for whatever be it of her life in Albania, for sacrificing herself for the people of the third world it makes the West feel better that 'one of us again rescuing the third world'".

According to journalist and author Douglas Robertson, 'Mother Teresa wasn't a saintly person – she was a shrewd operator with unpalatable views who knew how to build up a brand'.[68] English journalist Kitty Wenham also said, 'Mother Teresa's Sainthood is a Fraud, Just Like She Was'.[69]

According to Dr. Aroup Chatterjee, a London-based physician, 'the Missionaries of Charity ran inadequate facilities and often offered little comfort to those it was trying to help.' And he asserted that the whole system was a fraud.[70]

Many Indians do not know or appreciate scores of organizations such as Bharat Sevashrama Sangh, Seva International, Ramakrishna Mission Seva, Azim Premji Foundation, and numerous Indian organizations that serve the needy and poor without much media hype.

References

1. George Gheverghese Joseph, George Joseph, "The Life and Times of a Kerala Christian Nationalist", Orient Longman, New Delhi, 2003.
2. Farmer, David Hugh (2011). "The Oxford Dictionary of Saints", Fifth Edition Revised (5th ed.). Oxford: University Press. 2011, p. 418.
3. M.M.Ninan (2011). "Acts of the Apostle Thomas", Global Publisher, San Jose, CA. p.113.
4. David C. Sim(1998). "The Gospel of Matthew and Christian Judaism", p. 182.

5. Joseph, "Kerala Christian Nationalist", Orient Longman, 2003.
6. Christian Castes Archived 2006-11-29 at the Wayback Machine Encyclopædia Britannica
7. Simon J. Joseph (2012). "Jesus in India? Transgressing Social and Religious Boundaries", Journal of the American Academy of Religion Vol. 80, No. 1, pp. 161-199, Oxford University Press.
8. BBC Documentary: Did Jesus Die on the Cross? http://www.usislam.org/jesus/bbc_documentary.htm
9. Russell Goldman, "Jesus Christ May Not Have Died on Cross: No evidence in Ancient sources backs up defining symbol of Christianity", ABC News, 2 July 2010 https://abcnews.go.com/GMA/jesus-christ-died-cross-scholar/story?id=11066130
10. Comments On Ahimsa (Nonviolence), Bryan Teixeira https://atpweb.org/jtparchive/trps-19-87-01-001.pdf
11. Knitter, Paul F. "Without Buddha I Could not be a Christian", Oneworld Publications, 2009.
12. "Armed Pilgrimage", Vincent Ryan, October 06, 2008, https://www.americamagazine.org/issue/culture/armed-pilgrimage
13. John Shertzer Hittell,"A Brief History of Culture", (1874), p.137.
14. John M. Robertson,"A Short History of Christianity" (1902), p. 278.
15. Peters, Edward (1989). "Inquisition", University of California Press, p. 54.
16. Benjamin Keen and Keith Haynes (2000). "History of Latin America: Independence to the present", Houghton Mifflin Company, p. 106.
17. Hamnett, Brian R. (1999). "Concise History of Mexico". Port Chester NY USA: Cambridge Univ. Press. pp. 63–95.

18. Jose Rogelio Alvarez (ed.). "Inquisicion". Enciclopedia de Mexico (in Spanish). VII (2000 ed.). Mexico City: Sabeca International Investment Corp.
19. Chuchiak IV, John F. "The Inquisition in New Spain, 1571–1820: A Documentary History", Baltimore: Johns Hopkins University Press, 2012, p. 236.
20. The Medieval Christian Church: Holy Office of the Inquisition https://www.histclo.com/chron/med/church/mc-inq.html
21. Reuven Faingold (2013). "Judeus ibéricos deportados a São Tomé entre 1492-1497". Morashá: História Judaica Moderna, p.79.
22. Yosef Hayim Yerushalmi; Elisheva Carlebach; "Jewish History and Jewish Memory: Essays in Honor of Yosef Hayim Yerushalmi", 1998, UPNE.
23. Lowenstein, Steven (2001). "The Jewish Cultural Tapestry: International Jewish Folk Traditions". Oxford University Press. p. 36.
24. History of Goa, Britannica https://www.britannica.com/place/Goa/History
25. De Souza, Teotonio R. (1989). "Essays in Goan History". Concept Publishing Company. pp. 13–14.
26. Bradnock, Robert W.; Bradnock, Roma (2000). "Goa handbook". Footprint Handbooks. pp. 214, 253.
27. "The New Cambridge History of India: Science, Technology and Medicine in Colonial India"
28. Findly, Elison B. (1988). "The Capture of Maryam-uz-Zamani's Ship: Mughal Women and European Traders", Journal of the American Oriental Society, (108 (2). p. 227–238.
29. "Goa Inquisition was most merciless and cruel". Rediff. September 14, 2005.

30. Saraiva, Antonio Jose, (1985), Salomon, H. P. and Sassoon, I. S. D. (Translators, 2001), "The Marrano Factory. The Portuguese Inquisition and Its New Christians, 1536–1765", (Brill Academic, 2001)
31. K. V. Krishna Iyer, "Zamorins of Calicut: From the earliest times to AD 1806". Calicut: Norman Printing Bureau, 1938.
32. Elaine Sanceau (1936) "Indies Adventure: The Amazing Career of Afonso de Albuquerque, Captain-general and Governor of India (1509–1515)", Antiquity Publications Ltd.
33. Neill, Stephen, "A history of Christianity in India (1760–1858) – The Recovery of Catholic Missions", Cambridge University Press, 1985, p. 304.
34. Manohararāya Saradesāya, "A history of Konkani literature: from 1500 to 1992", Sahitya Akademi, 2000.
35. "India Inscribed: Development of printing technology in India 16th–18th centuries", Jose Kalapura. Proceedings of the Indian History Congress, Vol. 68, Part One (2007), p. 436-463
36. Controversy Intensifies Over Alleged Racism of India's St. Francis Xavier, L.A. Times Archives, Dec. 31, 1994https://www.latimes.com/archives/la-xpm-1994-12-31-me-14847-story.html
37. An Account of the Inquisition at Goa in India, Translated from the French by M. Dellon, published by R. Patterson & Lambdin. Buller & Lambdin, printer, 18I9. https://archive.org/details/accountofinquisi00dell/page/n6/mode/1up
38. The Portuguese Inquisition in Goa: A brief history, India Facts http://indiafacts.org/the-portuguese-inquisition-in-goa-a-brief-history/
39. Copland, Ian, "Christianity as an Arm of Empire: The Ambiguous Case of India under the Company,c. 1813-

1858", The Historical Journal, Vol. 49, No. 4 (Dec., 2006), pp. 1025-1054, Cambridge University Press.

40. Ahmadiyyas were at the forefront of creation of Pakistan, an Ahmadiyya Unit fought against India in Kashmir in 1947-48, 9 December 2019 https://www.opindia.com/2019/12/how-ahmadiyyas-were-at-the-forefront-of-creation-of-pakistan-islam-all-you-need-to-know/]
41. Clingingsmith, David,; Williamson, Jeffrey G., "India's Deindustrialization in the 18th and 19th Centuries", https://www.lse.ac.uk/Economic-History/Assets/Documents/Research/GEHN/GEHNConferences/conf7/Conf7-Williamson.pdf
42. "The Beautiful Tree – Indigenous Indian Education in the Eighteenth Century", Biblia Impex, Volume III, 1983.
43. Bellenoit, Hayden J. A., "Missionary Education, Religion and Knowledge in India, c. 1880-1915", Modern Asian Studies Vol. 41, No. 2 (Mar., 2007), pp. 369-394, Cambridge University Press.
44. "The Complete Works of Swami Vivekananda", Volume 3: Lectures from Colombo to Almora 'The Future of India' in 1897.
45. 12 October 1836: pp. 192-193; MacAulay, T., & Pinney, T. (1976). The Indian Legislator, 8 February 1835–17 January 1838. In The Letters of Thomas Babington MacAulay (pp. 127-240). Cambridge University Press. http://www.columbia.edu/itc/mealac/pritchett/00generallinks/macaulay/txt_letters_later.html
46. Global Christianity – A Report on the Size and Distribution of the World's Christian Population, Pew Research Centre https://www.pewforum.org/2011/12/19/global-christianity-exec/
47. Hackett, Conrad, "By 2050, India to have world's largest populations of Hindus and Muslims", Pew Research

Centre 21 April 2015. https://www.pewresearch.org/fact-tank/2015/04/21/by-2050-india-to-have-worlds-largest-populations-of-hindus-and-muslims/

48. Ibid.
49. "Census of India – Religious Composition". Government of India, Ministry of Home Affairs.
50. Melton, J. Gordon (2005). "Encyclopedia of Protestantism". Infobase Publishing. pp. 284–285.
51. "Enrichment Section: Who Is the God of the Old Testament?", Church of Jesus Christ https://www.churchofjesuschrist.org/study/manual/old-testament-student-manual-genesis-2-samuel/enrichment-section-a-who-is-the-god-of-the-old-testament?lang=eng
52. Bentley, David, "The 99 beautiful names of God", William Carey Library, 1999.
53. Creation of the Sun, Moon and Plants, Mvsei Vaticani http://www.museivaticani.va/content/museivaticani/en/collezioni/musei/cappella-sistina/volta/storie-centrali/creazione-degli-astri-e-delle-piante.html
54. "What Is Idolatry in the Bible? Its Definition and Significance", Christianity.com https://www.christianity.com/wiki/christian-terms/what-is-the-definition-of-idolatry-in-the-bible.html
55. "Reclaiming India's Stolen Cultural Heritage: Indian activists seek to recover missing idols, the victims of colonial plundering and contemporary thievery", Angel L. Martínez Cantera, The Diplomat, October 23, 2019 https://thediplomat.com/2019/10/reclaiming-indias-stolen-cultural-heritage/
56. Bosworth and Toller, Anglo-Saxon Dictionary, "weorþscipe".
57. Kay, William K., "Religion in education", Gracewing Publishing, 1997.

58. Vernon Whaley, "Called to Worship: The Biblical Foundations of Our Response", 2009.
59. Worship, Jewish Virtual Library https://www.jewishvirtuallibrary.org/worship
60. Ljakić, Zijad. "Upotreba riječi "obožavam"" – Use of word "worship" in Islam. n-um.com (in Bosnian).
61. Sengupta, Nitish K., "Land of Two Rivers: A History of Bengal from the Mahabharata to Mujib". Penguin Books India. 2011. pp. 96–98.
62. Guhathakurta, Meghna; Schendel, Willem van, "The Bangladesh Reader: History, Culture, Politics". Duke University Press. 2013. pp. 17–18.
63. Roshan Kishore; Ishan Anand. "Who are the beef eaters of India?", Live Mint, 20 Oct 2015 https://www.livemint.com/Politics/RhPVLUFmclIDWRIiSoTC7N/Who-are-the-beef-eaters-in-India.html
64. "Alexander the Great: Monster of Macedonia", Richard Gabriel, History Net https://www.historynet.com/alexander-the-monster.htm
65. Aboul-Enein, H. Yousuf and Zuhur, Sherifa, "Islamic Rulings on Warfare", Strategic Studies Institute, US Army War College, Diane Publishing Co., Darby PA https://www.researchgate.net/publication/346932310_Did_Islam_spread_by_the_sword
66. Abdul Qadir Baudauni, "Muntakhab-ut-Tawarikh", trans. by G. S. A. Ranking, W. H. Lowe, and Sir Wolseley Haig (Calcutta, 1884–1925), III, p.279-80.
67. "Hell's Angel" (1994) –Christopher Hitchens' Documentary on Mother Teresa – YouTube
68. Douglas Robertson, "Mother Teresa wasn't a saintly person – she was a shrewd operator with unpalatable views who knew how to build up a brand", Independent, 4 September, 2016 https://www.independent.co.uk/voices/mother-

teresa-wasnt-a-saintly-person-she-was-a-shrewd-operator-with-unpalatable-views-who-knew-how-a7224846.html

69. Kitty Wenham, "Mother Teresa's Sainthood is a Fraud, Just Like She Was", Medium, 7 September 2016 https://medium.com/@KittyWenham/mother-teresas-sainthood-is-a-fraud-just-like-she-was-eb395177572

70. "Mother Teresa: The Final Verdict", Meteor Books, India, 2002, The New York Times https://www.nytimes.com/2016/08/27/world/asia/mother-teresa-critic.html

❑

CHAPTER

3

THE ADVENT OF MUHAMMAD AND ISLAM

What is the meaning of Islam?
Who is a Muslim, and what does it mean?
Why is iconoclasm a common feature among all three Abrahamic religions?
Who is Allah? An ancient deity adopted by Muhammad or a new invention?
Is worshiping the stones in Kaaba the same as 'idol worship'?
Is Quran unaltered, and who compiled it?
How many Hadiths are there?
How many 'gods' were there in the Middle ast before Islam?
Was Mecca the original place of Kaba or Petra in Jordan?
What is the Islamic meaning of sahid (martyr)?
What do insallah and mashallah mean?
Is the title Ghazi given to a jihadi conqueror?
What is halal?
Does nikah in Arabic mean 'sexual intercourse'?

In the Arabian Peninsula, there was a tribe called Quraysh.[1] Amr al-'Ulā was born in this tribe around 464 CE and followed a religion of the ancient tradition established by Abraham, perhaps a mixed form of Judaism and Christianity. Later Amr changed his name to Hashim (name of God used for Abraham) ibn Abd Manaf, and his wife was Salma bint 'Amr, a celebrated woman of the Jewish faith. His clan Banu Hashim (the members are called Hashemites or al-Hashimi)[2] was named after him and had control over the region's key cities and territories. Their son was Abd al-Muttalib Shaybah ibn Hashim (497–578 CE), and he had six known wives, including Fatimah bint Amr of the Makhzum clan. Abdullah (*Abd Allah: 'slave of Allah'*) ibn Abd al-Muttalib (546–570 CE) was born to Abd al-Mutalib and Fatimah, and he was married to Āminah bint Wahb. Aminah's son Muhammad, the Prophet of Islam, was Abdullah's only child.

Muhammad was born in 570 CE to Aminah and Abdullah and was soon orphaned at six. He was raised by his paternal grandfather Abd al-Muttalib. Muhammad was very much into the 'other world'. He would periodically seclude himself in a mountain cave named Hira for several nights of prayer. When he was 40, Muhammad reported being visited by the celestial angel Gabriel in the Hira cave and claimed to have received his first revelation from *Allah*. Around 610 CE, three years after receiving these 'revelations', Muhammad began preaching these to the public. He then proclaimed that 'Allah is one and only one' and told his followers for complete "submission", the meaning of *Islām in Arabic* to only Allah as '*Dīn*'.[3] *Dīn*, in Arabic and anglicized as deen (e.g. *Deen-e ilahi* of Akbar) has three components: judgment, custom, and religion – hence was preached as the 'right way of life'. He also proclaimed that he was a prophet and the last messenger of Allah, in the line of other Abrahamic prophets of the past. While *islām* is a verbal noun, *muslim* is its active participle. Today people who follow *islām* are called *Muslim* or *Moslem, and* a female follower is called *a Muslima.*

Muhammad started by preaching to his close associates and family members but met with much resistance from society and even persecution of his followers. He moved to Medina and then took up the sword to fight the opposition to his new ideology.

The Quran

Quran or *Koran* is the holy book of the followers of the religion *Islām*. Originally written in Arabic, it is mandatory for a devout Muslim to regularly read and recite from the Quran and follow the Islamic practices and rules as prescribed in Hadiths. The origin of the word is an Arabic verb qara'a which means 'he read' or 'he recited', and *qur'ān* means 'act of reciting'.

It is said that the revelations from *Allah* to Muhammad were compiled into the Quran. It is also claimed that this is the only holy book in the world that has been unaltered. Muhammad preached these 'revealed' messages orally, and he never wrote those down himself. Quran denotes him as *'ummi'* which means illiterate person. Another interpretation of the term *ummi* is 'a community without scriptures'.[4] It is evident that there were as many as 17 scribes, many companions of Muhammad wrote down various verses of the Quran[5], the first one being of Khaalid ibn Sa'eed ibn al-'Aas. According to Ṣaḥīḥ al-Bukhārī, one of the six major hadith collections called *Kutub al-Sittah* of Sunni Islam, (by Persian scholar Muhammad al-Bukhari), Quran was first compiled into a book by Zayd ibn Thabit under the first caliph Abu Bakr Siddiq. However, Shia Muslims believe that Ali ibn Abi Taḷib was the first to compile the Quran into a written text shortly after the death of Muhammad.[6]

There were many copies of the Quran scattered at different places. Uthman ibn 'Affan, the third Caliph of Islam, oversaw the collection and compilation of the many verses of the Quran, written on skin, leaf, bone, and parchment. He then ordered the destruction of any remaining text containing verses of the Quran after he declared the completion of collections between 650 CE and 653 CE called the Uthmanic codex.[7] Uthman burned many remaining copies of the Quran, and his version was introduced to the world, which is most likely the version available today.[8] It is very much possible that many original verses were lost, and interpolation and addition may have happened during the compilation process led by Uthman.[9] Islamic scholar Professor Francis Edward Peters suggested that omission and commission occurred. The final work became extremely conservative during the recompilation process, as the content was selectively added or retained.[10]

It is widely believed that the *Sanaa palimpsest* or Sanaa Quran discovered in Yemen in 1972 is one of the oldest manuscripts of the Quran in existence.[11] Using a radiocarbon test, the age of the original document was set between 578 CE and 669 CE with a 95% accuracy.[12] A palimpsest is a manuscript page on a material such as skin, re-used by scraping off or overwriting the previous writing. Sanaa has two layers of text. Scholars suggest that the 'upper text' (overwritten) is primarily a copy of the 'Uthmanic' Quran, and the 'lower text' (the original text that was erased and written over by the upper text), contains text which is different from the Uthman text[13] and perhaps was written within a few decades after the death of Muhammad and clearly proves that modern-day Quran and the oldest versions may not be the same.[14]

What is Islām

In recent days, since the 2001 9/11 event, massive information was spread that *'Islām* means peace' and that *Islām* is the 'religion of peace'. In the Arabic language (which pre-dates Muhammad by hundreds of years), *Islām* meant 'submission or surrender to the Supreme being', which initially was 'voluntary submission'.

According to WikiIslam, the word *Islām* derives from the Arabic triconsonantal root *sīn-lām-mīm*, which means 'surrender', a pre-Islamic term. The Wiki notes that: "Lissan al-Arab, one of the most authoritative lexicons of the Arabic language, mentions that the word *Islām* is derived from the root verb *istaslama* which means 'to submit' or 'give in' or 'surrender',"[15] but Muhammad added a new meaning – 'submission to Allah, the only God'.

According to Quran (2:136)

"Say (O Muslims): We believe in Allah and that which is revealed to us and that which was revealed to Abraham, and Ishmael, and Isaac, and Jacob, and the tribes, and that which Moses and Jesus received, and that which the prophets received from their Lord. We make no distinction between any of them, and to Him we have surrendered. [Arabic "Muslimoon"]"

Quran (3:19) says Islam is absolute submission to Allah:

"The Religion before Allah is Islam (submission to His Will): Nor did the People of the Book dissent therefrom except through envy of each other, after knowledge had come to them. But if any deny the Signs of Allah, Allah is swift in calling to account."

Quran (3:83) says Islam is the religion of Allah:

"Do they seek for other than the Religion of Allah? While all creatures in the heavens and on earth have, willing or unwilling, bowed to His Will (Accepted Islam), and to Him shall they all be brought back."

Hadith

Hadīth in Arabic means narrative or report, or a speech of a person. In reality, Hadith is the 'practice book' of Islam and is said to have been based on how the prophet lived. There are six major collections (called *Kutub al-Sittah*) of the Hadith. The *'Ṣaḥīḥ al-Bukhārī'* is one of the most respected books for the Sunni Muslims. It was compiled by Persian scholar Muhammad al-Bukhari around 846 CE, more than 200 years after Muhammad's death (632 CE). Below is what it has to say about the term *Islām*:

"...Then he further asked, "What is Islam?" Allah's Apostle replied, "To worship Allah Alone and none else, to offer prayers perfectly, to pay the compulsory charity (Zakat) and to observe fasts during the month of Ramadan." (1:2:48)

"This letter is from Muhammad, the slave of Allah, and His Apostle, to Heraculius, the Ruler of the Byzantine. Peace be upon the followers of guidance. Now then, I invite you to Islam (surrender to Allah), embrace Islam and you will be safe." (4:52:191)

"While we were in the mosque, Allah's Apostle came out and said, "Let us proceed to the Jews." So we went out with him till we came to Bait-al-Midras. The Prophet stood up there and called them, saying, "O assembly of Jews! Surrender to Allah (embrace Islam), and you will be safe!" "Know that the earth is for Allah, and I want to exile you from this land, so whoever among you has property he should sell it; otherwise, know that the land is for Allah and His Apostle." (009:092:447)

"By Allah! I consider him a believer." The Prophet said, "Or merely a Muslim (Who surrender to Allah)." (1:4:247)

Some Muslim sects, such as Süleymaniye Vakfı (Turkey) and Quran Sunnat Society (India), called Ahle Quran or Quarnists, do not follow Hadith as much and follow only Quran. The founder of Ahle Quran, Abdullah Chakralawi (India), described the Quran as *"Ahsan Hadith"*, meaning 'most perfect hadith' and claimed that there was no need for any additional texts such as the Hadiths, besides Quran. [16]

Iman or 'Islamic Articles of Faith'

According to Quran (33:35): *"Iman is that you believe in Allah and His Angels and His Books and His Messengers and the Hereafter and the good and evil fate [ordained by your God]."*

According to Hadith, Muhammad introduced six fundamental 'Iman' in Islam.

1. Belief in the existence and oneness of one and only creator God Allah (all other 'gods' are false).
2. Belief in the existence of *farishta* or angels.
3. Belief in the existence of the books of which Allah is the author: the Quran (revealed to Muhammad), the Gospel (revealed to Jesus), the Torah (revealed to Moses), and Psalms (revealed to David).
4. Belief in all prophets' existence, Muhammad is the last of them, the penultimate, and others sent before them.
5. Belief in the the 'Day of Judgement'. On that day, humanity will be divided into two groups and will be sent to paradise or hell based on their faithfulness to their prophet and Allah.
6. Belief in the existence of Allah's predestination, whether it involves good or bad.[17][18]

On the other hand, there are five *arkāns,* which means pillars or basic acts for a true Muslim:*1. Shahadah* or the declaration of faith*, 2. Salah* or daily prayers *(namaz), 3. Sawm* or fasting during *Ramadan, 4. Zakat* or donation, *5. Hajj* – the pilgrimage to Mecca.

Within a few centuries, the army carrying the banner of Islam took over most Middle East, Africa, and parts of Europe, and finally, many parts of Asia. It was brutal warfare of conquest, conversion, and destruction of native cultures and civilizations. Millions were killed, sold in the slave markets, numerous great architectures, including temples, institutes of learning, and statues of local deities were broken into dust, and Islamic monuments, mosques, and mausoleums were built atop the ruins of many. But how was the Middle East before the arrival of Islam? Let us find out.

The Middle East before the Advent of Islam

The entire Middle East from Iran (Persia) to Egypt was a great center of culture and trade until 600 CE. Thamud's ancient civilization around the 8th century BCE is attributed to the people who migrated from south to north of the Arabian Peninsula. According to Arab Historian Ibn Khaldun: *"The Yemen, al-Bahryn, Oman and* the *Jazirah have long been in Arab possession, but for thousands of years, the rule of these areas has belonged to different (Arab) nations in succession. They also founded cities and towns (there) and promoted sedentary culture and luxury to the highest degree. Among such nations were the 'Ad and the Thamud. There was a long period of royal authority and sedentary culture."*[19]

Let us look back to the 8th century BCE.

Little is known about the Thamud's, but most likely, their descendants, the Nebatheans, have left indelible pieces of evidence of a great civilization in the desert of Arabia. It was the far north-west part of the peninsula called Petra (currently in Jordan).[20][21] Petra was a great city-civilization of 400 square miles. The hustling and bustling of traders from southern Arabia to the north and further happened through this city. The Nebatheans curved out palaces, monuments, and living quarters, cutting out rocks from the mountains. Their architecture and craftsmanship defy common sense and are shrouded with mystery as to how they carved those out, what technology they had to create 130-feet tall columns and the smoothness of the columns and walls. They had an elaborate water collection, preservation, and distribution system, including making the desert land food-sufficient by using the water wisely. It is believed that current-day Arabs, especially in Mecca (the Banu Thaqif tribes) and Medina, are descendants of these Thamuds and Nebatheans.

Some believe that all attributes of Islamic holy sites, including Kaaba, belonged to the pre-Islamic city Petra when Mecca was not well-known yet. Kaaba means 'cube' or a cubic-shaped 'sacred house' in Arabic that housed numerous deities of that period. During the birth of Islam, old maps did not figure Mecca prominently,[22] and it was not even on the trade route. It was Petra, which was one of the most prominent cities on the trade route. When Petra fell due to earthquake or volcanic eruptions and perhaps meteorite showers, causing the sacred black rock possibly dedicated to Hubal, which was worshiped by the local tribes, fragmented into five pieces. This represented one form of generic God or Allah among many deities. It is possible that once Muhammad and his followers migrated to Mecca after being forced to abandon Petra, they secretly carried the rock or pieces of the original black rock as it was their clan deity. Did they re-established Kaaba in Mecca as a sacred shrine that originally resided in Petra? It is to be noted that the description of 'Mecca' in the Quran talks about water, trees, fruits, etc.

"*We sent down water from the sky, blessed water whereby We caused to grow gardens, grains for harvest, tall palm-trees with their spathes, piled one above the other – sustenance for (Our) servants. Therewith We gave (new) life to a dead land. So will be the emergence (from the tombs).*" *(Quran* 50:9-11)

"*We sent down water from the sky in measure and lodged it in the ground. And We certainly are able to withdraw it. Therewith for you We gave rise to gardens of palm-trees and vineyards where for you are abundant fruits and of them you eat.*" (Quran 23: 18-19)

Yet, there is not even one iota of archaeological evidence that current day Mecca had any major green pastures or trees; the description in Quran perfectly matches Petra. Some historians believe that the story of Mecca is a fairytale because of a lack of solid evidence and are pointing to Petra as the original 'Mecca'.[23] According to Dan Gibson, a controversial scholar of Islamic history, the ancient mosques built between 622 CE and 876 CE if faced west, geo-locations suggest that those point to Petra and not Mecca.[24]

No matter how advanced or backward in today's standards, every civilization, while trying to celebrate earthly life, set aside what is called higher than themselves – the 'divine' presence. The word divine has most likely been derived from the Sanskrit word *'divya'*, which means giver of light – or knowledge, vision, and direction. And each culture has its sacred objects called 'deities'. 'Devata' represents nourishing and self-illumination powers and energy-giving sources.

The Nabataeans had two major deities – *al-Dushwa* and *al-Lat*, sun and moon gods. *Dhu al-Shara* or *Dushara* is a mountain probably originating as an aspect of *Ruda*; he is associated with the sun and the planet mercury.[25] Generally, Arabs were known to be Nomads and Bedouins. While a large part of Arabia was a harsh and hot desert and many people remained nomads – moving from one place to another, several cities flourished and were noted by Ibn Khaldun and other scholars. Damascus (in Syria), Yathrib (current Medina), Karbala, etc., are some examples. These cities were famous for global trade. About 1400 years ago, Mecca, where the current Islamic holiest place Kaaba is located, became the center of attention for all Muslims worldwide as it took the role of Petra, once known as the 'wonder of the land' destroyed by an earthquake or volcanic eruption. The civilization suddenly vanished into antiquity. Mecca took over from Petra and became the center of all trade and culture of Arabia.

In a shocking revelation by Marshall Hodgson, professor of Islamic studies and historian at the University of Chicago, that Arab Christians made a pilgrimage to the Kaaba, a pagan temple at that time, honoring *Allah,* a generic term used for God the Creator in that region and era.[26] If that was the case, it is up to the historians to figure out whether the original Kaaba was situated in Mecca or Petra and the antiquity of Allah.

Based on some other archaeological evidence and discoveries of some pre-Islamic inscriptions and tombs of Arab Christians, especially in the ruins of Umm el-Jamal, a Church in northern Jordan contained references to *Allah* as 'the proper name of God'.[27]

Kaaba included an ancient cluster of shrines and sanctuary for a multitude of religious practices. Pre-Islamic Arabia had major pilgrimages from all over the region for devotees who came to Petra or Mecca, where 360 deities of different tribes and clans were installed in the shrine complex of Kaaba. According to Islamic sources, Ibrahim and his son Ismael laid the foundations of Kaaba around 2130 BCE, [28][29] long before the advent of Islam as a religion.

There is some evidence indicating that Petra might have been the original birthplace of both Muhammed and Islam. Later after the destruction of Petra,[30] the center of all attractions moved to current Mecca.

Before 600 CE, there were numerous shrines in all significant cities in Arabia, including Kaaba and Hejaz. Arabs performed rituals similar to the Hindus and the so-called Pagans and also had the practice of sacrifices. Pilgrims from all over flocked to these shrines, and festivals were celebrated. Many believe that there were as many as 360 different deities and shrines as well near Mecca belonging to various tribes.[31][32] Arab tribes forever lost their ancient sacred places and deities after the advent of Islam, as introduced by Muhammad.

As noted already, 'Allah' was a generic term to denote the creator god or deity in Arabic and was used by many groups, Arabs and non-Arabs, before the Islamic era, which today means 'the God of Islam'. The word is related to the Abrahamic traditions — *il, El*, and *Elah or Eloah* (found in the Old Testament) in Hebrew and Aramaic languages. According to the Encyclopedia Britannica, Allah is a contracted form of *al-Illah*, meaning 'the God'. Some people think Allah represents an older form of the moon god (Hubal), and Islam's usage of the crescent symbol has a link to the old deity, and they use a lunar-based calendar.[33][34]

Arab scholar Hisham Ibn Al-Kalbi's *Book of Idols* (*Kitāb al-'Aṣnām*)), written in 737 CE–819 CE, has details of worship and ritual ceremonies in ancient Arabia before the birth of Islam. According to the book, almost every household had a deity similar to the concept of Hindu *'kula devata'* or 'deity of the clan'. According to some, the 'Chief God' of Arabia was the 'moon god' Hubal and most likely connected to the black stone(s) of Kaaba,[35] which was revered by several tribes and cults in pre-Islamic Arabia. The rituals to worship Hubal were unique. On various important occasions, similar to Hindu *Samskaras* such as virginity, conception, birth, marriage, and death, there was a practice of throwing arrows in front of the image of Hubal, which was a key deity managed and controlled by the Quraysh tribe in which Muhammad was born.[36][37] In ancient Syria, Hubal was also the moon god.

Hubal's name also appears in a Nabataean inscription in *Mada'in Saleh* and other deities such as *Dushara,* who had three daughters. The main female deities were *Allāt, Al-'Uzzá, and Manāt*. *Allāt* was the goddess associated with the underworld. *Al-'Uzzá*, "The Mightiest One" or "The Strong", was a fertility goddess, and she was evoked during a war for protection and victory. *Manāt* was the goddess of fate, and the *Book of Idols* describes her as the most ancient of these deities.[38][39]

According to Belgian scholar Koenraad Elst, "The pre-Islamic religion was also largely star worship (next to ancestor worship and the worship of special stones like the Black Stone in Mecca's *Ka'ba*). Thus, the three Meccan goddesses of *Satanic Verses* fame, *al-Lāt*, *al-Uzza* and *al-Manāt*, are roughly the Sun, Venus and the Moon. The *Ka'ba* was dedicated to the moon-god *Hubal*, and housed a stone fallen from heaven."[40]

During the advent of Islam, it is most likely that Muhammed destroyed all the temples,[41] killed all the 'idolaters', Islamized 'Allah', and established the *'Majhab'* called Islam in 610 CE. Moon and Sun worship, as it was prevalent in many ancient traditions, was condemned by Muhammad. Quran (41:37) reads:

"And of His signs are the night and day and the sun and moon. Do not prostrate to the sun or the moon, but prostrate to Allah, who created them, if it should be Him that you worship".

The story goes like this:

The elegant city of *al-Ka'bah al-Yamaniyah* (the 'Southern Ka'ba') was a prosperous city rivaling Mecca. There was *Dhul-Khalasa*,[42][43] a pristine temple with columns, pillars, and crown top which perhaps could be compared with a Jain temple or a Shiva temple built using marble or quartz, using pillars and the top of which was embroidered with a stone crown.

Once the primal deity Allah was taken over by Muhammad's forces, they said no other deity could exist. They set on a mission to destroy all structures and statues relating to any pre-Islamic worshipping practices, especially of the *Al-Aws* and *Al-Khazraj* tribes of Arabia.

The story goes like this:

One fine day, Arabs in the town *Al–Mashallel* were home after the summer was over. After celebrating the ritual ceremonies of their revered deity, they were resting at home. There was a beautiful temple of Manāt. She sat on a lion with two female companions, perhaps daughters. Suddenly, a large herd of horsemen with sharp weapons invaded the town at dawn. It was a chilly night.

Khalid ibn al-Walid was sent, most likely by Muhammad himself, to destroy the 'statues'.[44][45]

According to Hadiths Al-Bukhaari (3020) and Muslim (2476) as narrated that Jareer ibn' Abd-Allaah al-Bajali said: The Messenger of Allah said to me: "O Jareer, will you not relieve me of Dhu'l-Khalsah (the temple and deity)?" That was a house (in Yemen) belonging to the (tribe of) Khath'am, which was called Ka'bat al-Yamaaniyyah. I set out with one hundred and fifty equestrians. I used not to sit firm on horses, and I mentioned that to the Messenger of Allah. He struck me on my chest with his hand and said, 'O Allah! Make him firm and make him one who guides others and is guided on the right path'." So Jareer went and burned it (the temple) with fire, then Jareer sent a man called Abu Artaat to the Messenger of Allaah. He said, "I did not come to you until we had left it like a scabby camel". Then the Messenger of Allaah blessed the horses of (the tribe of) Ahmas and their men five times.

Then *Sa'd bin Zaid al-Ashhali*, a recently converted Muslim whose ancestors also worshiped *Manat*, was also dispatched. While they tried to destroy Manat's statue, a naked dark-skinned woman with long hair came to protect the deity. She was beating on her chest, wailing and telling the horsemen with swords not to destroy the shrine and the statue. But alas, as Sa'd was instructed, drew his sword and, without any mercy or pity, full of disgust, put his sword into her chest; blood oozed out, and then they cut her into pieces. According to Muir, Muhammad said that the woman slain in this incident was the Goddess of the Al-Aws and Al-Khazraj tribes, i.e., *Manat*.[46]

Then the troops were instructed first to break the nose and deface the statues. They broke several other parts. Nobody knows the statues' exact fate and the shrine which was located between Mecca, Medina, and the Red Sea. A millennia-old shrine of faith of the Arabs was destroyed forever, along with all the devotees and followers' lives, to send a stern message to the rest of the Arabs.[47][48]

It is said that Muhammad himself meticulously planned the execution of destroying all ancient shrines, statues, and in general, any pre-Islamic heritage in Arabia.[49]

According to Al-Haafiz Ibn Hajar, as quoted in the Hadith named *Hisn al-Muslim*, it is prescribed to remove things that may tempt or confuse the people, whether they are buildings, people, animals, or inanimate objects.

According to the book *Ar-Raheeq Al-Makhtum*, *Memoirs of the Noble Prophet*, by Saifur Rahman al-Mubarakpuri in the chapter *'Conquest of Makkah'* Muhammad sent Sa'd ibn Zayd al-Ashhali on a campaign to destroy Manaat (venerated by both Al-Aws and Al-Khazraj tribes), Khaalid ibn al-Waleed on a campaign to destroy *al-'Uzza* (revered by Quraish and Kinanah tribes) and 'Amr ibn al-'Aas on a campaign to destroy *Suwaa* (venerated by *Hudhail* tribe). All of that happened after the Conquest of Mecca by Muhammad in 630 CE.[50]

Arab Deities

As noted earlier, over 360 deities belonged to different tribes, cults, and sects before Islam's advent.[51] We will mention a few most important ones here.

Goddess Manat

In Arabic, *mana* means 'to determine', and Arabic *maniya,* which also means fate. Manat was the deity of destiny or fate and most ancient of all Abrahamic tribes such as Banu Aws and Banu Khazraj. Some of her statues were made out of wood, and it is said that the one in al-Mushallel was carved out of stone. People would flock from faraway places, shave their heads before visiting the shrine of Manat. There were animal sacrifices made to her.[52] A poem which is supposed to have been written by Abd-al-'Uzza ibn-Wadi'ah al-Muzani gave significance to the Khazraj:

"An oath, truthful and just, I swore By Manāh, at the sacred place of the Khazraj".

Many believe that a statue of Manat was among the 360 idols in the Kaaba, which initially may have been in Petra and not in Mecca. According to Ibn al-Kalbi, when worshipers would circumambulate the Kaaba, they would chant her name along with that of her sisters, *al-Lat* and *al-Uzza*, seeking their blessings and interception.[53]

Additionally, Manat was believed to be watching over the graves. Some tomb inscriptions read:

"And may Dushara and Manat and Qaysha curse anyone who sells this tomb or buys it or gives it in pledge or makes a gift of it or leases it or draws up for himself any document concerning it or buries in it anyone apart from the inscribed above".[54]

'Manasik' in Arabic means a set of rites and ceremonies that have to be performed by Muslim pilgrims in and around

Kaaba in Mecca, which are residual practices from the days of worshiping goddess Manat.[55]

Based on Herodotus (5th century BCE) in Greece, *Allat* was the same as *Aphrodite* [56][57] and was worshiped throughout the ancient Near East. People of Mecca and the nearby areas believed that the goddesses *Al-Lat*, *Al-Uzza*, and *Manat* were the daughters of Allah.[58][59][60][61]

Al-Lat is also considered the feminine form of Allah.[62] Al-Lat was used as a title for the goddess Asherah or Athirat.[63] Al-Lat is also mentioned in pre-Islamic Arab poetry, such as in *'al-Mutalammis'* satire of Amr ibn Hind:[64]

Thou hast banished me for fear of lampoon and satire.
No! By Allat and all the sacred baetyls (ansab)
thou shalt not escape.

A poem by the pre-Islamic monotheist Zayd ibn Amr mentions al-Lat, along with al-'Uzza and Hubal:[65]

Am I to worship one lord or a thousand?
If there are as many as you claim,
I renounce al-Lat and al-Uzza, both of them,
as any strong-minded person would.
I will not worship al-Uzza and her two daughters...
I will not worship Hubal, though he was our lord
in the days when I had little sense.

In the early days of Islam, Muhammad took some precautions before destroying older deities. The people of Mecca were allowed to continue worshiping the ancient deities for some time (apparently suggested by Gabriel). But one day, the angel Gabriel appeared and 'rebuked him, telling him that the earlier verses (allowing the worship of various deities) came not from God but rather from Satan'. According to the Abrahamic faith, Satan or the Devil is the one 'that seduces humans into sin or falsehood'. It is worth noting that famous author Salman Rushdie used the title *The Satanic Verses* for his controversial book. Perhaps alluding to the Islamic religious texts was instead 'satanic'; hence, the wrath of the fatwa was followed to him.

Afterward, Angel Gabriel is said to have revealed a new passage to Muhammad condemning the worship of these deities (Quran 53:19-23):

"Have ye thought upon Al-Lat and Al-'Uzza

And Manat, the third, the ot her?

Are yours the males and His the females?

That indeed were an unfair division!

They are but names which ye have named, ye and your fathers, for which God hath revealed no warrant. They follow but a guess and that which (they) themselves desire. And now the guidance from their Lord hath come unto them."

Thus, the ancient Arab world's old deities found space not even in the museums – unlike the Hindu/Buddhist murthys which were stolen by the colonists; they are dimly noted just in some history books today!

Allah

Allah is critical in Islam because everything in a Muslim's life revolves around the power, likes, and dislikes of this compelling icon of Islam. Originally, the term Allah is not of Arabic origin, as related and similar terms like "Al-ilāh" existed in Hebrew and Aramaic languages (El and Elah, respectively), as noted earlier.[66][67]

In Aramaic, the language said to have been spoken by Jesus Christ, God is Elah or Elaha, (Ĕlāhā/Ilahi) and in Syriac languages, it is 'Alâhâ' which was used by the Church in both of which meant "God".[68][69] The old Biblical Hebrew language used the plural form Elohim and, in some cases, the singular form Eloah.

According to Shahid, on the authority of 10th-century Muslim scholar Al-Marzubani, "Allah" was also mentioned in pre-Islamic Christian poems by some Ghassanid and Tanukhid poets in Syria and Northern Arabia. Many variants of the term Allah were found in pre-Islamic inscriptions.[70]

Arabic-speaking Christians and Jews also used Allah for God.[71] Some of them use the term Allah and not God to date. Some of them, while describing the Trinity of 'God' also use the words such as 'Allāh al-ab' for God the Father, 'Allāh al-ibn' for 'God the Son' and 'Allāh ar-rūḥ al-Quds' for 'God the Holy Spirit'. They also used the Muslim term *bismillāh* around the 8th century CE. The Muslim concept of bismillāh means – "In the name of Allah, the Compassionate, the Merciful". The Arab Christian concept, on the other hand, is: "In the name of Father and the Son and the Holy Spirit, One God".

Assyrian Christians use 'Ĕlāhā, or Alaha for the same. Maltese, the main language of Malta, the last land between Europe and Africa – related to Arabic used by predominantly Roman Catholic inhabitants, uses *Alla* for God.[72]

According to the Julius Wellhausen version of the *Documentary Hypothesis*, one of the models used by biblical scholars to explain the origins of Biblical literature, there was a tribal federation headed by the Quraysh tribe. Muhammad and his clan belonged to this tribe, and Muhammad's father's name was ʿAbd-Allāh, meaning "the slave of Allāh".[50] Allah was the supreme deity of the federation, whereas specifically for the Quraysh tribe, Hubal was the supreme one over all others, and Allah and Hubal were two distinct deities.

According to the disputed Wellhausen hypothesis, "the Kaaba was first consecrated to a supreme deity named Allah and then hosted the pantheon of Quraysh after their conquest of Mecca, about a century before the time of Muhammad."[73] Some inscriptions seem to indicate Allah's use as a name of a 'polytheist' deity centuries earlier, but we know nothing precise about this use. Interestingly, there was no image of Allah in Arabia.

According to *Kitab al-Aghani*, a 10th century encyclopedic collection – quoted by Irfan Shahid, pre-Islamic Arab Christians invoked the following battle cry, "Ya La Ibad Allah" (O slaves of Allah). This is very similar to Islamic *'Allahu Akbar'*, which means 'Allah is greater' (than other gods), a tribal expression, which would claim "my god is stronger than yours".[74]

Another evidence of Allah's antiquity is a Christian leader named Abd Allah ibn Abu Bakr ibn Muhammad who died in a battle in Narjan around 523 CE, had a ring with an inscription: "Allah is my lord". This is based on the biography of Ibn Ishaq.[75]

Iconoclasm

A term called aniconism prohibits any material representation of a natural and supernatural object of reverence. It may include 'god', saints, or even grave iconography. When the destruction of such images enforces this concept, it is called iconoclasm.

As noted earlier, 'idol' is the word that was introduced and used to denote any statue or image related to divinity in any culture. According to the *Merriam-Webster dictionary*, an idol is "a representation or symbol of an object of worship". The other meaning is 'a false conception'. According to Abrahamic theologies, an idol is a 'false god'. Idolatry is defined as the practice of worshiping an idol. In India, it is called 'murthy pooja'.

Etymonline defines 'idol' this way:

"From Latin 'idolum' "image (mental or physical), form," especially "apparition, ghost", but used in Church Latin for "false god, an image of a pagan deity as an object of worship".

A Greek word for an "image", *eidos*, meaning "form, shape; likeness, resemblance," used by Jewish and early Christian writers for "image of a false god," hence also "false god". The Germanic languages tended to form a word for it from the reverse direction, from "god" to "false god", hence "image of a false god".[76]

'Icon' is a similar term in English like idol, which came from the Greek word *eikon*, which means figure or image, and the Greek word kláō which means 'to break' later became 'klast'.

Thus, the breaker of an icon or idol is called an iconoclast. According to *Etymonline*:

"iconoclast" means "breaker or destroyer of images", from French *iconoclaste*, medieval Latin *iconoclastes*, and late Greek *eikonoklastes*.

Originally, the term iconoclasm was used about those in the Eastern Church in the 8th and 9th centuries CE. Their mobs of followers destroyed images, statues, and other (pagan) religious objects because they thought they were 'idols' – applied till the 16th and 17th centuries. Protestants in the Netherlands vandalized former Catholic churches on similar grounds. The purpose was "one who attacks orthodox beliefs or cherished institutions was first attested in 1842".[77]

In Judaism, 'idolatry' is prohibited, as can be found in the Hebrew Bible called Tanakh. For example:

"[Therefore,] do not make yourselves false gods. Do not raise up a stone idol or a sacred pillar for yourselves. Do not place a kneeling stone in your land so that you can prostrate yourselves on it. I am God your Lord." (Leviticus 26:1)

Also,

"Do not have any other gods before Me. Do not represent [such] gods by any carved statue or picture of anything in the heaven above, on the earth below, or in the water below the land. Do not bow down to [such gods] or worship them. I am God your Lord, a God who demands exclusive worship." (Exodus 20:3-6)

Iconoclasm is associated with all three Abrahamic traditions though the army of Islam widely practices it to date. Muhammad indoctrinated it in Islam as a duty of each Muslim to oppose 'idolatry' called *al-wathaniyyah*[78] in Arabic.

According to the Quran, here are the instructions on 'idols':

"Then, following misery, He sent down upon you a feeling of security, a slumber overcoming a party among you, while another party cared only for themselves, thinking false thoughts about God, thoughts fit for the Age of Idolatry." (3:154)

"Do they truly desire the law of paganism? But who is fairer than God in judgment for a people firm of faith?" (5:50)

"Remain in your homes, and do not display your adornments, as was the case with the earlier Age of Barbarism." (33:33)

"You only worship, besides Allah, idols, and you produce a falsehood. Indeed, those you worship besides Allah do not possess for you [the power of] provision. So seek from Allah provision and worship Him and be grateful to Him. To Him, you will be returned." (29:16-17)

"And [Abraham] said, You have only taken, other than Allah, idols as [a bond of] affection among you in worldly life. Then on the Day of Resurrection, you will deny one another and curse one another, and your refuge will be the Fire, and you will not have any helpers." (29:26).

Unequivocal instruction was given in the Quran for the destruction of every external icon for reverence and was made into a part of the Islamic conquests:

"Do not leave any image without defacing it or any built-up grave without levelling it." (Quran 21:25)

According to several historians, including Amin Faris and G.R.D. King, defacement, mutilation of affective parts of the face such as the eyes and nose was given as an alternative to complete destruction of an image. Evidence of these is found in the accounts of Muhammad's iconoclastic activities. The Book of Idols says: "When on the day he conquered Mecca, the Apostle of God appeared before the Kabah, he found the idols arrayed around it".[79] It was a common practice since the early days of Islam and by Muhammad to pierce their eyes with the point of his arrow first to 'destroy the power of these deities' to do any harm to them. And if time and resources permitted, he then ordered that they be knocked down, after which they were taken out to break into pieces or burned.[80][81]

It is evident from many temple remains (e.g., the Qutab Minar complex in Delhi) where whole murthys were not destroyed, but just the faces were broken. Thousands of temples were broken by the invading Islamic forces, first breaking the faces of the murthys and then breaking the whole murthy into pieces wherever was possible. If a mosque or mausoleum was built on top of it, the murthys were placed on the steps (upside down) so that people who would visit these places would have to step over the murthys, adding insult to injury.[82] In many cases, some broken sculptures of murthy's were intentionally kept within the occupied structures such as a mosque or a tomb to display the superiority of Islam.

Here are some examples from Islamic texts (Hadith) on the treatment of murthys.

Sahih Muslim, the *Book of Prayer* narrated that Abu'l-Hayaaj al-Asadi said: 'Ali ibn Abi Talib said to me: "Shall I not send you with the same instructions as the Messenger of Allah sent me? 'Do not leave any image without defacing it or any built-up grave without levelling it.'"

Muslim (832) narrated from 'Urwah ibn 'Abasah that he said to the Prophet: "With what were you sent?" He said, "I was sent to uphold the ties of kinship, to break the idols, and so that Allah would be worshipped alone with no partner or associate."

Muslim also quotes Al-Nawawi discussing the subject of image-making:

'They unanimously agreed that whatever casts a shadow is not allowed and must be changed.

Images that cast a shadow are three-dimensional images like these statues'.[83]

Ibn Khuldoon noted in al-Muqaddimah that the caliph Al-Ma'moon wanted to destroy the Pyramids in Egypt, and he gathered his men but failed.[84]

The destruction of the 6th century Bamiyan Buddha statues by the Taliban in Afghanistan in 2001 is perfectly in line with the iconoclasm practice of the Islamists. Regular news of desecration and destruction of murthys and temples in Pakistan, Bangladesh, and India is a stark reminder of the iconoclastic nature of the Islamists.

Celebration of Islamic Festivals by Non-Muslims

Post-Independence, the NeoCols started a narration that India's Muslim population was under threat as the Hindus were looking to avenge India's invasions and partition. These lies asserted that Muslims of India must always stay united and vote *en masse* for the Congress Party as their savior. This policy was later adopted by other regional parties such as the Samajwadi Party of Mulayam Singh and Mamata Banerjee's Trinamool Congress (TMC) party to create a 'vote bank' to win and control political power. The Communist party, especially the Nehru-influenced lobby or the left-Nehruvians, also used these tactics to win Muslim votes and appease them to keep them on their side; they allowed illegal Muslim migration, and even looking the other way for all sorts of criminal activities in Muslim neighborhoods. On December 9, 2006, then Indian Prime Minister Manmohan Singh, while addressing the 52nd meeting of the National Development Council, said: "We will have to devise innovative plans to ensure that minorities, particularly the Muslim minority, are empowered to share the fruits of development equitably. They must have the first claim on resources."[85] Indicating vote bank politics by the appeasement of the Muslim community.

It has been a fashion among some Hindus, especially the politicians, to don skull caps, hug a Muslim, organize or attend Iftar parties and celebrate Muslim festivals to celebrate in an effort of show-business for friendship and better understanding. But this has been going on only for the past few decades since the arrival of Mohandas Karamchand Gandhi in Indian politics. During invasions and Muslim rule periods, people were forced to convert or observe and respect the celebrations of Islamic festivals. The most notable one is *Eid or Id-Ul-Fitr*.

On the day of Eid, Muslim men take a bath and gather in an open place called Eid-gah or in mosque premises to attend the 'Eid Prayer Service'. After a prayer, the religious leader, Imam, delivers a sermon. Generally, people try to remember the sacrifices of the ancient prophet Abraham and his wife when he was ready to sacrifice his son Ishmael upon God's order. Now, they offer animal sacrifices.

On that day, millions of animals, including cows, are slaughtered globally to 'appease Allah'. Streams of blood flow from the veins of the animals. A river of blood floods the streets of Muslim habitats. The 'Halal' way of slaughtering the animal requires cutting the windpipe and the jugular veins, which keeps the animal alive until all the blood oozes out of the body and the animal suffers a slow and painful death. Their heads are severed off after their death instead of the other way around, which would be much less painful. In India, cows are slaughtered in the name of Allah, many times publicly, displaying to the whole world, including the non-Muslims. The prayer for the slaughter is: 'Say my prayer, and my sacrifice and my life and my death are for the sake of Allah, the lord of all worlds'. According to Islamic laws, there are two Arabic words related to animal sacrifice: qorbān and uḍḥiyah, the ritual animal sacrifice of livestock. The words mean offering or sacrifice.

Pre-Islamic animal sacrifice was offered to appease the deities or win their favor as an atonement of sins, as was the case with different cultures and their practices in the pre-Islamic world. In Arabia, animal sacrifice was rampant for their deities, including many of the Kaaba's 360 deities.

According to the Quran:

"For every people We have laid down a ritual of sacrifice (- although the purpose of the ritual is the same -) that they pronounce the name of Allah over the cattle He has provided them. Your Lord is One God; so submit yourselves to Him alone. And give, (O Prophet), glad tidings to those that humble themselves (before Allah)." (22:34)

"We have appointed sacrificial camels among the symbols of (devotion to) Allah. There is much good in them for you. So

make them stand (at the time of sacrifice) and pronounce the name of Allah over them, and when they fall down on their sides (after they are slaughtered), eat and also feed them who do not ask and those who ask. Thus have We subjected these animals that you may give thanks." (22:36)

According to Hadith (Volume 7, Book 68, Number 453 Narrated by Al-Bara):

The Prophet said (on the day of Idal-Adha), *"The first thing we will do on this day of ours, is to offer the ('Id) prayer and then return to slaughter the sacrifice." During the early days, while establishing Islam, initially, Muhammad took a strategic step to allow people to continue animal sacrifice and eat animal flesh even though their old deities were replaced with the only one, Allah.*

Quran says, 'Neither flesh nor blood of your sacrifices reaches Allah. But it is his righteous motive underlying them that reaches Him.' (22:37) Most likely, it was a bit of advice against the pre-Islamic practice of sacrifice. What do the Muslims pray on that day? 'Allah is the greatest; there is none worthy of worship except Allah. All praise belongs to Allah'.

As a Sanatani – Hindu, Buddhist, Jain, or Sikh, it is ironic that they condone and embrace this idea of exclusivity by celebrating Eid – and the message is unambiguous that non-Muslims' deities are not 'worthy of worship and prayer'! Muslims simply celebrate sheer disapproval of non-Muslims' objects of worship. That non-Muslims are *kafirs* according to the Islamic scriptures; they are objects of hatred and punishment! Billions are spent on these celebrations. This money supports the 'Halal Economy', which eventually helps the activities that ultimately hurt or undermine the kafirs, aka the Hindus, Sikhs, Buddhists, and Jains![86]

The term for the animal sacrifice is *'Qurbani'*, which may have originated from the Jewish word "corban", which means setting apart something in the name of God.[87] Non-Muslims also often use the term to denote any kind of sacrifice in general (not just animal slaughter) – but the real purpose of this sacrifice, according to Islam, is for Allah only.

The Arabic word *halal* means "permissible or lawful" to Muslims. Halal or kutha meat is flesh obtained from an animal after torture and slow bleeding and offering a Muslim prayer. Halal meat and many other 'halal-certified' products are imposed on all consumers globally, including Christians, Hindus, and Sikhs. This type of meat is forbidden – according to the *Rehat Maryada* of Sikh code of conduct.[88][89]

H.S. Singha, in his book, noted:

"According to the ancient Aryan Hindu tradition, only such meat as is obtained from an animal which is killed with one stroke of the weapon causing instantaneous death is fit for human consumption. However, with the coming of Islam into India and the Muslim political hegemony, it became a state policy not to permit slaughter of animals for food, in any other manner, except as laid down in the Quran – the kosher meat prepared by slowly severing the main blood artery of the throat of the animal while reciting verses from the Quran. It is done to make slaughter a sacrifice to God and to expiate the sins of the slaughter. Guru Gobind Singh took a rather severe view of this aspect of the whole matter. Therefore, he permitted flesh to be taken as food, repudiated the entire theory of this expiatory sacrifice and the right of ruling Muslims to impose it on non-Muslims. Accordingly, he made jhatka meat obligatory for those Sikhs interested in taking meat as a part of their food.*"*[90]

In a way, Jewish Kosher and Islamic Halal food habits are similar, but there are differences, and the main one being the Islamic prayer offered during the slaughter in case of halal. It also shows many practices in Islam, including forbiddance of pig in the diet and the practice of circumcision or *brit milah* (Judaism) and *khatna* (Islam), which has been practiced since the pre-Abrahamic period in Arabia. Around the time of the birth of Islam, both male and female circumcision was done by

Arabian tribes,[91][92] and this brutal practice continues to date, mostly in Africa and Muslim communities. Jewish tribes of Arabia practiced male circumcision,[93] which continues to date though there is no substantial scientific reason behind it.

Eid Milad-Un-Nabi is another Eid celebration of the birth anniversary of Muhammad. Many call it 'Nabi Divas' in many parts of India. According to Islam, that day is 'the most important event in the history of the world' – he was born to be the 'Chief of the Prophets'. According to the Quran (33:57) *'Allah sends down His blessings on the Prophet, and His Angels constantly invoke His blessings on him; do you, O believers, also invoke Allah's blessings on him and offer him the salutation of peace'*. On many occasions, non-Muslims are forced to observe the same in the Indian subcontinent.

Arabic and Islamic Terminologies

Many Arabic and Persian words entered into the Urdu language and other Indian languages, especially in Hindi, along with certain practices of Islam in the subcontinent, which are antithetical to the Dharmic traditions. Invasions of Islamic forces started in India around 712 CE. However, it took 500 years to establish Islamic rule in India due to fierce fighting and resistance by the Indian people. Later, for about 500 years, Indians had to deal with the brutal Islamic regime between the first Sultanate in Delhi in 1206 CE till the death of Aurangzeb in 1707 CE. Due to this reason and the co-existence of Arabs and Turks and other invading Islamic peoples, many Arabic terms and concepts and, more importantly, words significant for Islam have entered into the subcontinent vocabulary. Many Islamic images and practices are also innocuously respected or accepted and even used by non-Muslims. However, those terminologies are associated with ideas with a strong character of nonconformities to India's age-old tradition and culture.

How Indians have mixed up their ancient heritage with the outsiders' practices is part of a long history of the massive struggle for survival by the Hindus. Most of us know that Dharma is not a religion, and Ishwar is not equivalent to the Abrahamic concept 'God' or 'Allah'. But many such Islamic ideas have entered our vocabulary. Below are several important ones each Hindu should take cognizance of.

Saheed or Sahid

Shahid originates from the Arabic word, which is often found in the Quran, meaning "witness", and is generally used to denote an Islamic martyr or someone 'who dies for his faith' in Islam. [94] It is similar to the Greek term 'martyr', meaning "witness", which is also found in the New Testament. In the Islamic practice books or Hadiths, the term Sahid is a posthumous title and gets deeper significance.[95] Sahid is promised paradise, as noted in various Islamic texts, especially the Quran.

"Think not of those who are slain in Allah's way as dead. Nay, they live, finding their sustenance in the presence of their Lord; They rejoice in the bounty provided by Allah. And with regard to those left behind, who have not yet joined them (in their bliss), the (Sahid's) glory in the fact that on them is no fear, nor have they (cause to) grieve." (Quran 3: 169–170)

"Allah hath purchased of the believers their persons and their goods; for theirs (in return) is the garden (of Paradise): they 152. The Crash of a Civilization fight in His cause, and slay and are slain: a promise binding on Him in truth, through the Law, the Gospel, and the Quran: and who is more faithful to his covenant than Allah? Then rejoice in the bargain which ye have concluded: that is the achievement supreme." (Quran 9:111)

"Those who leave their homes in the cause of Allah, and are then slain or die — On them will Allah bestow verily a goodly Provision: Truly Allah is He Who bestows the best provision. Verily He will admit them to a place with which they shall be well pleased: for Allah is All-Knowing, Most Forbearing." (Quran 22:58–59)

Similarly, the Hadiths also further present the case for a Sahid.

It has been narrated on the authority of Anas B. Malik that the Messenger of Allah said: Who seeks martyrdom with sincerity shall get its reward, though he may not achieve it.[96]

Muhammad is reported to have said these words about martyrdom: *"By Him in Whose Hands my life is! I would love to be martyred in Allah's Cause and then get resurrected and then get martyred, and then get resurrected again and then get martyred and then get resurrected again and then get martyred".*

"Nobody who enters Paradise likes to go back to the world even if he got everything on the Earth, except a Mujahid who wishes to return to the world so that he may be martyred ten times because of the dignity he receives (from Allah)."[97]

A woman martyr is called a "shahida" or "sahida". The first martyr in Islam as recorded was a female named Sumayyah bint Khayyat, because she was stabbed to death by Abu Jahl, a strongman from the Quraysh tribe who opposed Islam.[98][99]

This exemplifies many women Jihadists found around the world.

As we can find these days, Jihadists are motivated by this idea of sahid. Many times, before going on a suicide mission, they record a 'martyrdom video' to leave behind evidence to inspire others to follow their path. However, according to some Islamic scholars, suicide (*aintahar* in Arabic) or killing oneself is forbidden in Islam, and thus 'suicide attacks' are not considered valid Islamic practice.[100]

Quran says: *"And do not kill yourselves, surely God is most Merciful to you." (Quran, 4:29)*

Hadith says: (Narrated by Abu Huraira): *"He who commits suicide by throttling shall keep on throttling himself in the Hell-Fire (forever) and he who commits suicide by stabbing himself shall keep on stabbing himself in the Hell-Fire." (Hadith, Sahih al-Bukhari, 2:23:446)*

But, suicide and death in a Jihadi mission are not the same.

The meaning and usage of the term martyr are also misplaced in the Indian subcontinent. Ancient Greeks and in the early days of Christianity, a witness who offered verbal or written testimony was called a martyr. In Christianity, it was particularly used for ideas related to the authenticity of the Gospel as the 'Word of God', sometimes followed by death by the opponent.[101] Later, it became more frequent that some testimonies were rejected, and the witnesses put to death, which then gained the meaning we have today [quote] 'dying for God', in the case of the Christian witnesses who followed Jesus himself – sacrificing their life for truth.

It is difficult to trace the source and history of the Jihadi suicides as we see them today. In the Indian subcontinent, many Hindus and Sikhs use the terms shahid or martyr without knowing the real meaning and historical context behind them. The alternative Hindu or Indian term for someone giving life for a great cause such as their tradition or country is called *'hutatma'* and *'veeratma'* in Sanskrit. The act of this supreme sacrifice is called to achieve *'veer-gatih'*.

Mazhab or Majhab

In Islam, the term mazhab is described as 'the straight path that leads towards Allah's pleasure, away from His anger; while guarding against the possibility of going astray.'[102]

Mazhab is a school of Islamic jurisprudence; a student is called Talab (male) or Taleba (female) — this is where the term Taliban originates from. When a student studies under a scholar or *alim* or listens to a jurist *faqīh* and follows his verdicts, they become known as that school's scholar or *'madhhab'* as used in original Arabic.[103] Mazhab has nothing to do with a typical religion as we understand it today, especially when it comes to the Hindu idea of Dharma.

Iman and Imandaar

Generally, it is used by all as 'trust' or trustworthy though the actual meaning has to do with faith in Islam and its laws.

Muhammad is narrated by some Islamic scholars about what Iman is:

Ibn Abbas narrates that the Angel Jibril once asked the Prophet: *"Tell me what is Iman?" The Prophet replied: "Iman is to believe in Allah, the Day of Judgment, His (Allah's) Angels, Books and Prophets and to believe in life after death; and to believe in Paradise and the Fire, and the setting up of the Mizan (scales) to weigh the deeds; and to believe in the Divine Decree, the good and the bad of it (all). Jibril then asked him: "If I do all this will I be with Iman?" The Prophet said: "When you have done all of this, you will be having Iman." "Iman is that you believe in God (Allah) and His Angels and His Books and His Messengers and the hereafter and the good and evil fate (ordained by your God)* "[104]

Hence Imandar is a person who is a devout follower of the Islamic faith. But in India, it is used frequently by non-Muslims to mean an honest person generally.

Ghazi

Bedouin nomads in the Arabic peninsula had the tradition of raiding established settlements, other tribes, and caravans, especially traders; this was called 'ghazw'. Ghazi has initially been a Bedouin term later adopted and used in Quranic Arabic for those who participated in *ghazw* or military expeditions and raids against the enemies, especially the non-Muslims. Ghazi was popularized by Muhammad for religious wars or Jihad and became an essential word in Islam to expand its territory.[105]

According to Ottoman historian Ahmedi the meaning of Ghazi is:

"A Ghazi is the instrument of the religion of Allah, a servant of God who purifies the earth from the filth of polytheism. The

Ghazi is the sword of God; he is the protector and the refuge of the believers. If he becomes a martyr in the ways of God, do not believe that he has died, he lives in beatitude with Allah, he has eternal life."[106]

According to Islamic texts, Muhammad participated in 27 such Ghazwa or expeditions. The first one was the Invasion of Waddan in August 623 CE, when he ordered his followers to attack a Quraysh caravan.[107][108]

The invader and founder of the Moghul rule in India Babur adopted this name: *Padshah Ghazi, Zahiru'din Muhammad Babur*. In his memoir called *Babur-Nama*, he wrote:

"As the Bajauris were rebels and at enmity with the people of Islam, and as, by reason of the heathenish and hostile customs prevailing in their midst, the very name of Islam was rooted out from their tribe, they were put to a general massacre, and their wives and children were made captive. At a guess, more than 3000 men went to their death; as the fight did not reach the eastern side of the fort, a few got away there. The fort was taken, we entered and inspected it. On the walls, in houses, streets and alleys, the dead lay, in what numbers! Comers and goers to and fro were passing over the bodies... With mind easy about the important affairs of the Bajaur fort, we marched, on Tuesday the 9th of Muharram, one kuroh (2m) down the dale of Bajaur and ordered that a tower of heads should be set up on the rising ground. On Wednesday, the 10th of Muharram, we rode out to visit the Bajaur fort. There was a wine party in Khawaja Kalan's house, several goat-skins of wine having been brought."

'After this success, Ghazi (Victor in a Holy-war) was written amongst the royal titles. Below the titles (tughra) entered on the Fath-nama, I wrote the following quatrain:

For Islam's sake,

I wandered in the wilds,

Prepared for war with pagans and Hindus,

Resolved myself to meet the martyr's death,

Thanks be to Allah! A ghazi I became.[109]

Like many other Jihadi Muslim rulers, Akbar also took on the title Ghazi: *Abul Fath Jalal-ud-din Muhammad Akbar Badshah Ghazi.* This indicates that, to the Hindu subjects how much contempt Akbar also had, though most historians hid it.

Throughout the Indian subcontinent, there are 'mazhars', 'dargahs' or memorials in these Ghazis' names, who conducted *ghazwa* against the kafirs, sometimes combined as Ghazi Peer. Ignorant Hindus unknowingly and reverently support such places and participate in festivals associated with them. Many towns and villages are also called 'Ghazipur' or 'Ghaziabad.'

Similarly, many so-called 'saints' who were engaged in many forms of human rights violations and spread hate and violence are also revered and, in many cases, by the Hindus. Prime examples are Xavier, popularly known as Saint Xavier, responsible for the Goa Inquisition and resulting brutal deaths of many non-Christians and destruction of many non-Christian places of worship. Mary Teresa Bojaxhiu, otherwise called 'Mother' Teresa, also has committed crimes against humanity. We have presented these in detail in Chapter II.

Manat

In the Indian subcontinent, the word *manat* is used for oblation to a deity to fulfill some prayers and wishes. People promise to offer something special after their wish being fulfilled. Was the idea of manat prevalent in large part of Asia during pre-Islamic times in connection to worshipping goddess *'Manat'*?[110] Or, was it an Islamic introduction? It is a matter for scholars to determine, but definitely, it is not a Hindu practice.

The Hindus use a similar term, *'manasik'*, which is identical to *'Sankalp'* or the oath they take before performing certain rituals.

Peer or Pir Baba

The term *Pir* is originally from Persian, which meant an elder or respected person. In Arabic, the word *Hazrat* is also used in the same context. Though there are subtle differences in meaning, *sheikh* or *shaykh* is also used for similar denotation. Generally, the term *pir* evokes the idea of a saint. This became popular in the Indian subcontinent as Sufism became prominent, and the Pir's role was typically personal 'spiritual guidance' to his followers. Two other commonly used terms for a Sufi leader are *murshid* and *Sarkar* (master or lord in Persian). The descendants of Ali are also called *Peer* in Alevism. Peer Baba is also a common term, and Baba is a Persian term meaning father.[111] But the majority of these so-called Sufi saints worked as the agents of Islam to covertly convert the Hindus[112] and spying for the rulers during the Islamic period in India.

Dargah, Mazhar, Maqbara

These are supposed to be holy or sacred memorials or tombs of famous Islamic icons from the past, especially professed spiritual leaders or healers during the Muslim period. But some research would reveal that similar to the so-called Christian 'saints' like Xavier – most of these people facilitated the conversion work for the Muslim rulers.

Many of these 'resting places', for preachers and visitors are attached to mosques or madrassas. An Arabic word *maqam* is also used to denote a living house, originally meant for the building adjacent to a dargah. However, a cursory look at the history will reveal the dark history behind these religious places because many of them were built after demolishing Hindu-Buddhist shrines after many fights.

A prime example is the Ajmer Sharif Dargah in Rajasthan, which was established by the so-called saint Moinuddin Chishti, a 13th-century Sufi who ultimately was Jihadi.

The historian M.A. Khan, in his book on Islam, noted: Khwaja Moinuddin Chisti (1141–1230), probably the second-greatest Sufi saint of India after Nizamuddin Auliya, demonstrated a deep-seated hatred toward Hindu religion and its practices.

On his arrival near the Anasagar Lake at Ajmer, Khwaja saw many idol-temples and promised to raze them to the ground with the help of Allah and His Prophet. After settling down there, Khwaja's followers used to bring every day a cow (sacred to Hindus) near a famous temple, where the king and Hindus prayed, slaughter it and cook kebab from its meat — clearly to show his contempt toward Hinduism. Chisti also came to India with his disciples to fight Jihad against the infidels and participated in the treacherous holy war of Sultan Muhammad Ghauri in which the kind and chivalrous Hindu king Prithviraj Chauhan was defeated in Ajmer. In Jihadi zeal, Chisti ascribed the credit for the victory to himself, saying: 'We have seized Pithaura (Prithviraj) alive and handed him over to the army of Islam".[113]

Devotional songs and music are performed at these sites, especially on *'urs'*, the Arabic word for the death anniversary of the founder. Many believe that this gave birth to *Qawwali* and *Kafi* forms of music. In Arabic, *qaul* means "utterance (of the Islamic prophet)", *Qawwāl* is someone who sings a *qaul,* and *qawwāli* is what a *Qawwāl* sings.[114] Qawwali texts exist in Persian, Urdu, and Hindi. Many Hindus get fascinated by such songs without knowing the actual meaning and the history behind them.

Salaam

In the Arabic lexicon, the word *salaam*, having Persian connections, means 'Peace, Safety, and Greetings'. Based on *Hadiths*, Muhammad was asked who should begin the greeting, and he said, "The one who is riding should greet the one who is walking, and the one who is walking should greet the one who is sitting, and the smaller group should greet the larger group". And also, one should give the salaam greeting upon entering a house".[115][116]

The Quran says: *"But when you enter the houses, greet one another with a greeting (salaam) from God blessed and good"*.[117]

The standard Arabic Muslim greeting *as-salāmu alaykum* or *salam alaikum* means "Peace be upon you" and is used chiefly as a religious salutation. It is also used by some other Arabic speaking non-Muslim communities, such as the Arab Christians. The reply to salam alaikum is 'alaykum was-salām', which means "peace be upon you, too". Another interpretation is: "Peace be upon you, as well as the mercy of Allah and his blessings".

It is clear the salutation to something is not the same as salaam. Hindus' universal greeting is *namaste* which has deep meaning.

Adaab

Originally the Arabic word *adaab* was meant to use for respect and politeness. Later, the term was adopted in Urdu along with a hand gesture for greeting others. Perhaps this was a compromise term adopted in the Indian subcontinent for a greeting to be used by the non-Muslims since *'salam alaikum'* was to be used only by the Muslims. In contrast, the majority of the people in the subcontinent have been Hindus. Adaab is not usually used in a Muslim country where the majority are Muslims.[118]

Inshallah

The Arabic word inshallah (*in sha Allah*) means "if *Allah* wills" or "*Allah* willing". The primary source of this term is found in the Quran (18:24): *"If Allah wills. And remember your Lord when you forget [it] and say, "Perhaps Allah will guide me to what is nearer than this to right conduct". It means nothing will happen without the will of Allah, which is above human will."*

In practical terms, *inshallah* actually means faith in 'Allah', who is the 'only God' of Islam. Any other ideas of God (including Jewish, Christian, and Hindu) are false ones.

Mashallah

As a result of the term *inshallah*, the Quranic Arabic word *mashallah* (*ma sha Allah*) is an Arabic phrase that means "*Allah* has willed it" or made it happen. Muslims use it to express joy and praise *Allah* in appreciation when an anticipated event or success comes to individuals.

Takbir

One of the essential Arabic phrases used by the Muslims, especially for the expansionism or jihadi purpose, is *'Allāhu Akbar'*, which means "*Allah* is greater [than everything]"; This phrase is called the *Takbir*.[119] The word is mainly used as a 'war cry' of the Islamists and Jihadists.

Mawla and Mawali

The word mawla has varied meanings based on interpretations of the Quran and Hadiths such as 'master', 'protector', 'lord', 'guardian', 'trustee', and 'helper'.

The word *mawla* is derived from the Arabic root *w-l-y* meaning "to be close to", "to be friends with", or "to have power over". People belonging to the Sufi sects use it for *Allah*.[120]

Originally, *mawāli* was used for clients of an Arab tribe; after the advent of Islam, it was used to refer to non-Arab Muslims and other client allies of the Muslim community. After Muhammad's death, the general designation for new converts to Islam was *mawla*. The plural form of *mawla* is *mawali*.

Mullah, Maulana and Maulavi

The word *'maula'na'*, rooted in mawla with the 1st person plural pronoun *'na'* (our) meaning 'our protector' is an attribute used for God in the Quran. Originally the term *maulavi* or *mawlvi* is also derived from the word *mawla*, and in Arabic, it is '*mawlawi*', a title given to a religious scholar, ulama, mullah or sheikh. One has to earn this title by studying in a madrassa.[121]

While *Mullah* is frequently used in the Middle Eastern Muslim countries as a title and respect for the religious leaders, in the Indian subcontinent, it has a derogatory connotation.[122] Muslims in these countries (the Indian subcontinent) use *maulana* more. Here the words maulvi and maulana are often used interchangeably; however, maulana is used for a religious leader with formal qualifications from a madrassa, and a maulvi is simply a priest or preacher. The term maulvi also has different levels – *maulvi* (basic), *alim* (intermediate), and *fazil* (advanced). These religious leaders and preachers are well-versed in Islamic scriptures and literature but may not have any orientation towards modern subjects such as science.

Dua

In India, the Arabic term *dua* has entered into the vocabulary of non-Muslims, though this term is exclusively for Muslims. Non-Muslims think that the word means prayer or blessings in general. But it is deeply associated with Muslim prayers, Muhammad, and Allah, and it is a way to express absolute surrender to Allah.

In Arabic, the term means 'request', and to a Muslim, it is an intense practice of prayer in Islam. Dua-related literature, poems, and songs have been created over the years, and devout Muslims follow or sing these in praise of how Muhammad prayed to Allah. The lyrical form of Dua is called *Munajat,* which in Islamic Arabic means 'intimate prayers to *Allah*'.[123][124]

There are several categories of dua. The first one is *Du'a al-mas'alah*, which is for asking something for a need from Allah. The other one is *Du'a al-'ibadah*, which is a simple surrender and worship of Allah. Dua includes various rituals in the Muslim community called *salat* or *salha,* including when a Muslim prays five times more popularly known as the *namaz* in the

Indian subcontinent. Quran prescribes – *"And establish regular prayers at the two ends of the day and at the approaches of the night: For those things, that are good remove those that are evil: Be that the word of remembrance to those who remember (Allah)."*[125]

There are various specified *suras* and *ayats* from the Quran and other Islamic literature which are used for Dua.

According to the *Book of 101 Duas,* the perfect Dua is:

"In the name of Allah the Beneficent the Merciful O Allah! O Allah! O Allah! The Security, the Security from the vanishment of the faith. O the Eternally Known! O the Eternally Obliging and O the Guide of those gone astray, Thee alone do we worship and of Thee (only) do we seek help. May Allah's blessings be upon His best creation Mohammed and all his (pure) progeny."[126]

And yet, not everybody in every situation can perform Dua among the Muslims. There are nine prerequisites to be eligible for any Dua to be accepted.

In India, Babur is said to have set Dua's standard among his followers and soldiers for the first time.[127]

The question arises: While even all Muslims may not have the right to perform Dua unless they strictly follow the nine standards outlined in Islam, why do Hindus use the word? Why can't they use words like *ashirwaad, prarthana*, etc., with different and much more profound meanings?

Islamic Prayers

There is no hard-fast rule on prayers for the Hindus. While prayer is important, it is only a part of their spiritual practice. Puja, meditation, archana are different ways to connect with divinity. Any Hindu can pray any time, anywhere. But that's part of Bhakti, one of many yogas for connecting with the supreme. Hindus, especially the Brahmins perform *japam* of the *Gayatri* mantra three times a day, called *Tri-Sandhya* or the three 'sandhi' periods of dawn, mid-day and night. Jewish people also pray three times a day. Although the Vedas are older than the Avesta, we find that the Zoroastrians have five daily prayer rituals, whereas the Hindus and Buddhists generally pray three times a day. It is not impossible that in ancient times Vedic people also prayed or performed fire rituals five times a day, which has been discontinued or lost. Yet the Zoroastrians are still following the same old practice.

As noted earlier, it is very much possible that while the Vedic practices influenced the Zoroastrian ones, they, in turn, influenced the Abrahamic ones. Most interestingly, both Zoroastrians and Muslims have almost identical prayer times. Below is the list of Prayer times and names.

Time of the day	Zoroastrian	Islamic
Dawn, before sunrise	*Hawan*	*Fajr*
Midday	*Rapithwan*	*Dhuhr* (Sanskrit dwiprahar?)
Afternoon (before sunset)	*Uziran*	*'Asr*
Evening to midnight	*Aiwisruthrem*	*Maghrib*
Midnight until the stars seen	*Ushahin*	*'Isha* (Sanskrit usha?)

One of five obligations in Islam is offering namaz or namaz prayer (also called s*alah* and *salat)* five times a day. Namaz can be offered anywhere, including at home or mosque. Generally, a mosque is a preferred venue for the congregation. Prior to the *namaz*, a call to the prayer is made from a mosque. This call is called *adhan* or *azaan*, recited in a loud voice by a person who is given the title of *muezzin* or *mu'adhdhin*.

In the early days of the advent of Islam, azaan was performed in the streets and from the rooftop of the highest houses and the (first)mosque of Medina. Later day mosques were built with tall towers called minarets from where the *muezzin* would recite the *azaan*. Currently, most mosques use loudspeakers sound of the azaan can reach people miles away.

The history behind this is collected in 'SALAT The Muslim Prayer Book' [2014 Islam International Publications Ltd. Published by: Islam International Publications Ltd Sheephatch Lane Tilford, Surrey United Kingdom GU10 2AQ]

The following is collected mostly from this book.

"In the early days of Islam, there was no prescribed way of telling people that the time for prayer had commenced, nor was there any means to call the Muslims to the mosque for congregational Prayers. The Holy Prophetsa was however, aware of the Jewish, Christian and pagan practices in this regard. He sought to counsel and asked his Companions as to what should be done to call Muslims to the mosque for congregational Prayers. One morning, Hadrat 'Abdullah ibn 'Aziz ra approached the Holy Prophetsa and related to him a dream which he had had the night before. He had seen someone announcing the Prayer time and calling people to the mosque for the congregational prayer in a loud voice. Hadrat 'Abdullah then related the words of the Adhan which he had heard in the dream."

They were as follows:

'I bear witness that there is none
worthy of worship except Allah.
Come to Prayer. (Recited twice)
Come to success.(Recited twice)
Allah is the Greatest.(Recited twice)
There is none worthy of worship except Allah.'

"During the azaan for Fajr Prayer, the mu'adhdhin should also recite the words given below twice after saying "Whenever you hear the Adhan, say what the mu'adhdhin is saying'. Hence, anyone who hears the azaan should repeat the same, phrase by phrase, after the mu'adhdhin has recited them but when the mu'adhdhin says the words '*Hayya 'alas-Salah and Hayya 'alal-Falah'* meaning 'Rush to success'. The person hearing the azaan should say: 'There is neither might nor any power except with *Allah*.'

The complete azaan is this:

Allahuu Akbar Allahuu Akbar
Allahuu Akbar Allahuu Akbar
Aashhadu Allaa ilaaha Illal-Laah
Aashhadu Allaa ilaaha Illal-Laah
Aashhadu Aanna Muhammadar rasulul-lah
Aashhadu Aanna Muhammadar rasulul-lah
Haiya 'Alas-salah
Haiya 'Alas-salah
Haiya 'Alal-falah
Haiya 'Alal-falah
Aasaalaatu Khaayrum Minan-Nauum.
Aasaalaatu Khaayrum Minan-Nauum.
Allahuu Akbar
Allahuu Akbar
Laa ilaaha Illal-Laah.

Meaning of azaan:

'Allah is most great. Allah is most great.
Allah is most great. Allah is most great.
I testify that there is no god except Allah.
I testify that there is no god except Allah.
I testify that Muhammad is the Messenger of Allah.
I testify that Muhammad is the Messenger of Allah
Come to prayer.
Come to prayer.
Come to success.

Come to success.

Prayer is better than sleep.

Prayer is better than sleep.

Allah is most great.

Allah is most great.

There is no god except Allah.'

After completion of the azaan, listeners should recite the following prayer:

"O Allah, Lord of this Perfect Call, and of the Congregational Prayer, make Muhammad a means of our access to You, and bless him with excellence and the lofty office, and grant him the most exalted station Thou hast promised him. Verily, Thou goest not back on Thy promise.'

"Iqamat (Iqamah): When the Prayer is about to commence, Iqamah is recited. This is an indication that the Imam (preacher) has taken his place facing the Ka'bah (west in case of the people east of Mecca) and is ready to begin the Prayer. The Iqamah is a shorter version of the azaan. Other differences between the azaan and the Iqamah are as follows: The Adhan is called aloud while the Iqamah is recited in a low tone. The text of the Iqamah is as follows:

'Allah is the Greatest, Allah is Greatest; I bear witness that there is none worthy of worship except Allah; I bear witness that Muhammad is the Messenger of Allah. Come to Prayer. Come to success. Salat is ready. Allah is the Greatest; Allah is the Greatest; There is none worthy of worship except Allah.'

After saying Takbir-i-Tahrimah, the following glorification called Thana' is recited individually in silence

'Holy art Thou, O Allah, and all praise is Thine; blessed is Thy name, and exalted is Thy state. There is none worthy of worship except Thee alone.'

When the Imam recites Surah Al-Fatihah loudly, the other worshippers should repeat it silently, verse by verse, during the short interval between the verses after the Imam recites those verses.[1]

'In the name of Allah, the Gracious, the Merciful. All praise belongs to Allah, Lord of all the worlds, The Gracious, the Merciful, Master of the Day of Judgment. Thee alone do we worship and Thee alone do we implore for help. Guide us in the right path— The path of those on whom Thou hast bestowed Thy blessings, those who have not incurred Thy displeasure, and those who have not gone astray.'

Thereafter, the Imam recites a portion of the Quran, at least three verses or a short chapter. Some examples are given below.

SURAH AL-KAUTHAR: *'In the name of Allah, the Gracious, the Merciful. Surely We have given thee abundance of good; So pray to thy Lord, and offer sacrifice. Surely, it is thy enemy who is without issue. [Alternative meaning: For he who makes you angry (O Muhammad), - he will be cut off (from every good thing in this world and in the hereafter)].*

After the second prostration, the faithful sits down in the same manner as he sat in the position called Jilsah. During this position Tashahhud is recited silently, which is as follows:

'All Salutation is due to Allah and all Prayer and everything pure. Peace be upon thee, O Prophet, and the mercy of Allah and His blessings; and peace be on us and on all righteous servants of Allah. I bear witness that there is none worthy of worship except Allah, and I bear witness that Muhammad is His servant and Messenger.'

SURAH SALATUL-VITR is offered after the 'Isha' Prayer. This prayer clearly differentiates between the faithful and the non-believer:

'O Allah, we beseech Thy help and ask Thy protection and believe in Thee and trust in Thee and we praise Thee in the best manner, and we thank Thee and we are not ungrateful to Thee, and we cast off and forsake him who disobeys Thee. O Allah! Thee alone do we serve and to Thee alone do we pray and make obeisance and to Thee we flee and we are quick and we hope for Thy mercy and we fear Thy chastisement, for surely Thy chastisement overtakes the unbelievers.'

Notice the repeated usage of the line, *'there is none worthy of worship except Allah'* which preaches an exclusive ideology, denies others' divine forms, and could be responsible for religious hatred, division, and violence. And the last line above *'surely Thy chastisement overtakes the unbelievers'*, that means non-believers would be punished creates fear. All non-Muslims are forced to listen to these every day five times.

According to the fundamental Vedic Hindu concept of omniscient, omnipresent, and omnipotent, Iswara is manifested and recognized in a multitude of ways. This is the foundation of a pluralistic, multicultural, and tolerant society. The prayers of azaan and namaz are an antithesis to pluralism and perhaps violations of basic human rights because these indirectly condemn the divinity of non-Muslims and indirectly incite discrimination, intolerance, and hatred. The belief and assertion of this idea *'there is none worthy of worship except Allah'* is basically a violation of 'good faith'. Non-Muslims are not bound to Islamic practices. Yet a) the non-Muslims are forced to listen to these discriminatory, intolerant and violence-promoting ideas. Non-Muslims, including aged and ill people, are forced to wake up very early in the morning and c) are told that 'your god is not true or invalid' d) instructing Muslims that all other deities and rituals are wrong and indirectly creating hatred towards the non-Muslims or indirectly telling the faithful the a) need to discriminate b) need to convert to Islam. These are not conducive ideas for the modern era and harmonious society.

According to the Indian constitution (Article 25 on Freedom of Religion in India and Article 26 on Freedom to manage religious affairs), every citizen has the right to his or her belief, practice, and follow their religious beliefs. However, the constitution does not approve of imposing one's beliefs and practices on other citizens. Article 26 also gives directives on Limits of Rights. In summary, 'if any religious practice is in contravention to any public order, morality, or health, then such religious practice cannot claim the protection of the state'.

Marriage Contract and Sexuality in Islam

Many Muslims and non-Muslims use the term *nikah* interchangeably with marriage or *shaadi* or *vivah*. While *shaadi* is a Persian word (sadi or shiyâti from Old Persian), *vivah* is a Sanskrit word. In Arabic originally, the word *nikah* meant 'sexual intercourse'.[128] While there are different types of marriages in the Muslim world, *nikah* is an easy way to take a woman for physical enjoyment. Lately, there has been a trend of wealthy Arab sheikhs coming to the Indian subcontinent to find underage girls to indulge in physical activities by paying a large sum to the agents.[129][130] This is not limited to Hyderabad or India; it happens in many countries around the world. This short-term arrangement is called *"mot'a" (nikah mut'ah* or *mutah*). According to the *Encyclopedia Iranica*, it means 'pleasure' in Islamic law and is used as a technical term in the sense of a marriage contracted for a definite period.[131]

According to Islamic Law or Jahiliyyah, there is no limitation for men to marry or divorce. In most cases, it allows men to have four wives at a given time, excluding concubines.[132]

The Sunnah and Hadith are supposed to contain the sayings and practices of Muhammad. When it comes to rights, the women have no rights over their bodies, but the man to be in bed with her does.

According to Sunan Ibn Majah Hadith: *"I enjoin good treatment of women, for they are prisoners with you, and you have no right to treat them otherwise unless they commit clear indecency. If they do that, then forsake them in their beds and hit them, but without causing injury or leaving a mark. If they obey you, then do not seek means of annoyance against them. You have rights over your women, and your women have rights over you. Your rights over your women are that they cannot allow anyone you dislike to tread on your bedding (furniture), nor allow anyone you dislike to enter your houses. And their right over you is that you should treat them kindly about their clothing and food."*[133]

According to the Quran (5:5 and 2:221), a Muslim can only marry a Muslim woman or a woman from the 'People of the Book' or *'Ahl al Kitab'* – the people of other Abrahamic faiths such as Christians and Jews. But they are forbidden to marry an 'idolater' and nonbeliever or *kufr*. If a Muslim man marries a woman from other traditions other than the people of the book, she first would have to convert to Islam, and the same rule applies to a man from other traditions marrying a Muslim woman.

On the other hand, the Hindu concept of *vivah* has a multidimensional meaning. It is a life partnership, divine conjugation performed as one of the 16 *'samskaras'*[134] in Hindu life, starting from conception till death. However, it is sometimes mocked by some modern feminist movements as the *vivah* companionship is supposed to be for seven births/ lives according to the Hindu tradition. A vivah is a lifetime vow to each other to stand by each other on all occasions. If one follows the vivah ceremony and the mantras, it will be evident that it is not a 'contract', but the partners are duty-bound to each other. Many cases of mismatch, domestic violence, etc., may happen in any marital relationship. Still, the unfair blame is placed on the system and the institution, while the individuals responsible, in most cases, the men.

Sexuality and Rape

Rape has been a tool in war and using women and children as war booties for sexual slavery has been in existence for the longest part of human history.[135] The introduction of three unfortunate terms – 'Love Jihad', 'Procreation Jihad', and 'Rape Jihad' are more recent. The former is converting non-Muslim women using honeytrap, and the latter two have to do with rape and impregnation, which aims to rapidly increase the number of converts.[136]

In Islam, like other cultures, generally, rape of women is forbidden and punishable, but that is mainly within Muslim society. However, since the beginning of the history of Islam, women and children of non-Muslims were permissible to be captured for sexual slavery, in reality, rape during Jihadi expeditions. This practice is called 'Sex Jihad' in recent times,[137] where child sex is also permissible.[138]

The rape of non-Muslim females is a norm in many parts of the world, including Africa, the Middle East, and Europe, to terrorize and convert non-Muslims. The prime example is the Yezidis in Iraq. Thousands of Yezidi girls and women were captured, raped, and sold as slaves.[139] In the Indian subcontinent, non-Muslim girls and women are regularly raped by the Muslim goons.[140][141][142]

If the beliefs of the Islamic State of Iraq and the Levant (ISIL) to be taken seriously, as per their digital magazine, *Dabiq*, they have clearly pointed out that the rape and enslavement of the 'idolators' such as the Yezidi women have sanctions in the Islamic scriptures, and they applied the shariah practice of spoils of war. According to them, verses from certain Hadith and Quran support their act of raping captured or kidnapped non-Muslim women.[143]

The magazine *Dabiq* noted, "enslaving the families of the kuffar and taking their women as concubines is a firmly established aspect of the Sharia's that if one were to deny or mock, he would be denying or mocking the verses of the Quran and the narration of the Prophet … and thereby apostatizing from Islam."[144][145]

In December 2014, the Research and Fatwa Department of ISIS released a pamphlet that focused on the treatment of female slaves. *Newsweek* quoted that "ISIS has released a list of rules about how female slaves, women, and children should be treated once captured by Jihadi warriors. The rules, published in the pamphlet, are written in the form of questions and answers and say, among other things, that it is "permissible" to have sexual intercourse with, beat and trade non-Muslim slaves, including young girls."[146]

According to the pamphlet, the Jihadis are allowed to have sex with adolescent girls and to beat the slaves to discipline. They can trade slaves, including for sex, 'as long as their owner has not impregnated them'.[147][148] Child sex with and without marriage, especially with 'enemy' children, has been prevalent with the Jihadis.[149] Now, equipped with some fundamental understanding of Islam and Islamic theology and culture, we will review how it evolved and expanded over the next 1400 years. The subsequent chapter will review the history of Islam and its impact on the Indian subcontinent.

The myth of a Composite Indian Culture

Many NeoCols would have us believe that there is a common or 'composite culture' in India. In reality, this is far from the truth. From a Western theological point of view, Indian adhyatmikata is completely different from all Abrahamic traditions. None of the core values of the Vedas, Upanishads, or Yoga can find any place in these traditions, especially Islam. So, there is nothing to really take from these religions, especially the ideas of exclusivity where 'my book, my prophet, and my beliefs are only true and absolute and if others don't adhere to it are infidels, targets of conversion'. At the same time, though the Dharmic System has much to offer to entire humanity irrespective of their belief systems, race, nationality, and religion. The practice of Yoga affects any individual if done properly, no need to 'believe'. While Hatha yoga works for many, there are many other forms of yoga that exist in the Dharmic or Yogic system of India. But most Abrahamic authorities, including the Vatican, reject yoga. So, all the citizens of India can live with the idea of coexistence, respecting unity in diversity. As long as freedom, peace, harmony, and progress of any individual or group are not disturbed, anyone can practice in their homes what they believe. Each individual has the right to pray and seek solace and peace in a higher power, whatever name it is called by.

Nobody has the right to impose one's ideas or ideology (in the case of communism) on others. The time has come to recognize that all attempts to religious conversions and push for 'isms' on millions by force are crimes against humanity, human rights violations, and civilizational offenses. God, Ishwar, and Allah are not and cannot be the same by definition. In conclusion, we can see that the Abrahamic traditions which were developed in the Middle East have a common base. Many deep connections and the terms related to each Abrahamic religion directly conflict with the Hindu ideas of divinity. Any attempt to find similarities or sameness is only a dishonest appeasement tactic. Hindus should understand that at the end of the day, Dharmic and Vedic ideas must prevail to re-establish India's leadership when it comes to the concept of Dharma, which represents laws and acts of harmonious existence and sustenance – both in the material (nishreyesha) and spiritual (abhyudaya or adhaytma) sphere of our existence. India is the mother of true spirituality, which many mistakenly denoted as 'religion'.

References

1. Watt, W. Montgomery (1986). "Kuraysh". Encyclopedia of Islam. Volume V: Khe–Mahi (New ed.). Leiden and New York: Brill. p. 434–435.
2. "Jewish Tribes of Arabia: Banu Nadir, Jews of the Jewish Tribes of Arabia, Yemenite Jews", Ofra Haza, Stamford Hill, Harel Skaat, Dor Daim LLC Books General Books, 2010.
3. John L. Esposito, ed. (2014). "Din". The Oxford Dictionary of Islam. Oxford: Oxford University Press.
4. Goldfield, Isaiah "The Illiterate Prophet (Nabi Ummi): An inquiry into the development of a dogma in Islamic tradition". Islam. 57: 58–68.
5. "Who were the scribes who wrote the letters of the Messenger

(peace and blessings of Allaah be upon him)? Question 20968". Islam Question and Answer. 17 August 2002.

6. Cenap Çakmak, ed. (2017). "Islam: A Worldwide Encyclopedia". ABC-CLIO. p. 1116–1120.
7. "The Qur᾽an – Introduction". Oxford Islamic Studies Online.
8. Nöldeke, Theodor; Schwally, Friedrich; Bergsträsser, Gotthelf; Pretzl, Otto (2013). "The Genesis of the Authorized Redaction of the Koran under the Caliph ʿUthmān". In Behn, Wolfgang H. (ed.). "The History of the Qur᾽ān. Texts and Studies on the Qur᾽ān". 8. Translated by Behn, Wolfgang H. Leiden and Boston: Brill Publishers. p. 251–275.
9. Leaman, Oliver (2006). "Ali". The Qur'an: an Encyclopedia. New York: Routledge. pp. 30–31.
10. F. E. Peters, "The Quest of the Historical Muhammad, International Journal of Middle East Studies", Vol. 23, No. 3 (August 1991), p. 297.
11. Lyons, Martyn (2011). Books: A Living History. California: J. Paul Getty Museum. p. 215.
12. "In the Sinai, a global team is revolutionizing the preservation of ancient manuscripts". *Washington Post* Magazine, September 8, 2012.
13. Metzger, B. M.; Ehrman, B. D., eds. (2005). "The Text of the New Testament: Its Transmission, Corruption, and Restoration". Oxford University Press. p. 20.
14. Sadeghi, Behnam; Goudarzi, Mohsen (March 2012). "Ṣan'ā' 1 and the Origins of the Qur'ān" (PDF). Der Islam. 87 (1–2): 1–129. doi:10.1515/islam-2011-0025. S2CID 164120434.
15. "The Meaning of Islam" https://stage.wikiislam.net/wiki/The_Meaning_of_Islam
16. Ahmad, Aziz, "Islamic Modernism in India and Pakistan 1857–1964". London 1967: Oxford University Press. p. 120-121.

17. "BBC – Religions – Islam: Basic articles of faith". 2011-07-19. Archived from the original on 2018-08-13.
18. Quran 2:285.
19. Ibn Khaldun, "Muqaddimah or Ibn Khaldun's Prolegomena" (1377).
20. Stephan G. Schmid and Michel Mouton (2013). "Men on the Rocks: The Formation of Nabataean Petra.
21. "A Short History". Petra National Foundation. Archived from the original on 4 December 2017.
22. Gibson, Dan (2004). "The Nabataeans: Builders Of Petra". Xlibris.
23. Gibson, Dan (2017). "Early Islamic Qiblas: A survey of mosques built between 1AH/622 C.E. and 263 AH/876 C.E. ", Vancouver: Independent Scholar's Press.
24. Ibid.
25. Javier Teixidor (8 March 2015). "The Pagan God: Popular Religion in the Greco-Roman Near East". Princeton University Press. p. 83.
26. Zeitlin, Irving M. (2007), "The Historical Muhammad", Polity.
27. Enno Littmann, Arabic Inscriptions, Leiden, 1949.
28. "The Kaaba" https://www.coursehero.com/file/p6m0ma0/Construction-of-the-Kaaba-dates-as-far-back-as-2130-BC-Muslims-also-believe/
29. "Islam: The Kaaba", Khan Academy https://www.khanacademy.org/humanities/ap-art-history/introduction-cultures-religions-apah/islam-apah/a/the-kaaba
30. Glueck, Grace (17 October 2003). "ART REVIEW; Rose-Red City Carved From the Rock". *The New York Times*.
31. Kaizer, Ted (2008), "The Variety of Local Religious Life in the Near East: In the Hellenistic and Roman Periods", Brill.
32. al-Kalbi, Hisham Ibn (2015), "Book of Idols", translated by Faris, Nabih Amin, Princeton University Press.

33. Robert Morey, "The Islamic Invasion: Confronting The World's Fastest-Growing Religion", 2001.
34. Jones, Prudence,; Pennick, Nigel, "A History of Pagan Europe". Psychology Press, 1995, p.77.
35. Robert Morey, The Moon-god Allah in the Archeology of the Middle East". Newport, PA : Research and Education Foundation, 1994.
36. Bismika Allahuma, "Hubal in the Worship of Pre-Islamic Arab Consciousness", 29 December 2006.
37. Hafiz Ghulam Sarwar, "Muhammad The Holy Prophet", 1969.
38. Al-Kalbi, 2015.
39. Karen Armstrong (2002). "Islam: A Short History. p. 11.
40. Koenraad Elst, "The Idea of God", 3 September 2016. http://koenraadelst.blogspot.com/2016/09/the-idea-of-god_5.html
41. Dermenghem, Émile (1930). "The life of Mahomet". G. Routledge. p. 239.
42. S. Salibi, Kamal (2007). "Who Was Jesus?: Conspiracy in Jerusalem". Tauris Parke Paperbacks. p. 146.
43. Robertson Smith, William (2010). "Kinship and Marriage in Early Arabia". Forgotten Books. p. 297.
44. Abu Khalil, Shawqi (1 March 2004). "Atlas of the Prophet's biography: places, nations, landmarks". Dar-us-Salam. p. 226.
45. "He sent Khalid bin Al-Waleed in Ramadan 8 AH", Witness-Pioneer.com Archived 2011-09-27 at the Wayback Machine.
46. "The Life of Mahomet and History of Islam to the Era of the Hegira".
47. Rahman al-Mubharakpuri, Saifur (2003). "Tafsir Ibn Kathir" (Volume 9). Dar-us-Salam. p. 321. See also "Tafsir Ibn Kathir", 53:19, Text Version.

48. Watt, W. Montgomery (1956). "Muhammad at Medina". Oxford At The Clarendon Press. p. 339–343.
49. Peter Welby, "Don't Be Surprised by ISIS Destroying History", Tony Blair Institute for Global Change, 6 July 2015. https://institute.global/policy/dont-be-surprised-isis-destroying-history#
50. "The Conquest of Makkah" https://web.archive.org/web/20110927030955/http://www.witness-pioneer.org/vil/Books/SM_tsn/ch6s6.html
51. "Culture and Religion in Pre-Islamic Arabia" https://courses.lumenlearning.com/suny-hccc-worldcivilization/chapter/culture-and-religion-in-pre-islamic-arabia/
52. Papaconstantinou, Arietta; Schwartz, Daniel L. (2016). Conversion in Late Antiquity: Christianity, Islam, and Beyond: Papers from the Andrew W. Mellon Foundation. Routledge.
53. Al-Kalbi, 2015.
54. Tate, Karen. "Sacred Places of Goddess: 108 Destinations". CCC Publishing. 2005.
55. "Manasik", Oxford Islamic Studies Online oxfordislamicstudies.com.
56. Corrente, Paola, "Dushara and Allāt alias Dionysos and Aphrodite in Herodotus 3.8", in Bernabé et al. 2013, pp. 265, 266.
57. Herodotus, "The Histories".
58. Berkey, Jonathan Porter (2003), "The Formation of Islam: Religion and Society in the Near East, 600-1800", Cambridge University Press.
59. Peters, Francis E. (1994), "Muhammad and the Origins of Islam", SUNY Press.
60. Peterson, Daniel C. (2007), "Muhammad, Prophet of God", Wm. B. Eerdmans Publishing.
61. Robinson, Neal (2013), "Islam: A Concise Introduction", Routledge.

62. Fahd, T., "al-Lat", in Bosworth et al. 1986, p. 692.
63. Monaghan, Patricia (2014), "Encyclopedia of Goddesses and Heroines", New World Library,
64. Al-Kalbi, 2015. p. 15.
65. Ishaq, Muhammad Ibn (1955), The Life of Muhammad: A Translation of Ishaq's Sirat Rasul Allah, with Introduction and Notes by A. Guillaume, Oxford University.
66. Zeki Saritoprak (2006). "Allah". In Oliver Leaman (ed.). The Qur'an: An Encyclopedia, Routledge p. 34.
67. Vincent J. Cornell (2005). "God: God in Islam". In Lindsay Jones (ed.). Encyclopedia of Religion. 5 (2nd ed.). MacMillan Reference USA. p. 724.
68. Christian Julien Robin (2012). "Arabia and Ethiopia". In The Oxford Handbook of Late Antiquity. OUP USA. pp. 304–305.
69. The Comprehensive Aramaic Lexicon – Entry for 'lh Archived 18 October 2013 at the Wayback Machine.
70. A. Amin and A. Harun, "Sharh Diwan Al-Hamasa" (Cairo, 1951), Vol. 1, pp. 478-480.
71. Irfan Shahîd, "Byzantium and the Arabs in the Fourth Century", Dumbarton Oaks Trustees for Harvard University-Washington DC, p. 452.
72. *Merriam-Webster*. "Allah" Merriam-Webster. Archived from the original on 20 April 2014.
73. Robin, Christian Julien, "Arabia and Ethiopia", in Johnson 2012, p. 304–305 https://www.cnn.com/2017/11/01/opinions/allahu-akbar-meaning/index.html
74. Alfred Guillaume & Muhammad Ibn Isḥāq, (2002 [1955]), The Life of Muhammad: A Translation of Ibn Isḥāq's 'Sīrat Rasūl Allāh' with Introduction and Notes. Karachi and New York: Oxford University Press, p. 18.
75. The Ten Commandments: First and Second Commandment.
76. "Idol", *Online Etymology Dictionary* https://www.etymonline.com/word/idol

77. "Iconoclast", *Online Etymology Dictionary* https://www.etymonline.com/word/iconoclast
78. "What is meant by al-wathaniyyah (idolatry)?" https://islamqa.info/amp/en/answers/307198
79. Nabih Amin Faris, "The Book of Idols", Princeton: Princeton University Press, 1952.
80. G.R.D. King, "The Sculptures of the Pre-Islamic Haram at Makka", in Ball and Harrow, p. 144-150.
81. "Obligation to Destroy Idols" https://islamqa.info/en/answers/20894/obligation-to-destroy-idols
82. Muhammad Saed Abdul-Rahman. "Islam: Questions and Answers - Divine Un", MSA Publication Limited. 2003.
83. "al-Muqaddimah" https://delong.typepad.com/files/muquaddimah.pdf
84. Quran 22:37
85. "Muslims must have first claim on resources: PM", PTI, Dec 9, 2006, https://timesofindia.indiatimes.com/india/Muslims-must-have-first-claim-on-resources-PM/articleshow/754937.cms
86. "How Islam Uses Halal Industry to Wage Economic Jihad", *Swarajya* Magazine https://www.swarajyamag.com/amp/story/politics%252Fhow-islam-uses-halal-industry-to-wage-economic-jihad
87. Rabbi Michael Skobac. "Leviticus 17:11". Jews for Judaism. Archived from the original on 30 March 2016.
88. Opinderjit Kaur Takhar (2016). "Sikh Identity: An Exploration of Groups Among Sikhs". Taylor & Francis. pp. 38–39.
89. Karen Pechilis; Selva J. Raj (2013). "South Asian Religions: Tradition and Today". Routledge. p. 242. The Sikh Rehat Maryada forbids hair cutting, adultery, the use of intoxicants, and the eating of kutha meat, or meat of an animal or fowl slaughtered slowly.

90. H.S. Singha, "Sikhism, A Complete Introduction" as mandated by the tenth Guru.
91. Bosworth, C.E.; van Donzel, E.J.; Lewis, B.; Pellat, Ch., eds. (1986). "Khitan". Encyclopaedia of Islam. 5. Leiden: Brill Publishers. pp. 20–22.
92. Šakūrzāda, Ebrāhīm; Omidsalar, Mahmoud (October 2011). "Circumcision". Encyclopædia Iranica. V/6. New York: Columbia University. pp. 596–600. Archived from the original on 19 January 2020.
93. Kueny, Kathryn (2004). "Abraham's Test: Islamic Male Circumcision as Anti/Ante-Covenantal Practice". In Reeves, John C. (ed.). Bible and Qur'ān: Essays in Scriptural Intertextuality. Symposium Series (Society of Biblical Literature). 24. Leiden: Brill Publishers. p. 161–173.
94. Khalid Zaheer (November 22, 2013) "Definition of a shaheed". Dawn.
95. Gölz, "Martyrdom and the Struggle for Power. Interdisciplinary Perspectives on Martyrdom in the Modern Middle East", Behemoth 12, no. 1 (2019): 2–13, 5.
96. Collected by Muslim ibn al-Hajjaj, "Sahih Muslim".
97. Collected by Muhammad al-Bukhari, "Sahih al-Bukhari".
98. Muhammad ibn Saad (2013), "Kitab al-Tabaqat al-Kabir", in Translated by Bewley, A. (ed.), The Companions of Badr, 3, London: Ta-Ha Publishers.
99. Razwy, Sayed A.A. (1997). "A restatement of the history of Islam & Muslims: CE 570 to 661". Stanmore, Middlesex: World Federation of KSI Muslim Communities
100. "What is the ruling on committing suicide? ", Dar Al-Ifta. https://www.dar-alifta.org/Foreign/ViewFatwa.aspx?ID=7149
101. "In Pursuit of Allah's Pleasure", Sheikh 'Aasim 'Abdul Maajid, Sheikh 'Esaam-ud-Deen Darbaalah, Dr. Naajeh Ibrahim, Dr. Sheikh Umar Abdur Rahman. Translated by: A. Ibrahim, Al-Arabi Ben Razzaq.

Davis, R. "Martyr, or Witness?" Archived 2011-05-11 at the Wayback Machine, New Matthew Bible Project.

102. Hussin, Iza (2014). "Sunni Schools of Jurisprudence". In Emad El-Din Shahin (ed.). The Oxford Encyclopedia of Islam and Politics. Oxford University Press.

103. Muslim, Al-Jami' al-sahih, 22, (no. 93).

104. Aboul-Enein, H. Yousuf and Zuhur, Sherifa,"Islamic Rulings on Warfare", Strategic Studies Institute, US Army War College, Diane Publishing Co., Darby PA, p. 6.

105. Afzalur Rahman (1993), "Muhammad As a Military Leader", Kazi Publications, p. 119.

106. Paul Wittek, (2013), "The Rise of the Ottoman Empire: Studies in the History of Turkey, thirteenth–fifteenth centuries", Royal Asiatic Society Books, p. 44.

107. Muhammad Husayn Haykal, "The Life of Muhammad", Islamic Book Trust, p. 195, 217.

108. "Babur-Nama", translated into English by A.S. Beveridge, New Delhi reprint, 1979, p. 370-71.

109. Al-Kalbi. 2015.

110. Newby, Gordon (2002). "A Concise Encyclopedia of Islam" (1st ed.). Oxford: One World. p. 173.

111. Jafri, Saiyid Zaheer Husain (2006). "The Islamic Path: Sufism, Politics, and Society in India". New Delhi: Konrad Adenauer Foundation. p. 4.

112. Khan, M. A., "Islamic Jihad, A Legacy of Forced Conversion, Imperialism and Slavery", Paperback – June 1, 2011, iUniverse. p. 90.

113. Monograph Series, Issues 20-23. Center for South and Southeast Asia Studies, University of California, 1979, p. 124.

114. Sahih al-Bukhari, 6234;

115. Muslim, 2160.

116. An-Nur 24:61

117. ahih Muslim, Hadith # 2167
118. Ratib An-Nabulsi, Muhammad (6 November 2017). "Allahu Akbar: Is Allah The Greatest in Our Lives?". About Islam.
119. A.J. Wensinck, "Encyclopedia of Islam", 2nd ed, Brill. "Mawlā", vol. 6, p. 874.
120. Roy, Olivier (1994). "The Failure of Political Islam". Cambridge, Massachusetts: Harvard University Press
121. 1975, Area Handbook for Bangladesh, p. 117.
122. John L. Esposito, ed. (2014). "Dua". The Oxford Dictionary of Islam. Oxford: Oxford University Press.
123. Gardet, L (2012). "Duʿāʾ". In P. Bearman; Th. Bianquis; C.E. Bosworth; E. van Donzel; W.P. Heinrichs (eds.). Encyclopaedia of Islam (2nd ed.), Brill.
124. The Oxford Dictionary of Islam. "Salat". Oxford Islamic studies.
125. "Book of 101 Duas" (Supplications), Printed by Ja'fari Propagation Centre (http://www.duas.org/101dua.htm)
126. "Courtly Culture Under Babur And The Early Mughals", Stephen P. Blake, Journal of Asian History, Vol. 20, No. 2, 1986, p. 193-214.
127. Vincent J. Cornell (2007), "Voices of life: family, home, and society". p. 59–60. (Marriage in Islam by Nargis Virani).
128. Srinivas Rao Apparasu, "Arabian nightmares: Hyderabad still a thriving bride bazaar for rich Sheikhs", Hindustan Times, 2 October 2017 https://www.hindustantimes.com/india-news/arabian-nightmares-hyderabad-still-a-thriving-bride-bazar-for-rich-sheikhs/story-dcLypwP6lk5l4Lh8dT5fYI_amp.html
129. "How Arabs buy 'wives' and dump them in a few weeks" https://www.ndtv.com/mumbai-news/how-arabs-buy-wives-and-dump-them-in-a-few-weeks-508764
130. "Mot'a", *Encyclopedia Iranica* https://iranicaonline.org/articles/mota

131. Qur'an, Sura 4 (An-Nisa), Ayah 3.

132. https://sunnah.com/urn/1261680

133. "The Sixteen Sanskaras In Hinduism", https://www.ritiriwaz.com/the-sixteen-sanskaras-in-hinduism/

134. Levinson, Bernard M. (2004). "Gender and Law in the Hebrew Bible and the Ancient Near East". p. 203.

135. https://www.meforum.org/60957/rape-as-jihad

136. Raymond Ibrahim, "Rape as Jihad", American Thinker, May 15, 2020.

137. Kern, Soeren (11 July 2013). "Britain: "Rape Jihad" Against Children". Gatestone Institute.

138. McLoughlin, Peter (March 2014). """Easy Meat": Multiculturalism, Islam and Child Sex Slavery". Law and Freedom Foundation. p. 222-258.

139. Ibrahim, 2020. https://www.meforum.org/60957/rape-as-jihad

140. Kathy Gannon, "Each year, 1,000 Pakistani girls forcibly converted to Islam", Associated Press, 29 December 2020. https://abcnews.go.com/International/wireStory/year-1000-pakistani-girls-forcibly-converted-islam-74930532

141. Rachel Avraham, "Op-Ed: World ignores mass rape of Hindu women and girls in Bangladesh", Foreign Policy Association, 8 November, 2019. https://foreignpolicyblogs.com/2019/11/08/op-ed-world-ignores-mass-rape-of-hindu-women-and-girls-in-bangladesh/

142. "Minor girl gangraped by 4 men for refusing to convert to Islam to marry one of them, say police", *Mirror Now*, Jun 11, 2021. https://www.timesnownews.com/india/article/minor-girl-gangraped-by-4-men-for-refusing-to-convert-to-islam-to-marry-one-of-them-say-police/769560

143. Sypher, Ford (28 August 2014). "Rape and Sexual Slavery Inside an ISIS Prison". The Daily Beast. Horror.

144. Kumar, Anugrah (13 October 2014). "ISIS Claims Islam Justifies Making 'Infidel' Women Sex Slaves". *The Christian Post*. Christian Post Contributor.

145. "ISIL seeks to justify enslaving Yazidi women and girls in Iraq". abril. *Today's Zaman*. 14 October 2014.

146. Amelia Smith, "ISIS Publish Pamphlet On How to Treat Female Slaves," *Newsweek*, 12/9/2014.

147. Abul Taher (13 December 2014). "Our faith condones raping underage slaves: ISIS publishes shocking guidebook telling fighters how to buy, sell and abuse captured women". *Daily Mail*.

148. Katharine Lackey, "Pamphlet provides Islamic State guidelines for sex slaves," *USA Today*, December 13, 2014.

149. Ibrahim, 2020. https://www.meforum.org/60957/rape-as-jihad

❑

CHAPTER 4

ISLAMIC WORLD AFTER THE DEATH OF MUHAMMAD

What is Caliphate, and who is a Caliph?
In which five countries in the world do the majority of Muslims live?
What is Wahhabism, and how has it impacted the world and India?
When was the state of Saudi Arabia created, and by whom?
What is the significance of Karbala?
How were the Shia and Sunni sects created?
What are the sects of Islam?
Who was Aga Khan?
What is Tablighi Jamaat and its impact?
What was the Two-Nation theory, and how it caused the partition of India?
What is the origin of the six pieces of stones in Kaaba?

A New Period

During his lifetime, Muhammad was the head of the Islamic empire called the Caliph. The Arabic word *khalīfah* meant "successor", but later it became a position as the head of the Islamic empire.

The story goes like this:

Muhammad, the founder of Islam, was both an ardent preacher as well as a fierce warrior. In March 632 CE Muhammad completed his first 'true Islamic pilgrimage' (and final one) to Mecca which is called the Farewell Pilgrimage *Ḥijjatu Al-Wadā* setting the tradition of annual Hajj. But within a few months, in June, he fell ill and suddenly died on his dearest wife Aisha at the age of 63.[1]

The Islamic world was within full control under the reign of Muhammad. His sudden death worried the immediate family members and administrators, fearing possible revolt to capture and control the empire. Muhammad had no son, thus no male heir.

People who gave shelter when Muhammad had to flee Mecca are the 'Ansar' tribe in Medina. The Ansars organized a meeting about the future of the empire. When *Abu Bakr as-Siddīq*, father of Aisha and close companion of Muhammad, and *Umar ibn al-Khaṭṭāb* son-in-law of Muhammad, heard about this meeting, they went to the gathering. A powerful army commander *Abu Ubaidah ibn al-Jarrah* delivered a passionate address. Abu told the Ansars that a leader should be selected from the family of Muhammad belonging to the Quraysh tribe; others won't be able to garner the authority and respect of people. He then asked the group to choose their leader between Umar and Ubaidah. But the Ansars argued that they would choose a leader from both Quraysh and their tribe Ansars and rule the empire jointly, which was followed by heated debate. Suddenly Umar held the hand of Abu Bakr and disclosed his allegiance to him.[2]

Finally, Abu was accepted by the majority and formally appointed as the Caliph though some other companions, including Ali ibn Abi Talib, a cousin, and son-in-law of Muhammad, raised issues initially who also could be the Caliph.

Shias believe that while Ali was in his mother's womb, while she was visiting Kaaba, and later, he was born inside the Kaaba.[3]

Ali apparently had support from a large section of the Ansars. Umar tried hard to get his support. A possible rebellion was brewing at the house of Fatimah, daughter of Muhammad and wife of Ali. Right after Abu Bakr assumed power, Fatimah and Ali protested against it where their followers gathered. According to Fatimah, Muhammad had previously wished Ali to be his successor. Abu then asked Umar and others to stop the protest and break up the gathering in a clear confrontation. But still, they did not accept Abu until the death of Fatimah. Sunnis suggest she died of grief, but the Shias say that she died in a second confrontation and due to a possible incident of miscarriage. Eventually, Ali made peace and accepted Abu as the leader. On his deathbed, Abu appointed Umar as the 2nd Caliph. Umar was killed by his opponent, a Persian. Then Uthman or Osman was elected as the next Caliph but was also killed by his enemy, and Ali finally became the Caliph – they are called the *Rashidun* Caliphs or the 'rightly guided' ones. Ali was also assassinated after five years of his rule when he faced the Islamic Civil wars called *Fitna,* resulting in the Battles of Jamel and Siffin.[4]

After the death of Fatimah, Ali had eight more wives with whom he had 33 children, including Hasan and Husayn.[5]

Caliphate and Ottoman Empire

After the advent of Islam in Saudi Arabia, organized armies set out for conquests — first into the Middle East and then towards Asia and Europe. The inheritors of the Islamic prophet Mohammed created an Islamic state called the Caliphate under the leadership of a Caliph who is supposed to be the head of the world's entire Muslim population called Ummah. The first four were called the 'rightly guided' (Rashidun) Caliphs since the prophet guided directly. Centuries later, the Turkish Ottomans established a Caliphate around 1517 CE. They were controlling the Muslim holy cities of Mecca and Medina and also conquered Egypt. The Ottoman Empire lasted till the beginning of the 20th century.

In India, there was a movement started by some Muslim leaders in support of the Ottoman Empire, which later was called the 'Khilafat Movement'.[6][7]

In World War I, which started in 1914, the Ottomans joined the Central Powers, including Germany, Austria, Hungary, and Bulgaria. The other side was Britain, France, and Russia. The war ended in 1918, and the Ottoman Empire was divided into parts. Mustafa Kemal Atatürk (the famous Bengali poet Kazi Nazrul Islam, also the national poet of Bangladesh, praised Ataturk and dedicated a poem for him), leading to the Turkish Republic. The Turkish Assembly abolished the Caliphate in 1924.

The current day Islamic State (ISIS) is founded on the idea of the Caliphate.[8][9]

Islamic Population in the Large Islamic Countries in the Middle East

In the modern days, after World War I, France controlled the Syrian portion of the former Ottoman Empire after the French soldiers left Syria in 1946, and they united with Egypt. They eventually became independent again in 1958. On the other hand, Iraq, also part of the former Ottoman Empire that Britain controlled during the World War, got independence in 1932 and became a 'republic' in 1958.

In Syria today, 87% of the population is Muslim – 75% Sunni and 13% Shīʻah. The rest of the population includes about 10% of Christians, some Jews, and local Druze communities. Before World War I, Christians were prominent in number, and like any other Muslim-majority nation, the number is rapidly dwindling.[10]

In Iraq, Muslims constitute about 95-98%, of which about 70% are Shī'ah, and the rest are Sunni. Christians are about 1% of the populace. A significant reduction of the Christian population happened after the fall of Saddam Hussein in 2003, primarily due to the rise of ISIS; many fled to neighboring countries such as Syria, Jordan, and Lebanon. Point to be noted here as a comparison, 90 % of Iran's people are Shī'ah and 10% Sunni.[11]

In Saudi Arabia, the majority of people are Muslims, and 75–85% of Saudi Arabian citizens are Sunni Muslims, and 10–15% are Shī'ah. Wahhabism, a Sunni sect of Islam that is said to be more fundamentalist in nature, is their state religion. Non-Muslims, Hindus, Christians, and even some other Islamic sects are forbidden to worship and follow their tradition in Saudi Arabia.[12][13] Any non-Muslim attempting to acquire Saudi Arabian nationality must convert to Islam.[14] Non-Muslims are not permitted to enter Mecca and Medina.[15][16]

However, due to pressure within society's freedom of women groups and freedom of practicing or not practicing Islamic mandate, the number of atheists is growing fast, perhaps as high as 5%.[17]

Global Muslim populations (top 5 countries roughly half of all Muslims: 2020 estimate)

Country	Muslim Population	Global Percentage
Indonesia	229,000,000	12.7%
Pakistan	200,400,000	11.1%
India	195,000,000	10.9%
Bangladesh	153,700,000	9.2%
Nigeria	99,000,000	5.3%

Interestingly, until the early part of the 20th century, after the Caliphate's dissolution, much of the Middle East, including Syria, Turkey, and Egypt, were controlled or occupied by two Western powers, Britain and France. Later America came into the picture mainly to control the oil in these areas, built friendship with Sunni Saudis by distancing with the Shīʿah majority countries such as Iran and Syria. Sunni majority Iraq became a battleground for America during the post-September 11 era.

In India, according to the 2011 census, there are about 15% or 172 million Muslims. However, a 2017 estimate puts the number of Muslims at 182 million. A 2020 report suggests that the number is around 195 million, making India's Muslim population the third-largest in the world.[18] Yet, Indian Muslims are considered a Muslim-minority community globally; although some parts of India, such as Kashmir, are Muslim-dominated, Muslims are still identified and treated as minorities. In contrast, non-Muslim minorities live in constant fear of violence in the Muslim-majority areas in India. Muslims are the majority in Lakshadweep (96%) and Jammu and Kashmir (68%). The majority of the Muslims live in six states – Assam (35%), West Bengal (27%), Kerala (27%), Uttar Pradesh (20%), Bihar (17%), and Jharkhand (15%). 85–90% of Muslims in India are Sunni.[19]

Shīʿah Muslims in India mainly live in a few metropolitan cities such as Lucknow, Hyderabad, Mumbai, Chennai, Bengaluru, Mysore, Bhopal, Kolkata, and Murshidabad, and the majority of them belong to the Twelver (Imamiyyah) sect. The other ones are the Bohra and Ismaili communities.[20]

Wahhabism

Najd or Nejd is the name of a region in Saudi Arabia where almost a third of the country's population lives; the capital Riyadh is located there. Before the advent of Islam, many tribes lived in the region, and Kindites were the most prominent. There was a flourishing trade from the Arabian Sea to the rest of the Middle East, especially between Yemen and Syria, and Jordan. But around the 5th century, some of these tribes in the Najd region were continually attacking the trading caravans.

In an attempt to bring order to the area, around 425 CE, the Kingdom of Najd was established as the first centralized state in that region. Later, the Kindites brought together various tribes to protect every tribe's interest and the trading route.[21]

Zayd ibn Haritha was the third individual after Muhammad's wife Khadija and his cousin Ali ibn Abi Talib to accept his new religion. Muhammad had made him the first commander of his army. Muhammad needed funds to support his religious expeditions. The easiest target was to raid the trade route. Meccan trade leader Safwan ibn Umayyah planned to travel to Syria with a massive caravan and many seasonal trade items to sell. Muhammad came to know about this and ordered Zayd to attack and capture these traders' wealth. It was his first such expedition, called the *Nejd Caravan Raid,* and it took place around 624 CE. With Zayd's leadership to attack Umayyah's caravan, their army raided and looted everything, and the booty was worth close to 100000 dirhams. He later invaded the entire region of Nejd the following year.[22][23]

Fast forward to 1700 CE. The ruins of ancient Nejd are scattered in that region. In 1703, Islamic preacher Muhammad ibn Abd al-Wahhab was born in Nejd. He started a new religious movement in that region. There was a widespread practice of honoring 'saints' near their tombs and shrines throughout the Islamic world. Wahab strongly advocated iconoclasm, destroying many such religious places and banning such practices to 'cleanse Islam' by getting rid of 'idolaters' and impurities.[24][25]

Taqī ad-Dīn Aḥmad ibn Taymiyyah was a Sunni Muslim scholar and theologian born in 1273 in Harran, Turkey. Because of his staunch iconoclastic view, he became very unpopular among the rulers and scholars during his lifetime. He was imprisoned several times. He belonged to the Hanbali school of jurisprudence. While Wahhabism's theology comes from Taymiyyah,[26][27] this movement's foundation in a big and organized way was started by ibn Abd al-Wahhab, popularly known as Wahabism.

Wahab alone could not accomplish these without the help of some political and funding support. He contacted the founder of the First Saudi State and the Saud dynasty, Muhammad bin Saud to seek political obedience to accept his variety of Islam for "power and glory" and the rule of "lands and men." Saud promised him to protect and propagate Wahhabism's doctrine, which has become a movement that is also the Saudi Kingdom's state religion. Wahhabism today stands for a polemic term. The followers call themselves *Salafi* or *muwahhid* because they follow the doctrine of *tawhid*[28] or exclusive access or rights to Allah. According to them, other faiths and other Muslims practice *shirk* or idolatry since they adore physical places of worship and their sacredness.[29]

It is a well-known fact that people worldwide think that Wahabis are not only ultra-orthodox and ultraconservative in their interpretation of Islamic texts and their practices; they are also radical in nature. Many even suggest that it is a "deviant sectarian movement" and a "vile sect", and they have "distorted Islam".[30][31]

The Advent of Modern Saudi Arabia

There was a town called Diriyah north of Riyadh, which is the current capital of the Kingdom of Saudi Arabia. Diriyah was an agriculture-based area. Muhammad I ibn Saud ibn Muhammad ibn Muqrin Al-Maridi was the king or Emir of the Diriyah region, and Diriyah was the capital of the 'Emirate of Diriyah'. He was the Banu Audi and Hanif tribes' descendant and was known as the 'desert warrior' and was the founder of the first Saudi state and the Saud dynasty or the 'House of Saud'. Muqrin died in 1725. The dynasty lasted till 1818.[32]

After World War I, the Ottoman Empire and the Caliphate collapsed. There was a power vacuum in the Arabian Peninsula. The fifth-generation descendant of Muhammad ibn Saud, Abdulaziz ibn Saud [33] found a great opportunity and started an expedition with a vision of conquering and ruling the Arabian

Peninsula around 1901. After his successful conquest, he established Saudi Arabia's kingdom as an Islamic state where Mecca and Medina, two cities most revered by the Islamic world, are also located. He ruled the kingdom as the first monarch from 1932 to 1953 though he established it in 1902 with parts of Arabia, including his family's ancestry home near Riyadh. It took him almost three decades to take over the entire peninsula. He is recorded to have fathered many children, including 45 sons, many of them later became kings. He got fortunate to discover massive deposits of petroleum in the country in 1938 to build his wealth, making him one of the wealthiest persons on earth.

After the initial pact between the Sauds and Wahab for over 150 years, that relationship became more robust with time. As the Kingdom of Saudi Arabia's official proclamation was announced in 1932, Wahhabism became the Kingdom's official religion.[34]

Abdulaziz ibn Saud (Ibn Saud) used the Wahhabi leadership and indirectly took control over religious institutions. Wahhabi ideas became social laws and rules of the Kingdom and even 'shaped the kingdom's judicial and educational policies'.[35]

This resulted in large-scale killings and punishment for those who did not accept Wahhabism. According to some estimates, the House of Saud conducted over 40,000 executions and over 350,000 amputations to establish Wahhabism.

After discovering oil in the country, the movement gained much more strength due to the royal family's substantial financial support. According to a US State Department report, Sauds have spent over $10 billion since 1970 to various foundations worldwide to spread Wahhabism.[36]

Wahhabism has another association – "Khawarij", a sect that vowed to "purify Islam". The word Khawarij in Arabic means to "exclude" the 'infidels' who do not comply with their idea of heresy and other beliefs.[37]

Around 1973 the price of crude oil suddenly jumped, and the oil producers in the Middle Eastern countries decided to stop oil export to the US for their direct support of Israel's state. It gave an edge to Saudi Arabia, an ally of America. With the new Petrodollar, a new Jihad was started by the Saudis.

A powerful organization called the Muslim World League[38] was established. Then they opened branches in almost every Muslim country where Sunni Islam was prominent. They printed the Wahhabi version of the Quran and distributed it globally in millions. They recruited some scholars from the Middle East and the Western world. They collected their writings to spread across the globe to reach out to the 'intellectual' class, including Sayyids Abul-A'la Maududi and Qutb, to Muslim communities throughout the Middle East, Egypt, Africa, Indonesia, Bangladesh, Pakistan, India, the United States, and Europe.

They built Saudi-style mosques and structures, sent trained Wahhabi preachers worldwide, like the Christian missionaries, and established madrassas and healthcare centers to provide free education and health care for the poor. Also, millions of migratory workers from many developing countries in South Asia who came to Saudi Arabia and Gulf countries for better fortunes were also indoctrinated into Wahhabism. They went back home to preach the same in their villages and towns. Often, they donated large sums to their local madrassas and mosques for the same purpose. This was engineered to spread Wahhabism to the remotest places on earth.[39]

Today the rise of terror organizations, including ISIS, Al Qaeda, and Boko Haram, is mainly because of Wahhabism.[40]

They are deadly against Western countries or non-Islamic states, and many other sects of Islam. These groups kill more Muslims than non-Muslims. Their main target is various Shiite sects, which is also the religion of the majority of the population in Iran and Iraq.

There is a perception that Wahhabism does not represent true Islam as preached by Muhammad. Yet, the Wahhabis, including the Saudi government, spent enormous funds to preach and establish this particular sect of Islam from South-East Asia to the Indian subcontinent to the Middle East and Africa.

A BBC report suggested that Wahabism is an "ultra-conservative form of Sunni Islam followed by the kingdom"[41] to which a prominent Islamic website replied and said that it is not really a separate 'ism' or a particular form of Islam followed only in the kingdom (of Saudi), rather it is true Islam:

"They call us Wahhabis, they call our way Wahhabism as if it is something specific [to us]; this is a clear error...

We are not a people of a new school of thought or a new creed. Muhammad Ibn Abdul Wahhaab did not come with anything new. Our creed is the creed of the righteous predecessors which has been narrated in the Book of Allah and the Sunnah of the Messenger. It is what the early righteous Muslims (the Salaf) were upon.

We respect and honour the four Imaams, with us there is no difference between Maalik, Shaafi'ee, Ahmad and Abu Haneefah." [In a sermon he delivered to the pilgrims in Hajj 11th of May, 1929][42]

In 2017, according to some news, it appeared that Crown Prince Muhammad bin Salman made some changes to Saudi religious policy and suggested: "Islamists throughout the world will have to follow suit or risk winding up on the wrong side of orthodoxy".[43]

Impact of Wahhabism in India

Apart from funding various Islamic charities worldwide, building thousands of mosques, and sending Islamic preachers, it has also created some new organizations and movements. One such movement is the Tablighi Jamaat, which means 'society of the preachers' and was established in India in 1926.[44]

This religious movement was founded by Muhammad Ilyas al-Kandhlawi, born in the Kandhla town of Muzaffarnagar,

UP, India. Later, he moved to Nizamuddin, near Delhi, with a close connection with the Deobandi school of Islam. He was a follower of Rashid Ahmad Gangohi Ansari Ayyubi family. His parents claimed to have been the descendants of Abu Ayyub al-Ansari, a close companion of Muhammad himself in Medina.

Kandhlawi preached that the Muslims were not following real Islamic teachings and wanted to bring about reform among various Muslim groups in India, which later spread to entire South and South-East Asia. The movement called for strictly following the practices of their prophet Muhammad. Their main activity is to train preachers and send them out to various parts of the world to teach the orthodox teachings to ordinary Muslims.[45]

Tablighi Jamaat

Like Wahabis, Tablighi is a Sunni Islamic missionary movement and onc of the most powerful Islamic movements.[46] It is said to have anywhere between 12 to 80 million followers globally in almost all countries,-especially in the Indian subcontinent – India, Bangladesh, and Pakistan.[47][48]

According to the book *Great Personalities in Islam*, "The Tablighi Jamaat was set up under British Rule in India. After closely watching the Jamaat for some time, the British realized that here was exactly what they were looking for, a movement that totally absorbed its members' energy and yet did not threaten British domination in any way as the doctrine of jihad was absent in this movement. Instead of directing Jamaat's energies outwardly towards their legitimate Kafir enemies or reclaiming the throne, it was now directed inwardly towards the rest of the Muslims. Therefore, it was a group that was allowed to flourish."[49]

According to a 2014 Indian Defence Review report, the fundamentalist group Jamaat-e-Islami (JEI), also a political party, has a plan to not only convert the entire population of Bangladesh into Muslims of their brand by eliminating the minorities such as Hindus, Buddhists, and Christians, taking over their properties and converting or killing the population. They have now expanded their network in several Indian states such as Assam, West Bengal, and Jharkhand. Their companion organizations include the Jama'at ul Mujahideen Bangladesh (JMB).[50]

According to the same report – "the JMB, another major Islamist group that shares the JEI ideology, is largely responsible for spreading violence and the fundamentalist ideology in Bangladesh. The JMB is reported to have a strong influence amongst the teachers and students of some 25,000 madrassas. Along with the JEI, the militants and activists from this group have been cooperating with al-Qaeda in the past."[51]

In India, apart from Tablighi Jamaat, some other organizations like Ahle-Hadith, the Gujarat Muslim Revenge Force, the Muslim Defence Force, and the Islamic Defence Force are very active. They all follow some form of extremist or Wahhabi ideology.

Apart from the personal interest of Ibn Saud, the West must be held responsible for the spread of this Wahhabism as an act of global deception. It was Britain, which after decimating the Ottoman Empire, established the rule of Wahhabism. As a first of its kind, Britain backed the Wahhabi Arabs in the Hejaz region. Later, the US took the cue to support these fundamentalists in Afghanistan to deploy them in the name of the Taliban against the Soviets.

In an interview with the *Washington Post* in 2018, Saudi Crown Prince Mohammed bin Salman in a historic confession, said, "The Saudi-funded spread of Wahhabism began as a result of Western countries asking Riyadh to help counter the Soviet Union during the Cold War." He added that "Wahhabism was spreading, of course, but with the support of the United States, rather than Saudi Arabia's efforts".[52]

According to a Turkish academician Ekrem Buğra Ekinci, the Wahhabi ideology, which used violence in the early days of its establishment, was transformed into an intellectual and missionary structure with the efforts of King Faisal. Saudi Arabia started to spend millions of dollars each year to establish dominance over poor Muslim communities, especially those that recently gained independence, with the claim of "bringing Islam back to its origin."[53]

"The Tablighi Jamaat and the Wahabis do not see eye to eye. This is, in fact, one of the major reasons why the Saudis banned the Tablighi Jamaat to give preference to the Wahabis."[54] Preachers from both these organizations come to India as tourists most of the time, and many never return.

Islamic Revivalism and Jahiliyyah

The Arabic word *jahala* means "to be ignorant or stupid, to act stupidly". *Jahiliyyah* refers to the state of societies before Muhammad's birth and is called the "Age of Ignorance".[55] Many interpret it as the 'Age of Idolatry' (before Muhammad) as the Quran stated :

"Then, following misery, He sent down upon you a feeling of security, a slumber overcoming a party among you, while another party cared only for themselves, thinking false thoughts about God, thoughts fit for the Age of Idolatry." (3:154)

"For the unbelievers had planted in their hearts a zealotry, the zealotry of lawlessness." (48:26)

Sayyid Qutb, an Egyptian Islamic scholar who was a crucial figure in Muslim Brotherhood, in recent times, popularized the term jahiliyyah and noted that if jahiliyyah is not stopped, "the Muslim community will be extinct within a few centuries." He viewed jahiliyyah as a state of domination of humans over humans instead of their submission to God.

According to him: "When a person embraced Islam during the time of the Prophet, he would immediately cut himself off from Jahiliyyah. When he stepped into the circle of Islam, he would start a new life, separating himself completely from his past life under ignorance of the Divine Law. He would look upon the deeds during his life of ignorance with mistrust and fear, with a feeling that these were impure and could not be tolerated in Islam! With this feeling, he would turn toward Islam for new guidance; and if at any time temptations overpowered him, or the old habits attracted him, or if he became lax in carrying out the injunctions of Islam, he would become restless with a sense of guilt and would feel the need to purify himself of what had happened, and would turn to the Quran to mold himself according to its guidance."

In his commentary on verse 5:50 of the Quran, Qutb wrote:

"Jahiliyya[...] is the rule of humans by humans because it involves making some humans servants of others, rebelling against service to God, rejecting God's divinity (ulahiyya) and, in view of this rejection, ascribing divinity to some humans and serving them apart from God. [...] People—in any time and any place—are either governed by God's shari'a—entirely, without any reservations—accepting it and submitting to it, in which case they are following God's religion, or a shari'a invented by humans govern them, in whatever form, and accept it. In that case they are in jahiliyya". [56]

Pakistani Islamist Abul Ala Maududi was the founder of the Jamaat-e-Islami, one of the largest Islamist organizations in the world, especially much influential in Asia. He introduced the idea of 'modern Jahiliyyah'. According to him, modern culture in the world, value system, lifestyle, and political systems are "the new barbarity" which is incompatible with Islam.[57] It is worth noting here that Maududi was against the partition of India with the hope that if Muslims remained within India, one day, it would be a Muslim-majority Islamic state. He argued that it would violate the Islamic doctrine of the *ummah*.[58] Afterward, he and his followers focused on making Pakistan a 'true Islamic state' and inspired the then Pakistani President General Zia-ul-Haq for the "Sharization" of Pakistan.

Later, a student of Maududi, Abul Hasan Naqvi from India, a strong proponent of pan-Islamism, was a critical figure in the Tablighi Jamaat. He wrote a book titled *What Did the World Lose Due to the Decline of Islam?* His writings are given credit for globally popularizing the term 'modern Jahiliyya'.[59] Even Syed Qutb was very impressed with his work to provide a broader definition of jahiliyyah that is applicable at any time in history (as opposed to pre-Islamic Arab) 'a state of moral corruption and materialism' the practice of idolatry. He was vehemently opposed to any idea of nationalism.

Today various Islamist jihadi groups use the idea of Jahiliyyah to fight against secular modern states and regimes.

Abrahamic Faiths: The Original Ones

All three Abrahamic faiths: Judaism, Christianity, and Islam, have numerous sects and cults created over many centuries. However, at least one sect in each claims to be the original and unaltered from their prophets' time for each faith.

Judaism

Karaite[60] Judaism or Karaism is a Jewish religious movement characterized by recognizing the written *Torah* (known as the *Tanakh*) alone as the supreme authority in Jewish religious law *halakha*. Karaites believe that God directly handed down the divine commandments to Moses, and these were recorded in the Torah (simply meaning 'instructions', to be interpreted as 'divine instructions') without any additional explanation or oral law. This is entirely different from Rabbinic Judaism, also called mainstream Judaism, which maintains that the Torah, originally an oral tradition, was codified in the *Talmud*. They also believe that all subsequent works are definitive and influential interpretations of the Torah. Due to this reason, the Karaites reject the Talmud. The *Talmud*, however, contains the history of the Jewish people and their beliefs and is necessary to understand their ethics and customs.

Christianity

Indulgence[61] is a practice of the Roman Catholic Church, which was defined as "a way to reduce the amount of punishment one has to undergo for sins". Indulgences meant severe penance, a form of punishment for the so-called sinners, including mandatory social services to support charities and hospitals. It gradually became an abusive system by the church authorities, which was commercialized and was a major challenge for the Church. Clergy abuse became rampant. 16th-century German theologist Martin Luther started a major reformation movement against indulgence-related extreme abuses and rejected many of the teachings and practices of the Church. According to him, salvation and eternal life were not necessarily granted to the churchgoer just for good deeds, and they required the 'gift of God's grace' through a strong faith in Jesus Christ as a redeemer from sin. He challenged the Pope's authority on this matter and claimed that the Bible is the sole source of divine knowledge. Those who follow Luther's teaching are called Lutherans.

Pope Leo X demanded the withdrawal of these alternative teachings, which Luther did not pay heed to. The Christian Roman Empire had a 'deliberative' body called the *Imperial Diet*, which was responsible for discussion, negotiation, and implementation of various ordinances of the Church, and King Charles V organized the *Diet of Worms* in 1521 CE to implicate Luther. This movement gave birth to Protestantism within the Christian churches.

Today there are three major sects of Christianity – Roman Catholicism, Protestantism, and Eastern Orthodoxy. The Protestant churches include Lutheranism, Calvinism, Anglicanism, the Quakers, etc.

Sola scriptura (means by scripture alone)[62] was a foundational doctrinal principle of the Protestant Reformation movement, which taught that the Christian scriptures are the sole infallible source of authority for Christian faith and practice. This doctrine maintains that the Bible is the first or original authority that is infallible or directly from God, and therefore, all subordinate authority has been deducted or concluded from the authority of the scriptures and is therefore subject to reform if they do not conform to the Bible.

Sola scriptura is still followed by several small churches that are offshoots of the Lutheran churches, Reformed churches, Baptist churches, and some Protestants, who call themselves "Bible-believing".

Islam

Quranism is a distinct sect of Islam that views that Islamic law and guidance for personal life and practice should be based on the Quran only, meaning partial or complete opposition to the authority of the Hadith. Quranists believe that Allah's message as revealed to Muhammad is recorded in the Quran, which is clear enough and complete, and there is no need to refer to any other texts or authorities.[63]

Quranists ignore the Hadith and some other texts as having some historical value. Later-day texts after the Quran, such as Hadith and Sharia Laws, on jurisprudence and legislation, were shaped according to many regional powers and historical streams of conquering ideologies based on tribal, political and imperial considerations.

The Quranists believe in Quran only and don't accept the stories about Muhammad written over a period as authentic and holy. The Sunnis don't accept some Shia religious texts, and many Shia sects don't accept some Sunni texts.

Quranism has the potency to become a global movement to reject authorities like Caliphs. It also has the possibility of defying the propagators of deep-rooted divisiveness and extremism in the world of Islam and curb the organized efforts to dominate the world by overt and covert means.

Modern-day Sufism, which claims to be akin to mysticism as practiced in the yoga traditions, could also be a viable movement to counter the exclusivism and hatred of other faiths, granted that people are cognizant of various Islamist activities of early Sufism in India (during Muslim period) which was a platform, network and tool to aid the covert conversion work and the espionage activities for the rulers.

Family of Muhammad

The Islamic world was divided into two groups – Shīʻah (Shia) and Sunni, soon after the death of Muhammad. Before we get into the details of the significant events after his death, we need to understand his family tree clearly.

Family tree of Muhammad

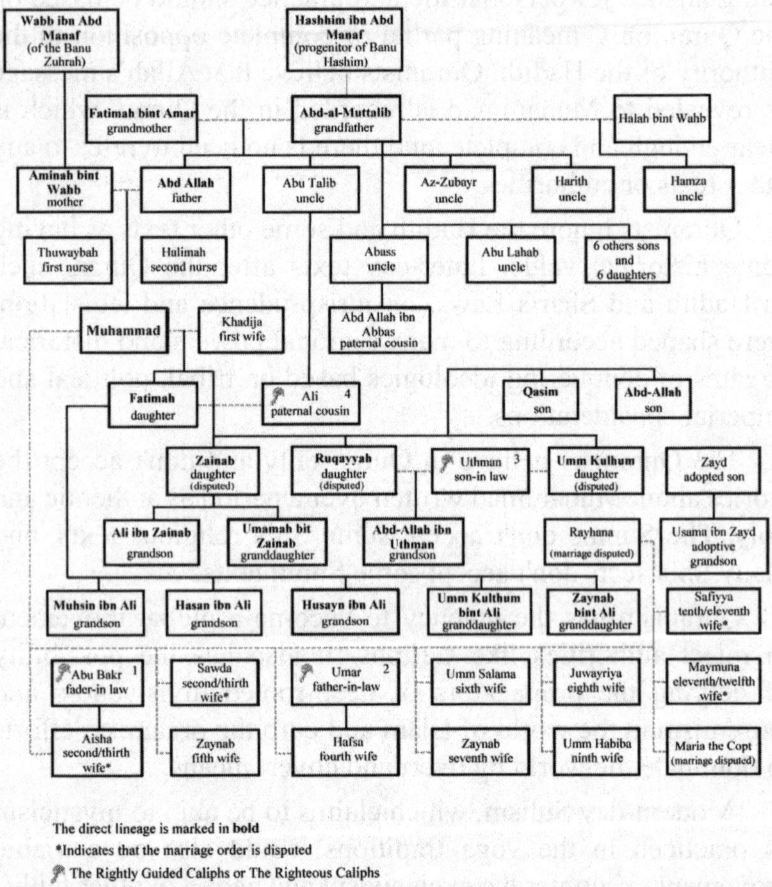

Muhammad's father was Abdulla, and Mother was Amina, and his paternal uncle was Abu Talib. When Abdulla died, he left behind five camels, a herd of sheep and goats, and Umm Ayman, also known as Barakah (the root of common Muslim name

Barkha) bint Tha'alaba, an Abyssinian slave who was to take care of Muhammad[64] and later was owned by Muhammad.[65]

Muhammad had three sons (all died infant) and four daughters – Zainab, Ruqayya, Kulthum, and Fatimah; The youngest daughter Fatimah became a prominent figure in Islam's history, and her descendants are called *sharīf*s and *sayyid*s. Sayyid is the Arabic title of respect, and Sharif is for "noble" or "high-born".

Zainab and Ruqayya married Uthman or Osman.

Ali ibn Abi Talib was a cousin of Muhammad and married to Fatimah. They had three sons: Muhsin, Hasan and Husayn and two daughters: Um Kulthoom, Zainab.

We can clearly see that endogamy was prevalent in the early Muslim society for many reasons – most important ones being keeping the power, property, and wealth within the clan of small set of families. Endogamy is prevalent in most Muslim societies. But Endogamy has its own negative effects as well. Is it possible that the 'mob' psychology is connected to endogamy? Is this possible that the negative psychological effects such as hatred towards other groups were acquired via epigenetics during the periods of genocide, conversion, and associated trauma?

Uthman ibn Affan, also known as Osman, a son-in-law, married the second daughter of Muhammad, Ruqayya. He played a crucial role in early Islamic history and is known for having ordered the compilation of the standard version of the *Quran*. He ordered a committee to use the version of the Quran belonging to Abu Bakr around 650 CE and ordered that the text be the standard version. All other existing texts of the Quran were destroyed.[66] While the Shī'ah uses the same Quran as Sunni Muslims, they do not accept that it was first compiled by Uthman. The Shī'ah believe that the Quran was gathered and compiled by Muhammad himself during his lifetime.

Is it possible that the original Quran, scattered in fragments, was destroyed or lost, and a new version was created later with many verses added specifically against other faiths and waging wars against non-Muslims? Or should we believe theologian Prof. Ian Paul who suggested: "there is mounting evidence that the Qur'an, or at least the bulk of it, predates Muhammad. A number of manuscript fragments have been found which can be dated (by carbon dating of parchment) to well before the time Muhammad was active. It is also packed with agricultural and geographical references, which are out of place in the arid Arabian Peninsula, and written in a dialect of Arabic, which even early Muslim scholars agreed was not the dialect of Muhammad's tribe in Mecca. Current thinking is still far from settled, but some evidence suggests it may have originated in the southern Levant or northern Arabia."[67]

Or, is it possible that a set of pre-existing verses from ancient Abrahamic traditions were initially used and then modified and expanded by Muhammad and perhaps later by his followers, including Uthman?

After the death of Ruqayyaa, Uthman married the third daughter of Muhammad, Kulthum. Under his leadership, the Islamic empire expanded into today's Iran and Afghanistan between 650 CE and 651 CE. There were major discords, protests, and rebellions during his reign, which culminated in armed revolt, and eventually, he was assassinated. He was also the brother-in-law of the fourth *Rāshidun* Caliph Ali ibn Abi Talib, whose wife, Fatimah, was Muhammad's youngest daughter. Ali lived with Muhammed and his family since he was five years old. At the age of ten, Ali was the first male to have accepted Islam and the second person after Khadija to accept Muhammad as the prophet. Ali was the bodyguard of Muhammad from an early age and took part in almost all the battles fought by the early Muslim forces. After the death of Fatimah, he married Muhammad's granddaughter Umamah bint Zaynab. He was appointed Caliph by Muhammad's companions in 656 CE after Caliph Uthman's death. He was also assassinated by a Kharijite while praying in a mosque of Kufa. Ali is the central figure in Shī'ah Islam and is considered as the rightful immediate successor (as an *Imam* or religious teacher) of prophet Muhammad by Shī'ah Muslims. He was the fourth Caliph according to the Sunni Muslims and the first imam of Shī'ah Muslim sect.

After the death of Uthman, Ali assumed the responsibility of the empire. Uthman's cousin Muawiya (602-680 CE), who was the governor of Syria, and later Muawiya I (661-680 CE), did not accept Ali's leadership. Soon, an intense civil war known as the First Fitna (656-661 CE) broke out. This war ended with the death of Ali and, at the same time, ended the era of the Rashidun Caliphate.

This complex family feud, which erupted after the death of Muhammad, caused the schism between the Shī'ah and Sunnis. It violently erupted in the next generation as well, which continues to date.

Hasan and Husayn were the grandsons of Muhammad and sons of Ali and Muhammad's youngest daughter Fatimah. Like his father, Husayan was a member of the 'Household of Muhammad' (*Ahl al-Bayt*) and the 'People of the Cloak' (*Ahl al-Kisā*), as well as the third Shī'ah Imam.

In the pre-Islamic period, the *Umayyads* were a prominent clan within the Quraysh tribe. They were the descendants of Umayyad ibn Abd Shams, who was the son of Abd Shams and is the progenitor of the line of the Umayyad Caliphs.[68][69] After the advent of Muhammad and Islam, many of them, including Abu Sufyan, a distant cousin of Muhammad, and his son Mu'awiya staunchly opposed both. But eventually, they embraced Islam during the lifetime of Muhammad. There were various governors for running the Caliphate. Governor Mu'awiya[70] in 661 CE established the 'Umayyad Caliphate' as a hereditary dynasty, and they chose Damascus in Syria as their capital till 750 CE. The capital later shifted to Spain from 756 CE till 1031 CE.[71]

After the death of Ali, Hasan temporarily took over his father's position. But he gave it up to Mu'awiya in return for some handsome financial gain and a pension. Before his death, in a big ceremony, Mu'awiya appointed his son, Yazid I (647-683 CE), as the new Caliph and wanted Husayn to accept his authority, to which Husayn did not agree and left Medina to take refuge in Mecca instead. While Yazid was on the throne, he was not given any importance by Husayn and others on Yazid's side.[72]

Karbala

The story goes like this:

The Iraqi city of Kufa on the Euphrates river banks has significant Islamic history attached, especially for the Shīʿah's, which surrounds cities such as Samarra, Karbala, Kadhimiya, and Najaf. Kufa was the last capital of Ali, the father of Husayn.

Some strongmen in the city of Kufa in Iraq, loyal to Ali, were the main strength of Ali's rule as a Caliph. They sent messengers to Husayn stating their allegiance and offered to help him fight Yazid to overthrow the Umayyads. He thought, with the help of the people of Kufa, he would fight Yazid. He then set out for Kufa, with a small caravan along with his close relatives and followers. But Yazid was keeping an eye on Husayn's movements, and once they reached near the city of Karbala, his caravan was attacked by Yazid's army.

Husayn then proceeded to Kufa with about 70 people, including his family members. Yazid's spies informed him about his plan and then sent an army of about 1000 people to take charge of Husayn. Husayn came to know about it and headed north to escape the fight. They reached Karbala, a plain with a beautiful landscape. But by then, Yazid sent a larger consignment of troops – about 4000 of them. Husayn's forces dug ditches in front of their camp tents, where they would set fire once Yazid's forces attacked. Husayn reached out to the local governor Ubayd Allah and requested a safe passage which was denied.

By the time, within ten days after their arrival, the troops attacked Husayn's group. During the dawn, Yazid's soldiers tried to attack Husyan's people, who then set fire in the ditches. But soon, the opposite side overwhelmed Husyan's people. Eventually, they set Husyan's camp to fire and his companions were mercilessly killed. His eldest son Ali Akbar was cut into pieces in front of his family members by Yazid's general Jarrar. Then they went after the other son Ali Ashgar. They decapitated him and put his head on a spear and displayed it in public. Almost all of Husayn's close relatives were brutally killed, including his two sons, one only six months old. Then Yazid demanded Husayn's surrender and submission to him. He declined and was shot at by arrows but continued to fight. And while he was still alive, Yazid's army men trampled over him to humiliate him. Ali was assassinated by a Kharijite called Abd al-Rahman. [73] All the surviving women and children were captured and presented to Yazid along with the heads of Husayn and his soldiers. After the battle, residents buried the dead without their heads in the field of Karbala, which is one of the holiest sites of the Shī'ahs; to the Sunnis, it is not as important an event or place.

The news of Husayn's death angered many in that part of the world, and it became a rallying reason to question the Umayyad Caliphate's legitimacy, which was ultimately overthrown.[74][75]

Muslim Sects: Shīah and Sunni

The Battle of Karbala caused an outcry in the global Islamic community divided the entire Islamic population into Shī'ah (Shia) and Sunni. The Arabic term *Shī'ah* is an abbreviation of *Shī'atu 'Alī*, meaning "followers, partisans or faction of Ali". Shī'ahs consider Ali to have been appointed by Allah as the successor to Muhammad and considered the first Imam of Islam.[76][77] On the other hand, Sunni is derived from the term *'Ahl-as-Sunnah'*, meaning people of the tradition who were Yazid's supporters.

About 85% of Muslims who live primarily in Southeast Asia, South Asia, China, part of the Arab World, and Africa are Sunni, and the rest, 15%, are Shī'ah in the world.[78]

Most Shī'ahs belong to the Twelver tradition (twelve 'divinely ordained Imams'),[79][80] and the rest are divided between many other groups. The majority population in Iraq, Iran, Bahrain, and Azerbaijan are Shī'ahs. They have a significant presence in Pakistan, Lebanon, Syria, Yemen, and Kuwait.[81]

Shī'ahs, in their tradition, literature, and practice, made Husayn immortal. As an ideal, his suffering, death, and sacrifice are remembered on the day of Muharram through a public procession of mourning, chest-beating, and sometimes hitting the body with sharp objects to the point it bleeds; inflicting severe pain and injury with the cry 'Hai Husayn'. They take out a makeshift vehicle called *Tazia* (to carry the body of

Husayn symbolically) displayed during Muharram in the Indian subcontinent. It is said that the Turkic Islamic Invader Timur, after coming to India, was very much impressed with the chariots or *rathas*. He was supposed to have carried with him a copy of an ancient copy of the Quran and some relic (hair) of Muhammed and some soil from the grave of Husayn and put in the Tazia with a precession, which is continuing till date.[82] Sunni Muslims also observe it as a day of the *sahid* or martyr and observe it as a non-obligatory day of fasting.

This division between the two sects among the Muslims is set in the war stage. From the days of Muhammad – severe violence, fights, battles, and wars started among various Muslim sects and communities, against the Jews and Christians and other ancient local traditions, and later, the Hindus and Sikhs in India. While fighting the non-Muslims, sometimes this sectarian division among the Muslims disappears. Various Muslim groups might not be seeing eye-to-eye among these sects and sub-sects. Yet, history is a testament to Muslims' uniting when fighting against other religious groups or races.

Another important historical fact that the world sometimes forgets is that the initial battles of Islam were fought near Mecca and Medina – the battle of Karbala (located in central Iraq) and other conflicts happened far and beyond, as we will see later. The battle of Karbala, in reality, was the battle between Syria and Iraq, and today the same fault lines are mapped mainly between Iran and Saudi Arabia.

Past decades have seen an increase in extreme conflict between the Sunnis and Shī'ahs around the world. The world has been polarized between Sunni Saudi Arabia and Shī'ah

Iran. Violence between these two sects has been set on the boil in many parts of the world.

Sunni is the largest sect of Islam, and its population is close to 90% of the 1.7 billion Muslims around the world. People that follow Sunni Islam are known as Sunnites or simply Sunni Muslims or Sunnis.

There are many countries where Sunni is the dominant religion. Most notably is Algeria, where Sunnis constitute more than 99% percent of the total population. Other countries where over 90% of the Muslims are Sunnis include Maldives, Libya, Jordan, Morocco, Sudan, Turkey, Egypt, Comoros, Somalia, Uzbekistan, Tajikistan, Afghanistan, Pakistan, Saudi Arabia, and Syria.[83]

The majority of the Shī'ah Muslims live mostly in four countries: Iran, Pakistan, India, and Iraq. Iran has about 70 million Shī'ahs, which is about 40% of the world's Shī'ah population. Iraq, India, and Pakistan have at least 16 million Shī'ahs. Many Shī'ahs also live in Turkey, Yemen, Azerbaijan, Afghanistan, Syria, Saudi Arabia, Lebanon, Nigeria, and Tanzania. Shī'ahs are a majority in these countries: Iran, Iraq, Azerbaijan, Lebanon, and Bahrain. In India, about 15% of the Muslim population is Shī'ah.[84]

Little Doubt

Is it possible that the Islamic history as we know about and Prophet Muhammad's origin are later-day interpretations, additions, or interpolations? Is it possible that the original Islam and, for that matter, the original prophet has been obliterated in the dust of struggles between later-day powers-to-be, like what happened to the history of Christianity, which was overtaken by the empires which used the power to propagate their conquests and expansion of their reign?

University of Oregon professor of Religious Studies Stephen Shoemaker has argued that Muhammad may have been alive beyond the common belief of 632 CE since there is some evidence of him invading Palestine after that. *Doctrina Jacobi* or the 'Teaching of Jacob' is a text written by a non-Muslim who recorded the earliest events in the Middle East. It is considered a reliable source by historians and was written by a newly converted Jew and a devout Christian named Jacob in Palestine between 634 CE and 640 CE. One paragraph reads: "What can you tell me about the prophet who has appeared with the Saracens?" And he said to me, groaning loudly, "He is false, for prophets do not come with a sword and a war-chariot."[85]

Is it possible that someone other than the original saintly Muhammed was a proxy warrior set out for conquest? How is it possible that right after the most influential religious leader's death, a major feud in the house split the Islamic world? Youngest wife of Muhammad Aisha, who was a daughter of Abu Bakr supported her father to be the Caliph over the son-in-law of Muhammad and husband of his daughter Fatimah who expected Ali to be the Caliph as according to her, Ali was 'wished by the prophet to be his successor' as the Caliph. Even the son-in-law of the prophet, Ali was feared and opposed by her mother-in-law Aisha, Muhammad's youngest wife? Hard to believe.

Imam

The term Imam traditionally represented a Muslim religious leader. In the Indian subcontinent, it is normally used by the Sunni Muslims as a title of a preacher or the worship leader of a mosque.

But for the Shī'ahs, an Imam is a leader of the Islamic community, similar to the idea of a Caliph, also called *Ummah*. It is also used to pay respect to the family members of Muhammad, especially by the Twelver sect. According to the Shī'ahs, the first Imam was Ali ibn Abu Talib and their sons Hasan and Husayn were 2nd and 3rd Imam. According to some sects such as the Twelvers, there were 11 Imams, and the 12th one would be the final one.[86]

While there are two main sects of Islam, Shī'ah, and Sunni, there are many sub-sects of Islam globally and in India. Below are some notable ones. There are four main Sunni schools: Hanafi, Maliki, Shafi'i, and Hanbali.

Different sects of Islam

Hanafi

The Hanafi school is one of the four main Sunni sects, named after the Islamic scholar Abū Ḥanīfa an-Nu'man from the 8th century. Patronized by the Abbasid Caliphs, the Hanafi school first flourished in Iraq. The Turkic invaders first brought this sect to the Indian subcontinent, which the Ottoman Empire also adopted. This sect is most prominent among Bengali Muslims. The Hanafi school has the largest number of followers, which is roughly a third of the world's total Muslim population, mostly in Turkey, India, Pakistan, Bangladesh, Central Asia, and Afghanistan.

Hanbali

The Hanbali school of Sunni Islam is named after the 9th-century Iraqi scholar Ahmad ibn Hanbal and is the strict traditionalist school of jurisprudence in Sunni Islam. Followers of this sect are found mostly in Saudi Arabia and Qatar, where it is the official state religion. Hanbalis are a majority in several parts of the UAE and are minorities in Bahrain, Syria, Oman, and Yemen.

The Hanbali school came to prominence and has become very powerful due to the Wahhabi-Salafist movement.[87]

Among the other Sunni sects, the Shafi'i school was founded by the Arab scholar Muhammad ibn Idris Al-Shafiʿi in early 9th century, and Malik ibn Anas founded the Mālikī school in the 8th century.

Barelvi

In Uttar Pradesh, India, there is a town called Bareilly. The founder of the Sunni Hanafi sub-sect called Barelvi, Ahmed Raza Khan, lived here, hence this name. It started as a movement (*Ahle Sunnat wal Jama'at*, or "People of the traditions [of Muhammad] and the community") of synthesis of Sharia and Sufi traditions, including reverence to Muslim godmen; it claims to be the only legitimate Sunni sect in the Indian subcontinent and currently has over 200 million followers in the Indian subcontinent. The majority of Muslims in India and Pakistan are Barelvis (and Hanafis)[88] and are in the opposite camp of Deobandi and Salafis. According to a report by *India Today*, over two-thirds of Muslims in India are estimated to follow the Barelvi movement and the vast majority of Muslims in Pakistan.[89]

Zaidiyyah

Zaidiyyah is a Shīʿah sect from the 8th century and was named after Zayd ibn ʿAlī, the son of the fourth Imam Ali ibn ʿHusain. The majority population in Yemen today is Zaydi, and the Houthis mostly belong to the same sect. They're the oldest branch of the Shīʿah sect and are the largest after the Imamiyyah or the Twelvers.

Alawites

The Alawis or Alawites are a 9th-century Shī'ah sect and revere Ali (Ali ibn Abi Talib), the first Imam of the Twelver school. It is also called the Nusayris sect from founder Ibn Nusayr. Sometimes they are also called Ansari, perhaps a corruption of "Nusayri". However, the Ansaris in India is a Sunni sect, may be connected to the Ansars of Medina.

The Arrival of the Final Prophet

The Arabic word *Mahdi* means "the Rightly Guided One"; according to Islam, *Mahdi* is a future prophet who will appear during the final judgment day. Many believe that he will appear together with Jesus Christ to establish the Kingdom of God to defeat the false Messiah or the Antichrist. There is no reference to *Mahdi* in the Quran but Hadith.[90] This is not a fundamental doctrine of the Shī'ahs or Sunnis, but it is a popular belief for both sects.

The Persian term *maẓhar ẓohūr (*some resemblance with Zoroastrian *Ahura Mazda)* is a concept related to God's manifestation, which resembles the idea of 'avatar' in Indic traditions. In Abrahamic traditions, it denotes a prophet. The Bábi Tradition, which in Persian is called *Babiyye* ('bab' means gate) was founded by Ali Muhammad Shirazi in Iran in 1844 and assumed the title of Báb. He believed and preached that he was the 'gate' to the Twelfth or final Imam Hujjat Allah ibn al-Hasan al-Mahdi.[91] The Babis believe that the creator is unknowable and incomprehensible, similar to the Vedic concept of Iswara, who manifests in an 'unending series of appearances' of *maẓhar ẓohūr* or prophets.

Babis broke away from the Shiite tradition due to disagreements with the Islamic clerics and the Government. Báb, originally a Persian merchant, believed and preached *maẓhar ẓohūr* and the coming of the next prophet. Babism became an underground movement; it eventually emerged as the modern Bahá'í Faith. Bab fell into the Islamic clerics and Government's wrath, and he was considered a rebel and even apostasy. Prime minister of Iran, Amir Kabir, ordered the execution of the Báb. Thousands of Babs are believed to have been executed by the Iranian authorities.[92] Only a few thousand Babis are surviving who live mostly in Iran.

Bahá'u'lláh, a son of a governor of an Iranian province, became a follower of the Báb. In 1848, he attended a conference of the Babis where there was intense discussion on whether to maintain Islamic law or adopt Bab's new message. Bahá'u'lláh supported the latter group and opted for reform and change.

Bahá'ís believe that Bahá'u'lláh was the prophetic *maẓhar ẓohūr*. According to Bahá'u'lláh, *maẓhar ẓohūr* is not 'an incarnation of God; they reveal God's attributes, not God's essence'.[93]

According to the *World Christian Encyclopedia,* in 2010, there are about 7.3 million Bahá'ís in the world, [94] representing 218 countries and the largest religious minority in Iran, Panama, and Beliz.

The Jafari or Twelvers, the Ismaili Sect, and Aga Khan

In 713 CE, Muhammad al-Baqir also known as *Abu Ja'far* became the 5th Shi'ite Imam whose mother was Fatima, the daughter of Hasan and a direct descendant of the grandsons of Muhammad – Hasan, and Husayn. After his death, his son Ja'far al-Sadiq became the 6th Imam. After he died, on the question of his successor, Shi'ites were divided. One group wanted his eldest son Ismail to be the Imam, and the others wanted his 3rd son Musa al-Kadhim. The first group became known as the Ismailis, and the later one was called Ja'fari or the Twelvers.

The Twelvers believe in twelve Imams known as *Davâzdah Emâm* and are the only school to comply with the Hadith of the Twelve Successors or the *ḥadīth al-ithnā ʿashar* khalīfa where Muhammad prophesied that he would have twelve successors.

Around the 9th century, the Ismailis became a recognizable large sect based in Syria. The Fatimid dynasty (909–1171 CE) was established around an area in Africa and Egypt, Arabian Peninsula including Mecca and Medina, and the capital being Cairo by an Ismaili leader named Ubadulla. The name was taken from the daughter of Muhammad – Fatimah – who was the wife of Ali and claimed their ancestry to Shī'ah Caliph Ali. They strongly opposed the Abbasid Caliphs in Baghdad.

Towards the end of the Fatimid Caliphate, around 1094 CE, a dispute erupted on who should be the next Caliph. The Fatimids in Egypt selected one, and the Ismailis in Persia and Syria named Nizar to be Caliph. The Nizari became a new sect that was extremely violent. The Nizari Fida'i is said to have introduced terrorism and murder for their goals to take over territories and are known as 'Assasins'.[95]

Ismailis have several sub-sects, including the Nizārī, Sevener, Mustaali, Dawoodi Bohra, Hebtiahs Bohra, Sulaimani Bohra, and Alavi Bohra.

Followers of the Tayyibi Isma'ili-Musta'li sub-sect of Ismailism believe that Al-Ṭayyib Abū'l-Qāsim was the twenty-first Imam and the last Caliph of the Fatimid Caliphate. In 1592, the Taiyabi sect was divided in a dispute over who should become the twenty-seventh Da'I or Imam between Dawood Bin Qutubshah or Sulayman bin Hassan. Dawood's followers came to know as the Dawoodi Bohra, and the other one is called the Sulaymani of Yemen. Again, in 1637 CE, the Alavi Bohra sect took birth after they came out of the Dawoodi Bohra sect. On the other hand, the Hebtiahs Bohra also came out of the Dawoodi Bohra sect in 1754 CE, and some of them live near Ujjain, India.

The common profession of the Bohras in India is trading, and the name came from the Gujarati word *vohrvu* or *vyavahar*, meaning "to trade". The majority of Dawoodi Bohras live in India, Pakistan, Yemen, East Africa, and the Middle East. It is estimated that there are about one million Bohras globally.

In Gujarat, a large number of Bohras converted to Hanafi Sunni sect in the 15th century, a conversion movement led by Jafari Bohras and Patani Bohras. In general, they are called Sunni Bohras using their last name as Vora or Vohra (not Bohra) and are commonly known as Sunni Vohra. A few families use the slightly different spelling of "Vora" or "Vohra" as their surname, which the Hindus also use.[96]

The Musta'lī Ismaili sect originated in Egypt; believes al-Musta'li as the 19th Fatimid Caliph and distinctly different from the Nizari sect that follows Mustali's brother Nizar. Mustalis are found today, mostly in Yemen and some in Western India.

The common understanding of the origin of the term 'assassination' is based on Venetian merchant and explorer Marco Polo, who understood the name was derived from the term hashish, a cannabis drug as the Arabic term *hashishin* means "users of hashish". There is a theory that Nizari *fida'is*, were given hashish as part of their training and during suicide missions.[97][98]

The Nizari Ismaili sect is also known as Assassins or Hashashins, who lived in Persia and Syria between 1090 and 1275. They adopted a terror strategy via murder to defeat their opponents in the Middle East – both Muslims and Christians; hence the term assassination came into use. There is also a theory that the 'Hasaneens' was a follower of Hasan, and during the initiations to his army, and during wartime, they were fed with hashish. But there is not enough evidence found to support this.

The Arabic words *fedayeen* or *fedayi or fida'i are* a term used to refer to people who would be ready to sacrifice themselves for religious and military campaigns implying "those who sacrifice themselves".

The Assasins were finally subdued by the 12th century by the Mameluk Sultans of Egypt and the Mongols, led by Hulagu.

Their descendants are the Nizari Ismailis, a 'heretic' sect, who claimed their ancestry to Ali and Fatimah via Nizar. In 1818, one prominent Nizari was given the title 'Aga Khan' by the Shah of Iran.

In 1840 the Nizaris attempted an uprising against the Shah, which failed, and Aga Khan escaped to Sind, India. He is also said to have helped the British conquer Sind in the first Anglo-Afghan war in exchange for a good amount of pension.[99]

The Aga Khan III, originally Sultan Mahomed Shah, became the 48th Imam of the Nizar Ismaili sect. He was one of the key founding leaders of the All-India Muslim League (AIML). Aga Khan appealed to the British Raj to consider Muslims to be a separate nation within India, the so-called 'Two-Nation Theory'. Based on some de-classified secret documents, Aga Khan III is said to have offered to have the services of "30,000 armed Arabs to Adolf Hitler" to back a Nazi occupation [100][101] of Egypt, Syria, and Palestine during the Second World War.

Daily Mail quoted from a memo attributed to Khan read: "If you give me 10 to 15 days warning, I will have for you 30,000 armed Arabs, amongst my most faithful disciples, who will shoot the Gaullists in the back."[102] He evaded a treason trial for a long time. Finally, Britain compromised, and the trial was never allowed to happen, fearing that it would anger Muslims worldwide.

The current Aga Khan IV, born in 1936 in Geneva, is Karim Aga Khan, the grandson of Aga Khan III, who is regarded as the Imam of around 15-18 million Nizari Ismaili Muslims globally. Harvard-educated Khan was brought up in Nairobi, Kenya, and is currently a British Citizen.

Khan lives a luxurious life, owning expensive properties, yachts, private jets, and spending a good lot on horse racing. According to *Forbes* magazine's list of richest royals,[103] Aga Khan's assets were worth US$800 million in 2010. He is known as a philanthropist, and his multiple organizations, including

Aga Khan Development Network, are engaged in promoting Islamic culture, arts, and architecture, especially in India and Pakistan.

The current residence of Khan is the historical and vast Aiglemont Estate in France. He also owns a private island in the Bahamas.

He has married three times so far with several British aristocrat women who converted to Islam. His second wife was Gabriele Renate Thyssen, whose Muslim name is *Begum Inaara Aga Khan*, who was 27 years younger than Khan. Khan fathered his son Aly Mohammad at the age of 64.

It may be worthwhile to mention that Gandhi served his last 'prison sentence' during the colonial reign in the Aga Khan Palace of Pune, a luxurious residence.[104]

The 'Lands' of Islam

Before we get into the descriptions of Islam's various land occupational statuses, let us remember the actual meaning of the term Muslim and Islam. Arabic word *Muslim* means "one who submits", and the verbal noun *Islam* means "submission". Islam is all about submission to '*Allah*', the ancient deity of the Arabs. Most translators mistakenly translate *Allah* into 'God', which are not the same.

In Arabic, *dar* means house or abode and also can be interpreted as land or country. This idea of *dar* is not found in the Quran directly. However, it mentions *"the abode of the hereafter and the abode of the earthly life, with the former described as clearly superior to the latter"*.[105]

According to Islamic Law *Sharia,* there are several major designations of land, based on the status and presence of Islam:[106]

dar al-Islam means the territory of Islam (voluntary submission to Allah), denoting regions where Islamic law prevails, generally a Muslim-majority nation where Islam is the official religion.

dar al-sulh or *Dar al-'Ahd*; 'the territory of a treaty', representing all non-Islamic lands which have ceasefire conciliation, a treaty or truce with a Muslim government for peace with Muslims.

dar al-harb, a territory of war, adjoining non-Islamic lands whose rulers are asked to accept Islam.

These terms were introduced during the early conquests of Islam and are still in use, especially groups promoting Islamic Caliphate through *Jihad* (holy war), such as the Islamic State (ISIL).

A sanction for the *dar al-sulh* has reference in the Quran, and Muslims are directed on how they should act in a Jihad or holy war:

"Excepting those who join a people between whom and you, there is a treaty or such as come to you with hearts reluctant to fight you or to fight their own people. Had Allah wished, He would have imposed them upon you, and then they would have surely fought you. So if they keep out of your way and do not fight you, and offer you peace, then Allah does not allow you any course [of action] against them." (Quran 4:90)

According to *The New Encyclopedia of Islam*, the *dar al-harb* is:

"the territories where Islam does not prevail. During colonial rule in India, the 'uluma' decided that as long as the laws of Islam were not prohibited, or as long as the peculiar institution of Islam existed, the country could be considered to lie within dar al-islam ("abode of Islam"). Symbolically, the dar al-harb is the domain, even in an individual's life, where there is a struggle against or opposition to, the Will of God".[107]

It also explains that jihad is a "Divine institution of warfare to extend Islam into the *dar al-harb* or to defend Islam from danger," and the final goal is to convert it into a *Dar ul-Islam*.[108]

Among the extremist Islamists, the Hanafi School is most prominent. An 8th-century Sunni religious scholar, jurist Imam Abu Hanifa is the founder of this school, which is followed by the majority of Sunni Muslims in the world. According to a Hanafi doctrine, *Bada'us-Sanaai':*

"There is no disagreement among the scholars of the Hanafi *maddhab* that *Dar al-Kufr* becomes *Dar al-Islam*, when the rules of Islam become dominant. They only dispute how *Dar al-Islam* transfers to become *Dar al-Kufr*. Abu Hanifa said, '*Dar al-Islam* becomes *Dar al-Kufr* in three (situations):

When law and order become *Kufr* (ruled by non-Muslim people or law),

When the state has a border with a *Kufr* (state),

There is no longer any security for the Muslims or the dhimmi (citizens)'.

Abu Yusuf and Muhammad, however, argued *Dar al-Islam* transfers to become *Dar al-Kufr* only when law and order become *Kufr*.[109] So is democracy and a democratic state *Dar al-Kufr?*

According to Abu Hanifa, it does not become *dar al-harb* until three things come together therein:

— it being contiguous with *dar al-Harb* and nothing of *dar al-Islam* exists between it and *dar al-harb,*

— second, the rule of the people of disbelief is enforced therein,

— third, that no Muslim or dhimmi remains secure there [based on the amnesty granted by Muslim powers].

When these three things come together therein, it becomes *dar al-harb,* and when anyone's condition falls short, it will not be *dar al-harb*.[110]

An Indian Sunni Islamic scholar Muḥammad Shafī', a Hanafi, was part of the Deobandi school in Deoband, Uttar Pradesh, India. He graduated from the Islamic School called the Darul Uloom Deoband Islamic University in 1917. This school was responsible for the Sunni Deobandi Islamic movement in the Indian subcontinent. Shafi was an important Islamic religious leader in the movement in the creation of Pakistan. He went around the country to give sectarian speeches and issued *fatwas* to create a separate Muslim state. The movement organized by the Deobandi leaders between 1913 and 1920 is called the *Silk Letter Movement.*[111] It aimed to end the British rule by allying with Ottoman Turkey, Germany, and Afghanistan to help create Caliph. There was a chain of letters shared among the Deobandi leaders – the letters were written on silk cloth, hence the name. British police came to know about this and arrested a few leaders in Punjab, Afghanistan, and Iran.

When Shafī ‘ was asked:

"Is Hindustan Dār al-Ḥarb, Dār al-Islām or Dār al-Amān? Is Dār al-Amān a subset of Dār al-Ḥarb?"

He responded:

"At present, Hindustan, according to our scholars, is Dār al-Ḥarb. Although Dār al-Amān is not a subset of Dār al-Ḥarb, it is permissible to make a peace-agreement with those in Dār al-Ḥarb according to Sharī'ah. In the case of a peace agreement, maintaining peace would be necessary. Thus, if a Dār al-Ḥarb, at the time of a peace-agreement, is called 'Dār al-Amān', there is no problem."[112]

Indian Sunni Islamic scholar named Shah Abdul Aziz Dehlavi (1746–1824 CE) followed the Naqshbandi school of Sufism. This sect stands strongly against any reform or modernization of Islam, sometimes violently. Sunni Islamist leaders such as Aziz's father, Shah Waliullah, belonged to this camp as well. It was Aziz who declared 'Hindustan' (India) as *dar-al-Harb.*[113]

So, two ideas are responsible for forming a separate nation for Muslims in the Indian subcontinent. Those are: a) India is a *Dar-ul-Harb*, and Muslims cannot live under *Dar-ul-Kufr* or 'Kafir Rule' (non-Islamic, non-Sharia secular democratic laws). Eventually, the country should become a *Dar-ul-Islam*. So, according to them, the Muslims needed a *Dar-ul-Islam* immediately, and the idea of Pakistan is rooted in this Hanifite-Deobandi thoughts. b) To create a global *Dar-ul-Islam*, it needed a global power center, and the best option they found was the Ottoman Caliph and Empire. Saudi Arabia came into the scene with Wahhabisim after the Ottoman Empire (established in 1299 CE) was dissolved after World War I in 1922. But the Khilafat Movement or Indian Muslim Movement (1919–1924), with which Gandhi, along with Maulana Azad, threw all their support, pushed the Indian National Congress and some of its leaders to join the movement.

Indian Muslim leader Syed Shahabuddin had, however, explained that *Dar-al-Harb* does not apply in the modern 'democratic' world, especially for India, which has a secular constitution and allows religious freedom to all groups equally. In an article in 2009, he wrote:

"Muslim Indians enjoy equal political and legal rights. They have the freedom to place their grievances before the legislature and the executive or take recourse to the judiciary. So far from being 'Dar-ul-Harb', India is a 'Dar-ul-Aman' (land of peace) and a 'Dar-ul-Muwahida' (land of compact). India is a secular state and the essence of Indian secularism is non-discrimination by the state among its citizens on ground of religion and equal treatment of all religions and religious groups as equal before law. That is why secularism as an essential character of the Indian state has a theological significance. So long as India remains true to its secular ideals, it shall remain a 'Dar-ul-Aman' and 'Dar-ul-Muwahida' and cannot be depicted as 'Dar-ul-Harb'."[114]

As a matter of fact, Muslim men and women enjoy maximum freedom and privilege in India than any other nation on earth. No democratic government, including the USA and UK, allows any law other than prescribed by the constitution, including Shariah. In India, Muslims have separate personal laws for family matters – marriage, divorce, inheritance. Many Islamist leaders would like to have Shariah laws in India for all citizens. Though a large number of Muslims live in poverty due to historical reasons, and now since millions of Muslims study in the religious schools or Madrassas, they do not learn modern subjects such as science enough to choose a profession other than becoming religious clerics. They depend on funds from religious groups for their livelihood.

It is well-known that the Shīʻahs in Iran are directly in severe conflict with Sunnis globally, especially the Arabs. However, lately, the power center of Sunni Islamic expansionism is torn between Saudi Arabia and Turkey. The old Turkey with past Caliphate pride is slowly reemerging as a hub of terror along with Qatar and Malaysia.

Two-Nation theory and the Muslim League

When the 3rd Mughal emperor, Akbar, was the ruler in Delhi, he introduced a new religious body called '*Din-I Ilahi,*' which means "Religion of God". According to historian Mubarak Ali, emperor Akbar did not use the term *Dīn-i Ilāhī* and called it called *Tawhid-i-Ilāhī* ("Divine Monotheism").[115] His claim is based on the writings of Abu'l-Fazl, the court historian of Akbar. It was contrary to the common belief that Akbar introduced a new 'syncretic' religion based on key elements of Islam, Hinduism, and Zoroastrianism; Akbar wanted to establish Islam as a superior 'monotheistic' religion finding parallels in Hindu and other traditions.

A Hanafi Islamic jurist Ahmad al-Fārūqī al-Sirhind and a member of the Naqshbandī Sufi order opposed Akbar's Din-i Ilahi.

Some scholars in Pakistan believe that *Din-i Ilahi* was the seed for the birth of the 'Two-Nation Theory'. Islamist leader Shah Waliullah (1703–1762) is in a way the father of the Pro-

Arab Islamist revival movement, whose goal was to regain the 'glory of Islamic rule' in the Indian subcontinent. He asked the Muslim rulers to ban Hindu and Shī'ah religious practices. He strongly advocated the segregation of Hindus and Muslims and commitment to Arab Culture. He wrote:

"Muslims, no matter where they live, wherever they spend their youthful days, they should in any case be completely separated from the natives of that country in their culture, traditions and mannerisms. And wherever they are, they must be immersed in their Arabic splendor and Arabic trends."[116]

In another letter, he wrote:

"Strict orders should be issued in all Islamic towns forbidding religious ceremonies publicly practiced by Hindus such as the performance of Holi and ritual bathing in the Ganges. On the tenth of Muharram, the Shī'ahs should not be allowed to go beyond the bounds of moderation, neither should they be rude nor repeat stupid things in the streets or bazars."[117]

Some experts point to Haji Shariatullah, as one of the early proponents of the 'Two-Nation Theory'. He was the founder of the Faraizi movement (1819 CE) in Bengal and asked the Muslims to abandon all un-Islamic practices and act upon their religious duties called *fard*. The other person also given credit is Syed Ahmad Barelvi, a Muslim revivalist from the Sunni Hanafi Maturidi sect known as Barelvi. Ahmad, a Wahhabist, was one of the extreme critics of the Shī'ahs and was credited as "the first person to realize the necessity of a movement which was at the same time religious, military and political". He also was the first to directly address the general Muslim population in his call for *jihad*.[118]

According to French scholar Prof. Olivier Roy, Barelvi was key to the 'reform movement started with the idea of Wahhabist understanding of monotheism, and the fight against the local interpretations and customs which 'had corrupted Islam' in a way.

Pakistani-American academic Akbar Salahuddin Ahmed noted that "reformers like Waliullah, Barelvi, and Shariatullah were not demanding a Pakistan in the modern sense of nationhood. They were, however, instrumental in creating an awareness of the crisis looming for the Muslims and the need to create their own political organization. What Sir Sayyed did was to provide a modern idiom in which to express the quest for Islamic identity."[119]

In an 1883 speech, Sayyed preached the idea of two nations:

"Friends, in India there live two prominent nations which are distinguished by the names of Hindus and Mussulmans. Just as a man has some principal organs, similarly these two nations are like the principal limbs of India".[120]

In another speech in 1887, he said:

"Now suppose that all the English were to leave India – then who would be rulers of India? Is it possible that under these circumstances, two nations, Mohammedan and Hindu, could sit on the same throne and remain equal in power? Most certainly not. It is necessary that one of them should conquer the other and thrust it down. To hope that both could remain equal is to desire the impossible and inconceivable".[121]

Generally, the NeoCols first blame the Congress for Muslims to feel alienated from the mainstream because of their 'idolatry' (*Vandemataram*) approach, or that the British used the 'divide and rule' strategy to keep the two communities divided and gave birth to the idea that 'Muslims cannot live with the majority Hindus' – the key propaganda phrase of the 'Two-Nation Theory'. We can see how the roots of Muslim separatism are not only found in inherent theological inspiration, but it goes back to the period of Akbar and Ahmad al-Fārūqī al-Sirhind. But more than any other Muslim leader, Allama Iqbal contributed maximum from the educated section of the Muslim polity and inspired Jinnah to opt for Pakistan.

Well-known historian Prof. Mohibbul Hasan studied at the Aligarh Muslim University and obtained an M.A. and Ph.D. from the University of Cambridge. He later became a Professor in the Department of History and Culture, Jamia Millia Islamia. He also served as the Vice-Chancellor of Jamia Millia Islamia and was appointed as the President of the Indian History Congress in 2002.

According to his second son Mushirul Hasan, the intellectual and young activists for the Pakistan movement were recruited from the Aligarh Muslim University (hinting at during his father's tenure), which has been a hotbed of separatist activities till now. He also wrote that before 1939, Aligarh provided support to the nationalist freedom movement. But soon after, they moved toward the Muslim separatist movement; students and faculty, both, rallied behind Jinnah and the Muslim League.[122] Since those days, Aligarh has remained a hotbed of separatists.

Invasion of Muslim holy sites by the Saudis

The story goes like this:

The original prophet of the Abrahamic faith, Abraham, and his son Ishmael were instructed by 'God' to build a sacred 'house' near the 'Well of Zamzam', which today is identified as the sacred structure called Kaaba.[123]

After the structure was built, an angel brought a black stone. It was said to have come from heaven, the celestial object (most likely a meteorite origin) which fell on the Abu Qubays hill in that area. Abraham placed the stone in the eastern corner of Kaaba. Later, he and his followers announced to the world about this 'great pilgrimage of mankind'.[124]

While the Kaaba may have undergone changes, the black stone is believed to be the original remnant of Abraham. The most sacred mosque of Islam, Masjid al-Haram of the Great Mosque of Mecca, surrounds the Kaaba structure, the holiest structure for Muslims in Mecca. Kaaba means 'cube' in Arabic since the structure is built in a cube form. As noted earlier, before the advent of Islam, the original Kaaba may have been situated in Petra, where 360 deities were worshiped. After the advent of Muhammad and Islam, only one deity, namely Allah, is worshiped. Though Islamic tradition forbids any icon, the black stone is a notable exception. The rest of the 359 deities and their icons were destroyed by Muhammad and his followers, as noted earlier.[125][126]

Millions of Muslims from all over the world go to Mecca for pilgrimage. The most important one is the *Hajj*, and the other one is *Umrah*. While Hajj involves multiple rituals and can be performed during specific days only, Umrah is ritually less involved and can be performed any time of the year. According to *Insidesaudi.com* roughly 20 million people come to Mecca for pilgrimage every year.[127]

It also noted: "Both pilgrimages produce $12 billion annually – $8 from *Hajj* and $4 from *Umrah*, almost 3% of non-oil GDP. This figure is forecast to increase to $150 billion by 2022, and the current $51.2 billion investments in local transport and infrastructure could result in 100,000 more jobs. The goal is to attract pilgrims from higher value Muslim minority countries and reduce waiting time by encouraging pilgrims to come for *Umrah* instead."

The site also shows that roughly 25% of the pilgrims are domestic, and 75% are international. In 2019, 4 million pilgrims were from Arab countries and 11 million from Asia.

Before we move on to the next chapter, which is about the entry of Islam into India, we may take note of how Saudi Arabia systematically removed and destroyed many ancient historical sites and monuments of Islam in Arabia. These include ancient mosques, burial sites, homes, and historical sites associated with Muhammad, family members, and companions.

According to several sources, including the 'History of the Cemetery of Jannat al-Baqi' inspired and guided by Wahhabism's iconoclasm zeal, no 'icon' could be 'worshiped' by the Muslims, thus Saudi monarchs took up many demolition tasks. Some most notable ones as listed here:

"The house of Mawlid where Muhammad is said to have been born, the house of Khadija, Muhammad's first wife, and his children Kulthum, Fatimah, Qasim, and Abd-Allah were born. "[128]

Other sites include the house of Islam's first Caliph, Abu Bakr (Hilton Hotel stands there), the house of Muhammed in Medina, Dar Al-Arqam, the first Islamic school where Muhammad taught, and the house of Ali where Hasan and Husayn were born.

Some notable mosques were also destroyed, including al-Manaratain, the mosque and tomb of Imam al-Uraidhi (destroyed in 2002), four mosques at the Battle of the Trench in Medina, and mosques of Abu Rasheed, Salman al-Farsi Mosque in Medina. Cemeteries and tombs destroyed include Jannat al-Baqi in Medina, Jannat al- Mu'alla in Mecca, Tomb of Eve in Jeddah (destroyed in 1975), and the grave of the father of Muhammad, Abdulla in Medina (destroyed in 1978).[129, 130, 131]

The story of the sacred Black Stone of Kaaba

Even earlier, during 1801–1806, the Saudi monarch's forces invaded Mecca, Medina, and Karbala when many ancient structures were destroyed, including the tomb of Husayn, the grandson of Muhammad and son of Ali, Muhammad's son-in-law.

And the greatest significant one was the most sacred icon of Islam, the black stone. Some say that the stone was broken into eight pieces during this invasion. 19th-century Czech-Austrian scholar on the Middle East, Alois Musil, in his book *Al-Saud*, reported this shocking event. Musil also noted that the forces desecrated the grave of Muhammad and took away a good amount of treasures, including gifts from the Ottoman ruler Othman Sultan Ahmed. Among many valuable items, the most precious was a diamond called al-Kawkab ad-Durri, which means the 'Priceless Planet'.[132]

The self-appointed caretaker of Islam did all these. Today, when Muslims go for Hajj, after circumventing the Kaaba structure wherein is placed the black stone, they kiss the black stone. In reality, they don't kiss the stones but the gum that holds together the eight stones in a silver container.

Perhaps the real reason for Sauds for removing sacred structures is about business – to make space for a maximum number of Hajj pilgrims near Kaaba. A massive amount of income from the Hajj pilgrims as well as a show-off of the power of the Sauds, may be part of the game.

In India, thousands of Hindu temples were destroyed during the invasions, and Islamic structures were built on top. The most notable ones are Ram Mandir in Ayodhya, Shiva Temple in Kashi or Varanasi, and the Mathura Mosque built after destroying the Krishna Janmabhoomi temple. Many Hindu saints and organizations requested the Muslim leaders to hand over these three sacred places to the Hindus. Yet, it has been hugely communalized and politicized, mostly by the NeoCols.

However, the Saudi kingdom did it in Islam's most sacred land; destroying or removing some of the most sacred structures to the Muslims did not generate any major hue and cry in the world. The majority of Sunni Muslims in India are under the spell of Wahhabism, an Arab version of Islam, which is, at the end of the day, in a way Arab Imperialism. The knowledge above is kept secret for the average Muslims by forcing the submission of Indian Muslims to Arab hegemony on Islam. No Muslim leader or Communist leader has the courage to even talk about it, and protesting is too much to expect. Once Muslims of India are made aware of these, they are expected to release these historical Hindu sacred places and monuments back to the Hindus, which may create strong goodwill.

References

1. Lewis Lord, "The Last Prophet", U.S. News & World Report, April 7, 2008, p. 3.
2. Madelung, Wilferd (1997). "The Succession to Muhammad p. 31, 32.
3. Nasr, Seyyed Hossein."Ali". *Encyclopædia Britannica Online.*
4. Al Qalqashandi Ma'athir al-inafah fi ma'alim al-khilafah qtd. in Hassan, Mona. "Conceptualizing the Caliphate, 632–1517 CE. ", Longing for the Lost Caliphate: A Transregional History, Princeton University Press, 2016, pp. 98–141, http://www.jstor.org/stable/j.ctt1q1xrgm.9
5. "Ali ibn Abi Talib", New World Encyclopedia, https://www.newworldencyclopedia.org/entry/Ali_ibn_Abi_Talib
6. "Shi'a Islam" (book) by Muhammad Husayn Tabatabaei.
7. "Pan-Islam In British Indian Politics: A Study Of The Khilafat Movement", 1918 1924 (Social, Economic And Political

Studies Of The Middle East And Asia) M. Naeem Qureshi, 1999, p. 88 https://1lib.us/book/5541174/c9780d?id=5541174&secret=c9780d
8. Alex Hanton, "10 Dark Secrets Of The Ottoman Empire", 13 July 2016, https://listverse.com/2016/07/13/10-dark-secrets-of-the-ottoman-empire/
9. History of Arabia – Kindah. *Encyclopædia Britannica.*
10. The CIA World Factbook.
11. World Population Prospects – Population Division – United Nations. population.un.org
12. https://www.goabroad.com/articles/teach-abroad/10-things-banned-in-saudi-arabia
13. Freedom House 2006 Report.
14. 2013 Report on International Religious Freedom: Saudi Arabia". state.gov. Washington, D.C.: United States Department of State. 28 July 2014.
15. Sandra Mackey's account of her attempt to enter Mecca in Mackey, Sandra (1987). The Saudis: Inside the Desert Kingdom. W. W. Norton & Company. pp. 63–64.
16. Cuddihy, Kathy (2001). "An A To Z Of Places And Things Saudi". Stacey International. p. 148
17. Max Fisher & Caitlin Dewey (23 May 2013). "A surprising map of where the world's atheists live". *Washington Post.* Archived from the original on 23 July 2018.
18. https://worldpopulationreview.com/country-rankings/muslim-population-by-country
19. Census2011.co.in.
20. Mahmood, Tahir (11 December 2006). "Reform Friendly". *The Times of India.*
21. Hawarey, Dr. Mosab (2010). "The Journey of Prophecy; Days of Peace and War (Arabic)". Islamic Book Trust. [This

book contains a list of battles of Prophet Muhammad, but it is in Arabic. The list of battles in English is available on this website: https://www.webcitation.org/5zLhjeYyz?url=http://military.hawarey.org/military_english.htm

22. Mubarakpuri, "The Sealed Nectar", p. 153.
23. Haykel, Bernard (2013). "Ibn 'Abd al-Wahhab, Muhammad (1703-92)". In Böwering, Gerhard; Crone, Patricia; Kadi, Wadad; Mirza, Mahan; Stewart, Devin J.; Zaman, Muhammad Qasim (eds.). The Princeton Encyclopedia of Islamic Political Thought. Princeton, New Jersey: Princeton University Press. pp. 231–232.
24. Brown, Daniel W. (2009). "The Wahhābī Movement". A New Introduction to Islam.
25. Kepel, Gilles (2003). "Jihad: The Trail of Political Islam.
26. Wiktorowicz, Quintan (2005). "A Genealogy of Radical Islam". Studies in Conflict & Terrorism.
27. "Tawhid", Oxford Islamic Studies http://www.oxfordislamicstudies.com/article/opr/t125/e2356?_hi=0&_pos=2
28. V. G. Julie Rajan "Al Qaeda's Global Crisis: The Islamic State, Takfir and the Genocide of Muslims", Routledge, 2015, p. 76.
29. Valentine, Simon (9 January 2015). "Force and Fanaticism". Oxford University Press. pp. 16–17.
30. Commins, David (2009). "The Wahhabi Mission and Saudi Arabia.
31. Historical Memorandum on the Relations of the Wahabi Amirs and Ibn Saud with Eastern Arabia and the British Government, 1800-1934. Qatar Digital Library: British Library: India Office Records and Private Papers. 1934. p. 2.
32. *Current Biography* (magazine), 1943, pp. 330–34.
33. Robert Murray Thomas "Religion in Schools: Controversies Around the World", Greenwood Publishing Group, 2006, p. 180.

34. Blanchard, Christopher M. "The Islamic Traditions of Wahhabism and Salafiyya", Congressional Research Service. pp. 2–3.
35. Dr. Abdullah Mohammad Sindi, "Britain, the Rise of Wahhabism and the House of Saud", Kaanaan Online, 20 January 2015, https://kanaanonline.org/en/2015/01/20/britain-the-rise-of-wahhabism-and-the-house-of-saud/amp/
36. "What is Wahhabism? The reactionary branch of Islam said to be 'the main source of global terrorism". *The Telegraph.*
37. Glasse, Cyril (2001). "Khārijites". The New Encyclopedia of Islam. California: Altamira Press.
38. "Muslim World League and World Assembly of Muslim Youth". Pew Research Center.
39. https://www.newstatesman.com/world-affairs/2014/11/wahhabism-isis-how-saudi-arabia-exported-main-source-global-terrorism
40. "The Popular Discourses of Salafi Radicalism and Salafi Counter-radicalism in Nigeria: A Case Study of Boko Haram", In: Journal of Religion in Africa, Online Publication Date: 01 Jan 2012.
41. Funeral of King Abdullah of Saudi Arabia, 23 January 2015, *BBC News* https://www.bbc.com/news/av/world-middle-east-30949575
42. A message to the BBC: It is Islam, not 'Wahhabism', 25 January 2015, Abul Abbaas, Naveed Ayaaz https://www.madeenah.com/a-message-to-the-bbc-it-is-islam-not-wahhabism/
43. Daoud, Kamel "If Saudi Arabia Reforms, What Happens to Islamists Elsewhere?", *New York Times*. (16 November 2017).
44. Johny, Stanly , "Explained, Who are the Tablighi Jamaat?", *The Hindu*. (2 April 2020.)
45. Ayoob, Mohammed (2007). "The Many Faces of Political Islam: Religion and politics in the Muslim world". Ann Arbor: University of Michigan Press.
46. Burki, Shireen Khan (2013). "The Tablighi Jama'at: Proselytizing Missionaries or Trojan Horse?". Journal of

Applied Security Research: An International Journal of Police – Security Operations & Practices. London: Routledge 8 (1): 98–117

47. Kuiper, Matthew J. (22 February 2018). "Tablighi Jamaʿat – Oxford Islamic Studies Online". www.oxfordbibliographies.com. Oxford University Press.
48. Masoodi, Ashwaq (16 September 2013). "Inside the Tablighi Jamaat". *Live Mint*.
49. "Great Personalities in Islam" Chapter on Maulana Ilyas Kandhlavi compiled by Badr Azimbadi, Adam Publishers, 2004.
50. Maj.Gen.Afsir Karim, "Wahhabism in South Asia", IDR, 13 September 2014 http://www.indiandefencereview.com/news/wahhabism-in-south-asia/
51. Ibid.
52. Karen DeYoung, "Saudi prince denies Kushner is 'in his pocket'", *Washington Post*, 22 March, 2018 https://www.washingtonpost.com/world/national-security/saudi-prince-denies-kushner-is-in-his-pocket/2018/03/22/701a9c9e-2e22-11e8-8688-e053ba58f1e4_story.html
53. Ayşe Betül Baldec, "US, Saudi Arabia try to throw off 'Wahhabi-linked' mess they created", *Daily Sabah*, 09 December, 2019 https://www.dailysabah.com/mideast/2019/12/09/us-saudi-arabia-try-to-throw-off-wahhabi-linked-mess-they-created/amp
54. Vicky, "Wahabis vs Tabligi Jamaat: How the battle has entered India", *One India,* 29 May, 2015, https://www.oneindia.com/feature/wahabis-versus-tabligi-jamaat-how-the-battle-has-entered-india-1761572.html
55. Eleanor Abdella Doumato (rev. Byron D. Cannon) (2009). "Jāhilīyah". In John L. Esposito (ed.). The Oxford Encyclopedia of the Islamic World. Oxford: Oxford University Press.
56. Sayed Khatab, "The Political Thought of Sayyid Qutb: The Theory of Jahiliyyah", Routledge, 2006.
57. Doumato, 2009.

58. Rasheed, Nighat. "A critical study of the reformist trends in the Indian Muslim society during the nineteenth century".
59. Doumato, 2009.
60. "Karaites and Karaism", *Jewish Encyclopedia* https://www.jewishencyclopedia.com/articles/9211-karaites-and-karaism
61. Peters, Edward (2008). "A Modern Guide to Indulgences: Rediscovering This Often-Misinterpreted Teaching", Hillenbrand Books, p. 13.
62. John MacArthur, "What Does Sola Scriptura Mean?", 27 August 2021 https://www.ligonier.org/blog/what-does-sola-scriptura-mean/
63. Jens Zimmermann, "Hermeneutics: A Very Short Introduction", Oxford University Press, 2015, p. 90.
64. Muhammad ibn Sa'ad, "Kitab al-Tabaqat al-Kabir", Translated by Haq, S. M. (1967). Ibn Sa'd's Kitab al-Tabaqat al-Kabir, Volume I Parts I & II, pp. 99-100. Delhi: Kitab-Bhavan. p. 109.
65. Ibn Sa`d, Mohammed, al-Tabaqat al-Kubra, Dar Sader, vol. 8, p. 223; Baladhuri, vol. 1, p. 96.
66. Stephen J. Shoemaker, "The Death of a Prophet: The End of Muhammad's Life and the Beginnings of Islam", University of Pennsylvania Press, 2012, p. 22. Full text of "The Death of a Prophet - The End of Muhammad's Life and the Beginnings of Islam" (archive.org)
67. Ian Paul, theologian, author, speaker, academic consultant. Adjunct Professor, Fuller Theological Seminary: https://www.psephizo.com/life-ministry/who-really-wrote-the-quran/ 2018.
68. Duri, Abd al-Aziz (2011). "Early Islamic Institutions: Administration and Taxation from the Caliphate to the Umayyads and ʿAbbāsids". Translated by Razia Ali. London and Beirut: I. B. Tauris and Centre for Arab Unity Studies.

69. Dixon, 'Abd al-Ameer (August 1969). "The Umayyad Caliphate", 65–86/684–705: (A Political Study) (Thesis). London: University of London, SOAS.

70. Bosworth, C.E. (1993). "Muʿāwiya II". In Bosworth, C. E.; van Donzel, E.; Heinrichs, W. P. & Pellat, Ch. (eds.). "The Encyclopaedia of Islam", New Edition, Volume VII: Mif–Naz. Leiden: E. J. Brill. pp. 268–269.

71. Muslim Spain (711-1492), 2009-09-04 http://www.bbc.co.uk/religion/religions/islam/history/spain_1.shtml.

72. "Caliphate", *Britannica* https://www.britannica.com/place/Caliphate.

73. Veccia Vaglieri, Laura. "Ibn Muldjam". *Encyclopædia of Islam*, Second Edition. Brill Online.

74. Rasul Ja'fariyan, "History of the Caliphs", Al-Islam https://www.al-islam.org/history-of-the-caliphs-rasul-jafariyan/imam-alis-imamate.

75. Madelung, Wilferd (1997). "The Succession to Muhammad: A Study of the Early Caliphate". Cambridge University Press.

76. "Islamic Beliefs, Practices, and Cultures". Marshall Cavendish Reference. 2019.

77. "A Shi'ite Anthology" by Muhammad Husayn Tabatabaei.

78. "Islamic World" https://www.nationsonline.org/oneworld/muslim-countries.htm

79. Guidère, Mathieu (2012). "Historical Dictionary of Islamic Fundamentalism". Scarecrow Press. p. 319.

80. Newman, Andrew J. (2013). "Introduction". Twelver Shiism: Unity and Diversity in the Life of Islam, 632 to 1722. Edinburgh University Press. p. 2. Archived from the original on 1 May 2016.

81. "Quick guide: Sunnis and Shias". *BBC News*. 11 December 2006. Archived from the original on 28 December 2008.

82. "Anatomy of a Tazia", 7 December 2011, https://www.dawn.com/news/678714/anatomy-of-a-tazia
83. Percent Sunni Muslim – Country rankings, The Global Economy https://www.theglobaleconomy.com/rankings/sunni/
84. Pew Research Center's Forum on Religion & Public Life • Mapping the Global Muslim Population, October 2009.
85. Shoemaker, 2012.
86. al-Fadl ibn Shadhan, "The Return of al-Mahdi", Bilal Muslim Mission of Tanzania, 1996.
87. Zaman, Muhammad (2012). "Modern Islamic thought in a radical age". Cambridge University Press. pp. 15–17, 62–95.
88. Curtis, Lisa; Mullick, Haider (4 May 2009). "Reviving Pakistan's Pluralist Traditions to Fight Extremism". The Heritage Foundation.
89. Sandeep Unnithan and Uday Mahurkar (31 July 2008). "The radical sweep". *India Today*.
90. Madelung, Wilferd (1986). "al-Mahdī", Encyclopaedia of Islam. 5 (2nd ed.). Brill Academic Publishers, 1986, pp. 1230–8.
91. Saiedi, Nader (2008). "Gate of the Heart: Understanding the Writings of the Báb". Canada: Wilfrid Laurier University Press.
92. Smith, Peter (2000). "Báb". A concise encyclopedia of the Bahá'í Faith. Oxford: Oneworld Publications. pp. 55–59.
93. Adamson, Hugh (2007). "Historical Dictionary of the Bahá'í Faith". Oxford, UK: Scarecrow Press.
94. https://www.thearda.com/QL2010/QuickList_40.asp . "Most Baha'i Nations (2010)". QuickLists > Compare Nations > Religions >. The Association of Religion Data Archives. 2010.

95. Daftary, Farhad (1998). "A Short History Of The Ismailis: Traditions of a Muslim Community". Edinburgh, U.K.: Edinburgh University Press.
96. N. Hanif, "Islamic Concept of Crime and Justice: Political justice and crime", Sarup & Sons, 1999, p. 283.
97. Bernard Lewis (1967), "The Assassins: a Radical Sect in Islam", Weidenfeld & Nicolson, p. 59-61.
98. "The Ismaili sect: from the 9th century" http://www.historyworld.net/wrldhis/plaintexthistories.asp?historyid=ab17#ixzz6UmWOv7HF
99. "Aga Khan I", *Britannica* https://www.britannica.com/biography/Aga-Khan-I
100. "Aga Khan III 'offered to help Adolf Hitler'", *Hindustan Times,* 9 March 2008, https://www.hindustantimes.com/world/aga-khan-iii-offered-to-help-adolf-hitler/story-OgaCmuJOnlxyI0JVxqhNvM.html
101. "How the Eton-educated wartime Aga Khan offered '30,000 armed Arabs' to help Hitler - but still evaded treason trial", *Daily Mail*, 08 Mar 2008 https://www.dailymail.co.uk/news/article-528720/How-Eton-educated-wartime-Aga-Khan-offered-30-000-armed-Arabs-help-Hitler--evaded-treason-trial.html
102. Ibid.
103. In Pictures: The World's Richest Royals, Forbes https://www.forbes.com/2010/07/07/richest-royals-wealth-monarch-wedding-divorce-billionaire_slide.html?sh=cb074783e78e
104. Vinay Lal, "A Reputation, and More, in Ruins: Gandhi at the Aga Khan Palace, Pune", UCLA Social Sciences http://southasia.ucla.edu/history-politics/gandhi/gandhi-aga-khan-palace-pune/
105. Abou El Fadl, Khaled (January 23, 2007). "The Great Theft: Wrestling Islam from the Extremists". HarperOne. p. 227

106. "Dar al-Harb", Oxford Islamic Studies http://www.oxfordislamicstudies.com/article/opr/t125/e490

107. Glasse, Cyril. (2002). "The New Encyclopedia of Islam": Revised Edition of the "Concise Encyclopedia of Islam". Walnut Creek, CA: AltaMira Press, pp. 111, 240.

108. Ibid.

109. Bada' us-Sanaai', Vol. 7, p. 130.

110. "Dar al-Harb" http://www.oxfordislamicstudies.com/article/opr/t125/e490

111. "Pan-Islam in British Indian Politics: A Study of the Khilafat Movement, 1918-1924". (Social, Economic and Political Studies of the Middle East and Asia), M. Naeem Qureshi. pp. 79 –82.

112. Muftī Muḥammad Shafī, I Imdād al-Muftīn, 2:745.

113. John Kelsay (2015). "Jihad". Islamic Political Thought: An Introduction. Princeton University Press. pp. 86–104. JSTOR j.ctt1287ksk.8.

114. Syed Sahabuddin, "Is India a 'Dar-ul-Harb'? Are Hindus 'Kafirs'?", Mainstream, 2 May 2009 https://www.mainstreamweekly.net/article1331.html#

115. Abu'l-Fazl ibn Mubarak (2010) [1902–39]. "The Akbarnama of Abu'l-Fazl". Delhi: Low Price Publications.

116. Dr. Mubarak Ali, "Almiyah-e-Tarikh", ch. 9 – 10, Fiction House, Lahore, 2012, pp. 95–105.

117. S. Athar Rizvi, "Shah Waliullah and His Times", Ma'rifat Publishing House, Canberra, 1980, p. 227.

118. Roy, Olivier (1985). "Islam and Resistance in Afghanistan". Cambridge University Press. pp. 57–8.

119. Akbar S. Ahmed (1997). "Jinnah, Pakistan and Islamic Identity: The Search for Saladin", Psychology Press, p.11.

120. Khuda Bakhsh Library, Sir Syed Speaks at Patna in 1883, August 23, 2020. https://www.kblpublications.com/amp/the-two-eyes-of-india

121. Balbir Punj, "The real Sir Syed: A British agent", *The Pioneer*, 22 October 2018. https://www.dailypioneer.com/2018/columnists/the-real-sir-syed--a-british-agent.html
122. Hasan, Mushirul (March 1985). "Nationalist and Separatist Trends in Aligarh, 1915–47". The Indian Economic and Social History Review. 22 (1): 1–33. doi:10.1177/001946468502200101
123. And remember Abraham and Isma'il raised the foundations of the House (With this prayer): "Our Lord! Accept (this service) from us: For Thou art the All-Hearing, the All-knowing". Quran 2:127.
124. Quran 20:27 "And proclaim to the people the Hajj [pilgrimage]; they will come to you on foot and on every lean camel; they will come from every distant pass – and Quran 20:29 declared "Then let them end their untidiness and fulfill their vows and perform Tawaf around the ancient House.""
125. "Mecca: From Before Genesis Until Now", M. Lings, Archetype, p. 39.
126. Ibn Ishaq, Muhammad (1955). Ibn Ishaq's "Sirat Rasul Allah – The Life of Muhammad" Translated by A. Guillaume. Oxford: Oxford University Press. pp. 88–9.
127. "How Much Money Does Saudi Arabia Make From Hajj and Umrah?" https://insidesaudi.com/how-much-money-does-saudi-arabia-make-from-hajj-and-umrah/
128. "History of the Cemetery of Jannat al-Baqi", [History of the Shrines, Al-Islam.org (Ahlul Bayt Digital Islamic Library Project)
129. Salah Nasrawi, Mecca's ancient heritage is under attack – Developments for pilgrims and the strict beliefs of Saudi clerics are encroaching on or eliminating Islam's holy sites in the kingdom, *Los Angeles Times*, September 16, 2007.
130. Jerome Taylor, "Medina: Saudis take a bulldozer to Islam's history", *Independent,* 24 September 2014 https://

www.independent.co.uk/news/world/middle-east/medina-saudis-take-bulldozer-islam-s-history-8228795.html

131. Irfan Ahmed, "The Destruction of Holy Sites in Mecca and Medina", p. 1, Archived 2011-07-13 at the Wayback Machine, *Islamica* Magazine, Issue 15. p. 71.

132. Ali Al-Ahmed, "Saudis Destroyed Islam's Holiest Stone", Gulf Institute, August 24, 2017 https://www.gulfinstitute.org/2017/08/24/book-saudis-destroyed-islams-holiest-stone/

❑

CHAPTER

5

ENTRY OF ISLAM IN INDIA AFTER MUHAMMAD

When and how did the first Muslims come to India?
How is Afghanistan connected to India?
Where is Bamiyan who built the Bamiyan Buddhas?
How did Raja Jayapala, the Hindus Shahi King, protect the western front of India from invasions?
Who is the Taliban?
What is the role of America, Russia, Britain, China, Pakistan, and Saudi Arabia in creating the Afghan mess?
What is the cost of the Afghan war?
Where was Kafiristan, and could India be named Kafiristan?
How did Raja Dahir protect Sind from the invaders?
What is the connection between the Kaaba and Somnath Temple?
Why did Genghis Khan never invade India?
What is the origin of Khan title?
Who was Timur and Sha Rukh?

Of all the foreign forces, the invaders carrying the banner of Islam have caused the most massive and long-term damage to the foundation of Indian civilization. This chapter will review the entry and impact of forces that used Islamism as their guiding principle.

African traders visited India as early as 130 BCE, traveling almost 3000 km across the Arabian Sea.[1]

African and Arab traders used to come to India's southern coast, mainly in the Malabar region and Konkan–Gujarat region via this sea route. The trade between India and the Arabs was in existence since long before the birth of Islam. Greeks figured out the best route to visit India; they had to go by the sea with the wind behind them northeastward, starting in late spring, and reached India mid-summer. They would return when the wind was behind them again, this time southwestward with the end of the monsoon. At that time, when the African pied cuckoos flocked together and flew towards rainy India, the sailors would follow their trail. And after the monsoon was over, the birds would return to their native places. When these 'monsoon birds' arrived on India's western and southern coasts, the Arab traders would also arrive there with their dates, herbs, and other products and return with Indian spices, jewelry, metal, and silk commodities. This trade travel was going on for centuries before the advent of Islam in Arabia. Even after Arabs were Islamized, the trade continued. Many Muslims who migrated to India as merchants and settled were generally non-proselytizing, and through local marriage relations, some conversions happened. Many of these Arab traders visited the Malabar region during the lifetime of Muhammad, even before Islam got a strong foothold in Arabia itself.[2]

Newly converted Malik Bin Dinar was one such converted Persian preacher and traveler who visited Malabar. Along with 20 others, he boarded in one of the India-bound ships pushed by the monsoon breeze. They ended up landing in Kodungallur, Kerala. Dinar and his group were welcomed as traders by the local ruler as he did so for centuries and provided them royal patronage to settle and even build mosques. The local ruler gifted Dinar an abandoned Jain temple, where he established the first mosque in the Indian subcontinent between 612 and 629 CE.[3] According to some, this mosque is the second one in the world that offered Friday Prayer after the Saudi mosque in Medina. Essentially Dinar was a missionary preacher who later built many more mosques and converted many Hindus.[4]

The earliest known community converted to Islam in the Malabar region was the Mappilas, later known as Moplah,[5] connected to the infamous Moplah massacre of 1921. Some historians suggest that the first mosque of the subcontinent, Juni Masjid or Barwada Masjid, was built in the ancient port town of Ghogha, on the Gulf of Khambhat, Gujarat between 610 CE to 623 CE.[6]

However, starting from the early 700s, invaders from newly Islamized Persia (Iran) and other neighboring countries united their armies under 'Persian' ethnicity and Islam as religion. Sindh was attacked first, and it fell in the hands of the invaders in 712 CE. The invasions, plunder, killings, selling of Hindu girls, boys, and women in large numbers in global slave markets, destruction of temples and educational institutes continued for centuries and virtually ended only after Aurangzeb died in 1707 CE.

Let us review the impact of a millennium of Islamic presence on India's socio-cultural history and economy. These observations of the famous American historian Will Durant summarize that part of India's history with lessons learned (or not):

"The Mohammedan Conquest of India is probably the bloodiest story in (world) history. It is a discouraging tale, for its evident moral is that civilization is a precarious thing, whose delicate complex of order and liberty, culture and peace may at any time be overthrown by barbarians invading from without or multiplying within. ...The Hindus ... had failed to organize their forces for the protection of their frontiers and their capitals, their wealth and their freedom, from the hordes of Scythians, Huns, Afghans, and Turks hovering about India's boundaries and waiting for national weakness to let them in.

For four hundred years (600-1000 AD.) India invited conquest; and at last it came."[7]

"It was not easy to be a Hindu during the last 800 years,"[8] he added.

Before we go to India, let us review the power structure in Islamic Arabia after Muhammad's death in 632 CE described in detail in the previous chapter. During his lifetime, much of Western Arabia or Hejaz was conquered and converted.

The day's order was that there would be a strong man called Caliph, the social, religious, and political successor to Muhammad as the 'leader of the ummah' or the entire Islamic world. A caliphate is 'an Islamic state ruled by a Caliph or Khalifa'.

Four successive Caliphs came after the prophet's death and were called the Rashidun Caliphate as part of the Sunni sect. Shias do not honor the first three leaders as Caliphs.[9]

The first Rashidun Caliph was Abu Bakr, the father of Muhammad's youngest wife, Aisha, and a trusted commander in Muhammad's army. Umar or Omar became the second Caliph after Abu Bakr, and then came two more, Uthman and Ali, a cousin and son-in-law of Muhammad. Hasan or Hassan was the eldest son of Ali and Muhammad's (and his first wife Khadija) daughter Fatimah and was the older brother of Husayn and the fifth Caliph.

Abu Bakr and Omar were able to expand their dominion to Palestine and Mesopotamia. By then, the Roman and Sasanian or Persian empires had become very weak. In 636 CE, the Battle of Yarmouk and then the Battle of Qadisiya saw Islam conquer parts of the Roman Empire and Iran.[10] Moreover, in 642 CE, the Battle of Nahavand, known as 'Victory of Victories'[11] in the Muslim world, sealed Iran's fate forever as the Sassanids fell and Persia was captured by the Muslims.

The Caliphs were ruling the entire Arab Peninsula. The first four Caliphs focused on the expansion of their rule around the neighboring lands with around 100,000 soldiers in their army.[12] During this period, they conquered the Levant, a large area in the Eastern Mediterranean. The Levant was the historically greater Syria, including present-day Syria, Lebanon, Jordan, Israel, Palestine, and most of Turkey and Transcaucasia, which corresponds to modern-day Georgia, Armenia, and Azerbaijan. In the north, from Egypt to Tunisia in Africa, Iran and some parts of Central and South Asia in the east were conquered.[13]

As noted earlier, the second Rashidun Caliph Omar or Umar, a commander and old-time trusted companion of Muhammad, became very powerful after the prophet's demise and the one who also succeeded the first Caliph Abu Bakr.

Omar had heard of India's wealth and had dreamt of jihad against the 'infidels' and planned for expeditions into India as early as around 640 CE.[14] Several governors were appointed to the Indian frontier and instructed to attack India with armed force. But the forces faced strong and robust resistance from the Indian side and were not much successful. Many of the governors were defeated and killed by the Hindu kings. Only during the rule of the caliphate of Mu'awiyah around 661–680 CE, Makran (coastal region of today's Baluchistan) could be defeated, and they established a military garrison there.[15] As they gained more power, they slowly conquered some other parts of Baluchistan.

History lost in Afghanistan

Today, Afghanistan is in everyone's consciousness. But how was Afghanistan before?

The legend goes like this:

The Princess of Gandhar, known as Gandhari, wife of blind Dhritarashtra and mother of the Kauravas, including Duryodhana, is a significant personality in the Mahabharata. No, Gandhari was not a bad character at all. Princess Gandhari was 'most beautiful of her times', a great scholar and a virtuous person. She was said to be the incarnation of Devi *Mati*, the deity of intelligence.[16]

Brother Shakuni was unhappy that her sister was forced to marry a blind person and waited for revenge. His vengeful acts are an intricate part of the Mahabharata.

We find in Mahabharata that Subala was the king of Gandhara[17], and his children included Shakuni (original name was Saubala), Gandhari, Achala, Vrishaka, and Vrihadvala.[18]

It is said that post-Mahabharata war, where Gandhari lost all her 100 sons, she cursed Krishna so that he won't have any ancestors left. If we take the most recent research work, we can say that the Mahabharata story unfolded a little more than 5000 years ago. Arjuna, who coordinated the Asvamedha Yajna of his elder brother Yudhisthira, did a royal campaign to this region after the Mahabharata war and defeated Shakuni's son.[19]

Even before the Mahabharata period, we find references of Gandhar from the Ramayana and some other ancient texts. There were various *Janapadas* or federated nations in the Indian subcontinent called *Bharat Varsha* from very ancient times. Commonly 16 such Janapadas are mentioned. Gandhara and Kamboj were two of *Janapadas* that were part of current Afghanistan.

According to various ancient texts and Puranas, the Gandhara janapada was founded by Gandhāra, son of Aruddha, a descendant of Yayati.[20]

The name of the capital of Afghanistan, Kabul, comes from the Kabul River. The ancient name of the river in Sanskrit and Avestan was *Kubhā*. The local settlement was also called Kubha.[21, 22]

In ancient times, the Rigveda and Avesta both mention the Kabul River and its area as Kubha. According to the Rigveda, 'Kubha was an "ideal city" and a vision of paradise set in the mountains and is full of poems in praise of the city'.[23, 24] The name later changed to *Kābul*.[25, 26]

Between 550–330 BCE, Kabul was a major center of learning for Zoroastrianism and subsequently Buddhism.[27]

The main cities within Gandhara kingdom were Puruṣapura (Peshwar), Takṣaśilā or Taxila, Sagala or Shakala (Sialkot), and Pushkalavati (Charsadda), the capital.[28]

In the Ramayana, famed King Bharata, brother of King Ram, had two sons, Taksha and Pushkala. According to legends, Taksha is said to have founded *Taksa-sila* (Taxila), and Pushkala founded Pushkalavati.[29]

Similarly, the modern city of Lahore's name is associated with King Ram's son Prince Lava, who founded this city Lavapuri[30] (the modern-day city of Lahore[31]), which is named after him.[32] Kasur was founded by and named after Lava's twin brother, Prince Kusha.[33] The city of Kasur was described as being situated somewhere on the right bank of the Beas (Sutlej) opposite the city of Lahore.[34] Kasur is located 50 kilometers south of Lahore.

In ancient times there were eight adjacent cities called *Aṣṭanagaram* or Hashtnagar and Ashnaghar in the Pashto language.[35, 36] Modern-day Charsadda and Ashnagar are part of these eight cities, as was the capital city of Pushkalavati in the olden days. An ancient sacred place called Prang also was part of these eight cities, which resembles Prayag or Sangam because of the confluence of Swat and several branches of the Kabul River. Locals also support this legend and comparison with Prayag.[37]

Due to the Afghanistan war, we are familiar with the Swat valley in Afghanistan. It is named after the river Swat. In ancient times in Sanskrit, it was called Srivastu or Suvāstu[38] and mentioned in the Rigveda as the *Suvāstu.*[39] The Suvastu (now Swat) meant river "of fair dwellings".[40][41]

Pushkalavati (Charsadda) was the capital of the Gandhara Kingdom. The Greeks called it *Peukelaotis*.

The sons of King Bharat had kingdoms that flourished on either side of the Indus River[42]. Bharat's descendants ruled this region for a long time until we find Raja Subal during the Mahabharata period.

The oldest archaeological evidence is in Bala Hisar Mound dating between 1400 BCE and 800 BCE.[43, 44] This area is also called Shaikhan Dheri; these ruins are located near today's Charsadda, 28 kilometers northeast of Peshwar. Hiuen Tsang, during his visit in the 7th century, noted it as Po-shi-ki-lo-fa-ti.[45]

According to Zoroastrian *Avesta*, *Gandhara,* especially the area of *Pushkalavati,* described as *Vaēkərəta,* the seventh 'most beautiful place on earth' created by *Ahura Mazda,* and according to Encyclopedia of Britannica, it was known as the "crown jewel" of that region.[46]

In 1001 CE Ghazni invaded this area, and since then, *Gandhara* lost its pride name and got the new one *Shaikhan Dheri* (*dheri* means mound or hill in Pashto).[47]

Purushapura or Peshwar (currently in Pakistan) was another great city of the Gandhara kingdom which is described in detail elsewhere. According to the Arab historian and geographer Al-Masudi, by the mid-10th century, the city was known as *Parashāwar*. Persian scholar Al Biruni called it *Purshawar* and *Purushavar.*[48]

Sagala, Sakala, or Sangala (current Sialkot in Pakistan) was another great city in the Gandhar region.[49, 50]

The Mahabharata described that Arjuna defeated the kings of Shakala in his Rajasuya conquest along with 33 other northern Janapadas and cities.[51]

Kamboja kingdom was located in the region northwest of Gandhara, which was also prominently recorded in the Mahabharata.[52]

The cis-Hindukush region from Kafiristan (today's Nuristan) up to southern Kashmir, including Rajauri/Poonch districts and shared borders with the Daradas (today's Gilgit) and the Gandhara, constituted the Kamboja country. [53, 54]

The *Kamboja Mahajanapada* of the Buddhist traditions refers to this cis-Hindukush branch of ancient Kambojas. [55] The capital of *Kamboja* was probably *Rajapura* (modern Rajori) in the southwest of Kashmir. Buddha statues were built in this region during the reign of Emperor Ashoka.[56] Ptolemy's Geography mentioned Kamboja settlements.[57]

Karpasika and Kapisa are same as Kamboja.[58] Today's Bagram (airfield) was a great city capital of Kamboja called *Kapiśi*.[59]

Who are the Pakhtoons? Most likely, they are the descendants of the tribe Pakthās mentioned in Rigveda. They were one of the Vedic tribes that fought against King Sudas in the Battle of the Ten Kings (dāśarājñá), recorded in the Rigveda:

"Together came the Pakthas, the Bhalanas, the Alinas, the Sivas, the Visanins. Yet to the Trtsus came the Ārya's Comrade, through love of spoil and heroes' war, to lead them."

— (Rigveda, Mandala 7, Hymn 18, Verse 7)[60]

The Bamiyan Story

We heard much about the Bamiyan Buddha statues, which were destroyed in March 2001 by the Taliban barbarians, on orders from leader Mulla Omar[61] after the Taliban declared those were idols of the kafirs and needed to be removed.[62] And the world watched helplessly!

Bamiyan is 130 kilometers northwest of Kabul, lies in the Bamiyan valley near the Hindu Kush Mountain range on the Silk Road. It became a prominent Buddhist center for religion, philosophy, and arts between the 2nd century CE and 770 CE, with a brief decline during the Islamic invasion by al-Mahdi (770 CE). The inhabitants, primarily monks, lived in small caves carved into the side of the Bamiyan rock cliffs with bright colored murals which are among the oldest oil paintings in the world, reflecting the Gandhara culture and arts in those days. The Buddhist culture again flourished after 100 years of the raid of al-Mahdi but lost to the conquests of the Ghaznavids around 977 CE.[63]

The world has forever lost great treasures, classical blended style of Gandhara Art form[64] the Buddhas of Bamiyan, which were the two largest Buddha statues in the world; Vairocana Buddha (the larger one, also called western Buddha) and Gautama Buddha (the smaller one, also called eastern Buddha) were carved into the side of a sandstone cliff in the 6th century CE. Carbon dating of the statues has determined that the larger 55 m (180 ft) statute was built around 618 CE, and the smaller 38 m (125 ft) one was built around 570 CE.[65, 66]

The murthys were decorated with gold and fine jewels.[67] which were looted perhaps by Mahmud Ghazni. The so-called progressive Government of Afghanistan honored Mahmud by releasing a postal stamp called 'National Unity' to commemorate him in 2007.[68]

Afghanistan

Along with modern-day Pakistan, Afghanistan was part of the so-called Harrapan, Indus Valley, or Sarasvati civilization before 3000 BCE. All pieces of evidence indicate that it was part of early Vedic civilization.

How did the name of this land become Afghan? Stan is Sanskrit *sthan* and means place or land. Scholars suggest that this land had bred and supplied the best horses in the world in ancient times, hence the name *Aśvaka* meaning breeder of horses.[69] Other variations included Ashvakan (the Sanskrit speaking Vedic people named it), Aśvakayana, or Asvayana, and Latinized as *Aspasioi*. Perhaps inside the ethnonym Afghan, *Aśvaka* is hidden, which was famous for 'breeding, raising, and training warhorses, as also in providing expert cavalry services'. Later, Asvaka evolved into new forms, including Assakan, Asgan, and Avagan.

Some people suggest that the name "Afghanistan" comes from "Upa-Gana-stan" which means in Sanskrit "the place inhabited by allied tribes".[70]

Philologist J.W. McCrindle noted: "The name of the *Aśvaka* indicates that their country was renowned in primitive times, as it is at the present day, for its superior breed of horses. The fact that the Greeks translated their name into "Hippasioi" (a horse) shows that they must have been aware of its etymological signification".[71] Historian R.C. Majumdar also attested the same.[72] When Alexander invaded this part of the world around 327 BCE, the *Aśvaka* people, called Assakenoi by the Greeks, fielded against him 2,000 cavalries, 30 elephants, and 30,000 infantry as recorded their valor by the Greek historian Diodorus Siculus, but were eventually defeated. A very important aspect of the people here to remember is that even Diodorus recorded that the women took up arms along with the men and preferred "a glorious death to a life of dishonour".[73] Later, we will present the valor of the Kalash people of Nuristan/Chitral, who did not surrender till the 19th century.

Between the 7th century and 3rd century BCE, the nomadic Sakas or Scythians occupied a vast land around the Caspian Sea.[74] Generally, historians suggest that they are of Iranian origin. And their language was also from Eastern Iran. In terms of religion, they also followed certain Iranian religions, most likely Zoroastrianism.

Parts of this land in Afghanistan were called "Sakastan" which means "the land of the Sakas", who went to India around the 1st century BCE.[75] They established a new kingdom called Bundhahishn, which, according to the Zoroastrian scripture written by Pahlavi, was denoted as "Seyansih". After the Arab invasions of Persia, it was first called Sijistan and later as Sistan bearing the same name today as part of Iran.[76]

Sistan or Sakastan in those days was comprised of the eastern part of modern Iran and the southern part of Afghanistan, including Nimruz, Helmand, Kandahar, and Baluchistan provinces. Many Arab Muslims, mainly traders, settled in this region. However, many parts of Afghanistan were not yet part of the Caliphate, and Kandahar or ancient Gandhar, a Hindu and Buddhist cultural seat, was still independent. In 652 CE, Herat, part of Afghanistan, fell to the Arab army. The name Herat most likely comes from the river Hari.[77, 78] A famous pillar in the riverbank could be an astronomical observation tower called the Minaret of Jam. While the mainstream historians would have us believe that it is a religious tower. But is it possible that Qutab Minar, which is said to have been 'inspired' by the Minaret of Jam, can be contemporary and was built by the same people as Qutab as an astronomical tower; though historians would say that 'the authenticity of the ensemble of the Minaret of Jam and the vestiges that surround it has never been questioned'.[79]

The land north of the Hindukush Mountains and south of the Amu Dariya River was called Bactria or Tokharistan, and it covered parts of Afghanistan, Tajikistan, and Uzbekistan. The Zoroastrian Avesta noted that it was one of the sixteen perfect lands Ahura Mazda created. Although later it was ruled by the Arabs, Buddhism was still actively followed there.

In 705 CE, Qutayba ibn Muslim, an Arab commander of the Umayyad Caliphate, conquered Balk, a key area in Afghanistan. A Buddhist monk Hui'Chao from Silla, Korea, visited this area around 726 CE, mentioned that though the Arabs ruled the region, all the inhabitants were Buddhists.[80, 81]

On the other hand, Zabul or Zabulistan in southern Afghanistan, which today belongs to the provinces of Zabul and Ghazni, was called *Jāguḍa*; it was the Sanskrit name in ancient India that meant saffron. The Chinese traveler and monk Xuanzang, around 644 CE, called it *Tsau-kü-ta*.[82]

Both Kabul and Zabul were centers for Hindu and Buddhist studies. For over two centuries, the people of Kabul and

Zabul resisted the Islamic invasions. The kings of this region, especially the Bamiyans, were called 'Sher' or tigers (or lions) due to their valor noted by Arab geographer Ya'qubi.[83]

The Conquests of Mahmud Ghaznavi between 1001 CE and 1027 CE[84] devastated the region, and the Hindu kings were defeated and were either killed or converted.

The mountain range that separates this region from mainland India was called the Hindu Kush, meaning "slayer of Hindus" or "killer of Hindus",[85][86] named by the 14th century Muslim scholar Ibn Battuta, where a large number of Hindu slaves being dragged died in this treacherous mountain range. Is the time ripe to change the name of this mountain range to 'Dard-e-Hind', meaning the agony of Hindustan?

It can be noted here that the founder of the Mughal Empire came from Fergana in eastern Uzbekistan and conquered Kabul from the Turco-Mongol Afghan dynasty before entering India.

The Birth of the Taliban and Islamic Emirate of Afghanistan

Fast forward to 1709 CE; the Hotak Empire was formed by Mirwaris Hotak together with various Afghan tribal chiefs in the region who fought against the Mughals and the Persians.[87,88,89]

The Hotaks were engaged in continuous wars. Ahmed Shah Abdali or Durrani founded the Durrani Empire and took over the reign as the king in 1747 CE.[90,91]

The empire collapsed in 1823, and the Emirate of Afghanistan was formed by the Barakzai clan. In 1926 the Emirate transformed into the Kingdom of Afghanistan. Mohammed Zahir Shah was the last ruler of the Kingdom and was overthrown in the 1973 coup, led by his cousin Mohammed Daoud Khan. Daud abolished the monarchy and established the Republic of Afghanistan, of which he became the first Premier.[92,93]

In 1978, the Saur Revolution was started by the Communist People's Democratic Party, and a military coup took place, in which Daoud and his family members were killed. Eventually, the Republic was transformed into the Soviet-supported Democratic Republic of Afghanistan.[94]

Mohammad Najibullah Ahmadzai was the pro-Soviet leader of the Democratic Republic of Afghanistan from 1986 to 1992 and the President from 1987 until his resignation in April 1992, shortly after which the Taliban took control of Kabul. He lived in the United Nations headquarters, and when the city fell to the Taliban, he was captured and was hung in public.[95]

In Arabic and Pashto languages, Taliban means students or seekers.[96, 97] In Afghanistan, these Islamists, mostly Pashtun tribesmen, identified and associated with the Islamic Emirate of Afghanistan (IEA).[98]

Who is a mujahideen? A Jihadi fighter for the cause of Islam.

It was basically a political movement and military organization in Afghanistan, empowered by the Deobandi Islamist ideology; many governments and organizations designated them as terrorists.[99] The Taliban are inspired by Sharia, Islamic practice, and law based on the scriptural interpretation and propagation by the Deobandi fundamentalist school, which started in India and is associated with global Jihad.[100]

It is also a creation of Pakistan's notorious Inter-Services Intelligence or ISI. The story began in 1994 when ISI used the Taliban to install a government in Afghanistan, which would be at the beck and call of Pakistan and ISI for its regional and global interests, especially in Kashmir and other parts of India. ISI provided all kinds of support – logistic, financial, and military.[100,101,102,103]

According to Ahmed Rashid, a Pakistani Afghanistan expert, "between 1994 and 1999, an estimated 80,000 to 100,000 Pakistanis trained and fought in Afghanistan" on the side of the

Taliban. American diplomat Peter Tomsen noted that up until 9/11, Pakistani military and ISI officers along with thousands of regular Pakistani armed forces personnel had been involved in the fighting in Afghanistan.[104, 105, 106]

The Six Nations on Afghanistan

The bloody history of Afghanistan since the 1970s involves six countries – Soviet Union, the USA, Pakistan, Saudi Arabia, UK, and China. After the 1978 coup and the killing of Daud Khan, there was a civil war in Afghanistan. In this chaos, the Soviet Union intervened in Afghan affairs and occupied Afghanistan in 1979.

But the story starts even much earlier with the British plan to partition India long before in 1947. As a matter of fact, the map of the partitioned subcontinent was drawn by experts as early as 1945. Churchill feverishly believed in the 3-nation theory: Pakistan, Hindustan, and 'Princestan' (the conglomeration of the 'Princely states'. Churchill and his England never imagined Princestan could not become a reality, thanks to Sardar Vallabhbhai Patel and other strong nationalist Indian leaders. As a matter of fact, India, with immense diversity, more diverse than Europe, remains one nation till now, which is a surprise and significant challenge for those forces who hoped and still wish to be balkanized and disintegrated.

Britain left India but left behind a major geopolitical mess that is haunting the whole world along with India even now. Britain did not give freedom to India because of Gandhi's brilliant Satyagraha. Britain was already struggling after World War II even to survive. They had no capability to govern India anymore. The final blow was the INA-inspired Naval Revolt in Bombay and army revolts in every major city. But Britain wanted to leave India with some long-term gain which Narendra Singh Sarila, the aide-de-camp to Earl Mountbatten of Burma, the last Viceroy of India called 'The Great Game'. [107] Churchill asked Wavell to 'keep part of India' for Britain before leaving India, and a game plan was scripted to protect Anglo-American interests, both geopolitics and oil and gas. The partition happened according to that plan without considering the gruesome tragedy that would unfold during the partition with death, rape, and displacement of millions.

Post partition, constant military and terrorist interventions, and even wars between Pakistan and India played out as the fruit of this plan. As we know, the British's love for Islamists, including Churchill himself (almost converted to Islam), the plan was executed with key players including Jinnah, Nehru, and Gandhi. Earlier, the British directly and indirectly promoted Islamist leaders and groups and also the communists to keep India fighting within. As a result, Islamic fundamentalism in the region, including Afghanistan and Pakistan, was emboldened. A far-reaching outcome of that game was the September 11 attack on the World Trade Center. According to the pretext of this plan, the British always feared the Russians and wanted to keep them beyond the Oxus River located north of Afghanistan. According to this British strategy, they needed access to India's northwest region of India. If India was not divided and no Pakistan was created, it would be very difficult to twist the arms of India to do the dirty job for them, such as the Afghan Taliban did to fight the Russians.

According to Sarila, "…the feeling with both the Churchill and Attlee governments in Britain that Partition of India was necessary to protect British interests."[108]

Fast forward to 1976, Britain is no more a superpower, and America has overtaken them. Pakistan President and Prime Minister Zulfiqar Ali Bhutto started the nuclear program in Pakistan in 1976. In March 1976, Pakistan signed an agreement with France for the purchase of nuclear fuel reprocessing plant. This drew international attention, and America was also not happy about it.

In a twist of destiny, Bhutto was hanged in March 1979 under the direction of the Islamist military dictator of Pakistan

Zia ul Haque. A new era of the Jihadi movement ushered in Pakistan, which would soon expand into Afghanistan and India. The ISI started lobbying with the US, especially the CIA and Saudis, for material assistance to the Islamist groups. Because of the nuclear program, the US relationship with Pakistan was at a low ebb. It appears that the lobbying worked – in January 1979, President Jimmy Carter noted that it was vital to "repair our relationships with Pakistan" in light of the Iran unrest.[109]

While Carter was much engaged in the Cold War, Iran was the top agenda of America. Soviets have not arrived in Afghanistan yet, but the CIA already planned a secret mission there using the backdrop of Iran's problems called Operation Cyclone, one of the CIA's longest and most expensive covert operations.[110]

Mullah Omar founded the Taliban group in September 1994 in his hometown of Kandahar with 50 students.[111,112,113] Mullah Abdul Ghani Baradar was the co-founder.

To start with, President Carter authorized the CIA to spend half a million dollars for "non-lethal" aid to the Mujahideen,[114,115] which was the beginning of US/CIA involvement in Afghanistan. In January 1980, the first shipment of US weapons for the Taliban was unloaded in Pakistan.[116,117,118]

In America, a former Navy Officer Texas Congressman, Charlie Wilson, a Democrat who was obsessed with Afghanistan, led US Congress into supporting Operation Cyclone. He directly worked with the CIA on this project. Upon becoming the President, Ronald Reagan entered the Cold War Era and augmented the 'Reagan Doctrine'. Under which, the US provided military and other support to anti-communist resistance movements in Afghanistan, Angola, and Nicaragua.[119]

Wilson became close to Reagan and was able to expand the scope of the project to work with the Mujaheeds directly. The USA and Saudi governments provided the finances and weapons. The US State Department and Pentagon were also directly involved.[120,121]

In October 1985, a meeting was organized in the White House where Reagan publicly met several major mujahideen leaders, including their commanders Yunus Khalis and Abdul Haq.[122,123]

Initially, in an effort to aid the anti-Soviet insurgency, the US government provided schoolbooks promoting militant Islamic teachings with photographs of weapons and soldiers to indoctrinate the youth into Jihad. The US Agency for International Development (USAID) gave millions of dollars to the University of Nebraska, Omaha, in the 1980s to design and publish the textbooks in local languages.[124]

According to a Washington institute report (March 1, 2002): In 1980, the Carter administration allocated $30 million for the Afghan resistance, though under the Reagan administration, this amount grew steadily.[125]

With the design and gameplan of Pakistan, aided by ISI and multiple countries by 1994, the Taliban movement was established fully.[126,127]

Zia ul Haque was killed in August 1988. Still, his inspiration remained with his military disciples, especially General Naseerullah Babar and Jamaat Ulema-e-Islam leader Maulana Fazal-ur Rehman whose group "represented Deobandism and aimed to counter the influence of the Jamaat-e-Islami and growing Wahhabism" of Saudi Arabia.[128]

Rehman is a staunch follower of Mahmud Hasan Deobandi. Mahmud's father, Zulfiqar Ali Deobandi, co-founded the Darul Uloom Deoband and the Jamia Millia Islamia school. He was responsible for launching the "Silk Letter Movement" for the freedom of India from the British and to join the Ottoman Caliph, which is known as the failed Khilafat movement.

According to Michael Rubin and Daniel Benjamin of the Washington Institute,[129] people in Kabul saw Pakistanis involved in Jihad. A training camp in Rish Khor, near Kabul, a Pakistani-supported terrorist group Harakat ul-Mujahideen ran a training camp for terrorism activities in India.[130,131]

Jalaluddin Haqqani became a top warlord and commander during the Soviet-Afghan conflict. He supported the Afghan Taliban. Haqqani was a close associate and one of the key mentors of Osama bin Laden when he founded al-Qaeda. Haqqani's group has created a link between various terror groups, which is called the Haqqani Network. Haqqani was one of the major beneficiaries of the CIA along with Gulbuddin Hekmatyar – both close to bin Laden.[132,133,134,135]

Haqqani received direct cash payments from CIA agents without the mediation of the ISI in the 1980s. This funding enabled Haqqani to have great command over the mujahideen.[136]

The Haqqani Network played an important role in the formation and growth of al-Qaeda, which allowed bin Laden to work with and train terrorists, especially new recruits, and build infrastructure for the purpose of global terrorism in the regions where the network is influential.[137]

Hamid Gul was a General with the Pakistani Army and the Director-General of the ISI. He played a major role in providing ISI support to Afghan Taliban groups against Soviet forces. In return, they received funds and weapons from the USA during the Soviet-Afghan war in cooperation with the CIA.[138]

Hamid dreamt of a trans-national Islamic revolution within Pakistan, Afghanistan, Central Asia, and Indian Kashmir. Once bin Laden arrived at the scene, he connected with Hamid. Although the US provided the money and weapons, the training of militant groups was entirely done by the Pakistani Armed Forces and the ISI.[139]

Bin Laden's first trainer was US Special Forces commando, Ali Mohammed.[140] With the cooperation of many quarters, including Western powers, Laden formed al-Qaeda in 1988.

In 1999, an Air India flight from Nepal to Kandahar was hijacked by the same group. The Taliban mediated the release of the hostages in exchange for the release of the terrorists in Indian judicial custody, including Masood Azhar, who soon after was given shelter in Pakistan. Azhar then started a new outfit named, Jaish-e-Mohammed (JeM), which is also known as the Army of Mohammed, Khudamul Islam, and Tehrik ul-Furqaan. With the support of ISI, Afghan Taliban, Osama bin Laden and other terror groups in Pakistan, he has created a major base. JeM has become a family enterprise with the patronage of many groups. Jamia Binoria Madrasa linked JeM with the Afghan Taliban.[141]

JeM, with Azhar's leadership, is involved in many terrorist attacks on India, including the 2001 Indian Parliament attack (in coordination with LeT),[142,143] 2008 Mumbai attacks,[144] 2016 Pathankot attack,[145,146] the army camp at Uri, Kashmir[147] and 2019 Pulwama attack.[148]

He has been suspected of the murder of American journalist Daniel Pearl in Karachi.[149,150] The US State Department also admitted that Pakistan is giving protection and support to Azhar.[151]

According to *Washington Post*, Afghanistan provided a useful base not only to train pro-Pakistani militants and terrorists but also to give them field experience.

British Involvement

The responsibility of Britain was very crucial and played a direct role in combat, especially by providing Special Air Services to support the Mujahideens on the ground.[152] British intelligence agency MI6 helped the CIA in its operations in Pakistan.[153] MI6 supported the Islamic group commanded by Ahmad Shah Massoud, an Afghan politician and military commander.[154]

Saudi Involvement

Islamic Mujahideen or Taliban were positioned to fight the Soviets. Pakistan President Zia ul Haq created a fear psychosis stating that the Soviets were planning to also invade Balochistan, Pakistan. He then worked with Saudi Arabia to support the Afghan resistance against Soviet forces. And in the meantime, the CIA and Saudi Arabian General Intelligence Directorate (GID) started funding the Taliban for training, military equipment, and weapons through the Pakistani ISI. ISI trained over 90,000 Taliban, including their leader Mulla Omar during the 1980s.[155]

Thousands of Arabs called 'Arab Volunteers' were also involved in the war, and Osama was one such 'volunteer'. Martin Ewans, former Head of the British Chancery in Kabul, stated that the Afghan Arabs "benefited indirectly from the CIA's funding, through the ISI and resistance organizations,"[156] and that "it has been reckoned that as many as 35,000 'Arab-Afghans' may have received military training in Pakistan at an estimated cost of $800 million in the years up to and including 1988".

Chinese Involvement

In 1978, when the pro-Soviet Afghan communists seized power in Afghanistan, the relationship between China and the Afghan communists turned hostile. The Afghans supported Vietnam (enemy of China then), and blamed China for supporting Afghan anti-communist forces. China started supporting the Mujahideen and significantly increased its military presence in the Xinjiang province, bordering Afghanistan. In an excuse to defend itself from Soviet attack, China even acquired military equipment and weapons from America.[157]

The Chinese People's Liberation Army trained and supported the Afghan Mujahideen during the Soviet-Afghan war. The training camps were moved from Pakistan into Chinese-controlled territories. Anti-aircraft missiles, rocket launchers, and machine guns, valued at hundreds of millions, were given to the Mujahideen by the Chinese. Chinese military advisors and army troops were present with the Mujahideen during training.[158]

Chinese military advisers and army troops trained several thousand Mujahideen inside Xinjiang and along the Pakistani border throughout the war.[159]

The funds that were given to the Islamist groups in Afghanistan between 1979 to 1992 by the US, Saudi Arabia, and China were anywhere between US$ six to twelve billion. This financial support and supply of weapons via ISI to thousands of Mujahideens[160] created a situation so that the Taliban's take over of Afghanistan became possible in 2021.

The September 11 and after

Rest is history: September 11, 2001, World Trade Center attack in New York and the 'Crusade' (as George Bush put it),[161] on terrorism by the West, 20 years later, which has left the world less peaceful, less safe.

After the fall of the Najib regime, there was a civil war in the country. In November 1994, the Taliban suddenly captured the city of Kandahar[162] and Kabul in September 1996 when they established the Islamic Emirate of Afghanistan. By then Taliban became a 'proxy force' to support Pakistan's regional interests.[163, 164, 165,166, 167]

In October 2001, the US, with allies including the Afghan Northern Alliance, invaded Afghanistan, drove out the Taliban regime, and their leadership fled to Pakistan.[168]

After the invasion of Afghanistan by the US and allied forces, the Taliban government was dissolved, which was supported by the majority of Afghan citizens.[169, 170]

In December 2001, the new Afghan government was formed with the leadership of Hamid Karzai. The UN Security Council formed the International Security Assistance Force (ISAF) to support the new government and provide basic security to the Afghans.[171, 172]

But within a few years, by 2009, a Taliban-led shadow government began to form in many parts of the country and imposed their own Sharia law and court.[173] In 2014, Ashraf Ghani was elected to be the president of Afghanistan and was re-elected in 2019.

In August 2021, the US and the allied forces withdrew from Afghanistan, which allowed the Taliban to make great progress in occupying a vast part of the country. On August 15, 2021, as the Taliban took over Kabul and President Ghani fled to UAE, the Afghan government collapsed.[174]

According to *AP News*, when the Trump administration opened negotiations with the Taliban in 2016, Ghani was asked a strong united team that could do tough negotiations with the Taliban. But Ghani was not able to deliver.[175]

The US decided to negotiate with the Taliban for a deal directly. Ghani was not kept in the loop. Apparently, due to a deal with the Taliban, Ghani was forced by the US to release 5,000 insurgents from Afghan jails.[176]

US Special Representative for Afghanistan Reconciliation Zalmay Khalilzad met Taliban co-founder Mullah Abdul Ghani Baradar and signed a 'peace agreement' between the US and Taliban in Doha, Qatar, on February 29, 2020. However, no aspect of the Doha agreement (including terms laid out for the withdrawal of American forces) was made public though some members of US Congress were allowed to review them. Yet the Taliban have dismissed and denied the talk and any agreement. [177]

According to *BBC*, Baradar was also the first Taliban leader to communicate directly with a US president after having a telephonic conversation with Donald Trump in 2020.[178]

AP News sources suggested that "The agreement provided significant legitimacy to the Taliban, whose leaders met with Pompeo, the first secretary of state to have such interactions. There were also discussions of them coming to the US to meet with Trump."[179]

The world only looks at the output of various terror networks and organizations each time an act of terror happens in the world. But they, especially the USA and UK, either forget or ignore these facts:

The terrorists, irrespective of their organization or affiliations, always quote Islamic books – the Quran and Hadis as their inspiration and guidance for their terror activities.

While a few countries, including the USA, Saudi Arabia, Turkey, and Qatar, have funded many of these groups, Pakistan is the actual factory for global terrorism.[180, 181]

No terror organization is better than others – all terror groups are bonded by Islamist-brotherhood, despite their apparent conflicts on the surface, for the cause of dar-al-Islam they are together.

Dozens of organizations are given incubation centers and shelters in Pakistan with the government and ISI support. The only way out for the world is to work on their real problem, the source – the Islamic military nation of Pakistan, then only much of the global challenges will significantly be reduced.

Unfortunately, the terrorists have gained great and unexpected opportunities to grow in Afghanistan now since over $83 billion is spent by America for the Afghan army. A huge amount was spent on military equipment, and killing machines left for the Taliban to potentially spread their terror globally.[182, 183]

It is a great mystery why President Joe Biden hurried – did his administration and or CIA have a secret deal with the Taliban or was it just obduracy on his part to rush the departure? Or the world is fooled, and the US/CIA did and got exactly what they wanted? The 'War Machines' are satisfied, the war businesses are happy, and the war contractors have no more business left there after getting a large pie of the taxpayers' money of America and Britain!

Thus, a country with great heritage almost goes back to the Middle Ages as framed by Timur, Ghazni, and Ghori. And the Afghans, who were even the most non-violent Hindu-Buddhist, are now the victim of ideologies of most violent fundamentalism and intolerance. The term freedom is obliterated from the Afghan vocabulary, at least for an unforeseen period.

Cost of Afghan War

As of April 2021, 20 years after the US attack on Afghanistan, here is the cost of the war, according to the *AP News*.[184]

American service members killed in Afghanistan through April: 2,448.

U.S. contractors: 3,846.

Afghan national military and police: 66,000.

Other allied service members, including from other NATO member states 1,144.

Afghan civilians: 47,245.

Taliban and other opposition fighters: 51,191.

Aid workers: 444.

Journalists: 72.

Estimated amount of direct Afghanistan and Iraq war costs that the United States has debt-financed as of 2020: $2 trillion.

Estimated interest costs by 2050: Up to $6.5 trillion.

Kafiristan

Are the people of India fortunate that the country's name is still Hindustan, Bharat and India? Was it possible that the country would be called Kafiristan (the land of the infidels)? Perhaps efforts were made at some point, and most probably settled invaders did not feel comfortable calling their new homeland Kafiristan; instead, they called it Hindustan and may have hoped someday it would become 'Mughalistan' or something similar.[185] However, the other side of the border today is Pakistan or the 'land of the pure'.[186]

Most people have forgotten that the Nuristan province in Afghanistan today and its surroundings, which borders with

Chitral district in Pakistan and surrounded by the Hindu Kush Mountains, was called Kafiristan or 'the land of infidels' the non-believers of Islam and Allah. The people of this area followed some form of Hindu practices mixed with Buddhist and Zoroastrian traditions. According to historian Richard Strand, around 1895–1894, these people were converted to Islam by force, and then they changed the name of the place from Kafiristan to Nuristan.[187] One can surely assume that these people must have been strong fighters; otherwise, how could they have resisted waves of invasions for so many centuries!

Ancient Kalash People

These people's origins can still be traced to the Kalash people,[188] who miraculously survived centuries of onslaughts just near Nuristan. Kalashas, 'a fiercely independent people' live in the incredibly scenic and fertile land in the Chitral district of Pakistan occupied Kashmir (PoK). Chitral means picturesque. The Kalashas' language is also called Kalasha,[189] belonging to the Indo-Aryan language family.

The whole area was a center of Buddhist culture in ancient times, and the Chinese called it Kapisa. The Chinese pilgrim Xuanzang who visited Kapisa in 644 CE called it Kai-pi-shi(h) [190] and described as a flourishing kingdom ruled by a Buddhist Kshatriya king and holding sway over ten neighboring states, including Lampaka (current Langman Province), Nagarahara (present-day Jalalabad), Gandhara (Kandahar) and Bannu (Bannu District in southern Khyber Pakhtunkhwa in Pakistan). Many think that these are descendants of the people of Gandhar.

Western historians would have us believe that the Kalash inhabitants were descendants of Greeks via Alexander's invasions. Some Muslims also claim that they are a sect of Islam. However, looking at their facial features, one can tell that they have more similarities with the Indian people[191] in Himachal and Kashmir than the Greeks, though it is not impossible to have some racial mix. But more importantly, in any introduction of Kalash people to the world, their socio-religious practices are not exposed or discussed.

They practice some form of ancient Hindu tradition. Some of their deities are Mahandeo or Mahadev, Imra (Yama – Mara is also a word for death in the local language), and Indr or Varendr (Indra). There is supposed to be a shrine of Sajigor (Indra's dressing room) in Rumbur valley. Kalashas call their Gods' rules Devalog (Dewalók). In December, they celebrate the festival called Chawmos, perhaps related to the Vedic practice of cāturmāsyá when Hindus perform penance, austerities, fasting, bathing in holy rivers, and religious observances for all.[192][193]

Fortunately, or unfortunately, the surviving few Kalasha people today are the 'smallest ethnoreligious group in Pakistan' with a population of less than 4000.[194] Proselytizing forces are at work to convert them and to submerge their culture into mainstream Islam, thus destroying their original practices. Numerous Christian Missionaries and Islamic preachers are at the job. How long can the world wait as one of the world's lasting indigenous cultures be forced to shut down by such efforts?

The Government of India also has a significant responsibility. According to the official Indian stand, Baltistan, Saksham Valley, and Aksai Chin are part of India; strangely, Chitral is not, though it was also an integral part of Kashmir even till Maharaja Hari Singh's tenure.[195]

Chitral was being ruled by the Kator dynasty, which Muhtaram Shah Kator founded. Kator was most likely a Kushan title of nobility. They reigned for almost four centuries, from 1570 until 1947. The ruler's title was Mitar or Mehtar.[196]

During the Second Anglo-Afghan War in the 1870s, the British put pressure on the then Mehtar of Chitral to join Kashmir and encouraged Hari Singh to accept Chitral as part of his rule. In 1878 a treaty was signed so that the Mehtar was to accept Hari Singh as their King and pay taxes to Kashmir.

Government of India (GOI) has also chosen to ignore this treaty though it was in good standing until the partition in 1947.[197]

According to the Government of India Act 1935, it was an integral part of Kashmir as per the Aitchison Treaties (Vol. XI Page 428). The British Indian government amended the 1935 Act to avoid complications and was in a hurry to 'finish the job somehow in 1947', which stated: "…territory which was under the suzerainty of, but did not belong, to the ruler of Indian state shall, for the Government of India Act of 1935, be deemed not to form a part of the State".[198] And Britain later would encourage Pakistan to invade Kashmir so that they did not have to take any more responsibility for this region, including Chitral; what a blunder on both sides to propose and accept it – because Prime Minister Nehru was in a hurry too!

The hope of the indigenous peoples of both sides of Kashmir and the area is that someday, the entire POK will join with its natural home – India. Chitral and the Kalash people and their culture can be liberated from the Islamist corporate conglomerate in the short term.

Raja Dahir and Loss of Sindh

Sindh or Sind was known as Sindhu-desh according to ancient Indian history and was part of greater India called Bharat-Varsha. It had borders with Makran, Silistan, Turan Multan, and the Thar Desert. And beyond Sindh to the east was mainland India, or Hindustan as the Islamic world would call it.

The *Arabian Nights'*-famed character Sindbad, the sailor, hailed from Baghdad. In the fictional story, he once visited Bassorah, a hustling and bustling city. Around 224 CE, the Iranian Empire was established by Ardashir I, which is known as the Sassanid Kingdom. The Islamic Caliph's army's long march to conquer nations led to this ancient land of Iraq and finally invaded Basra, which in Arabic means "the over watcher". After the Islamic forces occupied the city, they had to keep an eye on other areas in the vicinity as a permanent army base; perhaps this name was chosen because of that reason. The first Military camp was established here by Utbah ibn Ghazwan on the orders of Omar ibn al-Khattab.[199]

On the other side of the Arabian Sea, Debal, which meant a city of temples or *devalayas,* was a significant port city in Sindh located near modern-day Karachi in Pakistan. The Rai Dynasty kingdom ruled this place for 143 years, between 489 CE and 632 CE. Their territory covered over 60,000 square miles, and their influence extended from East Kashmir, from west Makran, and Debal from the south Surat, north Gandhar (Kandahar), and Kikanan hills.[200] After this incredible period of prosperity, the Brahman dynasty was established. Raja Dahir was the last king of this Kingdom of Sindh (663 CE–712 CE).

According to some sources, the predecessors of the Dahir dynasty were ruling Greater Sindh since 58 BCE[201] and were contemporaries of Vikramaditya of Dharanagar. The name of their first king was Adi Rai. His son was Dev Rai. Much later, Sukhdev Singh Charak became a Maharaja after defeating the Sassanids – the Iranian forces. Raja Sukhdev's kingdom was prosperous from about the seventh century CE. It is said that his reign extended from Sindh to the eastern borders of Kashmir and the west to Makran and south of the river Tigris to the Sri Lankan coast.[202]

The Caliphates' armies' expeditions starting in 634 CE, just after Muhammad's death, were directly faced by the people of Sindh around 700 CE.

A book called *Chach Nama* or the *"Story of the Chach"* which is also called the '*Fateh Nama Sindh*' (*"Story of the conquest of Sindh"*), and also, as '*Tareekh al-Hind*' or *"History of India and Sindh,"* which has recorded the history of Sindh including the invasion of Muhammad bin Qasim in the 8th century CE.[203]

Hajjaj was one of the most important governors within the Umayyad reign under the Caliph Abd al-Malik and later under his successor al Walid between 685 CE and 705 CE. First, he was given the position of *shurta* or the head of the security forces. Then he became the governor of Hejaz, the western part of Arabia, and Basra.

According to *Chach Nama*, Yusuf got into a major conflict with a maritime incident. There was a community called Med or Bawarji, most likely a Saka remnant, in Baluchistan's coastal area in current-day Pakistan. They were involved in piracy in the Arabian Sea and the Indian Ocean. They used to attack the ships from their bases in Kutch and Kathiawar in Gujarat and Debal in Sindh. They attacked a vessel coming from Sri Lanka. King Serendib from Sri Lanka had sent some gifts to the governor, which were arriving by this ship. The pirates attacked the ship and took all the gifts. Though Basra was far away from Debal – a dispute erupted between the two.

At that time, Ummayads were not yet ready for expeditions beyond Afghanistan, but now they found a reason to attack Sind. Raja Dahir's kingdom was well-known for both justice and prosperity. The Raja was not much aware of what was brewing on the other side of his borders. A sudden attack came on Sind by Umayyads' forces led by bin Qasim in 711 CE as ordered by Hajjaj and caught the Raja off-guard. First, he freed the captives from previous expeditions by the forces of the Caliph. Then he consulted the chieftains in the neighborhood of Debal to co-opt them and coerced some defectors using fear and betrayal. First, the Buddhist governor of Nerun surrendered to Qasim, perhaps had no army or weapons to protect the kingdom, alas they were 'Ahimsa-wadis' (non-violent)! Then they focused on Siwistan (Sehwan) on several tribal regions of Bajhra, Kaka Kolak, and got their allegiance without any fight! He then put together a combined force with these chieftains and captured the fort at Sisam – that means he captured the entire western part of the river Sindhu. Then he approached the army of Raja Dahir in Debal.

Raja Dahir tried to prevent Qasim from crossing the Indus River, moving his forces to its eastern banks. However,

Qasim crossed over and defeated his forces at Jitor, led by Raja Dahir's son Jai Singh. Qasim fought Dahir at Aror (near modern Nawabshah) in 712 CE, where he was killed in the Battle of Aror on the banks of the river.[204]

The Umayyad army, led by Bin Qasim, suddenly attacked and conquered the unguarded eastern part of Sindh to make it part of the Umayyad Caliphate. Raja Dahir reached out to all other kings in the neighboring countries to create a united front to stop the Umayyads. But the Buddhist governor surrendered to the forces of Caliphates without a fight.[205]

When the forces attacked Debal, Raja Dahir consulted the army chiefs and held a secret meeting with some friendly neighbors. His minister opined that the Umayyad forces were more powerful and that the chances were slim to win the battle. He also recommended that he and his family members escape to Rajputana and take refuge in another king's territories. "You should say to them, 'I am a wall between you and the Arab army. If I fall, nothing will stop your destruction at their hands.'" Then the minister suggested at least to send his family members away in safety. Raja Dahir replied: "I cannot send away my family to security while the families of my thakurs and nobles remain here. Tomorrow not only me but my entire dynasty will be branded as a traitor's family. This is against the tradition of India. Hence I will not resort to this."[206]

Raja Dahir declared to his family and army thus: *"I am going to meet the Arabs in the open battle and fight against them as best as I can. I and my army will put up a grand show. I hope to destroy the Arabs. If I do that, my Brahmin dynasty will be established on a firm footing, and perhaps this will be an eye-opener to all contemporary and future historians. If I and my army are destroyed, we will get Veera Swarga (honourable place in heaven) and if my army wins, the future history will record it in golden letters that a Brahmin dynasty had the determination and power to destroy the army of Arabs."* [207]

Further, he also declared that if he were to be killed on the battlefield, it would be recorded in the books of Arabia and India. This will bring permanent glory to his dynasty and kingdom. Then he organized his small yet extremely patriotic army. Before getting into the battle, he spoke to his army men and said: *"This land is not only mine, but it belongs to every Hindu and hence let us all fight together."*

His army wanted the forces of Qasim not to be allowed to cross the Sindhu River and was deployed on the eastern banks. But due to sheer numbers, Qasim's forces were able to cross the water and defeat Raja's army, which was led by his son Jai Singh. This was the battle of Jilar in 712 CE, and the army of Sindh was defeated. Raja Dahir was then captured and beheaded to display the head to demoralize the king's army and finally was sent to Hajjaj as a gift.

The memories of Queen Ladi and her beautiful daughters Suriya and Preemal are folk tales of the Sindhis to date. *Chach Nama* vividly documented their story, which was a part of the resistance against the invading Islamic forces. These three courageous women were taken as war booty after the death of Raja Dahir and were sent as gifts to the Caliph for keeping in his harem. To take revenge, they falsely narrated to the Caliph that bin Qasim already has violated their chastity. The Caliph was outraged to know this since he was expecting some 'virgin unspoiled booties' of war and ensured Qasim's death in a very novel way. He was wrapped and stitched in oxen hides[208] and sent to Syria, and he died on the way. Later the Caliph ordered the two sisters to be buried alive inside a wall,[209] drawing parallels with the actions of Aurangzeb on the young sons of Guru Govind Singh centuries later. His son Zorawar was nine years old, and Fateh was just seven. The young boys were offered to convert to Islam to save their lives, but they refused, so Wazir Khan sentenced them to be buried alive.

According to some other historical accounts, Qasim was killed due to a family feud with Sulayman, Iraq's governor.[210]

There are two districts called Shanbag and Nawabshah near Pakistani Hyderabad, and Raja Dahir's clan – descendants, called the Dahris remain there.

After bin Qasim's death, Raja Dahir's son Jai Singh recaptured Brahmanabad around 720 CE; later, Junayd ibn Abd al-Rahman al-Murri fought a battle killed Jai Singh, and captured Sindh.

But around the 10th century, Multan was captured by Ismailis, who set up an independent Fatimid state. The southern parts of current-day Pakistan resisted further Islamic invasions for almost three centuries due to several Hindu kings' dominant power.

The Arab historians documented the state of this part of India during this critical juncture of history very vividly: [211]

"It may be conceded that the Arab conquest of Sind was an insightful event in Islam's history, from the political point of view. But the effects of this conquest upon Muslim culture were profound and far-reaching. Then the Arabs came to India; they were astonished at the superiority of its civilization. The sublimity of Indian philosophical ideas and the richness of India's intellect were a strange revelation to them. The cardinal doctrine of Muslim theology that there is one God was already known to the Indian painters and philosophers. The Arabs found that the nobler arts, which enhance man's dignity, the Indians far excelled them. The Indian musician, the mason, and the painter were as much admired by the Arabs as the philosopher and the man of learning."

"Tabari records that Khalifa Harun once sent for an Indian physician to cure him of an obstinate and painful disease. The Arabs learned from the Indians a great deal in the practical art of administration. The employment of Brahmana officials on a large scale was due to their better knowledge, experience, and fitness for efficiently discharging the duties of administration. A great many of the elements of Arabian culture, which afterward had such marvelous effect upon European civilization, were borrowed from India. Arab scholars sat at the feet of Buddhist monks and Brahman pandits to learn philosophy, astronomy, mathematics, medicine, chemistry, and other subjects of study. The court at Baghdad extended its patronage to Indian scholarship. During the Khilafat of Mansur (CE 750–774), Arab scholars returned from India to Baghdad carrying with them two books, the *Brahma Siddhanta* of Brahmagupta and his *Khand Khadyaka*. These works were translated by Al Fazari into Arabic with the help of Indian scholars. It was from these two works that the Arabs learned the first principles of scientific astronomy. There is ample reason to endorse Haveli's view that it was India, not Greece, that taught Islam in the impressionable years of its youth, formed its philosophy and esoteric religious ideals, and inspired its most characteristic expressions in literature, art, and architecture."[211]

Raja Jayapala and the Ghaznavids

The British, Islamic, and Marxist historians would have us believe that Islam was inevitable for India, and the land crumbled upon the forces of Islam. Eminent scholar Arun Shourie wrote: "In regard to matter after matter like the Aryan Dravidian divide, the nature of Islamic invasion, the nature of Islamic rule, the character of the freedom struggle, we find this trait *suppreso veri suggesto falsi*. This is the real scandal of history writing in the last thirty years."[212]

In reality, the invading forces used the Quranic dictum:

"Fight in the cause of Allah those who fight, you but do not transgress limits for Allah loves not the transgressors."(Quran 2:190)

And,

"Kill them wherever you overtake them and expel them from wherever they have expelled you, and fitnah is worse than killing. And do not fight them at al-Masjid al-Haram until they fight you there. But if they fight you, then kill them. Such is the recompense of the disbelievers."(Quran 2:191)

While the Islamic forces were following their holy book, the Hindu Kshatriya kings' *raj dharma* was at work in India for centuries before political and imperial Islam could find a foothold in India. Disunity among the Hindu kings was always blamed as the major reason for the invasions to be successful. Yet, there were only a few exceptions to Islam's conquests of other lands, India is the most prominent one. After 1000 years of Islamic subjugation and systematic destruction of vital institutions – India is still a country of Hindu majority. In contrast, most other lands and cultures were subdued, destroyed, and converted to Islamic forces' allegiance. While almost all other nations lost their ancient culture, heritage, and traditions, India still maintains much. Was it because of the magnanimity of Akbar or the mercy of Aurangzeb? Neither. It was the Hindu system's inherent power; the power of her philosophy safeguarded; it was the power of the Hindu sword that kept most parts of India retaining and following the Sanatan Dharma. Hindus were fully aware of the power of shastras, and knowledge through their scriptures, and they understood the knowledge and requirements of power to protect and sustain their land and knowledge. Here we will see how the Hindu sword safeguarded the western border due to its valor for several centuries, which led to a great fight against the barbarians. There were some 'war codes of conduct' the Hindu kings followed. But in many cases, the betrayal of the Islamic-Turkic barbarism took them by surprise, and yet they defended the glory of their land, clan, and people.

The Hindu Shahi[213] dynasty was ruling over the Kabul Valley (Northeastern Afghanistan), Gandhara (Kandahar), and present-day Northwestern India between 850 CE and 1026 CE. "Parama Bhattaraka Maharajadhiraja Sri Jayapaladeva"[214] was the ruler of the Hindu Shahi dynasty from 964 CE to 1001 CE. His kingdom stretched from Laghman (current-day Jalalabad in Afghanistan) to Kashmir and Sirhind to Multan, with Peshawar being in the center. He was the son of Maharaja Hutpal and the father of Maharaja Anandapala.[215] Both kings defended the land heroically against the invasions of the Ghaznavids. The name of the capital of the Gandhara kingdom was Hund,[216], whereas Hund was also known as Waihind. In ancient times, it was called Udbhandapur, which is currently Ohind in Pakistan on the banks of the Sindhu (Indus). When Alexander attacked India, the king of Takshashila, Ambi, had a truce with Alexander in this place. The birthplace of the legendary grammarian Panini Shalator was located in a place between Lahore and Udbhandapur.

The Sunni Iranian Empire, which ruled between 819 CE to 999 CE, was called Samanid (Sāmāniyān in Persian).[217] Their territory extended between Khorasan (parts of Iran, Afghanistan) and Transoxiana (which includes modern-day Tajikistan, Uzbekistan, Kazakhstan, Kyrgyzstan) and modern-day Pakistan.

The city of Ghazni, which means *'jewel'* is an ancient city in Afghanistan. Achaemenid king Cyrus II invaded the city around the 6th century BCE, and it became part of the Persian empire. The Zoroastrian culture was prominent in Ghazni before the Islamic armies' invasion around 683 CE when they brought Islam to the region.

The Ghaznavids made the city and region dazzling between 977 CE and 1163 CE by invading and plundering wealth from Indian cities and temples and creating the Ghaznavid Empire. It stretched from Afghanistan, Turkmenistan, Pakistan, parts of Eastern Iran, and Rajasthan, India. In reality, though Islam arrived in India long before, imperialist Islam was brought to India by the Ghaznavids. A few centuries later came the Khwarizmi Empire; around 1215 CE, the Mongol army led by Genghis Khan's son Ögedei Khan invaded the region.[218]

The nomadic Turks became victims of slavery and were sold in Bukhara markets during the reign of the Samanids, which was their capital. Alptigin, a young man from the nomadic Turkic group, was brought as a slave to Bukhara and was raised in the Samanid royal house. He later became the commander-in-chief (*sipahsalar*) of the Samanid army in Khorasan and finally the governor of Ghazna from 962 CE until he died in 963 CE.

A young Turkic-origin boy from Kyrgyzstan named Abu was sold in the slave market. Alptigin was his master who invaded and seized Ghazna, the Ghazni province in modern Afghanistan. Abu later ruled the region between 977 CE to 997 CE and married the daughter of his master Alptigin. After the death of Alptigin, the slave boy Abu, known as Sabuktigin, took over the reign of the kingdom, which expanded its territory to the Neelam River in Kashmir and Sindhu River in current-day Pakistan.

According to Minhaj al-Siraj Juzjani, a 13th-century Persian historian:

"A merchant of the name of Nusr-Hajy having purchased Sabuktigin while yet a boy, brought him from the Turkic steppes to Bukhara, where he was sold to Aluptugeen, who, perceiving in him the promise of future greatness, raised him by degrees to posts of confidence and distinction, till, at length, on his establishing his independence at Ghazni, he conferred on him the title of amir al-umara (chief of the nobles), and also that of Vakil-i-Mutluk, or Representative."[219]

Once he sat on the throne, Sabuktigin expanded his reign beyond Alptigin's territories; under his control was the land between Ghazna to Balkh in the north, Helmand in the west, and the Indus River in what is today Pakistan.[220]

Eventually, Sabuktigin was made the governor of Baghdad by the Caliph of Baghdad. His younger son Ismail of Ghazni took charge after the death of Sabuktgin in 997 CE. Sabuktigin's older son, Mahmud, did not accept this since he was older, and he fought with his brother to become the emir of Ghazna.

Maharaja Jayapala kept an eye on Ghazni's developments, which saw a future challenge for the Hindu Shahi kingdom and the Hindus. Eventually, they came face to face in a battle.

According to Persian historian Firishta (Muhammad Qasim, *Hindu Shah):* "Sabuktigin had already begun raiding Lamghan under Alptigin. He crossed the Khyber Pass many times and raided the territory of Jayapala. He plundered the forts in the outlying provinces of the Kabul Shahi and captured many cities, thus acquiring huge war booty. He also established Islam in many places. Jayapala, in retaliation, marched with a larger force into the valley of Lamghan (Jalalabad), where he clashed with Sabuktigin and his son Mahmud. The battle went on for several days until a snowstorm affected Raja Jayapala's strategies, forcing him to vie for peace".[221]

Raja Jayapala then returned to his capital Udbhandapur also known as Waihind. Later he broke the treaty and declined to give taxes. Sabuktigin then retaliated against the king. At this time, Sabuktigin attacked Lamghan and burnt down hundreds of houses of the "infidels," destroyed numerous temples, and converted many people to Islam,[222, 223] and collected substantial war booty. Raja Jayapala was furious upon hearing this news and declared war against the Turkic forces of Sultan Mahmud in 1001 CE. According to Ferishta,

"The two armies having met on the confines of Lumghan, the Maharaja ascended a hill to view the forces of Sabuktigin, which appeared in extent like the boundless ocean, and in numbers like the ants or the locusts of the wilderness. However, Jayapala considered himself as a wolf about to attack a flock of sheep: calling, therefore, his chiefs together, he encouraged them to glorify, i.e., magnify, the orders issued to each of his commander. His soldiers, though few, were divided into squadrons of five hundred men each, which were directed to attack successively, one particular point of the Muslim line, so that it might continually have to encounter fresh troops. However, the army was hopeless in battle against the eastern forces, particularly against the Punjabis".[224]

The Raja was initially captured by Mahmud's soldiers. At this point, as a Kshatriya King, he felt humiliated by two consecutive defeats to an alien Islamic force, so he handed over his throne to his son and committed suicide by funeral pyre.

[225] This event gave a new gateway to Mahmud for many more battles and raids into India in the future to expand his Ghaznavid Empire into the heartland of India.

Ibn Battuta, the well-known Moroccan traveler and scholar who visited Ghazni in 1333 CE wrote:

"We travelled thence to Parwan, where I met the amir Buruntayh. He treated me well and wrote to his representatives at Ghazna enjoining them to show me honour. We went on to the village of Charkh [Charikar], it being now summer, and from there to the town of Ghazna. This is the town of the famous warrior-sultan Mahmud ibn Sabuktagin, one of the greatest of rulers, who made frequent raids into India and captured cities and fortresses there. His grave is in this city and is surmounted by a hospice. The greater part of the town is in ruins and nothing but a fraction of it remains, though it was once a large city. It has an exceedingly cold climate, and the inhabitants move from it in the cold season to Qandahar, a large and prosperous town three nights journey from Ghazna, but I did not visit it."[226]

Moving on to 1401 CE, Tamerlane's grandson, Muhammad bin Djinhangir, became the governor of Kabul, Kandahar, and Ghazni. Babur, the founder of the Mughal dynasty, conquered the region in 1504 CE and lived here. This region stayed under Mughal control until 1738 CE, after Nader Shah, an Iranian king, invaded it.[227]

In his memoir, *Baburnama*, Babur noted how beautiful the hillsides were, and the land was fertile. *Baburnama* also noted that Kabulistan or Kabul was independent during the Mughal era, and "Greater Lamghanat" included the Muslim-settled part of Kafiristan. Mughal emperor Akbar's younger brother Mohammad Hakim, then the governor of Kabul, led several Jihads against the 'non-believers' of this region.

Mahmud of Ghazni was the first independent ruler of the Ghaznavid dynasty, who ruled from 999 to 1030 CE. By the time he died, he had extended his kingdom from northwestern Iran to the Punjab region, Khwarazm in Transoxiana, and Makran.[228]

Mahmud, at the age of 27, after occupying his father's throne, took the title "Sultan" (which means authority) in 998 CE. Mahmud led 17 expeditions into India. The first one being the above-mentioned battle in 1001 CE and the last one in 1027 CE. He had two motives – plundering the riches, especially temples and palaces of the land, and terrorizing and converting the local populations into Islam. He went deep into India's heartland, starting from Sind, and then Kabul, Delhi, Kanauj, Mathura, Kangra, Thaneshwar, Kashmir, Gwalior, Malwa, Bundelkhand, Tripuri, Bengal, and Punjab.[229] He died in 1030 CE. His tactics were 'surprise shock attack' and 'hit and run'. The peaceful kingdoms were unprepared for such out-of-the-blue attacks. However, they gave heroic resistance and often defeated the encroaching enemy. Muslim and Marxist historians would call his attacks 'battles' and 'wars' – but many of his attacks were just sudden raids like an organized band of robbers and pirates.[230]

Kaaba to Somnath

Mahmud's last conquest in India was in 1027 CE when he attacked the famous Somnath temple in Gujarat. Somnath was famous for the *jyotirlinga* established there. The brave Hindu Rajputs fought hard and defended it for a long time, and the enemies could not make any dent due to the Hindu heroic resistance. However, after three days of fighting, over 5000 Hindus gave their lives to protect the temple. Some Muslim literature boasted that Mahmud had killed 50,000 people who tried to defend the temple[231] and were simple devotees. Mahmud Ghazni's troops finally broke into the mandir to plunder and destroy the Shiva Linga as typical iconoclasts. Mahmud's forces looted all the treasures of the temple, and according to some sources at that time, it was worth 20-million dinars,[232] the maximum amount of war booty he ever got, more than all other invasions and raids combined.

This attack may have been inspired by the belief that the deity from a temple of Manat in Saudi Arabia was smuggled to

Somnath in Gujarat.[233] According to the Ghaznavid court poet Farrukhi Sistani, who claimed to have accompanied Mahmud on his raid, 'Somnat (in Persian) was a garbled version of sumanat referring to the goddess Manat'. According to Farrukhi and another later-day historian, Abu Sa'id Gardezi, the images of most deities were destroyed in Arabia, but the one of Manat was secretly sent away to Kathiawar (in modern Gujarat) for safekeeping by the devotees.

It is said that Manat's image was a large black stone and could be confused with the Shiva Lingam in Somnath Temple. After all the killing, mayhem, and loot were completed, his final task was to break the Shiva Linga. It was made of meteoric rock and was extremely hard to break. One wonders if the origin of the stone was Petra? With: The miraculous lingam is said to have been suspended in the air without any support. Mahmud then used the hot and cold treatment alternatively and finally was able to break it. He brought the broken parts of the Lingam with him as loot and placed them in his palace in such a way so that people would be forced to walk over it. According to Marxist historian Romila Thapar, this event may not have taken place at all, and she argued that 'in his letters to the Caliphate, Mahmud exaggerated the size, wealth and religious significance of the Somnath temple, receiving grandiose titles from the Caliph in return.'[234]

Scholar Meenakshi Jain concurred that the attack and loot happened for sure, but she believes Mahmud could not damage the body of the mandir since there are records of pilgrimages to the temple in 1038 that make no mention of any damage. However, Islamic writers and chroniclers created legends to glorify Mahmud and the power of Islam in Turko-Persian literature.[235] However, the mandir was damaged during successive invasions.

Mahmud

The ruthless raider and plunderer Mahmud ruined and looted not just some temples but many cities and the architectural and artistic wonders of that era in Mathura, Kanauj, and Thaneshwar. Among the temples, Somnath was not destroyed due to the resistance of the Hindus but was looted; on the other hand, many other marvelous temples were destroyed and had to be rebuilt – including Jwalamukhi, Maheshwar, Narunkot, and Dwarka.[236]

Mahmud intended to plunder and not settle on Indian soil. However, his multiple raids weakened Indian defense and later helped the other invaders to come deep inside India. With the wealth looted from India, he built a vast empire covering Samarkand in the north, Gujarat in the south, Punjab in the east, and the Caspian Sea in the west. It included Persia (Iran) and Afghanistan. Many Muslims in the Indian subcontinent consider him as an Islamic Hero.[237][238]

Due to the 17 invasions of Mahmud starting from 1001 CE, Ghori in 1175 CE, then the devastating carnage of Bakhtiyar Khilji beginning in 1193 CE, and finally Timur in 1398 CE, Indian history and society were significantly impacted for centuries to come. According to Persian historian Alberuni: "He (Mahmud) utterly ruined the prosperity of the country (of India) and performed those wonderful exploits by which the Hindus became like atoms of dust scattered in all directions, and like a tale of old in the mouth of the people."[239] Indian defense and economy nearly collapsed because a large amount of wealth was looted from India. Human resources were seriously impacted due to rampant killing and capturing millions as slaves. Indian arts, cultural and architectural marvels, along with beautiful murthys, were destroyed. Islamic reign got a foothold, education, scientific innovation, culture, society, and human values of freedom were significantly compromised and set the rapid downfall of civilization. Due to Mahmud's attacks, India's western front, especially Afghanistan and Punjab, was overrun with much destruction and bloodshed. Similarly, Khalji destroyed many of India's great centers of learning and innovation, such as Nalanda.[240]

The Advent of Genghis Khan

The story goes like this:

Temüjin Borjigin was born near Ulanbator, the current capital of Mongolia, in 1162 CE. Legend says that he was born with a blood clot in his fist; the Mongols considered it as a sign of a great leader. His father was the chief of a tribe called Kyad, part of a confederation of many tribes and part of the Mongol Empire. Young Temüjin fell in love with a beautiful girl named Börte, and his father Yesügei arranged for their marriage. But they were not meant to enjoy each other's company for long, and their happiness came to an abrupt end as one morning, an opposing tribal group attacked them and kidnapped Börte. Borte was given to one of the warriors of the tribe as a gift or spoil of war. Temüjin was deeply distressed by his wife's abduction and remarked that his "bed was made empty", and his "breast was torn apart".

This event brought one of the key crossroads in Temüjin's life, which moved him along the path toward becoming a conqueror, the future Genghis Khan, the Emperor of the Mongol Empire.

The Secret History of the Mongols narrates the story like this: *"As the pillaging and plundering went on, Temüjin moved among the people that were hurriedly escaping, calling, 'Börte, Börte!' And so he came upon her, for Lady Börte was among those fleeing people. She heard the voice of Temüjin and, recognizing it, she got off the cart and came running towards him. Although it was still night, Lady Börte and Qo'aqčin both recognized Temüjin's reins and tether and grabbed them. It was moonlight; he looked at them, recognized Lady Börte, and they fell into each other's arms."*[241]

The story continues to tell that Börte was held captive for eight months and gave birth to her first son Jochi after she returned to Temüjin's home. The doubt about the father of Jochi was in *Temüjin*'s mind. He suspected that her captor had most likely impregnated her. However, Temüjin accepted Jochi as his son and was allowed to be part of his family.

History now knows of the brutality of his campaigns: *Temüjin,* who became known as Genghis Khan, is considered by many to have been one of the most brutal genocidal rulers in human history. Nobody is sure what is the root or meaning of Genghis. According to some, in Chinese, Zheng means "right", "just", or "true", which was probably a title that became the Mongolian adjectival modifier *-s*, creating "Jenggis" or "Chinggis". In the Mongolian language, over a period, the name universally became "Genghis".[242]

Genghis never entered India, though his indirect descendant Timur would wreak havoc in India a few centuries later.

Why did Genghis Never Enter India

On the western bank of the Indus River, there was a beautiful town of Kalabagh in the Punjab province, currently in the Punjab province of Pakistan. Kalabagh was full of dark green mango trees where birds sang all day long. But nature observed a painful episode of Kalabagh's history. In the year 1221, the forces of Jalal ad-Din Mingburnu or Jalâl ad-Dîn Khwârazmshâh, the ruler of Turkic Khwarezmian Empire, were destroyed by Genghis Khan along with his army of 50,000 soldiers. He nearly decimated the Islamic rule from modern-day Iran, Iraq, Afghanistan, and more. He destroyed many Islamic centers, including libraries. Samarkand and Basra were in complete ruins. Yet, he replaced Islamic structures with Buddhist temples.[243]

If we deeply study his conquests, without the excesses of his brutality and devastation, a logical pattern emerges, which is of two types. First, a sense of nationalism saw the emergence of a new national identity where all their tribes were perpetually engaged in in-fighting for a long time. He gave them a mission to be united as one nation, created a vast army, gave jobs to thousands, which kept them occupied. The second reason was revenge. His near relative Ambaghai was captured and killed by the Chinese, who interfered in Mongolian affairs for centuries. He invaded Xia and Jin Empires. The Chinese Qara Khitai rulers killed his grandson-in-law after capturing a Mongolian city. As retaliation, he attacked them.

What was the reason behind his furious attack on the Khwarazmian Empire? Genghis sent a large delegation to Khwarazm with a proposition for a trade relation. Shah Ala ad-Din Muhammad II massacred the delegation of 500 odd members, and their goods were auctioned off in Bukhara.[244]

An angry Genghis then sent three ambassadors to the Shah to demand that the Governor of Otrar, who caused the massacre, be handed over to him. The Shah's reaction was brutal. He humiliated them and then beheaded one. After this, Genghis invaded Khwarezm and devastated it.[245]

Shah Muhammad fled the country, and his son Jalal-Ad-Din was made the new Shah. But Genghis did not want to spare him either; his army was completely decimated in the Kalabagh battle in 1221.[246] Jalal escaped to India. He had asked for asylum from Iltutmish, which was intelligently denied, thereby escaping the wrath of Genghis.

After conquering China and other countries, he was nearly undefeatable, as he had not lost any battle in his life. He could have crossed the Indus, and Delhi was not very far from where the Mamluk Delhi Sultanate would have been too feeble in front of his army.

We all know how rich India was, from economy to culture to natural beauty. Invader after invader came to India to loot her wealth. Genghis was too close to mainland India. But he decided not to invade India. Why?

There is not much information about his personal life to be found in reliable documents, including a biography. Mongolia had some form of nature worship akin to Paganism called Tengrism. Along with ancestor worship, these Animistic and Shaminstic ancient practices pervaded Central Asia, and their chief deity was Tengri.[247] Together with Tengri, the Heavenly-Father and the Earth Mother were at the core of their tradition, which has many similarities with the Hindu tradition; Genghis' grandson, Kublai Khan, who ruled China and became a Buddhist.[248] Buddhism was, in a way, the religion of later-day Mongol empires, and most people in Mongolia today are Buddhists. However, the descendants of Khan in the Middle East were converted to Islam. Timur was the cruelest and most ruthless one.

Some NeoCols would suggest that Alauddin Khilji may have saved India and Hinduism from Mongol attacks (a century after Genghis Khan's demise). "...one can safely argue that Alauddin Khilji, for all his faults, actually saved the syncretic culture of the Indian subcontinent of that time – which included Hindu, Muslim, Buddhist, and Jain subcultures – from enormous destruction, even if preserving the culture of India may not have been what motivated his resistance to the Mongols… in fairness, be seen as the saviour of Hindustan that he unwittingly ended up being, by repelling the formidable and ruthless Mongol hordes."[249] This argument is not only laughable, but it shows their true color. It is very much possible that he may have admired and respected India's heritage and culture. Also, instead of giving much credit to Islamist fanatic Khalji, it might be a better idea to speculate that if Genghis indeed invaded India, he could easily have gotten rid of India's barbaric Islamic rule during the early years of Islam in India. It would have allowed Hindu-Jain-Buddhist tradition to flourish uninhibited, and if that was the case, we could call it a great missed opportunity for India.

Why was Khan so brutal? It appears from all sources, including the *Secret History of the Mongols*[250] that from the abduction of his young wife to the Chinese invasion after killing of his grand-son-in law and finally killing of his traders and ambassadors by the Khwarezmians, his key motivator to invade these countries were more or less retaliatory. It is not impossible that he hated Islamist barbaric forces; thus, the maximum brutality was displayed against them. The stark contrast can be found in all other conquerors and invaders, including Alexander. According to Prof. Ali Ansari, Institute of Iranian Studies, St. Andrews University, though his conquest of Persia was justified as the revenge of past atrocities of Persians on Greece, the real reason was the greed of wealth, power, and fame.[251]

India did not provoke Genghis, especially Iltutmish ruling Delhi at that time. In 1221, Genghis invaded Punjab and, in the Battle of Indus, defeated Turkic ruler Jalal-ad-Din who fled to India. But Iltutmish did not allow Jalal in his territory to avoid the wrath of Khan.[252]

The Khans

How did the Khan title get added to Genghis' name? The Mongolian Xianbei tribe were most probably the first to use the title 'Khan' for their kings or chiefs, an equivalent of the term King in Mongolian tradition. Genghis announced himself to be a 'Khan' of his empire. During his conquests, he impregnated hundreds of women, and from Mongolia to Turkey, Khan became a popular family name. Later it became the surname of millions of people globally, especially in the Indian subcontinent.

Khan's conquests caused massive demographic alteration in Asia, especially in countries like Iran. According to senior CIA officer Steven R. Ward, "Overall, the Mongol violence and depredations killed up to three-fourths of the population of the Iranian Plateau, possibly 10 to 15 million people. Some historians have estimated that Iran's population did not again reach its pre-Mongol levels until the mid-20th century."[253] The 13th-century Iranian historian Rashid al-Din noted that Khan's army reduced the population in Iran from 2,500,000 to 250,000 through war and subsequent famine.[254]

In Iran and many other countries of the Middle East, the Khans are despised, the way Hitler is despised by the Jews.

China also suffered a drastic decline in population during the 13th and 14th centuries. Before the Mongol invasion, Chinese dynasties reportedly had approximately 120 million inhabitants; after the conquest was completed in 1279, the 1300 CE census reported roughly 60 million people. Europe, especially Russia and Hungary, also met a similar fate. Much of pre-Mongol literature was destroyed in China.

Like many other civilizations, there was a so-called golden age in the history of Islam. During this golden age, Islam occupied the largest territory under the rule of the Caliph. Around 800 CE Harun Rashid was the Abbasid Caliph who is said to have built the House of Wisdom in Baghdad. Science, economy, arts, and literature significantly flourished.[255] War booties from various lands enriched the empire, and slaves, including beautiful women, were abundant in the region. Food and drinks were plentiful, the bazaars of Baghdad, Samarkand, and Istanbul, and many major cities were crowded with rich and poor alike, including many tourists. Many believed that Baghdad was one of the world's largest cities. The mighty river Tigris was flowing around Baghdad in a zig-zag motion as the source of life providing water, trade, and transport. Scholars of various subjects, including Islamic studies and other secular subjects worldwide, including the Hindus, gathered here. Arabs learned many subjects from the 'Brahmins' of India, which later transmitted to Europe. The Abbasid Caliphate ruled the Islamic world around the mid 13th century, and the Caliph was *Al-Musta'sim*. Baghdad had 36 libraries housing numerous books and manuscripts from all over the world. And the Grand Library of Baghdad, or the 'House of Wisdom' was the attraction of scholars from around the world that also stored many historical documents. Baghdad was a center of learning for science, astronomy, medicine, and literature besides Islamic studies, providing a liberal atmosphere for learning.

But misfortune befell on this land, and a sudden end to this peak of Islamic civilization dawned after the Siege of Baghdad in 1258 CE,[256] which spread terror across the region.

Around that era, the Mongol Khans were not following Islam yet. In terms of religion, Genghis Khan belonged to a Shamanic tradition. The Ilkhanate clan, called Khanate at that time, was ruled by the Mongol House of Hulagu named after Hulagu Khan, who was the son of Tolui and the grandson of Genghis Khan. Hulagu Khan's brother, Möngke Khan, demanded Caliph Al-Musta'sim for submission to the Mongol Empire and to pay tribute in the form of military support for Mongol forces in Persia. But the Caliph refused, and the Khan army attacked Baghdad in 1258 CE. Similar to Genghis, this was also a retaliatory conquest of Hulagu and Möngke Khan.

Heart-wrenching screams and cries of fleeing citizens filled the atmosphere, and they were killed randomly like insects. Women were dragged out of their homes and harems; even the children were not spared. According to Professor Martin Sicker, close to 90,000 people may have died.[257] The blood of royals, scholars, and learned people flew into Tigris, and the river turned red.

The brutal invaders looted stores and houses, destroyed mosques, palaces, and hospitals. Then they did what the invaders did to India around the same time – burning all the books from these libraries, and the Mongol barbarians used the leather covers of the books to make shoes without realizing how they were to deprive the world of knowledge preserved here for centuries. So many books were thrown into the Tigris, the water in that part of the river became black from the ink of the books.[258]

Caliph Al-Musta'sim was finally captured and was forced to helplessly watch as citizens were murdered, and his treasury was plundered. He was then killed in the most barbaric manner, as his body was wrapped in a carpet and trampled by horses.

Once a hustling bustling great city in the world began stinking rotten corpses, and the city lay in ruins. It is said that the Khans had to move their camps far away from the city to avoid the stench. This reminds us about what happened after Timur, by then an Islamist, took control over the Chagatai Khanate, the Ilkhanate, a few decades later and set out for world conquest. Timur played a reverse role during the invasion of Delhi in 1398 – days after the destruction, people could not enter the city due to the decaying of dead bodies and other ruins. It took years to rebuild the city,[259] and the same was true for Baghdad.

During these campaigns, the Khans destroyed much of Iran and Iraq – including their irrigation system, which caused a major setback for the agriculture and food sources, and it took a long time to recover.

The marauding soldiers of Islam that were led by the Caliphs to terrorize and conquer country after country met the same fate as a reversal of destiny. But unfortunately, as a result of this turbulence, once more, much of the knowledge was lost for good in just 13 days! It is always with these barbarian attacks that children, women, and knowledge suffer the most.

The Story of the Jats

Who are the Jats? There is no straight answer on who the 'Jat' people of India are. But it is well-known that and they were instrumental in forming the Khalsa Panth under Guru Govind Singh's leadership to fight the Islamic onslaught on the Hindus when there was no formal Sikhism established, and they fought against the Mughal army for freedom. The name of their *gotra* (the original ancestor) was Jhakhar or Jhakad. Jats are called various names in Afghanistan, such as Jaki/Zakarya/Zakar/Zigar/Jakar. Chinese traveler Xuangzang noted visiting a place called Jaguda in 644 CE, perhaps a territory named Zabul. The name Ghazni has some connection to this Jaguda.

The story continues like this: The city of Uch, currently located in the Pakistan part of Punjab, was called *Deogarh*[260]

("Stronghold of Giants") before the era of Islamic invasions. Deogarh and Lahore were Hindu cities of pride. A famous Central Asian Muslim Sufi named Jalaluddin Surkh-Posh Bukhari, came to Uch. As the early Sufi tradition and practice go, he used soft conversion methods – Sundandapuri, a Buddhist, was the ruler of Deogarh. Bukhari enticed and converted Ucha Rani, the daughter of *Sunandapuri.* Afterward, Bukhari asked her to build a fortress, and he named it *Uch* or "High". Another story suggests *Ucha Rani*, and she and her sister *Sita Rani,* rulers of Uch and Sitapur, both married Bukhari. And the city was named after *Ucha Rani*, which is called Ucha Sharif today.

Muhammad Ghori

Born in 1149 CE, as Shihab ad-Din, Mu'izz ad-Din Muhammad Ghori or Muhammad of Ghor was the Sultan of the Ghurid Empire and ruler. Ghori virtually opened the gates for Muslim rule in the Indian subcontinent after the fall of Ghazni in 1173 CE. In addition to some parts of India, he also ruled Iran, Tajikistan, and Turkmenistan. Two years after capturing Ghazni, he invaded and captured Multan and Uch in 1175 and Lahore in 1186. Qutb al-Din Aibak, a slave of Ghori, later became the first Sultan of Delhi in 1206.

Timur

Timur, also called Taimur or Tamerlane, was an infamous conqueror; he had mixed Mongol and Turkish ancestry. He was the founder of the Timurid Empire, ruling parts of Central Asia and Iran. Timur was a dreaded name in three continents – Asia, Africa, and Europe. It is estimated that about 5% of the world population at that time, around 17 million, were killed or perished because of Timur.[261] Timur was the great-great-great-grandfather of Babur (1483–1530), founder of the Mughal Empire.

Though Timur was not a direct descendant of Genghis Khan, he dreamed of re-establishing the legacy of Genghis

Khan. He claimed to be the heir of Khan and planned to restore Khan's Mongol Empire. Timur referred to himself as the "Sword of Islam" and called himself a *ghazi*. After defeating the Christian army in Smyrna in 1402, he was responsible for converting the remaining Mongol leaders to Islam. As a result, India encountered 100 years of Turko-Arab-Afghan and then 200 years of Mughal (Turko-Arab-Mongol) tyranny.

American historian Beatrice Forbes Manz writes, "in his formal correspondence, Timur continued throughout his life to portray himself as the restorer of Chinggisid rights. He justified his Iranian, Mamluk, and Ottoman campaigns as a re-imposition of legitimate Mongol control over lands taken by usurpers."[262]

Timur tried to accomplish what Genghis Khan could not – the invasion of India; he invaded India from the west in 1398. Though there was great resistance, his forces took over Multan, Attock, and Meerut after destroying many villages and cities and mercilessly massacring the population. He finally reached Delhi, where Nasiruddin Mahmud Tughlaq was the Sultan. It is said that after a brief battle, Timur took over Delhi and then put to death over 100,000 people, causing massive destruction of Delhi, one of the world's wealthiest cities at the time. After the raid, the city's condition was not livable anymore and was so bad that it took weeks for people to come back and almost a century for Delhi to re-establish its glory.

The infamous 'lame' Khan Timur left Kabul to invade India's heartland. He looted and terrorized many cities and arrived with his barbaric army at Delhi in winter 1398 during the reign of Sultan Mahmud Shah of the Tughlaq dynasty, who fled the capital. Timur ordered a general massacre and plunder, which continued for 15 days. According to Sharaf-ud-Din and Mir Khud, about one hundred thousand people were put to death in Delhi by Timur.[263]

British orientalist Stanley Lane-Poole noted, "The victory was complete and Timur, pitching his camp by the tomb of Firoz

Shah gave thanks to God with tears of joy in his eyes for three days." [264]

Poole also writes about Timur's invasion of Delhi: "Unhappy city was turned into a place of bloodshed, ruin and destruction…There were immense spoils of rubies, diamonds, pearls, gold and silver ornaments and vessels…Only the followers of Muslim religion escaped the general sack."[264]

Timur did not settle in the 'land of Kafirs' and returned westward after immense loot of wealth in 1399. On the way, he destroyed and plundered many places, including Meerut, Hardwar, Kangra, and even Jammu.

Shah Rukh

A mystic Persian 'Sufi' and poet named Hallaj (858 CE) or Mansour Hallaj was born in a Zoroastrian family. His famous doctrine of unity with the Supreme Being was similar to Zoroastrian or Vedic thoughts. He preached: "I am the Truth" or 'I'm also part of God', which is akin to the Hindu idea of 'Aham Brhamashmi' and 'Satyam Shivam Sundaram'. That means that each person can reach God without any intermediaries. Hallaj and his movement became very popular, and innumerable followers came under the radar of the Abbasid Caliphs.[265] He was put to confinement for a long time and finally executed because of *zindiq* or blasphemy. But before we discuss more about Shah Rukh, let us explore part of Islamic history from that era. In the early days of Islam, the term zindīq was used to denote individuals who did not follow central Islamic dogmas and practices.

Hallaj's ideas later became the Hurufi movement around 1370 CE, led by Persia-born Fazlallah Astarabadi in Iran and Azerbaijan. He was also a follower of Jalāl ad-Dīn Muhammad Rūmī (1207–1273 CE), a famous Persian poet, Islamic theologian, and jurist and was influenced by Sufism. Rumi's father was Bahā ud-Dīn Walad, who was the head of a madrassa, and Rumi inherited his father's position as Maulvi of the Konya Mosque. Later he became a scholar of Sharia laws. As an Islamic jurist, he gave sermons and taught Islam.

Timur had four sons, and the youngest one was Shah Rukh, who was a Timurid Sultan between 1405 and 1447 CE. Fazlallah was executed by Shah Rukh's son, Miran Shah, on Timur's order due to his 'crime' of zindiq.[266] According to historians Thomas W. Lentz and Glenn D. Lowry, "unlike his father, Shahrukh ruled the Timurid empire, not as a Turco-Mongol warlord-conqueror, but as an Islamic sultan. a model Islamic ruler who repaired much of the physical and psychological damage caused by his father."[267]

References

1. "The Geography of Strabo" published in Vol. I of the Loeb Classical Library edition, 1917.
2. "Islam in India", New World Encyclopedia. https://www.newworldencyclopedia.org/entry/Islam_in_India
3. Menon, A. Sreedhara. "Cultural heritage of Kerala: an introduction", East-West Publications, 1978, p. 58.
4. Freeman, Orien. "Invitation to Sociology, A Humanistic Perspective", 2019, p. 191.
5. West, Barbara A. (19 May 2010). "Encyclopedia of the Peoples of Asia and Oceania". Infobase Publishing.
6. Oldest Indian mosque: Trail leads to Gujarat. *The Times of India.* November 6, 2016.
7. Will Durant, The Story of Civilization", (Vol.1, Our Oriental Heritage, Chapter XVI, From Alexander to Aurangzeb).
8. Ibid.
9. Sowerwine, James E. (May 2010). "Caliph and Caliphate", Oxford Bibliographies Online Research Guide. Oxford University Press, USA. p. 5.
10. Akram, A.I. (1975). "5". The Muslim Conquest of Persia.
11. Iran, Arab Conquest of (636-671), Adam Ali, Conflict and

Conquest in the Islamic World: A Historical Encyclopedia, Vol.1, ed. Alexander Mikaberidze, (ABC-CLIO, 2011), p. 406.

12. Fratini, Dan (2006-04-01). "The Battle Of Yarmuk, 636. Military History Online.
13. A. I. Alkram. Chapter 19: The Battle of Chains - Chapter 26: The Last Opposition. Khalid bin Al-Waleed: His Life and Campaigns. The Sword of Allah. p. 1.
14. Al-Hind, the Making of the Indo-Islamic World: Early Medieval India and the Expansion of Islam 7th-11th Centuries. Brill. 2002. pp. 131–132, 136
15. Gabrieli, Francesco. "Muhammad ibn Qasim ath-Thaqafi and the Arab Conquest of Sind." East and West 15/3-4 (1965): 281–295.
16. Mahabharata Sambhava Parva, Chapter 67, Verses 161-162 https://archive.org/details/TheMahabharataMNDutt/page/n4/mode/1up?q=sambhava
17. Sambhava Parva, Chapter 110, Verses 9-19.
18. Resham Sengar, "Does Afghanistan have a link with Mahabharata?", *The Times of India*, 10 September 2019 https://timesofindia.indiatimes.com/travel/destinations/does-afghanistan-have-a-link-with-mahabharata/as71065831.cms
19. The Mahabharata, Book 14: Aswamedha Parva/Anugita Parva Chapters 83 verses 18-20 and 84 Verses 1-24 https://archive.org/details/dli.granth.118372/page/98/mode/1up?q=gandhara
20. Ancient Gandhara Kingdom (Kandahar, Afghanistan), Books Fact, 9 February 2016 https://www.booksfact.com/history/ancient-gandhara-kingdom-kandahar-afghanistan.html
21. Adamec, Ludwig W. (2012). "Historical Dictionary of Afghanistan". Scarecrow Press. p. 231.
22. Nancy Hatch Dupree / Aḥmad *'Alī* Kuhzād (1972). "An

Historical Guide to Kabul – The Name". American International School of Kabul. Archived from the original *on 2010-08-30.*

23. "Kabul: City of lost glories". *BBC.* 2001-11-12.
24. Adamec, p.231.
25. Ramesh Chandra Majumdar, Achut Dattatrya Pusalker, A. K. Majumdar, Dilip Kumar Ghose, Bharatiya Vidya Bhavan, Vishvanath Govind Dighe Published by Bharatiya Vidya Bhavan (1962). "The History and Culture of the Indian People : The Vedic age". p. 247.
26. Muir, John. "Original Sanskrit Texts on the Origin and History of the People of India". p. 352.
27. del Castillo, Graciana (2014-04-02). "Guilty Party: The International Community in Afghanistan". Xlibris Corporation. p. 28.
28. Sagar, Krishna Chandra (1992). "Foreign Influence on Ancient India". Northern Book Centre.
29. Dwaraka Prasad Sharma. "Shrimad Valmiki Ramayan - Sanskrit Text with Hindi Translation- DP Sharma 10 volumes"
30. Bombay Historical Society (1946). Annual bibliography of Indian history and Indology, Volume 4. p. 257.
31. Baqir, Muhammad (1985). "Lahore, past and present". B.R. Pub. Corp., pp. 19–20.
32. Masud-ul Hasan (1978). "Guide to Lahore". Ferozsons.
33. Nadiem, Ihsan N. (2005). "Punjab: land, history, people". Al-Faisal Nashran. p. 111.
34. Cunningham, Sir Alexander (1871). "The Ancient Geography of India: I. The Buddhist Period, Including the Campaigns of Alexander, and the Travels of Hwen-Thsang". Trübner and Company.
35. Raverty, Henry George (1867), "A dictionary of the

Puk'hto, Pus'hto, or language of the Afghans" (2 ed.), Williams and Norgate, p. 33.

36. Asiatick Society (Calcutta; India) (1812). Asiatick researches, or, Transactions of the society instituted in Bengal, for inquiring into the history and antiquities, the arts, sciences, and literature of Asia. John Murray. pp. 383.
37. https://www.thenews.com.pk/tns/detail/556515-travelling-to-charsadda/
38. Susan Whitfield (2018). "Silk, Slaves, and Stupas: Material Culture of the Silk Road". University of California Press. p. 136.
39. Macdonell, Arthur Anthony (1900). "A History of Sanskrit Literature". D. Appleton.
40. Vidyalankar, Satyakam (1977). "R̥gveda Saṃhitā". Veda Pratishthan.
41. Roy, S. B. (1989). "Early Aryans of India, 3100-1400 B.C. ", Navrang.
42. Dwaraka Prasad Sharma. "Shrimad Valmiki Ramayan - Sanskrit Text with Hindi Translation- DP Sharma 10 volumes"
43. Petric, Cameron, (2013). "Charsadda", in D.K. Chakrabarti and M. Lal (eds.), History of Ancient India III: The Texts, Political History and Administration til c. 200 BC, Vivekananda International Foundation, Aryan Books International, Delhi, p. 515.
44. Coningham, R.A.E. and C. Batt, (2007). "Dating the Sequence", in R.A.E. Coningham and I. Ali (eds.), Charsadda: The British-Pakistani Excavations at the Bala Hisar, Society for South Asian Studies Monograph No. 5, BAR International Series 1709, Archaeopress, Oxford, pp. 93-98.
45. Beal, Samuel, (ed. & trans.), (1884). "Si-yu-ki: Buddhist Records of the Western World", Volume 2, Author: Hiuen Tsang, London.

46. "Gandhara" *Encyclopœdia Britannica*: Gandhara
47. https://glosbe.com/ps/en/%D8%BA%D9%88%D9%86%DA%89%DB%8D
48. "Ancient Peshawar:Historical Review of Some of its Socio-Religious and Cultural Aspects". *www.asc-centralasia.edu.pk.*
49. Rapson, Edward James (1960). "Ancient India: From the Earliest Times to the First Century A.D." Susil Gupta (India) Private Ltd., p. 88.
50. Kumar, Rakesh (2000). "Ancient India and World". Classical Publishing Company. p. 68.
51. "The critical edition of Mahabharat" translated by Bibek Debroy. Section 23, 254(29) Digvijay Parva *https://archive.org/details/the-mahabharata-set-of-10-volumes/page/257/mode/1up?q=volume+2*
52. Mahabharat VII. 7.91.39
53. Mahabharat VII.4.5; II.27.23
54. "The History and Culture of the Indian People", 1977, p. 15, Dr. Ramesh Chandra Majumdar, Dr. Achut Dattatraya Pusalker, Dr. Asoke Kumar Majumdar; "An Advanced History of India", 1973, p. 54, Dr. Ramesh Chandra Majumdar; "The Soul of India", 1961, p. 56, Amaury De Riencourt.
55. "Problems of Ancient India", 2000, pp. 5-6; cf: Geographical Data in the Early Puranas, p. 168.
56. Encyclopaedia Indica, "The Kambojas: Land and its Identification", First Edition, 1998 New Delhi, p. 528.
57. Ptolemy's Geography mentions Tambyzoi located in eastern Bactria (Ancient India as Described by Ptolemy: Being a Translation of the Chapters ... 1885, p. 268, John Watson McCrindle - Geography, Ancient; Barrington Atlas of the Greek and Roman World, History - 2000, p. 99, (editors) Richard J. A. Talbert) and Ambautai people located to south of Hindukush Mountains (Geography 6.18.3; See map in McCrindle, p. 8). Dr. S. Levi has identified Tambyzoi with Kamboja (Indian Antiquary, 1923, p. 54.

58. "Geographical and Economic Studies in the Mahābhārata: Upāyana Parva", 1945, p. 44, Dr. Moti Chandra.
59. "Comparative Study of Thirty City-state Cultures: An Investigation", 2000, p. 388, Dr. Hansen, Mogens Herman (ed).
60. Rig Veda: Rig-Veda, Book 7: HYMN XVIII. Indra. (sacred-texts.com)
61. The Telegraph, March 12, 2001: After 1,700 years, Buddhas fall to Taliban dynamite (telegraph.co.uk)]
62. "Why the Taliban are destroying Buddhas". Usatoday.com. 22 March 2001.
63. Blänsdorf, Catharina (2015). "Dating of the Buddha Statues – AMS 14C Dating of Organic Materials"
64. Morgan, Kenneth W. (1956). "The Path of the Buddha". p. 43.
65. "Dating of the Buddha Statues – AMS 14C Dating of Organic Materials".
66. Petzet (Ed.), Michael (2009). "The Giant Buddhas of Bamiyan". Safeguarding the remains (PDF). ICOMOS. pp. 18–19.
67. "Bamiyan", Britannica *https://www.britannica.com/place/Bamiyan*
68. Stamp: Sultan Mahmud of Ghazni (971-1030), Ghaznavid Empire ruler *https://colnect.com/en/stamps/stamp/159490-Sultan_Mahmud_of_Ghazni_971-1030_Ghaznavid_Empire_ruler-National_Unity_Emperors-Afghanistan]*
69. Gupta, Parmanand (1989). "Geography from Ancient Indian Coins & Seals". Concept Publishing Company. pp. 17–18.
70. "The untold Hindu history of Afghanistan! " https://globalpress.hinduismnow.org/heritage/temple/untold-hindu-history-afghanistan/

71. John Watson McCrindle (1896). "The Invasion of India by Alexander the Great: As Described by Arrian, Q. Curtius, Diodoros, Plutarch and Justin". University of Michigan: A. Constable. p. 333-334.
72. Majumdar, Ramesh Chandra (1977) [1952]. "Ancient India", (Reprinted ed.). Motilal Banarsidass. p. 99.
73. Dani, Ahmad Hasan; Masson, Vadim Mikhaĭlovich; Harmatta, János; Litvinovskiĭ, Boris Abramovich; Bosworth, Clifford Edmund (1999). "History of Civilizations of Central Asia" (PDF). UNESCO. p. 76.
74. Hambly, Gavin. "History of Central Asia: Early Western Peoples". Encyclopædia Britannica Online. Encyclopædia Britannica, Inc.
75. Bailey, H.W. (1996) "Khotanese Saka Literature", in Ehsan Yarshater (ed), The Cambridge History of Iran, Vol III: The Seleucid, Parthian, and Sasanian Periods, Part 2 (reprint edition), Cambridge: Cambridge University Press, pp 1230–1231.
76. Bosworth, Clifford Edmund (1997). "Sīstān". The Encyclopedia of Islam, New Edition, Volume IX: San–Sze. Leiden, and New York: BRILL. pp. 681–685.
77. "Early Aryans of India, 3100-1400 BC." By S. B. Roy, p. 76.
78. Shroder, John F. (2016), "Hari Rud – Murghab River Basin". Transboundary Water Resources in Afghanistan: Climate Change and Land-Use Implications. Saint Louis: Elsevier. pp. 410–412.
79. "Minaret and Archaeological Remains of Jam" https://whc.unesco.org/en/list/211/
80. 'Wang Ocheonchukguk Jeon' "Memoir of the pilgrimage to the five kingdoms of India." by Hui Chao (Hyecho) (http://idp.bl.uk/database/oo_scroll_h.4d?uid=5251819708;bst=1;recnum=60867;index=1;img=1)

81. Sen, Surendranath (1956). "India Through Chinese Eyes: Sir William Meyer Endowment Lectures 1952–53". University of Madras.
82. "The History and Culture of the Indian People: The Vedic age". By Ramesh Chandra Majumdar, Achut Dattatrya Pusalker, A. K. Majumdar, Dilip Kumar Ghose, Bharatiya Vidya Bhavan, Vishvanath Govind Dighe Published by Bharatiya Vidya Bhavan, 1962, p. 247.
83. Peter Marsden (1998-09-15). "The Taliban: War, Religion and the New Order in Afghanistan". Palgrave Macmillan. p. 12.
84. Minorsky, V. (1937), "Ḥudūd al-ʿĀlam" (The Regions of the World), Great Britain: The E. J. W. Gibb Memorial Trust.
85. "Kitab al-Buldan" (Book of the Countries) by Ahmad al-Ya'qubi.
86. Barua, Pradeep P. (2005). "The State at War in South Asia". University of Nebraska Press.
87. "An Outline Of The History Of Persia During The Last Two Centuries (A.D. 1722-1922)". Edward Granville Browne. London: Packard Humanities Institute. p. 29.
88. Otfinoski, Steven (2004). Afghanistan. Infobase Publishing. p. 7.
89. Malleson, George Bruce (1878). History of Afghanistan, from the Earliest Period to the Outbreak of the War of 1878. London: Elibron.com. p. 227.
90. "Afghanistan". The World Factbook. Central Intelligence Agency. Ahmad Shah DURRANI unified the Pashtun tribes and founded Afghanistan in 1747.
91. "Last Afghan empire". Louis Dupree, Nancy Hatch Dupree *and others*. Encyclopædia Britannica *Online Version*.
92. "Afghan King Overthrown; A Republic Is Proclaimed". The New York Times. 18 July 1973.

93. Barfield, Thomas (25 March 2012). "Afghanistan: A Cultural and Political History" (Princeton Studies in Muslim Politics). Princeton University Press.

94. Afghanistan - DAOUD'S REPUBLIC, JULY 1973- APRIL 1978 (countrystudies.us)

95. White, Terence (15 October 2001). "Flashback: When the Taleban took Kabul". BBC.

96. Imtiaz Ali, "The Father of the Taliban: An Interview with Maulana Sami ul-Haq", Spotlight on Terror, The Jamestown Foundation, Volume 4, Issue 2, 23 May 2007.

97. Haroon Rashid (2 October 2003). "The 'university of holy war'", *BBC Online*.

98. Mark Magnier (30 May 2009). "Pakistan religious schools get scrutiny", *Los Angeles Times*.

99. Tom Hussain (4 August 2015). "Mullah Omar worked as potato vendor to escape detection in Pakistan". McClatchy news.

100. Gunaratna, Rohan; Iqbal, Khuram (2012), "Pakistan: Terrorism Ground Zero", Reaktion Books, p. 41,

101. Giraldo, Jeanne K. (2007). "Terrorism Financing and State Responses: A Comparative Perspective". Stanford University Press. p. 96. "Pakistan provided military support, including arms, ammunition, fuel, and military advisers, to the Taliban through its Directorate for Inter-Services Intelligence (ISI)".

102. Jones, Owen Bennett (2003). "Pakistan: eye of the storm". Yale University Press. p. 240. "The ISI's undemocratic tendencies are not restricted to its interference in the electoral process. The organisation also played a major role in creating the Taliban movement."

103. Boase, Roger (2010). "Islam and Global Dialogue: Religious Pluralism and the Pursuit of Peace". Ashgate.

p. 85. "Pakistan's Inter-Services Intelligence agency used the students from these madrassas, the Taliban, to create a favourable regime in Afghanistan".

104. Maley, William (2009). The Afghanistan wars. Palgrave Macmillan. p. 288.

105. Pape, Robert A (2010). "Cutting the Fuse: The Explosion of Global Suicide Terrorism and How to Stop It". University of Chicago Press. pp. 140–141.

106. Tomsen, Peter (2011). "Wars of Afghanistan". PublicAffairs. p. 322.

107. Narendra Singh Sarila, "The Shadow of the Great Game: The Untold Story of India's Partition", Carol and Graff Publishers New York, 2006. https://ia801208.us.archive.org/12/items/AzadIndiaWinsFreedom/The%20Shadow%20of%20the%20Great%20Game_%20The%20Untold%20Story%20of%20India_s%20Partition.pdf

108. Ibid.

109. Riedel, Bruce (2014). "What We Won: America's Secret War in Afghanistan, 1979–1989". Brookings Institution Press. pp. 98–99.

110. "The Oily Americans". *Time*. 13 May 2003. The Oily Americans - TIME

111. Maley, William (2001). "Fundamentalism Reborn? Afghanistan and the Taliban". C Hurst & Co. p. 14.

112. Matinuddin, Kamal, "The Taliban Phenomenon, Afghanistan 1994–1997", Oxford University Press, (1999), pp. 25–26.

113. Rashid, Ahmed *(2000),* "Taliban: Militant Islam, Oil and Fundamentalism in Central Asia", New Haven: Yale University Press, p. 25.

114. Gates, Robert (2007). "From the Shadows: The Ultimate Insider's Story of Five Presidents and How They Won the Cold War". Simon & Schuster. pp. 142, 144–145.

115. Coll, Steve (2004). "Ghost Wars: The Secret History of the CIA, Afghanistan, and Bin Laden, from the Soviet Invasion to September 10, 2001". New York: Penguin Press. p. 46.
116. Blight, James G.; et al. (2012). "Becoming Enemies: U.S.-Iran Relations and the Iran-Iraq War, 1979-1988". Rowman & Littlefield Publishers. pp. 19, 66.
117. Coll, Steve. "Ghost Wars: The Secret History of the CIA, Afghanistan, and Bin Laden, from the Soviet Invasion to September 10, 2001". New York: Penguin Press. p. 58.
118. Harrison, Selig S. *(1995). "Soviet Occupation, Afghan Resistance, and the American Response"*. Out of Afghanistan: The Inside Story of the Soviet Withdrawal. Oxford University Press. p. 53.
119. Crile, George (2003). "Charlie Wilson's War: The Extraordinary Story of the Largest Covert Operation in history". New York: Atlantic Monthly Press. p. 243.
120. Mann, James; Mann, Jim (2004). "Rise of the Vulcans: The History of Bush's War Cabinet". Penguin Books. p. 122.
121. Mashal, Mujib. "Hekmatyar's never-ending Afghan war". *www.aljazeera.com.*
122. Khalilzad, Zalmay (22 March 2016). "The Envoy: From Kabul to the White House, My Journey Through a Turbulent World". St. Martin's Publishing Group. via Google Books.
123. Tomsen, Peter (2013). "The Wars of Afghanistan: Messianic Terrorism, Tribal Conflicts, and the Failures of Great Powers. PublicAffairs". p. 16.
124. *Washington Post*, 23 March 2002, "From U.S., the ABC's of Jihad".
125. Michael Rubin, "Who Is Responsible for the Taliban?", Washington Institute, 1 Mar, 2002 https://www.washingtoninstitute.org/policy-analysis/who-responsible-taliban

126. Shaffer, Brenda (2006). "The Limits of Culture: Islam and Foreign Policy". MIT Press. p. 267. *Pakistani involvement in creating the movement is seen as central.*

127. Giraldo, Jeanne K. (2007). "Terrorism Financing and State Responses: A Comparative Perspective". Stanford University Press. p. 96. Pakistan provided military support, including arms, ammunition, fuel, and military advisers, to the Taliban through its Directorate for Inter-Services Intelligence (ISI).

128. Alex Strick van Linschoten and Felix Kuehn, "An Enemy We Created: The Myth of the Taliban-Al Qaeda Merger in Afghanistan", Oxford University Press (2012), pp. 121–122.

129. Michael Rubin and Daniel Benjamin, "The Taliban and Terrorism: Report from Afghanistan," Policywatch, The Washington Institute for Near East Policy, No. 450, April 6, 2000.

130. Pamela Constable. "Pakistani Agency Seeks to Allay U.S. on Terrorism," *The Washington Post*, February 15, 2000, p. A17.

131. Raman, B., International Institute of Counter Terrorism March 20, 1999 https://www.ict.org.il/Article.aspx?ID=761#gsc.tab=0

132. Bergen, Peter; Tiedemann, Katherine (14 February 2013). "Talibanistan: Negotiating the Borders Between Terror, Politics, and Religion". OUP USA.

133. "The Haqqani History: Bin Ladin's Advocate Inside the Taliban". nsarchive.gwu.edu.

134. Gopal A, Mahsud MK, Fishman B (2013). "The Taliban in North Waziristan". In Bergen P, Tiedemann K (eds.). Talibanistan: Negotiating the Borders Between Terror, Politics, and Religion. USA: Oxford University Press. pp. 132–142.

135. Elias-Sanborn B, ed. (11 Sep 2012). "The Haqqani History: Bin Ladin's Advocate Inside the Taliban". National Security Archive.

136. Brown, Vahid; Rassler, Don (4 July 2013). "Fountainhead of Jihad: The Haqqani Nexus, 1973-2012". Oxford University Press.

137. Cassman, Daniel. "Haqqani Network - Mapping Militant Organizations". web.stanford.edu

138. Afghanistan War Infoplease.com, 22 July 2007

139. Hiro, Dilip (January 28, 1999). "The Cost of an Afghan 'Victory' ". The Nation.

140. Interview with FBI special agent Jack Cloonan ArchivedMarch 21, 2012, at the Wayback Machine, Frontline, PBS, October 18, 2005.

141. "India fortifying case to put Jaish on ban list". The Hindu. 4 March 2019.

142. Pathak, Shekhar Gupta Rahul (15 May 1994). "Specter of subversion looms over India as Pakistan sponsored arms, mercenaries and funds from Muslim world pour in to destabilise Kashmir". *India Today*.

143. Bruce Riedel (5 January 2016). "Blame Pakistani Spy Service for Attack on Indian Air Force Base". The Daily Beast.

144. Maha Siddiqui, "US Report Punches Holes in Pakistan's Claim that Terrorist Masood Azhar is 'Missing'", News 18, 24 June 2020 https://www.news18.com/news/world/us-report-punches-holes-in-pakistans-claim-that-terrorist-masood-azhar-is-missing-2685785.html

145. "Pathankot attack: First terrorist was killed while he was climbing 10 ft high wall". The Indian Express.

146. "NIA registers case in Pathankot terror strike". Rediff.

147. "Viewpoint: How far might India go to 'punish' Pakistan?". 15 February 2019

148. "Jaish terrorists attack CRPF convoy in Kashmir, kill at least 40 personnel". The Times of India. 14 February 2019.
149. "Jaish-e-Mohammad: A profile". BBC News. 6 February 2002.
150. Shah, Saeed (13 September 2009). "Terror group builds big base under Pakistani officials' noses". McClatchy newspapers.
151. "US says Masood Azhar enjoys 'state protection' in Pakistan", Hindustan Times, 24 June 2020 https://www.hindustantimes.com/world-news/us-says-masood-azhar-enjoys-state-protection-in-pakistan/story-Q5StShJZy73Bp1bTSGdr5L.html
152. "Declassified files reveal Britain's secret support to Afghan Mujahideen". Times of Islamabad. 30 January 2018.
153. Bowcott, Owen. "UK discussed plans to help mujaheddin weeks after Soviet invasion of Afghanistan". The Guardian.
154. Marcela Grad, "Massoud: An Intimate Portrait of the Legendary Afghan Leader", (Webster MO: Webster University Press, 2009).
155. "Pakistan: A Plethora of Problems" (PDF). Global Security Studies, Winter 2012, Volume 3, Issue 1, by Colin Price, School of Graduate and Continuing Studies in Diplomacy. Norwich University, Northfield, VT.
156. Ewans, Martin (1 December 2004). "Conflict in Afghanistan: Studies in Asymetric Warfare". Routledge.
157. S. Frederick Starr (2004). "Xinjiang: China's Muslim Borderland" (illustrated ed.). M.E. Sharpe. p. 157.
158. Ibid p. 158.
159. Ibid . 157–158.
160. Coll, Steve (2004). "Ghost Wars: The Secret History of the CIA, Afghanistan, and Bin Laden, from the Soviet Invasion to September 10, 2001". Penguin Group. pp. 144–145, 238.
161. "Crusade' Reference Reinforces Fears War on Terrorism Is Against Muslims", By Peter Waldman and Hugh PopeStaff,

The Wall Street Journal, Sept. 21, 2001 https://www.wsj.com/articles/SB1001020294332922160

162. 'The Taliban'. Mapping Militant Organizations.Stanford University

163. Matinuddin, Kamal, "The Taliban Phenomenon, Afghanistan 1994–1997", Oxford University Press, (1999), pp. 25–26.

164. Amnesty International. "Document – Afghanistan: further information on fear for safety and new concern: deliberate and arbitrary killings: civilians in Kabul". 16 November 1995 Accessed at Amnesty.org

165. "Documents Detail Years of Pakistani Support for Taliban, Extremists". George Washington University. 2007.

166. UNSC Resolution 1333, 19 December 2000 (sanctions against Taliban territory).

167. Rashid, Ahmed *(2000),* "Taliban: Militant Islam, Oil and Fundamentalism in Central Asia", New Haven: Yale University Press, p. 107.

168. 'The Taliban'. Mapping Militant Organizations. Stanford University.

169. "WPO Poll: Afghan Public Overwhelmingly Rejects al-Qaeda, Taliban". 30 January 2006.

170. "Afghan Futures: A National Public Opinion Survey" *(PDF). 29 January 2015. p. 4.*

171. United Nations Security Council Resolution 1386.S/RES/1386(2001) 31 May 2001. (UNSCR 1386).

172. "United States Mission to Afghanistan". Nato.usmission.gov.

173. Witte, Griff (December 8, 2009). "Taliban shadow officials offer concrete alternative". *The Washington Post.*

174. Gall, Carlotta; Khapalwak, Ruhullah (2021-08-15). "Afghanistan Live Updates: Government Collapses as President Flees, and Taliban Enter Kabul". *The New York Times.*

175. Kathy Gannon, "Afghan president was isolated before slipping into exile", AP News, 16 August, 2021 https://apnews.com/article/race-and-ethnicity-2901e54d6268341d3caf936fef6313db

176. "The rise and fall of Afghan President Ashraf Ghani", France 24, 15 August, 2021 https://www.france24.com/en/live-news/20210815-the-rise-and-fall-of-afghan-president-ashraf-ghani

177. Rezaul H. Laskar, August 25, 2021 https://www.hindustantimes.com/analysis/in-the-us-taliban-peace-deal-the-mystery-of-the-secret-annexes-101629868569003.html

178. "Afghanistan: Secret Kabul talks between CIA and Taliban - US media", BBC https://www.bbc.com/news/world-asia-58320516

179. Matthew Lee, Eric Tucker, "Was Biden handcuffed by Trump's Taliban deal in Doha?" AP News, August 19, 2021 https://apnews.com/article/joe-biden-middle-east-taliban-doha-e6f48507848aef2ee849154604aa11be

180. Fareed Zakaria, "Pakistan is 'epicenter of Islamic terrorism'", CNN, May 5, 2010 http://www.cnn.com/2010/OPINION/05/05/zakaria.pakistan.terror/index.html

181. "Pakistan must introspect why it's universally acknowledged as epicentre of terrorism: India", Economic Times, 8 July 2020 https://economictimes.indiatimes.com/news/defence/pakistan-must-introspect-why-its-universally-acknowledged-as-epicentre-of-terrorism-india/articleshow/76851599.cms

182. US Spending Billions on Afghan Army https://time.com/6090830/us-spending-afghan-army-billions/

183. Adam Andrezejewski, "Staggering Costs – U.S. Military Equipment Left Behind In Afghanistan", Forbes, 23 August 2021 https://www.forbes.com/sites/

adamandrzejewski/2021/08/23/staggering-costs--us-military-equipment-left-behind-in-afghanistan/

184. Ellen Knickmeyer, "Costs of the Afghanistan war, in lives and dollars", AP News, August 17, 2021 https://apnews.com/article/middle-east-business-afghanistan-43d8f53b35e80ec18c130cd683e1a38f

185. "Mughalistan: IB unearths SIMI's latest obsession", Zee News India, 31 July 2004, https://zeenews.india.com/news/nation/mughalistan-ib-unearths-simis-latest-obsession_170769.html

186. "Mughalistan – An undivided Islamic nation in the Indian subcontinent", Bodoland Watch https://bodolandwatch.wordpress.com/2015/07/16/mughalistan-an-undivided-islamic-nation-in-the-indian-subcontinent/

187. Richard F. Strand, "Peoples and Languages of Nuristan". 2005 nuristan.info.

188. "The kalaṣa of kalaṣüm", Richard F. Strand.

189. Bashir, Elena, Jain, Danesh; Cardona, George (editors). "The Indo-Aryan languages". 2007 p. 905.

190. Su-kao-seng-chaun, Chapter 2, (no. 1493); Kai-yuan-lu, chapter 7; Publications, 1904, p. 122-123, published by Oriental Translation Fund (Editors Dr. T. W. Rhys Davis, S. W. Bushel, London, Royal Asiatic Society).

191. Ludwig W. Adamec, ed. Historical and Political Gazetteer of Afghanistan: Volume 6. Akademische Druck- u. Verlagsanstalt Graz. 1985, p. 349.

192. Witzel, Michael (2004), "Kalash Religion (extract from 'The Ṛgvedic Religious System and its Central Asian and Hindukush Antecedents')" (PDF), in A. Griffiths; J. E. M. Houben (eds.), The Vedas: Texts, Language and Ritual, Groningen: Forsten, pp. 581–636.

193. Jamil, Kashif (19 August 2019). "Uchal — a festival of shepherds and farmers of the Kalash tribe".

194. "Earthquake was Allah's wrath for Kalash community's immoral ways"". *The Express Tribune*. 10 November 2015.

195. Marsden, Magnus (2010). "A tour not so grand: mobile Muslims in northern Pakistan". In Osella; Filippo; Soares; Benjamin (eds.). Islam, Politics, Anthropology. Chichester, England: Royal Anthropological Institute by Wiley-Blackwell. pp. 57–75.

196. "History of Civilizations of Central Asia" (vol.4, part-1). Motilal Banarsidass. 1992-01-01. p. 219.

197. Marsden. 2010. p.58.

198. https://www.legislation.gov.uk/ukpga/Geo5and1Edw8/26/2/part/XII/crossheading/interpretation/enacted?view=plain

199. Bruce Stanley (2008), "Basrah", in Michael R.T. Dumper; Bruce E. Stanley (eds.), Cities of the Middle East and North Africa, Santa Barbara, USA: ABC-CLIO.

200. Bireshwar Nath Srivastava, "Harsha and His Times: A Glimpse of Political History During the Seventh Century A.D.", (Chowkhamba Sanskrit Series Office, 1976), p. 78.

201. "A Short History of Jammu Raj: From Earliest Times to 1846 A.D.".Ajaya Prakashan, 1985, p. 44.

202. Raja Dahir Forgotten Hero https://www.starofmysore.com/king-raja-dahir-forgotten-hero/

203. Friedmann, Y; et al. (1981), P. Bearman (ed.), "ČAČ-NĀMA in Encyclopedia of Islam", Second Edition, Brill Academic Publishers

204. Manan Ahmed Asif, "A Book of Conquest". Harvard University Press. 2016.

205. Chapter I, Sind Under The Arabs, The Arab Conquest www.aurobindo.du.ac.in

206. Asif, 2016.

207. DAWN The Review, "Rajah Dahar of Sindh", 17-23 May 2001. http://pakistanspace.tripod.com/khurram/dahar.htm

208. Aḥmad Shujāʻ Pāshā, "Pakistan, the cultural heritage", by Sang-e-Meel Publications, 1998, p. 43.

209. "The Chachnamah", An Ancient History of Sind, Giving the Hindu period down to the Arab Conquest. (1900). Translated from the Persian by Mirza Kalichbeg Fredunbeg. Karachi: Commissioners Press.

210. Nicholas F. Gier, "From Mongols to Mughals: Religious violence in India 9th-18th centuries", Presented at the Pacific Northwest Regional Meeting American Academy of Religion, Gonzaga University, May 2006.

211. Malik Mohamed, "The Foundations of the Composite Culture in India; Early Arab contact and the advent of Islam in India". Aakar Books, New Delhi 2007, p. 58-59.

212. Arun Shourie, Eminent Historians: Their Technology, Their Line, Their Fraud, Harper Collins; 1999

213. Yogendra Mishara, "The Hindu Shahis of Afghanistan and the Punjab AD 865-1026", p. 4.

214. Sailendra Nath Sen. "Ancient Indian History and Civilization". New Age International. p. 342.

215. D. W. Macdowall, "The Shahis of Kabul and Gandhara" Numismatic Chronicle, Seventh Series, Vol. III, 1968, pp. 189-224.

216. "Hund" https://www.jatland.com/home/Hund

217. Frye, R. N. "The Sāmānids". The Cambridge History of Iran, Volume 4: From the Arab Invasion to the Saljuqs. Cambridge: Cambridge University Press. pp. 136–161.

218. Richard Ernest Dupuy, Trevor Nevitt Dupuy "The encyclopedia of military history", p. 336.

219. Mohamed Kasim Ferishta, John Briggs MRAS (translator), "History of the Rise of the Mohammedan Power in India", Volume 1: Section 15. Packard Humanities Institute.

220. Ibid.

221. K. A. Nilakanta Sastri. "A Comprehensive History of India" Vol. Two, Orient Longman, 1957. p. 10.

222. Al-Utbi, Tarikh Yamini https://www rarebooksocietyofindia.org/book_archive/196174216674_ 10153404411876675.pdf p.349

223. Elliot and Dowson, "The History of India, as Told by Its Own Historians - The Muhammadan Period", Vol 2, Trubner London, pp. 18–24. The history of India : as told by its own historians. The Muhammadan period : Elliot, H. M. (Henry Miers), Sir, 1808-1853 : Free Download, Borrow, and Streaming : Internet Archive

224. Ferishta, Briggs.

225. P. M. Holt; Ann K. S. Lambton; Bernard Lewis, eds. (1977), "The Cambridge history of Islam", Cambridge University Press, p. 3,

226. Ibn Battuta (2004). "Travels in Asia and Africa, 1325–1354" (reprint, illustrated ed.). London: Routledge. p. 179.

227. Trudy Ring, Robert M. Salkin, Sharon La Boda (1996) "International Dictionary of Historic Places: Asia and Oceania", v.5, Taylor & Francis, p. 279-282.

228. Mahmud of Ghazni's Invasions of India, Maps of India https://www.mapsofindia.com/history/battles/mahmud-ghazni-invasions-of-india.html

229. Mahmud of Ghazni, UCLA Social Sciences Manas https://southasia.ucla.edu/history-politics/mughals-and-medieval/mahmud-of-ghazni/

230. "Mahmud Ghazni, The Pillager of Enormous Wealth From India", Adil Firdous Wani: http://www.ijsred.com/volume3/issue1/IJSRED-V3I1P69.pdf

231. Catherine B. Asher, Cynthia Talbot (2006). "India before Europe". Sterling Publishers. p. 42.

232. Yagnik, Achyut; Sheth, Suchitra(2005), "The Shaping of Modern Gujarat: Plurality, Hindutva, and Beyond", Penguin Books India, p. 39.

233. Akbar, M. J. (2003-12-31). "The Shade of Swords: Jihad

and the Conflict between Islam and Christianity". Roli Books Private Limited.

234. Thapar, Romila (2004). "Somanatha: The Many Voices of a History". Penguin Books India.

235. Meenakshi Jain "Review of Romila Thapar's "Somanatha, The Many Voices of a History"". *The Pioneer.* (21 March 2004).

236. "Mahmud Ghazni", Maps of India https://www.mapsofindia.com/history/battles/mahmud-ghazni-invasions-of-india.html

237. Neil Aggarwal (2018), "Representations of Mahmud of Ghazni in the Islamic State's texts, Contemporary South Asia", 26:1, 86-96, DOI: 10.1080/09584935.2018.1430747

238. "Mahmood Ghaznavi", History Pak https://historypak.com/mahmood-ghaznavi/

239. E. C. Sachau, "Alberuni's India", London, 1914, Vol I, p. 22.

240. Arun Shourie, "How history was made up at Nalanda", Indian Express, 28 June 2014 https://indianexpress.com/article/opinion/columns/how-history-was-made-up-at-nalanda/

241. Rachewiltz, Igor de (December 2015). "The Secret History of the Mongols: A Mongolian Epic Chronicle of the Thirteenth Century". Western Washington University.

242. "The Islamic World to 1600". The University of Calgary, The Applied History Research Group, https://web.archive.org/web/20070512201848/http://www.ucalgary.ca/applied_history/tutor/islam/mongols/

243. "Genghis Khan", Britannica https://www.britannica.com/biography/Genghis-Khan

244. "The Islamic World to 1600". The University of Calgary, The Applied History Research Group, https://web.archive.org/web/20070512201848/http://www.ucalgary.ca/applied_history/tutor/islam/mongols/

245. *Leo de Hartog (2004).* Genghis Khan: Conqueror of the World. *Tauris Parke. p.* 86–87.

246. Prawdin, Michael. "The Islamic World to 1600: The Mongol Invasions (The Il-Khanate)". University of Calgary. 2013. The Mongol Empire.

247. Heissig, Walther (1992). Fragen der mongolischen Heldendichtung: Vorträge des 6. Epensymposiums des Sonderforschungsbereichs 12, Bonn 1988 (in German). Otto Harrassowitz Verlag.

248. Mark Cartwright, "Religion in the mongol Empire", World History Encyclopedia, 1 November 2019 https://www.worldhistory.org/article/1469/religion-in-the-mongol-empire

249. Seshadri Kumar, "India Should Be Grateful to Alauddin Khilji for Thwarting the Mongol Invasions", The Wire, 9 December 2017 https://thewire.in/history/india-grateful-alauddin-khilji-thwarting-mongol-invasions

250. Igor de Rachewiltz, "The Secret History of the Mongols: A Mongolian Epic Chronicle of the Thirteenth Century" (Brill: Leiden, The Netherlands).

251. Alexander the not so Great: History through Persian eyes. https://www.bbc.com/news/magazine-18803290

252. Sverdrup, Carl (2010). "Numbers in Mongol Warfare". Journal of Medieval Military History. Boydell Press. 8: 109–17 [p. 113].

253. Madsen Pirie, "Genghis Khan, Warlord and Conqueror, Adam Smith Institute", 18 August 2019 https://www.adamsmith.org/blog/genghis-khan-warlord-and-conqueror

254. Mongol Invasions and Conquests: https://figipedia.weebly.com/uploads/7/2/6/3/7263810/mongol_articles.pdf

255. Jim Al-Khalili (2011). "The House of Wisdom: How Arabic Science Saved Ancient Knowledge and Gave Us the Renaissance". Penguin Publishing Group. p. 53.

256. Six Essays from the Book of Commentaries on Euclid, https://www.wdl.org/en/item/7465/

257. Sicker, Martin. 2000. "The Islamic World in Ascendancy: From the Arab Conquests to the Siege of Vienna". Westport, Connecticut: Praeger.

258. James Raven, "Introduction: The Resonances of Loss, in Lost Libraries: The Destruction of Great Book Collections since Antiquity", ed. James Raven (New York: Palgrave Macmillan, 2004), p. 11.

259. Marozzi, Justin, "Tamerlane: Sword of Islam, conqueror of the world". HarperCollins, 2004.

260. Imperial Gazetteer of India: Provincial Series, Volume 22, Superintendent of Government Printing, 1908, Great Britain Imperial gazetteer of India: provincial series

261. J.J. Saunders, "The history of the Mongol conquests", Routledge & Kegan Paul Ltd., 1971, p. 174.

262. Forbes Manz, Beatrice (April 1998). "Temür and the Problem of a Conqueror's Legacy". Journal of the Royal Asiatic Society. Third. 8 (1): 21–41. doi:10.1017/S1356186300016412. JSTOR 25183464.

263. *Beatrice F. Manz (2000). "Tīmūr Lang". Encyclopaedia of Islam. Vol. 10 (2nd ed.). Brill.*

264. Lane-Poole, Stanley, The Story of the Nations: Mediaval India under Mohammedan Rule, GP Putnam's Sons, New York 1903 pp. 156-158

265. "Al-Ḥallāj Islamic mystic". Encyclopedia Britannica.

266. Bashir, Shahzad (2012). "Fazlallah Astarabadi and the Hurufis". Oneworld Publications. p. 34.

267. Lentz, Thomas W.; Lowry, Glenn D. (1989). "Timur & Princely Vision". Smithsonian. p. 80.

❑

CHAPTER

6

HISTORICAL CENTERS OF EXCELLENCE AND LEARNING

Who destroyed the oldest university of the world – Huns or Alexander?
How many major (known) universities were there in India?
How were the Indian centers of learning destroyed?
What is the fate of one of the oldest centers for excellence in ancient India – Sharada Peeth?
How was the last class of Nalanda?
Where was the great grammarian Panini born?
What is the origin of the term Zen?
What was the unique method of test for graduating students at Mithila University?
Who introduced zero, negative numbers, and the positional number system?
Which university competed with Nalanda?

Dating of Indian Historical Events

There is a great new debate about many of the dates and timelines of Indian history which Western scholars propagated. Unlike Egypt, Indian texts such as Puranas, along with recorded genealogy of many important dynasties and astronomical records related to the position of celestial bodies connected to many important events, have been ignored for a long. Some scholars like Raja Ram Mohan Roy (not to be confused with the historical figure from the 18th century), and Dr. Subhash Kak are bringing their scientific background to challenge the dating of some of these historical events, which seem to be off by several hundred years.

The current chronology of Indian history is based on two key base factors. First, the Greek accounts tell that Sandrokottos, contemporary of Alexander, was the same as Chandragupta Maurya. The second one has to do with Emperor Devānāmpriya Priyadarśī Ashoka. Some researchers like Raja Ram Mohan Roy suspect that Sandrokottos is Gupta king Chandragupta I, not Chandragupta of the Maurya dynasty. A new analysis of these texts reveals that most likely Devānāmpriya Priyadarśī was Kumargupta I of the Gupta dynasty. If this is accepted, then the entire chronology of Indian history from Buddha to Alexander's period will require re-writing. According to this proposition, the Vikrama Samvat calendar was instituted to commemorate the death of Emperor Yaśodharmā Vishṇuvardhana Vikramāditya in 57 BCE.[1]

According to Subhash Kak, Indian history can be traced back to at least 150 generations.[2] Various dynasties in Magadha (an ancient kingdom in modern Bihar) alone had more than 100 generations/kings listed. He also noted that India's earliest calendar system, called *Saptarsi,* is still used in India, and the beginning of the current cycle started in 3076 BCE.[3]

This book does not have the scope to discuss and dispute the historical timeline, and commonly accepted dates are used in most cases. Another critical point to be noted, as we will see in a later chapter, Hindu, Buddha, Jain, and Sikh – all are part of the more extraordinary Indic tradition and civilization. Each is a limb of India's perennial heritage, and the terms such as Buddhism, Sikhism, etc., are discussed separately in some places in this book for contextual purposes only.

Centers of Excellence and Learning

Foreign invaders and the Islamic rulers not only plundered and destroyed thousands of temples and treasures, but they also destroyed many of the world's most ancient and essential places of learning across India, including the great University of Taxila (now in Pakistan) and Nalanda. Very few people even remember many other great universities[4][5] such as *Sharada Peeth (now in Pakistan Occupied Kashmir), Varanasi, Kanchipuram (Tamil Nadu), Vallabhpur (Gujarat), Vikramshila, Telhara, and Odantapuri in Bihar, Somapura in West Bengal, Bikrampur and Jagaddala (now in Bangladesh), Lalitgiri, Pushpagiri and Ratnagiri in (Odisha), Avantikpuri in Ujjain.* People flocked to these places from all over the world, including the Arabs, Greeks, Persians, and Chinese people, to learn Mathematics, Astronomy, Ayurveda, Metallurgy, among some of the critical subjects along with philosophy.

India has been a knowledge society for many millennia. We have read in the Upanishads and Jataka stories how various scholars studied at the ancient universities. Svetaketu was a noted scholar of Varanasi, which was a renowned center of learning. He later went to learn at the famous Takshasila University. Svetaketu had traveled all over India and met with 500 ascetics in a village, teaching various subjects.[6][7] Princess of Mithila also are said to have studied at Takshasila.[8]

How was the educational system and the infrastructure then? Much of the education and training of *adhyatma* (spiritual science), arts, social sciences, language, grammar, logic, weaponry, and numerous material sciences, technology, chemistry, sculpture, ayurveda, etc., were imparted in a Gurukul model. Each gurukul size differed significantly. Most of these gurukuls were located in the villages within a natural setting. There was another model where an entire city was full of gurukulas, and where general and specialized subjects were taught. Varanasi was such a center of learning, as well as

Kanchipuram. Many of these centers were attached to a temple complex. For example, Kanchi is known as the *ghatikasthanam*, or "place of learning".[9] During the "Golden Period" of Indian history, for about 500 years between the 4th and 8th centuries, under the patronage of the Gupta emperors, Harshavardhan and their descendants, India witnessed the rise of numerous educational institutes, including Nalanda. These gave rise to various knowledge sectors, including science, mathematics, astronomy, metallurgy, and various *adhyatmic* sciences.

Apart from Takshashila and Sharda, the two oldest, and Nalanda, the largest and longest-serving one, there were numerous other learning institutes across India. Invaders and the Islamic rulers destroyed multiple ancient and vital places of learning, universities, and libraries. As a result, once the architect of most pillars of our current civilization, India slowly weakened. By the end of Islamic rule in the 18th century, very few of these institutes remained. Some of the educational traditions survived in the form of *pathasalas* and *'tols'* or small academic centers that ensured a high literacy rate until the British arrived. But the original innovation, which was the hallmark of Indian genius, was mostly ceased.

According to the *Encyclopedia of Britannica*:

"These were the main developments in education before the Muslim invasions, beginning in the 10th century. Nearly every village had its schoolmaster, who was supported by local contributions. The Hindu schools of learning, known as *pathasala*s in western India and *tols* in Bengal, were conducted by Brahman *acarya*s at their residence. Each imparted instruction in an advanced branch of learning and had a student enrollment of not more than 30.

Larger or smaller establishments, specially endowed by rajas and other donors to promote learning, also grew in number. The usual learning centers were either the king's capital, such as Kanauj, Dhar, Mithila, or Ujjayini, or a holy place, such as Varanasi, Ayodhya, Kanchi, or Nasik. In addition to Buddhist viharas (monasteries), Hindu residential *mathas* and temple colleges rose in different parts of the country. There were also *agrahara* villages, which were given in charity to the colonies of learned Brahmans to enable them to discharge their scriptural duties, including teaching."[10]

Later, the British replaced the entire system with a corrupt form of India's old system.[11] The purpose was to create 'loyal clerks' to support the imperial and colonial administration in the country. But when they realized that they needed native engineers and doctors, mainly for their welfare, they established several modern Western model institutes.[12]

We will now review some of the ancient institutes that were either destroyed by the invaders or ruined due to lack of patronage and support from rulers (the Hindu kings were replaced by the Muslim ones, who won't support these institutes – Vallabhi is an example of that). Some of these universities were interlinked or had multiple campuses. Nalanda had a few other contemporary and sometimes competing institutes such as Vikramshila, Odantapuri, and Kanchipuram. Odissa's Pushpagiri had several branches, including Ratnagiri and Udaygiri.

It can be noted that these centers of learning had many unique contributions and specialties. Takshasila was well-known for education in the military sciences and also had a medical institute. Nalanda was famous for the number of manuscripts and books in its immense library. Kashi-Varanasi and Mithila excelled in Nyaya, whereas Vikramshila was well-known for Tantra. Navadwip specialized in Hetuvidya, or logic, and Tarka or debate.

Even after India's British conquest, the remnants of her excellent education system were still found all over the country. According to F. E. Keay, India had "a widespread, popular, indigenous system. It was not confined to one or two provinces, but in various parts of India, though some districts were more advanced than others."[13]

He also noted: "In Benares, Ward found 83 *mathas* and 1371 pupils. The average number of pupils to each teacher was 16 or 17. Some of these schools studied the Veda, some only grammar, some studied poetry, some the Vedanta, some logic and law, and some astronomy. Ward also listed schools at Nadia and Calcutta and mentions many other places where Sanskrit schools existed."[14]

Much research is needed to discover many more such lost centers of excellence throughout India. Rudimentary evidence is found about Multan, Tirhut, and Thatta (400 students) in Sindh. The subjects of the study included theology, philosophy, and politics. Multan was famous for the study of astronomy, astrology, mathematics, and medicine. Sirhind in Punjab was recognized for its school of Ayurvedic medicine from where doctors went to many parts of India.

Because of numerous great centers of learning, India excelled in every possible field for centuries. After these individual schools ceased to exist, India's leadership in all these fields and trade and manufacturing fell to the ground. The Europeans took over in the form of the industrial revolution.

We now introduce a list of such known great centers of excellence throughout India.

1. Sharada Peeth, POK Kashmir

Apart from being a prominent sacred Shaivite region, Kashmir is also famous for Sharada, another name for the Devi of Knowledge, Saraswati. Kashmir is also called Sharda Desh. Sharada Stotram, believed to be originated at this very place, is chanted by Hindus all over the world to date:

नमस्ते शारदादेवि कश्मीर पुरवासिनि ।
त्वामहम् प्रार्थये नित्यं विध्य दानञ्च देहिमे ॥

Namaste sharada devi Kashmira puravaasini |
twamaham prarthate nityam vidya danancha dehime||

Meaning: Namaste-Salutations; sharada devi-Goddess of wisdom; Kashmira puravasini-one who abides in Kashmira;

twamaham prarthate nityam- I pray to you every day; vidya danancha dehime-bestow me with wisdom.

In the picturesque mountainous region of Kashmir (currently occupied by Pakistan), just 80 miles northwest of Srinagar (6 miles from the LOC), Sharada is a beautiful town on the banks of the Neelam and Kishenganga rivers. There lies the millennia-old Sharada Peetham, one of the eight Maha Shakti Peeth (center of Shaktism). Sharada was one of the most prominent temple universities in India. It was famous for its library, where scholars worldwide traveled long distances to study specific texts not found anywhere. Sharada Script is said to have originated here and became popular in North India.

According to some, the site is at least 5000 years old.[15] The temple complex existed as early as the 4th century CE and around mid 8th century during King Lalitaditya's reign.[16]

Sri Gyan Atish Dipankar (982–1054 CE) is worshiped in Tibet and China as an *Avatar*.[17] Most likely, he was born in Bikrampur in current Bangladesh. He studied at the famous Vikramshila University in Magadha, Bihar. He moved to Tibet. Later his disciple, known as a 'Mahaguru' Lochen Rinchen Zangpo (958–1055 CE), visited the Sharada Peeth. He is credited with building more than 100 monasteries in Tibet and Tabo in Spiti,[18] Poo in Kinnaur in Himachal Pradesh, and Rinchenling monastery in Nepal. Lonchen visited Sharada Peeth around the 7th century CE. Buddhist scholar Thonmi Sambhota has visited and perhaps learned at the Sharada Peeth and created the Tibetan alphabet.[19] Alternatively, Kumarajiva (344–413 CE) is credited with the creation of the Tibetan script. His father, Kumarayana, was a Kashmiri scholar who traveled to Tibet and China to preach Bodhi dharma, and his mother was of Chinese origin.

Sharada or Saraswati is also associated with Buddhist practices, and numerous Buddhist scholars and pilgrims visited the Peeth. Bodhi dharma was prevalent in Kashmir between the 3rd and the 8th century. Some of the famous people who visited and stayed at the Peeth include Adi Shankaracharya. Vaishnava saint Swami Ramanuja's commentary on Brahma sutras, *Sri Bhasya,* was composed here. Historian Kalhana Pandit who in his 12th-century epic, *Rajatarangini,* respectfully talks about Sharada Peeth:

"There, the goddess Saraswati herself is seen in the form of a swan in a lake [situated] on the summit of the Bheda hill, which is sanctified by the Ganga source.

When visiting the goddess Sharada, one reaches at once the river Madhumati and [the river of] Saraswat worshipped by poets."[20]

Sharada Peeth was one of Asia's most significant learning seats for centuries and turned into ruins during the Islamic rule started by Sikandar Butshikan from 1389 CE till 1413 CE. His original name was Sikandar Shah Miri and later came to be known as Sikandar Butshikan, meaning "Sikandar the Iconoclast". He created the office of *Sheikh-ul-Islam* (scholars of the Islamic sciences) and established strict Sharia law for all inhabitants under his rule. He converted many Hindus and Buddhists into Islam through brutal torture and imposed the Jizya Tax on non-Muslims, payable annual tax of four tolas of silver.[21] Butshikan also banned any form of arts and aesthetics, including dance, drama, and music. Hindus could not wear tika or tilak on their forehead – no prayers, no conch shell, or mandir bells could be heard in his regime. If these tyrannies are not enough, crying over dead bodies and cremation were banned.[22] He invited several 'Sufis', including Mir Muhammad, the advisor to Sikandar, for advising and implementing his brutal Islamic laws.

Well-known Kashmiri chronicler and Sanskrit poet Jonaraja composed *Dvitīyā Rājataraṅginī* , which is believed to be the continuation of Kalhana's Rajatrangini. In *Dvitīyā Rājataraṅginī*, Jonaraja documented how Islam arose in the Kashmir valley. He wrote:

"The good fortune of the subjects left them and the king forgot his kingly duties and took delight, day and night, in breaking images.[23]

The temple was destroyed [by Sikander]. Sikander burnt all books the same wise as fire burns hay. All the scintillating works faced destruction in the same manner that lotus flowers face with the onset of frosty winter."[24]

Long after, Maharaja Gulab Singh Jamwal (1792–1857), the founder of the royal Dogra dynasty, the princely state of Jammu and Kashmir, restored the temple complex. But in 1947, Pakistani forces occupied it and continue to remain in the POK to date. One may conclude that the Sharada Peeth, which was the epitome of a knowledge society of Indian civilization, fell under the Islamic brutality, and India's further decline hastened. It is hoped that someday in the near future, Sharada Peeth will become an integral part of India again, and it is only a matter of time.

2. Kashi-Varanasi, Uttar Pradesh

Varanasi, also known as Kashi and Benaras, has been India's spiritual capital since time immemorial. The temple city has been a great center of learning, and seekers and scholars from all over the world flocked here both for spiritual solace and for learning various subjects.[25] Many compared the city to an 'Assembly-Hall' of scholars. It is unknown whether there were any large building complexes like some other universities, but it is clear that in almost every other house, there was a *gurukula.* Education was imparted in *Guru-Shishya* tradition. A teacher could have between 4 and 15 students, and some students spent 10 to 12 years in the *gurukulas* to learn specialized subjects. Education of Sanskrit and various *shastras*, including the Vedas, was prevalent here. Subject matters such as *darshanas,* Ayurveda, *jyotisha,* geography, grammar, logic, etc., were taught here. Starting from Bakhtiyar Khilji around 1194 CE, there was massive destruction of the temples and institutes of learning.[26] Many of the scholars were either killed or driven out of the area. By the 16th century, after the death of Aurangzeb, Varanasi regained its glory as a center of elite Sanskrit institutions, and many scholars who had moved out of Varanasi, especially to the south, started to return. Students from all over the subcontinent started to come again to Varanasi for higher learning.

Xuanzang visited Varanasi in 635 CE. He wrote this about the city: "is densely populated. The families are wealthy, and in the dwellings are objects of rare value. The disposition of the people is soft and humane, and they are earnestly given to study ... The climate is soft, the crops abundant, the [fruit] trees flourishing, and the underwood thick in every place."[27] He estimated that the city had about 100 temples with 3,000 priests, who mostly honoured Shiva – one of whose statues he saw as "full of grandeur and majesty".

Persian scholar, Abu Rayhan al-Biruni, visited India in 1017 CE and wrote about it as the leading center of the "Hindu sciences". He wrote: "The Hindus have some places which are venerated for reasons connected with their law and religion, e.g., Benares (Varanasi). They want to live there to the end of their lives, that their reward after death should be the better for it. They say that a murderer is held responsible for his crime and punished with a punishment due to his guilt, except in case he enters the city of Benares, where he obtains pardon."[28]

While it was still recovering from these severe setbacks, another big wave of attacks came during the rule of Aurangzeb, who destroyed the famous Kashi Viswanath temple and built a mosque (Gyanvapi) atop it.[29]

Edwin Greaves writes, "At the back of the mosque and in continuation of it are some broken remains of what was probably the old Vishwanath Temple. It must have been a right noble building; there is nothing finer in architecture in the whole city than this scrap. A few pillars inside the mosque appeared to be very old also."[30]

After the death of Aurangzeb in 1707 CE and the Mughal dynasty's rapid fall, Varanasi found its soul back with support from various kings.

Great saints like Kabir and Tulsidas, Guru Nanak, and Sri Chaitanya came to Varanasi to learn and spread their teachings. A good example of great scholars who came to Varanasi and spread their knowledge is Vaman Pandit. Vaman Pandit (1608–1695), originally from Bijapur, Karnataka, a contemporary of Maharaj Shivaji, came to Varanasi and studied for 12 years.[31] He was a Krishna devotee who studied *Srimad Bhagavatam* and composed a commentary on the *Bhagavad Gita* called *Yatharth Deepika*. Later, Pandit traveled to different parts of India and settled at Koregaon in Satara District, Maharashtra. He met with Samartha Ramdas and Tukaram, two well-known saints of the Maharashtra Bhakti movement, significantly impacting his life.[32]

Francois Bernier, a French physician, and traveler came to India in the mid 17th century. He became a personal physician to Mughal Prince Dara Shikoh, the eldest son of Shah Jahan, and traveled to many places in India. He called Varanasi "the Athens of the East" for its giddy confluence of ideas. In his book *Travels in the Mughal Empire*, he wrote: "The town of Benares, seated on the Ganges, in a beautiful situation, and amid a wonderful and rich country, may be considered the public school of the Gentiles. It is the Athens of India, whither resort the Brakmens (brahmins) and other devotees, who apply their minds to study. The town contains no colleges or regular classes, as in our universities, but resembles rather the schools of the ancients; the masters being dispersed over different parts of the town in private houses, and principally in the gardens of the suburbs, which the rich merchants permit them to occupy."[33]

3. Ujjayani or Avantikapuri, Madhya Pradesh

During the Mahabharat period, Sandipani Muni came to Ujjain, then called Avanti, after leaving Kashi, and founded the 'Sandipani Ashram', which soon became a great seat of learning during the Mahabharata period, and maybe even earlier. Maharshi Sandipani was the Guru of Sri Krishna and Balaram and their friend Sudama. Krishna and Balaram learned many subjects so quickly that the sage thought, 'he was educating the Sun and the Moon'. The story does not end here. After the completion of their scheduled studies, Krishna requested the sage what *'gurudakshina'* he wanted. The sage said that his son was lost in the ocean and asked if Krishna could bring him back. They went to a place called Prabhaas in Gujarat and found out that a demon called *Shankhasur* (who lived in a *shankh*, or conch shell) had kept the sage's son hostage in a place in the ocean. Krishna and Balaram picked up the whole conch and took it to Yamaraj, who blew into it, and the sage's son came out of it. As the sage got his son back, Krishna kept the conch, which is the famous *panchjanya,* in his hand.

The legendary emperor of India, Chandragupta II, also known as *Vikramaditya*, founded his Mauryan dynasty and the kingdom Magadha around the 4th century BCE in Avanti or Ujjain. It has been one of the holiest cities of the Hindus, Buddhists, and Jains – as par with Varanasi, Prayag, and Kanchi. Avanti was one of the world's most beautiful and wealthy cities ever. Since the time of Vikramaditya, it was a major seat of learning for spirituality, culture, Sanskrit literature, and science, including geography and astronomy. Vikramaditya's 'Nine Jewels' or nine great scholars who attended the court are of great stature in Indian and world history, including the famous poet Kalidasa. Ujjain was marked as the first meridian of longitude for the Indian geographers.[34]

As the tradition of scientific culture continued, in the 6th and 7th centuries, Ujjain became a significant center of mathematical and astronomical research. Some of the most famous mathematicians and astronomers used to work there.

There is a considerable dispute on the age of Chandragupta,

Ashoka, and Varahamihira. Based on astronomical and other evidence, the dates may need to be pushed back by 700 years.

Varahamihira (commonly proposed date: 505 CE – 587 CE) composed his seminal work, the *Brihat Samhita*, an encyclopedic composition that covered a whole array of topics like planetary motions, eclipses, timekeeping, season change, cloud formation, rainfall, agriculture, mathematics, architecture, temples, astrology, gemology, perfume making to name a few. He did not take original credit for many of his discoveries; rather, he suggested that some of the ideas he propagated in his work were just a summary of earlier existing literature on astronomy and *Shilpa Shastras*.[35] He was the first to discover many trigonometric formulas. Many believe that he might have introduced the zodiac signs, predicted calculations for auspicious ceremonies, and astrological computations.[36] It is also a possibility that the so-called Qutab Minar was one of his observatories along with 27 temples as research centers next to it.

Brahmagupta (598 CE – 668 CE), the great mathematician and astronomer, in his *Brāhmasphuṭasiddhānta* introduced zero, negative numbers, and the positional number system, which later went to Europe via Arab scholars. His famous work, the *Brāhmasphuṭasiddhānta* (literal meaning: "correctly established doctrine of Brahma"), was published in 628 CE, is a theoretical treatise. Belgian-American historian George Alfred Sarton is considered the founder of the history of science as an independent field of study. George Sarton thought Brahmagupta was "one of the greatest scientists of his race and the greatest of his time."[37]

Bhaskaracharya, or Bhaskara II (1114 CE–1185 CE), was the greatest mathematician of medieval India and was also an astronomer. His four-part work *Siddhānta-Śiromani,* ("Crown of Treatises"), especially *Lilavati,* broke new ground in many mathematical areas. Ujjain was famous for astronomical observatories, and he was the head of an observatory there. His book's four sections dealt with arithmetic, algebra, the planets' mathematics, and spheres, respectively.

It is presently an accepted fact that Bhāskaracarya's work on calculus predates Newton and Leibniz by about five centuries.[38] He is also credited with discovering differential calculus principles and their application to astronomical problems and computations. According to Susantha Goonatilake, strong evidence suggests that Bhāskara II was a pioneer in some differential calculus principles. Perhaps he was the first mathematician to conceive the differential coefficient and differential calculus.[39]

Sadly, this great seat of learning and tradition of mathematics, astronomy, and science was destroyed by Muslim ruler Iltutmish in 1235 CE; many temples, observatories, and learning institutes were systematically destroyed.[40] Ujjain had a very similar fate to other major universities, which were destroyed by Turkic Muslim invader Muḥammad Bakhtiyar Khalji just a few decades earlier.[41]

4. Kanchipuram, Tamil Nadu

Kanchi was the capital of the Pallava dynasty's kingdom between 275 CE to 897 CE, and via the patronage of the kings, education, arts, and sciences flourished.

Modern-day Kanchi Puram or Kanchi is a temple city in Tamilnadu, located on the Vegavathy riverbanks, about 45 miles from Tamil Nadu's capital, Chennai. Kanchi Puram means 'abode of Lord Brahma.' It has been a center of learning for many centuries apart from being a famous spiritual center for the Hindu, Jain, and Buddhist scholars. It was rightfully adorned as the *ghatikasthanam*, or "place of learning". In a way, Kanchi has a similar trait to Varanasi. Numerous small institutes flourished, specialising in different subject areas where the Buddhist monasteries offered Buddhist education. Later, Vedic education became more prominent during King

Mahendra Varman I, who made Sanskrit the kingdom's official language. It is believed that the Theraveda Buddhist ideas went to Myanmar and Thailand from the Buddhist institutions in Kanchi. Kanchi was known as the 'Kashi of South'.[42]

Acharya Bodhidharma is said to have spread the Zen or Mahayana Buddist tradition. Chan means dhyana or meditation in Chinese, *dhyan* in Sanskrit, and Zen is a distortion of that. In Tibet, he is described as a 'dark-skinned *siddha* from South India'.

At the Varadharaja Perumal Temple, Kanchipuram, the tradition is that the murthy of the famous Lord Atthi Varadar (a form of Lord Vishnu) is immersed in a pond and is brought out of water for 40 days and put back into the pond for 40 years. Though it is unclear exactly why the murthy is immersed in a pond, locals think that the tradition was started to protect it from Muslim invaders. A similar incident happened at Kashi Vishwanath Temple, where the Shivalinga was thrown into a well to protect from Muslim attacks on the great temple on which Aurangzeb built a mosque (Gyanvapi) 1669 CE in its place.[43]

Pakṣilasvāmin Vātsyāyana (not the author of *Kama Sutra*), the author of *Nyāya Sutra Bhashya*, an important commentary on Gautama's *Nyaya Sutras,* is said to have been an Acharya at Kanchi.[44]

Some suggest that Chanakya or Kautilya also may have been born in Kanchi, though according to Jain legends, he was born in Chanaka village in Golla either in Gandhara or Orissa, And Buddhist legends suggest his birthplace was Takshashila. Xuanzang came to Kanchi in 642 CE and noted that almost all major sects of Indian tradition were part of the education system, including the Vaishnavas, Shivas, Digambara Jains, and Mahayana Buddhists. In about 100 Viharas, there were about 10000 residential students and teachers.[45]

It appears no significant foreign attacks happened here, or it is possible that the attacks were successfully repulsed. Kanchi never ceased to be a great center of learning, even today.

5. Manyakheta, Karnataka

Located on the Kagina riverbanks, Malkheda or Malkhed is a town in Karnataka which was initially known as Manyakheta or "Mannakheḍa" in Prakrit. During the 9th-10th century, it was the capital of the Rashtrakuta dynasty. This ancient center of learning became famous during the rule of King Amoghavarsha I. He wrote one of the earliest Kannada classical, *Kavirajamarga*. During this time, he and scholars such as mathematician Mahaviracharya, Ajitasenacharya, Gunabhadracharya, and Jinasenacharya helped spread the Jaina tradition.

Later in the 13th century, seer and scholar Madhavacharya, born near Udupi, became a very prominent personality. He called his philosophy *Tattvavada* which means "arguments from a realist viewpoint". Later it became known as the *Dvaita Vedanta*. He and his disciples established numerous *mathas*, including Udupi Sri Krishna Math, to propagate his *Dvaita Vedanta*.

Sri Jayatirtha or Teekacharya was a great seer, dialectician, polemicist, and one of the most eminent scholars in Dvaita Vedanta's history, next to Madhavacharya. He headed the Madhavacharya Peetha around the middle of the 14th century. He is a respected seer of the *Dvaita darshan* along with Madhavacharya and Vyasatirtha. *Nyaya Sudha*, an essential commentary of Jayatirtha on Madhavacharya's famous text *Anuvyakhyana* is considered a commentary on the *"Brahma Sutras"*.

Malkhed is the Madhavacharya Peetha, which has two *mathas* or ancient institutes – Shri Uttaradi Matha and the Jain Bhattaraka Matha.[46] Shri Uttaradi Matha was established to propagate the Dvaita Vedanta philosophy along with learning other subjects. This matha has been instrumental as a learning center of the Vedas, Sanskrit literature, Madhava tradition, and several satellite institutions in Southern India. The matha also has been the host of a library that preserved many important Sanskrit manuscripts.[47]

The Jain Bhattaraka Matha, along with the 9th century impressive temple of Neminath, hosted the murthys of 24 Tirthankaras and Nandishwar Dvipa. Also, it is said that there is a famous *panchdhatu* (five metals) shrine with 96 murthys. In the Digambara Jain tradition, the head of a Jain institute is called a Bhattaraka, whose primary duties apart from managing and running the matha include training scholars, maintaining libraries, managing endowments, and presiding over installation ceremonies.

Among the various *Puranas, Maha Purana* (also called *Adi Purana* and *Uttara Purana*) is said to have been composed in this matha by Acharya Jinasena and his disciple Gunabhadra in the 9th century. It was also a significant learning center where *Gaṇitasārasaṅgraha,* one of the earliest Indian texts entirely devoted to mathematics, was composed by Mahaviracharya around 850 CE. This work was on par with Aryabhatta's *Arya-siddhanta* in 499 CE and Brahmagupta's *Brāhmasphuṭasiddhānta* in 628 CE. He is said to have separated astrology from pure mathematics. He used a specific form of Algebra and helped to develop various Algebraic problem-solving techniques. Modern-day mathematicians give him credit for the introduction of mathematical terminologies to describe concepts like an equilateral and isosceles triangle, rhombus, circle, and semicircle. He is credited with having discovered algebraic formulations like $a^3 = a(a + b)(a - b) + b^2(a - b) + b^3$. He also discovered the ${}^nC_r$ formula, which goes as: $[n(n - 1)(n - 2) \ldots (n - r + 1)] / [r(r - 1)(r - 2) \ldots 2 * 1]$ and devised a formula that approximated the area and perimeters of ellipses and found methods to calculate the square of a number and cube roots of a number. He also concluded that the square root of a negative number does not exist.[48]

6. Odantapura, Bihar

The Pala (Pala means 'protector') dynasty ruled large parts of India between the 8th and 12th centuries. Emperor Gopala established the Pala kingdom in the splendid capital city of Gaur in Bengal in 750 CE. The Palas were patrons of the Mahayana and Tantric schools of Bodhi Dharma. The most famous emperor of the dynasty was Dharmapala. He established several new cities along with numerous centers of excellence and learning. Along with Gaur, during this period, they found and turned a few existing towns such as Vikrampura, Pataliputra, Monghyr in Bihar, and Ramvati (Varendra), Tamralipta, and Jaggadala, in Bengal, very prosperous.

Odantapura or Odantapuri, also called Uddanapura,[49] was an ancient complex of learning, a Buddhist Mahavihara. It is located in Bihar Sharif in the Nalanda District of Bihar. Pala emperor Gopala established this in the 7th century in Magadha.

According to the Tibetan records, including *Kalachakra Tantra*, there were about 12,000 students[50] at Odantapuri, situated at a mountain called Hiranya Prabhat Parvat and by the bank of the river Panchanan. Students from across the globe came here, including the Arabs, and studied various subjects, including Mathematics, Astronomy, Ayurveda, Metallurgy, and Vedic and Buddhist scriptures. According to the same Tibetan source, during the reign of King Rāmapāla, a thousand monks belonging to both Hinayana and Mahayana traditions lived in Odantapuri, and occasionally over twelve thousand monks congregated there.

Nearly 400 years after it was established, it was destroyed in 1193 CE by the same Muslim invader Bhakhtiyar Khilji as were Nalanda and Vikramshila Universities.

7. Vikramshila, Bihar

About 50 kilometers east of Bhagalpur in Bihar (historically Magadha), Vikramshila University was established on a hill near the banks of Ganga in the late 8th century by Emperor Dharmapala, son of Gopala, who established the Odantapuri Vihara. It was in proximity of the Nalanda University and, in a way, competed with the same. Though it was smaller in size, it was very famous in its heyday. There were approximately 1000 students and about 100 teachers. It was most famous for the Tantrika Buddhist system's learning center where Sri Gyan Atisa Dipankara studied before he went to Tibet and established the 'Sarma' tradition, thus reviving the declining Bodhi Dharma there.[51]

The university complex was spread over one hundred acres of land. Six college buildings surrounded a large building at the Vigyan Bhawan center, and all were connected via six gates. [45]

Subjects studied here ranged from Sanskrit grammar, Logic, Metaphysics, Philosophy to Tantra Shastra. Some believe (based on the accounts of Tibetan pilgrim monks) that it was at Vikramshila where the tradition of awarding degrees and formal recognition with titles first started. Honorary titles like *'Pandit' and 'Mahapandit'* were granted on the basis of merit to those who completed their education with distinction. Even the portraits of famous alumni were painted on the walls of the University. It also had great libraries full of ancient texts.

There were 108 scholars appointed as Acharyas and the custodians of the University and temples.[52]

The center spread knowledge to the world for over four centuries. Bakhtiyar Khilji, the same barbarian who destroyed Nalanda and Odantapuri, also destroyed Vikramshila University in 1203 CE after killing thousands of monks and students.

8. Somapura, Bengal

Emperor Dharmapala set up Somapura in the 7th century CE, which was established on 27 acres of land as a primary learning center in the eastern part of the subcontinent. In addition to Buddhist and Hindu scriptures, Jain studies were an important subject here. Located in Paharpur in the Naogaon district of Bangladesh, Somapura was connected with Nalanda. It is said to have influenced Buddhist architecture as far away as Cambodia.[53]

The Somapura Mahavihara remained the main center of learning in this region for nearly four centuries before being abandoned in the 12th century following repeated attacks and was burnt to the ground in the 11th century by plunderers.[54]

9. Bikrampur, Bengal

Until very recently, in 2013, the existence of this great center of learning was hidden; remains of the Bikrampur University were excavated at Munshiganj, presently in Bangladesh. Emperor Dharmapala also established it in the late 7th or early 8th century.

This University was also flocked by students from all over India and beyond, from China, Tibet, Nepal, and Thailand. The center taught a wide range of subjects with particular importance to Buddhist education. It may have attracted around 8000 students. It is not clear how it was ruined, but it is very much possible that the Pala dynasty's patronage ended after the end of their rule. Multiple attacks by Muslim iconoclasts may also have caused decline and destruction.

10. Jagaddala, Bengal

The successors of Emperors Gopala and Dharmapala of the Pala dynasty continued their patronage for educational institutes throughout India. Emperor Rampala established the city of Ranavati on the banks of Ganga. He created the monastic Jagaddala Vihara in the early 11th century in Varendrabhumi in North Bengal, now in Bangladesh. According to some Tibetan sources, Jagaddala was one of the five great ancient universities along with Nalanda, Odantapuri, Vikramshila, and Somapura. It is also noted that these five ancient universities had a network alliance under state administration and were interlinked. It is said: "all of them were under state supervision" and there existed "a system of co-ordination among them ... it seems from the evidence that the different seats of Buddhist learning that functioned in eastern India under the Pāla were regarded together as forming a network, an interlinked group of institutions."[55]

The subjects which were taught at Jagaddala included Sanskrit and Vajrayana Buddhist scriptures. Notable scholars were Dansheel and Bibhuti Chandra, who were also well versed in the Tibetan language.[56] Many Tibetan sacred books were either composed or copied from this University by Tibetan and Chinese students and pilgrims. One of the oldest anthologies of Sanskrit verses, called *Subhāṣitaratnakoṣa*, is believed to have been compiled by Vidyakara, a Buddhist scholar at this University. After remaining a major learning center for a century, it was thought to be overrun by the Muslim plunderers around 1207.

According to Sukumar Dutt, "The ruins of the temple and monasteries at Pāhārpur do not bear any evident marks of large-scale destruction. The downfall of the establishment, by desertion or destruction, must have been sometime amid the widespread unrest and displacement of population consequent on the Muslim invasion."[57]

The list of educational institutes presented here is far from a complete list of ancient Indian universities. Dharmapala alone is said to have established around fifty Maha vihara or mega learning centres across his kingdom.[58] Many of them are lost in history, and some are being discovered recently, like Bikrampur.

11. Vallabhi, Gujarat

Bhatraka, the Gupta empire's military general in India's western part, Saurashtra, also the Governor, established the Maitrika Dynasty around 475 CE. This empire lasted for nearly 300 years, and their capital was Vallabhpur or Vallabhi, near modern-day Bhavnagar in Gujarat. The world-famous Vallabhi University was established by the Maitrikas, set up in line with Nalanda. The Kings were the chief patron of the center as well as the libraries for several generations. It was an important center of Buddhist learning, especially the Hinayana branch and Vedic sciences, between 600 CE and 1200 CE. Many non-spiritual subjects taught at the University included Nīti (Political Science, Statesmanship), Vārtā (Business, Agriculture), Administration, Law, Economics, Accountancy, Ayurveda (Medical Sciences), Book-keeping, Literature, Vyakaran (Grammar) and had a large library.[59][60]

Chinese traveler and pilgrim Xuanzang visited Vallabhi in the 7th century and noted that more than 6000 students were studying there. Yijing, towards the end of the century, described Vallabhi as 'at par with the Buddhist monastic center Nalanda'.

Arab Tajjikas invaded Saurashtra in 776 CE. According to King Agguka I of the Saindhava dynasty's inscription, after losing the battle, Tajjikas retreated. Perhaps because of repeated attacks, the Maitraka dynasty weakened and finally ended by 783 CE. Hence the patronage of Vallabhi University dried up, which caused a significant setback in running the institute. However, the educational activities continued in a limited way for a few hundred more years until the 12th century.

12. Vidyapeeth or Nagarjunakonda (Vijayapuri), Andhra Pradesh

Famous Buddhist philosopher Nāgārjuna, renowned for his contributions in *'Rasayana'* shastra (Alchemy or Chemical Sciences) and metallurgy, lived around 150–250 CE. According to some accounts, Nāgārjuna, originally from some other part of southern India, was the Guru of Satavahana king Yajña Śrī Śātakarṇi and was appointed the Chancellor of Nalanda University.

Nagarjuna Vidyapeeth was established on the Krishna riverbanks near Vijaywada, Andhra Pradesh, and was named after this great personality of ancient Asia. The University reached its peak in the 7th century. Its great library was housed on the five-story building's top floor had an enormous collection of Buddhist philosophy, geography, botany, metallurgy, various sciences, and medicine.[61]

It attracted scholars from various parts of the country, who were originally from other ancient Indian universities and even scholars from other countries, like China, Burma, and Ceylon. It is unknown how this magnificent institute came to an end.

13. Kanthalloor Shala, Kerala

Kerala or Chera-land has a great cultural and educational history. Chera or Aye kings ruled the region between the 9th and 12th centuries. The state also flourished in educational prowess. There was a great temple university at Valiyasalai near Thiruvananthapuram in Kerala between the 9th and 12th centuries CE. The Kanthalloor Shala was a famous Vedic residential center of learning. It was called the 'Nalanda of South'.[62] Students and scholars from all over India and Sri Lanka came here. The center offered a vast array of subjects; it is believed that over 64 subjects were taught here, including the Vedas, Jyotish, Chemistry, Goldsmithy, Medicine, Weaponry, Music, dance, drama, and Nastika philosophy.[63] There were four halls within the temple-university complex: Palaya Sala, Arya Sala, Valiya Sala, and Chinna Sala. There are places in the region with the same names, which indicates that it was a well-distributed center. It was a unique institute for training in weaponry. There was an arsenal center that produced many great warriors[64] as a military academy. A strict educational and disciplinary code was enforced here.[65]

It is not very clear how the center stopped functioning after the 12th century. One theory says that the conflict between Chola and Chera kings drew attention to the weaponry program and was destroyed by the Chola kings to weaken the Aye kings.

14. Telhara, Bihar

Just 33 kilometers away from the famous Nalanda University complex, there was an even older educational institute in

Telhara, Bihar. The site is also known by a few other names, e.g., 'Tilas-akiya' or 'Tiladhak'. Though long forgotten and discovered very recently after Nalanda and Vikramshila, Telhara was famous for higher education and research. Some evidence indicates that it was much older than Nalanda.[66] At some point in history, each competed to woo the best students and scholars from around the world.

Archaeologists found clay evidence dating back to the Kushana period. According to Vedveer Arya, the Kushana empire flourished between the 12th to 8th century BCE (common history suggests the period was between 30 CE and 375 CE).[67] If this is true, then Telhara University is over 3000 years old.

Xuanzang wrote about a three-storeyed structure, prayer hall, and a platform to seat over 1,000 monks and students following the Mahayana Buddhist sect and was also a center for Tantric Buddhism. Here is Xuanzang's description of Telhara. "…Telhara or Tilas-akiya as containing several monasteries or viharas, about seven in number, accommodating about 1,000 monks studying in Mahayana. These buildings had courtyards, three-storeyed pavilions, towers, and gates crowned by cupolas with hanging bells. The doors and windows, pillars and beams have base relieves (sculptures in gilded copper). In the middle vihara is a statue of Tara Bodhisatva and to the right (is) one of Avlokiteshwar".[68]

According to the Director of Archaeology, Department of Art and Culture (Bihar), Atul Kumar Verma, "Since the excavations suggest that Telhara might have been a contemporary of Nalanda, it is quite possible that it was either an independent university for specialised education or that students graduating from Nalanda University would come here for specialised study."[69]

The University was set on fire by Bakhtiyar Khilji after killing the residents at the campus. This barbaric act was committed during the same period when his army destroyed Nalanda University, i.e., between 1193 CE–1203 CE.

15. Pushpagiri, Odisha

In the ancient kingdom of Kalinga, modern-day Odisha, Kelua River flows northeast of the Pushpagiri hill (mountain of flowers) along with the other three hillsides – Lalitgiri, Ratnagiri, and Udaygiri, creating a picturesque heavenly setting. The Pushpagiri University for higher learning was established here in the 3rd century[70] and was spread over three campuses on three hills known as the 'diamond triangle of Odisha'.

The University may have been established by Emperor Ashoka, which lasted for about 800 years. Some believe that it was established in the first century BCE and older than Nalanda. Some even think it was built even earlier (a stone iconographic analysis indicates that Lalitgiri had already been established during the Sunga period in the 2nd century BCE). The vihara complex is compared with other great universities such as Nalanda, Vikramshila, Odantapuri, Takshashila, and Vallabhi. The architecture here is similar to the Gupta period and resembles that of Gandhar and Mathura.

Chinese traveler Xuanzang visited the center in 639 CE. He noted that Pushpagiri was an important Buddhist site in ancient India. Xuanzang wrote:

"In the south-west of the country was the Pu-sie-p'o-k'i-li (Pushpagiri) monastery in a mountain; the stone top of this monastery exhibited supernatural lights and other miracles, sunshades placed by worshippers on it between the dome and the amalaka (the notched stone disk, usually with ridges on the rim, that sits on the top of a Hindu temple's shikhara or main tower) *remained there like needles held by a magnet."*[71]

Some believe that prominent Tantrik Buddhist scholar Rahula probably studied at Pushpagiri and later became the Chancellor of Nalanda University around the early 9th century.[72]

When Muslim invaders attacked Nalanda, Vikramshila, and other centers, killed students and monk teachers, thousands of them fled to different parts of the world, including Tibet, Nepal,

Bhutan, and Odisha. They are said to have taken shelter in places like Jagaddalavihar Mahayana center and other monasteries.

In 1202 AD, the Chancellor of Vikramshila University, Sribhadra, also took shelter in Odisha. Muslim attacks were repulsed in Odisha till the 16th century due to strong resistance by great warriors.[73]

Lack of patronage caused the decline, and subsequently, Muslim invasions destroyed this great University.

16. Mithila, Bihar

The *Ramayana*-famed Janaka dynasty was established in the Mithila region. The concept of *Rajarshi*, meaning the king with *'rishi'* qualities, is exemplified by King Janaka, father of Sita. King Janaka Vaideha was very knowledgeable about many different subjects and a great philosopher. Kuru-Panchala was said to be a great center of learning. He organized a conference and invited all the prominent learned people of that era from that region. An award was announced for the best scholar who would receive one thousand cows with horns plated in gold. While this conference was on, Yajnavalka drove away all the Brahmins but had to face the great scholars like Uddalaka, Aruni, Ashvaḷa, and Gargi Vachasnavi, a great woman scholar in debates. Yajnavalka, with his knowledge and skill, defeated all of them.[74] Such was the spirit and tradition of India's education system.

Varanasi-Kashi, Prayag, Ujjain, and Mithila were great centers of learning from ancient times. It is said that Mithila University was as old as the *Ramayana* from the time of King Janaka. While there is not much archaeological evidence of the *Ramayana* period in general, the legend is that various subjects, including the Vedas, Upanishads, Nyaya, Tarka Shastra (Logic). etc., were taught here. For centuries, Buddhist thoughts influenced the establishment and subject matters at various universities in India. Around the 12th century, Mithila got prominence again when the Buddhist influence waned and Vedic knowledge reemerged. A robust *gurukula* system formed the basis of Mithila's education system.[75]

Great mathematician, philosopher, and author of *Tattva Chintamani*, Gangesha Upadhyaya's school of New Logic (*Navya-Nyaya*) was well renowned[76] and further enriched by scholars Vardhamana, Pakshadhara Misra, and others. Poet Vidyapati also hailed from Mithila, whose Maithili songs and *Padavali* have influenced generations of poets, including the Vaishnava poets of Bengal.[77] Vidyapati's student Raghunandanadasa Raya was also a well-known logician. He went around the country for a very successful intellectual debate conquest (*digvijaya*). Another great personality from Mithila was Vachaspati Misra, around the mid-15th century.

Earlier in India, famous personalities like Kanad (6th century BCE), Akṣapāda Gautama, Kapil, and Jamini introduced Vaisiseka, Nyaya, Sankhya, and Mimamsa darshanas. Mithila became a renowned center for Nyaya and Mimamsa. Great scholars such as Vachaspati, Prabhakara, Mandana, Kumarila, and Udayana were also from Mithila.

Unlike any other historic place of learning, Mithila had a unique method of testing the students required for graduation, called *Shalaka Pariksha*. It was described as: 'A needle was pierced in the book, and the student was asked to explain the page where the needle stopped'. It possibly meant a random test of an entire book.[78]

17. Morena Golden Triangle University, Madhya Pradesh

Within the Chambal River valley of Madhya Pradesh, there is a temple complex called Bateswar. Legend says at the nearby Bateswar temple, the rays and shades of the sun were used for specific calculations of time and other astronomical measurements. At the Bateswar temple complex, 200 small temples were dedicated to Shiva, Vishnu, and Shakti and were the center of the 'Golden Triangle University'. According to German scholar Gerd Mevissen, the temple complex was believed to have been built by the Gurjara-Pratihara kings. Bateswar was once a hub for temple-related arts and artists.[79] The Gurjara-Pratihara kings who ruled India around the mid-8th to the 11th century were mighty and for a long time contained Islamic invaders moving east of the Sindhu River. Nagabhata I defeated the Muslim armies of Junaid and Tamin during the Caliphate regimes in Arabia.

The temple complex was in total ruins. A good number of these temples were restored by the Archeological Society of India (ASI), led by K.K. Mohammed, Regional Director (North) of the ASI. The unique feature of this learning center was temple architecture and arts. These temples were a fusion of different building styles, and it is suggested that the 'artists and students fused and experimented with a variety of temple building ideas'.[80]

The *Kachchhapaghata* royal family was a Rajput dynasty of the Chambal-Gwalior region in Madhya Pradesh that came into existence after the Gurjara-Pratiharas' downfall. Towards the end of the 10th century, these kings became powerful and were great builders and architects.

In the district of Morena, in a village called Mitaoli (Mitavali), there was a famous temple complex called the Chausath (meaning the number 64) Yogini temple, located 40 kilometers from Gwalior.[81] An inscription was discovered from this temple dated to 1323 CE revealing that the temple complex was built by the Kachchhapaghata king Devapala (1055–1075 C.E). It also noted that the temple was a well-known center for providing education in various subjects, including astronomy and mathematics based on the movements of the sun. Three adjacent temples Mitavali, Padavali, and Bateswar in Morena, formed a Golden Triangle within which an excellent center for learning was established between the 8th and 12th centuries. Padavali temple complex was massive, where a large number of students and teachers were accommodated.

18. Nadia, Bengal

Mithila University's rule was that no student could take out or copy or even translate any books from the library. Basudev Sarvabhauma (1430–1540 CE), a multi-talented scholar from Navadwip, went to study Tarka Shastra at Mithila. His teacher was Mithila's famous scholar Pakshadhar Mishra. After the completion of his studies at Mithila, he got the title *Sarvabhauma*. *Tattva-chintamani* was one particular book related to the subject of Naya. Basudev memorized the whole book and part of another book named *Nyaya Kusumanjali* and headed for Nadia for further studies in Nyaya. But he had worries about his safety while going to Nadia and instead went to Kashi and studied Vedanta. Later he came to Nadia and established the Academy of New Logic there.[82] The famous philosopher of Nadia, Narahari Visharad was his father, who was also his teacher and became an expert in the *'navya naya'*. Mahaprabhu Sri Chaitanya was the disciple of Basudev. He was the court scholar of King Purushottam and Prataprudradev, the kings of Utkal (Odisha). Famous logician Raghunath Siromoni was his disciple as well.

The Sena (Sen) dynasty ruled Bengal from 1070 CE to 1230 CE. Originally called Navadwip, the city of Nadia is located at the confluence of the Ganga and Jalangi rivers in West Bengal. Nadia was the capital town of Laxman Sena (1178–1206 CE). Many teachers and students fled in different directions after the destruction of universities like Nalanda, Odantapur, and Vikramshila. Many may have also settled in a relatively safer location like Nadia in Bengal, accounting for its academic excellence in the 13th century. There were three primary centers at Navadwip, Santipur, and Gopal Para. Around the end of the

15th century, many famous schools were flourishing in Nadia. Some examples include Basudev Sarbabhouma's Nadia School of Philosophy, Raghunandan's Smriti school, Krishnananda Agamvagisa's school of Tantrism, and Ramrudra Vidyanidhi's school. Famous Indian philosopher and logician of the 15th century, Raghunatha Shiromani, had set up his school of logic here. For five centuries, Navadwip was referred to as *"Oxford of East"*.[83] These educational centers in Nadia were very much active till the end of the 18th century.[84]

In a way, Nadia became a substitute for all the universities destroyed in North India, including the Mithila University. Raghunandan, an eminent contemporary jurist, established a Chair of Smriti. Krishnananda Agamvagisa established the School of Tantrika Studies. Ramarudra Vidyanidhi headed the Chair of Astronomy and authored *Jyotisha-sara-samagraha*. Gadadhar Bhattacharya was called the 'prince of Indian Logicians', and his works are called *Gadadhari*.

During Raja Rudra's reign (1683–1694 CE), the total number of students at Nadia was 4000 and 600 teachers.[85] As the grand Indian tradition of learning was by asking questions and via debates since the Upanishadic times, Nadia followed the same. The teaching was deeply enriched by two teachers openly debating, and students engaged in various subjects.

Nyaya, Vyakaran, Politics, and Law were the main subjects among numerous others. Many students studied here for as long as 20 years. The University has produced many scholars, including poet Jaideva, who composed *Geeta Govinda,* poet Umapati Dhar, Law-giver Sulapani, and Gadadhar Bhattacharya (17th century) post-Shiromani Nyaya philosopher.

British missionary P. E. Keay observed the following about education at Nadia (1918): "At Nadia, the chief study is logic, but law and grammar are also taught. Rational discussions are frequently held, and the student's ambition is to gain success at one of these discussions held at a festival, and by adroit and hair-splitting arguments to silence his opponent."[86] Professor Cowell, who visited the schools at Nadia in 1867, said, "I could not help looking at these unpretending lecture-halls with deep interest, as I thought of the pandits lecturing there across generations of eager, curious minds. Seated on the floor with his 'corona' of pupils around him, the teacher expounds on those refinements of infinitesimal logic which make a European's brain dizzy to think of, but whose labyrinth a trained Nadia student will thread with unfaltering precision. I noticed during my visit middle-aged and even grey-haired men among the students."[87]

These excellent institutes produced and stored knowledge of multitudes of subjects and had carried them forward for centuries. The destruction of Taxila, Nalanda, and all other universities brought a significant decline in India's thought leadership and technological advancement. And as the British education system was introduced, replacing Indian traditional ones, the country slowly moved away from much of its own knowledge and teachings. The Western way of learning, thinking, and expressing became a norm, as is the case today.

The Silk Road Down South

Before we proceed further down history, let us look back a millennium at India's northwest part, where the Sindhu Civilization finds its origin. The Sindhu river originating in the Tibetan Plateau near the Kailash Lake, Manas Sarovar, flows through western Tibet, Ladakh, Gilgit, and Baltistan in India, and through Pakistan and down to the south to meet the Arabian Sea. It was part of the greater river belt noted in the Rigveda as Sapta Sindhu and the Zoroastrian Avesta as Hapta Hindu or land of "seven rivers". The famed kingdom of Gandhara, mentioned in the *Mahabharata,* was located in this region, Kandahar in Afghanistan.

The Silk Road was a trading network that started from China, moving through India while branching out in the east to Korea and Japan and the west to Persia, Arabia, Africa, East Africa, Egypt, and Europe between the 2nd century BCE and the 18th century CE.[88][89][90]

Much of these routes were on land, some had challenging roads, and some were through sea routes, especially the Arabian Sea, Indian Ocean, Persian Gulf, Red Sea, and the Mediterranean Sea. Most people refer to the land route as the Silk Road.[91][92]

One critical junction of this route fell in the northwest part of India. In India, it was known as the 'Uttrapatha' or the 'northern route'.

One of Tibet's westernmost cities was Kashgar, where the borders of China, Afghanistan, Kyrgyzstan, Tajikistan, and Pakistan coincide. The city was a critical post between China, West, and South Asia for almost 2000 years during the Silk Route existence. Several hundred miles south, there was a seaport called Barbarikon by the Greeks near present-day Karachi, Pakistan, near the Sindhu River's mouth.

The entire route was around various rivers flowing south, and the main one was Sindhu. A new tourism project is being developed between China and Pakistan to make this route a major tourist attraction, and China may have other ulterior motives as well.[93]

Once the journey goes down south in the route after the dangerous mountain ranges come to Gilgit, Baltistan, and the beautiful Chitral region, it finally ends in the Swat Valley. If one follows the Sindhu River here, about 60 miles west of the river's western side, there existed this beautiful city of Purushhapura or modern-day Peshawar. In the Gandhara Plains in the Valley of Peshawar, this city was in existence around the 5th century BCE.

According to Al-Masudi, the Arab historian and geographer, by the mid-10th century, the city was known as Parashāwar. And Al Biruni called it Purshawar[94] or Purushavar. Some suggest that the other origin of the name could be the Sanskrit name Poshapura for "The city of Flowers", found in an ancient Kharosthi inscription.[95]

Another theory holds its current name as a derivative of the Persian for "frontier town" or, more literally, "forward city". However, transcription errors and linguistic shifts may account for the city's new name. One theory suggests that the name is adopted from the Persian "Pesh Awardan",[96] meaning "place of first arrival" or "frontier city," as it was the first city in the Indian subcontinent after crossing the Khyber Pass.

This region was the birthplace of celebrated philologist and author of *Astadhaya*, the Sanskrit grammar of Panini around the 4th century BCE.

19. Takṣaśilā or Taxila, Pakistan

About a hundred miles east of Peshawar, after crossing the Sindhu River, Takdhu Ri was situated. According to Arial Glucklich, Takshashila was one of the oldest cities in the entire sub-continent.[97]

Takṣaśilā was a renowned ancient city in the western part of the Indian subcontinent standing between India and Central Asia. The Greeks called it Taxila. The meaning of the name is "City of Cut Stone." It was located in the current Punjab province of Pakistan, about 20 miles northwest of Islamabad. According to some historians, the city's known history goes back to at least 1000 BCE.[98]

The *Ramayana,*[99] *Mahabharata,*[100] *Shatapatha Brahmana,*[101] *Vayu Purana*, and even Panini's *Astadhyayi* [102] have mentions of Taxila. Buddhist and Jain literature also have honored the city. This can take the date back to 3600 BCE. When the trade via the Silk Road almost vanished, the city's importance and prosperity diminished. Western historians claim that the nomadic Huns destroyed the city and the University in the 5th century.[103]

The most important legacy was the University of Taxila, the world's first known real university with global connectivity. Established at least as early as the 10th century BCE,[104][105] and after almost 500 years, it gave the light of knowledge to the whole world before it was destroyed between the 4th and 5th century CE.

Thousands of students from across the world studied here.[106] The students were mostly from the elite and rich economic backgrounds, though everybody was welcome. Some of the most notable personalities who studied there are Indian luminaries such as Atreya, Pasenadi, Mahali, Patanjali, Jivaka, Charaka, Panini, Kautilya (Chanakya), and Prasenjita.[107][108][109]

Some students paid up to 1000 coins in advance to receive education[110] at Takshila University.

How the university came to an end is a matter of speculation. Based on scanty evidence, John Marshal declared that it was destroyed around 499 BCE by the White Huns. However, it is hard to find any revealing evidence from the Chinese, Persian, Indian texts supporting this hypothesis.

Marshall described that: *'the hordes of Ephthalites or White Huns which swept over Gandhara and the Panjab in the third quarter of the fifth century, carrying ruin and desolation wherever they went'*. And what was the compelling proof? *'Thirty-two coins, all of them silver, leave no room for doubt. It was the White Huns who were responsible for the wholesale destruction of the Buddhist sangharamas of Taxila ... several skeletons of those who fell in the fight, including one of White Hun, were lying.'*[111]

Almost all contemporary historians followed Marshal though there is enough room to dispute and discard the theory that the Huns hated Buddhism and that they would destroy such an excellent institute because of that.

On the other hand, Kurt Behrendet suggested:

"Although the exact relationship between the Buddhist communities of the Peshawar basin and the new Hun dynasty

is not entirely clear, there is considerable evidence to suggest that Buddhism continued under Hun rule ... (there is) textual evidence to show that Chinese Buddhist pilgrims continued to visit Gandharan sites in the Peshawar Basin into the early sixth century CE; the Bhamala main stupa can be compared to the 7th to 8th-century cruciform stupas in Kashmir, Afghanistan, and other parts of Central Asia."[112]

So, who really destroyed the university? Could it be 'Great' Alexander? It would be hard for Western historians, especially the Greek enthusiasts, to accuse Alexander of that horrible act.

When Alexander reached Indian soil, his main task was to find alliances through fearmongering tactics or bribery so that he did not have to 'fight'.[113] Typically, the famous conquerors fought to win lands. He met the King of Taxila Raja Ambhi. He found out that the king was mighty, and it would not be an easy battle with him. He paid 1000 *'talents'*[114] and gifted *'a wardrobe of Persian robes, gold and silver ornaments, and 30 horses, 1000 talents in cash'*.[115] It was pure bribery for alliance and not obeisance.

Alexander realized that the 'Brahmins' were key to the success of Indian society and the institutes. In *'The City of Brahmans'*, Greek historians wrote that Alexander massacred an estimated 8000-10,000 of these non-combatant Brahmins.[116][117] His question-answer sessions with the 10 Indian Brahmin prisoners (called Gymnosophists by the Greeks), related by Plutarch, show Alexander asking stupid questions – at sea, completely lost.[118]

Most Indian historians have forgotten that Alexander had earned an epithet for his killings and mayhems of the Indians, especially the unarmed Brahmins: *"...assigned* (to) *him by the Brahmins of India, The Mighty Murderer."* [119]

Were these Brahmins the ones who were massacred at the University of Taxila? Most likely. Perhaps the center was not completely destroyed but severely damaged. Thus, the entire Indian civilization was fractured by this big blow from the Greeks.

So why was John Marshal not honest enough? Because he was *"interested in Alexander's campaign and Graeco-Buddhist monuments at Sanchi and Taxila."* Marshal, who was *"filled with enthusiasm for anything Greek"* and also knew *that "at Taxila Alexander the Great halted and refreshed his army before advancing to do battle with Porus."* [120] So, was it an attempt by Marshal to whitewash this part of this Greek shame?[121]

20. Nalanda, Bihar

The whole world knows about the destruction of the Library of Alexandria. Yet, it is oblivious to one of the most outstanding Universities and library infrastructures in the world, the Nalanda Mahavihara. Nalanda, located in the Indian state of Bihar, was India's second-oldest University after Takshila, the ruins of which are currently in Pakistan. But how old is Nalanda?

According to legends, Jain Tirthankara Mahavira spent 'fourteen rainy seasons at Nalanda', and Gautama Buddha and some of his key disciples also may have given sermons at Pavarika, a mango grove in Nalanda village.[122][123] Though archaeological evidence is sparse, if these legends are to be accepted, Nalanda existed long before the current university structure, perhaps around the 5th–6th century BCE. Some recent archaeological discoveries suggest that Nalanda may have existed even around 1200 BCE. Carbon-dating of one of the stupas points to the 5th or 6th century BCE.[124]

We can trace back Nalanda's history to the Gupta period (319 CE to 543 CE). The actual dates of these periods are disputed by some Indologists (Raja Ram Mohan Roy et al.) A seal of Gupta emperor *Śakrāditya* or Kumaragupta is found here, which may designate him as the founder of Nalanda.[125]

For at least 800 years, this great center of learning distributed knowledge to the whole world. It was not just a Buddhist or Hindu seminary – here, students studied fine arts, mathematics, astronomy, politics, logic, literature and medicine, and the art of war.[126] The great astronomer and mathematician Aryabhatta was said to have headed the university at some point. Students from across the globe – from Korea, Japan, Persia, Tibet, China, and even Greece came and studied here. It was spread over 14 acres of land with three distinct buildings for the world's grandest library during its era. Nalanda had three large multi-storeyed buildings and was called the Ratnasagara (Ocean of Jewels), the Ratnadadhi (Sea of Jewels), and the Ratnaranjaka (Jewel-adorned). Ratnodadhi was supposed to be nine storied high, and the most sacred and rarest manuscripts were stored there.[127]

The library had between several hundred thousand [128] and nine million manuscripts on multitude of subjects based on various claims. It was in itself a wonder what the classification scheme and borrowing methods were! These manuscripts were the most valuable treasures of a knowledge society, collected and retained for centuries. The University accommodated over 10,000 students and 2,000 teachers [129] and was considered an architectural masterpiece.

The entire University, along with its library, was burnt down by Turkish Islamist raider Bakhtiyar Khilji and his barbaric soldiers in 1193 CE. Bakhtiyar Khilji was a commander in Awadh. Some years later, the Persian historian, Minhaj-i-Siraj recorded Khilji's acts in his book *Tabaqat-i Nasiri*.

Minhaj-i-Siraj wrote:

"*Muhammad-i-Bakht-yar, by the force of his intrepidity, threw himself into the postern of the gateway of the place, and they captured the fortress and acquired great booty. The greater number of the inhabitants of that place were Brahmans, and the whole of those Brahmans had their heads shaven, and they were all slain. There were a great number of books there, and, when all these books came under the observation of the Musalmans, they summoned a number of Hindus that they might give them information respecting the import of those books; but the whole of the Hindus had been killed. On becoming acquainted [with the contents of those books], it was found that the whole of that fortress and city was a college, and in the Hindui tongue, they call a college Bihar.*"[130]

It is said that the libraries and the other buildings burnt, and smoke from the burning manuscripts hung for days 'like a dark pall over the low hills.'[131]

The world lost a treasure house of knowledge preserved for over a millennium. There was a flood of blood everywhere. The unarmed and non-violent teachers and students were all butchered by the Islamic hordes. Perhaps it was the most fateful day for the Hindus and India. The advancement in various fields, material, and inner sciences came to a sudden halt, and the entire civilization faced the millennium's biggest crisis.

What is even more shocking is that the invading monsters burnt down many more libraries throughout India. The NeoCols did a careful cover-up – rarely any history book talks about these losses. Later we will find out how these historians are still busy covering up these stories, including Nalanda University and Somnath temple. Numerous Tibetan and Chinese seekers have visited Nalanda for centuries. Before Nalanda's demise, some original works were either copied or taken to Tibet by pilgrims and students. However, even after the great tragedy, attraction to one of India's most venerable places at that time did not stop for a long time.

The Last Class at Nalanda

Buddhist Monk *Dharmasvamin* visited Nalanda[132] almost 40 years after Nalanda's great fire and destruction. Passing through the ruins of the Mahavihara, he finally entered inside of some still-functioning area. He then was in awe to see that an old teacher, nearly ninety years old, was teaching to a small group of students, and it was a class of Sanskrit grammar. The life of

Rahula Shribhadra was somehow saved from Khilji's tyrants, and he was secretly given shelter by a local Brahmin named Jayadeva, and the visiting monk *Dharmasvamin* became his student. But one day, someone warned them that over 300 Turkic tyrants were about to attack the village. Upon hearing this, the class was adjourned, and Dharmasvamin carried his teacher to a secret hiding place. When the raid was over – the blood of the beheaded students was flowing down. The old teacher told Dharmasvamin that he had taught everything he knew, and that he should head back to his home Tibet. Shaken and extremely saddened, Dharma packed a bundle of books, as much as he could carry along with his little belongings under his bright orange robe. Dharma touched the Guru's feet for the last time and, with a heavy heart, took off for his journey back. He was looking back many times to see that Rahula Shribhadra was in meditation. Nobody knows for sure for how long!

Historical documents tell that when the Tibetan translator Chag Lotsawa (Chag Lo-tsa-ba, 1197–1264) visited the site in 1235 CE, he found it damaged and looted, with a 90-year-old teacher, Rahula Shribhadra, instructing a class of about 70 students. During Chag Lotsawa's time, Turkish soldiers had an incursion that caused the remaining students to flee.[133]

Certain Marxian historical accounts, namely by Radhagovinda Basak (1967) in *The History of North-Eastern India Extending from the Foundation of the Gupta Empire to the Rise of the Pala Dynasty of Bengal (c. AD 320-760)* referred to a text belonging to the 12th century which mentions that Shashanka had destroyed some Buddhist stupas in Bengal and Bihar and was an oppressor of Buddhism.[134] Around the 7th century CE, Shashanka was also accused of cutting the legendary Bodhi tree of Bodh Gaya. However, historian Ramesh Chandra Majumdar contested these alleged acts of Shashanka. He said that the accusations were doubtful and most likely false because they were written centuries after the alleged events. [135] It is "unsafe to accept the statements recorded in this book as historical".[136] Also, except for that one text, this alleged event was not found in any other historical documents. It is an excellent example of an effort to whitewash atrocities of the invaders perpetrated on the Indian civilization to justify and cover up Islamic destructions.

References

1. Raja Ram Mohan Roy (2015), "India Before Alexander: A New Chronology", Amazon Digital Services LLC - KDP Print USA.
2. Subhash Kak, "The Mahabharata and the Sindhu-Sarasvati Tradition". https://www.ece.lsu.edu/kak/MahabharataII.pdf
3. Buddhike Sri Harsha Indrasena (2015).The Saptarishis Calendar: 'The Indian Tropical Zodiac', Journal of Astronomical History and Heritage 18(2):190–198, The World Academy of Medical Leadership.
4. https://www.postcard.news/how-these-ten-great-universities-of-india-were-destroyed-by-islamic-invaders/amp/
5. https://wikiislam.net/wiki/Educational_Institutions_Destroyed_by_Muslims
6. Satapath Brahman 11, 6.3.1.
7. Brihadaranyak Upanishad Ch. 3 I.1.
8. Volume 3 Jataka, Story 377.
9. K.V. Raman (1975). "Sri Varadarajaswami Temple, Kanchi: A Study of Its History, Art and Architecture". New Delhi: Abhinav Publications.
10. Education In Classical Cultures, Ancient India https://www.britannica.com/topic/education/Education-in-classical-cultures
11. Kalyani Tripathy Dubey & Akhilesh Arvind Nimje (2015), "A Study of Critical Comparative Analysis of Ancient Indian Education and Present Education System".

International Journal of Advance Research In Science And Engineering.

12. "The tormented Indian Spirit – Redemption or Regression. Ravi Kumar", Nivedita, B., 2016. Bharathi, IIT Madras. 1(1).
13. F.E. Keay, "Ancient Indian Education: An Inquiry Into Its Origin, Development, and Ideals", 1920, p. 154.
14. William Ward (1811). "A View of the History, Literature, and Religion of the Hindoos"
15. Nazki, Ayaz Rasool (2009), International Seminar: Society, Culture and Politics in the Karakoram Himalayas, Sher-i-Kashmir University of Agricultural Sciences
16. Rashid, Salman (April 1 2018). "Heritage: Goddess of the Mountains". Dawn. https://www.dawn.com/news/1398483/heritage-goddess-of-the-mountains
17. An imagination of Bikrampur Buddhist Vihara from the footprint of Atish Dipankar's travel. Ar. Sayed Ahmed Department of Architecture, Bangladesh University, Bangladesh. American Journal of Engineering Research (AJER) Volume-02, Issue 12, pp.276-295.
18. Rizvi, Janet. (1996). "Ladakh: Crossroads of High Asia". Second Revised Edition. Oxford University Press, p. 256.
19. R. A. Stein. (1972) "Tibetan Civilization", Stanford University Press. pp. 51, 58.
20. Kalhaṇa's Rājataraṅgiṇī. Vol. 3: a chronicle of the kings of Kaśmīr. 1. Kalhana, Stein, M. A. 2003. p. 182.
21. Kaw, K.; "Kashmir Education, Culture, and Science Society" (2004). Kashmir and Its People: Studies in the Evolution of Kashmiri Society. APH Publishing Corporation.
22. Hasan, Mohibbul (2005). "Kashmīr Under the Sultāns". Aakar Books. p. 59–95.
23. Baloch, N. A.; Rafiqi, A. Q. (1998), "The Regions of Sind, Baluchistan, Multan and Kashmir" (PDF), in M. S. Asimov;

C. E. Bosworth (eds.), History of Civilisations of Central Asia, Vol. IV, Part 1 — The age of achievement: AD 750 to the end of the fifteenth century — The historical, social and economic setting, UNESCO, p. 316.

24. "Khwãjah Nizamu'd-Dîn Ahmad bin Muhammad Muqîm al-Harbî: Tabqat-i-Akbarî" translated by B. De, Calcutta, 1973.
25. "Varanasi had been a seat of learning from time immemorial in Hindustan", Abul Fazl Allami, Ain-i-Akbari, trans. H. Blochmann. Volume 1 (1873; reprint Calcutta: The Asiatic Society of Bengal, 1993), and Abul Fazl Allami, Ain-i-Akbari, trans. H. S. Jarrett, Volume 2 (1891; reprint, Calcutta: The Asiatic Society, 1993).
26. Varanasi, Encyclopedia of Britannica.
27. "Land and the People India, Al-Biruni" - Abridged Edition of Dr Edward C. Sachau's English Translation Edited With Introduction and Notes by Qeyamuddin Ahmad National Book Trust, New Delhi, 1983. p. 234.
28. "History of India", Collected, Arranged and Edited by A. V. Williams Jackson. Volume 9 – Historical Accounts of India by Foreign Travellers Classic, Oriental, and Occidental, 1907. Chapter 4 – Al-Biruni's Arabic Account of the Hindu Religion, p. 199.
29. Akhil Bakshi (2004). "Between heaven and hell: travels through Sri Lanka, Bangladesh, Bhutan, Nepal, and India: An Account of the expedition hands across the borders". Odyssey Books.
30. Edwin Greaves, "Kashi the city illustrious, or Benares", 1909.
31. Jaquir Iqbal (October 2009). "Encyclopedic dictionary of Marathi literature". Global Vision Publishing House. p. 466.
32. S.G. Kanhere, "Waman Pandit - scholar and Marathi poet" Bulletin of the School of Oriental and African Studies, University of London v4, 1926, pp. 305-314.

33. "Travels in the Mughal Empire, 1656-1658", Humphrey Milford, Oxford University Press, London, Bombay, 1916. p. 334.
34. new world encyclopedia https://www.newworldencyclopedia.org/entry/Ujjain
35. Stella Kramrisch (1958), "Traditions of the Indian Craftsman", The Journal of American Folklore, Vol. 71, No. 281, Traditional India: Structure and Change (Jul. - Sep. 1958), pp. 224-230.
36. Sarma, K. V. (2008). "Varāhamihira". In Helaine Selin (ed.). Encyclopaedia of the History of Science, Technology, and Medicine in Non-Western Cultures. Dordrecht: Springer Netherlands. pp. 2184–2185.
37. Gupta, Radha Charan (2008), "Brahmagupta", in Selin, Helaine (ed.), Encyclopaedia of the History of Science, Technology, and Medicine in Non-Western Cultures, Springer, pp. 162–163.
38. Seal, Sir Brajendranath (1915), "The positive sciences of the ancient Hindus", Longmans, Green and co.
39. Goonatilake, Susantha (1999), "Toward a global science: mining civilisational knowledge", Indiana University Press.
40. Datta, Bimal Kumar "Libraries & Librarians Of Ancient and Medieval India", Atma Ram & Sons, 1960 p. 7.
41. André Wink (2002). "Al-Hind: The Slave Kings and the Islamic conquest, 11th–13th centuries". BRILL. pp. 146–148.
42. Gopal, Madan (1990). K.S. Gautam (ed.). "India through the ages". Publication Division, Ministry of Information and Broadcasting, Government of India.
43. Catherine B. Asher (September 24 1992). "Architecture of Mughal India". Cambridge University Press. pp. 278–279.
44. Sures Chandra Banerji. "A Companion to Sanskrit Literature". Motilal Banarsidass Pub., 1990, p. 104-105.

45. "History of education in India", N Jayapalan, Atlantic Publishers, New Delhi 2000, 2005. P.35
46. Jaina Studies NEWSLETTER OF THE CENTRE OF JAINA STUDIES, SOAS. University of London, March 2017. https://www.soas.ac.uk/jainastudies/newsletter/file119532.pdf A Rare Letter of a Bhaṭṭāraka of Malayādri Padmanabh S. Jaini, CoJS Newsletter, March 2017, Issue 12, pp. 28-33.
47. https://www.uttaradimath.org/origin
48. Puttaswamy, T.K (2012), "Mathematical Achievements of Pre-modern Indian Mathematicians", Newnes.
49. http://gyanpro.com/blog/great-universities-of-ancient-india/
50. https://www.britannica.com/topic/Odantapuri
51. Newman, Bruce (January 1 2004). "A Beginner's Guide to Tibetan Buddhism". Snow Lion Publications.
52. O. C. Handa, "Buddhist Western Himalaya: A politico-religious history", Indus Publishing, 2001, p. 337.
53. "A Past Glory of Buddhism: Ruins of the Buddhist Vihara at Paharpur" http://www.unesco.org/archives/multimedia/document-698
54. Dutt, Sukumar (1988) [First published 1962]. "Buddhist Monks and Monasteries of India: Their History and Their Contribution to Indian Culture". Delhi: Motilal Banarsidass. p. 376.
55. Ibid.
56. "History of Education in India", N. Jayapalan, Atlantic Publishers & Dist, 2005. p. 36.
57. Dutt, 1988.
58. Sailendra Nath Sen (1999) [First published 1988]. "Ancient Indian History and Civilization" (2nd ed.). New Age International. pp. 278–279.
59. D.G. Apte, Universities in Ancient India, Faculty

of Education and Psychology, Maharaj Siyajiraj University of Baroda. Cornell University Library https://www.rarebooksocietyofindia.org/book_archive/196174216674_10153420277166675.pdf

60. Prashant Ruperal, "Ancient Vallabhi University to be revived", *The Times of India*, September 24, 2017.
61. "Ancient universities of India: League of extraordinary lessons", *Utkal Today.* https://www.utkaltoday.com/ancient-universities-of-india/amp/
62. Sabloo Thomas, "Documentary on Kanthalloor Shala", *Deccan Chronicle,* Feb 8, 2018. https://www.deccanchronicle.com/lifestyle/viral-and-trending/080218/documentary-on-kanthalloor-shala.html
63. Aathira Haridas, "Kanthalloor Sala: The 1000-year-old university in Trivandrum you may not have heard of", 18 April 2018 https://www.edexlive.com/beinspired/2018/apr/18/kanthalloor-sala-the-1000-year-old-university-in-trivandrum-you-may-not-have-heard-of-2515.html
64. Virarajendra, "Medieval Chola Empire and it's relations with Kerala", July 2010. http://ponniyinselvan.in/forum/discussion/40927/medieval-chola-empire-and-its-relations-with-kerala/p1
65. "Chronicles of Kanthalloor Sala which got lost in the mists of time", New Indian Express, 17 April 2018 https://www.newindianexpress.com/cities/thiruvananthapuram/2018/apr/17/chronicles-of-kanthalloor-sala-which-got-lost-in-the-mists-of-time-1802832.html
66. "Telhara University's ruins older than Nalanda, Vikramshila", First Post, 14 December 2014. https://www.firstpost.com/fwire/telhara-universitys-ruins-older-than-nalanda-vikramshila-1849141.html
67. "The Chronology of Ancient India, A Victim of concoctions and distortions", Vedveer Arya. https://www.academia.edu/27780697/The_Chronology_of_Ancient_India_

Victim_of_Concoctions_and_Distortions_by_Vedveer_Arya

68. D. R. Patil. (1963) "The Antiquarian Remains in Bihar". K.P. Jayaswal Research Institute, Patna.
69. https://www.indianexpress.com/photos/picture-gallery-others/after-nalanda-and-vikramshila-bihar-unearths-telhara-university/lite/
70. Scott L. Montgomery; Alok Kumar (2015). "A History of Science in World Cultures: Voices of Knowledge". Routledge. p. 121.
71. Patra, Benudhar (2014), "Kalinga and China: A Study in Ancient Relations", Odisha Review, July 2014, pp. 46-50.
72. "Exploring Pushpagiri University of Ancient Odisha: Going Beyond the Eurocentric Knowledge System", Kamalakanta Roul, Odisha Review.
73. Ibid.
74. Brihadarnyaka Upanishad, Chapter 4, I 2-7.
75. "History of Mithila", Upendra Thakur, Darbhanga, 1988, p. 532-536). Eventually, the entire region of Mithila became a great university where students from all over India came to study.
76. Gangesha India Philosopher, Britannica https://www.britannica.com/biography/Gangesha
77. Vidyapati Indian writer and poet, Britannica https://www.britannica.com/biography/Vidyapati-Indian-writer-and-poet
78. "Education In Early Mithila: A Reappraisal", Bishwambhar Jha, Proceedings of the Indian History Congress Vol. 71 (2010-2011), pp. 160-164 Published By Indian History Congress.
79. Dietrich Boschung; Corinna Wessels-Mevissen (2012). "Figurations of Time in Asia". Wilhelm Fink. pp. 82–97.
80. Michael W. Meister (1976), "Construction and Conception:

Maṇḍapikā Shrines of Central India, East and West", Vol. 26, No. 3/4 (September - December 1976), pp. 415-417, context: 409-418

81. "Ekattarso Mahadeva Temple". Archaeological Survey of India, October 2017
82. "Ancient Universities of India from 3600 Plus Years Ago", My India My Glory https://www.myindiamyglory.com/2019/02/14/15-ancient-universities-of-india-from-3600-plus-years-ago/
83. Cotton, Sir Evan (1980). "Calcutta, Old and New: A Historical and Descriptive Handbook to the City". General Printers & Publishers. p. 1.
84. "Ancient Indian Education, An Inquiry Into Its Origin, Development, and Ideals", by F. E. Keay, Oxford University Press London Edinburgh Glasgow New York Toronto Melbourne Bombay "HumphreyY Milford 1918.
85. "Early Aryan to Swaraj – Volume-3, Indian Education and Rajputs", Editors Dr. S.R. Bakshi, Dr. S. Gajrani, Dr. Hari Singh, Sarup and Sons, New Delhi.
86. Keay (1918). p. 52
87. Simon Cowell, Quoted in Nadia Gazetteer, p. 182.
88. Jerry Bentley, "Old World Encounters: Cross-Cultural Contacts and Exchanges in Pre-Modern Times" (New York: Oxford University Press, 1993), P. 32.
89. Ulric Killion, "A Modern Chinese Journey to the West: Economic Globalisation And Dualism", (Nova Science Publishers: 2006), p. 66.
90. Xinru Liu, "The Silk Road in World History" (New York: Oxford University Press, 2010), p. 40.
91. Gan, Fuxi (2009). "Ancient Glass Research Along the Silk Road". Shanghai Institute of Optics and Fine Mechanics, Chinese Academy of Sciences (Ancient Glass Research along the Silk Road, World Scientific ed.). p. 41.

92. Silk Roads Programme, UNESCO https://en.unesco.org/silkroad/countries-alongside-silk-road-routes/republic-korea
93. Sheridan Prasso, "One of China's Most Ambitious Projects Becomes a Corridor to Nowhere", Bloomberg, 3 March 2020 https://www.bloomberg.com/news/features/2020-03-02/a-china-belt-and-road-project-becomes-a-corridor-to-nowhere
94. "al-Bīrūnī and the Political History of India", M. S. Khān.
95. Dani, Ahmad Hasan (1969). "Peshawar: Historic City of the Frontier". Khyber Mail Press.
96. Ibid.
97. "The Strides of Vishnu: Hindu Culture in Historical Perspective", By Ariel Glucklich Oxford Press 2008.
98. Raymond Allchin, Bridget Allchin, "The Rise of Civilisation in India". Cambridge University Press, 1982. p. 314.
99. Marshall, John. A guide to Taxila 1960.
100. Kosambi, Damodar Dharmanand (1975) [first published 1956]. "An Introduction to the Study of Indian History" (Revised Second ed.). Bombay: Popular Prakashan. p. 126.
101. Raychaudhuri, Hem Chandra (1923), "Political history of ancient India, from the accession of Parikshit to the extinction of the Gupta dynasty", pp. 17–18, 25–26.
102. Scharfe, Hartmut (2002). "Education in ancient India". Leiden [u.a.]: Brill.
103. Marshall, John (1951). "Taxila: Structural remains" – Volume 1. University Press.
104. Hartmut, 2002
105. Allchin, Bridget; Allchin, Raymond (1988). "The rise of civilisation in India and Pakistan". Cambridge University Press.
106. "Top 5 Oldest Universities around the World" https://www.

hellotravel.com/stories/top-5-oldest-universities-around-world

107. Gupta, Subhadra Sen (2009). "Ashoka". Penguin UK. p. 27.
108. Bakshi, S. R. (2005). "Early Aryans to Swaraj". Sarup & Sons. p. 47.
109. Schlichtmann, Klaus (2016). "A Peace History of India: From Ashoka Maurya to Mahatma Gandhi". Vij Books India Pvt Ltd. p. 29.
110. Lucien X. Polastron (2007), "Books on Fire: The Destruction of Libraries Throughout History", Inner Traditions, p. 107.
111. Taxila – an illustrated account of archaeological excavations" By Sir John Marshall (1940).
112. "The Buddhist architecture of Gandhāra" By Kurt A. Behrendt pp. 207-209.
113. "Alexander's Campaigns in Sind and Baluchistan and the Siege of the Brahmin", By Pierre Herman Leonard Eggermont p. 91.
114. Who's Who in the Age of Alexander the Great: Prosopography of Alexander's Empire Waldemar Heckel. Wiley 2006.
115. "Alexander the Great", Nigel Cawthorne, Haus Publishing 2004, p. 99.
116. "Alexander and the East: The Tragedy of Triumph", A.B. Bosworth Oxford University 1996 p. 95.
117. Ancient Siege Warfare Paul Bentley Kern, Indiana University Press, 1999, p. 231.
118. Greek history from Themistocles to Alexander, in a ser. of lives from Plutarch, revised and arranged by A.H. Clough, 1860.
119. "On the Practicability of an Invasion of British India: And the Commercial and Financial Prospects and Resources of the Empire", Sir George De Lacy Evans, p. 48 Publisher: JM Richardson, London.

120. "Taxila An Illustrated Account of Archaeological Excavations", Marshall John, Preface, Cambridge University 1951.

121. "Destruction of Takshashila – a defining moment" https://2ndlook.wordpress.com/2009/08/04/destruction-of-takshashila-a-defining-moment/

122. Hartmut, 2002.

123. Dutt, Sukumar (1962). "Buddhist Monks And Monasteries of India: Their History And Contribution To Indian Culture". London: George Allen and Unwin Ltd (Reprinted 1988).

124. Tewari, Rakesh (2016). "Excavation At Juafardih, District Nalanda". Archaelogical Survey of India. pp. 6–8.

125. Altekar, Anant Sadashiv (1965). "Education in Ancient India". Nand Kishore.

126. Bhatt, Rakesh Kumar (1995). "History and Development of Libraries in India", Mittal Publications.

127. Hartmut, 2002.

128. Khurshid, Anis (January 1972). "Growth of libraries in India". International Library Review.

129. Shreya Pareek, "The Ancient Indian University Which Is Taking Students Again After 800 Years!", The Better India, 2014 https://www.thebetterindia.com/13918/ancient-nalanda-university-reopens-monday-know-lesser-known-facts-great-university/amp/

130. Bibliotheca Indica, Part 1, "Tabaqat-i Nasiri". p. 552.

131. Ibid.

132. Chos-dar, Upasaka. "Biography of Dharmasvamin (Chag Lo Tsaba Chos-rje-dpal), a Tibetan Monk Pilgrim". Translated by George Roerich. Introduction by A.S. Altekar.

133. Steven Kossak; Jane Casey Singer, eds. (1998). "Sacred Visions: Early Paintings from Central Tibet". Metropolitan Museum of Art. p. 14.

134. Basak, Radhagovinda (1967). "The History of North-Eastern India Extending from the Foundation of the Gupta Empire to the Rise of the Pala Dynasty of Bengal (c. AD 320-760)". Sambodhi Publications. p. 155.

135. Majumdar, Ramesh Chandra (1943). "History of Bengal". University of Dacca

136. Ibid.

❑

CHAPTER

7

TURKIC-AFGHAN RULERS IN INDIA

How was Delhi named?
Who built the Red Fort and Qutub Minar?
For how many years did the Mughals actually rule Delhi?
What are the two most important and unfortunate deaths which changed the history of India?
What was India's share of world GDP before and after the British came to India?
Was Tipu Sultan a patriot or a fanatic Islamist?
Why is the Muslim population of Bengal proportionately higher than most parts of India?
Was Titumir a freedom fighter?

Oh Delhi

People today give a lot of importance to the great city of Delhi for multiple reasons; it is the capital of the largest democratic nation. The British moved their capital from Calcutta (Kolkata) to Delhi in 1911. During the medieval time, Delhi was vital for the Muslim rulers and not necessarily for the vast number of native Indians. Muslim Delhi never ruled India entirely; even Akbar and Aurangzeb did not. However, history textbooks sing the city's great glory to celebrate the slave Sultanates, the luxurious Mughals' romanticism, and Lutyen's architecture.

Today we are much familiar with the term 'Lutyen's Delhi', the New Delhi. The British moved its capital from Calcutta to Delhi, and one key reason was to stay far away from the revolutionary activities in Bengal against the British Raj. Edwin Lutyen (1869–1944) is credited with many architectural designs and buildings built during that period. He designed several bungalows for the Viceroy, the current Rashtrapati Bhavan. Another architect Herbert Baker designed the Government Secretariat Buildings (North and South Block), while Robert Tor Russell built the Connaught Place and the current Parliament building. Of course, for 46 years, Delhi was the center of colonial power who turned one of the wealthiest countries in the world into the poorest one by taking away much of its movable assets – all the planning done here by the looters to take as much as possible before leaving India. And then we have seen how Delhi has been the prime seat of the Congress-Raj, which became a dynastic rule until very recently, occupying some important land and buildings of Delhi by the family members.

How was Delhi before the arrival of the Turkic invaders and Turko-Mongol settlers? Why did the Turks come from far away to find Delhi as their center instead of Lahore, another beautiful city? It may be the case that the invaders could not occupy any other prosperous town in Rajasthan/Haryana or the South because of resistance from powerful kings. Due to King Prithviraj Chauhan's fall in 1192 CE, they could occupy a fine city built over centuries by the Rajputs from Rajasthan and Bundelkhand. The invaders found a dream city-state between Delhi and Agra with magnificent palaces and gardens, dams, and even reservoirs. What else did they need besides power and, more sadly, plenty of beautiful women snatched from their families to end up in their harems? After all, even Princess Jodha had to be gifted to Akbar by her father due to the Mughals' power of manipulation!

No matter what the NeoCol historians have to say, we are forced to question their assertions about the so-called Indo-Islamic architecture in the Delhi-Agra region for one simple reason: there are plenty of significant inconsistencies, and logic defies in many cases. Case in point, a good number of the magnificent 'Islamic' structures we see today in Delhi or Agra are most likely not built by the Muslim rulers and are usurped existing buildings upon their arrival. Yes, it is a very non-conventional bold assertion. The reason is that modern historians are yet to give good answers to many vital questions on the Delhi-Agra region's development in the medieval period.

Did Shah Jahan build the Red Fort? Historians tell us that it was built between 1632 and 1658. But what if any evidence shows that Red Fort was already there and used by Shah Jahan in 1632 itself? If the painting in the Bodleian Library, Oxford, showing Shah Jahan receiving visitors at the Diwan-I-Am in 1632, is authentic, it raises many questions.[1]

Also, most likely, the royal emblem of King Anangpal is found inside the Khas Mahal of Red Fort.[2] There are no Islamic inscriptions in the building. What does it indicate?

Was Lal Kot, the original main fort, known as Kila Pithora of Prithviraj, and what is called Lal Killa or Red Fort was only an extension?

Did Shah Jahan build Taj Mahal? When was it built? How much did it cost? Who were the architects? The answers may be sketchy. The primary source which almost all historians parrot about the story of Taj is *"Travels in India"* by J. B. Tavernier, a French jewel merchant who visited Agra in 1640. There are many inconsistencies in his information, such as no mention of the year when the 'construction' of the Taj was started, and there are no details found in Mughal documents about the planning and construction. Other accounts related to Taj that copied the same information are contradictory.

A Guidebook on Taj Mahal, which the Archeological Survey of India published in 1982 read: (Page 4) *"The site selected for the burial was an extremely pleasant and lofty land situated to the south of the city on which, till then stood the mansion (Manzil) of Raja Man Singh and which was, at that time, in possession of the latter's grandson, Raja Jai Singh."*[3]

What is their source?

On the other hand, the 'Munj Bateswar Edict', a rock inscription discovered by the celebrated archaeologist Alexander Cunningham is not known by many today. It reads:

> **BATESVAR CHANDELLA INSCRIPTION OF PARAMARDIDEVA.** **211**
>
> L. 19. २ ॥ —[24].
> [प्रा]सादो वैष्णवस्तेन निर्म्मितोन्तर्व्वसद्धरिम् ।
> मूर्ध्ना स्पृस(श)ति यो नित्यं पदमस्यैव मध्यमम् ॥[36]—[25].
> चकारय[च] स्फटिकावदातमसाविदम्म[न्दि]रमिन्दुमौलेः ।
> न जातु यस्मिन्निवसन्स दे-
> 20. वः कैलासवासाय चकार चेतः ॥[37]—[26].
>
> (25).—He erected a temple of Vishṇu, containing (*an image of*) Hari, which with its top always touches his own middle stride.[36]
>
> (26).—And he also caused this crystal-white habitation of the moon-crested (Śiva) to be built, residing in which the god has never turned his thoughts to dwelling on Kailâsa.

According to the edict, *"King Paramardidev built two magnificent temples with white marble, one for Lord Vishnu and the other for Lord Shiva. They were defiled later on by the Muslim invaders. Perhaps a farsighted man took the edict to a safer place at Bateswar and buried it beneath the ground".*[4]

Who was King Paramardidev?

The area known as Bundelkhand today comprises parts of southeastern Uttar Pradesh and parts of northwest Madhya Pradesh. Legend says that the Kings who ruled the region were from the Iksvaku dynasty of Sri Ram. Later this kingdom was ruled by the Chandelas, who were Rajputs, between the tenth and thirteenth centuries. The founder of the kingdom was Raja Nanuk (831 CE).

Raja Gauda (1002–1017 CE) built the two famous Khajuraho temples – the Jagdamba and Chitragupta temples.

The kingdom was so strong that they had repulsed most of the Muslim attacks. Proof of that dozens of Khajuraho temples built before the iconoclasts' invasions some are still intact.

Vidyadhara was one of the most celebrated Chandela kings. He repulsed attacks by the Afghan invader Mahmud of Ghazni. He patronized temple architecture and sculptures, especially in Khajuraho Temple and the Kalinjar Fort. The 19th king in the dynasty was Paramardidev (1164–1199 CE). The great warrior queen, Rani Durgavati (1524–1564 CE), daughter of King Keeratraj, was the last ruler who bravely fought the Mughals, including Khwaja Abdul Majid Asaf Khan, a general of Moghul emperor Akbar, and sacrificed her life in protecting her kingdom and people.

After that, a new Bundel[5] dynasty was established by King Rudra Pratap in 1501 CE, and were Chhatri Suryanvanshi Rajputs by origin. King Bharatichand gave Sher Shah strong resistance while he tried to capture the Kalinjer Fort, where Sher Shah was killed in 1545.[6]

It is the job of historians and archaeologists to tell us the truth. What happened to the two temples built by King Paramardidev of the Chandratreya dynasty in 1156 CE, as noted in the Bateswar Edict? Who was Paramardidev? According to the renowned historian R. C. Majumdar, 'the other name of the Chandratreya or Chandel King Paramardidev was Paramal, and their kingdom was known as Bundelkhand.'[7]

Where are those magnificent temples? Were those destroyed like many other temples by the invaders? Or were those too grand and too beautiful to be destroyed and were saved for other purposes?

If the edict is to be taken seriously, the historians must answer a few questions. Have they located those two magnificent temples, even the remains, in case these were destroyed? What happened to them? Could these be still existing? Is it possible that these two exquisite temples were saved by the iconoclasts and were mandirs turned palaces occupied by the Mughals and then used as a mausoleum or else?

Can the Vishnu temple be the Tomb of *I'timād-ud-Daulah*, a Mughal mausoleum in Agra? It is described as a "jewel box", also called the "Bachcha Taj" or 'baby Tajmahal'. Was an existing structure, perhaps a desecrated temple which was occupied to use as the mausoleum commissioned by Nur Jahan, the wife of Jahangir, for her father Mirzā Ghiyās Beg (his title was I'timād-ud-Daulah)?

And could the Shiva temple described in the edict be the Taj Mahal, taken over and refurbished?

Many chroniclers documented much about the period of Jahangir, Shah Jahan, and Aurangzeb. The most important ones are *Badshahnama* by Abdul Hamid Lahori, *Wakiyat Jahangiri* by Emperor Jahangir, *Shahjahan-nama* by Enayet Khan, *Tarikh-i-Mufajjali* by Mufajjal Khan, *Mirat-i-Alam* by Bakhtyar Khan, *Alamgirnama* by Muhammad Qazim and *Mustakhab-ul-Lubab* by Kafi Khan. There is no mention of Shah Jahan building the mausoleum for his wife 'Mumtaz Begum' (*Badshahnama* calls her 'Aliya Begam').

Badshahnama (p. 29) reads: "(in) 1040 (H) (1631 CE), died Nawab 'Aliya Begam, in the fortieth year of her age, to the great grief of her husband the Emperor…She had borne him eight sons and six daughters. The third child and eldest son were Muhammad Dara Shukoh, the fourth Muhammad Shah Shuja, the sixth Muhammad Aurangzeb, the tenth Murad Bakhsh."[8]

But for strange reasons, she has been called by multiple names, which creates more confusion: Aliya Begam, Arjumand Banu Begam, Mumtaz-uz-Zamani, and Mumtaz Mahal.

On the other hand, in a book called *Agra – Historical and Descriptive*, Syed Muhammad Latif, half a century before the independence, published in 1896, wrote:

"…on Friday, … 17th of Jamadiulawal, 1041 A. H. (1631 A. D.), the mortal remains of the deceased Empress were sent to Akbarabad (Agra), the DaruUhhilafat under the charge of Prince Mohammed Shah Shuja Bahadur, Bastiul-Nisa Khanam, the head of the Royal household in the time of the late Empress who enjoyed her fullest confidence, and in the words of Abdul Hamid, 'understood her temper,' and who now was the head of the Royal household affairs under the Begam Sahib, and Wazir Khan, the Physician Royal. Under orders of the Emperor, food and cash in silver coin were distributed to the poor and needy all the way from Burhanpur to Agra, the last resting place of the Empress. The site selected for the mausoleum was to the south of the city. It was originally a palace of Raja Man Singh; but here it was now the property of his grandson, Raja Jey Singh, and His Majesty gave the Raja a lofty edifice from the Khalsa estate in exchange for this building, and the spot was used for the mausoleum of the deceased Empress."[9]

Similarly, was Qutub Minar too grand to be destroyed by the Turks, hence survived the ultimate iconoclasm? Is there any actual document that says that a particular sultan ordered to build it? Is there any design document or, for that matter, documents of the engineers and experts? The answer is not very strong! We will revisit this subject in detail at another time in another place.

Nevertheless, no one can ignore Delhi today. But where did the name come from? There are many theories, speculations, and stories attached to the name Delhi.

The legends and history of Delhi go like this:

The exotic lands surrounding modern Delhi have lured outsiders for centuries. A dive into the history of Delhi tells us that on the banks of river Yamuna, many came to plunder. In contrast, others came with ambitions to rule Hindustan, making Delhi and surrounding areas their citadel of power.

Delhi is said to be a 'city of cities', built and destroyed several times. The legend of *Mahabharata* talks about the beauty and wealth of the mighty Indraprastha. The name relates to Devraj Indra, and was built by the Pandavas as their capital in this region over five thousand years ago.

Several thousand years have passed since then, and mysteriously, there is no more mention of Indraprastha to be found in the lost pages of history. If there is a link between the Pandavas and medieval clans, it would probably be the Tomars who are believed to be descendants of Arjun and his grandson King Parikshit.[10]

Some suggest that the Jat Dhillon title is rooted in the ancestry of Raja Dhilu, tracing back the ancestry to *Mahabharata's* fabled King Karna, who established the townships near Delhi around 800 BCE and continued to rule till the 3rd century BCE. Yet, it is not clear if they expanded the kingdom beyond the immediate surroundings of modern Delhi. Many such kings and kingdoms throughout India and Delhi were not the most important and famous ones. The name Delhi could have come from Dhilli, a corruption of Dhilu. This story has been noted in Arya Samaj founder Swami Dayanand Saraswati's *Satyarth Prakash*. Some others think King Dhilu was a descendant of the Maurya dynasty of the 1st century BCE.[11]

For a moment, let's visit the 6th century CE history theatre in India's western part, mainly Rajasthan. Agnivanshi Rajputs called Chauhans of Sambhar were the ruling dynasty in today's Rajasthan and surrounding areas. The original names of the Chauhans were the Chahamans of Shakambhari (their capital being in modern-day Sambha Lake Town), who ruled between the 6th and 12th centuries. King Ajayraja II moved their capital to Ajayameru (modern Ajmer) in the early 12th century.

A small kingdom of the Tomara's emerged in the 8th century in the Haryana-Delhi region. Some say they were the descendants of the Mahabharata-famed Pandavas. Some say that they descended from the Kabul Shahi or the Hindu Shahi dynasty in Gandhar, which existed around the 7th century CE. Yet others say the Tomars are also connected to the Jats in

Rajasthan and Haryana.[12] King Anangpal I created a small kingdom, collecting several villages in large parts of Haryana and modern Delhi.

The Tomar dynasty ruled in present-day Delhi and Haryana for 415 years between the 9th and 12th centuries CE. There were 19 kings in this dynasty, beginning with Ananga Pal I (736–754 CE) and ending with Akr Pala (1130–1151 CE) as per the list given in Abul Fazl's Ain-i-Akbari (Bikaner manuscript).[13]

Archaeological evidence suggests the city of 'Lal Kot' was founded by the first Tomar king, Anangpal I in 736 CE as one of the first townships, but the name Delhi has not been prominent yet. This township already had some ancient establishments, perhaps from the ruins of King Dhilu's time or even further back – the Mahabharata Period.[14]

Anangpal built numerous palaces and temples during his reign, but minimal trace remains today except for the Kalkaji Mandir. The legend says that there were two lion statues at the gate of this temple with a bell in their mouths. Anybody seeking justice from the king had to ring the bell, and justice was delivered.[15]

In the 8th century, the Anandpur Dam was built by King Anangpal I for rain harvesting using water coming down from the Aravalli hills towards Delhi. About 16 km from Delhi, the dam was 23 feet high and 164 feet long, which collected rainwater during the rainy season and supplied it to nearby areas for drinking and irrigation water.[16]

The township of about 99 acres surrounding the Surajkund, a reservoir built in the 10th century, is located on the southern Delhi Ridge of Aravalli range in Faridabad of Haryana, five miles from South Delhi.[17] Surajkund (literal meaning is 'Lake of the Sun') was built in the Aravalli hills' backdrop with an amphitheater-shaped embankment constructed in semicircular form. King Surajmal, son of Anangpal I built it. He was a worshipper of the sun, hence the lake's design – the shape of a rising sun with arcs looking eastward. Also, he had built a Sun temple on its western bank.[18] This area had hunting forest resorts in the past.[19] This reservoir of 427 feet diameter supplied water to Delhi and surrounding areas as the Anandpur dam did. While we do not know precisely how many other significant structures and buildings they may have built and were usurped or demolished by the later Muslim invaders and occupants, these two alone give testimony of their administration and the technological achievements of that time.

Anangpur (Anandpur) was established as a royal resort in about 1020 CE by Anangapala II. Anangapala later moved Anangpur some 6 miles westward to a walled citadel called Lal Kot. He built this city of forts and temples extending to the Mehrauli region, the current Qutab Minar complex. This fortified city was created to fight the raids of Muslim invaders, especially by Mahmud of Ghazni.[20]

After the last Tomar King Akr Pāla's (or Akhsal) demise, Prithviraj Chauhan took control of Lal Kot. Some say he was given the throne by his grandfather Anangpal Tomar II in 1180 CE, and others suggest that Prithviraj Chauhan forcefully captured the throne. However, he is credited with the Rajput forces' unification under one banner against the Muslim forces.

The Tomara kings controlled their territory from the Lal Kot for about 100 years. Prithviraj or locally known as Rai Pithora, in 1164 CE, extended the citadel by building massive ramparts around it; the city became known as Qila Rai Pithora after that.[21]

One wonders, where are the buildings, rooms, and apartments they lived in? Was it the same as the famous current Red Fort and the mansions inside it they used?

From the 11th century onwards, Delhi started facing Muslim invasions, the Ghaznavids, and then the Ghruids. The Chahamana or Chauhan kingdom reached its zenith under Vigraraja IV in the mid-12th century. The dynasty's power effectively ended in 1192 CE, after the demise of Prithviraj Chauhan. He ruled Rajasthan, Haryana, Punjab, parts of Uttar Pradesh, and a large region in northwest India.

He repulsed Muhammad Ghori several times, and the number is varied based on different accounts, ranging from two times to twenty-two times. According to the *Prithviraja Prabandha*, Muhammad was repulsed seven times, and the *Hammira Mahakavya* notes eight times.[22] The *Prabandha Kosha*, *Surjana Charita* , and *Prithviraj Raso* describe that Raja Prithviraj defeated and captured Muhammad twenty times but lost the 21st battle.[23] Another text called the *Prabandha Chintamani* noted that Prithviraj's army defeated Ghori twenty-two times and heroically sacrificed himself in the fateful 22nd battle in Tarain.[24]

However, the Muslim chroniclers such as *Tarikh-i-Firishta* noted two battles, and he was defeated in the 2nd battle. It may be that they wanted to glorify Ghori and Islam and mentioned a fewer number of battles.[25]

Each time, Prithviraj pardoned Ghori despite advice from his ministers against it. But the final battle in Tarain in 1192 CE between the two turned fatal for Prithviraj. He was captured unprepared and unexpectedly and brutally killed by Ghori, thus ushering in the Turkic rule in Delhi. Prithviraj was the last Hindu king in Delhi until later, the valiant Emperor Hemu challenged and defeated the Muslim rulers (1556 CE) and captured the Delhi throne for a short time.

Currently available evidence does not reveal if delhi was India's most important city since the end of the Mahabharata period (Indraprastha, which existed around 3500 BCE) but maybe during the period of Vikramaditya-Varahamihira. It gained prominence again during the rule of Tomars and Chauhans. The Tomar kings were present in Delhi around the 10th century and may have renovated many ancient structures and built some, including the Qutub Minar complex area. The Turk invaders destroyed 27 temples in that complex, either built or renovated by the Tomar Kings from centuries-old existing structures, which later fell under Prithviraj Chauhan's dominion.

As popularly suggested, the Delhi Sultanate ruled from Delhi and Lahore for 320 years and not 500 years. Their direct rule reached only parts of India, especially the north and northwest. In most cases, they acted like uneducated nomadic tribes, mainly to plunder and loot using mercenaries to maintain their luxurious lifestyle. Their army was mostly for that purpose, in addition to safeguarding their houses.

The Mughals ruled from Delhi and partly from Lahore and Agra at their peak from 1526 to 1707 CE until the death of Aurangzeb. The throne of Delhi remained powerful for these 181 years, but after Aurangzeb's death, Marathas, Sikhs, and others got rid of the Mughal rule in most parts of India. The Mughal kings became powerless figureheads.

During the Mughal rule also appeared the Afghan Sher Shah (Pashtun or Pathan), and during his reign between 1540 and 1545 CE, he was perpetually engaged in multi-front wars both with Mughals and other Hindu Kings. His Sur dynasty, which ended in 1556 CE, took control of much of Babur and Humayun's Mughal territories, which was again about half of the subcontinent at that time.

Maharaja Hemu defeated the army of Akbar in the battle of Delhi in 1556 after announcing himself as Hemchandra Vikramaditya and taking charge of Delhi.[26] He had a very humble beginning and became the general of the army and Chief Minister for Adil Shah Suri, a nephew of Sher Shah, through hard work and perseverance. He exemplified the Kshatriya spirit to challenge the enemies of the nation. He was a great strategist and warrior; he first fought against the Pashtun rebels from West to East. Then he fought the Mughals, including Humayun and Akbar, and was victorious in twenty-two battles.[27] But his reign could last only for a few weeks.

To recapture the throne, the Mughals gathered a large army near Panipat. Raja Hemu was wounded after a courageous battle by a chance arrow and was captured by the enemy while unconscious. It appears that young Akbar may have been in shock and hesitant to harm the great leader, but Bairam Khan, Akbar's regent, beheaded him. A great hero sacrificed his life for the motherland, who won more battles than Akbar himself.[28]

A great tragedy ensued in India, which sealed India's fate for worse for 150 years more. Still, the impact of these fateful years is enormous, and Indians will take a long time to recover from the losses and regain their past glories and their position as the world leader, world teacher, and world power.

If there was a real Mughal rule, it began with Akbar, who, through strategy and appeasement of Hindu powers, maintained his kingdom for 50 long years. (1556–1605 CE). His descendants, Jahangir, Shahjahan, and Aurangzeb, were on the Delhi Throne for another 100 years. But they never had complete control over entire India, even during Aurangzeb's period, and they were constantly faced with tremendous Hindu resistance. It so happened that Aurangzeb's treasury was nearly empty due to these wars, and his imminent collapse was stopped after employing Murshid Kuli Khan (1700), who collected huge sums of taxes from Bengal since other regions were not paying enough. Murshid, who later became the Nawab of Bengal, was a Brahmin child sold to the slave market and rose through ranks.

The power of Mughal Delhi collapsed after the death of Aurangzeb in 1707 CE. Britain entered the scenes in Delhi after 200 years of the ceremonial powerless Mughal throne in 1911. Subsequently, within 36 years, Britain handed Delhi over to mostly the Nehru-Gandhi dynasty in 1947 while the main seat of democracy, the Indian parliament, found its importance.

The Mughal Occupation of India

How did the term Mughal or Moghul come into existence? Moghul is a debased form[29] of the word Mongol in the Persian language. Therefore, the Mughals were initially the descendants of the Central Asian Mongols, which bear the infamous name of Genghis Khan. Turkic tribes were also rooted in Mongolian ancestry, especially Genghis Khan and his sons. So basically, Mughal ancestry encompasses Genghis, Timur, and Babur. Anyone taking pride in Mughal ancestry must be reminded of Genghis, Mahmud, Ghori, Timur, and Babur's role in destroying numerous societies and civilizations.

After almost 200 years of Timur's invasions, his great-great-grandson Babur set for India's conquest around 1526 CE, after defeating the Lodhi Delhi Sultanate. Ibrahim Lodhi, the last Sultan of the 'Slave Dynasty' in Delhi, was not a strong ruler. Due to sour relations with some of his subordinates, including his uncle, Babur, the then ruler of Kabul, was invited to India. In the famous battle of Panipat, Lodhi lost and was killed in 1526, thus ushering in the Mughal dynasty in Delhi.

The major Mughals ruled in Delhi between 1526 CE and 1707 CE. Though it was less than 200 years, the impact was horrific. The most significant effect was first by Babur and then by Aurangzeb. The destruction of temples, institutes of learning, forced conversions, mayhem, and the genocide of Hindus is unmatched in world history. Yet India managed to remain a Hindu nation after all. The key reason was India's martial class – the Kshatriyas – Rajputs, Sikhs, and Marathas fought valiantly against the foreign occupation. Persia, Arabia, and the entire Middle East, and even some parts of Europe surrendered to Islam's armies within a very short period. But India mostly survived all of it except for the British and Muslim conspiracy[30] to break the country in 1947 based on religion.

In the meantime, in 1756, Robert Clive took Mir Jafar as a puppet as the Nawab of Bengal and established the East India Company into a dominion of Britain. Many early Britishers identified themselves closer with the Muslims since Christianity has the same Abrahamic roots. They were fascinated with the royalty and flamboyance of the Muslim Nawabs and adopted a lifestyle akin to them. Some converted and exhibited their feelings against the Hindus.

How was India then

The Middle Eastern scholars had a close, cordial respectful relationship with India. Arabs learned the number system, mathematics, astronomy from India and exchanged each other's knowledge. However, that relationship turned into conflict soon after Islamic forces set off for invasions. The Arabs, the Persians, and all nations under Islamic rule lost their older culture, heritage, science, literature, arts, and other knowledge bases.

Ahmad al-Ya'qubi, or Ya'qubi, a Muslim geographer and historian around 9th century CE, wrote:

"The Hindus are superior to all other nations in intelligence and thoughtfulness. They are more exact in astronomy and astrology than any other people." [31]

Why did Italian explorer Christopher Columbus set sail for India (1480 CE onwards) and call it the 'golden bird'? Because of its wealth. How did India gather wealth? It was a knowledge society where material science and spiritual science flourished together. India's contribution to the world of mathematics, science, and technology was her strength. Indian products were the best globally, and Indian traders traded both to India's west and east for centuries. India still had better and bigger ships than Europe until the colonials arrived in India. When Columbus was dreaming of landing in India, India had already been invaded a thousand times by Timur, Abdali, Ghazni, and the Ghoris and Lodhis were occupying Delhi just before Babur's arrival who started the Mughal dynasty. Even after nearly 700 years of destruction and loot, India was still rich at that time. Hindu kings' and temples' wealth was looted continuously by foreign forces. Yet, it was rich, so Columbus and other explorers like Italian Amerigo Vespucci would set their expeditions to India.

How much the pre-invasion Arabs admired Indian knowledge, especially mathematics, is revealed by Abu'l Hasan al-Qifti, Arab scholar and author of *Chronology of the Scholars*:

"Among those parts of their sciences which came to us, the numerical calculation...it is the swiftest and most complete method of calculation, the easiest to understand and the simplest to learn; it bears witness to the Indians' piercing intellect, fine creativity, and their superior understanding and inventive genius."[32]

Renowned French writer Francois Marie Arouet Voltaire (1694-1774) also brought into light the contribution of the Hindus and wrote:

"It is very important to note that some 2,500 years ago at the least Pythagoras went from Samos to the Ganges to learn geometry...But he would certainly not have undertaken such a strange journey had the reputation of the Brahmans' science not been long established in Europe....We have already acknowledged that arithmetic, geometry, astronomy was taught among the Brahmans. From time immemorial, they have known the precession of the equinoxes and were in their calculation far closer to the real figure than the Greeks who came much later. Mr. Le Gentil (a French astronomer who spent several years in India) has with admiration acknowledged the Brahmans' science, as well as the immensity of time these Indians must have needed to reach a knowledge of which even the Chinese never had any notion, and which was unknown to Egypt and to Chaldea, the teacher of Egypt."[33]

India was the fountainhead of knowledge and technology in those days. Then came the invaders from the west side of India, starting with Alexander. When Columbus was going to India, according to Elphinstone Mountstuart, a Scottish statesman and historian, who became the governor of then Bombay province during the British rule of India, "The Hindu Kingdoms overthrown by the Moslems were so wealthy that the historians were tired of telling of about the immense loot of jewels and coins captured by the invaders".[34]

Lieutenant-Colonel James Tod, an English-born officer of the British East India Company, was also an Oriental scholar.

He saw India in her original tradition and said: "Where can we look for sages like those whose systems of philosophy were prototypes of those of Greece: to whose works Plato, Thales, and Pythagoras were disciples? Where do I find astronomers whose knowledge of planetary systems excites wonder in Europe as well as the architects and sculptors whose works claim our admiration, and the musicians who could make the mind oscillate from joy to sorrow, from tears to smile with the change of modes and varied intonation?"[35]

Many of the observations above were supported by the statistical figures presented by British historian Angus Maddison. He charted countries with significant contributions to the world economy in terms of GDP since the first year of the Christian Era – 1 CE.

Between 1 CE and 1600 CE, India and China dominated the global economy holding a 50% share between the two. Once India faced invasions, the economy was hard hit, especially after the Gupta and Malwa kingdoms' decline around 700 CE. Then massive invasions followed by Islamic imperial rule started in India around 1000 CE. India was still holding its position until about the 1400s, when China took over from India. But still, till the days of East India Company and British rule established, India was at par with China. Then the decline started as the Mughal Empire collapsed, and different European trading adventurers arrived in India. Even when the British came to India in the late 1700s, India's contribution to the global GDP was around 20%, while China had 30%, America 20%, and Britain was yet to be a significant trader in the world.

India's GDP share in the world between 1500 CE and 1600 CE was 22.7%; between 1600 CE and 1700 CE, it was 22.2%, and between 1700CE and 1820CE, it was 21%. By 1820, India's share had fallen to 16.1%, and in 1870, it went down to 12.2%. When the British left India in 1947, it was around 3%.[36][37] If we extrapolate backward, one can only imagine how high India's GDP was before the start of the Common Era when India was the key global player in terms of trade and economy.

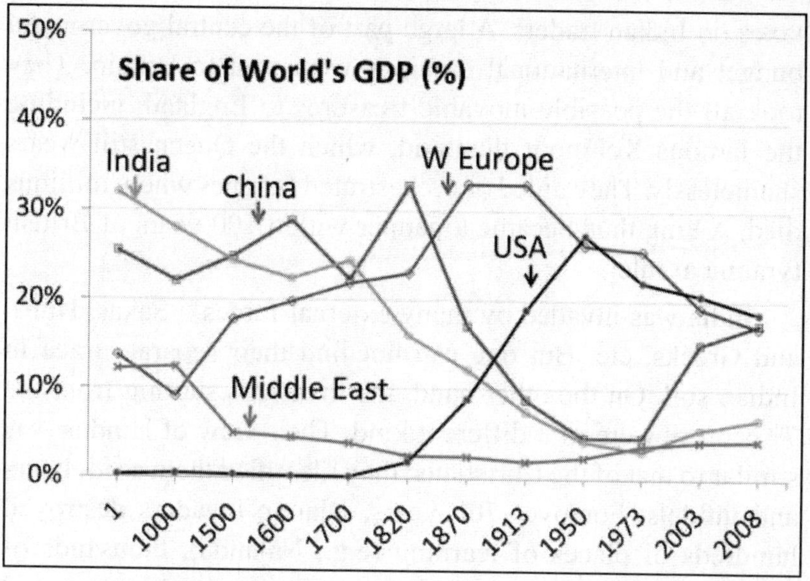

Source: [38]

When the British came to India around 1756, the Rupee had an excellent global economic standing. Due to Britain's financial crisis caused by the French Revolutionary wars and Napoleanic wars in 1816, to stabilize the economy, Britain introduced the 'Great Recoinage of 1816' [*A New history of the Royal Mint.* Christopher Edgar Challis]. Between 1816 and 1914, the Indian Rupee was at par with the US dollar; the exchange rate was one pound = 4.8 Indian Rupees.[39]

By the time the British left India in 1947, the British Pound exchange rate was at 13.50 (3-fold fall of Rupee value) rupees per pound; the exchange rate for the American dollar was 5.00 rupees per dollar.[40]

A recently published report from Columbia University Press by Utsa Patnaik et al. says that between 1765 and 1938, Britain looted wealth worth nearly US$ 45 trillion from India.[41][42]

So, it is only reasonable to say that Britain impoverished India severely via multiple means. They destroyed the education system and industries known to the whole world, including cotton, silk and muslin, brass, and iron products. They imposed taxes on Indian traders. A large part of the central government budget and international earnings were sent to Britain. They took all the possible movable treasures to England, including the famous Kohinoor diamond, which the Queen still wears shamelessly. They aided or orchestrated famines where millions died. A king thus became a pauper within 100 years of British tyrannical rule.

India was invaded by many external forces – Sakas, Huns, and Greeks, etc. But one can not find their separate trace in Indian soil. On the other hand, the invasions starting from the 7th century were of a different kind. Their view of Hindus was similar to that of the Christians; they identified them as idolaters and infidels. For over 700 years, Islamic invaders destroyed hundreds of places of learning (e.g., Nalanda), thousands of temples, built mosques over those structures, butchered around 100 million people. They also started to slaughter and eat cows mainly to insult the Hindus (who revere cows); all these tragic events went on until the death of Aurangazeb and the rise of the Sikh, Maratha, and Rajput empires. According to some Islamic scholars, killing cows is a sin.[43] As a matter of fact, most Arab world did not have any cows, and it was not a tradition there to kill cows for any occasion.

Belgian Indologist Koenraad Elst, in his book called *Negationism in India: Concealing the Record of Islam* noted:

"The Muslim conquests, down to the 16th century, were for the Hindus a pure struggle of life and death. Entire cities were burnt down, and the populations massacred, with hundreds of thousands killed in every campaign and similar numbers deported as slaves. Every new invader made (often literally) his hills of Hindus skulls. Thus, the conquest of Afghanistan in the year 1000 was followed by the annihilation of the Hindu population; the region is still called the Hindu Kush, i.e., Hindu slaughter. The Bahmani sultans (1347–1480) in central India made it a rule to kill 100,000 captives in a single day and many

more on other occasions. The conquest of the Vijayanagar empire in 1564 left the capital, plus large areas of Karnataka depopulated. And so on.[44]

"According to some calculations, the Indian (subcontinent) population decreased by 80 million between 1000 (conquest of Afghanistan) and 1525 (end of Delhi Sultanate)."[45]

The Boston to Bengal Story

On the other hand, the British kept the remnants of Mughals in good humor. After Aurangzeb died in 1707, the Rajput, Sikh, Marathas, and other Indian powers brought the Mughal Empire down. But they did not give up the royal throne. There were 14 more powerless Mughal kings installed as the descendants of Babur. The 18th Mughal 'emperor' Shah Alam II occupied the throne between 1760 and 1806. The East India Company struck a friendship with Shah with a plan to take over entire India. They went as far as to use the Company's seal on the Rupee, which acknowledged it as the Mughals' legal vehicle. The top Islamic clerics and Ulemas liked the British, who followed their ancient prophets – Musa (Moses) and Isa (Christ). They felt comfortable working with them over the Hindu powers such as the Marathas. Many British women converted to Islam and got married to Muslim high priests such as Muhammad Ismail Londoni.

David Ochterloney was born in Boston, USA, in 1758 to a father of Scottish and a mother of Welsh descent. His father was an American merchant and a soldier during the colonial period in America. David ventured on a voyage to India as a cadet in 1777 at the age of 18. He showed exceptional leadership and management skills.

He was commissioned into the East India Company's Bengal Infantry within a year and became a Lieutenant shortly after. He then led the Second Anglo-Maratha war. Later, in recognition of his outstanding service during the battles, he was promoted to the Major General and finally the "resident' in Delhi Mughal Darbar. Soon he adopted and thoroughly embraced the Mughal culture and lived like a Muslim ombudsman. In 1828 to honor his successes in Maratha and Anglo-Nepalese wars, a monument was constructed in Calcutta in his memory using public funds. It was designed by J. P. Parker and built by Martin & Co, which Rajendra Nath Mukherjee led; Mukherjee's company built many iconic buildings in Calcutta – from Victoria Memorial to Grand Hotel to Belur Math. He played a significant role in making the Howrah Bridge. Mark Twain called the monument the *"Cloud kissing Monument."* In 1969, the Indian Government renamed it Shahid Minar or the 'Martyrs' Monument.'

William Fraser was an assistant to David Ochterloney. He taught Persian, Arabic, and Sharia law to David. Fraser virtually led a Muslim life. David also had a similar lifestyle, wore Mughal attire, and had a mini harem of thirteen concubines. His favorite one was a Brahmin girl-child captured by the Mughals who ended up being a dancer at an early age. Her harem name was Bebee Mahruttun Moobaruck ul Nissa Begum, also called Generalee Begum. The children born to them were raised as Muslims. Mubarak Bagh in Delhi has David's residence, and her grave is called Randi ki Masjid[46] or the 'palace of whore'; some say because local Muslims disliked her for having a lofty lifestyle with an English man.

The Movement to White-Wash Islamic Atrocities

So, the invaders' theology or ideology was to look at Hindus as objects of hatred or cruelty. The invaders came to loot and destroy; what would motivate them to create something grand and unique in a foreign land? The arts, architecture, music, etc., are nothing but usurped, refurbished versions of existing Hindu art with an Islamic face. Today, buildings and monuments reveal these dark secrets of history that were attributed to Muslim kings, but slowly we are finding out that many of them were built long before they landed in India.

The effort to wipe off the history of Hindus is typically blamed on the British and Marxist historians. But in reality, it started 850 years ago when the invaders destroyed great institutions and architectural buildings, including thousands of temples. After independence, the Marxists, the opportunists of Nehru's Congress party, with the help of Muslim historians, worked meticulously to destroy India's positive history, sanitize, and cover up all destructions and atrocities of the Muslim invaders and rulers.

First, the colonist and then the Marxist historians had a game plan – white-wash all Islamic forces' atrocities on India and showcased the Muslim tyrants in a good light. A group of 'historians' led by William Dalrymple, Romila Thapar, Irfan Habib, Girish Karnad, and others took up the job of white-washing atrocities and destructions of the Turkic, Pathan, and Mughals; they wanted to show an image of benevolence these forces brought to India. They spoke positively about 'Islamic Contribution' to India. Still, they failed to give good examples of them patronizing science and technology or, for that matter, any excellent institute of learning which had been the backbone of India as India always had.

These NeoCols have created 'movements' against 'atrocities against the Dalits' in the past. But the maximum hatred and 'untouchability' towards the kafirs and killing them ruthlessly happened during the Islamic Jihads. Major manufacturing machinery for stories to white-wash and repaint the accounts of Islamic carnages in India was established. We will review these in detail soon.

For example, some leftist historians portray Aurangzeb as one of India's best rulers based on scanty pieces of evidence presented by people such as Audrey Truschke and Burjor Avari! Whereas the whole world knows what Aurangzeb did to India and the Hindus. He introduced the Fatawa-e-Alamgiri, established Sharia law in his empire in the Indian subcontinent, and banned music and other recreational activities.[47] He also introduced the *jizya* tax on the Hindus, destroyed numerous Hindu temples, including the Kashi Viswanath Temple in Varanasi, and executed the Sikh Guru Tegh Bahadur after a failed attempt at forceful force conversion to Islam.[48]

The Marxist historians would also project Babur as a tolerant and secular ruler. Yet, Babur himself has written in *Babur Nama*: *"Chanderi had been in the daru'l-harb (kaffir rule) for some years and held by Sanga's officer Meidini Rao with four or five thousand infidels, but in [Hijra] 934 [1527–28CE], through the grace of God, I took it by force within a ghari or two, massacred the infidels, and brought it into the bosom of Islam."*

In the *Babur-Nama* (Vol II), he records for posterity:

"After the success, Ghazi ['victor in jihad'] was written amongst the royal titles. Below the titles entered on the Fatehnama, I wrote the following quatrain:

For Islam's sake,

I wondered in the wilds

Prepared for war with infidels and Hindus

Resolved myself to meet the martyr's death

Thanks be to God, a Ghazi I became." [49]

Ram-Janmabhoomi temple (birthplace of Ram in Ayodhya, one of the most revered personalities by the Hindus, which is as essential as Jerusalem to the Abrahamic faith) was destroyed by instruction of Babur and was called Babri Mosque.[50]

The inscription on the structure read: 'By the command of Emperor Babur, whose justice is an edifice reaching up to the very height of the heavens, the good hearted Mir Baqi built the alighting place of angels. Bawad [Buwad] khair baqi (may this goodness last forever)'.[51]

Today, ample evidence is available that there was a grand Ram temple at the Babri structure site.[52]

It was not just a temple and sacred place of some 'believers', but it was vital for the entire Indian civilization. This temple's destruction was about the collapse of a millennia-old peaceful civilization, which contributed so much to the current world civilization. For centuries Hindus fought to have their mandir back, to take their civilizational pride and identity back. In recent times when a movement started to free the Ram Temple, there was a huge hue and cry – an unused mosque built on a Hindu temple could easily be given back to the Hindus. But such an act would only encourage the so-called 'Hindutva' forces – with that fear, and the NeoCols started a propaganda movement. And the Hindus, having so much evidence, played defensive until the structure was brought down through the anger and rage of a mob!

We are made to believe via our history books that perhaps it was a sad yet great thing that Babur defeated Ibrahim Lodhi at the battle of Panipat, and perhaps Babur was so great in founding the Mughal rule. While we not only know what Babur did to the Hindus was as bad as what Ibrahim Lodi did. Lodi also killed and converted numerous Hindus and destroyed Hindu temples. These are examples of Islam's sanitized history in India, which British and Marxist historians have supplied to us.

Can you imagine a statue of Hitler anywhere in the world? Lenin's statues are slowly being removed from all over the world. But the NeoCols would fight for a 'Babri' Mosque as a proxy for the Islamists! While Saudi Arabia has demolished and moved many holiest sites of Islam, including many ancient mosques and graveyards, Marxist intelligentsia provided fodder to the Islamist leaders of India against handing over the unused structure to the Hindus.

The communists and many Muslim historians tell us glorious tales of the Muslims' 'outstanding contribution' in India. It is the apologists' sugar-coated glorification of the horrific tragedy of millions of people over 500 years.

In reality, there was much more than the destruction of temples and other marvelous architectures and repurposing those as Islamic structures in the architectural contributions of the Arab-Turkic forces. The art of sculpting or *'shilpakari'* was banned, and the *shilpakar*s were banished except for the purpose of refurbishing many of the existing structures claimed as 'Muslim structures'. What was their unique contribution to art and music? The architecture they claim to have built was already in India. What noteworthy literature was produced during this period except for few panegyrics of the rulers and court chronicles?

The Grand Trunk (G.T.) Road's construction is attributed to Sher Shah! For much of his short-lived years as an empire – he was engaged in wars after wars. Where did he have time or resources to build such a grand highway? The G.T. road existed centuries before the arrival of Muslim invaders.[53]

Music and dance were banned under Islamic rules except in the harems and courts of the rulers. These arts mainly survived in Southern India and India's rural regions, where invasions did not impact as much. If we look at Mughal paintings, it was stuck in the 10th century – which is given way too much appreciation again by the NeoCols. Indigenous art forms starting from the Ajanta and Ellora, centuries before could have evolved further but were damaged, lost, and discouraged by the Islamists from further development. Yet, we find that the European arts have tremendously grown during the same period due to the freedom of the artists.

Music in India was kept alive either through persecution or patronage – because the music was 'haram' to the invaders' religion. Though there is no direct reference against music in the Quran, several Hadith calls music 'haram'.

Abu Hurayrah reported that the Messenger said: *"The bell is the musical instrument of the Satan."* [Muslim 2114, Book 37, Hadith 159]

Abu Malik Al-Ashari:

"The Messenger of Allah said, "Some people of my Ummah will drink wine, calling it by other than its real name, merriment will be made for them through the playing of musical

instruments and the singing of lady singers. Allah will cleave the earth under them and turn others into monkeys and swines".

[Ibn Ma'jah Vol.5 Hadith No.4020]

Abu Amir or Abu Malik Al Ashari heard the Prophet saying:

"From among my followers, there will be some people who will consider illegal sexual intercourse, the wearing of silk, the drinking of alcoholic drinks, and the use of musical instruments as lawful. And there will be some people who will stay near the side of a mountain, and in the evening their shepherd will come to them with their sheep and ask them for something, but they will say to him, 'Return to us tomorrow.' Allah will destroy them during the night and will let the mountain fall on them, and He will transform the rest of them into monkeys and pigs, and they will remain so till the Day of Resurrection." [Sahih Al-Bukhari Vol.7 Hadith No.5590]

Still, the Sultans needed entertainment, and the courtesans or *tawaifs* had to dance, sometimes nude in front of the sponsors, which created *mujra* and other similar forms of dance style. Islamic sculpture, arts, and music is nothing but a sad saga of India's musical history.

But one should remember that we have much to learn from some Muslim historians about what India had before and during the Muslim occupation. 9th-century Muslim historian Abū ʿUthman ʿAmr ibn al-Baṣrī, popularly known as al-Jāḥiẓ was an Arab prose writer who is credited with 140 different works. He is quoted to have said this:

"The Hindus excel in astrology, mathematics. They have a special Indian script. They excel in medicine and possess some wonderful secrets of that art. In particular those remedies that are of the greatest use in the most dangerous diseases. They have developed to perfection their art like sculptures, paintings and architecture. They are the inventor of chess. They make good swords and know all the tricks of fencing. They know charms that can remove poison and pain from the body. Their music is pleasant and they have all sorts of dances. They have collections

of poetry, philosophy, literature and science of morals. From India we received the book called Kalilah wa Dimnah. These people have judgment and are brave. They possess the virtues of cleanliness and purity. Contemplation has originated with them. In some virtues they surpass the Chinese." [54]

'Islamic Structures' in India

As noted earlier, many of 'Muslim architecture' was built on top of Hindu temples, captured palaces, and other pre-existing Hindu monuments. Even then, a large number of these architectures are just tombs or mausoleums. As we have noted elsewhere, the Taj Mahal may have been a Shiva temple[55] within a palace usurped by Shahjahan. The proper study of history in the truth-finding mission will reveal the real stories of many such structures, including the Qutub Minar in Delhi. The simple truth is that the tower was built along with the 27 temples destroyed by Aibak or Altatmas (Iltutmish), and someone named it the 'Qutub Minar' afterward. It is one of the biggest refurbishings in history. But this is considered a marvel of 'Islamic architecture,' and credit is given to a pauper like Aibak, who spent most of his time in Lahore and not in Delhi. He made a mockery of what was most probably a grand observatory center on earth for many centuries. It is like Delhi's great pre-existing garden (most likely created by the Tomars) was named 'Lodhi Gardens' after the Lodhis occupied Delhi! The nearby iron pillar is an excellent example of the antiquity of the surrounding structures and ancient Indian technology.

After Muhammad Ghori left India completing his raids, his general Qutb al-Din Aibak, a slave from then Turkistan, took charge of Ghori's territories. He invaded and occupied the northern part of India. A stable manager rose to the general's position and finally became the Delhi Sultanate founder in 1206 CE, later called the 'Slave Dynasty.' He was swamped in wars and mostly stayed in Lahore; no official documents prove that he had built the so-called Qutub Minar, attributed to him by the NeoCols.

The compound where this tower stands is called Mehrauli or Mihir-wali, which carries the name of famous mathematician astronomer Varahamira, who was a member of Emperor Vikramaditya's court of 'navaratna' or 'nine gems' around the first century BCE. Perhaps this was his research center and residence, and the tower was an astrological observation tower called *Vishnu Stambha*. Was the whole area the research center of Varahamihir or sage Mihir Acharya, along with 27 temples or research centers for each of the 27 nakshatras or stellar constellations?

The story becomes fascinating as we dig more into history. When Aibak, as a follow-up mission of what Ghori left, came to Delhi, he was in awe to see the architecture and temples in Delhi. Being an iconoclast true to Islam, he immediately thought of destroying different temples and murthys[56] everywhere.

Iltutmish, who was the 3rd Sultan of Delhi, was originally a slave in Aibak's time. He had an outstanding reputation as a faithful commander of Aibak's forces, and sometimes people thought of him as Aibak's son. After the death of Aibak, Aram Shah took over the throne in Delhi. But in a short time, Iltutmish took over Aram Shah's reign and ruled Delhi between 1211–1236 CE.

When he saw the broken temples and the magnificent tower, he thought there must be a reason why his predecessors spared it. He then named it after Qutubuddin, his former boss. Iltutmish tried to build another minar next to it called the Alai Minar. But where were those grand architects of the era when the complex was built? Neither had he the right technology nor the craftsmen to make it. It was eventually left as a primitive incomplete structure.

The NeoCol version of this story goes like this:

"The Qutub Minar was built simultaneously with the mosque but appears to be a stand-alone structure, built as the 'Minar of Jami Masjid', for the muezzin to perform adhan, call for prayer, and also as a *qutub*, an Axis or Pole of Islam."[57]

According to the 16th-century historian Abu'l-Fazl in his *Ain-i-Akbari*, who presented Delhi as the Chahamana capital, the old Rajput citadel called Qila Rai Pithora,[58] meaning Rai Pithora's Fort or the Fort of the 12th century Rajput king Prithviraj Chauhan was taken over by the Muslim invaders and rulers. To impose Islamic religious marks in his newly found territory, Aibak built the mosque after demolishing the temple complex and all institutions and schools there.

NeoCols make us believe that Aibak built a 'victory pillar' in Delhi. It is laughable – since he never won a battle himself – which victory are they talking about? And can anyone hear the sound of azan from a 240 feet tall tower?

But to fit their design and game plan, the NeoCols had to trivialize and sanitize the horror stories of Islamic imperialism in India. Systematically they had to show all positivity amid horror-ridden daily reports of Hindus living in fear every moment of their lives. They came up with the idea of 'contributions of Islamic culture in India'. First of all, what was 'Islamic' culture? Music? No. Arts? No. Because Sharia forbade it. Architecture? Most buildings ascribed to Islamic are built on top of an existing temple or palace; usurped broken temple materials. The inscription next to the mosque near Qutub Minar publicly displays to date, those 27 adjacent temples were destroyed and used the materials (but not the tower). The adjacent mosque called Quwwat-ul-Islam, ascribed to have been built by Aibak, is much more primitive than the ruined temples that remain visible today and not even comparable with the tower in terms of architectural grandeur. If one looks carefully, one will find that the mosque was built after razing the temple complex.

This horrific story of destruction is documented by none other than Quṭb al-Dīn Aibak's chronicler, Hasan Nizami, in *Taj-ul-Maasir*:

'The conqueror entered the city, and its vicinity was freed from idols and idol-worship; and in the sanctuaries of the

images of the gods, mosques were raised by the worshippers of the one God.'[59]

Thousands of captured Hindu women and girls as young as five years were kept in the harems. And those who were forced to work under the Muslim rulers, who spoke in some Indic languages such as Khariboli – suddenly had to deal with Arabic, Turkish or Persian languages. The new language Urdu took birth in battlefields, courts, and harems whose script is made Arabic, instead of Devnagari, as it was done for the Sindhi language. The Urdu language was later patronized and created a line of literature, especially poetry.

Was the veil, which Hindu women are supposed to wear, a Hindu custom? Looking at various sculptures depicting women, especially in temples, one can see that the practice of purdah or covering women was not there. Purdah is actually an Islamic practice. Child marriage? Another practice was created to save Hindu girls from lustful Muslim strongmen. The most celebrated of all occasions in life is the wedding. It should be performed during the daytime as done in Southern India. Why is it then done in the dead of night in North and East India? Muslim law forbids marrying a woman already married and not divorced (talaq). Their parents made the painful attempt to stop the strongmen of the Muslim ruling establishment who wanted to capture the most beautiful young Hindu girls by marrying them off in childhood and the dead of night in secrecy so that they could not be charged! Sadly, the tradition continues, though it is performed during the day in the southern parts of India.

Thousands of Hindu centers of culture and unique sculptures were destroyed forever, only to be replaced by the art forms as pleased by the rulers! If one sees the magnificent temples in southern India, Indonesia (Borobudur) and Cambodia (Angkor Wat), one can imagine what major architectural wonders India might have and lost. Luckily, classical music was saved because some dedicated classical music lovers continued the tradition and kept some of the conventions.

On a separate note, based on some rudimentary information, Iran or Persia had Hindu rule some millennia back as scholars like William Jones (Works of William Jones, London) suggested and Persian Architecture expert Arthur Upham Pope hinted at (Some interrelations between Persian and Indian architecture) deserves much research. Studying the ruins of Persepolis or Takht-e-Jamshid palaces, the capital of the Achaemenid Empire (550–330 BCE), may give some clues to a truth seeker. The pillars resemble those of Emperor Ashoka. One simple fact is that in order to build any structure, especially large, exquisite ones, one has to have deep knowledge of mathematics, geometry, and engineering. India gave all these to the rest of the world. Is it possible that what we call Persian architecture, or for that matter Islamic architecture, was also an original contribution of Indian Hindu experts?

Tipu Sultan

The NeoCols have glorified Tipu Sultan and Haider Ali as Indian patriotic heroes who fought against the British Raj. But little is revealed about their Jihadi contributions in terms of the anti-Hindu acts they committed. The NeoCols would say: "Tipu Sultan was secular, he fought against the British in three wars, in a sense, our freedom struggle began with Mysore wars – between the English and Tipu. He (Tipu) being called a fanatic or claims that he converted Hindus is baseless. He didn't do any such thing…"[60]

But there is direct proof of what kind of a Jihadi he was, which is obvious from the inscription in Arabic on the handle (hilt) of his sword :

"My victorious sabre is lightning for the destruction of the unbelievers. Haidar, the Lord of the Faith, is victorious for

my advantage. And moreover, he destroyed the wicked race who were unbelievers. Praise be to him, who is the Lord of the Worlds! Thou art our Lord, support us against the people who are unbelievers. He to whom the Lord giveth victory prevails over all (mankind). Oh Lord, make him victorious, who promoteth the faith of Muhammad. Confound him, who refuseth the faith of Muhammad; and withhold us from those who are so inclined. The Lord is predominant over his own works. Victory and conquest are from the Almighty. Bring happy tidings, Oh Muhammad, to the faithful; for God is the kind protector and is the most merciful of the merciful. If God assists thee, thou wilt prosper. May the Lord God assist thee, Oh Muhammad, with a mighty victory."[61]

In the Persian text called *The History of the reign of Tipu Sultan* by Mir Hussein Ali Khan Kirmani (translated by Colonel W. Miles), we find out the true nature of the Sultan as described below:

"Circa 1783, Zeinool Abidin Khan, Mehdivi, the Foujdar (Military Commander) of Coorg and an intimate confidante of the Sultan had been bestowed with complete and uncontrolled authority over the region of Coorg. He used this power bestowed by the benevolence of the Sultan to good effect. He indulged in wanton rape and plunder and was particularly severe on the women of the peasantry, compelling the most beautiful amongst them to submit to his lust and pleasure."[62]

The people in Coorg revolted against the tyranny and persecution which was led by Momuti Nair and Ranga Nair, who organized the peasants. They seized the fort of the local Fauzdar. Tipu himself set out to fight this revolt with a large army headed by the French commander Monsieur Lally. The army crushed the rebellion with the utmost cruelty, and even those who fled to the forest were chased. Over 80 thousand men, women, and children were forced to convert else they would be killed. In this sad saga of tyranny, many were killed for not converting, and others were converted and circumcised. The women were captured and distributed among the soldiers, and the most beautiful ones were sent to Tipu's harem.[63]

Alas, this was just one episode of the 'benevolent' and 'noble' Sultan. It will require more research and space to give further details of his other atrocious activities against the 'infidels'.

Bengal and Islamic Movements

Before dealing with this subject, let us review one of the Islamic movements relevant here for Eastern Bengal. A religious reform movement in some rural parts of Eastern Bengal called Faraizi was started by Haji Shariatullah in 1819. The purpose was to eliminate 'un-Islamic' practices of Bengali Hindus and focus on their duties and obligations as true Muslims for Allah, which in Urdu is called Farz; thus, the name Faraizi – and the followers were called Tawbar Muslim or Mumin. They belonged to the Hanafi school and banned all cultural activities which were not sanctions or references in Quran or Hadith called *bidah* or sins.[64] One of the movement's aims was to fight against the ban of cow slaughter by the Muslims in some areas by the Hindu landlords. After the death of Shariatullah in 1837, his son Md. Mohsin or Dudu Mian became the de facto leader.

There is also a major cover-up and whitewash of some Islamist personalities portrayed as freedom fighters. Like Tipu as Sultan, in Bengal, a key figure was Syed Mīr Nisār 'Alī , popularly known as Titumir, born in modern Bangladesh. Most history books present him as a 'peasant leader' who led an uprising against the East India Company and the British. But really? All information about him lead to one conclusion – he worked hard to re-establish strict Sharia among the followers. While he did fight against the persecution of the poor by the Britishers and landlords, his key inspiration was to reestablish the lost glory of Islamic rule in Bengal. Tutumir's family is said to be of Arab origin and were descendants of Ali, and one of his ancestors Saiyid Shahadat Ali came to India to preach Islam. Sahadat's son Mir Insaaf or Sayid Abdullah was appointed as the Qazi or Judge of an Islamic Sharia court.[65]

While in Mecca, in 1822, Titumir encountered Islamist preacher Syed Ahmad Barelvi, a key figure in the Deobandi Wahabi Islamist movement. Barelvi was known for advocating Jihad to 'purge all non-Islamic corruptions from sociopolitical life and enforce Sharia'.[66]

He also met, Haji Shariatullah who founded the 'Wahabi Farazi' movement. After he returned from a pilgrimage to Mecca, he started a Jahilya or Islamic purification movement and preached against deviating from Quran and asked his followers to have beards, women to wear burqas.[67, 68]

His main target was poor Muslim farmers (his followers) and the Hindu landlords (opponents) called zamindars. He told them that these landlords were working closely with the British and caused much oppression.

As a result, the poor Muslims and some neglected low-caste Hindus joined him. So, no 'large scale peasantry' followed him due to fighting against the rich, but against the Hindu kafir landlords where very few Hindus were involved; but the landlords, including Muslim ones, were against Titumir. He took advantage of this incident and announced himself as the leader of these mostly Muslim farm laborers with the title *Badsha* or king of the region of Narkelberia. He created resistance against zamindar Krishnadeva Rai with about a thousand followers. He rebelled against the zamindar forces and the local zamindars were compelled to either submit to his rule or vacate the land-holdings.[69]

While he could manage some of the zamindars, eventually, they had to face the East India Company forces since they were keeping an eye on Titumir for almost a decade for his rebellious activities. In anticipation before such a face-off occurred, he constructed a bamboo-fort (*Banser Kella in Bengali*) at Narkelberia. On 17 November 1831, Governor-General of India Bentinck asked several District Magistrates to lead forces with heavy weaponry along with private guards of Zamindars. The next morning the fort fell, and Titumir and 50 of his fellow soldiers were put to death by the bayonet; about 800 others were arrested.[70]

Fast forward to March 1971, before an important meeting took place between Maulana Bhasani and Mujibur Rahman. Prior to this meeting, it was decided in order to honor Titumir, the *Jinnah College* in Dhaka built in 1968 was renamed to Government Titumir College.[71] The naval base of Bangladesh Navy was named as 'BNS Titumir'. Many were surprised by this move to erase Jinnah's name. And the legacy of this falsification of history in glorifying the likes of Titumir and Tipu Sultan continues.

References

1. https://commons.wikimedia.org/wiki/File:Painting_of_Shahjahan%E2%80%99s_time_preserved_in_the_Bodleian_Library.jpg (This painting preserved in the Bodleian Library, Oxford, was reproduced in the *Illustrated Weekly of India* (page 32) of March 14, 1971.)
2. "Royal Emblem of King Anangpal in Red Fort", Tej Pratap Singh Solanki http://tejpratapsingh.blogspot.com/2013/01/royal-emblem-of-king-anangpal-in-red.html
3. Z.A. Desai, H.K. Kaul, Taj Museum (Annexure III, ASI Guide Book to Taj Museum), The Director General ASI, 1997 http://ip51.icomos.org/~fleblanc/projects/2001-2007_GCI/Taj%20Mahal/Taj%20Mahal%20Collaborative%202001/Taj_Mahal_2001_Annex-III_Guidebook.pdf
4. Epigraphia Indica, Volume 1, p. 238-239 https://archive.org/details/EpigraphiaIndicaVol1/page/n238/mode/1up

5. "Far East Kingdoms South Asia" https://www.historyfiles.co.uk/KingListsFarEast/IndiaBundelkhand.htm#
6. "Shēr Shah of Sūr". Encyclopædia Britannica. https://www.britannica.com/biography/Sher-Shah-of-Sur
7. R. C. Majumdar (Gen Ed), "History & Culture of the Indian People", Bharatiya Vidya Bhavan, Vol-5, p. 122
8. Shah Jahan, Elliot, H. M. Sir, Sh. Mubarak Ali, Lahore, 1875
9. Agra, historical & descriptive, Latif, Muḥammad (1896), Calcutta Central Press Co.
10. "Tomars of Delhi" by Harihar Niwas Dwivedi. Gwalior: Vidya Mandir Publication. 1983. p. 188.
11. A.C. Tuli, "For Delhi, the heart of India", The Statesman, 25 November 2016 https://www.thestatesman.com/features/for-delhi-the-heart-of-india-1480115730.html
12. Sociological Bulletin, Volume 53, Indian Sociological Society, 2004
13. Dhruvin Busa, "Sword & Scepter - Discover The History Of Delhi You Never Knew About", Homegrown, 27 Nov 2019 https://homegrown.co.in/article/803976/sword-scepter-discover-the-history-of-delhi-you-never-knew-about
14. Sailendra Nath Sen (1999). "Ancient Indian History and Civilization". New Age. p. 339
15. https://lighteddream.wordpress.com/2015/05/
16. "Tomars of Delhi" by Harihar Niwas Dwivedi. Gwalior: Vidya Mandir Publication. 1983. p. 188.
17. Sharma, Y.D (2001). Delhi and its Neighbourhood. Surjakund and Anagpur Dam. New Delhi: Archaeological Survey of India. p. 100.
18. Peck, Lucy (2005). "Delhi - A thousand years of building. Suraj Kund dam and Surajkund tank". New Delhi: Roli Books Pvt Ltd. p. 29.

19. "Ticketed Monuments – Haryana: Suraj Kund". National Informatics Centre, Government of India.
20. History of Delhi, Britannica https://www.britannica.com/place/Delhi/History
21. Ibid.
22. Cynthia Talbot (2015). "The Last Hindu Emperor: Prithviraj Cauhan and the Indian Past, 1200–2000". Cambridge University Press. p.53.
23. R. B. Singh "History of the Chāhamānas". N. Kishore. 1964, pp. 186–88.
24. Talbot, 2015, p. 51.
25. R. B. Singh (1964). p. 186–88.
26. Richards, John F. (1995). "The Mughal Empire" (The New Cambridge History of India). Cambridge University Press. p. 13.
27. Sarkar, Jadunath (1960). "Military History of India". Orient Longmans. p. 66–69
28. Tripathi, Ram Prasad (1960). "Rise and Fall of the Mughal Empire *(2nd ed.). p. 158–77.*
29. Dodgson, Marshall G.S. (2009). "The Venture of Islam". Volume 3: The Gunpowder Empires and Modern Times. University of Chicago Press. p. 62.
30. "The Hidden Story of Partition and its Legacies", Dr. Crispin Bates, http://www.bbc.co.uk/history/british/modern/partition1947_01.shtml
31. "Impact of Hindu Culture on Muslims", Mohsen Saeidi Madani, MD Publications New Delhi, 1993 p. 59.
32. The Universal History of Numbers - By Georges Ifrah p. 530 – 531.
33. Fragments historiques sur l'linde - By Voltaire p. 444 – 445.
34. Upendra Kachru (2011), India Land of a Billion Entrepreneurs, Pearson Education India.

35. Tod, James, Annals and antiquities of Rajasthan, or the central and western Rajpoot states of India. London, Smith, Elder and co., etc. 1829–32. p. 608–609.
36. Manas Chakravarty, "World history by per capita GDP", Livemint, 25 Aug 2010 https://www.livemint.com/Opinion/Nb7KkZ3yOVSNW3vHf9K1oM/World-history-by-per-capita-GDP.html
37. Wendell Cox, "500 Years Of Gdp: A Tale Of Two Countries", New Geography, 21 September 2015 https://www.newgeography.com/content/005050-500-years-gdp-a-tale-two-countries
38. Charles Wolf, Jr., Siddhartha Dalal, Julie DaVanzo, Eric V. Larson, Alisher Akhmedjonov, Harun Dogo, Meilinda Huang, Silvia Montoya, "China and India, 2025: A Comparative Assessment", NATIONAL DEFENSE RESEARCH INSTITUTE
39. Prepared for the Office of the Secretary of Defense, 2011 https://www.rand.org/content/dam/rand/pubs/monographs/2011/RAND_MG1009.pdf
40. 'The lowdown on the Indian rupee', https://www.travelex.co.uk/currency/currency-pairs/gbp-to-inr
41. Lala Lajpat Rai (1917), 'England's Debt to India: A Historical Narrative of Britain's Fiscal Policy in India', New York.
42. 'Agrarian and Other Histories', Essays for Binay Bhushan Chaudhuri, Edited by Shubhra Chakrabarti and Utsa Patnaik, 2018.
43. Sreevatsan, Ajai, "British Raj siphoned out $45 trillion from India: Utsa Patnaik", *Livemint,* November 22, 2018 https://www.livemint.com/Companies/HNZA71LNVNNVXQ1eaIKu6M/British-Raj-siphoned-out-45-trillion-from-India-Utsa-Patna.html
44. "Muslims should stop eating beef, cow meat 'haram' in Islam: Shia Waqf Board chief Waseem Rizvi", *Zee News,*

July 24, 2018, https://zeenews.india.com/india/muslims-should-stop-eating-beef-cow-meat-haram-in-islam-shia-waqf-board-chief-waseem-rizvi-2127298.html

45. Elst, Koenraad (1992), "Negationism in India: Concealing the Record of Islam", *Voice of India*, (2002, 2014).
46. Konrad, Mike "The Greatest Murder Machine in History". https://www.americanthinker.com/articles/2014/05/the_greatest_murder_machine_in_history.html#ixzz48Z66k9gV
47. Roychowdhury, Adrija "Masjid Mubarak Begum: The story behind 'Rundi ki masjid', built by an ambitious Mughal concubine", *The Indian Express,* 22 July 2020 https://indianexpress.com/article/research/masjid-mubarak-begum-the-story-behind-rundi-ki-masjid-built-by-an-ambitious-mughal-concubine-6514901/
48. Brown, Katherine Khuda Bakhsh extension Lecture, "Did Aurangzeb Ban Music?" Khuda Bakhsh Library auditorium. https://m.timesofindia.com/city/patna/Aurangzebs-ban-on-music-a-major-event/articleshow/929628.cms
49. Seiple, Chris (2013). "The Routledge handbook of religion and security". New York: Routledge. p. 96.
50. "Baburnama", translated/edited by A.S. Alridge. p. 574–75.
51. Hiltebeitel, Alf (2009), "Rethinking India's Oral and Classical Epics: Draupadi among Rajputs, Muslims, and Dalits", University of Chicago Press, p. 227.
52. "Babur Nama", translated by A.F. Beveridge, 1922, II, p. LXXVII.
53. Shekhar, Shakti "Ram temple existed before Babri mosque in Ayodhya: Archaeologist K.K. Mohammad", *The Times of India,* 1 October 2019, https://timesofindia.indiatimes.com/india/ram-temple-existed-before-babri-mosque-in-ayodhya-archaeologist-kk-muhammed/articleshow/71391712.cms

54. Elisseeff, Vadime "The Silk Roads: Highways of Culture and Commerce", pp. 159–162.
55. Madani, 1993. p. 59.
56. Oak, P.N. "Taj Mahal: The True Story", 1965.
57. Knapp, Stephen (2009), "Crimes Against India: And the Need to Protect Its Ancient Vedic Tradition", iUniverse.
58. William Pickthall, Marmaduke; Muhammad Asad, (1975). "Islamic culture", Volume 49. Islamic Culture Board. p. 50.
59. Abu'l-Fazl,"Ain-i-Akbari",fromhttps://archive.org/stream/kingsrodetodelhi00festiala/kingsrodetodelhi00festiala_djvu.txt
60. Hasan Nizami, 'Taj-ul-Maasir': Lal, K. S. (1994). "Muslim slave system in medieval India". New Delhi: Aditya Prakashan. Chapter 10,
61. "Tipu Sultan true secularist: Siddaramaiah", *The Indian Express,* 8 November 2015, https://indianexpress.com/article/india/india-news-india/tipu-sultan-true-secularist-siddaramaiah/
62. Mysore Gazetteer Volume II, C. Hayavadana Rao
63. "The history of the reign of Tipu Sultan", written by Mir Hussein Ali Khan Kirmani and translated from the original Persian by Colonel W. Miles: Chapter VI pp. 68–85.
64. Wenger, Estefenis, "Tipu Sultan, A Biography", Vij Books, 2017.
65. "Haji Shariatullah". Muslim Ummah of North America.
66. Khan, Muazzam Hussain. "Titu Mir". Banglapedia. Bangladesh Asiatic Society
67. Dasgupta, Atis (1983). "Titu Meer's Rebellion: A Profile". Social Scientist. 11 (10): pp. 39–48. doi:10.2307/3517042.
68. Khan, Titu Mir.
69. Dasgupta (1983).

70. Ibid.
71. Bose, Neilesh (2009). "Anti-colonialism, regionalism, and cultural autonomy: Bengali Muslim politics, c.1840s–1952", (Thesis). Tufts University. pp. 58–59.
72. Jagannath College – Banglapedia". en.banglapedia.org.

❑

CHAPTER

8

IMPACT OF MUSLIM LEADERS, INSTITUTES, AND MOVEMENTS

How many generations can the trauma of genocide continue for?
Why Gandhi wanted the rule of the Ottoman Empire and Caliphate in India?
What was the most significant impact on non-Muslims in the subcontinent after the failure of the Khilafat movement?
Why the Moplah pogrom of the Hindus was passed on as 'peasant rebellion'?
Who was responsible for establishing communist institutes in India?
How JNU and Aligarh were established, which are the hotbeds of anti-national and separatist tendencies?
Was Gandhi responsible for a secular Jinnah to become Islamist?

Psychological and Genetic Impact of Trauma

A fundamental human behavior is the fear of death when faced with danger or a life-threatening situation. It is very natural because we fear death most. Now imagine a day in prehistory. You are living in a cave, and on a dark night, a large black bear with sharp nails and teeth shows up out of nowhere – you are now face to face with imminent death. Remember, you neither have a flashlight nor a gun. Perhaps some stone weapons. What are you supposed to do? If you have courage and strength – you will try to slay the beast. But if not – you would try to run as fast as you can. Science calls it 'Fight or Flight Syndrome' and tells us that we are programmed (brain and genes) permanently or wired to behave like this. It is said that there is supposed to be a third way in the case of a bear – you lay down pretending to be dead, and the bear won't touch you. But it is not verified and is unlikely to work. However, there are two other possible reactions to threat – 'freeze' (to survive and thus surrender), which is involuntary – body's vital functions stop – you become immobile. The discovery of this third reaction has expanded the syndrome's scope to 'Fight, Flight, Freeze or Fawn (appease - voluntary)' – Four F's.[1][2] This also may explain why the wives of most abusive husbands still protect the abuser. In aggressive rape cases, the victim either 'freeze' or 'appease' the perpetrator to save her life.

The trigger of this syndrome can be real or perceived; for example, the war veterans returning to society from the battlefield sometimes find enemies everywhere and behave abnormally. What happened to them? While they might be programmed neurologically of particular memories, there is a very good chance that their gene expressions called 'epigenetics' has also been affected! So, when people go through trauma such as rape, murder, genocide, the experience of trauma may continue for not only the rest of their lives but also many generations after. The genetic imprint is transferred to the progenies. Besides the 'Ostrich Syndrome', where the potential prey or victim denies or hides its head in the sand while facing danger, the four F's and epigenetic changes together affect the behavior of all victims of trauma, especially enslaved people like the Hindus during Islamic and British rule, and even now.

When the British rule was established in India, they also came with a judicial system that was to some extent fair, especially for their own people – compared to what the Hindus went through for centuries under Islamic rule. The Hindus kind of heaved a sigh of relief as if their freedom was back. Soon the beast within the Brits were revealed. On the one hand, Hindus were trying to get out of the mess created over a few centuries by the invaders, and now suddenly, they realized that they had to fight another oppressing power! The majority of Muslims at that time thought that the Muslim rulers were still ruling the country, whereas the Mughals were merely Delhi aristocrats, to describe in the best way.

The majority of the Indian Muslims are converted Hindus, often brutally, and their epigenetics also changed due to the severe hardship they lived through for centuries. They not only 'appeased' the Islamist preachers or converters, but they also have developed a hatred towards their ancestors, perhaps not for saving and rescuing them from the clutches of Islamic rulers and clerics. The Islamic religious leaders preach to them about the superiority of the Mughals, Ghazni, Khilji, etc. Many of them buy it due to either some or many of these factors: fear of Allah and *dozhak* (hell), inferiority complex, and identity crisis. Due to traumatic epigenetic changes, they accept the preachers' assertions without question. The case with non-Muslims is different; along with their neurological conditioning of flight or freeze, their epigenetics, when active, experience the trauma that holds them from any defense or offense. Even among those who left East Pakistan and came to India, many of them suffer from these as well. There are many studies that prove these conditions.[3] Revelations of genetic research on the impact of the African slave trade are very poignant for the Indians also.[4] This may explain why a large number of Indians are docile when they come face to face with historical truth and violent events around them. Appeasement of their past tormentors has become a norm. You may say, well, is revenge the answer?

Definitely not; acknowledging, accepting, and healing through reconciliation is the answer, but not an outright denial. It will go a long way in taking the relationships of two communities. We will discuss definitive measures on this in the second book.

Sindh, Punjab, Rajasthan, and other parts of the country valiantly fought the invasions from the beginning of the first millennium CE. The legendary Hindu warriors, not just Shivaji, Ranjit Singh, or Rana Pratap – but millions fought against Islamic brutalities to protect their land, life, and culture – just because they were Hindus and refused to convert. But after Gandhi came to the scene, Hindus became utterly pacifists even in their fight against the British; extraordinary exceptions were the freedom fighters in Bengal, Punjab, and other parts of the country.

Seeing this pacifism, Subhas Bose left the country to bring a martial spirit among the people and launched a fight against the British from outside. Today many people acknowledge that India got freedom, not because of the non-violent movement, but the violent ones, including the heroism of the Azad Hind Fauj or Indian National Army (INA) and the Naval Revolt by the Indian soldiers in the British Navy and army which was influenced by the INA and Subhas Bose's activities.

India's partition happened based on the assertion that 'Muslims cannot live with Hindus' theory, inspired by the pan-Islamic expansionist ideology, that is, the 'Two-Nation Theory'.[5] based on the theological ideas of '*dar-ul-Harb*' and '*dar-ul-Islam*'.

But a peaceful population exchange did not occur along with the partition, and millions died in religious violence, thousands were raped. Even today, a tribunal could be and should be formed to assess one of the most treacherous and horrific episodes of human suffering in history. Although Hindus did not ask for the partition, they suffered tremendously during this transition. Both the British Government, key negotiators of partition and independence from the Indian side, should have been made accountable and given proper treatment and place in Indian history, even posthumously. The partition left the minorities in Pakistan vulnerable to persecution. As a result, the Hindu-Sikh population in West Pakistan and the Hindu-Buddhist population in East Pakistan dwindled down to a tiny percentage since 1947. According to *"Population & Housing Census-2011: Union Statistics" [Bangladesh Bureau of Statistics. March 2014. p. xiii]* in 1941, minority population was 28%, in 1951, 22%, and in 2011 it was 8.5%. Today the number is even less. Most parts of Pakistan, including Punjab and Baloch, Sindh, POK – Gilgit, Chitral, etc., are experiencing continuous ethnic cleansing to date.[6]

But what for? The minorities chose 'flight' over 'fight' and, in many cases, 'freeze' because the political leadership, law and enforcement, and the judicial systems of Pakistan and Bangladesh did not protect the helpless people.

Jaina and Buddha traditions preach and teach ahimsa, so does the Yoga philosophy, which is a great virtue. Especially in Bengal – there was a considerable impact on the population following Jaina and Buddha traditions. Bengal was Buddhist and Jain for a long time – the martial class vanished under the doctrine of ahimsa. Unfortunately, when the invaders came to these parts of India, they could not give a proper fight, surrendered, and converted. Just like what happened to many parts of India after Ashoka became pacifist and began rooting out the Kshatriya class. Post-Independence, Hindus turned to pacifism in all three divided parts. This pacifism was aided by none other than Gandhi and, of course, the effect of 4 F's and epigenetics.

The political and social system in India kept the majority of the Muslims illiterate and impoverished and was made into a 'vote bank' by various political parties. The economic backwardness has fueled extremism everywhere. ISIS recruits and recruiters are regularly found in the Madrassas. It is not because Hindus oppressed them, but Jihad's theology inspires many, incited by religious leaders and funded by countries like Pakistan, Turkey, Qatar, Malaysia, and Saudi Arabia.

So, when Hindus are attacked in the media, the judicial system and law enforcement apparatus in many cases fail to ensure justice to the Hindus, lies are spread by vested interest groups, including the Marxists, to create a situation that makes it seem like minorities are always the victims. As if all responsibilities lie on the 'big brother', the majority of Hindus. This situation makes the majority of the Hindus more docile ('flight' syndrome), some 'freeze' and very few 'fight'. But the media still color it as a communal riot 'started by the Hindus' with slogans like 'minorities are under threat' or 'Muslims are in danger' etc. That is the sad reality today. Hinduphobia has been created worldwide by vested interest groups like evangelists, jihadists, and leftover communists! They have fished in muddy waters to exploit the underprivileged people's sentiments by inciting hatred towards the rest and using the British- introduced divide and control mechanism.

So, for the Muslims, though they also suffered under British rule, very few were thinking of getting rid of the British to have an independent India rather than a global Islamic Caliphate. Most Muslims felt proud of their ancestors, such as the invaders or converts, whereas Hindu leaders, from Bankimchandra to Vivekananda, from Tilak to Aurobindo, all saw through the design and concluded that they had to assert that Hindus revoke the past glory to free India, recognize the pain of their ancestors and their contributions. So Bankim gave the *mantra* of *Vandemataram*, and Aurobindo saw Mother Durga and Mother India as the same and called the former *Bhavani* and the latter *Bharatmata*. This helped thousands of Hindus to unite to perform one duty – fight for freedom from British Rule.

In the meantime, Gandhi started his political career on the wrong foot. The Caliphate or Khilafat movement (Ottoman Turks) was trying to re-establish the global Caliphate including in India. Gandhi supported the movement and coerced Congress Party to do the same. That was instrumental in creating a further gap between the Hindus fighting for freedom and the ordinary Muslims who mostly rejected Indian nationalism. Though there were some Muslims who joined the freedom movement, the proportion was very much lacking. The seed of 'Muslim appeasement', meaning accepting their demands over majority wishes or national interest, was sowed by then in the 1920s.

The Khilafat Movement

The post of Caliph is the global head of the Islamic world, similar to the position of the Pope in the Vatican for the Catholic Christians globally. The First Islamic Caliph was Abu Bakr, son-in-law of Muhammad. The most recent one was Mullah Omar, founder of the Taliban and Islamic Emirate of Afghanistan.[7] During World War I, Muslim leaders worldwide rallied behind the Ottoman Empire and the Caliphate to fight against the British to recover the lost Islamic empire; this was called the Khilafat movement. In India, many of the Khilafat leaders were imprisoned for their sympathies towards the Turkish empire. Many of these leaders and some Hindu leaders of the Indian Independence movement, including Gandhi, supported and urged Indians (non-Muslims included) to join it. On January 19, 1921, in a public speech in Gujarat, Gandhi said: "I tell the Hindu sadhus, that if they sacrifice all for the sake of the Khilafat, they will have a great thing for the protection of Hinduism. Today the duty of every Hindu is to save Islam from danger. If you do this, God himself will inspire them to look upon Hindus as friends, and Hindus will look upon them as friends."[8]

One of the key leaders in this movement was Abul Kalam Azad, who later was appointed the first education minister of independent India. Manmohan Sharma, in his book 'ISIS History, Evolution and Contemporary Challenges' quotes historian Saradindu Mukherji, "... he (Azad) was then known as the ex-editor of Al-Hillal and was the founder of Hizbullah Society at the Dar-ul-Irshad College at Calcutta which was described as the 'pan-Islamist of extreme type, rabidly anti-British, and extremely fanatical'."[9]

The idea behind the Khilafat movement was to ensure the seat of the Ottoman Sultan and the Caliphate after the war was over. In reality, it had nothing to do with the Indian nationalistic movement; it was the opposite – to have a buy-in of the Indian leaders to support the pan-Islamist agenda. Or was it a British ploy to destroy the Khilafat movement, which was going to trouble them? The movement adopted the non-cooperation method called *Satyagraha,* which was the center of the general Independence movement method of Gandhi. It became a mass movement, and the British were worried. They suppressed the movement violently, and Gandhi suspended the campaign by 1922. Two birds were killed at once – Khilafat and Satyagraha! The new Turkish leaders, after their independence, abolished the Ottoman Sultanate – and with that, the last hope to salvage the Ottoman Caliphate and Sultanate was gone. Islamists lost much of its political significance very fast. The Deobandi movement was, in a way, a response to regain the loss of Muslim political power under British rule in India.

Mukherjee concluded with what was the long-term impact of this movement: "Besides the loss of innocent Hindu lives, it only confirmed the religio-cultural-political differences between the Hindus and Muslims at various levels. It was a blunder on the part of Gandhi to have systematically encouraged the Muslims to deepen their pan-Islamic solidarity and thus further their distance from their closest neighbours from whom came their not-too-distant ancestors. Gandhi had failed to anticipate the danger in playing up with the primordial forces, and he would be repeating the same blunder on a larger scale leading to the partition of India in 1947."[10]

Hand Shaking of Communism and Islamism

If Gandhi's support to the Khilafat movement was not enough, in the 1950s, M.N. Roy (original name Narendra Nath

Bhattacharya) indirectly changed the direction of the Hindu-Muslim relation narrative in Indian history. He introduced Marxism to the Indian elites, which in turn later would take the Marxist-Colonist-Islamist depiction of India's past.

M.N. Roy, who closely worked with Jatin Bhattacharya – a revolutionary freedom fighter, and Aurobindo Ghosh (Sri Aurobindo) tried to collect arms for the Indian independence movement from different countries but failed. Later he fled to and hid in Mexico, where he formed the Mexican Communist Party. Afterward, he was invited by Lenin and joined the International communist body of Comintern.[11]

He formulated how to make entire South Asia a 'communist block' and inspired forming the Communist Party of India (CPI – 1920).[12]

Roy's first set of recruits were several Muslim intellectuals (called ex-Muhajirs), including Mohammad Shafiq and Mohammad Ali. Later, Roy had a fallout with Stalin and returned to India. He escaped Stalin's purging as it happened to many Indian communists like Virendranath Chattopadhyay (brother of Sarojini Naidu), a prominent person outside India in India's freedom struggle.[13] He met with Nehru and Subhash Bose – rejoined the Indian National Congress (was welcomed by Nehru), and asked his communist friends to join Congress to 'radicalize the Congress party'. Nehru said: "I was attracted to him by his remarkable intellectual capacity."[14]

But later, Roy had a disagreement with Congress Party leaders, including Gandhi, and he formed his own Radical Democratic Party (1940).

It is apparent that Roy influenced Nehru's thoughts, and he became close to Russia. On the one hand, Nehru followed socialism, became an Islamist sympathizer, and embedded Western ideals on the other. Though he wrote *The Discovery of India*, he proved himself to be an amalgamation of communist and Western ideals.

He negated the atrocities of Islam on India and Hindus. He suggested that Islam 'was welcomed by the lower castes of India',[15] and any violence of the so-called 'progressive forces' against the 'reactionary forces' of the upper-class Hindus was justified. Yes, a good number of neglected lower caste people embraced Islam due to caste discrimination and oppression by the upper castes – but there is no evidence to prove that 'the lower caste people welcomed Islam as their savior', and that had no comparison to what Islamists did to the Hindus! There was no provision by the Islamic invaders to treat the upper and lower caste Hindus differently – to them, they all were idolaters and kafirs. This line of thinking became the cornerstone of subsequent communist movements in India to negate the Islamist barbarism in India. Jawaharlal Nehru picked it up later and had a glorious honeymoon period with the communists and Islamists for him to become the first-rate liar about Indian history. Why did Nehru act in this way? Was there a hidden pride in possible Muslim and Mughal links in his psyche? According to some, his grandfather was a Muslim (Ghiyasuddin Ghazi) and changed his name and religion to save him from British wrath after the 1857 uprising. According to M.K. Singh, author of *Encyclopaedia of Indian war of Independence*: "It is now quite clear, as you will soon see that Ganga Dhar (grandfather of Nehru) was an assumed name. The man we now know as the paternal grandfather of Jawahar Lal (son of Moti Lal) was, in reality, a Sunni Mohammedan; in fact, he was a Mogul nobleman." The book gives details of sources from which he came to this conclusion.[16]

Some people claim that Nehru said: "I am English by education, Muslim by culture and Hindu by accident". This author has not found any direct proof of this statement. But it is confirmed that when Nehru was the President of Congress in 1929, in his presidential address in Lahore, he said: "I was born a Hindu but I do not know how far I am justified in calling myself one or speaking on behalf of Hindus. But birth still counts in this country and by right of birth I venture to submit to the leaders of the Hindus that it should be their privilege to take the lead in generosity. Generosity is not only good morals but is often good politics and sound expediency. And it is inconceivable to me that in a free India the Hindus can ever be powerless."[17]

The Congress Party leaders, after his death, inherited Nehru's legacy of denial of Islamic atrocities, and it was taken over by the Marxist and Islamist historians of Delhi, most of whom belong to the Stalinist sect of communists. The NeoCols created necessary machinery to manufacture many socio-political narratives and myths from their viewpoint.

India's first education minister was Maulana Abul Kalam Azad – portrayed as a great nationalist freedom fighter, former President of Indian National Congress, appointed by Nehru. He was born in Mecca, which was part of the Ottoman Empire, and was a Muslim theologian. He founded the Jamia Millia Islamia University in 1920 along with Dr. Mukhtar Ahmed Ansari, Mahmud al-Hasan, and a few others. Dr. Ansari was a leader of Congress and the Muslim League, and both he and Hasan were staunch supporters of the Khilafat movement.

Is it possible that the economy of an undivided India could become more powerful than not only Britain but also Europe? So, first, the British authorities divided the country to make it weak and then looted the remaining wealth and left the land almost bloodless before departing. On the other hand, they wanted to have Pakistan in their hands so that they could control it to ensure access and dominance on the region west and north of Pakistan for strategic reasons. According to Narendra Singh Sarila, the aide-de-camp to Earl Mountbatten, "Partition of India may not have been totally unconnected with the British concern that the Great Game between them and the USSR for acquiring influence in the area lying between Turkey and India was likely to recommence with even greater gusto after the Second World War and the start of the Cold War. And to find military bases and partners for the same." [18]

According to him, "The British believed that the safety of their Indian empire and access to the oil fields in the Middle East lay in keeping the Russians at a distance beyond the Oxus River on the northern fringes of Afghanistan. British strategic interests demanded that they have access to and partners in the northwest of India even after India's independence. Indeed, the start of the Cold War even before India's independence made this even more imperative, and the USSR's invasion of Afghanistan nearly 30 years after independence confirmed British fears. … the feeling with both the Churchill and Attlee governments in Britain that the Partition of India was necessary to protect British interests".

While the Indian nationalists, mainly the Congress leaders, failed to see through the design and game plan of the British, it appears that Jinnah was aware of the key motive for the division of India and the creation of Pakistan. Sarila noted: "Jinnah's cooperation with the British dovetailed with their efforts to carve out a friendly sphere of influence in the North West."

Sarila's book revealed that Field Marshall Wavell, Viceroy of India, 1943-47, and predecessor of Mountbatten concluded that India had to be partitioned to preserve British interests and even drew maps (eerily similar to the Cyrill Radcliff division of India) as early as 1946 that showed the desired boundary demarcation. While in London, Wavell, on August 31, 1945, called on Churchill. According to Wavell's account: 'He warned me that the anchor [himself] was now gone and I was on a lee shore with rash pilots...His final remark, as I closed the door of the lift was: "keep a bit of India."'

Finally, the eternal fight between Pakistan and India would keep India weak and bleeding because they were very much aware that an Islamist nation born out of hatred toward the non-believers would not give up hope to convert the entire country into *Dar-al-Islam* through war and various types of terror activities as proxy-war.

Actually, history is slightly different. In the 1940s, Azad, then Congress President, propagated the idea of a 'United India' where the Muslims and rest (Hindus, Sikhs, Christians, and the 'Ambedkarites' meaning the lower caste Hindus) have 50% representation each in the parliament where the Muslim population was around 25% with veto power to the Muslims members. British bought the formula during their plan to hand over the power to the Indians; their secret support to Muslim League would not leave a real united India. In 1946, the Cabinet Mission was sent to India with Stafford Cripps, Pethick-Lawrence, and A.V. Alexander, who wanted a 'united India' as formulated by Azad. Azad had a secret deal with the British,[20] and even Gandhi was kept away though the design was leaked and could not be made into an Act. All this was to ensure creating a Muslim state in all of India in the long term, and the designer was none other than Maulana Abul Kalam Azad, later an entrusted member of the Nehru cabinet. Although many important works were done during his ministership, how much was his own idea is questionable. He was posthumously awarded India's highest Award 'Bharat Ratna'. While Nehru called him a 'Caravan Leader' and eulogized, saying, "a very brave and gallant gentleman, a finished product of the culture that, in these days, pertains to few"[20] and Gandhi praised him as "a person of the calibre of Plato, Aristotle and Pythagoras".[21]

Maulana Abul Kalam Azad was the true inheritor of the pan-Islamist design along with his sinister plan to further diffuse any attempt to blame the Muslim invaders and rulers for atrocities against the Hindus, glorify the Muslim rulers, and Nehru made him the education minister!

Great efforts were made to create institutes to make Islamic ideas polished and propagate Islamism using Western methods. An orthodox Sunni theologian school called Deoband was established in 1886, led by Maulana Maudoodi. He saw India as a 'house of Islam', according to him, needed to be re-established; actually, Maudoodi wanted the entire British Empire to be ruled by Islamic power. Maudoodi was the founder of Jamaat-e-Islami, the largest Islamist organization in Asia. After independence, he moved to Pakistan and worked all his life for this mission. His close disciple, Pakistani President Mohammad Zia-ul Haq, who was assassinated, was instrumental in 'shariaization' of Pakistan. Using the notorious spy agency ISI he started his mission to decimate the Hindu population in Pakistan and covertly invade India. Maulana Azad worked closely with the Deobandis. One can only conclude that the 'united India' was just a ploy to create an Islamic state in India by the so-called moderate nationalist leader!

Two centers were established in India for Muslim learning and propagation of Islamic ideas and theology.

An Islamic university was formed in India in 1866 called Darul Uloom Deoband in the town of Deoband in Uttar Pradesh. The institute belongs to the conservative Hanafi school, and it emerged as a major Sunni Islamic platform and movement called 'Deobandi', which influences thousands of Madrassas globally.[22]

Many from the Sunni sect worked against the partition of India because they supported the Khilafat movement; the idea was an indirect rule of India by Muslims to bring back the glory of the Mughals and Pathans. A key Deobandi leader Hussain Ahmad Madani whose father claimed to be the descendant of Muhammad was instrumental in having the Congress-Khilafat Pact. And it either escaped Gandhi's imagination, or he did not mind a pan-Islamic design in the Khilafat movement. And the same Madani got India's first Padma Bhushan Award in 1954!

Deoband frequently issues fatwa or religious edict. A few recent ones include banning Salman Rushdie's book and barring his entry to India in 2012; in 2010, they issued a fatwa that men and women cannot be together in public offices unless women are 'properly' dressed. Another fatwa in 2013 banned photography as un-Islamic.

The second institute was a semi-western structured school, Aligarh Muslim University, established to ensure the propagation of Islam in a modern era by removing all negatives associated with their religious books and history. Muhammadan Anglo-Oriental College (MAO) was established in 1875 by Syed Ahmed Khan to modernize education for the Muslims of India. He was very attracted to Western education and culture, wanted to reform Muslim society in India, and dreamt of Muslim education institutes in the model of Oxford and Cambridge. He worked for the East India Company. MAO College was renamed[23] to Aligarh Muslim University in 1920. Donations came from Governor-General Thomas Baring and many rich Muslims and some Hindu kings. Two key funding trustees were Aga Khan III and Ali Mohammad Khan Dehlavi. Both of them were President of the All-India Muslim League (AIML), which promoted the idea that Muslims had to have a separate nation within India, the so-called 'Two-Nation Theory', which later led to the partition of India. Khan also believed in Syed Ahmed Khan's vision of equipping Muslims with contemporary modern education methods.

Muslim poet Allam Iqbal, who is remembered for one of his early poems, wrote that *'Ye Hindustan hamara, sare jahan se accha',* meaning this Hindusthan or India is the best in the whole world. Jawaharlal Nehru made it popular and is still used by many Indians in their 'national' celebrations. But few people know that Iqbal turned to be a much stronger Islamist than Jinnah himself.

Also, many people forgot that though highly educated and accomplished in the British system, his 'Hindustan' was not truly his favorite land. He touted that in a democracy, 'heads are counted but not weighed,' and he opted for a separate land for the Muslims.

Iqbal wrote in *Payam-i-Mushraq* 'that you seek the treasures of our alien philosophy from the common, poor of mind and low grade people, as the crawling ants on the ground, can not attain the heights of wisdom of Hazrat Sulayman (The Prophet of God). You should avoid democracy and become within the bond of perfect man (the Holy Prophet), as two hundred donkeys can not have combined the brain of a man.'[24]

Explaining the quantitative aspect of the Western democracy, Iqbal added that a European gentleman had disclosed this secret that men of wisdom do not disclose what they have in their mind; and democracy is a kind of government, in which 'individuals are counted and not weighed.'[25]

He differed from people like Azad and realized that the dream of a Muslim rule in an undivided India was not possible due to the democratic setup. In the short term, he settled with a Muslim Pakistan and had a dream that India would be Islamized using the power of Pakistan in time.

While leaders like Maulana Azad felt that since India has a secular constitution and allows religious practice freedom to all, Muslims are as free as any Muslim country to observe their religious activities and India was not a *Dar Ul Harb*. However, his activities proved that he had a long-term pan-Islamist vision: India would become a Muslim state or *Dar ul Islam* one day. But Iqbal very clearly advocated that India was a *Dar Ul Harb*. His poem states:

"Mullah Ko Jo Hai Hind Mein Sajde Ki Ijazat,

Nadan Ye Samajhta Hai Ke Islam Hai Azad!"

It translates to,

In Hind, if the Mullah is allowed to prostrateHe thinks Islam is free.[26]

It means that by just being able to offer prayers, Islam is not free in India and that India was not an Islamic state (yet).

Iqbal was one key architect of Pakistan, especially by inspiring Jinnah. Alas, he could not dwell in this *'sare jahan se accha'* land; he chose Pakistan after the partition to become Pakistan's national poet. What really happened to him? Victim of Islamism?

Aligarh University soon deviated from the original goals of modern education and became the hotbed of these separatist ideas. A historian from Aligarh, Mohammed Habib, in 1920, took up a major project to rewrite the history of Islam in India, especially the subject of the Hindu-Muslim conflict in India, basically to justify the atrocities by the invaders and occupant imperial Muslim rulers. His thesis later became cannon fodder for communist historians. He propounded ideas that a typical 'Dalit' apologist would love. They would assert because Islam had no caste – everybody was equal, and lower-class Hindus accepted Islam gleefully as their savior. They would suggest that the motive of the Muslim persecutors was not necessarily religious, though there are plenty of documents by Muslim historians and chroniclers giving gory details of killings and atrocities as the jihad against the infidels and would call 'excesses' by the authors to please their patrons. As if these invaders were tribals and thus were barbarians, not due to inspiration from their scriptures, but the hatred towards non-Muslims. And we all know today, nothing can be hidden due to the information era – all above could have been exceptions, but in almost all cases – the norm was precisely the opposite.

The Moplah Massacre

We will now spend some time describing the first large-scale atrocities on Hindus, which would become a norm after the pan-Islamist Khilafat movement failed. According to Manmohan Sharma, "The most important and the most disastrous consequence of the utterly misguided Khilafat movement in India was the horror let loose on the hapless Hindus of Kerala, who suffered in the worst possible way at the hands of the Muslims suffused with the Khilafat spirit. Sought to be passed off as a Moplah 'rebellion', it was one of the most horrific anti-Hindu pogroms of the colonial times and all in the name of Islam."[27]

Mapilla is the oldest Muslim community in Kerala, whose ancestors are believed to be the first converts in India. The Moplah carnage, which is generally passed as a 'peasant rebellion', was a massive genocide of the Hindus. In 1921, over 10,000 Hindus were killed in this horrific massacre,[28] and thousands were forcibly converted; what happened here repeated in Noakhali and Calcutta in 1946. The mob was involved in the widespread destruction of railway properties, telephone lines, and looting and destruction of thousands of Hindu houses. For about six months, there was no rule of law.[29]

The NeoCol version of this massacre was portrayed as a rebellion against landowners who 'happened to be' Hindus. It was a meticulously planned event. A large number of swords and knives were distributed to the rioters before the event started. Congress leader Annie Besant's report[30] noted that more than 000 Hindus were killed, thousands of homes destroyed, and ndreds of families were dishonored and converted through rd and plunder. It was not against just the 'high-caste us', but all Hindus were killed; infants were slaughtered their mothers because they were born of Hindu parents. of interpreting that history, it would be much evident in the es of various authoritative sources.

The news of this horrific carnage committed by the Moplah Islamists quickly spread across India, especially all over southern India. It created an additional feeling of horror when certain Khilafat leaders passed a resolution saying, "congratulations to the Moplah on the brave fight they were conducting for the sake of religion." Gandhi joined them and praised the Moplahs, "brave God-fearing Moplahs who were fighting for what they consider as religion and in a manner which they consider as religious." [31]

While Gandhi supported the Khilafat movement to establish a Muslim Caliphate, visited Noakhali after the genocide there, he gave plenty of advice to the Hindus only. Arya Samaj conducted refugee rehabilitation camps, and later Swami Anand wrote a book called *Aryasamaj and Malabar*, which documented details of the riots. Veer Savarkar also wrote his novel *Moplah* based on the real events of Malabar. No Muslim leader condemned the massacre either. Instead, Maulana Modini called the looting and killing of Hindus was a 'military necessity'.[32]

Commenting on the silence of the Muslims, Gandhi had to say this to the Hindus:

"The Hindus must have the courage and the faith to feel that they can protect their religion in spite of such fanatical eruptions. A verbal disapproval by the Musalmans of Moplah madness is no test of Musalmans friendship. The Musalmans must naturally feel the shame and humiliation of the Moplah conduct about forcible conversions and looting, and they must work away so silently and effectively that such a thing might become impossible even on the part of the most fanatical among them. My belief is that the Hindus as a body have received the Moplah madness with equanimity and that the cultured Musalmans are sincerely sorry of the Moplahs perversion of the teaching of the Prophet." [33]

But this is what Swami Shraddhanand said:

But some of the Muslim leaders could not bear this even. Maulana Fakir and other Maulanas, of course, opposed the resolution, and there was no wonder. But I was surprised, an out-and-out Nationalist like Maulana Hasrat Mohani opposed the resolution on the ground that the Moplah country no longer remained Dar-ul-Aman but became Dar-ul-Harab and they suspected the Hindus of collusion with the British enemies of the Moplahs. Therefore, the Moplahs were right in presenting the Quran or sword to the Hindus. And if the Hindus became Musalmans to save themselves from death, it was a voluntary change of faith and not forcible conversion." [34]

Annie Besant recounted:

"Can you conceive of a more ghastly and inhuman crime than the murder of babies and pregnant women? ... A pregnant woman carrying 7 months was cut through the abdomen by a rebel, and she was seen lying dead on the way with the dead

child projecting out ... Another baby of six months was snatched away from the breast of the mother and cut into two pieces. ... Are these rebels' human beings or monsters?" [35]

C. Sankaran Nair wrote:

"The horrid tragedy continued for months. Thousands of Mahomedans killed, and wounded by (British) troops, thousands of Hindus butchered, women subjected to shameful indignities, thousands forcibly converted, persons flayed alive, entire families burnt alive, women it is said hundreds throwing themselves into wells to avoid dishonor, violence, and terrorism threatening death standing in the way of reversion to their own religion. This is what Malabar, in particular, owes to the Khilafat agitation, to Gandhi and his Hindu friends."[36]

The Viceroy Reading reported,

"Their wanton and unprovoked attack on the Hindus, the all but wholesale looting of their houses in Ernad, etc, the forcible conversion of Hindus in the beginning of the Moplah rebellion and the wholesale conversion of those who stuck to their homes in later stages, the brutal murder of inoffensive Hindus without the slightest reason except that they are 'Kafirs' or belonged to the same religion as the policemen, who entered their mosques, burning of Hindu temples, the outrage on Hindu women and their forcible conversion and marriage by the Moplahs."[37]

A report before the Congress Working Committee said:

"The families, which have been forcibly converted into Mohammedanism, lived in the neighborhood of Manjeri. It is clear that conversions were forced upon Hindus by a fanatic gang which was always opposed to the Khilafat and Non-co-operation Movement, and there were only three cases so far as our information goes."[38]

A very carefully crafted Congress Working Committee resolution of January 16, 1922 on the Moplah massacre stated:

"The Working Committee places on record its sense of deep regret over the deeds of violence done by Moplahs in certain

areas of Malabar, these deeds being evidence of the fact that there are still people in India who have not understood the message of the Congress and the Central Khilafat Committee, and calls upon every Congress and Khilafat worker to spread the said message of non-violence even under the gravest provocation throughout the length and breadth of India.

"Whilst, however, condemning violence on the part of the Moplahs, the working Committee desires it to be known that the evidence in its possession shows that provocation beyond endurance was given to the Moplahs and that the reports published by and on behalf of the Government have given a one-sided and highly exaggerated account of the wrongs done by the Moplahs and an understatement of the needless destruction of life resorted to by the Government in the name of peace and order.

"The Working Committee regrets to find that there have been instances of so-called forcible conversion by some fanatics among Moplahs, but warns the public against believing in the Government and inspired versions."[39]

Swamy Shraddhanand further commented:

"The first warning was sounded when the question of condemning the Moplahs for their atrocities on Hindus came up in the Subjects Committee. The original resolution condemned the Moplahs wholesale for the killing of Hindus and burning of Hindu homes, and the forcible conversion to Islam. The Hindu members themselves proposed amendments till it was reduced to condemning only certain individuals who had been guilty of the above crimes. ...Well, even the harmless resolution condemning some of the Moplahs was not unanimously passed but had to be accepted by a majority of votes only. There were other indications also, showing that the Musalmans considered the Congress to be existing on their sufferance and if there was the least attempt to ignore their idiosyncrasies, the superficial unity would be scrapped asunder."[40]

Congress leader Annie Besant expressed her sorrow about the 'Malabar Agony': "...as from that date [August 1] onwards thousands of the forbidden war-knives were secretly made and hidden away, and on August 20, the rebellion broke out; Khilafat flags were hoisted on police stations and government offices. …The misery is beyond description. Girls, wives, pretty and sweet, with eyes half-blind with weeping, distraught with terror; women who have seen their husbands hacked to pieces before their eye, in the way "Moplahs consider religious", old women tottering, whose faces become written with anguish and who cry at a gentle touch and a kind look, waking out of a stupor of misery only to weep, men who have lost all, hopeless, crushed, desperate.

…I have walked among thousands of them in refugee camps, and sometimes heavy eyes would lift as a cloth was laid gently on the bare shoulder, and a faint watery smile of surprise would make the face even more piteous than the stupor. Eyes full of appeal, of agonized despair, of hopeless entreaty of helpless anguish, thousands of them camp after camp. Two Pulayas, lowest of the submerged classes were captured with others and were given the choice between Islam and Death. These, the outcaste of Hinduism, the untouchables, so loved the Hinduism which had been so unkind a step-mother to them that they chose to die Hindus rather than to live Muslim. May the God of both Muslim and Hindus send His messengers to these heroic souls, and give them rebirth into the Faith for which they died."[41]

According to *The Manchester Guardian*, "…India broods the horror of the coldblooded massacres by the Moplahs, still daily showing how Hindus fare in the hands of fanatical Mohammedans. The public obscurely but rightly connects the holocaust of Hindu lives and property with Khilafat preachers and realizes that the rule even of the arrogant British is better than no rule."[42]

In 1924, a similar incident happened in Kohat, Northwest Frontier Province. The rioting and massacre lasted for three days, and the fanatic Muslim mob killed a number of Hindus and Sikhs. Over 3000 Hindus who lived there for generations had to flee after they could sense that the whole exercise of ethnic cleansing was to make the region free of Hindus and Sikhs.[43]

Great freedom leader Lala Lajpat Rai commented, "Is it that the Kohat Hindus are being punished for participating in the Khilafat movement? Are the Frontier Hindus being held responsible for the help rendered towards the Khilafat by Amirchand Bamwal and other Hindu leaders? When the Kohat incident happened, Mahatmaji's heart was so struck that he cried out in agony: "I had persuaded Hindus to render help to have the Muslim temple of Khilafat, and today my own temples are being destroyed by the Mohammedans."[44]

According to Nair and Mukherji, "Any history of Khilafat Non-co-operation movement that leaves out the Moplahs' roles in the horrible genocide of Hindus can never be taken as an authentic historical narrative. Thus, in the official historiography that we have since Nehru's days, the dominant view is that India's struggle for independence was primarily non-violent, and it was thus entirely Gandhian. In this framework, many episodes, many personalities, many substantive issues—like the long history of violence-ridden Muslim separatism-communalism and much relevant explanations were strictly avoided".[45] In the absence of the Islamic Caliphate or an Islamic rule in the subcontinent, the fight with native Hindu-Sikhs was now in the hands of Islamist leaders such as Iqbal, Jinnah, and Suhrawardy, with active intellectual and human resources provided by Deoband and Aligarh.

References

1. "Responses To Threat: Freeze, Appease, Flight, Fight" https://www.psychologytools.com/resource/responses-to-threat-freeze-appease-flight-fight/
2. DRM, "Trauma Response and Complex PTSD: Fight, Flight, Freeze, Appease", *Medium*, 3 February 2020, https://

medium.com/fearless-she-wrote/trauma-response-and-complex-ptsd-fight-flight-freeze-appease-2da4cf76a8be

3. Jiang, Shui; Postovit, Lynne; Cattaneo, Annamaria; Binder, Elisabeth B.; and Aitchison, Katherine J. "Epigenetic Modifications in Stress Response Genes Associated With Childhood Trauma", Review Article, Front. Psychiatry, 08 November 2019, https://doi.org/10.3389/fpsyt.2019.00808 https://www.frontiersin.org/articles/10.3389/fpsyt.2019.00808/full%20,
4. "Genetic impact of African slave trade revealed in DNA study", *BBC News,* 24 July 2020 https://www.bbc.com/news/world-africa-53527405
5. Khan, Liaquat Ali (1940), "Pakistan: The Heart of Asia", Thacker & Co. Ltd.
6. ANI | Washington D.C. [USA], "Pakistan Army carrying out ethnic cleansing of minority groups: Nadeem Nusrat", *Business Standard,* 15 March 2018 https://www.business-standard.com/article/news-ani/pakistan-army-carrying-out-ethnic-cleansing-of-minority-groups-nadeem-nusrat-118031500602_1.html
7. "Mullah Mohammed Omar: Co-founder and leader of the Taliban who fought the Soviets before presiding over a brutal Afghan regime", *Independent,* 30 July 2015 https://www.independent.co.uk/news/people/mullah-mohammed-omar-co-founder-and-leader-taliban-who-fought-soviets-presiding-over-brutal-afghan-regime-10428546.html
8. Mahatma Gandhi Complete works Vol XIX p. 254.
9. Sharma, Manmohan (2015). "ISIS History and Evolution of Contemporary Challenges", India Policy Foundation, p. 11.
10. Ibid. p. 22.
11. "M.N. Roy Dead", https://www.livemint.com/Sundayapp/GWgU2wPzQ2vx9qLm4lusFK/Stalins-young-man-MN-Roy-and-the-Russian-Revolution.html

12. "Formation of the Communist Party of India at Tashkent (1920)", cpim.org https://cpim.org/history/formation-communist-party-india-tashkent-1920
13. "Stalin's shooting lists", Stalin Documents, Russia website.
14. Nehru, Jawaharlal "An Autobiography", The Bodley Head, London, 1936; pp. 154, 218, https://sreenivasaraos.com/tag/letters-from-jail/
15. Mohammad, Raees "Why I converted to Islam and buried my Hindu identity: Dalit Camera founder", *The Print*, 5 February 2020, https://www.theprint.in/opinion/why-i-converted-to-islam-and-buried-my-hindu-identity-dalit-camera-founder/359849/
16. Singh, M.K. "Encyclopaedia of Indian War of Independence 1857–1947", Hardcover, 2009, Vol. 13, Anmol Publications Pvt Ltd. pp. 3–4.
17. Mukherjee, Rudrangshu "Great Speeches of Modern India", Vintage Books, 2011
18. Sarila, Narendra Singh "The Shadow of the Great Game: The Untold Story of India's Partition", Carol and Graff Publishers, New York, 2006. https://ia801208.us.archive.org/12/items/AzadIndiaWinsFreedom/The%20Shadow%20of%20the%20Great%20Game_%20The%20Untold%20Story%20of%20India_s%20Partition.pdf
19. Maryam, Hajira "How Abul Kalam Azad's idea of united India was defeated in 1946", *TRT World,* 13 August 2021 https://www.trtworld.com/magazine/how-abul-kalam-azad-s-idea-of-united-india-was-defeated-in-1946-49169
20. Azad, Abul Kalam (2010). "Ghubar-e-Khatir". New Delhi: Sahitya Akademi. pp. 5, 7.
21. Speech by Education Minister Kapil Sibal, 2009: http://www.education.nic.in/Speeches/NED09.pdf
22. Hamid, Myra (2005). "The Political Struggles Of The Ulama Of Dar-Ul-Uloom Deoband: Identifying And Operationalizing The Traditionalist Approach To Politics".

23. Muhammad Moj, (2015). "The Deoband Madrassah Movement: Countercultural Trends and Tendencies". Anthem Press. p. 47. Archived from the original on 4 February 2016.
24. Iqbal : "Payam-i-Mushraq", p. 135.
25. Iqbal : "Zarb-e-Kaleem", p. 150.
26. Iqbal : "Zarb-e-Kaleem" 030 Hindi Islam Poem.
27. Sharma, 2015. p. 16.
28. Papers by command: Volume 16, Great Britain. Parliament. House of Commons – 1922 P. 20
29. Nair, C. Gopalan (2020). "The Moplah Rebellion, 1921", Aditya Prakashan, Foreword by Saradindu Mukherji.
30. Nair, C. Sankaran. "Malabar's Agony", Annie Besant. *New India.* Quoted in "Gandhi And Anarchy". pp. 133–6.
31. B.R. Ambedkar (1945), "Pakistan Or the Partition of India".
32. "Congress and Gandhi Ji's Silence on Moplah Riots", *Arya Samajam Kerala,* 29 June, 2020, https://aryasamajkerala.org.in/congress-and-gandhi-jis-silence-on-moplah-riots/
33. Ambedkar (1945).
34. Shraddanand, Swami. *The Liberator,* Issue 26 August 1926.
35. Ambedkar (1945).
36. Nair, C. Sankaran (1995), "Gandhi and Anarchy". Mittal Publications. pp. 45–47.
37. Lord Reading's Report, Calicut, Dated 7/9/1921.
38. Ambedkar (1945).
39. Ibid.
40. Shraddanand, Swami, (1926).
41. Besant, Annie "Malabar's Agony", *New India*, 29 Nov 1921.
42. Sampath, Vikram, "Savarkar, Echoes from a Forgotten Past, 1883–1924", (2019) quoted from

43. *Manchester Guardian*, 1 Sept 1921–12 Dec 1921.
44. McGinn, Patrick (1 November 1986). "Communalism and the North-West Frontier Province: the Kohat Riots, 9–10 September 1924". South Asia Research. Vol. 6 (No. 2) p. 139–158.
45. Nanda, B.R. (2008), "The Collected works of Lala Lajpat Rai". Vol.II, Manohar, Delhi. p. 192–193.
46. Nair, C. Gopalan (Author); Mukherji, Saradindu (Foreword), "The Moplah Rebellion, 1921", Aditya Prakashan, 2020.

❑

CHAPTER

9

THE LEFT TURN – THE COLONIST-MARXIST PLOY

Why is communism called 'a religion without god'?
What did Marx say about India and Indians,
and how did it affect the psyche of Indian communists?
Why did Karl Max write Das Capital?
How Mao initiated the Naxal movement
by giving guerilla training to communists from Bengal
What did top physicists in the world say about
India's spiritual heritage?
How JNU became a center of anti-national activities
How is the communist term 'communal' used by
the Indian communists against the 'nationalists'?

Understanding Marxism

Marxists, especially their 'theologians' and academics, connived on a major scale to prove Marx correct and relevant and establish themselves proposing a contrary view that often matches the colonists' mindset.

French philosopher and sociologist Raymond Claude Ferdinand Aron wrote his famous book *The Opium of the Intellectuals* in 1955. In a chapter called "Intellectuals in

Search of a Religion," in his book, he suggested the Soviet Communists found a replacement religion for Christianity in Marxism:

"[Marxism] provides true Communists with a global interpretation of the universe; it instills sentiments akin to those of the crusaders of all ages; it fixes the hierarchy of values and establishes the norms of good conduct. It fulfills, in the individual and in the collective soul, some of the functions which the sociologist normally ascribes to a religion."[1]

He continued that the new religion called Marxism as a church where *"the people could be disciplined while ushering in the final cure for mankind's misery. It promised salvation through violence and revolution and demanded total submission to the Party."*[2]

An overhyped 'scientific theory of politics and economics' propagated globally has caused the decimation of populations and cultures and eventually became a cult that attracted millions. Cult leaders and followers alike ignore science and the latest evidence contrary to their 'belief system'. Like the Islamists, they use brute force, the power of the gun, otherwise called a revolution. They establish state power and use the state machinery to eliminate 'non-believers,' calling them various names such as the bourgeoisie, counter-revolutionary, etc.

Aron has summarized the ironies and contradictions of Marxism in this manner:

"Revolutionaries tend to exaggerate both the margin of their freedom and the power of destiny. They imagine that prehistory will end with them, that the proletariat, transfigured by its struggle, will give human societies a new look. Uplifted by their faith beyond the humdrum lessons of wisdom, they expect perpetual peace to flower from unlimited violence. They proclaim the inevitability of their triumph, because the cause which embodies so much hope cannot possibly fail. As time passes, as they in their turn assume the burden of power,

as the immemorial essence of human collectivities reasserts itself through all the upheavals, confidence is corroded by disillusionment. As belief in the classless society begins to wane, they must profess to believe more and more in the necessity which mocks mankind and its futile struggles. Once the mainstay of optimism, belief in destiny becomes the alibi of resignation."[3]

The Communist Manifesto of Karl Marx and Frederick Engels was published in 1848. Karl Marx published the first volume of *Das Capital* in 1867. Later, two other volumes were edited and published in 1883 after the death of Marx. These are like the holy Bible or Quran to the believers of communism.

Today, there is a global epidemic of Opioid addiction. In reality, the 'opioid addiction' of mind and intellect was introduced by Marx and Lenin. Marxism's opium affected numerous thinkers, which caused at least 100 million valuable human lives globally in the past century through tremendous agony, trials, and tribulations! The Marxist romantics wanted to prove certain prophecies of Marx, which never came to be true. According to Richard M. Ebeling of Foundation for Economic Education (FEE): "Marx not only misinterpreted capitalism's 'birth pangs' for its 'death rattle', but he totally misread how capitalism had actually evolved, considering that as an economic system it was just emerging when Marx wrote and was not ending. "Bad timing" is the most polite way to express Marx's misconception of where capitalism was on the timeline of modern history." He continued: "Being blunt, every one of Marx's 'predictions' has failed to come true. In the 150 years since the publication of volume one of Marx's *Das Capital*, there has been an immense increase in capital investment that has led neither to a concentration of ownership of wealth in fewer and fewer hands nor has it resulted in the growing 'misery' of the general public. Nor has it resulted in society being more and more polarized into two classes – the 'owning class' and the 'property-less proletariat'."[4]

The Communist Prophet: Karl Marx

Karl Heinrich Marx, ethnically Jewish, was born in Germany in 1818. His father converted from Judaism and joined a Christian Church. Karl studied law and philosophy. Jenny von Westphalen, daughter of a 'noble' family, four years older than Karl, met when they were very young. They became close friends as teenagers. Both were well-read and literary and had deep romanticism for each other. According to Marx, she was the 'most beautiful girl in the town of Trier'. Her father was a friend of Karl's father. Karl avoided military duty due to what is referred to as a "weak chest" at 18. Jenny and Karl became engaged in 1836 and got married in 1843 in the Kreuznach church of Saint Paul. Later at the University at Bonn, Marx joined the radical Poets' Club, which was regularly monitored by the German police. He joined the Trier Tavern Club drinking society and served as club co-president. It was "a society of about thirty university students from his hometown whose main ambition was to get drunk as frequently and riotously as possible." He enjoyed partying, getting drunk, and kept 'unkempt hair' to look cool.[5]

Soon, because of his publication of ideas and articles, which were radical in those days, he had to leave Germany and take exile in London[6] with his wife and children and struggled in poverty every day. In front of his eyes, three of their six children died. These miseries and abject poverty made him hate the capitalist system. In his *Communist Manifesto* and later *Das Capital*, he finally expressed that anguish and disappointment in life.

He started to hate the rich and, thus, the system of capitalism. As a solution to the 'evils of capitalism', Marx wanted to propagate the complete upheaval of capitalism by the workers of the world. He believed that capitalism was fated to fall and was at the point of collapse. Marx wanted to festinate this process. Marx envisioned the workers abolishing private property and then abolishing the state too in the future.

However, socialism was only a temporary stage for Marx. It was supposed to set the stage for an even perfect political and economic system – communism. Marx foresaw a day when his socialism, with state ownership of the property, would be replaced by communism, in which the state would no longer exist.[7] But Marx's wishes were never fulfilled. The reality of his theories shaped up to be quite the opposite: Marxism, Communism, Socialism all not only have failed everywhere but have created more tyrannical and oppressive regimes. Unlike liberalism, what in theory was supposed to minimize state power, in reality, ended up giving the state more power and led to complete subjugation of the individual. Erstwhile USSR, China, and North Korea have been prime examples.

Marxism in India

The ideas of Karl Marx influenced many parts of Europe. After several failed revolutionary attempts to create communist states in Europe, only in 1917, the Russian Revolution gave birth to the first communist state and communist 'religion', almost as a replacement of Christianity followed by the Czars. For about a thousand years since the 10th century CE, the Czars, starting with Prince Vladimir I, who adopted Christianity as the official religion for Russia, which later came to be known as the Russian Orthodox Church.[8]

The idea of a communist party in India was hatched in Russia around 1920, which later helped create the Communist Party of India (CPI) in 1925.[9] CPI split in 1964, with support from China created the Communist Party of India – Marxist (CPI-M) in 1964. They have formed elected state governments in the states of West Bengal, Tripura, and Kerala (still in power as of 2021) through the violence and tyranny of cadres. And later, as if because CPI-M was not doing the job right, to create a large number of cadres in India fast, China designed and indoctrinated a number of young people and peasant leaders of West Bengal and started the 'Naxal movement' or Communist Party of India Marxist-Leninist (CPIM-L) in 1967.

The story goes like this:

According to Chinese historian Li Danhui, the CPI (Communist Party of India) Darjeeling County Committee sent four trainees to China to initiate the revolution. They were Kanu Sanyal, Dipak Biswas, Khudan Mullick, and Khokan Majumdar (alias Abdul Hamid), and the group was named the 'Darjeeling County Committee Study Group,' and the birthplace of the movement was Naxalbari in Darjeeling district of West Bengal, after which the movement was named Naxal. According to Li, they were taught tactics of guerrilla warfare at Changping Military School near Peking and were trained to manufacture ammunition, handle explosives, and even practiced military maneuvers in Tibet.[10]

Mao met with Naxal leaders led by Kanu Sanyal on December 13, 1967, and told them: "We (The proletariat) do not rely on Gandhi, Nehru… and so on to solve the problem... They are temporary; only heroes are workers, farmers, they are the leaders of the future… use surprise attacks to seize weapons from policemen, and use superior forces to annihilate a small group of police force at each battle." In that 80-minute long meeting, high profile people, including premier Zhou Enlai, vice-chief of the general staff of People's Liberation Army Yang Chengwu, and CPC's internal security and intelligence in-charge Kang Sheng were present. Mao's final words were: "When the CPI leftists come to power and establish revolutionary people's government, China would sign a treaty with them and return all the land south of the McMahon Line to them."[11] So, the Naxals decided to go for a violent revolution.

The mouthpiece of Chinese communists called *People's Daily* wrote an editorial on July 5, 1967, entitled *"Spring Thunder over India"*.[12] And the effect was, "A peal of spring thunder has crashed over the land of India. The revolutionary peasants in the Darjeeling area have risen in rebellion. "[13]

Naxals introduced a slogan – 'China's Chairman (Mao) is our Chairman', thus acquiring the title Maoists.

Hundreds of schools, government offices, and police stations were attacked by the Naxalites. They resorted to killing police, businessmen, and teachers. Among them was the Vice-Chancellor of Jadavpur University Gopal Sen and the Headmaster of a school in Durgapur – Bimal Dasgupta, who was tied to a chair and burnt to death.[14] P.C. Bhattacharya, Head of Department of Physics at University Science College, was stabbed at his office.[15] Desecration of the statues of leaders and even killing cadres of CPI(M) became a norm. Naxals labeled CPM in West Bengal as "neo-fascist." And leaders were called "the neo-revisionist scab of a police minister named Jyoti Basu."[16]

The Congress Government under the Chief Ministership of Siddharth Sankar Roy took extreme measures to destroy the CPIM-L and its 'revolution'.

Jyoti Basu was a London-educated barrister and an elite whose family moved to West Bengal due to Islamic persecutions. Later, the top leader of CPI-M Basu soon snatched the power from Congress to form their communist-based Left-Front government. While their main ideological leader Pramod Dasgupta said that the parliamentary democracy is just the first step towards a full communist revolution. In 1969, Dasgupta asserted, 'We have adopted democracy in order to strengthen the democratic struggle, but we firmly believe that we would not be able to reach our goal through parliamentary democracy. Our goal is socialism and for that is required the bloody revolution. We want to reach the state of clash between the Centre and the State through the path of parliamentary democracy to such a level that it would spark off the bloody revolution.'[17] Naxals rejected Parliamentary democracy as "semi-feudal and comprador bourgeois" and believed only in armed struggle.

However, CPI-M came to power by introducing a series of violent events – the most notable one was the 'Sain Bari

Murders' where brothers belonging to the Congress Party were brutally killed, and their mother was fed rice with her sons' blood![18] While the legacy of communist rule in India (West Bengal, Tripura, and Kerala) is on its way out, the only state that still clings to it is Kerala, due to very complex demographic deadlock. Left-over communists still has some influence in academics and media.

How did all of this happen? British fed the Indian freedom fighters in the jails with communist literature to divert their attention from nationalism to global communism, as propagated by the Communist Party of Britain! These newly converted communists created many groups of students, laborers, writers, journalists, and historians in India. Encouraged by none other than Prime Minister Jawaharlal Nehru, under his very nose, some say with his patronage, a generation of historians and writers were nurtured to promote the Marxist-Leninist ideology in India and create a large number of followers and 'comrades'.

History has taught us that whether you call it imperialism, fascism, colonialism, expansionism, religion-based institutes including Caliphate and Papal-Church systems, at the end of the day, they belong to the same groups who dominate and control land, wealth, and masses for their self-interest, power, and luxurious life as is the case with almost all communist leaders.

To fulfill Indian Marxist forces' mission, Marxist sympathizers, intellectuals, and cadres, in unison, have been working against the Indian nation-state to deviate from the 'spirit' envisioned by the seers like Aurobindo and other great luminaries. They fail miserably when both science and spirituality, more completely, *adhaytma vidya* stare at them with a threat since they cannot think beyond materialism. When many modern-day Western scholars and scientists praise India's age-old knowledge system, the Marxists and 'secularists' hide behind their image as the saviors of the tribal or Dalit people who have been sadly facing social oppressions. After all, that's where some of their support bases are reduced to now by providing some immediate benefits such as schools and medical camps. However, their propaganda is no more effective enough to disillusion the general public in India, be it the lower 'castes' or, the lower economic strata groups.

When Hindu socio-religious leaders of all eras attempted and succeeded in reforming and 'course correct' the general society, they were termed as bourgeois or reactionaries. They have coined two terms for people who they think are the biggest obstacles to their sinister designs to destroy the soul of Indian civilization, culture, and heritage. One is 'communal,' and the other is 'Hindu Right'. Both these ideas stem from Europe (example: Leftist and Rightist political terms) and do not fit the definitions in the Indian context. Hindus are taken aback by this attack because now they are forced to respond on their terms, which is foreign to them! But it is a straightforward task to explain Hindutva's idea to anybody, which will be addressed in the next book in detail. Simply speaking, the identity of being a Hindu, feeling, and living as a Hindu is Hindutva. Following Hindu traditions, reforming and empowering Hindu society, taking pride in Hindu Dharma and fight for their rights is Hindutva. Any attempt to correct the injustices meted out to the Hindu-Sikh-Jain population of India, the NeoCols will designate them as 'communal'. Nationalist Indians, no matter what religious path or political-ideological path they follow, must not be afraid or intimidated anymore – the nefarious designs of the NeoCols stand exposed!

And the World Knew India Differently

The American philosopher-poet Ralph Waldo Emerson commented about the *Bhagavad Gita*:

"I owed – my friend and I owed – a magnificent day to the Bhagavad Gita. It was the first of books; it was as if an empire spoke to us, nothing small or unworthy, but large, serene, consistent, the voice of an old intelligence which in another rage and climate had pondered and thus disposed of the same questions which exercise us."[19]

American essayist, poet, and philosopher Henry David Thoreau, on the other hand, would share his experience with the philosophy of India:

"In the morning I bathe my intellect in the stupendous and cosmogonal philosophy of the Bhagvat Geeta, since whose composition years of the gods have elapsed, and in comparison with which our modern world and its literature seem puny and trivial; and I doubt if that philosophy is not to be referred to a previous state of existence, so remote is its sublimity from our conceptions. I lay down my book and go to my well for water and lo! There I meet the servant of the Brahmin, priest of Brahma and Vishnu and Indra, who still sits in his temple on the Ganges reading the Vedas, or dwells at the root of a tree with his crust and water jug. I meet his servant come to draw water for his master, and our buckets as it were grate together in the same well. The pure Walden water is mingled with the sacred water of the Ganges."[20]

American writer Mark Twain who is thought of by many as 'the father of American literature' said these profound things about India:

"India is the cradle of the human race, the birthplace of human speech, the mother of history, the grandmother of legend, and the great grandmother of tradition. Our most valuable and most instructive materials in the history of man are treasured up in India only."

And Will Durant would say:

"India was the mother of our race and Sanskrit, the mother of Europe's languages. She was the mother of our philosophy, mother through the Arabs, of much of our mathematics, mother through Buddha, of the ideals embodied in Christianity, mother through village communities of self-government and democracy. Mother India is, in many ways, the mother of us all." [21] The India he spoke of was mostly a Hindu India.

That is the universal essence of Indian civilization expressed by a person living nearly 10,000 miles away, in a time without television, radio, or telecommunication.

Marxists won't find any meaning or purpose in Emerson's self-realization and grand expression; they have more reverence for the Volga or Huang Ho than the Ganga! For many decades they influenced the education system and polity of the country. They would dismiss Thoreau and Emerson summarily because Karl Marx said so:

"*...If we knew nothing of the past history of Hindostan, would there not be the one great and incontestable fact that even at this moment India is held in English thraldom (*the state of being a thrall; bondage; slavery; servitude*) by an Indian army maintained at the cost of India? India, then, could not escape the fate of being conquered, and the whole of her past history, if it be anything, is the history of the successive conquests she has undergone. Indian society has no history at all, at least no known history. What we call its history, is but the history of the successive intruders who founded their empires on the passive basis of that unresisting and unchanging society. The question, therefore, is not whether the English had a right to conquer India, but whether we are to prefer India conquered by the Turk, by the Persian, by the Russian, to India conquered by the Briton.*"[22]

Do the Marxists care about 'Hinduism'? Hindu religious gurus and institutions, politicians, and politics do have many social and religious anomalies to fix. But the Marxists' game has been to use the weaknesses of the society creating confusion among Hindus and then making the Hindus feel bad about their own traditions just like the colonists did. The Marxists, however, have no respect for Hinduism – the effort to show that 'Hindutva' is narrow and Hinduism is 'great' and different is just a façade! The act of respecting and adopting a Hindu way of life is Hindutva. When it comes to science, one would at least expect them to come to terms. Quantum Physics has been the new frontier of material science. Three names stand tall for their contributions: Nobel Laureate Danish physicist Niels Bohr, Nobel Laureate Austrian-Irish physicist Erwin Schrödinger, and German physicist Werner Karl Heisenberg. They came in touch with the Hindu philosophy and scriptures and expressed the greatness of the same in many ways, and perhaps their lives and work were deeply impacted.

Neils Bohr said, *"I go into the Upanishads to ask questions."*[23]

Schrödinger said, *"The unity and continuity of Vedanta are reflected in the unity and continuity of wave mechanics. This is entirely consistent with the Vedanta concept of All in One."*

"The multiplicity is only apparent. This is the doctrine of the Upanishads. And not of the Upanishads only. The mystical experience of the union with God regularly leads to this view, unless strong prejudices stand in the West."

"There is no kind of framework within which we can find consciousness in the plural; this is simply something we construct because of the temporal plurality of individuals, but it is a false construction... The only solution to this conflict insofar as any is available to us at all lies in the ancient wisdom of the Upanishad."[24]

Heisenberg said, *"Quantum theory will not look ridiculous to people who have read Vedanta."*[25]

Several of these scientists met India's modern sage poet Rabindranath and discussed Hindu philosophy at length. Another great scientist Nicola Tesla who invented an Alternate Current (AC) and dreamed of giving free 'power' (energy) for all our machines to run, became close to Swami Vivekananda. Tesla said: *"All perceptible matter comes from a primary substance, or the unity beyond conception, filling all space, the akasha or luminiferous ether, which is acted upon by the life giving Prana or creative force, calling into existence, in never-ending cycles all things and phenomena."*[26]

Then Marx Plays

Marx could not ignore India either; he praised the Indians from a labor-economics point of view: *"...Mr. Campbell himself, greatly influenced as he is by the prejudices of the East India Company, is obliged to avow "that the great mass of the Indian people possesses a great industrial energy, is well fitted to accumulate capital, and remarkable for a mathematical clearness of head and talent for figures and exact sciences." "Their intellects," he says, "are excellent."*[27]

"At all events, we may safely expect to see, at a more or less remote period, the regeneration of that great and interesting country, whose gentle natives are, to use the expression of Prince Soltykov, even in the most inferior classes, "plus fins et plus adroits que les Italiens" [more subtle and adroit than the Italians], whose submission even is counterbalanced by a certain calm nobility, who, notwithstanding their natural langor, have astonished the British officers by their bravery, whose country has been the source of our languages, our religions, and who represent the type of the ancient German in the Jat, and the type of the ancient Greek in the Brahmin."[28]

The Marxists and the colonial historians called the Vedas poems of the 'pastoral nomads'.[29] Part of the reason is the uneducated (in Sanskrit literature), and uninitiated (in Hindu tradition) translators delivered their 'masterpieces' to their masters. To those readers, it may have appeared to be primitive literature and fed the same to the gullible and equally uneducated 'scholars', and westernized elites about India's past as useless stuff! Anglicized Indians easily got detached from the age-old traditions of India, got attracted towards Marxism in the guise of socialism, and produced many leaders, including Nehru, who actually took India further to the direction as Marx suggested: *"England has to fulfill a double mission in India: one destructive, the other regenerating the annihilation of old Asiatic society, and the laying of the material foundations of Western society in Asia."*[30]

As we can see today, both Russia and China are the new expansionists and colonists of the modern era. You may question America for that, but at the expense of trillions of dollars of the taxpayers' money, America has not been successful in controlling any nation fully. Nehru was influenced by both communism and the Western colonist mindset. Through Gandhi, Britain handed over the ruling power to him so that 'their' India was in 'safe' hands! So, instead of calling this ideology an apologist, defeatist and destructive, many Indian leaders at that time were forced to accept him. It is too much to give all credit to Nehru alone as 'Nehruvian' ideology; in reality, it is a neo-colonist idea. We can call the followers, including Nehru, as Neo-Colonists of India, in short – NeoCols.

While the West has a vested interest in finding great markets in countries like India, at the same time, the American politicians are engaged in regime changes and installing puppet governments and starting wars – not as much for western hegemony as much as for economic reasons. American war machines and military-industry leaders are the key benefactors of wars, as we have seen in Iraq and Afghanistan.

However, Western media is fed by the same NeoCol 'scholars' and journalists about Indian affairs. The West's attempt to follow the thoughts and propaganda or the Indian NeoCols is not suitable for the West either. Eventually, they have to come to terms with finding and tell the truths about India, not through their borrowed lips but their own research. West will only gain if they make friends with India, the Hindus, to see a more peaceful and prosperous world.

A letter of Karl Marx published in – *New-York Daily Tribune*, August 8, 1853 is an eye-opener for any reader to understand his thoughts on India.[31]

He called India 'Hindostan' the people 'Hindoos' in 1853: *"Arabs, Turks, Tartars, Moguls, who had successively overrun India, soon became Hindooized, the barbarian conquerors being, by an eternal law of history, conquered themselves by the superior civilization of their subjects."*

Later, Marx hesitantly gives some credit to the 'Hindoos' belonging to a 'superior civilization', contradicting his earlier statements. And then recommends how to destroy that civilization:

"The British were the first conquerors – superior, and therefore, inaccessible to Hindoo civilization. They destroyed it by breaking up the native communities, by uprooting the native industry, and by levelling all that was great and elevated in the native society. The historic pages of their rule in India report hardly anything beyond that destruction. The work of regeneration hardly transpires through a heap of ruins. Nevertheless it has begun." And this was written 94 years before India became independent from the colonists![32]

However, Marx did not see much value in propagating Marxism in India at that time, British historian and politician Thomas Babington Macaulay picked up the task and tried to create 'brown sahibs' by introducing a 'clerk making' educational system and would not show anything good in India. The Marxists, the followers of the new materialist religion, called communism, whose prophet is Marx, actually took over the task from the British colonists to make sure Indian people suffer from an inferiority complex, remain divided, and pitted one against the other just in the name of the great illusion and grand mirage called *'samyavaad'*, translation in Indian language denotes a theory of 'equality for all' that is communism.

Thanks to Sardar Vallabhbhai Patel, who persuaded hundreds of princely states not to remain independent states to fulfill the dream of Churchill to create the third country called Princestan after Hindustan, Pakistan, and remain within the Indian Union.[33] And thanks to the failures of the communist leaders to balkanize, break India into small pieces ruled by communist or Muslim rulers – India has rejected communism. India, fortunately, avoided the great danger of 'purging' millions in the name of the rule of proletariats as it happened in the communist states. Otherwise, another Stalin or Pol Pot would be shining in the pages of Indian and world history books.

But that is not it. As noted earlier, freedom fighters in India, especially in Bengal, were fed with communist literature – as a result, many people fell for it. Even within Congress Party, the so-called 'socialists' were finding space, and they also had a conflict with mainstream communist leaders, or they at least pretended to be different! The first key move by this group was by Yusuf Maher Ali, who founded the Congress Socialist Party (CSP) in 1934. He was credited with coining the terms 'Quit India'[34] and 'Simon go back'.[35] Many members of the Indian revolutionary groups, including the Anushilan Samiti and Jugantar, also were influenced by Marxist literature and some of them became part of CSP. Jayaprakash Narayan was also a key member of the same though he was introduced to Marxism in Wisconsin, USA, and was deeply influenced by M. N. Roy.

In 1936, the All India Students Federation (AISF) was formed in a convention in Lucknow, Mohamed Ali Jinnah presided over the convention, and Jawaharlal Nehru inaugurated it.

During World War II, the Soviet Union, led by Stalin, joined the Allied Powers – both with a stated goal to protect from the invasion of the Axis powers and safeguard communism. The communists in India, because of their affiliation with Russia, called the war 'People's War', and by virtue of that, they could not take part in the fight against 'British Imperialism'. Yet, the Russian interest needed to be protected through all their activities. AISF had many internal conflicts, and in 1970, under the coverage and patronage of communist rules in several states, including West Bengal – the Student Federation of India (SFI) was formed out of AISF.

The JNU Connection

A new chapter at the well-intentioned Jawaharlal Nehru University (JNU) was about to start. Centre of Russian Studies was established in 1965. The most popular courses JNU offered at that time were in linguistics; many students were engaged in writing and spreading Russia's revolutionary and socialistic history in particular and socialism in general. The communists were delighted to have a fertile campus in Delhi's heart to propagate Marxism and dreamt of occupying academics in such a way so that a generation of Marx-infected intellectuals and professionals could be created. A firebrand 22-year old student named Prakash Karat joined JNU in 1970. At that time, communist leader A.K. Gopalan was in Delhi, and Karat became his most beloved disciple (aide). Gopalan joined Indian National Congress and took part in the Khilafat movement as well. He was also a victim of communist literature propaganda by the British and became a hard-core communist. He first joined the Congress Socialist Party – CSP and finally, around 1939, joined CPI. When CPI-M was formed with the break-away CPI members, Gopalan became a very important member and critical ideologue of the new party. In 1970 the Student Federation of India (SFI), the student wing of CPI-M, was formed. Prakash Karat was a founding member of the SFI, India's Marxist student organization, while he was at JNU and a key person of JNU's Student's Union. He was the President of the SFI between 1974 and 1979. Later, he became the General Secretary of the CPI-M from 2005 to 2015.

If one Karat was not enough, communists at JNU got lucky to find another future leader in Sitaram Yechury. He joined JNU and did his M.A. in Economics and continued to do a Ph.D. in Economics, and stayed there for a long time. At JNU, he met Prakash Karat and other leftist groups and became 3-time president of the JNU Student's Union. During the Emergency in 1975, they went underground[36] and created a solid foundation for Marxist hotbed at JNU, which flourished fully after the end of Emergency in 1977-78. With the help of SFI, student member Yechury aptly created a power center and network at JNU, which in the future would be a ruthless pro-communist group and later breed anti-national activism by students. Yechury later took over the role of CPI-M General Secretary from Prakash Karat in 2015.

A remarkable ecosystem to promote Marxist ideology to undermine Indian democracy was created in just a few decades. The history of these groups is deceiving, violent, and supports and promotes anti-national sentiments. They closely work with academicians, journalists, media, foreign academics, and Marxist organizations in different countries connected with Islamist and Christian evangelist groups.

So, now one can easily understand what happened to a very well-intentioned university, JNU became a 'communist' education center. Only a few educational places like JNU and Jadavpur University (Kolkata) are the last bastions of these communist movements in the Indian subcontinent. Together with Aligarh and Jamia – two Muslim-dominated universities, JNU remains the fountainhead of anti-India, communist, and pan-Islamic activities. In other words, these are the NeoCols' final forts. They influence academia and media both, and Western academia and media either consciously due to some vested interests or unconsciously fall for the stories and ideas coming out of these places, ultimately undermining Indian democracy.

Can the communists be humanely trusted? After knowing the fate of innocent people during the communist revolutionary era in various countries, one can only be certain that violence is encoded in their bible *Red Book.* They have no ethics; even if you are comrades, they can hurt you at any time. Stalin purged many of his close associates mercilessly, including revolutionaries from India who ended up in Moscow with a dream of a revolution. Stalin liquidated hundreds of thousands of his own party workers brutally. The same goes with Lenin, Mao, Pol Pot et al. The Naxal movement in India is a sad history of losses of precious brilliant young minds. That NeoCols would create trouble at JNU, or Jadavpur is no news – actually, the fact that they are limited to small-scale inciting violent acts indicates success by the peace-loving greater Indian society and democracy.

Some people like New Zealand psychotherapist Bede Draper think that those who follow communism might have a mental or cognitive disorder. Some others say, "communism is nothing but just another Abrahamic cult minus a God. So the concept of brotherhood or ummah comes naturally to communists."[37]

There is a bad joke about the evolution of Western civilization. There was Aristotle, Plato, and the likes of Archimedes – they lived in the planes of intellect (head) and beyond. Then came Christ – his compassion came down from brain to heart. Marx took his followers down to the belly – food! Then came Freud, and he descended further below! West has significantly contributed to material science, but leaders like Marx and his key disciples Lenin, Stalin, Pol Pot actually brought tremendous pain and suffering in the world. If Hitler was not horrific enough, then the communists were 100 times worse. The same NeoCols never had anything to say about Pakistan and its monstrous general Yahya Khan killing millions of people, mostly Hindus in East Pakistan. Mired in crusades and religious fundamentalism, various Churches' confrontation with modern sciences gave the upper hand to a kind of secular scientific world. Church's religious authority does not necessarily control every moment of people's lives due to the impact of modern science, but communists ignore science and interfere in people's minds and lives.

In India, the great mathematicians and scientists were also *adhyatmic* or spiritual in the Indian sense. Bhaskaracharya, Sridhracharya, and many more – all of them were using different forms of Yoga in their lives. Even most recently, some top scientists like Satyen Bose (Boson famed) and Jagadish Ch. Bose were *adhyatmic*.[38]

J.C. Bose is one of the greatest scientists of modern India who has been finally given credit for his radio discovery, which he did before Marconi. Susmita Chatterjee has written about him: *'the scientist who brought the ancient Indian wisdom of spiritualism into the domain of science'*.[39] But some leftist historians cut him, dwarf, because of his association with spirituality and that he was a nationalist!

Here is what he spoke at Royal Institution in London in 1901 about his electrographic recordings or 'self-made records' of metal, muscle, and plant responses to various stimuli:

"It was when I came upon the mute witness of these self-made records, and perceived in them one phase of a pervading unity that bears within it all things – the mote that quivers in ripples of light, the teeming life upon our earth, and the radiant suns that shine above us – it was then that I understood for the first time a little of that message proclaimed by my ancestors on the banks of the Ganges thirty centuries ago – 'They who see but one, in all the changing manifoldness of the universe, unto them belongs Eternal Truth, unto none else, unto none else!' "[40]

The Western science-oriented groups have seen through the Church's rationale, lack of logic and science, and mostly stay away from Church. Yet ordinary people in the West are 'religious' – not necessarily all go to church, whereas the communists neither could digest science nor could accept a life beyond intellect and matter. Thus, they are stuck, in Indian literature called in the *'trishanku'* state. In India, the residues of the communists are in good numbers. They have been advocating against the Hindu System to throw the baby with the bathtub altogether for a long time. Their voice and the last communist generation are becoming fainter every decade. But the damage they can do anytime, anywhere just to prove a point that 'they are right' is still significant!

There are just five communist countries globally – China, Cuba, Laos, North Korea, and Vietnam. In 1991 the Communist Soviet Union collapsed along with the Communist Party of Soviet Union (CPSU), which had 18 million members. The birthplace of the first communist state is no more communist! As the first 'Russian' president, Boris Yelstin banned CPSU. In 1993 Russia adopted a new constitution and added Article 13, which states: "No ideology may be established as a state or obligatory one."[41] It is a stark joke on the Indian Communists!

Indian Council of Historical Research (ICHR)

The formation of the JNU NeoCol base, Islamists' platforms at Aligarh, Deoband, and Jamia was about to change India's 'intellectual' movement. Next, then Prime Minister Indira Gandhi made Nurul Hasan the Education minister. From 1971 to 1977, he was the Union Minister of State (with independent charge) for Education, Social Welfare & Culture. As India's education minister, he founded the Indian Council of Historical Research (ICHR). His maternal grandfather, Sir Syed Wazir Hasan, was a president of the Muslim League. His maternal uncle Syed Sajjad Zaheer was an eminent Marxist thinker. Hasan was appointed as a Professor in the Department of History at Aligarh Muslim University (AMU), of which he was a Chairperson. His father belonged to the Talukdars, aristocrats during the Mughal rule. In his early childhood, he attended the *Sultan ul Madaris*, in Lucknow, a leading Shia Islamic Madrassa in India.

According to historian Saradindu Mukherji: 'The educational system deteriorated further after an Aligarh Muslim University "Marxist" historian, Syed Nurul Hassan was appointed as the Minister of Education (1972-1977) by Indira Gandhi, which marked the quickening of the Nehruvian and Islamic framework was added the superficial "Marxist" veneer, without the academic rigor and depth of a Christopher Hill or a Eric Hobsbawm. What actually happened was suffusing the textbooks with unacceptable justification of anti-Hindu viewpoints, sanitizing the worst of religious bigotry, rationalizing, and then justifying every assault that had befallen on this country and its people (by the Islamist forces). It was a heady mix – meant to poison younger minds, generations after generations.' [42]

D. D. Koshambi was "the patriarch of the Marxist school of Indian historiography".[43] Currently, senior Marxist historiographers include R. S. Sharma, Irfan Habib, Romila Thapar, D. N. Jha, Suraj Bhan, and K. N. Panikkar.[44] R. S. Sharma was made the first Chairman of ICHR, and their office is inside the Marxist hotbed – JNU. Irfan Habib, a Marxist historiographer who, after returning from Oxford, joined AMU as a faculty member. He was a professor of history at AMU for 32 years (1969–91). He was the 5th Chairman of the ICHR during 1986–90, also served as the general secretary, Sectional President, and then the General President of the Indian History Congress (1981).

According to Amiya Bagchi, a Marxist political economist, Habib was "one of the two most prominent Marxist historians of India today and at the same time, one of the greatest living Marxist historians of India between the twelfth and eighteenth centuries."[45] Have you thought about this puzzle – a historian being a Marxist as opposed to being just a historian?

The Beef Controversy

'Beef eating was a common practice in ancient India' – this is a favorite subject of debate among the leftist intellectuals. Why did the debate have to be opened now? A few miscreants lynched some Muslims for carrying or eating beef. India has laws to deal with such criminal activities, and law and order of the country is responsible for punishing the guilty. After all, the majority of the country's population is Hindu, and the majority of the Hindus have a special place for cows. Any effort to undermine that sentiment is a violation of human and religious rights. People like D.N. Jha[46] were suddenly out to prove that beef-eating is sanctioned in ancient Hindu scriptures.[47] Without getting into a debate about the veracity and authenticity of those claims, and finding counter-evidence against it, let us ask why the Jhas of the world want to talk about it. Psychologically speaking, he was from a Brahmin family, yet perhaps his fondness of beef needed justification! Even an alcoholic comes up with many reasons to drink and proves that drinking is all pro and no con!

In reality, it is a convenient way to say that cow-slaughter should not be an issue, which encourages the Muslims and, to some extent, to the Christians by giving them a voice to have the 'rights' to slaughter cows in India against the wishes of hundreds of millions of Hindus. Another excuse is propagated that beef is a cheap source of protein, and poor people can afford it. A large population of India is still vegetarian – how do they get protein, and how come they don't perish without meat or fish? What is the purpose of this type of license-giving approach to encourage cow slaughter? To reduce Hindu-Muslim tension or to prove that Muslim invasions and the introduction of cow-slaughter to insult their culture simply were good for India?

Or simply, D.N. Jha wanted to be in the limelight beyond his leftist community? Perhaps! He taught history at Patna University and Delhi University without having a Ph.D. Yet, he authored many history textbooks for India's National Council of Educational Research and Training (NCERT), the organization which develops the textbooks and course curricula for Indian schools. He used the preferred methodology of writing the 'Marxist' history of India – selective lifting of sources, obfuscation, and intellectual compromise.

Did he have to prove in his last part of life what a dedicated NeoCol he was? Perhaps. After all, D.N. Jha was a true disciple of non-other than K.S. Sharma – a prominent 'Marxist' historian! Like Namboodriad and Randive, who used to quote and justify Marx in the late '70s to brainwash a generation of academics – how could Jha be an exception? After all, Marx said: "*We must not forget that this undignified, stagnatory, and vegetative life, that this passive sort of existence evoked on the other part, in contradistinction, wild, aimless, unbounded forces of destruction and rendered murder itself a religious rite in Hindostan. We must not forget that these little communities were contaminated by distinctions of caste and by slavery, that they subjugated man to external circumstances instead of elevating man the sovereign of circumstances, that they transformed a self-developing social state into never changing natural destiny, and thus brought about a brutalizing worship of nature, exhibiting its degradation in the fact that man, the sovereign of nature, fell down on his knees in adoration of Kanuman (Hanuman), the monkey, and Sabbala, the cow."*[48]

Anybody who is a professed Marxist, the time has come to desert them, abandon them, protest them, ban them, and bar them from any academic and media circles. They are the true fascists – they support Lenin, Stalin, Mao, Castro, and Pol Pot. One can rightly ask – should they actually be put to trial for bringing violent divisive ideologies to India. They hide behind freedom of speech; real fascists masked as socialists do not deserve democracy; they deserve what Stalin did, purging – socially and academically.

They claim to represent the poor, Dalit, and suffering people. In reality, they are stooges of Russia or China, many are on their payroll, or at least they are self-serving utopian communists who are counting their days to remain relevant.

The Communal-Secular Debate

Today, the establishment of Marxist academics and media persons are self-painted as 'progressive' scholars. Suppose one dares to criticize them, especially anyone who attempts to show Hindu history and identity in a positive light. In that case, many names such as 'communalist,' 'Hindu Right,' 'Hindu Nationalist,' 'Hindu supremacist,' etc., are heaped upon them.

The most slandering is 'communalist. 'Let's take a quick look at the source and meaning of 'communalism'. The term was first seen in use in the latter part of the 20th century. The purpose was to differentiate between the communist 'commune' based social structure and other similar political movements that were equivalent to 'anarchist', 'socialist', and 'communist'.

According to Murray Bookchin, socialist communalism is: "a theory of government or a system of government in which independent communes participate in a federation,"[49] as well as "the principles and practice of communal ownership." In this case, the term 'government' does not imply accepting a state of a top-down hierarchy.

There were 'utopian socialism' and 'anarcho-communism', which had 'communalist property ownership' and 'communalist rules of property' ultimately became modern 'commune-based' communism as propagated by Karl Marx.[50]

According to *Merriam-Webster dictionary*

Definition of communal

1: of or relating to one or more communes

2: of or relating to a community

3: of, relating to, or based on racial or cultural groups

Definition of communalism

1: social organization on a communal basis

2: loyalty to a sociopolitical grouping based on religious or ethnic affiliation.

But when it comes to the Indian subcontinent, the term has been given an entirely different meaning and connotation, which typically denotes 'allegiance to a particular ethnic or religious group rather than to a broader society', and religious sectarianism is equated with that. Any violence, customarily called 'religious riots' is termed as 'communal violence.'

In India, the opposite of 'communal' is 'secular,' meaning non-related to religion or group. In the West, secular means the separation between the church and the state, meaning the state should not favor any religion. It was first used by the

British writer George Holyoake,[51] an atheist, in 1851. He described it as a social order separate from religion, without dismissing or criticizing religious belief itself.

It, however, served the same purpose as the Marxists – putting down anyone having any religious affiliation or feeling. But Indian NeoCols went a step further – any time someone talks about the 'Hindu community' and tries to address their problems, that is invariably termed as 'communal'. But they make sure it is not applied to other religious communities – because Hindus have to be vanquished from India and the world – that is one of the missions of the NeoCols, especially the Marxists. Then only the Marxists will be able to control the population, eat beef and do away with any morality that the Hindu system propounds. *Ahimsa, satya*, etc. values, would have to be first removed from people's psychology so that they can annihilate millions directly or via proxy using various Abrahamic religious groups' missionary strategies.

References

1. Aron, Raymond Claude Ferdinand "The Opium of the Intellectuals", 1955. Calmann-Lévy. (English translation published in 1957).
2. Ibid.
3. Ibid.
4. Ebeling, Richard M., "How Marx Got on the Wrong Side of History", FEE Stories, June 16, 2017, https://fee.org/articles/how-marx-got-on-the-wrong-side-of-history/
5. Francis Wheen, (1999), "Karl Marx: A Life", W. W. Norton & Company. https://archive.nytimes.com/www.nytimes.com/books/first/w/wheen-marx.html
6. Karl Marx: Dictionary of National Biography. Volume 37. Oxford University Press. 2004.
7. Christian Worldview Handbook, David S. Dockery, Trevin Wax, B & H Publishing Group, 2019.

8. "Religion of Russia", *Britannica* https://www.britannica.com/place/Russia/Religion
9. https://sites.google.com/a/communistparty.in/cpi/ (Archived from the original on 9 December 2015.
10. Patranobis, Suthirtho, "Mao pushed Naxals for People's Revolution, encouraged surprise attacks: Scholar",
11. *The Hindustan Times*, May 28, 2017 https://www.hindustantimes.com/india-news/mao-encouraged-india-s-naxal-leaders-to-seize-weapons-from-cops-chinese-historian/story-2UwhuDQ9MgOa8rAzxFWa3O.html
12. Ibid.
13. Indian Vanguard, "30 Years of Naxalbari" https://naxalresistance.wordpress.com/2007/09/17/30-years-of-naxalbari/
14. Damas, Marius "Approaching Naxalbari", Calcutta: Radical Impression, 1991, p. 82.
15. "Bengal has a long and bloody history of campus violence. Sadly no lesson was learnt", *The Times of India,* Aug 27, 2015 https://timesofindia.indiatimes.com/city/kolkata/bengal-has-a-long-and-bloody-history-of-campus-violence-sadly-no-lesson-was-learnt/articleshow/48692024.cms
16. Hindustan Standard, 19th December, 1970; http://jpg.net.in/wp-content/uploads/2020/11/Koyel-Basu-.pdf
17. Franda, Marcus "Radical Politics in West Bengal", Cambridge, London: MIT Press, 1971, pp. 167–168.
18. Ibid.
19. "Sainbari massacre documentary to highlight perils of political", 19 March 2020, https://www.outlookindia.com/newsscroll/amp/sainbari-massacre-documentary-to-highlight-perils-of-political/1772794
20. https://quotes.yourdictionary.com/author/quote/563247
21. Thoreau, Henry D. "Walden" http://www.thoreau-online.org/walden-page154.html

22. "About India: Quotes from the Well Known from Around the World", Desh Videsh https://www.deshvidesh.com/about-india-quotes-from-the-well-known-from-around-the-world/
23. Karl Marx (1853). "The Future Results of British Rule in India, Written: on July 22, 1853, Source: MECW Volume 12, p. 217; First published in the *New-York Daily Tribune*, August 8, 1853; reprinted in the *New-York Semi-Weekly Tribune,* No. 856, August 9, 1853. https://marxists.architexturez.net/archive/marx/works/1853/07/22.htm
24. Prothero, Stephen, (2010). "God Is Not One: The Eight Rival Religions That Run the World and Why Their Differences Matter", Harper Collins, p. 144.
25. Schrödinger, Erwin (1944), "What is Life?", Cambridge University Press, p.129.
26. The Krishna Path, "Did Quantum Physics Come From the Vedas".
27. https://uplift.love/did-quantum-physics-come-from-the-vedas
28. https://www.goodreads.com/quotes/7468576-all-perceptible-matter-comes-from-a-primary-substance-or-tenuity
29. Karl Marx, "The Political Writings". 1853.
30. Marx. 1853.
31. Omvelt, Gail "Buddhism in India, Challenging Brahminism and Caste", SAGE Publications, 2003. p. 27.
32. Marx. 1853.
33. A letter of Karl Marx, published in *New-York Daily Tribune*, August 8, 1853, Reprinted in the *New-York Semi-Weekly Tribune*, No. 856, August 9, 1853. https://marxists.catbull.com/archive/marx/works/1853/07/22.htm
34. Marx. 1853.
35. Singh, Buta. "Role of Sardar Patel in the Integration of Indian States", Calcutta Historical Journal (July-Dec 2008).

36. https://www.aajtak.in/education/history/story/quit-india-slogan-75-years-mahatma-gandhi-history-yusuf-meherali-congress-457855-2017-08-09
37. Nauriya, Anil (31 October 2003). "'Simon Go Back' — 75 years after". *The Tribune*. Chandigarh, India. https://www.tribuneindia.com/2003/20031031/edit.htm#5
38. Phukan, Sandeep "Emergency's Class of 1975: Activists Then, Leaders Now", *NDTV,* 26 June 2015, https://www.ndtv.com/india-news/emergencys-class-of-1975-activists-then-leaders-now-775056%3famp=1&akamai-rum=off
39. Soti, D.K. (2020, July 4). "Communism is nothing but just another abrahamic cult minus a God. So concept of brotherhood or ummah comes naturally to…" [Tweet].Twitter. https://twitter.com/DivyaSoti/status/1279244836202319872?s=19
40. Brown, Mackenzie C. (2016). "Jagadish Chandra Bose and Vedantic Science", Trinity University.
41. Chatterjee, S "Acharya Jagadish Chandra Bose: Looking beyond the idiom", Research Gate, January 2009.
42. DOI:10.7135/UPO9781843317760.006 https://www.researchgate.net/publication/291879198_Acharya_Jagadish_Chandra_Bose_Looking_beyond_the_idiom
43. Bose, Jagadish Chandra "Response in the Living and Non-Living", Good Press, 1902.
44. The Fundamentals of the Constitutional System, Constitution of the Russian Federation http://www.constitution.ru/en/10003000-02.htm
45. Mukherjee, Saradindu, "The Citizenship Amendment Act, 2019, Some Reflections", Akshaya Prakashan, 2021, p. 110.
46. Sreedharan, E. (2004). "A Textbook of Historiography: 500 BC to AD 2000". Orient Blackswan. p. 469.
47. https://www.dharmadispatch.in/history/how-the-murky-

world-of-the-indian-council-for-historical-research-ichr-massacred-indian-history-and-triumphed

48. Bagchi, Amiya Kumar (1996). "Writing Indian history in the Marxist Mode in a Post-Soviet World", Vol. 24, No. 1/3 (Jan. – Mar. 1996), Social Scientist, p. 89-110. (https://www.jstor.org/stable/3520121)
49. Jha, Dwijendra Narayan "The Myth of the Holy Cow", Navayana, 2002.
50. http://vedicphilosophy.tripod.com/No%20beef%20in%20Vedas.htm
51. Karl Marx, "The British Rule in India", First published: in the New-York Daily Tribune, June 25, 1853.
52. Bookchin, Murray (August 27, 2006). "What is Communalism? The Democratic Dimension of Anarchism".
53. Marx/Engels "Collected Works", Progress Publishers, 1975.
54. Holyoake, G.J. (1896). "English Secularism: A Confession of Belief". Library of Alexandria. pp. 47–48.

❑

CHAPTER

10

INDIAN NATIONAL POLITICS DURING THE BRITISH ERA

How many political parties did India have before 1947?
What did Gandhi and Nehru have to say about Bhagat Singh and other revolutionaries?
What was the role of Hindu Mahasabha in India's Independence?
What was common among Netaji, Savarkar, and Rash Behari Bose?
Why the British left India in 1947 though there was no major movement in India?
What was the role of communists in the Indian independence movement?
What happened to the thousands of Azad Hindu Fauj Prisoners of War?
What is the difference between dominion status and independence?
What was one event that brought Bhagat Singh into action?

After the end of the Mughal era, the dynasty virtually collapsed after the death of Aurangzeb, and the British

East India Company took control of many parts of India. People everywhere were already suffering due to their manipulative and oppressive activities. In 1857, the War of Independence happened; the British-Indian soldiers revolted, which was ruthlessly crushed. Then Britain took charge of India as a formal ruler under the British monarchy and government.

In 1878 the Arms Act was passed banning Indians from possessing arms and the Vernacular Press Act to stop publishing any criticism of the British government.[1]

The Indian National Congress (INC)

Slowly many British-educated Indians in London, Mumbai, and Calcutta felt the need to form a platform to voice their concerns relating to British governance in India. As a result, the Indian National Congress (INC) was established with 72 delegates from all over the country who met at Bombay on December 28, 1885.[2]

The INC was founded by Dadabhai Naoroji, a businessman and British MP in London, along with a retired Imperial Civil Service officer, Alan Octavian Hume. Soon the INC assumed the role of the only political platform to deal with the British Raj. A question is raised nowadays, is it possible that after the lessons learned from the 1857 short-lived independence battle, Britain could have thought to use the INC behind the scenes to control the sentiment of the masses via a political platform and manage all movements with an aim 'to provide Safety Valve to the British Government'? Or did the educated class of Indians want a platform to launch their political career? Nevertheless, it became a mighty national organization within a few decades; hence the control of the party was very important for the British as well.

At that time, Congress leaders such as W.C. Banerjee, Gopal Krishna Gokhale, R.C. Dutt, Ferozeshah Mehta, George Yule, etc. 'had full faith in British Government' and in order to demand their rights, they just used 'Protest, Prayer, and Petition' methods. It was 'an assembly for politically-minded individuals who were interested in reform'.[3]

The British government announced to divide the Bengal province into two parts, citing the reason – 'Bengal was too large to be governed effectively.' On October 16, 1905, the then Viceroy Curzon declared to divide the province into two parts: Muslim-majority part on the east side and Hindu majority part on the west, thus sowing the seed for the future permanent separation of these two areas. This was nothing but a 'Divide and Rule' ploy by the British. Entire India was outraged by this, and it created a major mass movement involving protests, boycotts, and even an assassination attempt against the Governor of the new province of West Bengal. This changed the nature of the independence movement and had an impact on the 'soft' leadership of the INC. Non-political figures such as Rabindranath came forward and led protests on the streets. This became more or less a movement of the Hindus and did not gain much support from the Muslims. Perhaps Muslim leadership in East Bengal had hoped that a separate region would give them more control over their religion and livelihood, and hence, they opposed the movements.[4]

After almost six years of protests and movements, Bengal was reunited in 1911, but to be divided again only 36 years later in 1947.

The Hindu Mahasabha

The NeoCols, on any occasion, would attack any person or organization having any association with the term Hindu. The greatest example was the contribution of the Hindu Mahasabha in nation-building. They frequently quote Netaji Subhas Chandra Bose's criticism of Hindu Mahasabha, which may have been Bose's strategic political statement in those days. Here is the proof in the pudding.

Apart from Chitta Ranjan Das, the people Bose was very close to was his own brother Sarat Chandra Bose. Bose was deeply spiritual and is well known that he practiced many traditional forms, including Tantra. During his days with the INA, he regularly meditated, sometimes in a local temple. Their mother was a direct disciple of Ramakrishna Paramhansa.[5]

During his peak political life within India, Bose was very close to Hindu Mahasabha founder Pandit Madan Mohan Malviya. And of course, he was closely working with Veer Savarkar in preparation to organize an Indian Army outside of India, along with Rash Behari Bose in Japan, who was also the president of the Hindu Mahasabha Japan.

After the division of Bengal, Muslim League was formed with great support from the Muslim-majority East Bengal in 1906, which sowed the seeds of Muslim separatism and future division of India.[6] The British Indian Government created a separate Muslim electorate under the Morley-Minto Reforms of 1909.[7] This triggered the disappointed Hindu leaders to create an organization to protect the rights of the Hindus.[8]

In Punjab, Lal Chand and U.N. Mukerji founded Punjab Hindu Sabha in 1909 as a non-sectarian organization for an "all-embracing movement" that aimed to safeguard the interests of "the entire Hindu community". [9]

Punjab Provincial Hindu Conference was organized later, criticizing the INC for failing to protect Hindu interests and urging for Hindu-centered politics. Slowly Hindu Sabhas were formed in other parts of India.[10]

Then came the idea of an all-India-based organization, and in the Allahabad session of the INC in 1910, a formal proposal for the same was presented. In December 1913, during the Ambala session, the Punjab Hindu Sabha passed a resolution to create an All India Hindu Sabha, which proposed holding a general conference of Hindu leaders from all over India at 1915 Kumbh Mela in Haridwar. An umbrella organization called *Sarvadeshak* (All India) *Hindu Sabha* was formed in 1915 conference to work with regional Hindu Sabhas at the Kumbh Mela in Haridwar where Swami Shraddhanand and even Gandhi were present and were supportive of the formation of All India Hindu Sabha.[11]

In 1921, the *Sarvadeshak Hindu Sabha* was renamed to *Akhil Bharat Hindu Mahasabha* for Hindu solidarity and social reform and for a "united and self-governing" Indian nation.[12]

Pandit Madan Mohan Malviya, whom Rabindranath called 'Mahamana' is one of the most towering figures of India who has been more or less forgotten or rather made to forget in Indian history books. He is the person who suggested the motto *'Satyameva Jayate'* for India, which means 'Truth alone triumphs'. He selected this mantra from the *Mundaka Upanishad* [3.1.6]

सत्यमेव जयते नानृतं सत्येन पन्था विततो देवयानः ।
येनाक्रमन्त्यृषयो ह्याप्तकामा यत्र तत् सत्यस्य परमं निधानम् ॥

satyameva jayate nānṛtaṃ
satyena panthā vitato devayānaḥ
yenākramantyṛṣayo hyāptakāmā
yatra tat satyasya paramaṃ nidhānam

Meaning: Truth alone triumphs, not falsehood. Through truth, the divine path is spread out by which the sages whose desires have been completely fulfilled, reach to where is that supreme treasure of truth.

Is this sacred? Is this secular? It's up to you to decide. That is the power of India's idea of Dharma!

Malviya was a scholar, educationalist, social reformer, and politician. He joined the INC in 1886 and only person before 1947 to become the INC president four times. He was the key founder of the Hindu Mahasabha. The largest educational institute in Asia and one of the largest globally, the Benares Hindu University (BHU) was founded by him. Malviya was a strong proponent of Hindu political unity for the education and economic development of Hindus and the reconversion of Muslims to their ancestral Hindu faith. With these goals, he and Lala Lajpat Rai helped establish the Hindu Mahasabha. Soon after, revolutionary leaders Vinayak Damodar Savarkar and Balakrishna Moonje became prominent leaders of the Mahasabha. Savarkar and the Mahasabha strongly criticized the INC for its Muslim appeasement policy.

Revolutionary and founder of INA Rash Behari Bose became the president of the Japan unit of Hindu Mahasabha in 1938. According to Uday Mahurkar, 'Savarkar and Rash Behari were in secret correspondence with each other on the proposal to take the help of Axis powers to free India from 'British rule', which was later planned and executed by Subhas Bose.'[13]

Political Developments beyond Indian National Congress (INC)

While on the surface, the INC may appear as a great organization, at least till 1905, it was detached from any mass movement and acted as an elite club. But after the 1905 division of Bengal, the internal politics were changed significantly. Congress became more vocal and active in demanding substantial political reforms and eventually voiced demands for full independence from Britain.

Later came in more determined leaders around 1892 with the advent of 'Lal-Bal-Pal' trio: Lala Lajpat Rai, Bal Gangadhar Tilak, Bipin Chandra Pal. Thereafter Aurobindo Ghosh (later, Sri Aurobindo) came to the scene.

Brahmabandhav Upadhyay (born Bhavani Charan Bandyopadhyay), contemporary to and friend of Rabindranath and Vivekananda, is called the 'doyen of revolutionary movement'. According to his biographer, Julius Lipner, Brahmabandhab 'made a significant contribution to the shaping of the new India whose identity began to emerge from the first half of the nineteenth century…Vivekananda lit the sacrificial flame of revolution, Brahmabandhab in fueling it, safeguarded and fanned the sacrifice.' [14]

He and Sister Nivedita worked with many revolutionaries, including Aurobindo Ghosh, who took the initial steps to organize the revolutionaries joined with by Aurobindo's brother Barin Ghosh, elder brother of Swami Vivekananda Bhupendra Nath Datta, and Subodh Chandra Mullick, when they formed the Jugantar Party in April 1906. This was created as an inner circle of the Anushilan Samiti using the existing exercise and fitness clubs.

Soon after, using the occasion of the partition of Bengal in 1905, Lal Bal Pal mobilized Indians across the country against the Raj via demonstrations, strikes, and boycotts of British goods. But the movement was short-lived after the arrest of Tilak and the retirement of Pal and Ghosh. British would call Tilak 'The father of Indian unrest', and Pal is known as the 'Father of Revolutionary Thoughts in India'. Sri Aurobindo referred to him as one of *'mightiest prophets of nationalism.'* Pal expressed his disdain for Gandhi's ways, which he criticized for being rooted in "magic" instead of "logic".[15]

With the departure of Aurobindo from active politics in 1907, the death of Tilak, and the arrival of Gandhi, Pal also retired from politics in 1922.

In 1913 Lala Hardayal founded the Ghadar party with the help of Indians in America, with its headquarters set up in the Yugantar Ashram in San Francisco. For some time, Ghadar Party influenced many members of the independence movement and opposed the Gandhian path. But it did not last for too long.

The story goes like this:

While traveling by train in 1892, by chance, Tilak met Vivekananda. After finding out the greatness of the Swami, Tilak hosted Vivekananda in his house. A person who was present there (Basukaka), heard a conversation between the two that they came to a mutual agreement in terms of serving the nation. It was decided that Tilak would work towards nationalism in the "political" arena, while Vivekananda would work for nationalism in the "religious" arena.[16]

After the death of Vivekananda, grief-stricken, Tilak paid this tribute to Vivekananda:

"No Hindu, who has the interests of Hinduism at his heart, could help feeling grieved over Vivekananda's samadhi. Vivekananda, in short, had taken the work of keeping the banner of Advaita philosophy forever flying among all the nations of the world and made them realize the true greatness of Hindu religion and of the Hindu people. He had hoped that he would crown his achievement with the fulfillment of this task by virtue of his learning, eloquence, enthusiasm and sincerity, just as he had laid a secure foundation for it; but with Swami's samadhi, these hopes have gone. Thousands of years ago, another saint, Shankaracharya, who, showed to the world the glory and greatness of Hinduism. At the fag of the 19th century, the second Shankaracharya is Vivekananda, who showed to the world the glory of Hinduism. His work has yet to be completed. We have lost our glory, our independence, everything."[17]

An ardent follower of *Bhagvat Gita*, Tilak started the *Swadeshi* (meaning: of one's own country) movement in India. Jamshed Tata (who was inspired by Swami Vivekananda) and Tilak together established Bombay Swadeshi Stores to promote the national movement. In April 1916, Bal Gangadhar Tilak launched the Indian Home Rule League with the rousing slogan, "Swarajya (self-rule) is my birthright, and I will have it."

While Lala Lajpat Rai was carrying on the movement single-handedly, he died after James Scott, a police officer, hit him with a stick on November 17, 1928. The death of Lala became a major event and was raised in the British Parliament, but the government denied any role in Rai's death.[18]

From 1920 onwards, the INC was basically led by Gandhi and was engaged in a nationwide non-cooperation movement using Satyagraha attaching with the Khilafat movement.

The Chauri Chora incident which took place on February 4, 1922, in the Gorakhpur district of Uttar Pradesh, was a turning point of the Indian independence movement. A large group of protesters was fired upon indiscriminately by the British police. Then the protesters retaliated and set the Police station on fire which killed all inhabitants inside. It caused the death of three civilians and 22 policemen. Gandhi suddenly called off the movement without consulting any executive committee member of the INC. And yet, 19 civilians were sentenced to death and 14 were given a life sentence, and Gandhi announced a fast-unto-death to stop the movement. While Gandhi took a path of denial and avoidance, Pandit Madan Mohan Malviya took up the cause of justice for the protestors. The sessions court at Gorakhpur tried 225 persons for looting, arson, and causing death and gave a verdict to 170 persons to the death sentence. Malviya was able to free 151 accused after eloquent argumentation and received much praise from the chief justice.[19]

Many independent leaders were disappointed and even astonished that Gandhi unanimously announced the suspension of the movement, which could possibly bring the British government to its knees by demanding full independence. This aroused suspicion about the political acumen, judgment, and integrity of Gandhi. It is not unusual for people to question if there was a behind-the-scenes deal with Gandhi and the Raj.

Gandhi faced great opposition during the Gaya Congress of 1922, where he took a very hard stand on the withdrawal; as a result, the INC was divided. One young freedom fighter Ram Prasad Bismil was associated with the Arya Samaj founded by Swami Dayanand Saraswati. He also had worked with Lala Hardayal. Initially, Bismil (his pen name) participated in the INC. In January 1923, some seniors formed a new political party named Swaraj (self-rule) under the leadership of Chittaranjan Das and Motilal Nehru, and the youth members of the INC, including Bismil, opted for a revolutionary group called Hindustan Republican Association in style of Irish Republican Army (IRA). Later it was renamed to Hindustan Socialist Republican Association (HSRA). The key leaders included Sachindra Nath Sanyal, Bhagat Singh, Shivaram Rajguru, Sukhdev Thapar, and Chandrashekhar Azad, who later planned to kill James Scott to avenge the death of Lala. They were caught afterward in killing a mistaken police officer instead of Scott. And Gandhi called them "misguided souls".[20]

In the 1930s and early forties, thousands of revolutionaries were put in jail. The youngest person to sacrifice his life was 18-year-old Khudiram Bose of Medinipur, West Bengal, in 1908, who was praised by Tilak. For supporting Khudiram Bose, Tilak was arrested on sedition charges in 1908.

Jawaharlal Nehru was either totally ignorant or conveniently denied the revolutionary movements that started in India in the early 1900s. The very weapons used by many revolutionaries, especially in the Kakori Case, and even Bhagat Singh, who was connected to the revolutionaries in Bengal, were from the famous 'Rodda Arms Heist' in Kolkata on July 21, 1916.[21] G.D. Birla, the founder of Birla Industries, is said to have been involved in that as well. How could Nehru not know all these?

Here is what Nehru wrote in his autobiography:

'When Lalaji's death came soon after, inevitably it was connected with the assault, and sorrow itself gave pride of place to anger and indignation. It is well to appreciate this, for only so can we have some understanding of subsequent events, of the phenomenon of Bhagat Singh, and of his sudden and amazing popularity in north India. It is very easy and very fatuous to condemn persons or acts without seeking to understand the springs of action, the causes that underlie them. Bhagat Singh was not previously well known; he did not become popular because of an act of violence, an act of terrorism.'[22]

Notice the use of the term 'terrorism' by Nehru, which was used by the British to placate young revolutionaries. But how ignorant he was about the revolutionaries in Bengal and Punjab is evident here:

'Terrorists have flourished in India, off and on, for nearly thirty years, and at no time, except in the early days in Bengal,

did any of them attain a fraction of that popularity which came to Bhagat Singh. ...terrorism, in spite of occasional recrudescence, has no longer any real appeal for the youth of India. Fifteen years' stress on nonviolence has changed the whole background in India and made the masses much more indifferent to, and even hostile to, the idea of terrorism as a method of political action.'[22]

He further added:

'Terrorism is a dying thing in India and elsewhere, not because of Government coercion, which can only suppress and bottle up, not eradicate, but because of basic causes and world events. Terrorism usually represents the infancy of a revolutionary urge in a country. ...Bhagat Singh thus did not become popular because of his act of terrorism, but because he seemed to vindicate, for the moment, the honor of Lala Lajpat Rai, and through him of the nation. He became a symbol...' [22]

After the death of Tilak in 1920 and Lala Lajpat Rai in 1928, Gandhi became the focal point, only to convert the INC into a pacifist organization again and perhaps, with British support and strategy.

We can see that there were three major political parties in India before Independence. Some elite Indians headed the Congress party along with Hume, a British, as its secretary. Muslim League was created by some Muslim leaders and constantly supported and fomented by the British. Though founded virtually in Moscow, the Communist Party of India (CPI) was controlled by the Communist Party of Great Britain (CPGB), as they distributed communist literature to the revolutionaries in the jails. It is also well-known that the CPGB was used as a bridge not only between them and the CPI but also the INC. We may not have much information available yet about the deal Britain had with the CPGB.

In relation to their usage of revolutionaries to convert from nationalists to communists, it is very clear that the CPGB had many activities with the politics of the Indian subcontinent. The most prominent personality is Rajani Palme Dutt, who was an England-born journalist and communist theoretician, a member of the Executive Committee of the CPGB.[23] However, once he came close to Russian communist leaders, including Stalin, he got the role of supervising the communist party of India on behalf of the Comintern.[23] Wearing the journalism cap, he met with his communist counterparts in India, many prominent Congress leaders, including Gandhi, Nehru, and Patel in India.

In the *Journal of Communist Studies* via John Callaghan, we find the following: 'In spite of its small size, the British Communist Party was from its inception charged with responsibility for nurturing trade union and revolutionary organizations in the British colonies. In India, it played a notable role in this regard and no one in the British party worked harder or exercised more influence in connection with Communist politics on the subcontinent than R. Palme Dutt. '[24]

At this crucial juncture of the nation, only a few leaders could see through the British design and realized the need for a completely new and genuinely indigenous party to fight the British. Hardcore nationalist leaders were disillusioned by the soft approach towards the British, and the last straw broke after the suspension of the civil-disobedience movement by Gandhi and the INC after the Chauri Chora incident; thus, the birth of the first-ever truly indigenous political party called Swaraj Party happened on January 1, 1923. Initially, Khilafat was part of the name but later dropped.

This could have been a new turning point after the death of Tilak and the appearance of Gandhi in the Indian political scene. Many Congress leaders, including Motilal Nehru, flocked to the Swaraj Party. The most prominent one was Subhas Bose, who held C.R. Das as his political Guru. However, C.R. Das died at a very young age of 55 in 1925, and many suspect that there might have been foul play in his mysterious death.

This is what Sri Aurobindo had to say about C.R. Das in a telegraph:

"Chitta Ranjan's death is a supreme loss. Consummately endowed with political intelligence, constructive imagination, magnetism, a driving force combining a strong will and uncommon plasticity of mind for vision and tact of the hour, he was the one man after Tilak who could have led India to Swaraj." [25]

And Rabindranath gave his glorious tribute via his poem:

With thee came down the immortal breath.

This thou booned us with thy body's death.[25]

And with the demise of C.R. Das, the Swaraj Party slowly faded away.

Even Gandhi admitted: "Time cannot efface the memory of a man so great and good as Deshabandhu. At this time of trial for the nation there is no Indian who does not feel the void created by his death."[26]

The Winds of Change

In 1932, the so-called Communal Award or the MacDonald Award was created by the British prime minister Ramsay MacDonald who was to grant separate electorates to minority communities in Indian legislatures. In protest, Madan Mohan Malviya and Madhav Shrihari Aney separated from the INC and formed the Congress Nationalist Party, [27] which contested the 1934 elections to the central legislature and won 12 seats.

Indian independence movements were almost dead inside India in the 1940s after a few initial movements earlier. Today it appears that the last important movement by the INC was the 1942 Quit India movement which apparently was used like in the past to soften the stance of revolutionaries. But smelling a possible repeat of Chauri Chora, Britain nipped the movement in the buds by arresting most Congress leaders. Ultimately the independent movement had to take a completely different role, this time, fighting from outside of India. [28]

The Quit India movement was a misfire by the INC headed by Gandhi. It ended up in violence, and hundreds of people were killed by the British, and over 100,000 people were imprisoned, including top Congress leaders. The 'safety valve' called 'Satyagraha' or 'non-violent' movement that was helping Britain not to deal with violent freedom fighters worked well. Now, there was not much pressure on Britain to give freedom to India immediately.

World War II (WW II) started in Europe on September 1, 1939. Over 384,000 native British soldiers were killed in combat[29] in that war, a large part of the British Army was Indians. According to a BBC report, 'up to three million Bengalis were killed by famine, more than half a million South Asian refugees fled Myanmar (formerly Burma), 2.3 million soldiers manned the Indian army, and 89,000 of them died in military service.' [30] The war ended on August 14, 1945.

Much information regarding the transition or transfer of power between Britain and India is still not easily available. Secret discussions and deals between British and Indian leadership are still largely unavailable. Cambridge University historian Philip Nicholas Mansergh has given us plenty of detailed information of this period by researching, compiling, and editing the 12-volume work associated with Indian independence. It is called *Constitutional Relations Between Britain and India: The Transfer of Power 1942-7*. (London: Her Majesty's Stationery Office, 1971-1983).

By the end of WW II, the general public of Britain, just like the Vietnam-era war by America, was frustrated. The youth would not join the army anymore and demanded 'speedy demobilization' and revolted in some places to meet their demand.[31]

Britain was basically bankrupt after WW II. The British did not have the political will nor the resources to control

India anymore, with the 40,000 British troops to manage a vast country and another 2.5 million troops that were natives because of which 'they could not be trusted' anymore.

But Britain saw a great opportunity and a respectable exit route in leaving India gracefully. Really speaking, Britain felt it would be relieved from the complex task and stress to confront and manage Indians during their post-war frustration and yet, to be benefited indirectly as long as they could install their own friends in Delhi. And that is what exactly happened on August 15, 1947. So, they exited India with a 'high honor' with the hopes – a) Will have their own friends in Delhi to rule Indians; b) They will have access to Russia and Middle East (oil) via Pakistan and Afghanistan; c) Their economic, political, and strategic interests will remain in force directly or indirectly, via the Pakistani puppets and their friends such as the USA.

The shrinking of the British Empire, in reality, meant the emergence of the new 'American Empire'. While countering the Communist Soviet Empire, American political thinker James Burnham in 1947 in his book *The Struggle for the world* against the Soviet Union's plot he wrote: "The reality is that the only alternative to the Soviet World Empire is an American Empire which will be, if not literally world-wide in formal boundaries, capable of exercising decisive world control."[32]

While the Soviet Empire nearly dissolved, the American Empire, ditching much of the founding fathers' values and visions, really built an empire of wealth and power throughout the world. America even advised Britain 'not to abandon essential strategic positions in India' and wanted "to participate in the use and upkeep of some of these positions.[33]

It was Veer Savarkar whose far-sighted vision and action worked perfectly in this situation. In his book *Veer Savarkar: The man who could have prevented partition*[32] Uday Mahurkar wrote:

'Savarkar's national security vision is best reflected in the fact that on the one hand, he implored Bose to take the help of

Axis powers to overthrow the British, but on the other hand, he called upon Hindus to militarize themselves by taking advantage of World War II and enrolling themselves in the British army. The British, who had by far tried to keep Indians unarmed and unprepared out of fear and distrust, were now keen on encouraging them to join the army to cater to their war needs.'

In addition, Mahurkar writes:

'It was on the basis of an enlightened security vision rooted in the thinking that in the world arena, an enemy's enemy should be seen as a friend and that there were no permanent friends or permanent enemies on the platform of nations that Savarkar advised Subhas Chandra Bose to use World War II to India's best advantage. In a meeting with Bose in Bombay on June 22, 1940, Savarkar urged him to flee India and join hands with Japan and Germany in organizing an army (which later came to be known as the Azad Hind Fauj or INA) from amongst the Indian soldiers of the British army captured by the Axis Powers in the war.'[32]

Within six months, Bose's 'great escape' from his Calcutta home took place, and after traveling through many countries, he finally arrived in Japan and took over the Indian National Army's charge from Rash Behari Bose and others.

While Britain was responsible for the death of millions in famine, oppressed India for two centuries, and thousands of Indian soldiers sacrificed fighting for the British army, there was no reason to be sympathetic to Britain, as Gandhi insisted. This one event may suggest that Gandhi was working on behalf of Britain! Bose's idea was to hit the enemy during its crisis time to gain India's freedom.

Revolutionary leader Rash Behari Bose fled India and first organized the Indian Independence League and then the Indian National Army (INA) or Azad Hind Fauj in 1938 in Japan. Eventually, Subhas Bose took over the INA in 1943 when he reached East Asia from Germany, which gathered nearly 50,000 soldiers in a short time.[35]

According to Mahurkar, 'On July 8, 1943, in a private meeting with S.P. Mukherjee and other leaders at Delhi, Savarkar advised that if Subhas Chandra Bose landed in Bengal with his army, the Bengal Hindu Mahasabha should openly join him and officially disassociate with the Central Hindu Mahasabha as part of a larger strategy.'

Sadly, we also find some evidence of how in the name of fighting fascism how the communists opposed Bose. According to Rajani Palme Dutt - 'The Indian National Army which was headed by Subhas Chandra Bose, and which had the backing of Japanese fascism was regarded as functioning as the adjunct of Japan. The CPI took a leading role in the fight against Japanese imperialism.'[36]

And finally, they called Bose the 'dog of Tojo' (Japanese Emperor). In a 2010 event, at last, admission and apologies were issued by CPM leader A. B. Bardhan, though Prakash Karat was hesitant:

According to a report by Indian Express:

"Seven decades after his party denounced Subhas Chandra Bose as an "imperialist agent" and "Tojo's dog" (after Japanese Prime Minister Hediki Tojo), CPI general secretary A. B. Bardhan admitted at a function on April 5 that it was a "mistake on the part of the undivided Communist Party of India not to have recognised Netaji's indomitable spirit of patriotism". He added: "I have no hesitation in apologising for this lapse." However, CPM general secretary Prakash Karat, who was also present at the function, ignored Bardhan's reference to the "undivided" party's view of Netaji. While he paid rich tributes to Bose, he did not make any reference to the historical "mistake".'[37]

The Massacres of the INA Soldiers

By the end of the war, once Japan surrendered, INA's support system crumbled, and INA was forced to withdraw, and eventually, they were captured by the British as the Prisoners of War (POWs).

About half of the INA soldiers have perished in battles. The remaining INA soldiers were brought to India as POWs. There were over 23,000 INA soldiers captured as the POWs by the British Army and were kept in various army barracks, camps, and jails throughout India. The INA trials began at the Red Fort between November 1945 and May 1946, on various charges of treason, torture, murder, and abetment to murder, during WW II.

A war crime trial popularly known as the 'Red Fort Trial' of the INA members was set up. Many of them were court marshaled for working against British interest, and many were to be sentenced for sedition against the Raj.

But before the trials began, Britain violated all international laws and tortured and killed many. [38] In an effort to reduce the number of trials to avoid public furies, thousands of INA soldiers were killed in cold blood. We all are familiar with the Jallianwala Bagh massacre of April 1919, though the new generation's memory is fading where 1500+ innocent people were brutally killed. But what happened in Nilganj and Jhikargacha is equally heinous, if not more.

The unknown history of great sacrifices is yet to be told to the world, the British's cold-blooded killings of the INA POWs. When the Trial was announced, the British authorities were worried that the number of POWs would be too many and perhaps risky to bring to Delhi. To reduce the burden and to take revenge, British troops killed several thousand unarmed, helpless soldiers of the INA. In Jhikargacha, currently in Bangladesh, over 3000 INA members were killed, and in Nilganj, near Barrackpore, West Bengal, they killed 2300 soldiers. They were lined up at night outside the barracks and were killed by machine guns. Their bodies were dumped into nearby canals and ditches.[39, 40]

And possibly there were other such mass murders which we are yet to know. These are the most condemnable acts in the post-war scenario; great war-crimes committed by the British still await justice. The wails of these dead soldiers still echo even 80 years later. Would the Indian government open a full inquiry someday and honor every soldier who was murdered?

Reasons Behind the British Exit from India

Before we discuss the subject, we need to know the key players from the British side during the last decade of British rule in India. The British monarchy was established in the 10th century, which included medieval Scotland and Anglo Saxon England, and became the kingdoms of England and Scotland. From 1603, the English and Scottish kingdoms were ruled by a single sovereign. From 1649 to 1660, the tradition of monarchy was abolished by the formation of the republican Commonwealth of England. Colonies started to develop in many parts of the world, especially in Asia and Africa, mostly by the British traders. Around the 1920s, the Dominions evolved into self-governing countries within a Commonwealth of Nations. King George VI and Queen Elizabeth became the heads of the Commonwealth, with 'free association symbol of its independent member states', which included 14 countries.

The British monarch became the nominal head of the British Empire, which covered a quarter of the world's land area at its greatest peak in 1921. During the reign of Queen Alexandria Victoria (1837– 1901) the Empire doubled in size, and in 1876 the Queen became 'Empress of India', the 'Jewel in the Crown'. Victoria married her cousin Albert of Saxe-Coburg, and as we know from various sources, Victoria was a sympathizer of Islam.

George VI became the King (1936–1952 CE) of Britain. After that, Elizabeth Alexandra Mary became the Queen. She married her cousin Prince Philip, Duke of Edinburgh. King Philip was a naval officer who served during World War II when India was under British rule. Louis Mountbatten was the maternal uncle of Philip. Both were descendants of Victoria; Mountbatten was the great-grandson of Victoria. His elder sister, Alice, was the princess of Battenberg (Germany). Princess Alice was Philip's mother. Mountbatten is said to have introduced Prince Philip Mountbatten to Princess Elizabeth at a family wedding in 1934. [41]

A few figures are the most important in Britain's political leadership: First, Winston Churchill was the Prime Minister of Britain between 1940 and 1945 and Clement Attlee between 1945 and 1951. Archibald Percival Wavell was the Commander-in-Chief of India and later the Governor-General and the Viceroy of India between 1943 and 1947. The last Viceroy of India was Louis Mountbatten.

As millions of Indian soldiers were being decommissioned from the British Army, Britain was very much concerned about the publicity about the Free India Legion and the dedication and sacrifice and subsequent trials of the INA soldiers. They anticipated rebellion and its impact on Indian masses and armed forces and also in regions across the world under the control of Britain. In an effort to stop any information about the INA trials from leaking out, the British government ordered the British Broadcasting Corporation (BBC) not to broadcast anything related to the INA.[42] But once the Red Fort Trial proceedings were started, the government could not stop the leakage of the news,[43] which spread like wildfire throughout the country.

In any case, after the war was over, Bose first told his close associates that he would surrender, and his trial and possible execution would create massive outrage in India, which would overthrow the British Raj eventually. His colleagues disagreed, and he started to work on a plan to create another army again using Russian support.

But the very trial of the INA soldiers caused much outrage among Indians, more specifically, the men in uniform, including Navy, Air Force, and Army.

So, while there was no major Independence movement, why did Britain decide to leave India? Today, it is well known that some of the movements by the INC had some impact in terms of mass awakening. However, we also know today that the history was written completely imbalanced towards the less important parts of the independence movement.

It has been already noted earlier that the unfortunate and untimely demise of two historical personalities changed the course of the history of India – Prithviraj Chauhan and Maharaj Hemu. In recent times, a few more such unfortunate deaths also impacted India's recent history. The first one is Lokmanya Tilak, then Chittaranjan Das and Lala Lajpat Rai. In the post-1947 era, Syama Prasad Mookerjee's (SPM) death is not just shrouded with mystery, but we know today that he was murdered as was Prime Minister Lal Bahadur Shastri in Tashkent. To date, the Indian government and the people have not demanded a true inquiry yet about the deaths of SPM and Shastri.

The disappearance of Bose is today viewed differently than the official history of India as more and more information has come to light. It is an established fact now that Bose did not die in the plane crash; not only was the evidence unsatisfactory, but new information also suggests that the so-called plane crash was preplanned by Bose himself to fool the world so that they don't have access to him. Of course, his departure from Indian soil was a loss, and much blame for that goes to none other than Gandhi and his companions. But in hindsight, though he had no other option, it was a blessing in disguise because he could do what he wanted to do – fight the Brits with might and not appeasement and pacifism.

As noted earlier, the people of India suffered enormously economically due to WW II. And the soldiers in the British

Indian army were sick of the British Raj. The INA trials triggered anger and outrage among Indians in all three parts of the Indian Military.

According to some military intelligence reports, the Indian soldiers were so angry that they could not be relied upon to obey their British officers.[44]

Wavell, anticipating more trouble and insurgency within the British Indian armed forces and masses based on the intelligence reports, recommended to start negotiation with the relevant parties for the transfer of power and wrote to Churchill [October 24, 1944]:

'If we can secure India as a friendly partner in the British Commonwealth, our predominant influence in these countries [such as Burma and Malaya] will, I think, be assured; with a lost and hostile India, we are likely to be reduced in the East to the position of commercial bag-men. '[45]

First, thc Royal Indian Navy revolted in Bombay, Karachi, Madras, Vizag, and Calcutta in February 1946. The rebel naval soldiers were in control of 22 vessels in Bombay. A total of 78 ships, 20 onshore establishments were under their control, and about 20,000 of them were involved. It was followed by the Royal Indian Air Force and the Indian Army. At some places, such as Jabalpur, Madras, and Poona, (Pune) soldiers started ignoring orders from British superiors.

Mahurkar has noted: 'The 1946 Royal Indian Navy Revolt, though a brief incident from 18–23 February, has still not got its due place in Indian history. The revolt was the last trigger that sounded the death knell for British rule in India.... Two weeks after the revolt, the British prime minister met with the King, and the decision to free India was taken on 5 March 1946.'[46]

In a new awakening, people, especially the youth of Bombay, welcomed these rebellious soldiers, gave them food and water, erected barricades, and fought with armed policemen and with several British battalions who had tanks and armored cars.

There was a General Strike by the people of Bombay, which Patel and Jinnah and their parties opposed. After that, there was a street battle in Bombay, and over 200 people died.

The rebels and general public went around Bombay (Mumbai) carrying Netaji's portraits and forced the British to shout *Jai Hind* and other INA songs and slogans, including *'kadam kadam barhaye ja'*. They also brought down the Union Jack on their ships and refused to obey their British masters.[47]

These massive events terrified the British Raj. Viceroy Wavell's diary [February 19, 1946] is revealing:

'A day of alarms but not excursions. I saw Porter [Secretary, Government of India, Home Department], all for capitulation to the I.N.A.; Bewoor [Secretary, Posts and Air Dept.] about a postal strike; Carr [A.O.C.-in-C.] about R.I.A.F. mutiny; Griffin [Chief Commissioner of Railways] and Conran-Smith [Secretary, War Transport Department] about a railway strike; and finally the C-in-C., most gloomy of all, about the R.I.N. [Royal Indian Navy] mutiny at Bombay and the I.N.A. trials. What a cheerful day -- prospect or reality of three mutinies and two strikes!'[48]

Both Nehru and Patel, in a meeting in Bombay on February 26, 1946 condemned these spontaneous activities of rebellion and protest as "mass violence". In an interview Nehru, as if a British statesman speaking, said, "The R.I.N. Central Strike Committee had no business to issue such an appeal [for the strike]. I will not tolerate this kind of thing.'[49]

What was the reaction of Gandhi? He denounced it, saying it was an "unholy combination" between Hindus and Muslims and preferred to die rather than see India delivered over to "the rabble."[50]

Due to the negative campaign by Nehru and other INC leaders against the mass uprising, within a few months, public opinion was subdued though the process of Britain's departure was already set in motion. Slowly, the mass anger faded away, and so much so that by November 1946, sympathy for British people grew among many Indians. A great example is the admission of the INC leader Ashok Mehta himself during the Meerut session of the INC:

"A year ago, an Englishman could not show his face in Bombay or Calcutta; today he alone moves freely and even Indians move in English dress."[51]

And British politician Alan Campbell-Johnson who served on the staff of Mountbatten, wrote [June 1, 1947]:

"It should be noted that the fury is internal and fratricidal, and that the British are probably more popular with both Hindus and Moslems than at any time in living memory."[52]

The book *Bose: The Indian Samurai – Netaji and the INA, A Military Assessment by General G. D. Bakshi* [KW Publishers Pvt Ltd (April 2, 2018)] gives us a window into that grim past. The British Prime Minister Clement Attlee, who presided over the independence and partition of India, visited India in 1956 and stayed in Calcutta as the guest of the Governor of West Bengal P.B. Chakraborthy. Chakraborthy once wrote in a letter: "When I was acting Governor, Lord Attlee, who had given us independence by withdrawing British rule from India, spent two days in the Governor's palace at Calcutta during his tour of India. At that time I had a prolonged discussion with him regarding the real factors that had led the British to quit India." Chakraborthy added, "My direct question to Attlee was that since Gandhi's Quit India movement had tapered off quite some time ago and in 1947 no such new compelling situation had arisen that would necessitate a hasty British departure, why did they have to leave?"[53]

"In his reply Attlee cited several reasons, the principal among them being the erosion of loyalty to the British crown among the Indian Army and Navy personnel as a result of the military activities of Netaji," Justice Chakraborthy says. That's not all. Chakraborthy adds, "Toward the end of our discussion

I asked Attlee what was the extent of Gandhi's influence upon the British decision to quit India. Hearing this question, Attlee's lips became twisted in a sarcastic smile as he slowly chewed out the word, m-i-n-i-m-a-l!"[53]

Another direct proof comes from Frederick William Pethick-Lawrence, the Secretary of State for India and Burma from 1945 to 1947. On November 25, in reply to a letter of Wavell, he wrote: 'anything in the nature of reconquest and retention of India by force practicable from a political, military or economic point of view. Politically our party would not support such a policy nor do we believe that it would be practicable from an international point of view. From a military point of view we have not the forces sufficient to embark upon the holding down of India as a whole ... Nor from an economic point of view can we contemplate the great expenditure that would be entailed...'[54]

British Exit Plan

Realizing that the time was up for packing, Britain announced to form an interim government before transferring power to the Indian leaders of the INC and Muslim League. As proposed by the British, the INC and Muslim League agreed to participate in elections to form a constituent assembly. In March 1946, newly elected British government headed by Prime Minister Clement Attlee sent the Cabinet Mission to India to formulate a plan for the formation of a government that would lead to an independent India.[55]

The Cabinet Mission members met with the Executive Council of the Viceroy where, Edward Benthall, a member, said "the Council was unanimous that a change of government at the Centre was imperative ... It is due to the uncertainty of Indian troops and police to whom they must look for defense and support in the future."[56]

According to this plan, elections were held for the first time for the Constituent Assembly. The Constitution of India was drafted by the Constituent Assembly on May 16, 1946. The total number of members of the Constituent Assembly was 389, of which 292 were representatives of the provinces, 93 represented the Princely States, and four were from the chief commissioner provinces of Delhi, Ajmer-Merwara, Coorg, and British Baluchistan. The elections for the 296 seats were completed by August 1946. Congress won 208 seats, and the Muslim League 73.

Many of these INC members were taken into the Viceroy's Executive Council in the form of an Interim Government, which virtually silenced any voice of dissent so that the silent, behind-the-scenes transfer of power happens without any further mass uprising.

On February 20, 1947, Attlee announced in Parliament their "definite intention" to transfer "power to responsible Indian hands" by June 1948. Mountbatten told the British Cabinet on May 8, 1947, that Patel and Nehru expressed "a desire for a form of early Dominion Status (but under a more suitable name)." Mountbatten noted: "This is the greatest opportunity ever offered to the Empire."[57] On May 10, Nehru had a meeting with the Viceroy and his staff where he said: "…himself was most anxious, apart from sentimental reasons, to have the closest possible relations with the British Commonwealth.... He did not intend to talk about 'Dominion Status' openly because of the many suspicions. He wanted to prepare the ground."[58]

On September 2, 1946, nearly six months after the revolts, the Interim Government of India, or the Provisional Government of India, was formed from the newly elected Constituent Assembly of India, which was assigned to assist the transfer of power and it got resolved after August 15, 1947.[59] The executive branch of the interim government was served by the Viceroy's Executive Council headed by the Viceroy of India.

At this point, it seemed like a peaceful and silent transfer of power was to happen, perhaps without the division of the country and ensuing bloodbath.

However, after this election, the Muslim League was on a crash course with the INC. Hindu-Muslim riots erupted in many places, and the Muslim League demanded a separate constituent assembly for Muslims in India. Under pressure, or more likely pretense, hence it was pre-planned, on June 3, 1947, Mountbatten suddenly announced to scrap the Cabinet Mission Plan and with the speedy passage in the British Parliament of the Indian Independence Act 1947 under which two separate nations of India and Pakistan would be created. The Act codified British withdrawal and the partition of India.[60]

The Act was passed on July 18, 1947, and, although it was earlier declared that India would become independent by June 1948, the creation of two nations happened on 14th (Pakistan) and 15th (India) August 1947. While the Constituent Assembly met for the first time on December 9, 1946, it reassembled for the last time on August 14, 1947 as a 'sovereign body and successor to the British parliament's authority in India'.

Just imagine, you are living in a relatively peaceful place. You wake up in the morning and hear that your country has changed. If you are a Hindu, Sikh, or Buddhist, you find out that the new name of your country is not India but Pakistan. And if you are a Muslim, your country is no more India, but Pakistan if you lived in the areas known as Pakistan and Bangladesh today. And then you are told that you don't belong in your land; you must migrate to your newly named country, leaving all your belongings and generational memories. And then you leave the birthplace with much grief only to be attacked by the goons, looters, and rapists. You would be lucky if you could reach the other side of the border. Your daughters and wife would be lucky if they were not raped, and even their body parts were not severed afterward. This is what happened to millions in August 1947.

Already, Britain caused millions of deaths via manufactured famines in the eastern parts of undivided India. For nearly 200 years, they looted all the wealth out of India. They siphoned out wealth worth over US $45 trillion from India[61] and also funded the industrial revolution. As a result, they left the vast majority of Indians in abject poverty, and the average life expectancy at that time was only 30 years.

How was the demarcation of borders of the three countries done? Cyril John Radcliffe, a retired British judge, was appointed as the chairman of the two boundary committees set up with the passing of the Indian Independence Act. He had no knowledge of India's geography, history, culture, and society, and it was his first and only visit to India. He basically sat in his office, put his marker on the map called the 'Radcliffe line' of the subcontinent, and decided the borders lines. This so-called Radcliffe Award was delivered to the most unfortunate people of the subcontinent so quickly, and it shows the map must have been already drawn before Radcliffe came to India, perhaps months or even years before his arrival. After Radcliffe returned to England, when he came to know about the deaths and miseries of millions of people on both sides of the Radcliffe divide, he was so much grief-stricken that he refused to accept the remuneration for the work done and never returned to India.[62]

All the players in this disastrous game of partition knew what was to come. J.D. Tyson, the Secretary to the Bengal Governor, wrote to the authorities in England on July 5, 1947:

"Mountbatten is a hustler; ever since he came out he has pursued shock tactics.... I believe, now, we shall withdraw in fairly peaceful conditions – whatever may happen after we have gone .... I think there will be very unsettled conditions in India for some time to come... but the trouble will be primarily between Hindus and Muslims – not anti-European."[63]

And Penderal Moon, a British official then serving in India, wrote: 'So with a quick unprecedented unanimity all [Britain, INC and Muslim League] set forth together on a path leading straight to mass slaughter.'[64]

Dominion Status and the Commonwealth

All the reports from the pre-independence era tell us that it was very painful for Britain to leave India. But they had very little choice. So, within the limit of choices, they wanted to make sure that India remained under British influence and control as much as possible. One was the idea of 'dominion' status, and the other was the idea of the 'British Commonwealth', which India is part of to date. Why? India celebrates with pomp-and-show the Commonwealth Games. Why?

The Indian Independence Act of 1947 basically was a great tool to divide India, not just into three parts but many. Of course, it was the craziest idea and formation in known history to have two different land areas were made into one country – West and East Pakistan – a 2000-km-distance between Dacca (Dhaka) and Islamabad. And the other hidden sinister design was that 562 princely 'states' were given a choice to join either India or Pakistan or remain independent – thus the possibility of India being broken into 500-plus pieces. No thanks to Nehru, but thanks to Sardar Patel, India soon became one united nation except Hyderabad and Goa, which was settled later.

Prime Minister Nehru and Deputy Prime Minister Sardar Vallabhbhai Patel invited Mountbatten to continue as Governor-General of India. He was replaced in June 1948 by Chakravarti Rajagopalachari. The princes and 'kings' of the princely states had the option to either remain independent or join either nation. Thus, India's leaders faced the prospect of inheriting a nation fragmented between medieval-era kingdoms and provinces organized by colonial powers. Under the leadership of Sardar Vallabhbhai Patel, the new Government of India employed political negotiations backed with the option of military action to ensure the primacy of the Central Government while a constitution was being drafted. The Constituent Assembly adopted the Constitution of India, drafted by a committee headed by B.R. Ambedkar, on November 26, 1949. India became a federal, democratic republic after its constitution came into effect on January 26, 1950. Rajendra Prasad became the first President of India, taking over from Governor-General Rajagopalachari.

A 'dominion' was an autonomous region within the British Empire, was "equal in status" but had an "allegiance to the Crown". Virtually, King George VI continued to reign as the Emperor of India, and 'Lord' Mountbatten was the country's first Governor-General. Nehru was sworn in as the premier but served on the command of the British Governor-General, and unelected Indian nationalist leaders were administered oaths in the name of the British King-Emperor. It also meant that a British field marshall led the Indian army, and judges appointed by the British continued to be part of the high courts and the federal court.[65]

The idea of the Commonwealth was to create a new semi-colony of the Empire. The British Chief of Staff's Committee noted: 'From the military point of view, and on the grounds of our future strategy and the security of the British Commonwealth, our aim must be to retain India constitutionally within the British Commonwealth of Nations and to direct all our endeavor towards persuading her to this end. If in these endeavors we were successful, a formal Treaty would probably be unnecessary, and our strategic requirements could be met by Staff conversations and liaison arrangements similar to those in force with the other Dominions.'[66]

Initially, the British were unsure of India's dominion status, and even some dominions did not want to share this status with a non-white polity. "Objections to India getting dominion status came not only from within the British parliament but also from the leaders of the other dominions (Canada, Australia, New Zealand, and South Africa), who did not want to be placed on a status of equality with a non-white polity."[67]

Finally, the heads of Commonwealth states agreed that 'India's continuance in the Commonwealth was extremely important to the interests of Britain and the dominions.'[68]

There was a sense of jubilation in both British and Indian camps. On June 3, 1947, Alec Joyce of the India Office wired this to Mountbatten's press attaché Alan Campbell-Johnson:

'A packed House of Commons listened with intense interest to Prime Minister's announcement this afternoon. Proposals and first reaction from India undoubtedly created profound gratification among all Parties. Sense of unity and recognition of tremendous issues and possibilities involved were comparable only with most historic moments during war.... This has been a great day for us all.'[69]

How was the reaction on the Indian side? Key INC and Muslim League leaders expressed much happiness and gratitude for this 'gift' to India by Britain. Rajendra Prasad, President of the Indian Constituent Assembly, described the transfer of power as "the consummation and fulfillment of the historic tradition and democratic ideals of the British race."[70] Does he appear as a British apologist?

This is how a key Commonwealth member country's 'white' head Field Marshal Smuts, then Prime Minister of South Africa expressed to console themselves: "This does not look like quitting..."[71] In May 1949, a resolution was moved for the ratification of the Commonwealth Prime Ministers' decision to accept the "sovereign, independent republic" of India as a member of the Commonwealth of Nations in the Indian Constituent Assembly. Although some other 'white' nations had reservation about India joining the Commonwealth – so much for the hatred of 'white race' on the 'kala aadmis'.

Britain was only giving 'dominion' status to India and Pakistan and not complete freedom. It was only ratified in 1950 after the British-inspired constitution was introduced.

Nehru commented: '...yet we have seen that even out of that prickly thorn of frustration and despair, we have been able to pick out the rose of fulfillment.'[72]

It appeared to be a very proud and happy moment for Nehru for his country to become part of the Commonwealth, in reality, the British Monarch. He said:

"We join the Commonwealth obviously because we think it is beneficial to us and to certain causes in the world that we wish to advance. The other countries of the Commonwealth want us to remain there because they think it is beneficial to them. It is mutually understood that it is to the advantage of the nations in the Commonwealth and therefore they join."[73]

The Final Call and Announcement

On February 20, 1947, it was announced by Prime Minister Attlee, based on the Indian Independence Act, that Britain would grant full self-government to British India by June 30, 1948, at the latest and the future of the Princely States within India would be decided after the date of final transfer is decided.[74] Thc Act caused the repeal of the use of the term 'Emperor of India' as a title for the British Crown and ended all treaties with the princely states. Mountbatten continued as Governor-General, and Jawaharlal Nehru was appointed India's first Prime Minister. On the other side, Muhammad Ali Jinnah became Pakistan's Governor-General and Liaquat Ali Khan it's Prime Minister.[75]

Interestingly, before Mountbatten left for India to take over the office of Viceroy, it is evident that Britain had full confidence in him. As noted before, he was part of the family of the British monarchs. Attlee and members of the Cabinet Mission had told him that he 'was, in fact, to regard himself less as the last British Viceroy than as the first head of the new Indian State.'[76] Mountbatten, the last British Viceroy, also became the first head of the new Indian state at the invitation of the Congress. Nehru and Patel 'wanted him to stay on [in that capacity] as long as he would.'[77]

Subsequently, the Indian British military officers did not get a chance to become heads of the three defense services of

India as well as of Pakistan. To keep full control, the post of the Supreme Commander of the armed forces of the two new newly formed countries was given to the former Commander-in-Chief of the Indian Army, Claude Auchinleck.[78]

Most Indians may not be aware of the fact that Mountbatten designed flags for the new states with the Union Jack in the upper part of the flag. Even the flags of the Governor-General and governors, and the Navy and the Air Force were suitably designed, and it was decided not to publicize these matters. It appears that Gandhi, Patel, and others knew about this and were willing to accept it, but finally decided to persuade Mountbatten to not to do so as there was a "general feeling among Congress extremists… that Indian leaders were pandering far too much to the British." However, they agreed to fly the Union Jack on certain occasions.[79]

The apparent end of the British Empire with a 'tryst of destiny' staged in Delhi on August 15, 1947, while the British flag, the Union Jack, was still flying as the Indian national flag was unfurled, playing the British anthem "God Save the King" which Indian anthem 'Jana Gana Mana' followed. Nehru toasted for the health of the British King and Mountbatten toasted the Dominion Government.[78] The "programme had originally included a ceremonial lowering of the Union Jack," but it was changed, and the Union Jack was not brought down because it might offend "British susceptibilities."[80]

Remnants of the British flag and design are still found in the Indian Naval Ensign (also known as the Indian White Ensign) used by ships of the Indian Navy. On can see it on the Indian Navy's official website: https://indiannavy.nic.in/

The Naval Ensign of India has a white ensign, with a horizontal red stripe and a vertical red stripe intersecting at the center of the flag (Cross of Saint George), the emblem of India superimposed on the intersection, and the national flag in the upper canton next to the staff (used to be Union Jack before). The most recent version of the ensign was adopted in 2014 after adding the inscription "Satyameva Jayate". The Pennant (flown from the ship masthead) is still a red cross with Ashok Chakra on it.

The newly appointed President of the Indian Constituent Assembly, Rajendra Prasad, requested Mountbatten, who was still the head of the new state, to convey "a message of loyal greetings from this House" to the British King. It said: 'That message will serve as an inspiration in the great work on which we launch today ... I hope and trust that the interest and sympathy and the kindness which have always inspired His Majesty will continue in favour of India and we shall be worthy of them'.[81]

In reality, India and Pakistan acquired dominion status; India remained a dominion till 1950. It was only on January 26, 1950, that the country was able to truly break free from the monarchy and transform into a sovereign democratic republic after its constitution came into effect, though the constitution is more or less a colonial construct and the key author Ambedkar himself did not have faith in it!

On January 24, 1947 the Director of the Intelligence Bureau, Government of India, noted: 'The game so far has been well played, in that (a) both Congress and the League have been brought into the Central Government; (b) the Indian problem has been thereby thrust into its appropriate plane of communalism.... Grave communal disorder must not disturb us into action which would reproduce anti-British agitation. The latter may produce an inordinately dangerous situation and lead us nowhere. The former is a natural, if ghastly process, tending in its own way to the solution of the Indian problem.'[82] Copies of this note were sent to the private secretaries of Attlee, Lord Alexander and Stafford Cripps.

When Wavell convened the Shimla Conference after the war in Europe had ended, the Congress, as V.P. Menon wrote, came in for cooperation without any conditions. Congress President Maulana Azad wrote to Wavell, "the contacts established between the Congress and the government, had largely allayed past bitterness, and marked the beginning of a new chapter of confidence and goodwill".[83]

On May 23, Attlee, in a wired message to the Dominion Prime Ministers, conveyed:

"They [the INC leaders] said that though, in order to secure assent of their party, they would have publicly to stress fact that it is inherent in Dominion status that Dominion can secede from Commonwealth whenever it wishes, in their view Hindustan would not ultimately leave the Commonwealth, once Dominion status had been accepted. This most unexpected development opens up new possibility of whole of India, although divided into two or possibly three independent states, remaining in the Commonwealth after the effective transfer of power has taken place.'[84]

Attlee hoped that others would follow India but recommended maintaining secrecy about it:

'Example set by India would be likely to influence Burma, and probably later other parts of the Empire to remain in the Commonwealth. I must emphasize the need for extreme secrecy on this matter because if it became known that Congress leaders had privately encouraged this idea, the possibility of their being able to bring their party round to it would be serious[ly] jeopardized.'[84]

Churchill was delighted to observe this development and told Mountbatten that if he could achieve Dominion status for both Hindustan and Pakistan, 'the whole country would be behind him'. [85]

How about Gandhi? He must have been very happy since Mountbatten noted that "even during the war he had expressed himself as not being against it [dominion status]".[86] Gandhi's view about accepting the British proposals said: "to help and not hinder the Allied war effort".

So, was it true Independence that Indians got, or land with a Dominion status under the British Crown's Commonwealth?

References

1. https://ncert.nic.in/textbook/pdf/hess209.pdf
2. https://ncert.nic.in/textbook/pdf/hess209.pdf
3. https://www.open.ac.uk/researchprojects/makingbritain/content/indian-national-congress]
4. https://www.indiatoday.in/education-today/gk-current-affairs/story/partition-of-bengal-1905-divide-and-rule-protests-1368958-2018-10-16]
5. Sinhal, Meenu "Biography of Netaji Subhas Chandra Bose", Prabhat Publications, 2015, https://www.netajisubhasbose.org/early-life]
6. Bapu, Prabhu (2013). Hindu Mahasabha in Colonial North India, 1915-1930: Constructing Nation and History. Routledge. p.16.
7. Ibid. p. 3.
8. Ibid. p.16.
9. Ibid. p.17.
10. Jaffrelot, Christophe (2011). "Religion, Caste, and Politics in India". C. Hurst & Co. p. 43.
11. Bapu, Prabhu (2013). "Hindu Mahasabha in Colonial North India, 1915-1930: Constructing Nation and History". pp. 17-20.
12. Ibid. p. 20.
13. Mahurkar, Uday, "Veer Savarkar: The man Who could have prevented partition", Rupa Publication, India, 2021.
14. Lipner, Julius, (1999), "Brahmabandhab Upadhyay: The Life and Thought of a Revolutionary", Delhi: Oxford University Press, India, p. xv.
15. "Bipin Chandra Pal: As much a revolutionary in politics, as in his private life".
16. Mohan, Brij "Gita Today: A Common Man's Approach to Shrimad Bhagwad Gita", Notion Press, 2019.

17. Bhagwat, A.K.; Pradhan, G.P. (2015), "Lokmanya Tilak – A Biography", p. 226.
18. Rana, Bhawan Singh (2005). "Bhagat Singh". Diamond Pocket Books. p. 36.
19. https://internet.bhu.ac.in/mahamana/mahamanaasalawyer3.php
20. https://www.dailyo.in/politics/bhagat-singh-mahatma-gandhi-sukhdev-rajguru-freedom-struggle-british/story/1/2704.html
21. https://www.livehistoryindia.com/story/cover-story/a-great-robbery-that-shook-the-raj/
22. https://ia802904.us.archive.org/20/items/towardfreedomthe000770mbp/towardfreedomthe000770mbp.pdf Nehru Toward freedom: The autobiography of Jawaharlal Nehru, The John Day Company, New York, 1941.
23. Journal of Communist Studies Volume 6, 1990 - Issue 1, Rajani Palme Dutt, British Communism, and the Communist Party of India, John Callaghan, pp. 49-70.
24. Beckett, Francis "Enemy Within: The Rise and Fall of the British Communist Party", London: John Murray, 1995, Published online: 12 Nov 2007, https://www.tandfonline.com/doi/pdf/10.1080/13523279008415006?needAccess=true
25. https://www.yogaofsrichinmoy.com/sri-chinmoy-speaks/world-figures/indians/chitta-ranjan-das/
26. https://www.srichinmoylibrary.com/ils-6
27. Beck, Sanderson. "South Asia 1800-1950".
28. https://revolutionarydemocracy.org/rdv11n2/dutt.htm
29. https://www.parliament.uk/business/publications/research/olympic-britain/crime-and-defence/the-fallen/
30. https://www.bbc.com/news/world-asia-india-33105898
31. Mansergh, Nicholas. "Constitutional Relations Between

Britain and India: The Transfer of Power 1942-7". (London: Her Majesty's Stationery Office, 1971-1983). VI, p. 1055.

32. Hitchens, Christopher "For the Sake of Argument", p. 144 Verso, 1933.
33. Mansergh, VI, p. 644; VII, p. 931.
34. Mahurkar, Uday, "Veer Savarkar: The man Who could have prevented partition", Rupa Publication, India, 2021.
35. Belle, Carl Vadivella (2014), "Tragic Orphans: Indians in Malaysia", Institute of South-East Asian Studies, p. 199.
36. Record of the Discussions of Dutt with Gandhi, Patel and Nehru (revolutionarydemocracy.org)
37. http://archive.indianexpress.com/news/bardhan-admits-comrades---mistake--on-netaji/616627/
38. http://www.hindustantimes.com/news/specials/Netaji/images/nov_2_45.gif
39. https://www.myindiamyglory.com/2019/10/08/1945-nilganj-massacre-how-british-shot-2000-ina-soldiers-in-det-camps/
40. https://zeenews.india.com/video/india/why-is-the-history-of-nilganjs-massacre-unheard-2337421.html
41. https://www.indiatoday.in/world/story/how-prince-philip-was-related-to-lord-mountbatten-the-last-viceroy-of-india-1789194-2021-04-09
42. Hitler's Secret Indian Army Last Section: "Mutinies"
43. http://www.hindustantimes.com/news/specials/Netaji/images/nov_2_45.gif
44. https://www.indiatoday.in/india/story/exclusive-attlee-told-bengal-governor-netaji-not-gandhi-got-india-freedom-claims-book-305512-2016-01-25
45. Mansergh, V, p. 127.
46. "Veer Savarkar: The man Who could have prevented partition" (Rupa Publication India, 2021)
47. https://www.indiatoday.in/india/story/exclusive-attlee-

told-bengal-governor-netaji-not-gandhi-got-india-freedom-claims-book-305512-2016-01-25]

48. "Wavell: The Viceroy's Journal", ed. by Penderel Moon, (Delhi, 1977), p. 215.
49. Jawaharlal Nehru, Selected Works XV, New Delhi, 1981, pp. 4, 13.
50. "The Collected Works of Mahatma Gandhi", Vol. 83, (Delhi, 1981) p. 304.
51. Mansergh, IX, p. 133.
52. Campbell-Johnson, Alan "Mission with Mountbatten", (London, 1951) p. 98.
53. https://www.indiatoday.in/india/story/exclusive-attlee-told-bengal-governor-netaji-not-gandhi-got-india-freedom-claims-book-305512-2016-01-25]
54. Mansengh, IX, p. 174.
55. Chaurasia, Radhey Shyam (2002). "History of Modern India, 1707 A. D. to 2000 A. D.", Atlantic Publishers & Distributors. pp. 300–400.
56. Mansergh, VII, p. 7.
57. Mansergh, X, p. 699.
58. Mansergh, X, p. 735.
59. Chaurasia, Radhey Shyam (2002). "History of Modern India, 1707 A. D. to 2000 A. D.", Atlantic Publishers & Distributors. pp. 300–400.
60. https://indianexpress.com/article/research/independence-day-dominion-status-august-15-1947-6555454/
61. [https://historyofyesterday.com/how-britain-looted-45-trillion-from-india-2e923dfb2efb]
62. [https://www.timesnownews.com/india/article/heres-why-the-man-who-drew-the-partition-map-of-india-never-returned-for-a-visit/635563]
63. Mansergh, XI, p. 940.
64. Penderal Moon, Divide and Quit, (London, 1961) p. 70.

65. https://indianexpress.com/article/research/independence-day-dominion-status-august-15-1947-6555454/
66. Mansergh, VIII, pp: 53-57.
67. https://indianexpress.com/article/research/independence-day-dominion-status-august-15-1947-6555454/
68. Mansergh, X, p. 829.
69. Edwards, Michael "The Last Years of British India", (London, 1963) p. 181.
70. Alan Campbell-Johnson, Mission with Mountbatten, (London, 1951) p. 159; V.P. Menon, The Transfer of Power in India, (Bombay, 1957) p. 415.
71. Mansergh, X, p. 988.
72. Resolution Re Ratification of Commonwealth Decision May 16, 1949. https://www.constitutionofindia.net/constitution_assembly_debates/volume/8/1949-05-16]
73. Ibid.
74. Ghose, Sankar (1993). "Jawaharlal Nehru: a biography", New Delhi, Allied Publ. p. 151.
75. https://www.parliament.uk/about/living-heritage/evolutionofparliament/legislativescrutiny/parliament-and-empire/collections1/collections2/1947-indian-independence-act/
76. Mansergh, X, p. 243.
77. Mansergh, XII, p. 36.
78. Alan Campbell-Johnson, p. 765.
79. Mansergh, XII p. 164.
80. Mansergh, XII, p. 772.
81. Alan Campbell-Johnson p. 158
82. Mansergh, IX, pp. 542-43.
83. Wavell: The Viceroy's Journal, 51. IbM, XII, pp. 790-91. 52. Ibid, VI, p. 455.

84. Mansergh, X, 974-75.
85. Ibid, X, p. 945.
86. Ibid, XI, p. 132.

❑

CHAPTER

11

THE CURTAIN DROPS

Was the partition of India preplanned by the British long before 1947?
Was Jinnah indirectly the creation of Gandhi?
Was Jinnah's grandfather a brahmin, and how did he get converted?
How did Syama Prasad Mukherjee manage to retain West Bengal and East Punjab within India?
Which one vote determined the creation of West Pakistan?
Who envisioned the 1971 war, Indira Gandhi or someone else?
Did Mujibur Rahman really fight for Bangladesh to become the president of Pakistan?
How many people died during the partition?
How many women were raped during the 1971 war?
What is the relationship between Yahya Khan and Nader Shah, who looted India?

The Plot for Division

After nearly 1000 years of foreign invasions and occupation and more than 100 years of colonial rule, the 'wounded civilization', as V.S. Naipaul[1] would call it, arrived at a point when vivisection of the ancient nation was about to happen. While Muslim League and Muslim leaders, including Jinnah, started campaigning for a Muslim homeland cut out of India, the major theatre was set in the East. In this tragic historical drama, Bengal ended up playing a key role before the Brits left India. And a key factor in this role had to do with the demography. If not for sheer numbers, no Islamist leader could exploit the Muslim population to fulfill their personal dreams, both political and religious. While Jinnah dreamt of becoming the head of the new country of Pakistan, Muslim leaders like Suhrawardy and in future Mujibur Rahman also had their dreams. And the majority of Muslims fell for it along with the clerics. Many parties fueled the volcano of this Islamist design. This chapter will see how the full drama was staged until the curtain for this part of history finally dropped on August 15, 1947.

Will and Ariel Durant, the authors of *The Story of Civilization*, felt like a duty to write a short booklet after seeing the gruesome state of Indians during his visit; the booklet is called *The Case for India.* Will wrote: “The British conquest of India was the invasion and destruction of a high civilization by a trading company utterly without scruple or principle [...] bribing and murdering, annexing and stealing, and beginning that career of illegal and legal plunder”.

In a chapter called ‘The rape of a continent’, he painfully noted that Britain profited enormously by severely exploiting India and that at the time of their departure, the vast majority of Indians were living in poverty. He expressed his sadness, saying the British committed “the most sordid and criminal exploitation of one nation by another in all recorded history...I had come upon the greatest crime in all history”. And, “I saw such things in India as made me feel that study and writing were frivolous things in the presence of people – one-fifth of the human race – suffering poverty and oppression bitterer than any to be found elsewhere on the earth. I was horrified. I had not thought it possible that any government could allow its subjects to sink to such misery.”[2]

When Nehru, his family, and other benefited leaders of India celebrated the 'freedom' were they aware of what Durant saw? Did they feel even an iota of sadness and accountability for those butchered and uprooted due to their unplanned and selfish decision to divide India and letting millions of people down when the leaders went to sleep on a royal bed!

As noted in Chapter VIII, the division of India was part of the 'Big Game Plan' Britain had. Narendra Singh Sarila, the aide-de-camp to Earl Mountbatten, the last Viceroy of British India in his book concluded: "Once the British realized that the Indian nationalists who would rule India after its independence would deny them military cooperation under a British Commonwealth defense umbrella, they settled for those willing to do so by using religion for the purpose. Their problem could be solved if Mohammed Ali Jinnah, the leader of the Muslim League Party, would succeed in his plan to detach the northwest of India abutting Iran, Afghanistan and Sinkiang and establish a separate state there – Pakistan. The proposition was a realizable one as a working relationship had been established between the British authorities in India and Jinnah during the Second World War and he was willing to cooperate with Britain on defense matters if Pakistan was created."[3]

The Volcanic Eruptions in the East

Everything was moving in the right direction as planned by Britain. In order to understand the religiopolitical developments in the Eastern part of the Indian subcontinent in those days, we first need to know of the key players, especially from the Muslim community. Most Hindu leaders played a very positive role, both from Hindu Mahasabha and Congress; because of them, West Bengal and Assam remained with India. Lest we forget, Hindus of India owe a lot, not only to Rammohan Roy, Bankim Chandra, Vivekananda, Aurobindo, and Rabindranath for their original contributions for India's rebirth but also to Swami Pranabananda, the founder of Bharat Sevashram Sangha, a great spiritual leader and reformer in undivided Bengal. Because of his vision, Bengal and India entrusted a great leadership role in Syama Prasad Mookerjee (SPM). Details will be presented in the next book; in the meantime, let us traverse through the pages of India's history unfolding in the East in the 1940s.

The Muslim Leadership

Muhammad Ali Jinnah

Jinnah is called the father of Pakistan. Many feel that compared to any other figure in India, including Gandhi, Jinnah impacted the Indian civilization more than anybody else in modern times.

His father was originally from Gujarat, India, and was born in Karachi. Many Pakistani historians like Akbar S. Ahmed have sought to gloss over Jinnah's Hindu ancestry. They claim that Jinnah's father, born as a Rajput, married into the Ismaili Khoja family and converted to Islam. Ahmed suggested that Jinnah's ancestors were Rajput from Punjab. Some of the family names – Valji, Mumbai, and Nathoo – were even 'akin to Hindu names'.[4]

Another source suggests that "Jinnah's grandfather Premji Bhai Thakkar's decision to get into the fish business in the coastal town of Veraval, Gujarat got him ostracised and excommunicated from his strict vegetarian community of Lohanas, a sub-caste of Dhudhi Rajput and they may not have converted to Islam."[5]

Virendra Pandit, in his book *Return of the Infidel* claimed that 'It is not Gandhi but Jinnah who was the Father of modern India,' and also noted that his ancestry belonged to King Ram's Raghuvansh clan[6]:

"For three generations, the Jinnah family struggled to find its Islamic identity after being ex-communicated from their Hindu caste, Lohana-Thakkars, of the Saurashtra region. This caste was believed to have had a Raghuvanshi descent from the family tree of Lord Rama, and some thought they were Bhatia Rajputs."

But after he converted, the local Brahmin priests would not take him back to the community. Hence Premjibhai remained 'a nominal Muslim'. His son and father of Jinnah, Poonjabhai was thin and wiry (*Jhinia* in Gujarati) and had the nickname Jhiniabhai. Jinnah derived his surname from his father, Jhinia. And also, it is most likely the case that Jinnah's grandfather Prembhai did not convert to mainstream Shia or Sunni sects but belonged to rather a new localized sect at that time, called the Khoja-Ismailia sect of Aga Khan.

It appears that even after conversion, "Premjibhai continued to worship the family deity Shrinathji, an incarnation of Lord Krishna, and Thakorji, besides the Tulsi tree. Outside, he would, however, go to the mosque. Premjibhai had joined the Khoja sub-sect, thanks to Adamji Khoja, his friend, philosopher, and guide who had brought him into the fish trade and then into the Aga Khan fold."

Jinnah's father, Jhinia, whose real name was Poonjabhai Premjibhai Thakkar, later moved to Karachi.

Pandit also noted that Jhinia named his first son 'Mamad' due to the hesitation of revealing his Muslim identity and hiding the Hindu identity as a first-generation convert. Jinnah's original name was Mamadbhai Jhiniabhai Thakkar or MJ Thakkar. In 1893, Mamad went to England to study. There he tried to change his name several times. First, he played with "Mohammedali Jhiniabhai of Karachi", then as "Muhammad Z. Thakkar", by changing Jhinia into Zina, and, finally "Muhammad Ali Jinnah" or M.A. Jinnah.

Pandit also noted that 'Gandhi hailed from the Modh Vania/ Bania caste, and Jinnah, despite his grandfather's conversion to Islam, inherited his Lohana-Thakkar caste's obstinate habits. Both these rival castes were seen as great achievers, innovators, and business-minded'.

Would this caste-rivalry become a key factor why they disliked each other, perhaps as competitors? At some point, Jinnah gave up on Gandhi and went for a self-exile in London. But once people like Iqbal and Liaqat Ali aroused his Islamic identity, he returned to India and spent the rest of his life for an Islamic nation, Pakistan. Like his dream project of Pakistan, he was himself 'half quail, half partridge', a personality split to the core, asserted Pandit.[7]

Jinnah studied in England and became a well-known barrister, and he completely devoted himself to law practice. He began political life by joining the Congress party in 1904.[8] During his early political career, he closely worked with Dadabhai Naoroji and Gopal Krishna Gokhale.[9] When Bal Gangadhar Tilak was being tried by the British on sedition charges in 1908, he asked Jinnah to represent him.[10]

He joined the Muslim League in 1913 though he emphasized "greater national cause", the independence of India. He tried to bring the Congress and Muslim League together for the 'greater cause'.[11] Gokhale said that he "has true stuff in him, and that freedom from all sectarian prejudice which will make him the best ambassador of Hindu–Muslim Unity".[12]

When Gandhi came to the Indian political scene, he supported the Khilafat movement. But Jinnah criticized Gandhi for the endorsement of 'religious zealotry'. He publicly criticized Gandhi for this and suggested that Gandhi's *Satyagraha* was 'political anarchy'. Jinnah was not happy with Congress's move and wanted to start a new political party. Eventually, he worked with Swaraj Party.

It was not Jinnah, but Muhammad Iqbal in 1930 who demanded a separated state for Muslims in British India, and in 1933 a pamphlet advocating Pakistan was published by Choudhary Rahmat[13] when Jinnah was no longer active in politics and was in London.

Gandhi gradually took center stage of Indian politics after the untimely death of Tilak in 1920. Jinnah disagreed much with the strategies and actions of Gandhi. Jinnah felt sidelined and neglected. He tried his best to find his place in Indian politics, but after the 1929 Congress session where he was insulted by the Gandhians (similar to the case of Subhas Bose), he thought of leaving politics for good, and after his wife died a broken heart Jinnah left for London with tearful eyes, in a way a self-imposed exile, and started his law career again, and became one of the highest-paid lawyers in Britain. The story could have ended here. But two people influenced him heavily to restart his political career.[13,14] The first person is Iqbal and the second one is Liaquat Ali Khan.[15][16] Although Jinnah and Iqbal were opponents at one point, Iqbal later became Jinnah's mentor, who sowed the seed of Islamic separatism in his mind.[17]

According to historian Akbar S. Ahmed, Jinnah abandoned hope of reconciliation with the Congress as he "rediscover[ed] his own Islamic roots, his own sense of identity, of culture and history, which would come increasingly to the fore in the final years of his life".[18] Akbar also noted that Jinnah formulated his ideas "directly from Iqbal – including his thoughts on Muslim unity, on Islamic ideals of liberty, justice and equality, on economics, and even on practices such as prayers".[19, 20]

On the other hand, Balraj Puri suggested that Jinnah as the Muslim League president, after the 1937 vote, turned to the idea of Partition in "sheer desperation".[21]

Iqbal died in 1938, but Jinnah's return to India in 1934 and the influence of Iqbal caused a great shift in ideology for Jinnah, and he 'discovered' 'deeper appreciation' for Muslim identity.[22] He adopted a new policy and strategy for a separate homeland for Muslims.[23]

For the rest of his life of a decade, Jinnah was devoted entirely to the cause of the 'Two-Nation theory' and the creation of a Muslim homeland in the form of Pakistan. He was responsible for the 'direct action' and many other atrocities on Hindus with the help of local Islamists leaders such as Suhrawardy and finally successfully pushing for the creation of Pakistan.

According to Praful Goradia, "Jinnah did not qualify to be, by any means, an ideal Muslim.... Jinnah was a brilliant courtroom advocate but remained only that. To him, the Muslim League and his Muslim followers were clients; his final fee was a place in the hall of fame in history as the founder of a new country for his community. The Muslim desire for a separate homeland existed before Jinnah, but he was its effective articulator, winning it for them after unleashing violence on Hindus and convincing the British of the imperative for Partition."[24]

Regarding his lifestyle being a Muslim, it is commonly known that he ate pork and drank alcohol which is forbidden in Islam. According to Hussain Haqqani, a former Pakistani diplomat, Jinnah 'was an ostensibly liberal, cigar-smoking, whisky-drinking, pork-eating'.[25]

Goradia concluded: "Jinnah did not belong to Islam nor to thc cause of Pakistan. He was their advocate, came and did his duty with immaculate competence. As we have said, he was for Pakistan, an alien leader. Little wonder, he left behind a country with more faults than strengths."[26]

Fazlul Huq

Born in Barisal, Bangladesh, Fazlul Huq was a very talented and educated personality. He was a very famous jurist as well. Being advised by Sir Ashutosh Mukherjee, he joined the bar council of the Calcutta High Court and practiced law for nearly forty years. Once the British annulled the first Partition of Bengal, the Bengal Provincial Muslim League was formed and, of which Huq became secretary. Later he was elected to the Bengal Legislative Council from the Dacca Division in 1913. He was given the post of the All India Muslim League president in 1916 and Joint Secretary of the Indian National Congress in 1917. Later he became a popular leader in Bengal with strong connections to Delhi. His Krishak Praja Party was the third-largest party after the Bengal Congress and Bengal Provincial Muslim League. He formed a coalition government with the

Muslim League and later with the Bengal Congress to become the leader of the Legislative Assembly and Prime Minister of the Province twice.

Khilafat movement was aimed at ending British rule by replacing it with the Ottoman Caliphate rule in the subcontinent. Huq did not support the Khilafat movement. He became the Education Minister of Bengal for a short time and promoted a reservation system for Bengali Muslims.

Though he had a difference with the Muslim League, he supported the League's Lahore Resolution in 1940, which called on the British government to allow the Partition of the eastern zone of the Indian subcontinent for a potential Muslim homeland. The resolution initially seemed to support the notion of an independent state in Bengal and Assam.

"That geographically contiguous units are demarcated into regions which should be constituted, with such territorial readjustments as may be necessary that the areas in which the Muslims are numerically in a majority as in the North Western and Eastern Zones of (British) India should be grouped to constitute 'independent states' in which the constituent units should be autonomous and sovereign".[27][28]

Huseyn Shaheed Suhrawardy

Suhrawardy served as the third and last Prime Minister of undivided Bengal until the Partition of India. Suhrawardy's family claimed their family tree to the first Caliph of Islam, Abu Bakr. His early education was done at the Calcutta Madrassa and later at St. Xavier and Oxford. His political career started with the Swaraj Party of Chitta Ranjan Das, like Subhas Bose. Later Suhrawardy joined the All India Muslim League and led the Bengal Provincial Muslim League.

While he was the Prime Minister of Bengal, many large-scale massacres of Hindus happened in the Undivided Bengal, including the Great Calcutta Killings. He was also instrumental in proposing and nearly succeeded in creating a united Free

State of Bengal as an independent country separate from India and Pakistan. His plans were foiled mainly by Syama Prasad Mukherjee (SPM),[29] and after the Partition, he moved to Pakistan and became a leader of the Awami League party. In 1956, Suhrawardy became Pakistan's fifth Prime Minister. His close aide was Sheikh Mujibur Rahman and was part of Suhrawardy's Islamist activities, including the Great Calcutta Killings.[30] Later, Mujib wrote about Suhrawardy: "Bengalis had initially failed to appreciate a leader of Mr. Suhrawardy's stature. By the time they learned to value him, they had run out of time".[31] After the Calcutta massacres, a senior British intelligence officer reported: "There is hardly a person in Calcutta who has a good word for Suhrawardy, respectable Muslims included. For years he has been known as "The king of the goondas" and my own private opinion is that he fully anticipated what was going to happen, and allowed it to work itself up, and probably organised thc disturbance with his goonda gangs as this type of individual has to receive compensation every now and again."[32]

Khwaja Nazimuddin

Nazimuddin was a Bengali Muslim League politician educated at the Aligarh Muslim University. He was the Prime Minister of the Undivided Bengal in 1943 and Chief Minister of East Bengal. Later he contributed significantly to the formation of Pakistan. He became the Governor-General and later the Prime Minister of Pakistan in 1951.

Sheikh Mujibur Rahman

Sheikh Mujib was born in Gopalganj of today's Bangladesh. He came to Calcutta and joined Islamia College (Currently Maulana Abdul Kalam College) to study law. His political career began by joining the All India Muslim Students Federation in 1940. Later he joined the Bengal Muslim League in 1943 and worked closely with Huseyn Suhrawardy, and worked actively for a separate Muslim state of Pakistan. He was part of the team of Suhrawardy during the Great Calcutta Killings in 1946. After the Partition of India, he, like his mentor Suhrawardy, also moved to East Pakistan and joined the University of Dhaka to study law. There he founded the East Pakistan Muslim Students' League.

He had the experience of Islamist politics via his association with the League and people like Suhrawardy and Bhasani; at Dhaka University, he also came in touch with socialistic ideologies. After Pakistan announced Urdu to be the national language instead of Bengali, he organized protest movements against it. Following Suhrawardy's death in 1963, Mujib headed the Awami League. Eventually, Bangladesh was created after the largest genocide of mostly Hindus in East Pakistan. Thousands of women were raped, over three million killed, and about 10 million refugees moved to India,[33] mainly to West Bengal, and Assam, and Mujib became the head of the new Government.

Was the Bangladesh war lead by Mujib? Mujib was in a Pakistani jail from March 26, 1971, to January 8, 1972 and also was not a military man. While the liberation movement started on March 26, 1971, the real 13-day war with the participation of India happened between December 3 and December 16, 1971. Who fought the Bangladesh war? The Eastern Rifles of the Pakistan Army, led by Muhammad Ataul Goni Osmani, together with the Regular military (Mukti Fauz) and the Muktibahini (or Gonobahini) fought the war.[34]

Was Mujib fighting for an independent country, Bengali nation, Bangladesh? Or was he positioning himself for the Prime Minister of entire Pakistan through his movement? The answer is 'yes'. Based on eminent Indian columnist Kuldip Nayar's book *Scoop! Inside Stories from the Partition to the Present* (which recorded his interviews with Mujib and Bhutto) we can find some details. On December 15, 1971, when Bhutto met Mujib after freeing him from jail, Rahman first thought he was to be executed and was surprised to meet Bhutto in person instead. He was expecting to become the President of Pakistan since his Awami League party was victorious in the 1970 election. Instead, he was asked to head the newly formed nation, Bangladesh. This was a major surprise for Mujib, and he surely was disappointed. He had no choice but to accept the reality and went on to Dhaka to take charge of the newly formed government.[35]

Nayar interviewed Bhutto and Mujib, Bhutto first in 1971.

Bhutto told Nayar: "On December 23, when we (he and Sheikh Mujib-ur-Rahman) met for the first time, Mujib took out the Quran and said: 'I am a good Muslim. I still want defence, foreign affairs, and communication to be central subjects between the two regions (of Pakistan).' "

Mujib's version was different. Mujib told Nayar: "Within a couple of days of my arrival at the dak-bungalow, Bhutto appeared there one afternoon. I asked him: 'Bhutto, how are you here?' He said: 'I am the president of Pakistan.' I began laughing and said: 'You, Bhutto, Pakistan's president! That place belongs to me; you know I won the majority of seats in the Pakistan National Assembly.' "

A slightly different version of this conversation appeared in New York Times:

At another point, when Mr. Bhutto had been contending that the two wings were still united by law and tradition, Sheik Mujib – reminding him that the Awami League won a national majority in the last election, the results of which were never honored – said: 'Well, if Pakistan is still one country, then you are not President and chief martial-law administrator. I am.'[36]

The story of the meeting between Mujib and Bhutto after the release of the former from the Pakistani jail, according to R. Chowdhury, goes like this[37]:

After greeting each other, Bhutto sat on a sofa. Mujib sat by his side. Mujib started the conversation.

Mujib: *Ap kaise*? (What brings you here?)

Bhutto: I am the President and Chief Marshal Law Administrator of Pakistan.

Mujib: How come?

Bhutto: East Pakistan has fallen. India won victory and Pakistanis surrendered to India. General Yahya Khan resigned.

Mujib was outraged. He sprang to standing position and scornfully demanded.

Mujib: How can it be? How can you be the president? You are a loser, a minority (in the elections). I am the majority leader. I have the right to those positions, not you. Take me immediately to a radio or TV station, I will denounce all these and keep East Pakistan as before. I will nullify all these and fix everything.

Bhutto: Please calm down. This is the reality now. Sit down, please.

Mujib sat down. After a silence, Mujib expressed his disgust at Tajuddin Ahmed, Secretary-General of Awami League and wartime Prime Minister based in India and said that he suspected he would end up with something like this (in collaboration with India).

This corroborates with the assertion of Prof. Aftab Ahmed of Dhaka University. Prof. Ahmed wrote in his book that upon landing in Dhaka on January 10, 1972, Mujib rebuked Tajuddin saying, "শেষ পর্যন্ত তোমরা পাকিস্তান ভাইঙ্গাই ফেললা? - So, in the end you all have divided Pakistan?"

After Bhutto left, Mujib locked himself in his room. Raja Khan (Mujib's fan and caretaker in the jail) and others were worried that Mujib might do something in desperation, given his earlier tantrums at the breakup of Pakistan and Bhutto becoming the new leader. Khan finally succeeded in getting the door opened after repeated knocks and appeals to his "Baba". Mujib then fell prostrate on a prayer mat and cried out (in

Bangla), "Ya Allah, why all these happened? I never wanted it to be like this…"

It testified that Mujib remained committed to a united Pakistan, refused to accept the surrender of Pakistanis, and of course, did not seem happy with the creation of an independent Bangladesh. Until then, his sole aim was to be the supreme leader of Pakistan while gaining full autonomy for East Pakistan.

According to this author Sharmin Ahmed, daughter of Tajuddin Ahmed, the first Prime minister of Bangladesh, had to say about her Mujib Kaku (uncle): "মুজিব কাকু প্রচন্ড ক্ষমতালোভী, সুবিধাবাদী ভীতু মানুষ ছিলেন। তিনি কখনও বাংলাদেশের স্বাধীনতা চাননি। তিনি পাকিস্তানের প্রধান মন্ত্রী হতে চেয়েছিলেন। - 'Mujib uncle was highly power-hungry, opportunist and a coward. He never wanted the independence of Bangladesh. He wanted to be the Prime Minister of Pakistan"—Sharmin Ahmed (from her book *Tajuddin: Neta o Pita*).

So, what would one deduce about Sheikh Mujibur Rahman: a trickster, confused, or a true Pakistani? Stanley Wolpert in his book *Zulfi Bhutto of Pakistan*, wrote, in a meeting on December 27, 1971, Mujib assured Bhutto that their two countries would have a Confederation relationship. "I told you it will be confederation," said Mujib. "This is also between you and me… You leave it to me… Absolutely leave it to me. Trust me… My idea is we will live together, and we will rule this country. You know the occupation (Indian) army is there."

Mujib said similarly to Anthony Mascarenhas in an interview in London on January 8, 1972, *'Going to keep some link with Pakistan'*. (Ref: *Bangladesh: A Legacy of Blood*). Earlier in a jail room conversation with Khan, Mujib blamed President Yahya Khan for destroying Pakistan. On the other hand, in his Affidavit for the Hamoodur Rahman Commission, Yahya credited Mujib to be a patriot and blamed Bhutto for breaking Pakistan. "It was Bhutto, not Mujib, who broke Pakistan", Yahya wrote. When the time came for Mujib to leave, he wanted to go to India first. Why? Was it Mujib's political trickery, a quick change of mindset, and game plan? He had earlier denounced Tajuddin's India collaboration that materialized Bangladesh, and now he became an India lover overnight. Reasons are not far to seek. Despite Mujib's best efforts to keep Pakistan united and finally keeping himself out of trouble, Bangladesh became a reality. India was instrumental in the process (he had little idea about the Mukti Juddho fought by the Bengalis). He, therefore, had to reorient and readjust his political strategy and loyalty. Under the changed circumstances, he needed India's blessing to reassert himself. Otherwise, he would probably soon lose ground to Tajuddin.[37]

So, did Mujib really fight for an independent Bangladesh? In reality, after winning the election, he thought he would be the President of entire Pakistan. It now appears that instead of killing him, Bhutto had a compromise plan. At the same time, Yahya wanted to kill Mujib on the day when East Pakistan became Bangladesh. It was Bhutto who saved him. Some cite one reason that he had a deal with Indira Gandhi that Mujib would be set free in exchange for the nearly 100,000 Pakistani POWs.

It is obvious from the above information that Mujib was dreaming of becoming the President of united Pakistan and not necessarily Bangladesh. Once he was freed, he had no choice but to accept a compromised role of being the head of Bangladesh only. Most likely, it was not a happy day for Mujib, though he had much to celebrate as he was still alive!

Although Mujib, once made the head of the state, had committed to creating Bangladesh as a secular nation-state, it wasn't long before Mujibur inclined towards political Islam through state policies and personal conduct. His Islamist heart was revealed slowly; after all, he was a disciple of Suhrawardy.

Mujibur, along with his mentor Suhrawardy, was always part of the Islam-based separatist political circles from the days of Jinnah.

He revived the 'Islamic Academy' (which had been banned in 1972 for suspected collusion with Pakistani forces) and banned the production and sale of alcohol, and banned the practice of gambling, not necessarily for a healthy society but simply catering to the demands of Islamic groups.[38] Rahman made an important trip to Lahore in 1974 to attend the Organization of the Islamic Conference's (OIC) summit, fixed Bangladesh's diplomatic and political relations with Pakistan, and sought membership for Bangladesh in the OIC and the OIC Islamic Development Bank. In his public speeches and appearances, Rahman began using more Islamic greetings and slogans and often made references from Islamic literature. In his final years, Mujibur Rahman pretty much abandoned the famous "Joy Bangla" (Victory to Bangladesh) salutation and replaced it with "Khuda Hafez", preferred by religious Muslims. This upset the communists of Bangladesh, making Mujibur even more politically insecure, and he sought the support of Islamist groups by declaring a common amnesty to the suspected war criminals. He declared, "I believe that the brokers, who assisted the Pakistanis during the liberation war have realized their faults. I hope they will involve themselves in the development of the country, forgetting all their misdeeds. Those who were arrested and jailed in the Collaborator Act should be freed before December 16, 1974."[39] Before his assassination, the country was failing in many ways, and his family members were accused of corruption.

The Pakistani forces had damaged the historic Ramna Kali Temple during the 1971 war. There was a massacre, killing over 100 people, mostly Hindus. But after the creation of Bangladesh, instead of helping to repair and restore it, Mujibur ordered to create a park at the same place (Ramna Race Course and Park) in the name of his lifelong mentor Suhrawardy.[40]

Abdul Hamid Khan Bhashani or Maulana Bhashani

Bhashani was a Deoband-educated Islamic scholar and political leader who was said to be a socialist and introduced what is called Islamic Socialism; for that reason, some called him 'The Red Maulana'.

He was a strong proponent of the Khilafat movement. When Bengal was partitioned in 1947, his movement pushed for including the Sylhet district of Assam into East Pakistan. After the Partition, he founded the Pakistan Awami Muslim League, became the first President, was later renamed to Awami League (AL). He was a strong opponent of Suhrawardy, opposing the cozy relationship of Pakistan with America. He played a vital role in the Bangladesh liberation movement by directly and indirectly supporting Sheikh Mujib.

Though he is portrayed as a 'socialist' leader, he could not hide his Islamist ideas. He said:

"Assam is ours, West Bengal is ours, Tripura is ours. Until we secure these from the clutches of India, Bangladesh's freedom will not be complete."[41]

While India gave all possible support to the freedom fighters of Bangladesh, slowly, a negative propaganda wave was created against India among the Muslim masses of Bangladesh. In 1976, Bhashani led the so-called Farakka Long March[42] to demolish the Farakka Barrage, and demanding more water from the Ganga into the Padma River.

Governance During the British Period

The East India Company (EIC) was formed to conduct trade in the Indian Ocean region, especially the Indian subcontinent, Southeast Asia, and parts of China. After the Battle of Plassey in 1757, EIC became the ruler of India, the beginning of the presence of the British Empire on Indian soil. Initially, EIC was founded in 1600 CE as a British joint-stock company. Slowly it took over large parts of India, created its own army, and took over administrative functions from the princely states and leftover Mughal empire. A hundred years from then, there was the great Indian War and the Rebellion of Independence in 1857. After the war, Britain introduced the Government of India Act in 1858, and Britain took direct control of India, which came to be known as the 'British Raj' henceforth. The fate of the company (EIC) was sealed in 1874 when it was dissolved, and the newly formed British Raj took over all the governmental functions and the army.

For ruling India under the British Raj, the Imperial Legislative Council was in charge from 1861 until Independence in 1947. After Independence, it became the Constituent Assembly of India. Finally, in 1950, after the adoption of the Indian Constitution, it became the Parliament of India, which has a Lower house and an Upper house.

In British Raj, the presidencies and provinces had legislative councils. The Imperial Legislative Council, the Chamber of Princes, and the Central Legislative Assembly was the legislative structure. A shared government structure called 'dyarchy' where the British Government shared responsibilities with legislative councils of various provinces. Britain then offered a self-governing option for Indian Provinces. In 1919, the Government Act of India was introduced and created a 'bicameral' legislature having central as well as revenue shares to provincial legislative bodies, which continued for a decade.

There were three major Indian political organizations set up in India at that time. Alan Octavian Hume, a British member of the Imperial Civil Service upon retirement, proposed in 1883 to form a political organization for the greater role of Indians in the government and have a civic and political dialogue with the British Raj. Indian National Congress was formed in 1885, and Umesh Chandra Banerjee became the first President.[43]

In 1905, All India Muhammedan Conference was held in Dhaka, from where the All India Muslim League took birth.

In 1923, the Swaraj Party was formed as the Congress-Khilafat Swaraj Party, where Chitta Ranjan Das was the President and Motilal Nehru, father of Jawaharlal Nehru, was Secretary. Swaraj Party's main demand was greater self-government, and the Party disintegrated after the death of Chitta Ranjan in 1925.

However, Congress and the Swaraj Party had a majority in the legislative councils. In a religion and caste-based divisive move, British Parliament, led by Prime Minister Ramsay MacDonald, announced the 'Communal Award' in 1932, which granted separate electorates for different castes among Hindus and Muslims, Christians, Buddhists, etc. This very controversial 'divide and rule policy' was justified to 'avoid civil war'.[44]

After many protests, the dyarchy in the provinces ended with the Government of India Act 1935, which allowed more autonomy. Bicameral legislatures were created in six provinces, and in 1937 elections were held for the first time with separate electorates, which allowed the formation of provincial governments by the largest party, with the head being a Prime Minister for the province.

The Legislative Assembly of Bengal was the largest legislature of British-occupied India, which served as the lower house of the legislature of undivided Bengal. Bengal Legislative Council was the upper house, and the 250-seat lower house of the Legislative Assembly was formed. Bengal Congress party captured the maximum vote share and became the majority. But Congress leaders did not form the government for various reasons. The regional anti-feudal Krishak Praja Party (KPP) and the Bengal Provincial Muslim League, with some independent legislators' support, formed the first such Government and elected Fazlul Huq (leader of KPP) as Bengal's first Prime Minister in 1937.

In 1941 Huq joined the Viceroy's Defense Council, and Jinnah did not like this, and soon Muslim League withdrew support of Huq's Government. He was able to convince Hindu Mahasabha leader SPM to support his government, and the second coalition government was formed. But in 1943, Huq's government fell again. This time a close aide of Jinnah, Khwaja Nazimuddin, formed the Muslim League Government, which also did not last for long for many reasons, including famines, riots, war, etc.

In the next election in 1946, the Bengal Provincial Muslim League became victorious in the general election. While compared to some other Muslim-majority provinces in India, Bengal Muslim League got a comparatively large vote share. A close compatriot of Jinnah, Suhrawardy became the Prime Minister of Bengal. The voice for creating a Muslim state became louder as Suhrawardy's dream of a 'United Free State of Bengal' took birth where there would be three countries – India, Pakistan, and United Bengal and they wanted the most important city in India, Calcutta, to be part of the new state of Bengal.

The 1946 (Great) Calcutta Killings

The dream of a revival of the Islamic Caliphate, which would also include India as part of the new Turkic Caliphate, did not materialize. Many pan-Islamist Muslim leaders, mostly from the Muslim League, felt that the dream was fading away. Muslims were divided into two camps for supporting a Muslim rule in India or parts of India. The Two-Nation theory was one that stated that Muslims cannot live together under the Hindu majority rule and should have a different country for the Muslims. On the other hand, a group of Muslims felt that if Muslims remained within India, the whole country would become a Muslim nation one day by a sheer increase of the number, and create a Muslim legislative body that would eventually rule the country. While Congress was a majoritarian political party, the Muslim League was the 2nd largest with significant support from the Muslim community. The 'Lahore Resolution' of the Muslim League in 1940 demanded that the Muslim-majority areas in the northwest and the eastern parts of India should be constituted as 'independent states'. Jinnah said that his dream was "either a divided India or a destroyed India".[45]

The undivided pre-partition Bengal was one of the most prosperous Provinces on all accounts, including education, agriculture, industry, etc. Hindus constituted 42%, and Muslims were the majority with 58%. Calcutta was a very important city for India till then, and Muslims were not the majority there, it had 64% Hindus. A sinister plot was hatched to ensure Calcutta's inclusion in a future United Bengal or East Pakistan and to make Calcutta a Muslim-majority place by killing and driving away Hindus and Sikhs from there. The Muslim League government was in power in Bengal. After the Lahore Declaration and Jinnah's call for the creation of Pakistan, the then Prime minister of Bengal, Suhrawardy, seized the opportunity to promote his dream to include Bengal and Assam as part of Pakistan. However, since Calcutta and surrounding industrial districts like Howrah and Hooghly were a Hindu majority, it did not logically fit to demand it to be part of Pakistan or United Bengal.

It began with Jinnah declaring a 'Direct Action Day' on August 16, 1946, where Muslims would observe a general strike in demanding the creation of Pakistan from Britain. August 16 was a Friday and the 18th day of Ramzan. On that day, the Islamic Prophet Muhammad waged the bloody Jihad called *Battle of Badr*, which resulted in his first decisive battle victory over the 'infidels' subsequent to the conquest of Mecca.

In Bengal, Suhrawardy and others from Muslim League gave fiery speeches to remind Bengali Muslims of the importance of the day of Badr victory. They charged them to follow their Prophet's footsteps so that the Bengali Muslims favor the Muslim League plan, and they become victorious. League leaders appealed to the Muslim clerics to encourage all faithful Muslims to gather at their mosques for the Friday prayer and 'use all means' to create Pakistan. To the fanatic clerics, 'direct action' meant perpetrating violence against the majority Hindus to kill and drive them away from Calcutta and surrounding areas to make these areas Muslim majority.

The August 13, 1946 issue of Muslim league mouthpiece *The Star of India* wrote: "Muslims must remember that it was in Ramzan that Allah granted permission for jehad. It was in Ramzan that the Battle of Badr, the first open conflict between Islam and heathens, was fought and won by 313 Muslims, and again it was in Ramzan that 10,000 Muslims under the Holy Prophet conquered Mecca and established the Kingdom of Heaven and the Commonwealth of Islam in Arabia. The Muslim League is fortunate that it is starting its action on this Holy month and day."[46]

Once some small-scale violence in the streets of Calcutta began, Suhrawardy and his puppet, Governor Frederick Burrows, announced it as a public holiday so that all businesses were closed. Congress leaders like Kiran Shankar Roy opposed it and asked the Hindus to keep their businesses and shops open. However, the violent Muslim mobs attacked many Hindu businesses. Along with the strike, Muslim League also organized a rally at the Monument. After the afternoon prayers, thousands of Muslims armed with different weapons gathered, and the crowd size was estimated by variously as low as 60000 and up to 200000. Then-communist leader Jyoti Basu also attended this event. Khwaja Nizamuddin delivered the first speech, falsely accused Hindus of attacking the Muslims earlier that day and instigated the Muslims to fight 'in self-defense'. Then it was Suhrawardy's turn to motivate the Muslim mob to fight for Partition and the creation of Pakistan and gave fiery slogans such as: "*Maar ke lenge Pakistan, lad ke lenge Pakistan, le kar rahenge Pakistan, Allahu Akhbar, nara-i-takhbir*".[47] (We will kill and fight to create Pakistan, we are determined to create Pakistan).

The whole event must have been pre-planned and with full knowledge of Jinnah since there were many activities, including recruiting hundreds of Muslims in the Police prior to August 16.

Bangladeshi historian Harun-or-Rashid supported the view that Suhrawardy pre-planned the events in such a way that it reveals the perfect 'engineering of riots against the Hindus in a pre-planned manner and shielding the Muslim marauders from the police.'[48]

Following is from the book by Dr. Tathagata Roy, which proves the long planning by the League leaders:

"...Hindu police constables... therefore, could not be trusted to carry out the designs that Suhrawardy had in mind.... The idea was to Muslimise the Calcutta Police. Why the Calcutta Police in particular? Because Calcutta had already been chosen by the Muslim League as the theatre of the bloodbath that had been scheduled on August 16, 1946, in what they would call 'Direct Action', and what the rest of the world would eventually call the Great Calcutta Killings.... Niaz Mohammed Khan, under Suhrawardy's orders, journeyed to the Northwest to recruit Punjabi Muslim and Pathan constables for the Calcutta Police."[49]

During this troubling time, Sheikh Mujibar Rahman was an ardent follower of Suhrawardy, and he played a major role in organizing the strike. According to his *The Unfinished Memoirs* written by Mujib himself: "Mujib's belief in the political leadership of Suhrawardy never wavered. As these recollections reveal, to the very end — until Suhrawardy's death in late 1963 — Mujib remained a devoted, almost stubborn Suhrawardy loyalist."[50]

So, this was The Direct Action Day of August 1946, also known as 'The Week of the Long Knives'.

On the morning of August 16, Muslim mobs started attacking Hindu homes and businesses. At first, it was a one-sided attack, and Hindus felt helpless. One Gopal Mukherjee, who owned a goat butcher shop (hence popularly known as Gopal Pantha), saw the Muslim mob approaching with lethal weapons. He quickly organized local Hindu youth, especially from various gymnastics clubs, and created the Bharat Jatiya Bahini.

Gopal's uncle was revolutionary Anukul Chandra Mukhopadhyay. According to historian Sandip Bandopadhyay, who interviewed Anukul Chandra, he (Gopal) "never bore a grudge against Muslims" but "was forced to turn violent when Muslim rioters approached central Kolkata".[51]

Years later, in an interview with Andrew Whitehead, who wrote for *Indian Express,* he said: "It was a very critical time for the country," he asserts. "We thought if the whole area became Pakistan, there would be more torture and repression. So, I called all my boys together and said it was time to retaliate. If you come to know that one murder has taken place, you commit ten murders. That was the order to my boys."[52]

Whitehead also noted: "Gandhi called me twice," Gopal says. "I didn't go. The third time, some local Congress leaders told me that I should at least deposit some of my arms. I went there. I saw people coming and depositing weapons which were of no use to anyone out-of-order pistols, that sort of thing." Then Gandhi's secretary said to me: "Gopal, why don't you surrender your arms to Gandhi?" I replied, "With these arms, I saved the women of my area; I saved the people. I will not surrender them. Where was Gandhi, I said, during the Great Calcutta Killings? Where was he then? Even if I've used a nail to kill someone, I won't surrender even that nail." During the Calcutta Killings, Gopal and Bharat Jatiya Bahini were hailed as saviors and heroes.

The counterattack by the Bahini eventually stopped the Muslim mob violence within a short period. League leaders eventually proposed a ceasefire process. Two people were selected as negotiators – a leader of the Muslim League student wing G.G. Ajmiri and Mujibur Rahman, then a member of the

Muslim National Guard; they said to have met Gopal, and the negotiation believed to have worked.

According to most conservative estimates, between 4,000 and 10,000 people, mostly Hindus and Sikhs, lost their lives, and over 100,000 residents were left homeless within 72 hours.[53]

This event sparked violent rioting in other parts of India, including the massacre in Noakhali and Tippera (current day Comilla) districts in October 1946.

The Noakhali Genocide

In the Noakhali district of then East Bengal, later East Pakistan, and now Bangladesh, in October-November 1946, fanatic Islamists launched a genocidal attack on the Hindus. Forced conversion, rape, killings, and arson on Hindu religious places and properties went on rampant for weeks in a large area that covers more than 200 square miles. The day was October 10, a very sacred day for the Hindus – the Kojagari Lakshmi Puja. It is estimated that over 5000 Hindus were killed who refused to convert, women were raped, and thousands of others were forcibly converted to Islam. Many were to give forcible confession statements that they willingly converted. Close to one hundred thousand survivors who left behind their homes and property took shelter in refugee camps in Comilla, Chandpur, Agartala (Tripura), and other places. A similar number of Hindus who did not leave their homes were surrounded by fanatic Muslim mobs. There was no support from the administration, and they even had to beg permission from the Muslim gangs to leave their villages. According to Dinesh Chandra, "Hindus were forced to pay subscriptions to the Muslim League and jiziyah, the protection tax paid by dhimmis in an Islamic state."[54]

Many tried to pass these incidents as regular Hindu-Muslim communal riots. SPM, the leader of Hindu Mahasabha and founder of Jan Sangh, said that these events were pre-planned and "concerted attack on the minority community by the majority community."[55]

After the Noakhali massacre, Gandhi toured the region and camped for about four months in an attempt to restore peace. He addressed the Hindus, saying: "if the Muslims want to kill us, we must face death bravely"…and continued... "We should dispassionately think where we are drifting. Hindus should not harbour anger in their hearts against Muslims, even if the latter wanted to destroy them. Even if the Muslims want to kill us all, we should face death bravely. If they established their rule after killing Hindus, we would be ushering in a new world by sacrificing our lives."[56] This type of fatalism has programmed generations of the Hindu population to become the ostrich that hides its head under the sand seeing any danger!

Similarly, Gandhi recommended the collective suicide of Jews in Nazi Germany. He said: "If there ever could be a justifiable war in the name of and for humanity, a war against Germany, to prevent the wanton persecution of a whole race, would be completely justified. But I do not believe in any war. A discussion of the pros and cons of such a war is therefore outside my horizon or province."[57]

Even during World War II, he wrote to the British: "This manslaughter must be stopped. You are losing; if you persist, it will only result in greater bloodshed. Hitler is not a bad man."[58]

And the advice to the victims of the holocaust was this:

"If I were a Jew and were born in Germany... I would claim Germany as my home even as the tallest gentile German may, and challenge him to shoot me or cast me in the dungeon.... And suffering voluntarily undergone will bring them an inner strength and joy.... The calculated violence of Hitler may even result in a general massacre of the Jews by way of his first answer to the declaration of such hostilities. But if the Jewish mind could be prepared for voluntary suffering, even the massacre I have imagined could be turned into a day of thanksgiving and joy that Jehovah had wrought deliverance of the race even at the hands of the tyrant."[59]

Later he said, "Hitler killed five million Jews. It is the greatest crime of our time. But the Jews should have offered themselves to the butcher's knife. They should have thrown themselves into the sea from cliffs. As it is, they succumbed anyway in their millions."[60] And recommended that had the Jews committed collective suicide, that would have been "heroism."

Lesson learned: A nation that is a victim of pacifism and fatalism must continue to suffer!

The Final Destiny of Bengal

The conspiracies in 1946 alone, which included the Calcutta Killings, Noakhali, Tippera (current Comilla), and other genocidal incidents, where over 10,000 Hindus lost their lives, thousands of women folks were raped. This real 'pogrom' proved that a United Bengal was not going to be as peaceful a nation as Suhrawardy preached. Some Congress leaders like Sarat Chandra Bose were convinced with the argument that a United Bengal would be 'a very prosperous state' where each part of Bengal would reciprocate in the production of food and raw materials and the other in manufacturing and distributing. And that the Hindus and Muslims would live in harmony. However, due to the visionary work of Hindu Mahasabha, led by SPM foiled the plan of Suhrawardy.

On April 7, 1940, in Assam's Sylhet (currently in Bangladesh), the dreamer of a 'United India' SPM warned and asked every concerned person to help in that mission: "The dangers in front of us are many; the latest addition in the shape of a movement for Pakistan should not be lightly brushed aside. The preposterous claim must be nipped in the bud by all lovers of Hindusthan....Jinnah is out to destroy the very soul of India".

At the North Bihar Provincial Hindu Conference of April 14, 1940, SPM said, "We shall rise, we shall unite. We shall live in a country whose destinies shall be in the hands of her children alone and where the flag of a tree and United Hindusthan shall proclaim forever the glory of peace and progress, of tolerance and freedom."

But the sinister designs of Suhrawardy and his cohorts would not let that dream be fulfilled. As a last resort, SPM opted for the division of Bengal and West Bengal's inclusion as part of India, the homeland of Bengali Hindus, and formed the 'Bengal Partition League' in 1946, which was supported by the majority of Hindus from all classes and castes. Also, he thwarted the Muslim League plan to include the whole of Punjab into West Pakistan. His campaign for West Bengal and East Punjab to be included and kept within divided India succeeded.[61][62]

There was the Bengal Provincial Hindu Conference at Tarakeshwar, Bengal, on April 5, 1947. This was presided over by SPM, and he passed a proposal to constitute a 'separate Bengali Hindu homeland' within India. It was attended by over 400 delegates from all over Bengal and a total of over 50,000 people. Nirmal Chatterjee, the head of Bengal Hindu Mahasabha, declared that the League was to "Sustain Bengali Hindu nationalism, carve out a separate homeland for the Bengali Hindu people and constitute it as a province within India, and preserve the Bengali culture and heritage."[63] Eminent Bengali leaders such as Kshitish Chandra Niyogi and Dr. Bidhan Chandra Roy attended the meeting.

Slowly the Bengal Partition League garnered support from many prominent leaders, including Hemanta Kumar Sarkar, revolutionaries like Upendranath Banerjee and Nalinaksha Sanyal, Major General A.C. Chatterjee, Jadab Panja, Dr. Shishir Kumar Banerjee, Subhodh Chandra Mitra, and Shailendra Kumar Ghosh. Soon the League came to be known as the Bengal Provincial Conference. In February, the Bengal Provincial Hindu Mahasabha constituted a committee for creating a separate province for the Hindus of Bengal and began their campaign in the districts. Soon, over 100,000 volunteers were recruited to mobilize mass opinion in favor of it.

In March 1947, SPM convened a meeting in Calcutta that was attended by many of Bengal's prominent personalities, including historian Dr. Ramesh Chandra Majumdar, famous linguist and educationist Dr. Suniti Kumar Chattopadhyay, Dr. Makhanlal Raychaudhuri, Pandit Ramshankar Tripathi, among others. At the meeting, SPM explained and proposed the need for a homeland for the Bengali Hindus. Dr. Suniti Kumar Chattopadhyay supported the same.

In May, a galaxy of eminent Bengalis, including scientist Dr. Meghnad Saha, historians Dr. Jadunath Sarkar and Dr. Ramesh Chandra Majumdar, and Dr. Suniti Kumar Chattopadhyay, demanded Bengali Hindu homeland on the ground of security of the Hindu population. Soon after, Hindu Mahasabha and Congress jointly organized a large public meeting, and Dr. Jadunath Sarkar presided over it to press for Partition. At the same time, 50 jurists from Calcutta High Court signed a statement demanding the Partition of Bengal.

SPM called for a general strike on April 23 to oppose the inclusion of the whole of Bengal into Pakistan, which was supported by the grassroots workers of the Communist Party and activists of the Calcutta Tram Workers' Union.

SPM also met Viceroy Mountbatten to first explain to him his formula to give due respect to the minority voices in Bengal and Punjab and convinced him in favor of the Partition. Soon after Dr. Bidhan Chandra Roy and Kiran Shankar Roy gave assurance to SPM, they would convince the Congress members about the division's necessity. The Chambers of Commerce Kolkata gave full support for the division of Bengal. Business leaders like G.D. Birla believed that the Partition was not only unavoidable but an excellent way to solve the communal problem. Nalinaksha Sanyal, who was the chief whip of the Bengal Assembly, worked closely with SPM during the Bengal Famine in 1943. He joined hands with SPM in the efforts to the creation of West Bengal and played a crucial role in the voting.

So, the role played by the Bengal Pradesh Congress in the Partition was significant, and it would not have materialized without their full support. There were over 76 meetings held to promote the idea of division of Bengal, of which the Indian National Congress reportedly organized 59.

Partition of India at Last

To oversee the Partition of India, Louis Mountbatten was sent to India by the British Government.

Mountbatten came up with a plan on June 3, 1947 (the '3rd June Plan') for the Partition. The plan contained these main provisions:[64]

First of all, it decided that India would be independent by August 15, 1947, and the creation of a separate independent United Bengal was ruled out. The legislators elected from the Hindu and Sikh majority and Muslim-majority areas of the assemblies of Bengal and Punjab would meet separately and vote to determine the fate of these provinces. If a simple majority of either group wanted Partition, then these provinces would be divided.

Sind and Baluchistan were to make their own decision. Later, both voted to join Pakistan.

Other provinces had different arrangements.

The fate of the North-West Frontier Province (NWFP – currently in Pakistan) and Sylhet district of Assam was to be decided via referendum. In NWFP, 51% of people went out to vote, and others, including Abdul Gaffar Khan, boycotted the referendum. The majority of those who voted favored joining Pakistan. The Sylhet referendum decided in favor of joining Pakistan, and the district's Karimganj subdivision chose to join India.

In the Punjab Province, while many Muslim clerics and groups opposed the idea of Pakistan, the Christian leaders wholeheartedly supported it, and the leader was prominent

Christian leader Dewan Bahadur S.P. Singha, who assured full cooperation with Jinnah. Were the Christian leadership, which became part of the 'Great Game' of British, as noted earlier, aware of these? Mr. Jinnah praised, "We will never forget your favour as you have cooperated with us." Dewan Singha and the Christian community in Punjab opted for Pakistan.[65]

What was the reason behind selecting August 15 for the 'Independence Day'? Does it have to do with the day Japan 'surrendered' to end the WWII? The so-called VJ Day or 'Victory over Japan Day' is August 15, 1945 when Japan's Emperor Hirohito broadcast the surrender (Hirohito did not use the word surrender rather he used these phrases: 'we have decided to effect a settlement', 'our empire accepts the provisions of their joint declaration' due to 'the war situation has developed not necessarily to Japan's advantage, while the general trends of the world have all turned against her interest.') to the Japanese people on radio. Is that the connection, to insult the real independence hero Bose who worked with the Japanese?

The Story of Master Tara Singh

Master Tara Singh was an ardent Sikh leader born in Rawalpindi and by profession was a teacher (hence the title 'master').[66] He was involved in the independence movement and was jailed 14 times. He was strongly against the Partition of India and led the Sikh community. A leader of the Shiromani Akali Dal (SAD), which condemned the Lahore Resolution of the Muslim League for the creation of Pakistan. He and SAD fought "tooth and nail" against the concept of a Pakistan.[67]

Master Tara Singh was instrumental in organizing the Shiromani Gurdwara Prabhandak Committee, an apex body that dealt with the Sikh gurdwaras. He was also a founding member of Vishwa Hindu Parishad (VHP) in 1964 along with RSS head M.S. Golwalkar, S.S. Apte, Swami Chinmayananda (first President) with the objective "to organize, consolidate the Hindu society and to serve and protect the Hindu Dharma." The delegation during the meeting also included Bharatiya Vidya Bhavan founder K. M. Munshi, Gujarati scholar Keshavram Kashiram Shastri, Satguru Jagjit Singh, Sir C.P. Ramaswamy Iyer, Swami Dayananda Saraswati as well as the Dalai Lama.

On June 23, a special meeting of the Punjab Legislative Assembly was convened for voting. The four Christian members were ready to vote for Pakistan. But Master Tara Singh took out his sword and told everyone that he could do anything to supporters voting for Punjab joining Pakistan. But ultimately, eighty-eight people voted for India and 91 people for Pakistan, which included votes of three Christian members, and Speaker Singha cast the 4th vote, which made it a majority. [68] After voting on both Western and Eastern sides, the Partition was declared; the Eastern part of Punjab went to India and the West to Pakistan.

The same Christians in Pakistan today whose ancestors helped create a separate country are persecuted daily along with Sikhs and Hindus, churches, and temples destroyed and converted forcibly on a regular basis.[69]

Division of Bengal and Punjab

At its joint session on June 20, 1947, the Bengal Legislative Assembly decided by 120-90 votes that it should remain united if it was to join the (new) Constituent Assembly of Pakistan. But legislators from Hindu-majority Western Bengal met separately and decided by a 58-21 vote that the province was to be partitioned, and West Bengal was to join the (existing) constituent Assembly of India. The 58 legislators supporting creating West Bengal as part of India were from Congress, Hindu Mahasabha, the Communists, and unlike Punjab, Christian members. In contrast, all members against it were from the Muslim League. In another meeting, legislators from Eastern Bengal voted 107-34 in favor of East Bengal joining the Union of Pakistan.

Still, there were certain dissatisfactions and uncertainties. Hindu-majority district of Khulna and Buddhist-majority Chittagong Hill Tracts was given to Pakistan. Hindu-majority areas such as Faridpur and Bakarganj were also given to Pakistan. Malda and Nadia districts were undecided till the last moment. SPM worked with Nalinaksha Sanyal to retain Nadia and with Atulya Ghosh to retain Malda within India. The Muslim-majority district of Murshidabad became part of West Bengal after much negotiation based on strategic and commercial reasons.

Finally, the Partition became a reality along with the creation of West Bengal, a homeland for Bengali Hindus in India. It was a historical struggle and movement of Bengalis to protect their land, life, language, religion, and culture, which was an extraordinary, united mission accomplished by the Bengali Hindus going above politics.

Famous Bengali litterateur Bibhutibhushan Bandyopadhyay wrote: "Good that Bengal was partitioned. Bengali Hindus will heave a sigh of relief."[70]

So, instead of three different countries, two countries were created – Pakistan (East and West) and India. In the largest migration in history, the total number of people displaced from their ancestral homes on both sides is estimated to be about fifteen million. In this hellish carnage of massacre, arson, loot, forced conversions, abductions of young girls and women, and unimaginable sexual violence of close to 100,000 rapes took place. As if rape was not violent enough, many were disfigured, dismembered, and then killed.[71]

In his book *Midnight's Furies* Nisid Hajari wrote: *"Gangs of killers set whole villages aflame, hacking to death men and children and the aged while carrying off young women to be raped. Some British soldiers and journalists who had witnessed the Nazi death camps claimed Partition's brutalities were worse: pregnant women had their breasts cut off and babies hacked out of their bellies; infants were found literally roasted on spits."*[72]

Though the exact number is hard to determine, it is estimated that about five million minorities, mostly Hindus, left East Pakistan and came to India, predominantly in West Bengal and Assam, and less than half of the Muslim population moved to East Pakistan from India, which is roughly estimated to be two million.

This was the beginning of the genocide of the Hindu, Buddhist, and Christian populations in East Pakistan. More than 3 million Hindu refugees came to West Bengal by 1960, causing massive housing, food, and sanitation problems in the ill-prepared state.

As the genocide continued, in 1964, over 135,000 Hindu refugees came to India. A law was enacted by the Pakistan government called 'Enemy Property Law', which was meant to take away the ownership rights of Hindus who took refuge in India, even temporarily.

Dhaka University Professor Abul Barkat's work provided a grim picture of the fate of properties left-back by mostly the Hindu refugees. He recorded about 925,050 Hindu households (40% of Hindu families in Bangladesh at that time) were impacted by this law, and the land loss was about 1.64 million acres or 6,640 square kilometers or 53% of all Hindu-owned land). He also noted that, between 1971 and 2013, at least 11 million Hindus fled to India due to religious persecution. He projected that if the condition did not change drastically, there would be no Hindus left in Bangladesh after 2030.

His research also documented the beneficiaries of these massive criminal land grabbing activities according to people belonging to various political parties, which showed that 44.2% of the land was grabbed by influential people from the Awami League and about 31.7% by the people of the Bangladesh Nationalist Party (BNP).[73]

The Indian Citizenship Amendment Act (CAA) of 2019 and the National Register for Citizens (NRC)

After the partition of India, minorities faced tremendous discrimination and atrocities in West and East Pakistan. On April 8, 1950, a bilateral treaty was signed between India and Pakistan called the Liaquat–Nehru Pact[74] to guarantee the rights of minorities. Both countries set up 'Minority Commissions' to monitor the conditions of the minorities. According to the treaty, 'refugees were allowed to return to dispose of their property, abducted women and looted property were to be returned, forced conversions were unrecognized, and minority rights were confirmed.'

Until 1950 India did not have a constitution. Once implemented, it guaranteed citizenship to all of the country's residents. The Citizenship Act was passed in 1955, which allowed foreign nationals to seek asylum and citizenship. It allowed people from parts of "undivided India" to become citizens after seven years of residency in India and from other countries, 12 years of residency. By the 1980s, a large number of illegal immigrants infiltrated various Indian states, including Assam, Tripura, and West Bengal. After some violent movements against this situation, the 'Assam Accord' was signed and amendments to the Citizenship Act of 1955 happened in 1985. The Indian government led by Prime Minister Rajiv Gandhi agreed to identify foreign citizens, remove them from the electoral rolls, and expel them from the country.[75]

As the systematic persecution of non-Muslims in Afghanistan, Pakistan, and Bangladesh continued, as we have seen earlier, the Indian Government further amended the Citizenship Act in 1992, 2003, 2005, and 2015. The notion of "illegal immigrants" was added to the Act, making them ineligible to apply for citizenship either by registration or naturalization and declaring that their children also were illegal immigrants. Illegal immigrants were defined as citizens of other countries who entered India without valid travel documents or who remained in the country beyond the period permitted by their travel documents. They can be deported or imprisoned.

The 2003 Amendment[76] mandated the creation and maintaining of a National Register of Citizens (NRC), which any nation would do. Nevertheless, it is never too late. On a rare occasion, non-partisan support was given by various political parties, including the National Congress and Communist Party of India (CPI-M) along with BJP, the then ruling party. Dr. Manmohan Singh, the then leader of the opposition, while participating in a parliamentary debate, noted that the 'refugees belonging to minority communities in Bangladesh and other countries had faced persecution, and requested that the government's approach to granting them citizenship be made more liberal.'[77]

The Parliament of India passed the latest Citizenship (Amendment) Act or CAA, 2019, on December 11, 2019. It amended the original Citizenship Act of 1955 by providing a pathway to Indian citizenship for persecuted religious minorities from three specific countries: Afghanistan, Bangladesh, and Pakistan, who are Hindus, Sikhs, Buddhists, Jains, Parsis, or Christians, who arrived in India before the end of December 2014.[78] As many as 31,000 such minorities were living in various parts of India with much suffering and were to be settled gracefully in India as citizens using this special Act.[79] The amendment also relaxed the residency requirement for naturalization of these particular migrants from twelve years to six.[80]

However, this Act did not change the general rights to seek asylum to anybody from any country, race, or religion. No nation on earth would welcome illegal immigrants with open arms. Countries like the USA allow citizenship to many asylum seekers from time to time. It is done due to humanitarian reasons and labor benefits from these migrants for the country. No nation can afford random migrant infiltration via borders. Yet, because of persecution of the minorities in these countries, an established fact, it is a great humanitarian gesture by the Indian Government to offer fast-track citizenship to a very small number of suffering people, such as the non-Muslim minorities from mostly these three countries. According to historian Prof. Saradindu Mukherji[81]: 'The NDA Government led by Prime Minister Narendra Modi has found a solution to one of the most serious humanitarian problems of post-independent India.'

He concluded: 'Anyway, the CAA 2019 is a *fait accompli*. All those who cherish human values and justice must welcome it since it is intended to give citizenship to all those Hindu, Sikh, Buddhist, Jain, Christian and Parsi refugees living in India who had fled Afghanistan, Pakistan and Bangladesh after facing persecution, discrimination, denial, deprivation and every other form of intimidation and humiliation.'[81]

Protests were organized in India mostly by the communist and Islamist groups in a meticulously planned way which proves that these are supporters of anti-national forces within and outside of the country. The impact on the economy due to these protests has been in hundreds of crores, but for whose benefits?

The War of 1971

The pogrom and genocide of Hindus and Buddhists which was going on since the 1940s, especially from 1946 continued till 1971. In 1950 there were three major massacres - Anderson Bridge, Sitakunda and Muladi massacres. In the 1960s there were many massacres including the Rajsahi massacres in 1962. But in 1971 alone it peaked and there were at least 35 documented massacres throughout East Pakistan. During the 1971 Bangladesh Liberation War, millions were killed, thousands were raped, houses destroyed, and properties confiscated by local Muslims; over seven million Hindu refugees crossed the border for safety and settled mainly in the districts of Nadia, Howrah, North 24 Parganas, and South 24 Parganas district of West Bengal.

It is to be noted here that the brutal military dictator Yahya Khan was the key player behind the 1971 war and genocide in Bangladesh. He was born to a Shia Qizilbash family of Persian descent who traced their military links to the time of Nader Shah. During his invasions of Delhi in 1739, he ordered a massacre of common men, and his army killed about 30,000 Delhites,[82] and about 10,000 women and children were taken as slaves.[83] Nader's idols were Genghis Khan and Tamerlane.

Nader looted some of the most famous jewels from India – the Peacock Throne, the Kohinoor, and Daryanoor diamonds, which are now with the British monarchy.

Michael Axworthy, a British academic and commentator, suggested that the success of Nader's Delhi invasion exposed to the world how weak the Mughals became at that time, which in a way inspired the East India Company to occupy India. According to him, without Nader, "eventual British Rule in India would have come later and in a different form, perhaps never at all – with important global effects".[84]

True to his ancestry of Nader, Yahya was responsible for hatching massive genocidal operations called Operation Blitz and Operation Searchlight,[85] a majority of the victims were Hindus.[86] While Nader Shah took 10000 women with him as slaves, in Bangladesh in genocidal rape carnage, between 200,000 and 400,000 women and girls were victims.[87, 88, 89] though the actual number may be more than a million, a large number of them were kept in the army cantonments and camps all over the country.[90] In these military camps and cantonments, the Pakistani soldiers kept the captive girls as their sex-slaves,[91, 92] mostly Hindu girls and women.[93, 94] It was not just the military, members and activists of various Islamic parties were involved in the abduction and rapes of women.[95]

In a brutal, barbaric display of stone-age behavior, many Muslim religious leaders called the women "war booty" in support of the rapes.[96, 97] According to Australian doctor Geoffrey Davis as reported by the *Forbes* magazine, the numbers are underestimated:

"...Probably the numbers are very conservative compared with what they did. The descriptions of how they captured towns were very interesting. They'd keep the infantry back and put artillery ahead and they would shell the hospitals and schools. And that caused absolute chaos in the town. And then the infantry would go in and begin to segregate the women. Apart from little children, all those were sexually matured would be segregated. And then the women would be put in the compound under guard and made available to the troops...Some of the stories they told were appalling. Being raped again and again and again. A lot of them died in those [rape] camps. There was an air of disbelief about the whole thing. Nobody could credit that it really happened! But the evidence clearly showed that it did happen."[98]

Was the creation of Bangladesh the brainchild of the then Prime Minister Indira Gandhi? Perhaps not. All records indicate that she was forced to retaliate against Pakistan's sudden attack of Indian bases on December 3, 1971, though a preparation to attack East Pakistan was already underway. Indira was not planning to launch a full-scale war against Pakistan and appealed to world leaders to stop Pakistan's aggression. On December 6, before the Indian Parliament, she announced the formation of Bangladesh and thus India's recognition for the new Bangladesh Government.[99]

On December 16, Pakistani Army surrendered in Dacca (Dhaka). Who was planning this less than two weeks' victorious war? It was General Manekshaw who oversaw everything along with General Jacob. Initially, the plan was to hit Jessore and Khulna (as per Indira Gandhi's knowledge), but suddenly the whole scenario changed as the war began. A mystery surrounds till date on how this significant historical event of the subcontinent developed. After all, immediately after the war ended all war-related documents kept at the Eastern Command in Kolkata were destroyed.[100] Perhaps, General Manekshaw died with lots of secrets! Why General Manekshaw's pension was stopped and was restored by none other than President Abdul Kalam near the time of his death is also a mystery.

All the credit for freeing East Pakistan and the creation of Bangladesh is given to former Prime Minister Indira Gandhi. However, much credit goes first to Rameshwar Nath Kao. He was the founder of India's premier intelligence body Research and Analysis Wing (RAW), is credited as the 'architect of Bangladesh' for his role in the 1971 war.[101] It appears that Kao was planning for this for some time and even told PM Gandhi as early as in 1969, which she may not have imagined. Kao was also responsible for the 1975 referendum of erstwhile independent country Sikkim to join India as a state. The people who executed the Bangladesh plan meticulously were Field Marshal Sam Manekshaw, Lieutenant General Jack Jacob, and other Indian military officials. It appears that Indira Gandhi wanted a quick and limited operation in East Pakistan to teach a lesson to Pakistan and not a full-fledged liberation war. However, Kao, Manekshaw, and others executed a larger game, which was to free East Pakistan.

According to social scientist and journalist Nalin Mehta, "Capturing Dhaka itself was not an official war objective for the Indian Army in 1971. As the Army prepared for war, Operation Instruction 53, issued by Army Headquarters on August 16, 1971, mandated Indian forces in the Eastern Sector to destroy Pakistani forces in Eastern Sector and to occupy the major portion of East Bengal, including the entry ports of Chittagong and Khulna.

The idea was to win and hold territory in a short war and then negotiate a favorable ceasefire. Conquering Dhaka was considered an option at the planning stage, but Army Headquarters never made it a formal war aim because it also had to worry about a possible Chinese threat from the north, the threat to Bhutan, the continuing insurgency in the North-East and possible American intervention.

Eventually, by November 30, Army Headquarters issued revised orders, mandating "the liberation of the whole of Bangladesh as the military task of Eastern Command." Lt. General Jagjit Singh Aurora, the Eastern Army commander, had made it clear that his strategy would be fluid, and after the Army made fast early advances in battle, the plan for a lightning strike to Dhaka now looked good – though formal orders for this were never issued."[102]

It appears that Indira Gandhi was not aware of this total plan, and General Jacob led the downfall of Dhaka and personally executed the surrender.[103]

After the 1971 war, Gen. Manekshaw became very popular throughout India. In a conversation with Indira Gandhi, it is said that that she asked Manekshaw if he was going to have a coup d'état against her with an apparent indication of his hidden plan and execution to free Bangladesh without the latter's knowledge and approval. Manekshaw was quoted like this: "Mrs. Gandhi called me to her office. She was very worried. 'Everybody says you are taking over. When are you taking over'?"[104]

The fact that Indira Gandhi was scared of Manekshaw is indirect proof that the entire 1971 war episode was beyond the planning and knowledge of Indira Gandhi.

In December 1971, the new Bangladesh Government strongly opposed to Indian plan to free the Pakistani POWs and wanted India to allow filing cases against the Pakistani military criminals for their 'crimes against humanity' and holding trials in courts.[105]

History must not ignore the fact that Indira decided to return more than 93000 Pakistani soldiers who committed the most heinous crimes in modern history. They were let to go scot-free and received a hero's welcome in Pakistan; many settled in

India who cannot be traced today. Experts speculate that Indira released them in exchange for sparing the life of Mujib, who was to be killed only three years later by the same Pakistanis via ISI operatives. This historical blunder haunts Hindus and Buddhists in Bangladesh today because the world, especially the Islamists, found that there is no voice for the Hindus, and anyone can do anything and not get punished.

But why did Indira release them instead of giving them to the hands of Muktibahini and the Bangladesh army, who suffered brutal persecution of unimaginable degree? And several thousand Indian soldiers also gave their lives in the 1971 war. Generally, it is propagated that Pakistan, through America, put pressure on India to ratify the Shimla agreement, and maybe Indira succumbed to that pressure. Other stories say that America conveyed to the USSR that if India took Pakistani land, which they had captured during the war, USA would consider it Indian occupation – an attack on their 'ally', and persuaded the Russians to convince Indira to accept the Shimla Agreement.

But perhaps the real story from Washington was narrated by *The New Yorker* magazine[106]:

On August 2, 1972 – eight months after the defeat of the Pak army, the two countries signed the Shimla Agreement under which India agreed to release all the 93,000 Pakistani prisoners of war (POW). The treaty, unfortunately, had a provision for Pakistan that they would recognize independent Bangladesh in exchange for the release of the POWs.[107]

During her time and today, many people believe that 'Indira Gandhi had squandered a golden opportunity to bargain with Pakistan and settle the Kashmir problem on India's terms.' India was completely in a dominant position to bargain with Pakistan for long-term peace in the region, including solving the Kashmir problem for good. According to a 2018 book *GP:1912-1995* (Publisher Academic Foundation) by Prof. Ashok Parthasarathi, former science adviser to PM Indira

Gandhi, though the majority of her close aides wanted to go after POK, Gilgit, Skardu, and Baltistan, she mysteriously decided, perhaps based on the advice from P.N. Haksar, her principal secretary. Haskar was one of the closest confidants of Gandhi and was part of her small inner coterie of bureaucrats, known as the "Kashmiri mafia". According to the book, Indira Gandhi received a secret telegram on December 16 from then-Soviet President Brezhnev, who congratulated her for war victory and pledged military support if she decided to 're-take PoK'. She sat on that telegram for more than a month.

Since then, India has been facing a proxy war in Kashmir, causing thousands of deaths and draining national resources.

According to a Defense update report:[108]

"Indira Gandhi, like father (Nehru), was not interested to solve the Kashmir issue and was more worried about Bangladeshi leader Sheikh Mujibur Rahman, who was in Pakistan's custody and was sentenced to death by Pakistan's military court on charges of treason. But the advice was to first solve India's problems and then find a diplomatic solution to the Bangladeshi leader's release. But Indira Gandhi was in no mood to take advice and was ready to pay any price for the release of Sheikh Mujibur Rahman for unknown reasons!"

India captured over 12,000 sq km of Pakistani territory in the West. Bhutto's biggest concern was that and, of course, the release POWs for saving grace after the humiliating defeat they had in 1971. He was desperate. However, the advisers of Indira and negotiators both miserably failed in assessing Bhutto's game plan and played into Pakistani strategists in Shimla.

The report noted:[109]

"Naivety of the Indian delegation can be seen from the fact that it allowed Pakistan to bluff its way through at Shimla. The Indian leadership was fooled into believing Pakistan's sincerity. Unquestionably, Pakistan never intended to abide by its promises, both written and verbal. Fruits of a hard-fought victory in the battlefield were frittered away on a negotiating table by bungling leadership."

Field Marshal Sam Manekshaw told in an interview about Indira after signing the Shimla Agreement: "She went to Shimla and Bhutto made a complete *** out of her. Bhutto apparently told Indira that 'I know, I have just taken over from Yahya Khan, if I yield anything now, they will throw me out. Give me a chance, in six months' time I promise you everything will settle, everything peacefully.' She came back and told me this, and I said he (Bhutto) had made a monkey out of you". [110] This is also reported in a book on Manekshaw.[111]

Notorious General Tikka Khan executed the plan for the Hindu Genocide and was known as the "Butcher of Bengal",[112] even he did not face any punishment!

According to Sashanka Banerjee, an Indian Diplomat, 'India wanted to keep the Pakistani soldiers in conditions of comfort that went over and above the provisions listed in the Geneva Convention...' and also added that, 'India ordered the release of all 93,000 Pakistani POWs under the Shimla Agreement of August 2, 1972. The world had never known such decency in international relations as India's conduct with Pakistan on the POW issue.'[113]

It remains a mystery to date what was the real reason why Indira, after capturing huge parts of POK and even West Pakistan, unilaterally declared a ceasefire and signed the Shimla Agreement, which had a provision to release all the POWs. According to Banerjee, Justice Abu Said Choudhury, who later became the president of Bangladesh, in his letter to Indira Gandhi, wrote on December 16, 1971 (the same day Indira received Brezhnev's telegram), that he warned her 'of dire consequences if she decided to go for a unilateral ceasefire on the western front. It would remain, he maintained, the half-finished business of the Bangladesh war'. His concluding line was, "When you chop off the tail of a cobra, its head becomes ten times more venomous."[114]

India and the minorities in Bangladesh, Pakistan, and Afghanistan continue to pay a heavy price of their life, liberty, and honor to date due to these decisions of Indira Gandhi.

In West Pakistan, according to the 1941 census, the Hindu population was about 14%, whereas, in East Pakistan, it was 28%.[115]

After the Partition, close to five million Hindus and Sikhs were forced to move to India.[116]

According to the 1951 census, the Hindus were 1.6% of the total population of West Pakistan (currently Pakistan), and 22% of East Pakistan (currently Bangladesh) and 18.4% in 1961.

Pakistan's 2017 Census counted 2.14% or 4.44 million Hindus. But others do not agree. For example, the Pakistan Hindu Council suggested that the number was nearly double the census number.[117] A 2021 *India Today* report suggested there were 7.5 million Hindus in Pakistan.[118]

The abduction of Hindu women, forced conversion, and economic challenges are causing a rapid reduction of the number of Hindus and Sikhs in Pakistan today. And it appears that the days are not too far away when these minorities would become extinct, just as it has happened in Afghanistan.[119, 120, 121, 122]

In the 1970s, there were more than 500,000 Hindus in Afghanistan.[123] Before the Taliban rule arrived in 1996, the number was still close to half a million Hindus in Afghanistan. Today, Afghanistan has only 0.3% minorities belonging to Hindu, Sikh communities.[124] In 2020, there were about 1,300 Sikhs and 600 Hindus.[125]

A 2010 survey by the Sikh Resource and Study Center reported 50,000 Sikhs living in Pakistan. But according to the Pakistan Government's National Database and Registration Authority (NADRA), there were 6,146 Sikhs registered in

Pakistan in 2012. According to the US Department of State, the Sikh population in Pakistan was reported to be as high as 20,000. An *India Today* report titled *'Sikhs on the verge of extinction in Pakistan''* reported: *'Sikh population in Pakistan has drastically come down within the past two decades – from around 40,000 in 2002 to 8,000.'*[126]

Drawing of the Curtain

Renowned historian Will Durant wrote: "India was the motherland of our race, and Sanskrit the mother of Europe's languages: she was the mother of our philosophy; mother, through the Arabs, of much of our mathematics; mother, through the Buddha, of the ideals embodied in Christianity; mother, through the village community, of self-government and democracy. Mother India is in many ways the mother of us all."[127] That means a great nation that has given so much to the world and world civilization, it is hard to even measure and fully appreciate by anybody.

The ancient land of Gandhar, later Kandahar – Kabul (870 CE), Zabul (963 CE), and the land of Afghanistan, were lost to invaders. Once a flourishing region of Zoroastrian-Hindu-Buddhist culture and traditions, very little trace of the legacy is left there today.

Sind or Sindhu is integrally associated with the name of the nation, race, and civilization. It is even mentioned in India's national anthem. Sind was first lost to the invaders in 712 CE and then finally in 1947 along with the rest of present Pakistan and Punjab. West Bengal and East Punjab were miraculously saved as part of India in 1947, and the Eastern part of the erstwhile 'Banga' or Bongobhumi or Bengal is now Bangladesh.

The entire nation, the oldest continuous living civilization, was inflicted severely and crushed, broken into pieces – figuratively, politically, and culturally. The crash is enormous.

But India ought to resurrect. Rabindranath prayed for the 'brahma-muhurta' or the perfect auspicious moment for India to give the light to the world again:

এই শ্মশানের মাঝে শক্তির সাধনা
তব আরাধনা নহে হে বিশ্বপালক।
তোমার নিখিলপ্লাবী আনন্দ-আলোক
হয়তো লুকায়ে আছে পূর্বসিন্ধুতীরে
বহু ধৈর্যে নম্র স্তব্ধ দুঃখের তিমিরে
সর্বরিক্ত অশ্রুসিক্ত দৈন্যের দীক্ষায়
দীর্ঘকাল— ব্রাহ্মমুহূর্তের প্রতীক্ষায়।

[Rabindranath (Naibedya 66)]

"Oh Lord, the operator of the universe, the worship of demonic force of materialism is not for you. The joy of light to flood the universe is most likely hiding in the East, to give new life to the tearful who has lost everything with infinite patience, humility – quietly in the ocean of suffering and sorrow, waiting for the perfect moment in history!"

And Sri Aurobindo gave hope and predicted:

"India of the ages is not dead nor has she spoken her last creative word; she lives and has still something to do for herself and the human peoples. And that which must seek now to awake is not an anglicised oriental people, docile pupil of the West and doomed to repeat the cycle of the occident's success and failure, but still the ancient immemorable Shakti recovering her deepest self, lifting her head higher towards the supreme source of light and strength and turning to discover the complete meaning and a vaster form of her Dharma." [128]

References

1. Naipaul, V.S. (1977). "India: A Wounded Civilization", Alfred A. Knopf (Publisher), New York.

2. Durant, Will "The Case of India", Simon and Schuster, 1930. https://www.vifindia.org/sites/default/files/139221701-The-Case-for-India-1930.pdf

3. Sarila, Narendra Singh, "The Shadow of the Great Game: The Untold Story of India's Partition", https://ia801208.us.archive.org/12/items/AzadIndiaWinsFreedom/The%20Shadow%20of%20the%20Great%20Game_%20The%20Untold%20Story%20of%20India_s%20Partition.pdf Carol and Graff Publishers New York , 2006.

4. Ahmed, Akbar S. "Pakistan and Islamic Identity, The Search for Saladin", Routledge, https://archive.nytimes.com/www.nytimes.com/books/first/a/ahmed-jinnah.html?_e_pi_=7,PAGE_ID10,1790062921]

5. Kidwai, Rasheed, "Fish to Blame for Partition? Congress Leader Claims 'Taboo' Business Pushed Jinnah's Grandfather to Convert", *News 18,* January 13, 2019, https://www.news18.com/news/india/fish-to-blame-for-indias-partition-book-claims-taboo-business-pushed-jinnahs-grandfather-to-convert-2000857.html

6. "A Muslim whose antecedents 'were' of Lord Rama's Raghuvanshi lineage", *Free Press Journal,* May 29, 2019, https://www.freepressjournal.in/cmcm/a-muslim-whose-antecedents-were-of-lord-ramas-raghuvanshi-lineage

7. Pandit, Virendra "Return of the Infidel", Vitasta Publishing, 2017.

8. Wolpert, Stanley *(1984)*. "Jinnah of Pakistan". New York: Oxford University Press. p. 20.

9. Singh, Jaswant *(2009)*. "Jinnah: India-Partition and Independence". Oxford: Oxford University Press. p. 41-42.

10. "Where Jinnah defended Tilak", *The Hindustan Times,* 3 March 2010, https://www.hindustantimes.com/mumbai/where-jinnah-defended-tilak/story-UV1H6DIIMzzuFx3kTXShgK.html

11. Malik, Iftikar H. (2008). "The History of Pakistan". The Greenwood Histories of the Modern Nations. Westport, Conn.: Greenwood Press. p. 120.
12. Wolpert, Stanley (1984). "Jinnah of Pakistan", New York: Oxford University Press.
13. Malik, Iftikar H. (2008). "The History of Pakistan". The Greenwood Histories of the Modern Nations. Westport, Conn.: Greenwood Press. p.121.
14. Ziring, Lawrence (1980). Pakistan: The Enigma of Political Development. p. 67
15. Aziz, Qutubuddin (2001). "Jinnah and Pakistan". p. 98.
16. Bolith, Hector (1954). "Jinnah: Creator of Pakistan". London: John Murray. OCLC 1001456192. p. 104-106.
17. Ahmed, Akbar S. *(2005)* "Jinnah, Pakistan, and Islamic Identity: The Search for Saladin". London: Routledge. p. 180.
18. Ibid. p.26.
19. Karim, Saleena (2010). "Secular Jinnah & Pakistan: What the Nation Doesn't Know". Checkpoint Press, p. 26.
20. Khan, Zamir (30 June 2010). "Iqbal and Quaid's Vision of Pakistan" (PDF). The Dialogue. V (2): 151.
21. Puri, Balraj (1–7 March 2008). "Clues to understanding Jinnah". Economic and Political Weekly. Bombay: Sameeksha Trust. 43 (9): 33–35. JSTOR 40277204. p.35.
22. Kazimi, M. (2005). "M.A. Jinnah Views and Reviews". Oxford University Press. p. 114.
23. Ahmed, Akbar S. (2005), "Jinnah, Pakistan, and Islamic Identity: The Search for Saladin", Routledge, p. 62-73.
24. *Pioneer.* 01 April 2019, https://www.dailypioneer.com/2019/columnists/jinnah---s-real-identity-jinnah---s-real-identity.html
25. Haqqani, Husain "Reimagining Pakistan: Transforming

a Dysfunctional Nuclear State", HarperCollins, India, 2018. https://www.indiatoday.in/lifestyle/culture/story/remagining-pakistan-talks-about-jinnah-gave-clerics-free-hand-in-political-mobilisation-1227905-2018-05-06

26. Totalitarian leaders (dailypioneer.com)
27. The Lahore Resolution, 1940.
28. Raynor, Brian, (2000), "John Frith, Scholar and Martyr: A Biography", Pond View Books, p. 145.
29. Sarkar, Avik (2020). "Syama Prasad Mukherjee And The Rescue Of Hindu Bengal From An Islamist Plot Called 'United Bengal'", *Swarajya,* 20 June. Available at: https://swarajyamag.com/politics/s-p-mookerjee-and-the-rescue-of-hindu-bengal-from-an-islamist-plot-called-united-bengal
30. Markovits Claude, Markovits (5 November, 2007). "The Great Calcutta Riots 1946". https://www.sciencespo.fr/mass-violence-war-massacre-resistance/fr/document/calcutta-riots-1946.html
31. Mazumdar, Jaideep (2017). "'The Butcher Of Bengal' And His Role In Direct Action Day", *Swarajya,* 21 August. Available at:https://swarajyamag.com/politics/its-a-crying-shame-that-the-butcher-of-bengal-has-a-road-named-after-him-in-kolkata
32. National Archives UK, Calcutta Riots, Extracts from a military report on the Calcutta riots, 24 August 1946 (WO 216/662), The Road to Partition (1939-1947).
33. How India responded to the influx of 10 million refugees – Governance Now. https://www.nationalarchives.gov.uk/education/resources/the-road-to-partition/calcutta-riots/
34. Raman, B., (29 August, 2006) Bangladesh: A Bengali Abbasi Lurking Somewhere?, South Asia Analysis Group, Paper No. 232. https://web.archive.org/web/20070611031127/http://www.saag.org/papers3/paper232.html

35. "In their words: Bhutto and Mujib, December, 1971", *The Daily Star,* 15 November 2014 https://www.thedailystar.net/in-their-words-bhutto-and-mujib-december-1971-50468
36. Schanberg, Sydney H. "He Tells Full Story of Arrest and Detention", *New York Times,* 18 Jan 1972, https://www.nytimes.com/1972/01/18/archives/he-tells-full-story-of-arrest-and-detention-sheik-mujib-describes.html
37. R. Chowdhury is a former soldier and a freedom fighter in the war of liberation of Bangladesh. http://southasiajournal.net/was-sheikh-mujib-for-an-unbroken-pakistan-or-independent-bangladesh-sensational-revelation-about-mujib-in-pakistan-in-1971-%EF%BB%BF/
38. Raman, B. (29 August 2006). "Mujib and Islam". Archived from the original (PHP) on 11 June 2007.
39. Madhukalya, Amrita (2014). "Bangladeshi Hackers Target BJP Punjab Website". *DNA India,* 30 April. Available at: https://www.dnaindia.com/india/report-bangladeshi-hackers-target-bjp-punjab-website-1983474
40. Rahman, Syed Sadiqur (2012). "Ramna Racecourse". In Islam, Sirajul; Jamal, Ahmed A. (eds.). Banglapedia: National Encyclopedia of Bangladesh (Second ed.). Asiatic Society of Bangladesh.
41. Haq, Enamul. "Bhasani's Farakka Long March". Maulana Abdul Hamid Khan Bhashani. Archived from the original on 10 September 2011.
42. Nanda, B. R. (2015) [1977], "Gokhale: The Indian Moderates and the British Raj", Legacy Series, Princeton University Press, p. 58.
43. Talbot, Ian; & Singh, Guharpal, (2009), "The Partition of India", Cambridge University Press.
44. Tunzelmann, Alex von (2012). "Indian Summer: The Secret History of the End of an Empire". Simon and Schuster.

45. 13 August 1946 issue of Muslim league mouthpiece *The Star of India,* quoted by Devendra Panigrahi, 'India's Partition: The Story of Imperialism in Retreat' , Routledge, 2004.
46. Suhrawardy Speech, 16/8/1946, https://www.opindia.com/2018/08/eye-witness-account-of-direct-action-day-great-calcutta-killing-of-16-august-1946/
47. "The Foreshadowing of Bangladesh: Bengal Muslim League & Muslim Politics: 1906-1947".
48. "My People Uprooted: A Saga of the Hindus of Eastern Bengal"; Ratna Prakashan, Kolkata, 2001.
49. Ahsan, Syed Badrul (2012). "Mujib, in his own words", *The Indian Express*, 7 July, Available at: http://archive.indianexpress.com/news/mujib-in-his-own-words/971272/2
50. Kolkata Bureau (2014). 'Celebrating the centenary of a "divisive" figure', *The Hindu*, 18 August, Available at: https://www.thehindu.com/news/cities/kolkata/celebrating-the-centenary-of-a-divisive-figure/article6326661.ece
51. Whitehead, Andrew (July 1, 1997). "Duty does not permit repentance --The butchers of Calcutta", *The Indian Express,* 1 July, Available at: https://web.archive.org/web/20131016133334/http://expressindia.indianexpress.com/news/ie/daily/19970701/18250453.html
52. Burrows, Frederick (1946). "Report to Viceroy Lord Wavell". The British Library IOR: L/P&J/8/655 f.f. 95, 96–107.
53. Sinha, Dinesh Chandra; Dasgupta, Ashok (2011). "1946: The Great Calcutta Killings and Noakhali Genocide". Kolkata: Himangshu Maity. p. 263.
54. Ibid.
55. Prayer meeting, April 6, 1947, New Delhi, CWMG Vol. 94, p. 249.

56. Gandhi, M.K., (1960). "My Non-violence", Compiled and Edited by : Sailesh Kumar Bandopadhyaya, Navajivan Mudranalaya, Ahemadabad, Chapter: 'The Jews', Available at: https://www.mkgandhi.org/mynonviolence/chap27.htm
57. "The Truth About Gandhi" (7 March, 1983). The Harvard Crimson, https://www.thecrimson.com/article/1983/3/7/the-truth-about-gandhi-pbtbhe-movie/
58. Gandhi (1960).
59. Mahatma Gandhi, June 1946, in an interview with his biographer Louis Fischer. https://www.jewishvirtuallibrary.org/gandhi-on-the-holocaust
60. Ibid.
61. Madhok, Madhuri "Shyama Prasad Mookerji ensured India got•parts of Bengal, Punjab", *Sunday Guardian*, 2 July 2016, https://www.sundayguardianlive.com/opinion/5556-shyama prasad-mookerji-ensured-india-got-parts-bengal-punjab
62. Eminent Parliamentarians, Monograph Series, Dr. Syama Prasad Mookerjee, Lok Sabha Secretariat, New Delhi, 1990 https://eparlib.nic.in/bitstream/123456789/58670/1/Eminent_Parliamentarians_Series_Syama_Prasad_Mookerjee.pdf
63. Chatterji, Joya (2002). "Bengal divided: Hindu communalism and Partition, 1932–1947", Cambridge University Press. p. 241.
64. "Remembering Mountbatten's June 3 Plan", *Tribune India,* 4 June 2018, https://www.tribuneindia.com/news/archive/comment/remembering-mountbatten-s-june-3-plan-599572
65. Kureshi, Salman Tarik "How four Christian votes made Pakistan possible", *The Friday Times*, 1 June 2018, https://www.thefridaytimes.com/how-four-christian-votes-made-pakistan-possible/

66. "Tara Singh", Britannica https://www.britannica.com/biography/Tara-Singh
67. Kudaisya, Gyanesh; Yong, Tan Tai (2004). "The Aftermath of Partition in South Asia". Routledge, p. 100.
68. Kureshi, Salman Tarik (2018). "How four Christian votes made Pakistan possible", *The Friday Times,* 1 June, https://www.thefridaytimes.com/how-four-christian-votes-made-pakistan-possible/
69. Roy Chowdhury Dipanjan (2020). "Minorities in Pakistan: A life under siege", *The Economic Times,* 20 June, https://economictimes.indiatimes.com/news/international/world-news/minorities-in-pakistan-a-life-under-siege/articleshow/76476124.cms
70. Bibhutibhushan Bandopadhyay's Letter of 25th June, 1947. (Bengali).
71. Doshi, Vidhi; Mehdi, Nisar (2017). "70 years later, survivors recall the horrors of India-Pakistan partition", *The Washington Post,* 14 August, https://www.washingtonpost.com/world/asia-pacific/70-years-later-survivors-recall-the-horrors-of-india-pakistan-partition/2017/08/14/3b8c58e4-7de9-11e7-9026-4a0a64977c92_story.html
72. Hajari, Nisid, "Midnight's Furies: The Deadly Legacy of India's Partition", Houghton Mifflin, 2015.
73. Barkat, Abul, An Inquiry Into Causes and Consequences of Deprivation of Hindu Minorities in Bangladesh Through the Vested Property Act: Framework for a Realistic Solution – Dhaka: PRIP Trust, 2000.
74. PA50B1228.pdf (mea.gov.in)
75. Jayal, Niraja Gopal (2019), "Reconfiguring Citizenship in Contemporary India, Journal of South Asian Studies", 42(1), pp. 34–36. (context: 33–50), doi:10.1080/00856401.2019.1555874
76. https://indiankanoon.org/doc/949775/

77. Parliamentary Debates Official Report, Volume 200, Number 13, Rajya Sabha Secretariat, Government of India, 18 December 2003, p. 383.
78. "Parliament passes the Citizenship (Amendment) Bill 2019". pib.gov.in
79. "How many immigrants will benefit from Citizenship Act? 25,447 Hindus, 5,807 Sikhs, 55 Christians, two Buddhists and two Parsis, says Intelligence Bureau". Firstpost.
80. "The Citizenship (Amendment) Bill, 2019" (PDF). PRS India.
81. "The Citizenship Amendment Act, 2019, Some Reflections", Akshaya Prakashan, 2021, p. 14.
82. Marshman, John Clark *(1863)*. "Nadir Shah". The History of India. Serampore Press. p. 200.
83. Dalrymple, William; Anand, Anita; (2017). "Koh-i-Noor", Bloomsbury Publishing. p. 52.
84. Axworthy, Michael "The Sword of Persia: Nader Shah, from Tribal Warrior to Conquering Tyrant", I.B. Tauris 2006 p. XVI.
85. Abu Md. Delwar Hossain (2012), "Operation Searchlight", in Sirajul Islam and Ahmed A. Jamal (ed.), Banglapedia: National Encyclopedia of Bangladesh (Second ed.), Asiatic Society of Bangladesh.
86. Boissoneault, Lorraine "The Genocide the U.S. Can't Remember, But Bangladesh Can't Forget", Smithsonian Mag, 16 December 2016 https://www.smithsonianmag.com/history/genocide-us-cant-remember-bangladesh-cant-forget-180961490/
87. Sharlach, Lisa (2000). "Rape as Genocide: Bangladesh, the Former Yugoslavia, and Rwanda". New Political Science. 22 (1): 89–102. doi:10.1080/713687893. S2CID 144966485. p. 92-93.
88. Sajjad, Tazreena (2012). "The Post-Genocidal Period and its

Impact on Women". In Samuel Totten (ed.). "Plight and Fate of Women During and Following Genocide" *(Reprint ed.). Transaction. pp. 219–248.*

89. Ghadbian, Najib (2002). "Political Islam: Inclusion or violence?" In Kent Worcester; Sally A. Bermanzohn; Mark Ungar (eds.). Violence and Politics: Globalization's Paradox. Routledge. P.111
90. D'Costa, Bina (2011). "Nationbuilding, Gender and War Crimes in South Asia". Routledge, p. 102.
91. *Christian Gerlach (14 October 2010). "Extremely Violent Societies: Mass Violence in the Twentieth-Century World". Cambridge University Press. p. 155.*
92. *Mookherjee, Nayanika, (October 23, 2015). "The Spectral Wound: Sexual Violence, Public Memories, and the Bangladesh War of 1971". Duke University Press. p. 159.*
93. Islam, M. Rafiqul (2019). "National Trials of International Crimes in Bangladesh: Transitional Justice as Reflected in Judgments". Brill. pp. 175–177.
94. Bartrop, Paul R.; Jacobs, Steven Leonard (2014). "Modern Genocide: The Definitive Resource and Document Collection" [4 volumes]
95. D'Costa, Bina, (2011). p. 108
96. Siddiqi, Dina M. (1998). "Taslima Nasreen and Others: The Contest over Gender in Bangladesh". In Herbert L. Bodman; Nayereh Esfahlani Tohidi (eds.). "Women in Muslim Societies: Diversity Within Unity". Lynne Rienner. p. 208.
97. D'Costa, Bina (2011). "Nationbuilding, Gender and War Crimes in South Asia". Routledge, p. 108.
98. Hossain, Anushay "1971 Rapes: Bangladesh Cannot Hide History", *Forbes*, 21 May 2012 https://www.forbes.com/sites/worldviews/2012/05/21/1971-rapes-bangladesh-cannot-hide-history/?sh=94a7ca416dfe

99. "1971 war: The story of India's victory, Pak's surrender, Bangladesh freedom", *Business Standard,* 16 December 2018 https://www.business-standard.com/article/current-affairs/vijay-diwas-how-india-ended-pak-s-atrocities-and-ensured-freed-bangladesh-118121600120_1.html
100. Joseph, Josy "Truth lost? Most military records of Bangladesh War Missing", *The Times of India,* 9 May 2010 https://timesofindia.indiatimes.com/india/truth-lost-most-military-records-of-bangladesh-war-missing/articleshow/5907855.cms
101. Bhalla, Gursharan, "Vijay Diwas 2020: Remembering The Heroes of 1971 War Who Led India To Victory Over Pakistan", *India Times*, 16 Dec 2020 https://www.indiatimes.com/news/india/heroes-of-india-pakistan-1971-war-vijay-diwas-529840.html#
102. Mehta, Nalin, "How 'Jake sweetie' conquered Dhaka for India", *The Times of India,* January 15, 2016, https://timesofindia.indiatimes.com/blogs/academic-interest/how-jake-sweetie-conquered-dhaka-for-india/
103. Singh, Zorawar Daulet, "Two yrs before 1971 war, RAW's R.N. Kao told Indira Gandhi to be ready for Pakistan partition", *The Print*, 1 December, 2019 https://theprint.in/pageturner/excerpt/2-yrs-before-1971-war-raw-chief-told-indira-gandhi-to-be-ready-for-pakistan-partition/325899/
104. "'When are you taking over', Indira asked Manekshaw", *Zee News India*, 27 July, 2008 https://zeenews.india.com/news/nation/when-are-you-taking-over-indira-asked-manekshaw_458236.html
105. Cloughley, Brian (2016). "A History of the Pakistan Army: Wars and Insurrections", Skyhorse Publishing, Inc.
106. Mishra, Pankaj, "Unholy Alliances: Nixon, Kissinger, and the Bangladesh genocide", *New Yorker,* September 16,

2013 https://www.newyorker.com/magazine/2013/09/23/unholy-alliances-3

107. "Indo-Pak Shimla Agreement: 40 years later – IBNLive". Ibnlive.in

108. "Golden opportunity lost! Why did Indira Gandhi release 93,000 Pakistani prisoners of war in 1972?!" *Indian Defence News* http://defenceupdate.in/golden-opportunity-lost-indira-gandhi-release-93000-pakistani-prisoners-war-1972/

109. Ibid.

110. Aashish, 'Sam Manekshaw on Indira Gandhi, "She went to Shimla and Bhutto made a complete *** out of her. She came back and I told her he has made a MONKEY out of you"' Twitter, 5 July 2020. https://twitter.com/i/status/1279667976086548480

111. Falki, Hanadi, "Field Marshal Manekshaw", Prabhat Prakashan, 2008.

112. "Muktijuddho (Bangladesh Liberation War 1971) – Butcher of Bengal General Tikka Khan takes charge in East Pakistan – History of Bangladesh". *Londoni*.

113. Banerjee, Sashanka S., "The True Story of India's Decision to Release 93,000 Pakistani POWs After 1971 War", *The Wire*, 16 December 2020 https://thewire.in/history/the-untold-story-behind-indira-gandhis-decision-to-release-93000-pakistani-pows-after-the-bangladesh-war

114. Ibid.

115. Ranganathan, Anand (2015). "The Vanishing Hindus of Pakistan – a Demographic Study", *Newslaundry, 9 January, https://www.newslaundry.com/2015/01/09/the-vanishing-hindus-of-pakistan-a-demographic-study-2*

116. Hill, Kenneth H.; Seltzer, William; Leaning, Jennifer; Malik, Saira J.; Russell, Sharon Stanton;

Makinson, C. (2004), "A Demographic Case Study of Forced Migration: The 1947 Partition of India "Session 44: Understanding the Forced Migration of Trafficked Persons and Refugees", Population Association of America 2004 Annual Meeting Program.

117. "Hindu Population (PK) – Pakistan Hindu Council".
118. PTI (2021) "Most of the revered Hindu sites in Pakistan in state of decay: Report", *New Indian Express*, 8 February, https://www.newindianexpress.com/world/2021/feb/08/most-of-the-revered-hindu-sites-in-pakistan-in-state-of-decay-report-2261178.html
119. Imtiaz, Saba (14 August 2017). "Hindu Today, Muslim Tomorrow". The Atlantic. https://www.theatlantic.com/international/archive/2017/08/hindu-muslim-pakistan/536238/
120. Sarfraz, Mehmal (13 April 2019). "In Pakistan, the problem of forced conversions". The Hindu. https://www.thehindu.com/news/international/in-pakistan-the-problem-of-forced-conversions/article26823108.ece
121. Husain, Shahid (15 July 2015). "1,000 girls forcibly converted to Islam in Pakistan every year". *The News International*. https://www.thenews.com.pk/print/51401-1000-girls-forcibly-converted-to-islam-in-pakistan-every-year
122. Abi-Habib, Maria; ur-Rehman, Zia (5 August 2020). "Poor and Desperate, Pakistani Hindus accept Islam to get by". *NY Times*. https://www.nytimes.com/2020/08/04/world/asia/pakistan-hindu-conversion.html
123. Kumar, Ruchi. "The decline of Afghanistan's Hindu and Sikh communities". aljazeera.com. https://www.aljazeera.com/features/2017/01/01/the-decline-of-afghanistans-hindu-and-sikh-communities/
124. The State of Minorities in Afghanistan pdf: https://www.misaal.ngo/wp-content/uploads/2019/02/afghanistan.pdf

125. Kumar, Ruchi, (26 March, 2020). "Solidarity for Sikhs after Afghanistan massacre". *Al Jazeera.* https://www.aljazeera.com/amp/news/2020/3/26/solidarity-for-sikhs-after-afghanistan-massacre

126. Harmeet Shah Singh (30 August, 2019). "Sikhs on the Verge of Extinction in Pakistan: Campaigner", *India Today*. https://www.indiatoday.in/india/story/sikhs-on-verge-of-extinction-in-pakistan-campaigner-1593674-2019-08-30

127. Durant, 1931.

128. Sri Aurobindo, "The Foundations of Indian Culture" // SABCL. Volume 14, pp. 363-381.

❑

CLOSING

Thus, a great civilization crashed and broke into pieces after the infliction of a series of tremendous injuries to its body and soul. By 2021, seventy-five years have passed since that last major upheaval, and the civilization is still bleeding. NeoCols are abundant everywhere, but the end of their influence seems to be near. The only way out for the civilization to heal and relive to 'give light (Bhar-rata)' is a revolution of minds. This revolution is not a political one but a psycho-cultural and *adhyatmic* one, reorganizing a society with a more responsible, more cooperative and awakened masses knowing their past (not as told by others) and potential more glorious future based on the Dharmic ideas of *rnas,* one's obligations to the society, and the dharmic systems of sustenance and growth. And of course, truly following the Upanishadic motto '*satyameva jayate*'- being truthful to our history, society and people. These are the responsibilities as true children of the soil.

The land where a river, Ganga, is revered like nowhere on earth, yet people don't hesitate to dump anything in it! The youth, who are supposed to be filled with patriotic ideas and ambitions to be the best in their fields, have only one goal –

somehow becoming wealthy. Prosperity is necessary for any nation to progress, but if it is at the cost of the rest, society will remain in peril and inimical forces will always take advantage to propagate their agenda.

The business of fakeness among the people who are supposed to be leaders, protectors, and benevolent, is so rampant that it is very difficult to trust one another. Extreme selfishness, jealousy towards even own family members, uncontrolled greed, together with a hunger for wealth – these are all symptoms of a morally decayed society. The land of *Bhagwat Geeta*, Ram, Sita, Krishna, and Draupadi has become most unethical in all spheres of life – politics, business, governance – everywhere.

Though many of the archaic laws of the land have been quashed, many more remain from the British Era. The Constitution is more or less a colonial one. The key author Ambedkar himself, after completion, suggested destroying it since it did not reflect/fit the ethos of the land. *"My friends tell me that I made the Constitution. But I am quite prepared to say that I shall be the first person to burn it out. I do not want it. It does not suit anybody."*[1]

The new generation of Indian leaders ought to focus on a few things, first, throwing away cheap mimicking of the West. People need to go to the root of their civilizational ethos, that is, Dharma; they need to study history beyond textbooks. This book aims to create awareness among the Next-Gen about how much history has been suppressed and concocted by the NeoCols to keep the Indians feeling inferior, non-confrontational, passive, selfish, and ashamed about their tradition and heritage, and no pride for their ancestors.

This book has revealed the true nature of various outside cultures, worldviews and forces and their impact. What are the weaknesses of the majority Hindu society, and how to infuse every aspect of living with Dharmic ideas? This book is not against anybody but an attempt to understand the true nature of others who have impacted the lives, societies, and the nation in the past and are still doing so. But equally important to know who you really are!

What is the difference between 'Hinduism' and 'Hindutva'? The term 'Hinduism' was imposed on a supposed set of 'religious' practices based on Western theological concepts, not applicable in the Indian situation. One does not have to be 'religious' to be Hindu. Even Swami Vivekananda said that he 'is an atheist if he does not believe in himself'. He also said that when you utter the word Hindu – it should send 'a galvanic shock' in you. Why? Because in his words, 'The debt which the world owes to our motherland is immense. Taking country with country, there is not one race on this earth to which the world owes so much as to the patient Hindu, the mild Hindu'. [2] This was also the assertion of Chandranath Bose, the author of the first book titled *Hindutva* (Bengali 1892) – he said, 'to talk about Brahman in you, one must experience it'. This is true Hindutva, and as long as Hindus follow the original ideas of the *Rishis* they can regain their own faith, heritage, history, and control their destiny.

The terms Hindu, Hinduism, Hindutva, etc., are vastly misunderstood, misused, and misappropriated, not just by the NeoCols, but also by the Hindus themselves. In order for the Hindus to regain their self-respect, inner strength, realize full potentials as individuals, as societies, and as a nation, must ask the question – 'what do I know about our history, tradition and heritage' and what one ought to do in order to understand the power of the great Hindu System which can transform any individual, any society and any nation irrespective of their nationality, race, and religion? Ultimately, Dharma means prosperity, progress, and sustenance – followed by peace and harmony.

Though I'm not an expert on the scriptures, I lead a conscious and practical Hindu life. Thus, I'm going to share my take on the idea of religion, 'Hinduism', 'Hindutva', spirituality, *adhyatma*, and Dharma in my next book. Note that I've used these apparently contradicting yet similar words for a reason – to raise your curiosity so that you read the book. The next book is about 'know thyself'! You are the children of immortals, '*amritasya putrah*'!

युजे वां ब्रह्म पूर्व्यं नमोभिर्विश्लोक एतु पथ्येव सूरेः।
शृण्वन्तु विश्वे अमृतस्य पुत्रा आ ये धामानि दिव्यानि तस्थुः॥

"Following only in the footsteps of the wise, I merge you both in the ancient Brahman by continued meditation. May the Glorious One manifest Himself! May the sons of Immortal Bliss hearken to me – even they who occupy celestial regions!" [3]

India is rising again to give the light of peace and harmony to the world, but it won't happen without millions of people wanting it, working for it, and dedicating and sacrificing many lives for the cause. That day is not that far, but what would be the cost? And a question to the reader – what would be your role in it?

References

1. Dhananjay Keer, "Dr. Ambedkar: Life and Mission". Bombay: Popular Prakashan, 1971, Ch. XXIV, p. 449-450.
2. Lectures from Colombo to Almora, Swami Vivekananda, p. 4.
3. *Svetasvatara Upanishad* – Chapter 2, Verse 5.

❑